OCCUPATIONAL SOCIOLOGY

Occupational Sociology

LEE TAYLOR

CORNELL UNIVERSITY

New York · Oxford University Press · 1968

Printed in the United States of America

For MICHELLE MARIA

PREFACE

Occupations in urbanized America are a major societal phenomena. They are also a central part of the concrete subject matter of sociology. Occupations constitute a primary laboratory for sociologists in the conceptual study of social organization. An understanding of occupations is central to systematic manpower planning by state and federal agencies. The sociology of occupations is a prerequisite for comprehensive labor force planning.

A knowledge of occupations is of prime importance to individual members of the labor force—to practically every male and a rapidly increasing proportion of females in urbanized societies. Youth need more occupational information in "choosing" a field of work. Adults who wish to change jobs, women who seek to combine home management and careers, and workers who face automation or retirement need to know more about the sociology of occupations. Regardless of ideolgy of work, sociology of work information is a helpful tool and a stimulating body of knowledge.

This book opens, in Part One, with a study of occupations in relation to social organization. Occupational characteristics and manifestations in urbanized society are examined. Multiplicity of occupations influences mobility, status, achievement, and production. Both individuals and planners are confronted by job multiplicity. Occupational conditions of work and job satisfaction are influenced by environments of bureaucracy, professionalization, and unionization. Status and prestige are important matters in urbanized society. Individuals most often obtain them in occupations, and occupations are in turn influenced by the society of which they are a part.

In Part Two the analysis is focused on internal occupational structures and institutions. These include aspirations, training, work entry, career patterns, types of payment, control of work behavior, occupational associations, and finally retirement from occupations. For individual members of the labor force and for students of sociology these elements of occupations—internal structures—are keys to individual achievement and to occupational production.

The meaning of occupations for individuals and for society are traced in Part Three. Here colleagueship, ideologies, and family life and work are analyzed. Chapters concerning the types of occupations ranging from professions to service jobs are included. Here the social characteristics of occupations are described and interpreted in terms of meaning, occupational structures, and social organization.

This book sets the meaning, structure, and characteristics of occupations firmly in the analysis of social organization.

My interest and research in occupations extends back for more than a decade. Roland Pellegrin did much to stimulate my early work. Arthur Jones is a close colleague in my study of occupations. His contributions influenced the outline of this book. Charles Glasgow, Charles Coates, Howard Bracey, William Kuvlesky, Philip Taietz, Ward Bauder, Theodore Caplow, and Archibald Haller as intellectual collegues have directly and indirectly raised occupational questions influencing this analysis.

Alvin L. Bertrand, Don Martindale, Paul Jehlik, Homer Hitt, Adrian K. Constandse, Nyle Brady, Joseph Metz, Harold Capener, William Reeder, Olaf Larson, Grace Horton, and Richard Klatt are professional colleagues who have contributed to an environment which has encouraged my work.

The manuscript was typed and retyped with care and scholarship by Mrs. Carol Markham. Time for concentration on the manuscript was increased by the elimination of pressures of daily work by staff members Mrs. Mollie Zall and Miss Frances Geherin.

Mr. Paul O. Whitfield, Editor in the Educational Division of Oxford University Press, is a deeply appreciated colleague whose insight and dispatch in relations between author and publisher have contributed greatly to excellence and scholarship.

Mrs. Jacquelin K. Taylor is a vital helpmate and constructive critic. Much academic publishing still remains in many characteristics a cottage industry, and the contribution, stimulation, and patience of my family cannot be over acknowledged.

Lee Taylor

Ithaca, New York
January 1968

ACKNOWLEDGMENTS

Acknowledgment is made to the following authors, publishers, and agents who have granted permission to reprint excerpts from copyrighted publications:

Aldine Publishing Company for Table, "1. Participants in American Chemical Society Activities," by Anselm L. Strauss and Lee Rainwater, *THE PROFESSIONAL SCIENTIST: A Study of American Chemists* (Chicago: Aldine Publishing Co., 1962).

The American Management Association, Inc., for excerpts from J. Donald Stauton, "I Didn't Raise My Boy to be a Salesman!," *Management Review*, 47 (March 1958).

Administrative Management Society Management Bulletins, for excerpts from Charles E. Ginder, "Unionization in the Office," *Office Executive*, 36 (January 1961).

American Psychological Association, for excerpts from Donald E. Super, "A Theory of Vocational Development," *The American Psychologist*, 8 (May 1953); and from Charles H. Mahoen, "Fear of Failure and Unrealistic Vocational Aspirations," *Journal of Abnormal and Social Psychology*, 60 (March 1960).

American Sociological Association, for excerpts from Nancy C. Morse and Robert S. Weiss, "The Function and Meaning of Work and the Job," *The American Sociological Review*, 20 (April 1955); from Elton F. Jackson and Harry Crokett, Jr., "Occupational Mobility in the United States," *American Sociological Review*, 29 (February 1964); and from Mapheus Smith, "An Empirical Scale of Prestige Status of Occupations," *American Sociological Review*, 8 (April 1943).

Basic Books, Inc., for excerpts from Dick Bruner, *Man, Work, and Society*, edited by Sigmund Nosow and William H. Form (Basic Books, Inc., New York, 1962); and from Theodore Caplow and Reece J. McGee, *The Academic Marketplace* (New York: Doubleday Anchor Book, 1965; Basic Books, Inc.).

Borenstein, Audrey Farrell, for excerpts from "The Ethical Ideal of the Professions" (Unpublished doctoral thesis), Louisiana State University, Baton Rouge, 1958.

Chamber of Commerce of the U.S.A. for Table, "Fringe Payments by Type of Payment, 1965" and for Table, "Comparison of . . . 86 Companies," *Fringe Benefits*, 1963 (Washington, D.C.: Chamber of Commerce of the U.S.A.).

Columbia University Press, for excerpts from Paul H. Douglas, *American Apprenticeship and Industrial Education*, (New York: Columbia University Press, 1921).

E. P. Dutton & Co., Inc., J. M. Dent & Sons, Ltd., for excerpts from Adam Smith, *The Wealth of Nations*. Vol. 1 (New York: E. P. Dutton and Co., 1957).

Harper & Row, Publishers, Inc., for excerpts from Russell Lynes, "How America 'Solved' the Servant Problem," *The Domesticated Americans* (New York: Harper & Row, Publishers, 1967).

Harvard University: Division of Research, for excerpts from Richard E. Walton, *The Impact of the Professional Engineering Union* (Boston, Division of Research, Harvard University Graduate School of Business Administration).

Harvard Business Review, for excerpts from David Mayer and Herbert M. Greenberg, "What Makes a Good Salesman," *Harvard Business Review*, 42 (July–August 1964).

Industrial Relations Research Association, for Table, "Social Status vs. Percent Unionized," by Bernard P. Indik and Bernard Goldstein: *Industrial Relations Research Association: Proceedings of the 16th Annual Meeting*, Publication No. 32, (Boston, Mass., December 27–28, 1963).

The Macmillan Company for excerpts from Emile Durkheim, *The Division of Labor*, Free Press, 1949; from Alvin W. Gouldner, *Patterns of Industrial Bureaucracy* (Glencoe: The Free Press, 1954); and from Paul F. Lazarsfield and Wagner Thielens, Jr., *The Academic Mind* (Glencoe: The Free Press, 1958).

McGraw-Hill Publishing Company, for excerpts from Maurine Clark, *Captain's Bride: General's Lady*, (New York: McGraw-Hill Book Co., Inc., 1956).

National Opinion Research Center, for excerpts from "Jobs and Occupations: A Popular Evaluation," *Opinion News*, IX (September 1, 1947).

Oxford University Press, Inc., for excerpts from H. H. Gerth and C. Wright Mills, *From Max Weber: Essays in Sociology*, (New York: Oxford University Press, 1946).

Pacific Sociological Review, for excerpts from Lionel S. Lewis and Joseph Lopreato, "Functional Importance and Prestige of Occupation," *The Pacific Sociological Review*, 6 (Fall 1963).

Pastoral Psychology, for excerpts from Robert Parks Rankin, "The Ministerial Calling and the Minister's Wife," *Pastoral Psychology*, 11 (September 1960).

Personnel Administrator, for Table, "Labor Force Participation Rates for Women," by Daniel H. Kruger, "Women at Work," *The Personnel Administrator*, 9 (July–August 1964).

Personnel and Guidance Journal, for excerpts from Odell Uzzell, "Influences of Occupational Choice," *The Personnel and Guidance Journal*, 39 (April 1961); and from Willa Freeman Grunes, "On Perception of Occupations," *The Personnel and Guidance Journal*, 34 (January 1956).

Society for the Study of Social Problems, for Table, "Total Central Life Interests," by Louis H. Orzack: "Work as a 'Central Life Interest' of Professionals," *Social Problems*, 7 (Fall 1959); and for excerpts from H. M. Blalock, Jr., "Occupational Discrimination: Some Theoretical Propositions" *Social Problems*, 9 (Winter 1962).

Sociology and Social Research, for Table, "Major Areas of Subject Matter in Occupational Sociology Articles," by Erwin O. Smigel et. al., "Occupational Sociology: A Reexamination," *Sociology and Social Research*, 47 (July 1963).

Time, Inc., for excerpts from: William H. Whyte, Jr., "The Wives of Management," *Fortune*, 44 (October 1951); from Ralph E. Lapp, "Where the Brains Are," *Fortune*, LXXIII (March 1966); and for Figure, "The Migratory Scientists."

University of Chicago Press for Table, "Forty Five Occupations Ranked According to Social Status," by George S. Counts, "The Social Status of Occupations, *The School Review*, Vol. XXXIII (1925); for Table, "Distributions of Prestige Ratings," by Robert W. Hodge et. al., "Occupational

Prestige in the United States, 1926–1963," *American Journal of Sociology*, LXX (November 1964); for excerpt from William H. Form and Delbert C. Miller, "Occupational Career Patterns as a Sociological Instrument," *The American Journal of Sociology*, 54 (January 1949); for Table, "Entering Dental Students. . . . ." by D. M. Moore and Nathan Kohn, Jr., "Some Motives for Entering Dentistry," *American Journal of Sociology*, 66 (July 1960); for excerpt from Paul K. Hatt, "Occupation and Social Stratification" *American Journal of Sociology*, 55 (May 1950); and for excerpts from Oswald Hall, "Types of Medical Careers," *American Journal of Sociology*, 55 (November 1949).

University of Michigan Press, for Table, "Employees' Reasons for Satisfaction with Job Activities," Lee E. Danielson, *Characteristics of Engineers and Scientists*, (Ann Arbor: University of Michigan Press, 1960).

University of Minnesota Press, for Table, "Occupational Mobility Rates. . . ." by W. Lloyd Warner and James C. Abegglen, *Occupation Mobility in American Business and Industry* (Minneapolis: University of Minnesota Press, 1955).

University of North Carolina Press, for excerpts from William A. Westly, "Secrecy and the Police," *Social Forces*, 34 (March 1956); from Raymond W. Mack, "Occupational Ideology and the Determinate Role," *Social Forces*, 36 (October 1957); from Charles M. Grigg and Russell Middleton, "Community of Orientation and Occupational Aspirations of Ninth Grade Students," *Social Forces*, 38 (May 1960); and for Table, "Methods Used to Advertise Vacancies," by David G. Brown, *The Market for College Teachers*, (Chapel Hill: University of North Carolina Press, 1965).

CONTENTS

Introduction   3

1 OCCUPATIONS AND SOCIAL ORGANIZATION

    I Occupations and Urbanized Social Organization   19
   II Multiplicity of Occupations   40
  III Occupations and Mobility   62
  IV Bureaucracy as an Occupational Environment   87
   V Professionalization as an Occupational Environment   115
  VI Unionization as an Occupational Environment   135
 VII Occupational Status and Prestige   164

2 OCCUPATIONAL STRUCTURES AND
   INSTITUTIONS

VIII Occupational Aspiration in Urbanized Society   189
  IX Preparing for an Occupation   220
   X Entering an Occupation   244
  XI Occupational Career Patterns   266
 XII Occupational Remuneration and Rewards   296
XIII Occupational Controls of Work Behavior   325
XIV Associations and Societies   344
 XV Retirement from Occupations   369

3 MEANING OF OCCUPATIONS FOR INDIVIDUALS
   AND SOCIETY

XVI Meaning of Work   395
XVII Colleagueship   413

XVIII   Occupational Ideologies   431

XIX   Occupations and Family Life   452

XX   Innovative Occupations: Professions and Executives   476

XXI   Clerical and Sales Occupations   492

XXII   Agribusiness Occupations   516

XXIII   Craft and Operative Occupations   537

XXIV   Service Occupations   563

Index   587

OCCUPATIONAL SOCIOLOGY

INTRODUCTION

Work is one of man's important social functions. Modern Western men are observed to work for sustenance, survival, status, and the avoidance of frustration. In recent times they have sought to make work respectable, indeed to glorify it. Leisure, work's presumed opposite, often has been viewed with suspicion or unacceptability. More persuasive than all of this, work in modern times has been a thing apart, largely separated from the remaining totality of life. One goes to the office, shop, store, factory, laboratory, and so forth. For most members of a modern industrial labor force the hours before and after work are precisely different in their nature and meaning from those hours devoted to work. The meaning of work has come to be a duty, privilege, responsibility, or something else, but always the means to accomplishment of some end which is nonwork. Few modern men experience work as a way of life.

Through the ages work has had different meanings.[1] For most men life and toil scarcely have been separated. With this historic integration of life and toil the number of separate and relatively distinct occupations has been few. In industrialized societies, where work and the rest of life are most distinctly separated, the number of occupations is observed to be greatly proliferated. In ages past the doctrine of work was seldom known. Moreover, work (including occupations) was held as a low estate. Most often work was viewed as brutalizing, dirty, or punishment for man's sinful nature.

The Greco-Roman view of work. The Greeks were forthright in their judgment. Work was a curse and little else. Emphatically their name for it was sorrow and their emotion for it was fatigue and burden. They believed that men had to work because the gods hated men and condemned them thus. Or, put another way, they believed that work was

3

the price that the gods charged for the goods of life. When faced with giving some hierarchy to the various occupations, agriculture was viewed as less unworthy of a citizen than other work because it contributed to livelihood and independence. Mechanical arts were lower and viewed as brutalizing to the mind. Artisans and craftsmen, even when free, were considered in a category little above the slave's, if that. Even the work of creative artists was held in low esteem. At the apex of the occupational hierarchy the Greeks placed pure science.

The Roman view of work was greatly similar to that of the Greeks. For free men the only occupations of value were agriculture first and big business second. But these were of high esteem only when they led the practitioners to honorable retirement as gentlemen in rural areas. All other skilled and managerial work was held to be regrettable even though necessary.

Hebrew and Persian notions of work. The Hebrew view of work contained much of the thought expressed by the Greeks and the Romans. There was concurrence in the expression that work was necessary to expiate Original Sin. But for the Hebrews there was also another dimension to the condition of man's toil. Work, they believed, was the law of man's existence and therefore more than punishment for sin. Work was man's duty in leading the world back from sin and into divine harmony. The world was not something for passive contemplation, but something to be realized most fully through man's efforts. There must be continued work to restore the harmony that was destroyed by Original Sin. This process of work was to end in justice and happiness, indeed the Kingdom of God on earth.[2]

Many of the prophets and rabbis went at length to undermine the prestige of economic work. Such materialism, they asserted, took time away from devotion to spiritual life. Beyond such activity, however, there was often praise for other work. It was expressed that work is cooperation with God and consistent with the route to salvation. The acceptable nature of work was no more clearly asserted than in the notion that idleness was offensive. It directed one to lasciviousness and in all manner it was lower than labor in its lowliest form. The Pharisees expressed the notion that manual labor was preferable to idleness and a part of the condition of health. Accordingly, they held a father was obligated to teach his son an honest occupation. In summary, the Hebrews believed that the forms of work, even if they resulted in condemnation, was a superior adjustment to man's plight than idleness.

Further east, the Persian view of work was even more positive than that of the Hebrews. The view was not clear or without its share of conjecture, but in essence it was a doctrine with relatively more praise for labor, thrift, and property. The owner of land was viewed as superior to the non-owner, the possessor of a house as superior to the non-possessor, the richer man as more desirable than the poorer man, the well-fed man as more acceptable than the hungry man. Vigor, labor, and work which led to all of these ends were in the main acceptable conditions to the Persian.

The Christian view: early and medieval. The teachings of Jesus were multiple and complex. On the one hand, he was recorded as saying, "Therefore I say unto you, Take no thought for your life, what ye shall eat, or what ye shall drink; nor yet for your body, what ye shall put on. Is not the life more than meat, and the body than raiment?" [3]

On the other hand, the early Christians believed that while work might be punishment for Original Sin, it was necessary to work to earn one's living; work was a form of behavior superior to the asking for alms. Even the acquisition of material goods was held as a value when the goods were shared in charity with one's brothers. In this manner work and occupation gained a respectability in early Christendom. Moreover, the early Christian view did not distinguish clearly between mental and manual work.

St. Augustine made it clear that work should be obligatory for monks. Occupation in handicrafts, tilling of the soil, and small commerce were all approved as long as the seller accepted only a just price and did not participate in usury. Big enterprise was condemned when it was conceived as an entity in and for itself. St. Benedict charged, "Work, do not despair." Work was not exulted in and for itself, but it was the mechanism by which one achieved purity, charity, and expiation.

In the medieval period work gradually gained respectability. St. Thomas Aquinas ranked the occupations. Agriculture was first, followed by handicrafts, and commerce was last, but regardless of rank work was considered necessary and acceptable. To the Scholastics work was a natural right and duty. St. Antoninus of Florence and St. Bernardin of Sienna spoke out boldly against idleness; they approved industry and activity. The genesis of capitalism was thus approved.

The Reformation: Luther and Calvin. Work has been largely established in the modern mind as a key to life itself through the mechanism of Protestantism. Its major spokesmen in this behalf were Luther
and Calvin. For Luther, work was natural and required. Indeed, a mo-
nastic, contemplative life was disdained as egotism and to be avoided.
Work was of the highest order of respectability when the goal and end
was self-maintenance and maintenance of society. Self-aggrandizement,
or climbing in the social hierarchy by one's own work effort, was heart-
ily disdained. The calling to work was an ordinance of God. All occupations, therefore, are important. To view them in hierarchy is to go
against the will of God and the blessedness of man.

The case for work as expressed by Calvin was clear and unrelent-
ing. God was absolute power and energy, man was nothing. Man's purpose was the glorification of God. Man by his own striving and occupational effort could in no way ensure his salvation. But man as the instrument of God would act, and the Calvinist would never rest as if his
election were certainly proven. Under this dictum all men were to
work, both rich and poor, because it was the will of God. This view of
work produced a new man—active, austere, and hard working. Ease
and luxury were denied as sinful. To dislike work was to suggest that
one's election was doubtful. Contemplation was thought to be insufficient, and work as a service to God was necessary.[4]

The importance of Calvin's view for modern times is the contribution of the idea of success. Achievement and success in one's occupation or work was the revelation that the activity was pleasing in the
sight of God. In striking contrast to Luther, Calvin viewed achievement and mobility in the hierarchy as a proper condition. Certainly,
satisfaction with one's lot was viewed as lazy and unrespectable.

The Renaissance. In the Renaissance a sensate view of occupational
endeavor became widely articulated. The trend was away from God
and the hereafter. One focused on oneself, accomplishment, and success. Of great importance was the high view and respect given to man
as a creator. Man himself had a right and responsibility to be innovative, imaginative, and productive. Achievement in material things, arts,
and inventions of all descriptions was held in a new and high esteem.
Notions of progress and the dignity of man were elevated to high and
lofty places. In sum, it was felt that civilization would be known as the
fruit of man, human activity, labor, and productiveness.

Modern doctrines of work: Bolshevism, Fascism, and the Protestant Ethic. In the modern view one finds from many sources the notion that a well-organized society should insure to its citizenry the right to work. Under these conditions the imaginations of men are pushed to points of highest dignity. Men are awarded for seeking to invent machines that will reduce human drudgery. Men should work, but their efforts should be directed to the construction of mechanisms for eliminating hardship and monotony from the toil of life. Leisure should be one of the rewards of work. In the modern view there is much need for social legislation to insure the rights of man and the dignity of work. Bolshevism is an example *par excellence* of such a position. In 1918 it was asserted by the Bolshevist government that parasitic classes were to be destroyed; work would be required of all people. The Union of Soviet Socialist Republics required that one work in order to eat.[5] The prominence of occupation in the character of such social organization is undebatable. The alternative seems to be: work if you want to, but if you want to exist you must work.

The Fascist view of work was similar to that of the Bolshevist, but broader. In 1922 the Fascist Co-operative Convention proclaimed in essence that: (1) work is the means by which men legally obtain full and useful citizenship in their society; (2) work is the appropriate mechanism for creating, perfecting, and increasing man's mental, moral, and spiritual well-being; (3) "workers" are all people who dedicate their activity to the above tasks and therefore they must all be admitted to work opportunities without discrimination; and (4) the nation is above all classes and categories of workers.[6] The Fascists viewed all forms of work as respectable and as a social duty. Man was encouraged in his technical, manual, and intellectual achievements. With all of these forms of work no special rights and privileges were achieved. The nature of work was an expectation and not a matter of reward.

The gospel of work in Protestant America has been a driving force, a synthesis of many of the traditions previously outlined for Europe. That gospel might be summarized as glorifying man's accomplishment by sweat and toil. Idleness, riches, and luxury were viewed with suspicion. The building of fortunes, capitalist monuments, were acceptable when accompanied by philanthropies.

Affluent society and automation. The most recent view of work is characterized by affluency and challenged—or frustrated—by automation. The affluent society is the expression of accomplishment, achievement for all, abundance for the many. But affluence in consort with automation reduces the amount of human sweat and toil that is prerequisite for high levels of occupational attainment. The high dignity that was placed on individual toil in the eighteenth, nineteenth, and early twentieth centuries is reduced in its importance. It is now often dysfunctional. Automation displaces men from toil in factories, offices, and fields. The material accomplishment is great, but the appreciation is often limited. Students of history understand that the ancient Greeks viewed toil as brutalizing to the dignity of man. But the average man of contemporary society has little knowledge of and less appreciation for the views of the ancient Greeks. He understands work more than he appreciates leisure. The paradox is largely that the affluent automated society has achieved to a great degree for the masses what the aristocrats of Greece held in high judgment for the few and were unable to achieve for the masses. One society had the ideology, another society has the achievement; the two have yet to meet for the establishment of a bold new social order.

A CONCEPT OF OCCUPATIONS

The term "occupation" is widely used, but with divergency of meaning. The character and meaning of occupation has changed considerably from one time and one place to another. From the point of view of occupational sociology a specific conceptual formulation is needed.

Occupational and non-occupational work. First, a distinction is necessary between occupational and non-occupational work. Salz has suggested that the notion of occupation must cover three sets of conditions, namely, technological, economic, and social. Accordingly, he defined occupation as "That specific activity with a market value which an individual continually pursues for the purpose of obtaining a steady flow of income; this activity also determines the social position of the individual." [7]

Occupation is one of the most revealing characteristics concerning individuals and the society of which it is a part. Yet all people do not have occupations. An occupation can normally be listed for those individuals who are gainfully employed in the labor force. But for children of a young age, full-time students, and aged, the infirm, housewives, and for the few privileged whose sustenance needs are provided without work, no real occupation can be objectively indicated. To confound the issue of occupation even more, it must be noted that some individuals will in quick serial order, if not simultaneously, participate in multiple types of work tasks; the occupation of a person may change over a period of time in his life. And finally some individuals may alternately work and be unemployed.

"Work" is a basic condition and a generic term. "Occupation" in its verb form, "to occupy," may also be viewed as basic or generic. From a sociological point of view, work in an occupation is more limited, precise, and specific. One man or woman carrying out a task of work in isolation, in a solitary way, and with little interaction or cognizance of other individuals who participate in a similar work, is not viewed as behaving occupationally by sociologists. Occupation, sociologically speaking, involves a degree of corporateness, a degree of consciousness of kind, and a reciprocity between the acting individuals in the occupation and the recognition of these individuals in the occupation on the part of the larger society. For example, one may observe that a flagpole sitter is occupied, but an occupation of flagpole sitters is yet to be identified. Flagpole sitters may be multiple in number or have existed from one time and place to another, but ideology, corporate knowledge, and interaction among flagpole sitters is seldom if ever a matter of record. Many men may work at jobs that are essentially unique and vitally important, as illustrated by new jobs in space science. Such jobs are nonoccupational work.[8]

Jobs and positions. Jobs may be distinguished as having a high degree of specificity. They have titles which describe the work and work area. For example, a job might have the title automatic screw machine set-up man, floor molder, punch press operator, typist I, file clerk, maintenance electrician, washroom attendant, receptionist, overhead crane operator, crane hooker, die sinker, gear hopper, fur beater, doughnut pumper, or grinding wheel dresser.[9] It is typical of such job titles that both the work and the area of work are largely illustrated.

Positions may be differentiated from jobs. A position title is less specific than a job title. Examples of position titles are foreman, supervisor, department head, administrative assistant, accountant, or engineer.[10] The title used in a position will normally indicate the work area, but often will not denote the specific content of the work. A foreman may work in a shoe factory, a chemical plant, or an automobile factory. The specific details of the work will vary considerably with the place of work.

Recruitment into jobs is normally uncomplicated. The tasks required even when complex are usually so specified that one may obtain the facility in a brief instruction period on the job. Movement of people into positions is typically more complicated. Some prior experience is normally required.

Initiative on the part of jobholders is usually abhorrent, a quality unsought. The task of a jobholder by nature is routine. Its dimensions are specified by some individual in a superior position in the hierarchy. Initiative on the part of jobholders will most often contribute frustration and lower efficiency rather than accomplishment and improvement in performance. Those who hold positions, on the other hand, are given some latitude for individual initiative. Indeed, they are to some extent expected by definition of their position to interpret, mold, and direct the character of the position itself.

In contrast to jobs and positions, occupations have an enduring superstructure character which continues on by tradition before and after specific individual participants hold the occupations. Occupations are corporate. Surrounding them there is some articulated or covert ideological notion. There is a consciousness of kind on the part of participants in a given occupation. An occupation is a complex normative system within which people act for production, economic sustenance, status, and the fulfillment of meaning.

Occupation as a sociological concept. The sociological concept of occupation may be defined as a patterned set of human relations having to do with specific work experiences. The integration of the patterned work relations precipitates the development of occupational structures and the manifestation of occupational ideologies. Ideology and identity are central to the sociological notion and experience of occupation.

Integral components of the sociological concept of occupation include career, status, prestige, mobility, images, clients, culture, structure, recruitment, remuneration, and control. One might study the career stages of an individual or individuals in an occupation. The career stages might be hierarchically organized so that one enters at a low level and under given conditions progresses through a hierarchy and by the normal expectation reaches a higher level prior to retirement from the occupation. The status and prestige of an occupation are reciprocally achieved by its participants and awarded by the society of which it is a part. Mobility may be observed on the part of practitioners within an occupation or between occupations. One might also observe that some entire occupations have been mobile from one status in the society to another. Occupational images are a matter of considerable concern in an urbanized society. The quality of practitioner performance may elevate or reduce the image of an occupation. Interaction between clients and occupational men is important. In some cases the clients are superordinate, in other cases subordinate. The culture within which occupational men work varies greatly from time to time and place to place. The social structure of a society and the original structure of an occupation are juxtaposed in power shifts as the occupation expands or contracts. The nature of recruitment into an occupation illustrates its importance, power, and contribution to society and individuals. The remuneration and rewards of occupational participants may contribute to hierarchy in the total society, or the obliteration of hierarchy. The control of occupations typically may be held by the practitioners themselves, as in the case of professions, or it may be external and largely a function of the greater society of which the occupation is an integral part. These norms of occupations express the sociological concept.

Occupation and way of life. The experience of occupation is most precise when work is clearly separated from the bulk of the remainder of life. For this reason the power and significance of occupations have been of paramount importance in the eighteenth, nineteenth, and twentieth centuries. More often than at other times in history most men during these periods have gone to work. That is, they leave their home or place of domicile and go to another location to work in a factory, store, office, etc. Throughout much of the earlier history of humankind work and the greater totality of life were little separated.

In the second half of the twentieth century some occupational experiences, most often in the professions, have been reverting back to type, and the participants are now unable to clearly distinguish their work experience from the balance of their totality of life. The work of professional men in the clergy, teaching, law, medicine, and so forth is so intertwined with their style of life, their income, their education, their place of residence, their size of family, and their amount of leisure that the separation of their life and work is more a matter of academics than perceived reality. For contemporary artists much of the same situation prevails; life and work are intensely integrated. Aside from the professionals the life and work experience of executives is also greatly integrated. In roles of other-directedness the leisure and family life of executives struggling for power often are wound through a great labyrinth with their occupational endeavor.

With the increase of professionals and executives in the occupational world it is suggested by some that the separation of occupation and life is becoming somewhat reduced in the second half of the twentieth century. Should this situation continue to obtain, the power and significance of occupations in social organization might well be contracted if not sharply reduced.

Boundary maintenance. One of the fundamental conditions for the vast majority of occupations in contemporary urbanized society is boundary maintenance. In order to distinguish several thousands of occupations it is necessary to specify in the process of categorization the boundary or points of separation. It is the nature of occupations for their boundaries to be malleable, indeed to change over a period of time, yet boundaries may also be stable and enduring over a considerable period, so that the notion of boundary among occupations is a viable one.

The genesis of a boundary is a matter of reciprocity and negotiation partly initiated by the participants of the occupation and partly issued by the society of which it is a part. And so it is in the mass urbanized society that occupations may grow in size and function and over the course of time experience a great shift in their character and meaning. Or occupations may be rigid in maintaining their boundaries, become nearly static in their character, and in many cases face contraction, if not obliteration. For example, medical doctors in the practice of their occupation may have the alternative of rigidly controlling the character of their field, or they may be expansive and allow the many new disciplines that border upon medicine to come within the domain of the parent occupation. If medicine becomes expansive its image and function may change. If it becomes rigidly restrictive it may exclude many of the new disciplines and thereby contribute to their becoming free-standing occupations over which the parent occupation has little or no control and with which the parent occupation may ultimately be thrust in vital competition. Although malleable and fluid the notion of boundary maintenance is one of the most persistent and important aspects of the concept of occupation.

DEVELOPMENT OF OCCUPATIONAL SOCIOLOGY

The sociologist's interest in man's work and occupations is of long standing. In much of the writing of sociology one finds both implicit and explicit reference to work, occupations, and professions. Empirical research in occupations, however, is of more recent origin; it has developed largely since the late 1940's in the United States. In recent years the amount of empirical inquiry into the nature and condition of occupations has been vast, and the body of information is more than sufficient for it to be distinguished as one of the important areas of sociological inquiry.

European antecedents. Division of labor is a central notion in occupational sociology. Important writings which stated the notion date from the early period of sociology in Europe; Emile Durkheim's *The Division of Labor in Society* (1893) is a signal example of this contribution. The working conditions of people in several occupations constituted part of the empirical inquiry of Frederick LePlay. Max Weber contributed to the understanding of occupations in his emphasis on political, scientific, and professional work. The salaried employee and the manual worker were studied in Germany.[11] These writings and others illustrate the questions concerning occupational man from an early time in European sociology.

American investigations: empiricism. The American sociological experience in the study of occupations is viable, colorful, and important. In the United States, occupational sociology reached high importance, indeed fashion, in the early years (1920 to 1930) at the University of Chicago. First, there were the studies of the low status occupations. These included hoboes, prostitutes, jackrollers, and taxi dance hall girls. Soon they were supplemented by studies of schoolteachers, salesladies, and waitresses. The study of occupations spread to other universities, and the range of inquiry also was broadened. It included studies of professionals—academic men, physicians, ministers, and others.

In addition to breadth, the subject of occupational sociology took avenues of depth. Inquiry was made not only into the totality of an occupation, but into the normative condition of occupations. Studies were made of careers, recruitment, ethics, clients, and many other aspects of occupations. The themes of inquiry in occupational sociology might be listed as follows: (1) the behavioral nature of work, (2) the structure of occupations, (3) the description and analysis of individual occupations, (4) the study of occupational mobility.

TABLE INTRO. 1

Major Areas of Subject Matter in Occupational Sociology Articles, 1946–52 and 1953–59

| | Per Cent | |
Area Studied	1946–52	1953–59
Career	23.2	12.9
Occupational status and mobility	14.1	21.0
Ethnic group and occupations	13.6	8.2
Working force	10.7	8.2
Occupational role and personality	8.5	16.4
Occupational images	6.8	5.1
Occupational comparisons	3.9	5.1
Methodology	3.9	7.7
Client-professional relations	2.8	1.0
Occupational culture and ethics	2.3	9.8
Miscellaneous	10.2	4.6
Total Per Cent	100.0	100.0
Total Number of Articles	177	195

Source: Erwin O. Smigel, et al., "Occupational Sociology: A Re-examination," Sociology and Social Research, 47 (July 1963), 475.

The subject areas in occupational sociology are illustrated in Table Intro. 1, which indicates an over-all increase in the total study of occupations. The subjects of occupational mobility, occupation role and personality, and career are numerically the most frequent.

When the studies of occupational sociology are classified according to the Alba Edwards Scale it is clear that inquiry into the professions is far more frequent than into other occupational categories. The second most frequent category of study includes the proprietors and managers. It is clear that those occupations on the upper half of the socio-economic continuum are researched more than, indeed, out of proportion to, those of the lower half of the continuum.

Contemporary European investigations. Modern, empirical occupational sociology is found in many areas, and European sociology is continually being enriched by inquiry into occupations. In France, England, Norway, Denmark, Germany, and other nations the report of occupational conditions is found with considerable frequency. There have also been cooperative international studies of occupations. The systematic comparison of education and income with size of family and occupation is available on an international basis; similarly, occupational status and intergenerational mobility is being researched internationally.

The development of occupational sociology is of recent origin. Intensive empirical inquiry is a matter of record both in Europe and America, and the findings are rich with insight. Man's knowledge of his occupations is multiplying.

NOTES

1. Adriano Tilgher, *Homo Faber: Work through the Ages* (Chicago: Henry Regnery Co., 1929–1958). This section draws heavily on this book.
2. Ibid. pp. 13–14.
3. *The Holy Bible* (New York: World Syndicate Company, Inc., 1923), Matthew, 6:25.
4. Tilgher, *Homo Faber,* p. 59.
5. Ibid. p. 116.
6. Ibid. pp. 119–20.
7. Arthur Salz, "Occupation," in Edwin R. A. Seligman (ed.), *Encyclopedia of the Social Sciences* (New York: The Macmillan Company, 1933), vol. 11, pp. 424ff.
8. Lee Taylor, "The Life Insurance Man: A Sociological Analysis of the Occupation" (Unpublished Ph.D. Thesis, Louisiana State University, Baton Rouge, La., 1958), p. 31; and Carroll L. Shartel, *Occupational Information* (2nd Ed.; New York: Prentice-Hall, Inc., 1953), p. 26.
9. Robert Dubin, *The World of Work* (Englewood Cliffs, N.J.: Prentice-Hall, Inc., 1958), pp. 85–6.
10. Ibid. p. 85.
11. Carl Dreyfuss, *Occupation and Ideology of the Salaried Employee* (New York: Columbia University Press, 1938); and Henri DeMan, *Joy in Work* (London: George Allen & Unwin, Ltd., 1929).

SUPPLEMENTARY READINGS

Materials suggested in the supplementary reading list at the end of each chapter are specifically selected for introductory students or persons to whom occupational subject matter is new. The lists are short because they are intended to be supplemental to the chapters. They include only the most basic materials for increasing depth in scholarship. The items are also selected for their availability to facilitate course organization.

READINGS FOR INTRODUCTION

Adriano Tilgher, *Homo Faber: Work Through the Ages* (Chicago: Henry Regnery Co., 1929–1958), paperback.
Arthur Salz, "Occupation," in Edwin R. A. Seligman (ed.), *Encyclopedia of the Social Sciences* (New York: The Macmillan Company, 1933), vol. 11.

OCCUPATIONS AND SOCIAL ORGANIZATION 1

Occupations are an integral part of society. They are directly related to the production and distribution of goods and services. When they become highly organized they may have sufficient power to influence societal organization, but in most cases societal organization makes definitive impacts on occupations. In Part One the various influences of society on occupations are examined.

Here we will discuss the relations of occupations to social organization. We will start with the phenomenon of urbanized society, and examine the fact that most workers are employees. We will then study the multiplicity of occupations, with the focus on division of labor and census enumerations. The mobility characteristics of American society are partly a function of the organization of occupations, and they also determine occupational structures.

Three chapters in Part One deal with the specialized environments of bureaucracy, professionalization, and unionization. Each of these environments are part of the urbanized society, and each makes a different impact on occupational organization.

Part One concludes with a chapter on status and prestige. Both of these phenomena are of major importance to American societal configuration. To a degree they are implemented by occupational structures, and to a degree occupational organizations create a propitious situation for the development of status and prestige norms.

OCCUPATIONS AND URBANIZED SOCIAL ORGANIZATION I

The occupational structures of a society are integrally related to the social organization of that society. Observations of agrarian society, industrial society, and employee society provide considerable insight into the occupational structures and social organization of a society. Alba M. Edwards has written:

. . . There probably is no single set of closely related facts that tell so much about a nation as do detailed statistics of the occupations of its workers. The occupations of the people influence directly their lives, their customs, their institutions—indeed, their very numbers. . . . And, were the figures available, the social and industrial history of a people might be traced more accurately through detailed statistics of the occupations of its gainful workers than through records of its wars, its territorial conquests, and its political struggles.[1]

The importance of occupations for understanding the social organization of modern Western societies is further illustrated when one observes that 50 to 60 per cent of the population of labor-force age (14 and over) is typically engaged in the world of work. The study of dependency ratios which relates the proportion of workers (people between the ages of 20 and 64) per 100 people in the pre-work and post-work periods indicates the amount of burden on occupational men. From 1820 to 1940 the burden on occupational men was lightened; the dependency ratio declined. By the middle of the twentieth century dependency of older people was increasing sharply. Following World War II the baby boom caused an increasing dependency for the pre-labor force ages. This greater dependency pressure on the labor force contributes to lower rates of unemployment, and, in the nature of United States social organization, more people become employees.

Peter Drucker refers to the United States as an employee society.[2] The observation is clear and revealing concerning the social organization. Most of the people who work in this society are employed by some large firm or government agency. This is in sharp contrast to the historical tradition of the United States, in which workers prided themselves in being owners of the tools of production, owners of their own land or stores; indeed, free entrepreneurs who directed their own work. As the nation has shifted rapidly from agrarianism to an urbanized social organization, its workers have shifted from a self-employed to an employee condition. The 1960 Census reveals less than 16 per cent of the labor force as self-employed and 84 per cent as employees.[3]

Salz has gone so far as to develop a typology of societal organization, ranging from corporate to occupational.[4] He identifies corporate social organization as a nearly static condition, most exemplified by caste systems of stratification. Occupational social organization, he asserts, is characteristic of an open or free societal development. Modern Western societies, according to this typology, are characteristically at the open or free occupational end of the continuum, but fall short of the ideal type. This is to say, modern society lies somewhere between the two extremes because many of the occupations in contemporary social life are developing something of a manifest corporate organization in and of themselves. Professions, exemplified by the ministry, law, teaching, and medicine, tend to take on a corporate existence as they manage to maintain a considerable boundary around their organizations. By contrast, in many other occupations there is a great fluidity as one moves into and out of the type of work.

Corporate organization of society is clearly illustrated on the European Continent as early as the twelfth century. The practice of an occupation was a matter of privilege or heredity more than of individual choice. Guild membership was central to the practice of an occupation, and membership was a function of social class. Moreover, town councils regulated occupations.[5]

With the Industrial Revolution the guild system declined in its occupational importance. In the seventeenth and eighteenth centuries occupational divisions of labor became characterized by their extreme proliferation and diversification. Working categories came into existence, so that in some places industrial managers and their employees stood in important contrast to each other. The social structures of bourgeoisie versus proletariat and of management versus union were a product of this phase of occupational organization.

OCCUPATIONS AND SOCIAL ORGANIZATION

Freedom of occupational choice and notions of *laissez faire* followed in the new industrial urbanized societies. Workers in the labor force were theoretically free to seek employment and sell their services at will. This was facilitated by a technology which provided rapid transportation and rapid communication of employment opportunities in various areas. From this period there developed the norm of mobility whereby people were expected to move for occupational opportunity.

Notions of occupational specialization, in contrast to occupational generalization, have grown from the writings and experiences of men like Adam Smith and Frederick Taylor. The first was concerned with the economic efficiency and the latter was concerned with the training and utilization of men much as if they were machines. Such notions of job specification were implicitly more addressed to societal conditions than to worker satisfactions. In the past century, job specialization was pushed to such a stage in the United States that by 1965 the *Dictionary of Occupational Titles* [6] listed 21,741 separate occupations. And although evidence is far from complete, that which exists suggests that rural youth consider 10 to 12 occupational alternatives while urban youth consider about 16 in the so-called free occupational type of society.[7] It is observed here that this extreme occupational diversification is dysfunctional from the point of view of the individual's effective choosing, if not for the society as a whole. While theoretically free to choose an occupation, there are no adequate mechanisms in the society whereby occupational aspirants are given a basis for understanding the multiple occupational opportunities, on the one hand, and for evaluating their occupational aptitudes, on the other. In short, most employees enter the job market with a limited range of knowledge and experience. One's choice of an occupation is more influenced by his immediate social space than by a rational approach to the total labor market. Hence, in the free society there is a considerable dilemma in the processes of recruiting highly capable and highly skilled manpower into those occupations where they are most needed for the societal organization. There is no ideological space whereby the political institutions are given power to assign men to specific jobs. The freedom-of-choice recruitment mechanisms often do not function in the greatest interest of individuals or the total society.

Recent research contributes new insights into the meaning of work. The findings suggest that the extreme job specification which leads to the identification of over 20,000 occupations often does not comparably lead to worker satisfaction. This minute specificity of job experience gives workers little basis for identifying with their work. Consequently, their work becomes a means for achieving the economic remuneration necessary for a gratifying life away from their job. Worker turnover, job mobility, high sickness rates, and so forth are all norms which confound the industrial organization of the urbanized society.

As gratification in the work experience has been reduced, there has developed a counterbalancing trend, both in Europe and the United States, referred to as job enlargement.[8] Along with job enlargement is an entire social structure identified as human relations in industry. To counter the dysfunctionalness of the Frederick Taylor tradition, efforts are now being made to incorporate the work space of employees into the entire fabric of the plant or industry where they are employed.

Where occupations are extensively organized their fluidity adds complexity to the total social organization. In the rapid changes of the contemporary United States some jobs have gone out of existence completely (e.g. beach-comber, coconut shaver, rumble seat assembler, wagon-smith) and new jobs have come into existence (e.g. accelerator operator, artificial inseminator, audiovisual specialist, shrimp-peeling-machine operator).[9] In other cases a job title may continue but the content of work that is in the job may be changed. Furthermore, the social prestige of an entire work category may be increased or decreased in accordance with other changes in the social organization. The configuration of a society is sharply changed when many hoe and dig jobs are replaced by industrial jobs.

Occupational fluidity in the United States has become so great in the second half of the twentieth century that the normal amount of vocational training which one receives in the public schools is no longer adequate to provide occupational skill for the complete duration of one's work years. In the eighteenth and early nineteenth centuries one largely gained occupational skill by the participant observation method. By the late nineteenth and first half of the twentieth century occupational skills were so diversified that much of the educational institution of the nation was in effect a vocational training mechanism. By the second half of the twentieth century it became apparent that vocational training must be a continuous experience throughout the employment years. This specific condition can be observed in the many vocational classes, programs for continuation of education, correspondence education, and a whole variety of so-called short courses which are aimed at enabling the on-the-job-labor force to maintain a current conversancy with the ever-increasing number of skills needed in the occupational world of the urbanized social organization.

Finally, one may learn much about the social organization of a society from the statistics which report the occupational categories of the labor force. The occupational statistics that have been variously reported since 1870 to 1960 constitute a penetrating review of the shift in the nation's social organization from agrarianism, a hoe and dig society, to industrial-professionalism, a trade and think society. Expressions like "white-collar workers" and "blue-collar workers" reveal much about the level of technology and the socio-economic conditions of the people in society.

During the first half of the twentieth century there were major shifts in the nation's labor force. During this period it became clear that owners of small farms, small businessmen, and fee-taking professionals were relegated more to the area of history and away from the dominance of the occupational organization of the nation. This era saw the end of the captains of industry and rugged individualism. They were replaced by the organizational men, other-directedness, and the employee society. White-collar workers were experiencing the greatest increase ever. These included the clerical, sales, and professional occupations.

Masses of schoolteachers, sales workers, and office employees dominated this category of white-collar workers. Old-line classical learned professions, including ministry, law, medicine, teaching, etc., had an increase in the number of practitioners, but it was minimal compared to that in the newer occupations. For example, these kinds of old-line professionals increased by some sixfold from 1870 to the 1950's. By sharp contrast, the number of engineers, chemists, designers, and draftsmen increased from a mere 9000 in 1870 to more than 700,000 in 1950.[10] Most of the white-collar workers, whose number increased most precipitously, were salaried rather than fee-taking. Similarly, there was a marked increase in the semi-professionals, including laboratory and X-ray technicians, engineering aides, electronics technicians, etc.

More recently, particularly since 1940, there has been a significant increase in the number of proprietors, officials, and managers. These are primarily salaried organizational men filling middle range managerial ranks in the expanding large corporations. They are employee managers of lower ranking employees, rather than owners of businesses and industries.

The proportion of manual workers remained almost unchanged between 1910 and 1950, 37 and 39 per cent, respectively. Within this category there were some important changes. Unskilled workers declined from approximately 12 to 6 per cent, operatives increased by 4 per cent, and craft workers showed little change, ranging from 12 to 13 per cent, respectively.

Changes in the labor force in the first half of the twentieth century further illustrate the movement of workers out of primary industries, namely, agriculture, lumbering, mining, and fishing, into secondary industries, namely, manufacturing and construction. Even more, they show the movement of people into tertiary industries, exemplified by those in various services, public administration, finance, real estate and insurance, entertainment and recreation services, and the professions. About half of the nation's labor force by the twentieth century was in occupations which relied heavily on education and which were characterized by customer or by client contact. By the middle of the twentieth century the nation's labor force was characterized by extensive occupational specialization. Occupational organization moved from hard physical work in the direction of more brain work.[11]

PRESENT OCCUPATIONAL STRUCTURE AND SOCIAL ORGANIZATION

By mid-century the occupational statistics for the nation illustrated a new kind of social organization. Idea people were coming rapidly to dominate both the occupational and social organizational structure of the nation. They included approximately 20 per cent of the labor force, about half of whom were professionals and technical experts and half of whom were managers, officials, and proprietors. To a great extent the work of all the remaining occupational people of the nation depends on and is ultimately directed by the idea people. They are directly supported by an adjacent but subordinate category of clerical and kindred workers (14 per cent) of the labor force. Under their technical and managerial direction another large segment of the labor force, more than 40 per cent, is engaged in specific jobs carrying out basic production, processing, and distributing the goods and services necessary for the operation of the urbanized society. This large category of workers includes farmers, craftsmen, operatives, and sales persons. At the bottom of the occupational hierarchy are another 20 per cent of the labor force. These workers are in service and laboring occupations. They are more directly related to the producing, processing, and distributing occupations immediately above them.[12]

By the 1960's the census data showed a continual expansion of the dominance of idea and white-collar people. The 1960 Census was the first to record that white-collar workers outnumbered manual workers in the nation, 43 per cent compared to 39 per cent, respectively.[13] More

TABLE I.1

Distribution of Employed Civilian Workers, by Occupational Groups and Selected Occupations, United States,[a] 1950 and 1960

Occupation groups and selected occupations	1960 Number	%	1950 Number	%	Per cent Change
All employed persons	64,639,247		56,435,273		14.5
Persons with occupations reported	61,455,572	100.0	55,692,340	100.0	10.3
White-collar workers	26,587,834	43.3	20,819,314	37.4	27.7
Professional, technical & kindred workers	7,232,410	11.8	4,921,272	8.8	47.0
Engineers, technical [d]	853,738	1.4	519,680	.9	64.3
Chemical	41,026	.1	32,543	.1	26.1
Civil	155,173	.3	125,125	.2	24.0
Electrical	183,887	.3	105,887	.2	73.7
Industrial	97,458	.2	40,278	.1	142.0
Mechanical	158,188	.3	112,440	.2	40.7
Sales	56,836	.1	24,734	(b)	129.8
Natural scientists	149,330	.2	116,918	.2	27.7
Biological scientists	13,937	(b)	9,215	(b)	51.2
Chemists	83,420	.1	74,637	.1	11.8
Mathematicians	7,527	(b)	1,691	(b)	345.1
Physicists	13,941	(b)	7,422	(b)	87.8

TABLE I.1 (cont.)

Occupation groups and selected occupations	1960 Number	%	1950 Number	%	Per cent Change
Medical & other health workers	1,305,901	2.1	1,007,515	1.8	29.6
Dentists	83,003	.1	75,355	.1	10.2
Dietitians & nutritionists	26,119	(b)	22,474	(b)	16.2
Nurses, student professional & professional	639,719	1.0	476,647	.9	34.2
Physicians & surgeons	228,926	.4	192,520	.3	18.9
Technicians, medical & dental	138,162	.2	76,662	.1	80.2
Teachers, elementary & secondary schools	1,521,590	2.5	1,042,809	1.8	45.9
Other professional, technical & kindred workers	3,401,851	5.5	2,234,350	4.0	52.3
Accountants & auditors	471,302	.8	378,055	.7	24.7
Lawyers & judges	212,408	.3	181,646	.3	16.9
Technicians, electrical & electronic	91,463	.1	11,738	(b)	679.2
Technicians, other engineering & physical science	183,609	.3	90,995	.2	101.8
Managers, officials, & proprietors except farm	5,409,543	8.8	5,036,808	9.0	7.4
Salaried	3,387,918	5.5	2,508,984	4.5	35.0
Self-employed	2,021,625	3.3	2,527,824	4.5	−20.0
Clerical & kindred workers	9,306,896	15.1	6,954,440	12.5	33.8
Secretaries, stenographers & typists c	2,178,641	3.5	1,507,649	2.7	44.5
Other clerical workers	7,128,255	11.6	5,446,791	9.8	30.9
Cashiers	468,950	.8	231,382	.4	102.7
Office-machine operators	307,828	.5	142,350	.3	116.2
Sales workers	4,638,985	7.5	3,906,794	7.0	18.7
Retail trade	2,694,745	4.4	2,449,760	4.4	10.0
Other than retail trade	1,944,240	3.2	1,457,034	2.6	33.4
Insurance agents, brokers & underwriters	364,557	.6	272,663	.5	33.7
Real estate agents & brokers	193,104	.3	141,003	.3	37.0

Occupation groups and selected occupations	1960 Number	%	1950 Number	%	Per cent Change
Salesmen & sales clerks, manufacturing	464,770	.8	328,084	.6	41.7
Manual workers	23,746,463	38.6	22,437,059	40.3	5.8
Craftsmen, foremen, & kindred workers	8,741,292	14.2	7,820,634	14.0	11.8
Foremen (not elsewhere classified) [d]	1,096,658	1.8	777,266	1.4	41.1
Construction craftsmen [d]	2,404,323	3.9	2,354,906	4.2	2.1
Brickmasons, stonemasons, & setters	185,909	.3	165,981	.3	12.0
Carpenters	818,835	1.3	918,753	1.6	−10.9
Electricians	337,147	.5	311,251	.6	8.3
Mechanics & repairmen [d]	2,197,193	3.6	1,708,812	3.1	28.6
Air-conditioning, heating & refrigeration equip.	61,997	.1	43,639	.1	42.1
Automobiles	682,103	1.1	654,350	1.2	4.2
Office machines	29,262	([b])	31,023	.1	−5.7
Metal craftsmen, except mechanics [d]	1,099,835	1.8	1,095,683	2.0	.4
Boilermakers	23,754	([b])	35,645	.1	−33.4
Machinists	498,688	.8	514,696	.9	−3.1
Molders	48,929	.1	60,676	.1	−19.4
Toolmakers, diemakers & setters	182,345	.3	152,658	.3	19.4
Other craftsmen	1,943,283	3.2	1,883,967	3.4	3.1
Locomotive engineers	56,630	.1	73,004	.1	−22.4
Locomotive firemen	37,087	.1	54,263	.1	−31.7
Operatives & kindred workers	11,897,636	19.4	11,180,315	20.1	6.4
Drivers & deliverymen	2,279,576	3.7	1,906,616	3.4	19.6
Other operatives, etc.	9,618,060	15.7	9,273,699	16.7	3.7
Laborers except farm & mine	3,107,535	5.1	3,436,110	6.2	−9.6
Service workers, including private household	7,170,784	11.7	5,708,178	10.2	25.6
Service workers, except private household	5,444,958	8.9	4,297,018	7.7	26.7
Protective service workers [d]	662,133	1.1	564,414	1.0	17.3
Waiters, bartenders, cooks, & counter workers	1,717,083	2.8	1,328,018	2.4	29.3
Other service workers	3,065,742	5.0	2,404,586	4.3	27.5
Private household workers	1,725,826	2.8	1,411,160	2.5	22.3

TABLE I.1 (cont.)

Occupation groups and selected occupations	1960 Number	%	1950 Number	%	Per cent Change
Agricultural workers	3,950,491	6.4	6,727,789	12.1	−41.3
Farmers & farm managers	2,505,684	4.1	4,310,979	7.7	−41.9
Farm laborers & farm foremen	1,444,807	2.4	2,416,810	4.3	−40.2
Occupations not reported	3,183,675		742,933		661.0

[a] Adjusted to include Alaska & Hawaii
[b] Less than 0.05 per cent
[c] Female only; the comparatively few men recorded in this group are included in the total for the major occupational group
[d] Male only; the few women recorded in this group are included in the total for the major occupational group

Note: Because of rounding, sums of individual items may not equal totals. Most totals include occupations not shown separately.

Source: Max Rutzick and Sol Swerdloff, "The Occupational Structure of U.S. Employment, 1940–1960," *Monthly Labor Review*, 85 (November 1962), 1211.

specifically, the trend showed the most dramatic increase occurring among those occupations that required the greatest amount of education and training (see Table I.1). The nation's labor force increased by 14.5 per cent between 1950 and 1960. White-collar workers increased by 28 per cent compared to a 6 per cent increase for manual workers. Within the white-collar category the greatest percentage increases were recorded for technicians in electronics (679 per cent), mathematicians (345 per cent), and industrial engineers (142 per cent). Professionals as a category increased by 47 per cent, compared to a 7 per cent increase for managers-officials-proprietors. Clerical workers increased by only 34 per cent and sales workers by 19 per cent. Within the white-collar category the professionals experienced the greatest increase. The professionals were still exceeded in number, however, by the clerical and kindred workers, 9.8 million and 7.5 million, respectively. Both the managerial and sales worker categories had a slightly smaller proportion of practitioners (see Table I.2).

Projections for 1975 indicate an anticipated 31 per cent increase in the nation's labor force. All of the white-collar occupational categories are expected to increase more than the average for the total labor force.

TABLE I.2

Employment by Major Occupational Group, 1960 to 1975

Major Occupational Group	Actual, 1960 Number (in millions)	Per cent	Projected, 1975 Number (in millions)	Per cent	Per cent change 1960–75
Total	66.7	100.0	87.6	100.0	31
Professional, technical, and kindred workers	7.5	11.2	12.4	14.2	65
Managers, officials, & proprietors, except farm	7.1	10.6	9.4	10.7	32
Clerical & kindred workers	9.8	14.7	14.2	16.2	45
Sales workers	4.4	6.6	5.9	6.7	34
Craftsmen, foremen, & kindred workers	8.6	12.8	11.2	12.8	30
Operatives & kindred workers	12.0	18.0	14.2	16.3	18
Service workers	8.3	12.5	12.5	14.3	51
Laborers, except farm & mine	3.7	5.5	3.7	4.3	—
Farmers, farm managers, laborers, & foremen	5.4	8.1	3.9	4.5	−28

Source: *Manpower Report of the President, 1963* (Washington, D.C.: U.S. Government Printing Office, 1963), p. 100.

The increases range from a high of 65 per cent anticipated for professionals to a low of 32 per cent anticipated for managers-officials-proprietors. In the manual occupational categories only the service workers are expected to exceed the national labor force rate of growth, 51 per cent compared to 31 per cent. The farmers and farm laborers are expected to decrease (by 28 per cent) between 1960 and 1975. In absolute numbers this will be a drop from 5.4 million to 3.9 million.

In juxtaposition to the decline in the farm labor force, the occupational structure in rural America is now dominated by non-farm jobs. As recently as 1940 farmers and farm managers constituted approximately one-half of the occupational individuals in rural areas. By 1960 only one-fifth of the occupational people in rural areas were in agricultural types of work.[14] In 1950 the census recorded that skilled and semi-skilled workers, blue-collar employees, outnumbered farm workers as the most numerous type in rural areas. The 1960 Census reported 5.5 million craftsmen, foremen, and operatives residing in rural areas, compared to some 3.5 million farmers and farm laborers. Moreover, the white-collar workers residing in rural areas numbered 4.8 million and also exceeded the number of rural workers. The differences between the rural and urban occupational profiles are declining precipitously. Nevertheless, rural occupational people are still disproportionately represented in the blue-collar occupations and in those types of jobs which require less formal education and less specific training.

Women continue to invade the once male world of gainful employment. During the 1950's the female labor force expanded more rapidly than the male category, 4.8 million compared to 3.5 million, respectively. This was primarily due to the influx of married women into the labor force. By 1960 more than half of the occupational women were married, and women constituted approximately one-third of the labor force. Beween 1950 and 1960 the rate of participation of women in the labor force increased from 33 to 37 per cent. For men the rate of participation decreased from 84 to 81 per cent. This decline was primarily a function of the lesser number of men working prior to age 19 and after age 65. Projections to 1970 show anticipated increases in the proportion of women in the labor force.[15]

Idea people of the contemporary labor force are exceedingly mobile. Unlike the self-employed workers of the nineteenth century and the captains of industry of the same era, the new idea people, both professionals and managers, are typically employees. Their importance occupationally and social organizationally is based on abstract knowledge and decision-making ability. In short, their occupational tools and social organizational property are brains. Their value seldom accumulates or appreciates by long residence in a specific area. Unlike the old physical property owners and the fee-taking professionals, their power is little based on building a clientele in a specific geographical area.

Idea occupational men are power-holders and power-wielders in the nation's social organization. They have, however, no political body of organization or representation, nor are they invested with political intrigue. To a great extent they are free occupational men. They render a high service to the urbanized industrial society. Accordingly, they are much sought after and competed for.

The mobility of idea people and the accompanying impact on national social organization is poignantly illustrated by the movement of research and development scientists and engineers out of the Middle West (see Figure I.1). These idea people are found in all sections of the nation. But the Middle West, which educates a disproportionate number of them, particularly at the Ph.D. level, is unable to retain them. The Far West, particularly California, attracts a great number of the research and development idea people. Social organizationally the states of the Far West are investing much in a Ph.D. economy. They are moving into the vanguard beyond states which calculate their resources in terms of topsoil or minerals.[16]

EMPLOYEE SOCIETY

The nation's employees have outnumbered the self-employed in the labor force for many decades, and the proportion of employees continues to increase. In 1960 over 83 per cent of the labor force participants were employees. Seventy-three per cent were in private employment and an additional 10 per cent were in government employment.[17]

The employee experience in the nation's labor force is a sharp departure from the historical and ideological tradition of rugged individualism. But the employer-employee relationship of the urbanized society is vastly different from the master-servant relationship found widely in Europe and America in the nineteenth century and earlier. In the urbanized society the employer is also usually an employee. In the contemporary employee society the components of the social organization involve extensive division of labor, free contract negotiation for conditions of work, and division or corporate control of property.[18]

The modern employer is most typically a corporation executive, manager of a government agency, or director of a nonprofit institution. The authority for such manager employers is vested in corporate charters or constitutions.

The employee society is organized in a hierarchy of occupations. The relationships between the occupational men in such a society are deter-

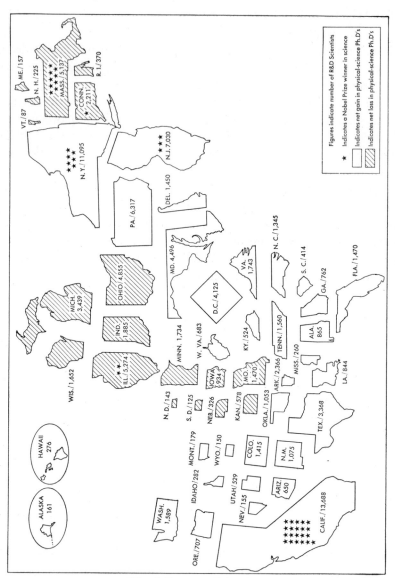

FIGURE I.1. The Migratory Scientists.

This "brain map" shows the geographic distribution of the top level of the U.S. scientific population—those individuals who are engaged in basic research, development, and design; and those no less important R&D contract getters, the scientifically trained administrators who propose and manage high-technology research projects. *Over a third of these scientists hold doctorates in the natural sciences or engineering.* The size of each state is proportional to population of R&D scientists, Rhode Island being the basic unit. Source: Ralph E. Lapp, "Where the Brains Are," *Fortune,* LXXIII, 3, (March 1966), 154–5.

mined by their statuses and the contribution of their work roles to the greater society. The new category of managerial rulers derive their authority from their functional positions more than from charisma and individual aggrandizement.[19]

In the employee society occupational status is ideologically achieved. To a great extent the open-class structure does in fact make possible the achievement of one's occupational space. The conditions of one's occupation are further negotiated for in the employee society by the mechanisms of labor unions and professional associations. Accordingly, the individual occupational man's interests as well as the national goals are furthered most by a cooperatively balanced division of social space. The interests of economic self-aggrandizement that characterized the social organization of the nineteenth century for the captains of industry have not been eradicated to any great degree. The rights to a job and the details of work environments are largely matters arranged by negotiation. Commitments to full employment and continuous occupational training bring the employee society into a closer and more harmonious organic whole.

SPECIALIZATION

The great advent of occupational specialization came with the beginning of the twentieth century. Late in the nineteenth century science emerged in a new occupational splendor. Chemistry led the way from the colleges to the factories. Physics followed in turn. By the twentieth century science teaching in the schools was designed with specific occupational objectives.[20]

With World War I mass production became effective, and occupational specialization was accelerated. Lewis and Maude write: "The twentieth century bred technologies and techniques, sciences and pseudo sciences, systems and knowhows, at an accelerating rate." [21] Henry Ford's assembly line and Frederick Taylor's notion of scientific management contributed to job specialization in the blue-collar level, in addition to that already cited in the new sciences.

Job specialization leads to so complex a division of labor that there is increasing reluctance on the part of workers to assume responsibility for their occupational roles. In many cases job definitions are so specified and partial that occupational practitioners are unable to understand where their work fits into the total social organization, and accordingly they are unable to assume responsibility.[22] "Buck-passing" is so much a part of the contemporary scheme of social organization that Hughes asserts that we in fact hire people to make mistakes for us. In other words, in the complex division of occupations we delegate work responsibility to others in many cases because we do not want to run the risk of error and face the guilt of failure. If we pay someone else and mistakes are made they can be blamed and we remain faultless.[23]

Still another dimension of occupational specialization is the dilution of skills. Much of the proliferation of work is accomplished by the breaking down of an occupation into its component parts and assigning a specialized worker to each part. In such cases it is often discovered that a loss of workmanship, a loss of craft pride, and a loss of meaningfulness in work results.[24] For example, in Walker's study of automobile plant workers it was discovered that the assembly line environment caused workers to view their tasks with overwhelming negativeness and with a sense of boredom and depersonalization.[25] In other cases this dissatisfaction with the meaning of work is shown to precipitate high rates of job turnover and high rates of absenteeism.

Job simplification and specialization in addition to diluting some occupations contributes to the rapid obsolescence of others.

Job enlargement has recently come into vogue to counter some of the excesses of job specialization.[26] Job enlargement generally has a threefold focus, including a more highly satisfied worker, a reduction in manufacturing costs, and a higher quality product. Job enlargement is not a retreat from specialization and a complex division of labor, but an incorporation of the human relations findings into the broad specializations of the occupational environments.

SUCCESS IDEOLOGIES AND MOBILITY

Success notions and mechanisms of achievement are central to the occupational specialization of the urbanized society. With an organization for occupational achievement and an open-class ideology, success becomes a primary mechanism for both distributing the labor force and for providing progressive career stages.[27]

Extensive educational and occupational training facilitate mobility and success achievement. Informal factors abound, but in the main occupations are open to those who aspire and who complete the appropriate courses of education and training for them. In a type of social organization where idea and white-collar occupations dominate over manual occupations, education is essential to success. Accordingly, the status and remuneration rewards are generally greater for those occupations which require the most extensive and rigorous amount of training.

TRAINING AND RETRAINING

Traditionally, occupational skills were gained by participant observation and by apprenticeship. With the ascension of the learned occupations rigorous and specific training is widely required. Moreover, with the rapid accumulation of knowledge precipitated largely by the idea occupational men, training becomes increasingly more continuous and less and less an experience completed prior to one's full-time entrance into the labor force.

The idea people and their technical specialists are faced initially with learning an extensive body of abstract knowledge along with their idea and abstract occupational tools. Both their body of knowledge and their occupational tools continue to be modified by their own research and development creativity. Accordingly, a course of initial training becomes progressively obsolete over the years unless the practitioner participates in a continual course of retraining.[28]

In addition to the training needs for research and development idea people there is a dramatic need for acceleration in the training and retraining of skilled, semiskilled, and unskilled workers. The nation's rapid shift from a labor force dominated by manual workers to one dominated by white-collar workers is hampered by an absence of occupational training for large numbers of people, and curtailed by outdated and inappropriate occupational training for many others. To accommodate to this changing situation the federal government is expanding a program of manpower training and development. The government's manpower training program is being supplemented by local agency programs and by numerous in-service training programs.

Automation is contributing to a vast relocation of workers from one type of occupation to another, and it is reducing the importance of many jobs and eliminating others. Indeed, automation contributes to the need for highly skilled technicians and technical assistants, while reducing the need for many unskilled workers.

OCCUPATION AND COMMUNITY

Occupation influences the totality of one's life to such an extent that residence locations often follow occupations. One may identify, for example, white-collar suburbs. These are status-conscious communities populated by affluent managers, professionals, and often less affluent sales and clerical workers. They are frequently progressive, avant garde, and often antiseptic in their observable details. In such white-collar communities one finds modern well-equipped schools, community churches that are both circumspect and well attended, country club facilities, etc. Occupational titles and other conspicuous displays characterize these neighborhoods.

By contrast there are vast blue-collar communities that are greatly homogeneous in much of their character.[29] In the blue-collar neighborhoods there is more of a prevailing concern with union membership and union participation. There is some suggestion that the blue-collar workers in suburban communities manifest little suburban life style.[30] In still more specific situations one will find communities dominated by members of medical occupations, executive communities, academic communities, and so forth. Indeed, as one moves up the occupational scale into the professions, occupation and way of life become so integrated that occupational residential communities are near necessities.

SUMMARY AND IMPLICATIONS

In the urbanized society occupations have become well organized, typically exercising considerable power in their own behalf or on behalf of their practitioners. Occupational specialization has been greatly accelerated since the end of the nineteenth century. The occupational world has become recently dominated by the idea people. They influence and direct the work of virtually all other occupational men in the society. Their innovation and direction has dramatically influenced the social organization of the society. In the employee society both idea people and manual workers typically have bosses. Success ideologies are mechanisms for distributing occupational people through the work world according to where they are needed and the contribution they may make best. Education and training are becoming central to occupational success as the white-collar work world becomes larger than the blue-collar one and as the idea people continue to expand their dominance.

Finally, as occupations become more diffused through the social organization of the society and into the life of its members, residential homogeneity follows occupational practice. White-collar and blue-collar suburbs are frequently segregated. Similarly, executive and academic communities are separated from medical communities, etc. Occupations and urbanized social organization are reciprocally related. The urbanizing society is a society of occupational specialization.

NOTES

1. Alba M. Edwards, *Population: Comparative Occupational Statistics for the United States, 1870–1940* (Washington, D.C.: U.S. Government Printing Office, 1943), p. xi.
2. Peter E. Drucker, "The Employee Society," *American Journal of Sociology*, 58 (January 1953), 358–63.
3. U.S. Bureau of the Census, *U.S. Census of Population: 1960, General Social and Economic Characteristics, U.S. Summary*, Final Report PC (1)-1C (Washington, D.C.: U.S. Government Printing Office, 1962), p. 215.
4. Arthur Salz, "Occupation," in Edwin R. A. Seligman (ed.), *Encyclopedia of the Social Sciences* (New York: The Macmillan Company, 1937), Vol. II, pp. 424–35.
5. Ibid. p. 427.
6. *Dictionary of Occupational Titles* (3rd Ed.; Washington, D.C.: U.S. Department of Labor, 1965).
7. John W. Banning, "Career Exploration Meets Youth Needs Directly," *Extension Service Review*, 32 (June 1961), 116.
8. Georges Friedmann, *The Anatomy of Work* (New York: The Free Press of Glencoe, Inc., 1961), chaps. 3 and 4.
9. A. B. Eckerson, "What's New in the D. O. T.?" *Employment Service Review*, 3 (March 1966), 9ff.
10. Harold L. Wilensky and Charles N. Lebeaux, *Industrial Society and Social Welfare* (New York: The Free Press, 1965), p. 91.
11. Ibid. p. 94.
12. Donald J. Bogue, *The Population of the United States* (Glencoe: Free Press, 1959), p. 472.
13. Max Rutzick and Sol Swerdloff, "The Occupational Structure of United States Employment, 1940–1960," *Monthly Labor Review*, 85 (November 1962), 1209–13.

14. Louis J. Ducoff, "Changing Occupations and Levels of Living of Rural People" (Talk presented at the 40th Annual Agricultural Outlook Conference, Washington, D.C., 1962).
15. "The U.S. Labor Force 1950–1960," *Population Bulletin*, 20 (May 1964), 64–5.
16. Ralph E. Lapp, "Where the Brains Are," *Fortune*, LXXII (March 1966), 155ff.
17. *U.S. Census of Population*, 1960, *U. S. Summary, General Social and Economic Characteristics*, PC (1)-1C US, p. 215.
18. Orme W. Phelps, *Introduction to Labor Economics* (New York: McGraw-Hill Book Co., Inc., 1955), p. 5.
19. Drucker, "The Employee Society."
20. Roy Lewis and Angus Maude, *Professional People* (London: Phoenix House Ltd., 1952), pp. 34–48.
21. Ibid. p. 34.
22. Robert K. Merton, *Social Theory and Social Structure* (Glencoe: The Free Press, 1949), chap. 13.
23. Everett C. Hughes, "Mistakes at Work," *The Canadian Journal of Economics and Political Science*, 17 (August 1951), 320–27.
24. Wilensky and Lebeaux, *Industrial Society*, pp. 59–60; see also Frank H. Cassell, "Manpower Program Implications of Skill Imbalance," *Proceedings of the 19th Annual Winter Meeting, Industrial Relations Research Association*, 1967.
25. Charles R. Walker and Robert H. Guest, *The Man on the Assembly Line* (Cambridge: Harvard University Press, 1952).
26. C. R. Walker, "The Problem of the Repetitive Job," *Harvard Business Review*, 28 (May 1950), 54–8; and Georges Friedmann, *Anatomy of Work*, see esp. chaps. 3 and 4.
27. C. Wright Mills, *White-Collar* (New York: Oxford University Press, 1956), pp. 265–86; and Talcott Parsons, "The Professions and Social Structure," *Social Forces*, 17 (May 1939), 457–67.
28. Neil W. Chamberlain, "Retooling the Mind," *Atlantic*, 214 (September 1964), 48–50.
29. Arthur B. Shostak and William Gomberg, *Blue-Collar World* (Englewood Cliffs, N.J.: Prentice-Hall, Inc., 1964).
30. Bennett M. Berger, *Working Class Suburb* (Berkeley: University of California Press, 1960).

SUPPLEMENTARY READINGS

Neil W. Chamberlin, "Retooling the Mind," *Atlantic*, 214 (September 1964), 48–50.
Dictionary of Occupational Titles (3rd Ed.; Washington, D.C.: U.S. Department of Labor, 1965).

Peter E. Drucker, "The Employee Society," *American Journal of Sociology*, 58 (January 1953), 358–63.

Alba M. Edwards, *Population: Comparative Occupational Statistics for the United States, 1870–1940* (Washington, D.C.: U.S. Government Printing Office, 1943).

C. Wright Mills, *White-Collar* (New York: Oxford University Press, 1956).

Arthur B. Shostak and William Gomberg, *Blue-Collar World* (Englewood Cliffs, N.J.: Prentice-Hall, Inc., 1964).

Harold L. Wilensky and Charles N. Lebeaux, *Industrial Society and Social Welfare* (New York: The Free Press, 1965).

MULTIPLICITY OF OCCUPATIONS II

Occupational multiplicity is one of the most abiding characteristics of urbanized industrial society. Most men through the centuries have lived simply and close to nature, with a few occupations. In urbanized societies, in the second half of the twentieth century, most men live with a multiplicity of occupations—more than 20,000 in the U.S. Never before have so many men lived with occupations so close to science, service, and people-oriented tasks.

The 1965 *Dictionary of Occupational Titles* lists 21,741 occupations. The list is so enormous that most persons never read it, and they would not recognize a majority of the occupations if they did. These occupations by which men live are numerous: some are exciting and challenging, others are frustrating, and routine; but most often they are obscure.

One of the great paradoxes of social organization and occupational organization of contemporary American society is the juxtaposing of an ideology for freedom of occupational choice with an absence of effective social mechanisms for disseminating knowledge of the characteristics of the nation's more than 20,000 occupations in such a way that occupations can be related easily to individuals' interests and abilities and, accordingly, freely chosen. In fact, a reasonable stability is achieved in the occupational organization of the nation by structural forces which pressure men to choose the occupation of their parental generation or an occupation immediately adjacent, above or beneath that of the parental work category. Few people experience extensive occupational vertical mobility. Consequently, the complex occupational diversities and related complex social organization of the nation are more phenomena for students of organization than they are behavioral realities in the lives of workers in the labor force.

Division of labor serves the organization of society in the provision of many goods and services, while most men have little real acquaintance with the labor divisions' occupational breadth or depth.

DIVISION OF LABOR

Societies everywhere manifest some forms of division of labor. Complexity in division of labor increases with industrialization and decreases with ruralization. For societies with extensive divisions of labor to function smoothly massive solidarity must be achieved.[1]

Some theoretical considerations. While the phenomenon of division of labor is old and basic, it was given little recognition until the end of the eighteenth century. One of the first scholarly theoretical statements concerning it was Adam Smith's *The Wealth of Nations* (1776). Abstract notions of division of labor in recent years have gained widespread currency. In recognizing its significance Adam Smith, John Stewart Mill, and others, held reservations concerning its ultimate impact on agricultural occupations. Smith wrote:

The nature of agriculture, indeed, does not admit of so many sub-divisions of labour, nor so complete a separation of one business from another, as manufactures. It is impossible to separate so entirely the business of the grazier from that of the corn-farmer as the trade of the carpenter is commonly separated from that of the smith. The spinner is almost always a distinct person from the weaver; but the ploughman, the harrower, the sower of the seed, and the reaper of the corn, are often the same.[2]

To a great extent the eighteenth- and nineteenth-century perceptions of men like Smith and Mill have been sustained in the second half of the twentieth century. Only now, in the scientific urbanized areas of the world, is agriculture crumbling as the last stronghold of the small family enterprise, and falling into a system of complex division of labor.

The function of the division of labor, according to the thesis developed by Durkheim and related students of social organization, is to contribute to a social solidarity. Division of labor is far more than a technology of expertise specifically designed to bring efficiency in production or differential prestige to occupations. The division of labor binds men to men and groups to groups. As the specialized producers in a diversified occupational organization contribute with expertise and efficiency to a small and specific goal, they are intensely bound to other occupational experts for the rendering of services outside of their own area of expertise. ". . . the most remarkable effect of division of labor is not that it increases the output of functions divided, but that it renders them solidarity." [3]

In another place Durkheim goes on to observe:

> . . . we must especially determine in what degree the solidarity that it produces contributes to the general integration of society, for it is only then that we shall know how far necessary it is, whether it is an essential factor of social cohesion, or whether, on the contrary, it is only an assessory and secondary condition.[4]

It is at the point of examining societal integration and social solidarity that the concrete subject of this book has its theoretical importance. Occupational diversification has forged ahead almost as if it were unilateral. Yet as disorganization and anomie become more frequent in the urbanized society, as the occupational aspiration of many young people is grossly inappropriate for the reality of the labor force, and as occupational work is abruptly challenged by retirement, the solidarity and integration of the society is threatened. This book, from one point of view, describes the occupational organization in a society which, to date at least, is deficient in developing adequate social mechanisms for disseminating systematic information concerning occupations and the labor force in such a way that individuals can aspire realistically in terms of their interests and abilities. As the occupational arena has become so broad, symptoms suggest that disintegration has occurred; this is illustrated by the hard-core unemployed, by frequent job changing, by reward-seeking away from work rather than in it, etc.

Division of labor differentiates specialist from generalist, and the urbanized society casts favor on the specialists. Those few occupations that remain in a generalist state—for example, subsistence farming and sect clergy—are in a precarious state. The generalist has no particular competency by which to demand respect of fellow citizens or with which to carry weight in the balance of social organization. At best the generalist appears as a dilettante, one praiseworthy in earlier times, but shunned by modern standards.

A contemporary norm of division of labor is expressed by specialization in the organization of schools. One is not simply trained for a general fulfillment of life, but trained to be proficient at a specific task which is different from other specific tasks. There are multiple curricula which are continually changing to keep up with the technology of the times. They prepare students to be specialists in specific occupational areas appropriate to the particular division of labor in the particular place at a given time.

We are all specialists now, asserts Lewis and Maude.[5] Specialization has favored industrialization and the growth of urbanization. Yet in the earlier stages of division of labor specialization, one had at least a general conception of the type of services rendered by other specialists in the society and of the relation of one's own service or specialty to the totality. Now as one examines the *Dictionary of Occupational Titles* few of the thousands of occupational specialties will be familiar. The merit and meaning of much of the specialization is at best difficult to evaluate. Many of the new occupations deal in the highest order of integrity with their subject matter. Others have changed their names and images in an effort to appear more professional or to gain prestige beyond their area of contribution. Licensing, boards of control, codes of ethics, etc., all attempt some regulatory effort to bring balance and integration out of the vast division of labor. Theoretically, one must ask if a division of labor that is extended beyond common recognition and consent is a force for social solidarity or a symptom of social disorganization. Or put another way, will the division of occupational labor in a society be limited by the ability of a modal number of actors in that society to recognize and evaluate the broad contributions of the several occupational specialties?

The norms and expressions of job enlargement may also be viewed as evidence of excessive occupational specialization.[6] Other evidence of this phenomenon is found in the scientific management movement of Frederick Taylor, which was followed by a strong human relations in industry movement.[7] In these instances one observes that the minute breaking down, as it were, of an occupation into its component parts is resisted when the individual loses a perception of the contribution his work makes to his total environment. Machine-like efficiency may be achieved for that brief period of time that a man will respond to simple routine. But from the empirical evidence integrity of occupation and meaning in work appear to be stronger than single measures of efficiency. It would appear, therefore, that the division of labor is achieved only up to that point where occupation and meaning are sustained, and only up to that point where an understanding of the total range of occupations is perceived by the adult members of the society. The division of labor pushed beyond these points appears to contribute to the deterioration of society rather than to produce social solidarity.

What is not yet understood in the above situations is the absolute or relative capacity of men to understand greater or lesser amounts of occupational division of labor. It remains to be discovered if the tendency toward job enlargement and the reduction of the number of occupations listed in the *Dictionary of Occupational Titles* are indexes of a human saturation, or oversaturation, or merely manifestations resulting from as yet undeveloped occupational and societal mechanisms for communicating the meaning of the vast specificity in the division of labor. It may be as men are socialized from an early age to live in contractual, sensate, urbanized societies that the now apparent anomie from an impersonal division of labor will be ameliorated.

In the United States the social organization is characterized by a society populated with the first generation of people born to and socialized in an urbanized environment. Still, there are significant numbers of individuals born and socialized in rural areas, and even more important, ideologies of the bucolic life with close personal relations are still widely heard, even if their position might be precarious. We are in effect still experiencing a society that is less than completely urbanized. As greater numbers of the society's people become saturated with the norms of automation, computerization, and cybernation, enormous new capacities for dealing with complex occupational divisions may develop. The impersonal planning, testing, and counseling that are variously viewed now as invasions of personal privacy may come to be heralded in the more completely urbanized society as norms for achieving greater individual freedom and vaster creative expression.

It is in this balance and with this prospective that the importance and intellectual excitement of the current multiplicity of occupations must be examined.

CONCEPTS

Throughout the history of most human existence there has been little real basis for differentiating between the labor force, the work force, and the adult population. In most subsistence societies all members work for sheer survival, and frequently at a nonmonetary level. It is only as societies become more urbanized and industrialized that a labor force and a working force are differentiated.

Labor force. "Labor force" in industrialized America is defined as persons age 14 and over who are gainfully employed, or unemployed and looking for employment. In this definition the minimum age for employment has varied. In earlier decades the ages of 10 and 12 were used. In the 1960's few members of the population are gainfully employed at age 14. Normatively, one now enters the labor force between the ages of 16 and 18.

Empirical measures of the unemployed who are seeking employment are complex. One may be in fact employed, but underemployed in terms of a normative forty-hour-week standard. Or one may work forty hours a week but under skill level or optium productivity desired by the worker. One may be an unemployed seasonal worker who is officially looking for a job but who in fact does not desire one until the next season of employment. In any event, the essence of the concept "labor force" is that of gainfully employed workers.[8]

Working force. The concept "working force" is distinguished from the concept "labor force." The working force is by definition all individuals in a society who are economically active, regardless of monetary remuneration. In primitive and subsistence societies the working force includes virtually all of the adult members of the population. In industrial urbanized America the working force is distinguished from the labor force primarily on the basis of its including housewives and other unpaid workers.

SOCIOLOGY OF THE LABOR FORCE

In dynamic and ever-changing America the labor force in the twentieth century has been a remarkably stable proportion of the total population. In each decade since 1900 the labor force has approximated 40 per cent of the national population. Proportionally, the labor force growth is approximately equal to the growth of the national population.

Internally the characteristics of the labor force record some notable and behaviorally significant changes. Women workers have increased, for example, while male workers have decreased. In 1900 approximately 20 per cent of the females over age 14 were reported in the labor force.

By 1960 the proportion of females in the labor force was nearly 35 per cent. During the war years of the 1940's female participation in the labor force reached a high of more than 37 per cent. By 1950 their proportion had dropped back to 32 per cent, but it is gradually increasing again. Most males have long participated in the labor force, but their proportion shows a slight decrease from approximately 88 per cent in 1900 to only 79 per cent by 1950 and only 77 per cent by 1960.

Only a minority of individuals between the ages of 14 to 20 are in fact in the labor force. Between the ages of 20 and 25 most males enter the labor force, and the second largest proportion continue on as students, typically in advanced graduate and professional study. Most females between the ages of 20 and 25 become homemakers, and the second largest, but nearly equal, proportion enters the labor force. Only a few females continue as advanced students. Males continue to participate normatively in the labor force until they reach the ages of 65 or 70. Then, with the increased longevity, the older category, mostly retirees, exceeds those in the labor force. Female participation in the labor force drops slightly after age 25 and does not increase again until age 35. The decrease represents the normative childbearing years, so that the participation in the labor force is essentially bimodal, or pre-childbearing and post-childbearing.

The multiplicity of occupations in the contemporary United States is combined with sufficient technology and sufficient substitutes for human energy input that labor force pyramids reveal a changing type of the population sustained outside of the world of work. The young and the aged are both increasingly excluded normatively from occupational participation. Indeed, much of the social space required for formal school attendance is achieved by the lack of need for young people to enter the labor force and by the accelerated need for entrants into the labor force to be highly educated and highly skilled.

Much of the sustaining of many older people in museum-like retirement is a function of the contracting of need of human energy input in the labor force. This is coupled with an acceleration of production in the 30 to 45 years of normative work of most male members of the population. Production is sufficient to sustain the non-employed younger and older persons.

The sociology of the labor force also has to do with the ordering, organizing, remuneration, status, and movements into and out of the labor force.⁹ Explanations for the division of the labor force into vast numbers of different occupations and for the distribution of workers among the occupations remain something of an enigma. Some of the many occupations are filled by selecting among aspirants who desire entry. Other occupations are filled by a residue of individuals who have few if any other occupational choices. In some cases occupational practitioners are attracted to dirty or dangerous work, such as extinguishing oil well fires or selling explosives, by being awarded high wages. In other equally dirty and dangerous jobs—for example, garbage collecting and coal mining—practitioners receive only modest rewards, but they have few alternatives.

In other cases, the labor force is manipulated artificially by the establishment of minimum wage laws for the lower end of the continuum and by the establishment of income taxes for the upper end of the continuum. The intent of such structuring is to level remuneration. Ideally, this should reduce striving for certain occupations and lift the stigma from others; in fact, it is hard to prove that major differences in the distribution of workers in the many occupations are achieved by this manipulation of incomes.

While much of the meaning of work is articulated as remuneration, important forms of remuneration exceed simple monetary returns. Prestige, rank, and status are major elements of sociological remuneration in occupations. Practitioners frequently report that their motivation and satisfactions in such medium-salary occupations as social work, nursing, and public school teaching lie in their opportunity to serve their fellow man, or some similar high-sounding ideological or moral explanation. In other situations it is reported that practitioners find gratification in their work by contact with their associates. This is exemplified by the case of secretaries to executives and administrators, assistants in scientific laboratories, and service workers in the glamorous occupations, for example, theater and recreation.

In other cases, distribution of participants in occupations can be explained by the routine of the work, which demands little creativity on the part of an individual. Many are gratified in such occupational situations where their work is a mechanism to an end outside of the occupational arena which is more important than the work in and for itself. And the opposite of this situation explains the participation of other workers in occupations which demand maximum creativity and put extensive pressure on the individual. Such practitioners are threatened by routine in occupation and challenged by unique experiences. In such situations ranging from the routine to the creative, monetary consideration may bear little weight in evaluating the importance of occupations.

It is from the sociology of the labor force that one understands the sagacity of the observation that to know a man's occupation is to know the single most important fact of his life. Many structures influence the occupation in which one will be a practitioner. They range from the social, economic, and biological, to the mental. Yet none of these determine the character and profile of the multiplicity of occupations in the urbanized industrial societies. Occupations are at once viable forms of social organization and components of societies. As components of societies, occupations are mechanisms through which practitioners are able to express themselves. As viable organizational entities, occupations determine many ways and set many limits within which human beings express themselves. As biological animals men express their character most clearly in primitive and subsistent societies. As social beings men express their character most articulately in the urbanized societies through the mechanisms of multiple and diverse occupations. Goods and services are produced in primitive and subsistent societies. In urbanized societies the variety of occupations are mechanisms for producing and distributing goods and services, but in addition they are the mechanisms for announcing who one is in a social sense. This is clearly exemplified by the deliberate efforts women make to be systematic participants in the urbanized industrial labor force.

WOMEN IN THE LABOR FORCE

By 1965 the profile characteristics for women in the labor force appeared as follows. They numbered 26 million, or 37 per cent of all women in the working ages. Working women constituted 35 per cent of the nation's labor force. Normatively, the age of working women has increased so that over half are reported at age 40 or over. Put another way, half of the women between the ages of 45 to 54 are in the labor force. Furthermore, of working women who are married, three out of five have their husbands present. Nearly 40 per cent of working women are also working mothers. And nearly 40 per cent of all women workers work full-time. The largest proportion of occupational women, 32 per cent, are in clerical positions. For full-time women workers the median income is $3,700 annually.[10]

As reported earlier, the proportion of women in the labor force has gradually increased since the turn of the century. But following World War II, from 1947 to 1964, there was a precipitous increase in female participation in the labor force. During this period women experienced a 53 per cent increase, or from nearly 17 million to nearly 26 million. During the same time span male participation in the labor force increased modestly, only 12 per cent, or from 43 million to 48 million.

Historically, women occupational participants have been employed most frequently in their late teens and early twenties. But by the middle 1960's the largest proportions of women workers were between the ages of 35 and 54. Furthermore, the greatest percentage increase between 1940 and 1965 was for women over age 55 (see Table II.1).

TABLE II.1

Women in the Population and Labor Force,[a] by Age, 1940 and 1965 [b]

Age	Labor Force 1965	Per cent distribution 1965	Per cent distribution 1940	Per cent increase 1940–65
Total	26,108,000	100.0	100.0	88.6
14 to 17 years	1,078,000	4.1	2.8	176.4
18 to 24 years	4,658,000	17.8	28.1	19.7
25 to 34 years	4,295,000	16.5	27.6	12.4
35 to 44 years	5,816,000	22.3	19.4	117.0
45 to 54 years	5,632,000	21.6	13.2	207.8
55 to 64 years	3,607,000	13.8	6.6	292.1
65 years and over..........	1,024,000	3.9	2.2	230.3

[a] Civilian non-institutional population and civilian labor force.
[b] Data are for March 1940 and April 1965.
Source: 1965 Handbook on Women Workers (Washington, D.C.: U.S. Department of Labor, Women's Bureau, Bulletin No. 290, 1965), p. 14.

An increasing proportion of married women in the labor force corresponds to the increased proportion of total number of women in the labor force. In the period between 1940 and 1964 the proportion of married and single women in the labor force reversed. By 1964 married women with husbands present outnumbered considerably single women in the labor force. The proportion of women workers who are widowed, divorced, or married with husbands absent has changed very little in the past quarter-century.

The increasing proportion of women in the labor force is one of the most notable features of change. The internal shifting profile of women workers—to increases in age and increases for the married—is equally notable. The increasing multiplicity of occupations, however, is little reflected in the distribution of positions held by working women. Clerical, domestic, and child-rearing occupations are historically dominant as the work in which women engage, and they continue to be dominated by women.

OCCUPATIONAL ENUMERATIONS AND PROJECTIONS

Early enumerations.[11] The first occupational data to be included in a decennial census were obtained in 1820. At that time the inquiry was simple and the details few. The data were reported in three so-called occupational classes: agriculture, commerce, and manufactures. The 1830 Census recorded no occupational information. In 1840 occupations were again reported, this time in the following categories: mining; agriculture; commerce; manufactures and trades; navigation of the ocean; navigation of canals, lakes, and rivers; and learned professions and engineers. From 1820 to 1840 the data were really more industrial than occupational.

In 1850 the first real occupational census analysis was made, although the base was limited to free males age 16 and over. The data were ordered into an alphabetical list of 323 occupations, and summarized into the following classes: commerce, trade, manufactures, mechanical arts and mining; agriculture; labor not agricultural; army; sea and river navigation; law, medicine, and divinity; other pursuits requiring education; government, civil service; domestic servants; and other occupations. In 1860 the occupational listing was expanded to 584 items.

From 1870 to 1900 census enumerators were asked to obtain occupational information for the total population. The instructions were to get both kind of work and nature of work, but only one space was provided on the schedule. Therefore, the information tended to be largely industrial. From 1910 to 1930 two places were provided on the enumeration schedules and more detailed industrial-occupational information was obtained. Between 1940 and the present, detailed occupational data have been collected.

Comparability between the early enumerations and the present is difficult. Extensive changes have come about in the national economy. Cobbling, a handicraft in the 1870's, has become the modern factory shoe industry. Other old occupations have gone completely out of existence, and totally new occupations have come into existence. The work content of some continuously existent occupations has changed.

Following the 1920 Census an alphabetical index of occupations was developed. It was used for the first time in the 1930 Census. This early Alba Edwards classification system designated 557 occupations and occupational groups.[12] Since 1930 the occupational enumeration in the census has been expanded both in breadth and in depth. The basic schema of occupational classification, however, has changed very little. It continues to be arranged essentially in a prestige hierarchy, from professional occupations at the upper end of the continuum to unskilled and laboring occupations at the bottom.

Contemporary enumerations. By 1960 the census provided the most detailed occupational statistics collected to that date concerning American workers.[13] The 1960 Census was the first to report a greater proportion of white-collar than manual workers. Within these two categories the kinds of occupations requiring the greatest amount of education and training grew more rapidly than those requiring less education and training. The detailed data on occupations in that census were collected from a 25 per cent sample of the total population.

The changing distribution of the multiplicity of occupations is illustrated in Table I.1 (see p. 25). In profile, the distribution of occupations shows 43 per cent in white-collar categories compared to only 39 per cent in manual categories. Professional occupations experienced the most rapid growth between 1950 and 1960. Their increase was 47 per cent, compared to a 14 per cent increase for all occupations. Within the professional category, electrical and electronic technicians experienced the most dramatic increase, 679 per cent. Mathematicians experienced a 345 per cent increase. Industrial engineers rose 142 per cent and sales engineers 130 per cent. Physicists increased by 88 per cent and medical technicians by 80 per cent. Indeed, most types of professional workers increased more rapidly than the average increase for the national labor force.

Clerical workers, another category of white-collar workers, increased by 34 per cent. Sales workers increased by only 19 per cent, and managers increased by only 7 per cent. Clearly, in the multiplying occupations the proliferation is at the white-collar level.

Workers in craft occupations increased by only 12 per cent. Operative workers rose only 6 per cent. Laborers, excluding farm and mine, decreased by nearly 10 per cent and agricultural workers decreased by a dramatic 41 per cent. An increase of some 25 per cent was recorded for service workers.

In terms of absolute numbers of workers, operatives total nearly 12 million and continue to be the largest single occupational category in the nation. The operatives constitute nearly 19 per cent of the labor force. Clerical workers are the second largest category, numbering over 9 million, or 15 per cent. Craft workers rank third, 8.7 million, or 14 per cent. Professional workers have increased to more than 7 million and constitute nearly 12 per cent. Service workers also total 7 million, or approximately 12 per cent. Managers, as a nearly stable occupational category, total a little more than 5 million, or approximately 9 per cent. Sales workers number 4.6 million, or 7.5 per cent of the labor force. Agricultural workers are the smallest occupational category, totaling less than 4 million—only 6 per cent of the labor force.

The nation's occupational distribution has not only shifted from hoe and dig to make and trade, but more recently to idea and service dominancy. This is illustrated most clearly by the dramatic increases in the professional and in the service occupations.

Dictionary of Occupational Titles. The most detailed empirical analysis of the multiplicity of occupations is found in the *Dictionary of Occupational Titles,* first released in 1939. A second edition was published in 1949, and a third in 1965.[14] When the nationwide federal-state employment services were established in 1933 there was no system of classifying occupations. In 1934 the first study was begun to provide an adequate classification system. This system reported occupational information in terms of tasks performed, knowledge required, machines, equipment, materials used, physical demands, working conditions, and worker characteristics. In the construction of the first dictionary literally thousands of jobs were visited and observed by occupational analysts.

The war years of the 1940's brought about many occupational changes. New occupations were created and some old ones went out of existence. Accordingly, there was need for a second edition of the *Dictionary of Occupational Titles,* which was developed and published in 1949.

With the continuing industrial dynamics of the nation new occupa-

FIGURE II.1

Type of Information Found in the *Dictionary of Occupational Titles,* *1965*

posing sensitized roller to images on film. (3) Transfers exposed roller to developing bath, using electric hoist. Turns roller in developing solution for specified time to dissolve sensitized coating from areas of roller that were exposed to light through film. Transfers developed roller to dye bath and turns roller in bath to dye unexposed area of roller. Transfers dyed roller to wash vat and rinses excess dye from roller. Dries roller with cloth.

COPYMAN (print. & pub.) II *see* COPY CUTTER.

COPY OPERATOR (r.r. trans.) *see under* DUPLICATING-MACHINE OPERATOR (clerical) III.

COPY READER (print. & pub.) **132.288. deskman; headline writer; rewrite man.** Edits and corrects newspaper or magazine copy and writes headlines preparatory to printing, in accordance with established format, style, and policy of publication and rules of syntax: Reads copy to detect errors in spelling, construction, continuity, punctuation, and facts. Refers to reference sources or newspaper files as necessary to verify facts, such as birth dates of persons mentioned in news stories. Marks corrections and rearrangement of story organization, using standard proofreading symbols. Writes headlines of specified size and type style to fit space allotted to individual story on dummy page. Attaches photographs and drawings to finished copy for preparation of printing plates. May write or rewrite stories. May supervise other workers engaged in preparing or editing copy, and may be designated COPY CHIEF.

    COPY READER, BOOK (print. & pub.) **proofreader.** Reads copy of manuscripts to be printed in book form and prepares copy for printing, indicating size and style of type to be used. May plan positioning of illustrations.

COPY READER (radio & tv broad.) *see* SCRIPT READER.

COPY READER, BOOK (print. & pub.) *see under* COPY READER.

COPYRIGHT CLERK (radio & tv broad.) *see* COPYRIGHT EXPERT.

COPYRIGHT EXPERT (radio & tv broad.) **963.288. copyright clerk.** Examines script of radio and television musical programs to be broadcast to ascertain that permission has been secured for use of copyrighted materials: Investigates musical compositions as to author, owner, and publisher to see that license has been granted company to use programmed material and to arrange for payment to copyright owner. Examines special musical arrangements to determine whether they constitute an infringement on other copyrighted

CORDING-MACHINE OPERATOR (any ind.) *see* EMBROIDERY-MACHINE OPERATOR.

—— (hat & cap; trim. & stamp. art goods) *see* TUCKING-MACHINE OPERATOR *under* SEWING-MACHINE OPERATOR, REGULAR EQUIPMENT (any ind.).

CORD PIPER (garment) *see* INSERTER *under* SEWING-MACHINE OPERATOR, REGULAR EQUIPMENT.

CORD-POCKET BUILDER (rubber tire & tube) *see* BAND BUILDER.

CORD-REEL OPERATOR (paper goods) *see* PAPER-REEL OPERATOR.

CORD SPLICER (rubber tire & tube) *see* SPLICER.

CORDUROY-BRUSHER OPERATOR (textile) **585.885. alternating-brush operator; comb brusher; treadle and crosser operator.** Tends machine that raises and sets pile of such fabrics as corduroy and velvet by action of series of brushing units: Pushes truck or roll of cloth into feeding position. Sews end of cloth to leader cloth in machine, using portable sewing machine. Turns crank to set width guides according to width of cloth. Starts machine and observes cloth to detect grease spots, holes, or torn selvages as cloth is drawn between rollers and brushes. Turns valve to admit water into trough of wet brushing unit. May doff cloth from swing-folding attachment onto handtruck.

CORDUROY-CUTTER OPERATOR (textile) **585.885. cutting-machine operator.** Tends one or more cutting machines that cut woven races in greige corduroy cloth: Sews end of cloth to lead cloth, using portable sewing machine. Places slotted wire guides under circular cutting blades so blades project into guide slots, and inserts guides into alternate races with fingers. Positions magnetic stop-motion bar that automatically stops machine when guides slip out of cloth races and rake contact with bar. Starts machine and observes cloth to detect inferior cutting. Notifies CUTTING-MACHINE FIXER of inferior cutting resulting from machine malfunction. Withdraws guides at seams, pulls seam through machine, and inserts guides into races behind seam to continue cutting process. Records lot number, piece number, yardage, and production. Delivers cloth from swing-folding attachment onto handtruck. Points guide tips and alines guides, using pliers and emery cloth.

CORDWOOD CUTTER (logging) **940.884. pulpwood cutter; wood chopper.** Fells trees in forest and cuts and splits logs into sizes suitable for stoves or fireplaces, using power or crosscut saw, ax, wedges, and maul. Stacks wood in ricks and cords. May load wood on

Source: *Dictionary of Occupational Titles, 1965,* 3rd Ed., vol. I (Washington, D.C.: U.S. Department of Labor, Bureau of Employment Security, U.S. Employment Service, 1965), 168.

FIGURE II.2
Illustration of the *Dictionary of Occupational Titles* Classification System

OCCUPATIONAL GROUP ARRANGEMENT OF TITLES AND CODES

0|1 PROFESSIONAL, TECHNICAL, AND MANAGERIAL OCCUPATIONS

This category includes occupations concerned with the theoretical or practical aspects of such fields of human endeavor as art, science, engineering, education, medicine, law, business relations, and administrative, managerial, and technical work. Most of these occupations require substantial educational preparation (usually at the university, junior college, or technical institute level).

00 01	**OCCUPATIONS IN ARCHITECTURE AND ENGINEERING** This division includes occupations concerned with the practical application of physical laws and principles of engineering and/or architecture for the development and utilization of machines, materials, instruments, structures, processes, and services. Typical specializations are research, design, construction, testing, procurement, production, operations, and sales. Also includes preparation of drawings, specifications, and cost estimates, and participation in verification tests.
001.	**Architectural Occupations** This group includes occupations concerned with the design and construction of buildings and related structures, and/or floating structures, according to aesthetic and functional factors.

001.081	ARCHITECT (profess. & kin.)
	ARCHITECT, MARINE (profess. & kin.)
	    architect, naval
	    naval designer

002.081
Con.
	STRESS ANALYST, AIRCRAFT (aircraft mfg.)
	    aircraft-structural engineer
	    stress engineer
	TEST ENGINEER, AIRCRAFT (aircraft mfg.)
	    flight-test engineer
	WIND-TUNNEL-TEST ENGINEER (aircraft mfg.)

002.168	INSPECTOR, MATERIAL TEST (aircraft mfg.)
002.187	COST-ANALYSIS ENGINEER (aircraft mfg.) FIELD-SERVICE ENGINEER (aircraft mfg.) service engineer MISSILE-TEST ENGINEER (aircraft mfg.)
002.188	ENGINEERING SCHEDULER (aircraft mfg.)

002.280	RESEARCH MECHANIC (aircraft mfg.) I
	    laboratory test mechanic
	    test analyst, aircraft

002.281	DESIGN DRAFTSMAN, RAM-JET ENGINE (profess. & kin.)
	DRAFTSMAN, AERONAUTICAL (profess. & kin.)
	ENGINEERING CHECKER (aircraft mfg.)
	    checker
	    drawing checker
	    engineering-drawings checker
	FLIGHT-TEST-DATA TRANSCRIBER (aircraft mfg.)

003.081
Con.
	INDUSTRIAL-ILLUMINATING ENGINEER (profess. & kin.)
	OUTDOOR-ILLUMINATING ENGINEER (profess. & kin.)
	POWER-PLANT ENGINEER (light, heat, & power)
	RADIO ENGINEER (profess. & kin.)
	RADIO-DESIGN ENGINEER (profess. & kin.)
	    Antenna Engineer (profess. & kin.)
	    Radar Engineer (profess. & kin.)
	    Television Engineer (profess. & kin.)
	RADIO-RESEARCH ENGINEER (profess. & kin.)
	    radio technician
	ROCKET-ENGINE-TEST ENGINEER (aircraft mfg.)
	TELEGRAPH ENGINEER (tel. & tel.)
	    Division-Plant Engineer (tel. & tel.)
	TELEPHONE ENGINEER (tel. & tel.)
	EQUIPMENT ENGINEER (tel. & tel.)
	LINE-CONSTRUCTION ENGINEER (tel. & tel.)
	    district engineer
	TELECOMMUNICATIONS-SERVICE ENGINEER

001.168 SCHOOL-PLANT CONSULTANT (education)
901.281 DRAFTSMAN, ARCHITECTURAL (profess. & kin.)
Draftsman, Tile and Marble (profess. & kin.)

002. Aeronautical Engineering Occupations
This group includes occupations concerned with the design and construction of aircraft, spacecraft, and missiles. Accessory techniques required are those used in mechanical, electrical, electronic, and powerplant engineering. Typical specializations are aerodynamics, design, electronics, flight-testing, structural dynamics, thermodynamics, and weapons-control research.

002.081 AERODYNAMIST (aircraft mfg.)
aerodynamicist
aerodynamics engineer
aerophysics engineer
Thermodynamics Engineer (aircraft mfg.)
AERONAUTICAL ENGINEER (profess. & kin.)
AIRCRAFT DESIGNER (aircraft mfg.)
airplane designer
design engineer, aeronautical
master-lay-out man
Wind-Tunnel-Model-Design Engineer (aircraft mfg.)
ENGINEER, CONTROLS (aircraft mfg.)
ENGINEERING DESIGNER, AIRCRAFT STRUC-TURES (aircraft mfg.)
designer
draftsman
engineering designer
engineer, lay-out
engineer, structures
ENGIN... aircraft

002.288 SPECIFICATION WRITER, AIRPLANES (profess. & kin.)
airplane-specifications engineer

003. Electrical Engineering Occupations
This group includes occupations concerned with the application of the laws of electrical energy and the principles of engineering for the generation, transmission, and use of electricity. Also includes the design and development of machinery and equipment for production and utilization of electric power. Accessory techniques needed are those used in mechanical, power, and process engineering. Typical specializations are power generation and distribution, atomic power generation, electrical and electronic equipment manufacturing, radio and television broadcasting, research, and telephone, telegraph, and electronic computer engineering.

003.081 ELECTRICAL ENGINEER (profess. & kin.)
ELECTRICAL-EQUIPMENT ENGINEER (profess. & kin.)
ELECTRICAL-PROSPECTING ENGINEER (petrol. production)
electrical engineer, geophysical prospecting
SIGNAL ENGINEER (profess. & kin.)
ELECTRICAL-RESEARCH ENGINEER (profess. & kin.)
ELECTRONIC ENGINEER (profess. & kin.)
Engineer, Instrumentation (profess. & kin.)
Systems Engineer (profess. & kin.)
Thermionics Engineer (profess. & kin.)
AUDIO ENGINEER (profess. & kin.)
acoustical engineer

(tel. & tel.)
planner, telecommunication service
services engineer
003.151 INDUSTRIAL-POWER ENGINEER (light, heat, & power)
power salesman
salesman, industrial power
SPECIAL-SERVICE REPRESENTATIVE (tel. & tel.)
003.168 SUPERVISOR, ELECTRONIC MAINTENANCE (gov. ser.)
003.181 ELECTRICAL TECHNICIAN (profess. & kin.)
electric-laboratory technician
ELECTRONIC TECHNICIAN (profess. & kin.)
Computer-Laboratory Technician (profess. & kin.)
Development-Instrumentation Technician (profess. & kin.)
Electronic-Communications Technician (profess. & kin.)
Electronic Technician, Nuclear Reactor (profess. & kin.)
SYSTEMS-TESTING-LABORATORY TECHNICIAN (profess. & kin.)
003.187 COMMERCIAL ENGINEER (radio & tv broad.)
traffic engineer
DISTRIBUTION-FIELD ENGINEER (light, heat, & power)
line inspector
ELECTRICAL ENGINEER, POWER (light, heat, & power)
DISTRIBUTION ENGINEER (light, heat, & power)
electric-distribution engineer
Overhead-Distribution Engineer (light, heat, & power)
B...

Source: *Dictionary of Occupational Titles*, 1965, 3rd Ed., vol. II (Washington, D.C.: U.S. Department of Labor, Bureau of Employment Security, U.S. Employment Service, 1965), 33.

55

FIGURE II.3

Occupational categories, divisions, and groups

OCCUPATIONAL CATEGORIES

0⎫ Professional, technical, and
 ⎬ managerial occupations
1⎭
2 Clerical and sales occupations
3 Service occupations
4 Farming, fishery, forestry, and

related occupations
5 Processing occupations
6 Machines trades occupations
7 Bench work occupations
8 Structural work occupations
9 Miscellaneous occupations

TWO-DIGIT OCCUPATIONAL DIVISIONS
PROFESSIONAL, TECHNICAL, AND MANAGERIAL OCCUPATIONS

00⎫ Occupations in architecture and
 ⎬ engineering
01⎭
02 Occupations in mathematics and
physical sciences
04 Occupations in life sciences
05 Occupations in social sciences
07 Occupations in medicine and health
09 Occupations in education
10 Occupations in museum, library, and
archival sciences

11 Occupations in law and jurisprudence
12 Occupations in religion and theology
13 Occupations in writing
14 Occupations in art
15 Occupations in entertainment and
recreation
16 Occupations in administrative
specializations
18 Managers and officials, n.e.c
19 Miscellaneous professional, technical,
and managerial occupations

CLERICAL AND SALES OCCUPATIONS

20 Stenography, typing, filing, and
related occupations
21 Computing and account-recording
occupations
22 Material and production recording
occupations
23 Information and message distribution
occupations

24 Miscellaneous clerical occupations
25 Salesmen, services
26⎫
27⎬ Salesmen and salespersons,
  ⎱ commodities
28⎭
29 Merchandising occupations, except
salesmen

SERVICE OCCUPATIONS

30 Domestic service occupations
31 Food and beverage preparation and
service occupations
32 Lodging and related service
occupations
33 Barbering, cosmetology, and related
service occupations
34 Amusement and recreation service
occupations

35 Miscellaneous personal service
occupations
36 Apparel and furnishing service
occupations
37 Protective service occupations
38 Building and related service
occupations

FARMING, FISHERY, FORESTRY, AND RELATED OCCUPATIONS

40 Plant farming occupations
41 Animal farming occupations
42 Miscellaneous farming and related
occupations

43 Fishery and related occupations
44 Forestry occupations
45 Hunting, trapping, and related
occupations
46 Agricultural service occupations

PROCESSING OCCUPATIONS

50 Occupations in processing of metal
51 Ore refining and foundry occupations
52 Occupations in processing of food, tobacco, and related products
53 Occupations in processing of paper and related materials
54 Occupations in processing of petroleum, coal, natural and manufactured gas, and related products
55 Occupations in processing of chemicals, plastics, synthetics, rubber, paint, and related products
56 Occupations in processing of wood and wood products
57 Occupations in processing of stone, clay, glass, and related products
58 Occupations in processing of leather, textiles, and related products
59 Processing occupations, n.e.c.

MACHINE TRADES OCCUPATIONS

60 Metal machining occupations
61 Metalworking occupations, n.e.c.
62
63 } Mechanics and machinery repairmen
64 Paperworking occupations
65 Printing occupations
66 Wood machining occupations
67 Occupations in machining stone, clay, glass, and related materials
68 Textile occupations
69 Machine trades occupations, n.e.c

BENCH WORK OCCUPATIONS

70 Occupations in fabrication, assembly, and repair of metal products, n.e.c.
71 Occupations in fabrication and repair of scientific and medical apparatus, photographic and optical goods, watches and clocks and related products
72 Occupations in assembly and repair of electrical equipment
73 Occupations in fabrication and repair of products made from assorted materials
74 Painting, decorating, and related occupations
75 Occupations in fabrication and repair of plastics, synthetics, rubber, and related products
76 Occupations in fabrication and repair of wood products
77 Occupations in fabrication and repair of sand, stone, clay, and glass products
78 Occupations in fabrication and repair of textile, leather, and related products
79 Bench work occupations, n.e.c.

STRUCTURAL WORK OCCUPATIONS

80 Occupations in metal fabricating, n.e.c.
81 Welders, flame cutters, and related occupations
82 Electrical assembling, installing, and repairing occupations
84 Painting, plastering, waterproofing, cementing, and related occupations
85 Excavating, grading, paving, and related occupations
86 Construction occupations, n.e.c.
89 Structural work occupations, n.e.c.

MISCELLANEOUS OCCUPATIONS

90 Motor freight occupations
91 Transportation occupations, n.e.c.
92 Packaging and materials handling occupations
93 Occupations in extraction of minerals
94 Occupations in logging
95 Occupations in production and distribution of utilities
96 Amusement, recreation, and motion picture occupations, n.e.c.
97 Occupations in graphic art work

Source: *Dictionary of Occupational Titles*, 1965, 3rd Ed., vol. II, (Washington, D.C.: U.S. Department of Labor, Bureau of Employment Security, U.S. Employment Service, 1965), 1–2.

tions are created and the demise of old ones continues. In the preparation of the third *Dictionary of Occupational Titles* the content and the definitions of over 45,000 individual jobs were studied and verified, and occupational analysts made a study of over 75,000 jobs.

The third edition of the dictionary is more complex than the preceding two. The first volume of the third edition contains the names and definitions, alphabetically listed, of 21,741 separate occupations. Figure II.1 illustrates the type of information contained in volume 1.

Volume 2 of the new *Dictionary of Occupational Titles* lists the occupations in a classificatory system. Occupations are classified into a six-digit code system. Jobs are first grouped by field of work, material, product, subject matter, service, or industry. This classification is recorded in the first three digits. Within this three-digit system, occupations are further classified according to the activities performed or skills required, and they are arranged in a descending order of complexity. This descending order of complexity is reflected in the last three digits. See Figure II.2 for a sample of the classification system for selected professional occupations. The total system of classification is reported in Figure II.3. There are nine basic categories, ranging from professional, clerical, service, farming, processing, machine trades, bench work, structural work, to miscellaneous occupations.

The *Dictionary of Occupational Titles* provides one systematic technique for ordering the multiplicity of more than 20,000 occupations into manageable categories. Still, it is the subdivisions within these categories where people find the occupations in which they may be employed. Individual practitioners work in occupations, not in occupational categories. There still is no effective mechanism for relating the worker's individual interests and ability with knowledge of the multiple number of occupations within the categories. The *Dictionary of Occupational Titles* is an important technical device, but it is barely known and little used by individuals aspiring to occupations.

Projections for 1975. In the *Occupational Outlook Handbook* trends and projections for the multiple occupations are continuously reported in a semitechnical to nontechnical language. The *Handbook* is for the intelligent layman as well as for the occupational specialist. It purports to answer questions concerning what occupations will be needed most a few years in the future. It reveals which occupational areas are expanding most rapidly and which are declining most.

Occupational changes between 1960 and 1975 are reported in Table I.2 (see p. 29). All occupational categories are expected to increase by nearly 31 per cent. Professional occupations will continue to increase more rapidly than all others, by 65 per cent. Service workers will experience the second greatest increase, 51 per cent. A 45 per cent increase is anticipated for clerical workers. Operative occupations will increase by only 18 per cent, considerably less than the average occupation in the nation. Labor occupations will show no appreciable change. Finally, farm occupations will continue to decline, by some 28 per cent through 1960 and 1970.

Projections for specific occupations and for occupations within specific regions are considerably more difficult to obtain. Smaller numbers of practitioners in specific idea occupations or technical occupations can be changed dramatically by shifting focuses in the areas of innovation and by inventions in technology. These total occupational categories will continue to show strong increases while numerous particular occupations will experience considerable fluctuation.

SUMMARY AND IMPLICATIONS

Men in urbanized America live in a society characterized by a greater multiplicity of occupations than ever previously known. Yet in the real work life of most members of the labor force their meaningful experience with and contact with occupations is sharply limited. There are a few well-known occupations, usually of the professional or entertainment type, whose images are widespread and popular. Most occupations, however, in the second half of the twentieth century are obscure in definition and meaning for most workers. Indeed they are so little known that they seldom become real or viable considerations in occupational choosing.

The division of labor in the urbanized society moves in the direction of saturation, perhap to the brink of disorganization rather than to the core of societal integration. In the abstract we all tend to be specialists and are dependent on a vast number of other occupational specialists for most of our goods and services. Yet the nature of social organization and of occupational organization is so complex that most people are inadequate judges of the proficiency with which vast numbers of occupational practitioners carry out their skills and services.

Labor force concepts themselves are complex. Definitions have changed in the course of time. Participation in types and categories of work also has changed. Most important in recent years have been the modifications of the labor force in terms of social norms and values. Even more particularly the labor force experience is truncated as married women move in hordes from the work force.

With the increasing complexity of occupation the importance of their census enumeration and related types of analysis have been recognized. Each decade the type of occupational information enumerated is more complete. Specific analyses of occupational data are made and systematically reported in dictionaries of occupational titles. Finally, occupational projections are made and disseminated in popular as well as technical forms to enable planning agencies and individuals to prepare for the changing world of work more systematically.

NOTES

1. Emile Durkheim, *The Division of Labor in Society* (Glencoe: The Free Press, 1949).
2. Adam Smith, *The Wealth of Nations*, vol. I (New York: E. P. Dutton & Co., Inc., 1957), p. 6.
3. Durkheim, *Division of Labor*, pp. 60–61.
4. Ibid. p. 64.
5. Roy Lewis and Angus Maude, *Professional People* (London: Phoenix House Ltd., 1952), pp. 34ff.
6. Georges Friedmann, *The Anatomy of Work* (New York: The Free Press of Glencoe, 1961).
7. Frederick Winslow Taylor, *Scientific Management* (New York: Harper and Brothers, 1947); and F. J. Roethlisberger and William J. Dickson, *Management and the Worker* (Cambridge: Harvard University Press, 1947).
8. A. J. Jaffe and C. D. Stewart, *Manpower Resources and Utilization: Principles of Working Force Analysis* (New York: John Wiley and Sons, 1951); P. M. Hauser, "The Labor Force and Gainful Workers: Concept, Measurement, and Comparability," *American Journal of Sociology*, 54 (January 1949), 338–55; W. E. Moore, "The Exportability of the 'Labor Force' Concept," *American Sociological Review*, 18 (February 1953), 68–72; and *Social Science Research Council, Labor Force Definition and Measurement* (New York: The Social Science Research Council, Bulletin No. 56, 1947).
9. Theodore Caplow, *The Sociology of Work* (Minneapolis: The University of Minnesota Press, 1954); and P. M. Hauser, "The Labor

Force as a Field of Interest for the Sociologist," *American Sociological Review*, 16 (August 1951), 530–38.
10. *1965 Handbook on Women Workers* (Washington, D.C.: U.S. Department of Labor, Women's Bureau, Bulletin No. 290, 1965), p. 2.
11. Alba M. Edwards, *Comparative Occupational Statistics for the United States 1870–1940* (Washington, D.C.: U.S. Government Printing Office, 1943).
12. *Alphabetical Index of Occupations* (Washington, D.C.: Fifteenth Census of the United States, 1930), p. 3.
13. Max Rutzick and Sol Swerdloff, "The Occupational Structure of U.S. Employment, 1940–1960," *Monthly Labor Review*, 82 (November 1962), 1209–13.
14. *Dictionary of Occupational Titles* (3rd Ed.; Washington, D.C.: U.S. Department of Labor, Bureau of Employment Security, U.S. Employment Service, 1965); and A. B. Eckerson, "The New Dictionary of Occupational Titles," *Occupational Outlook Quarterly*, 7 (September 1963), 31–3.
15. Cora E. Taylor, "The Occupational Outlook for 1970," *Occupational Outlook Quarterly*, 7 (February 1963), 7–13.

SUPPLEMENTARY READINGS

Theodore Caplow, *The Sociology of Work* (New York: McGraw-Hill Book Co., Inc., 1954, 1964).
P. M. Hauser, "The Labor Force and Gainful Workers: Concept, Measurement, and Comparability," *American Journal of Sociology*, 54 (January 1949), 338–55.
A. J. Jaffe and C. D. Stewart, *Manpower Resources and Utilization: Principles of Working Force Analysis* (New York: John Wiley & Sons, Inc., 1951).
W. E. Moore, "The Exportability of the 'Labor Force' Concept," *American Sociological Review*, 18 (February 1953), 68–72.
Max Rutzick and Sol Swerdloff, "The Occupational Structure of U.S. Employment, 1940–1960," *Monthly Labor Review*, 82 (November 1962), 1209–13.

OCCUPATIONS AND MOBILITY* III

The relations between occupations and mobility are of vital practical importance for labor force planners and of great theoretical interest for students of human relations. Over the past forty years numerous monographs have been written concerning occupational mobility.[1] Early writers dealt with the subject from an ideological point of view. They also reported empirical research findings which described the situations. Contemporary writers make trend comparisons.

INTRODUCTION

In an open-class society occupational mobility is greatly determined by the nature of social organization. Theoretically, occupation is a status to be achieved rather than ascribed. Given this position, occupations are determined more on the basis of merit than on the basis of inheritance, at least theoretically. It is an ideology of opportunity and an ideology of success and achievement. In a caste society occupation is primarily a matter of ascription. The historical caste societies of the Orient constitute examples of such social organization.

In urbanized societies in general and in the United States in particular, the number of occupations has increased to such an extent that individual participants in the labor force have little opportunity for perceiving the total range of occupations, assessing their ability and aptitude, and selecting accordingly. In fact, due to informal factors and limited recruitment mechanisms, most individuals are reported to enter those occupations which are similar to those of their parents, or an occupational category that is immediately adjacent to that of the

* Much of the material in this chapter was prepared for lectures for the Induction-Inservice Training Program for Personnel in the Division of Vocational and Technical Education, U.S. Office of Education, presented at the University of Maryland, June 30 and July 27, 1965.

parental generation.[2] The ideology of freedom in occupational choice is maintained while the integration of the ongoing society is achieved haphazardly and with a vast amount of occupational inheritance.

Three types of occupational mobility may be enumerated: a change in position in relation to one's colleagues, shifting from one occupation to another, and the increasing or decreasing in prestige of a total occupation.[3]

The main problems associated with occupational mobility concern its extent of increase or decrease. There is also a matter of concern about the techniques whereby an individual may achieve mobility. Factors which have historically contributed to increasing occupational mobility in the United States have been the frontier, mass of immigration, industrial growth, and increasing birth rates. In the main, all of these factors in recent years have been reduced in importance or obliterated completely. In short, many have argued that occupational mobility in the United States must decrease. The major empirical findings, however, provide no clear basis for asserting that occupational mobility has been reduced. There is, to be sure, only conjectural evidence that occupational mobility has expanded. It does appear that the avenues and mechanisms of occupational mobility have shifted.

The shifting of jobs and career achievement constitute an area of great significance in occupational mobility. Most research evidence suggests that participants in the American labor force change jobs on the average of every three to five years. The meanings of this vast occupational mobility are complex. From one point of view, the freedom to shift from job to job is one of the bulwarks of democracy. From another point of view, it contributes to a considerable amount of unemployment. Moreover, a significant amount of job changing is forced by the organization or disorganization of economic institutions rather than caused by the desires of the labor force participants. In any event, and regardless of its origin, job shifting is a major dimension of occupational mobility in the United States.

Career achievement and its less glamorous counterpart career decline are also important types of occupational mobility. In the prestige-status-oriented urbanized society the occupational norms, particularly in the professions, are organized in such a way that the practitioner is encouraged, if not required, to work toward career achievement.

An entire occupation may be shifted virtually from the top to a

point of near obliteration or from a point of obscurity up to prominence. This kind of occupational change is clearly seen in the downward movement of farming as it continues to be characterized as a
generalist occupation in an age of specialists; in the upward movement
of the military associated with an environment of international power
and world tension; in the downward movement of the importance of
the clergy in the face of advances made by many scientific occupations,
and in the upward movemennt of nuclear scientists in an atomic age.
Entire categories of occupational practitioners are, accordingly, thrust
into occupational mobility as the importance of their occupation is increased or decreased.

ASPIRATIONS AND MOBILITY

Various studies have shown occupational mobility to be related to
achievement motivation.[4] In the study of motivation and occupational
mobility an effort is made to analyze the differential behavior and
achievement of individuals from similar regional, occupational, and educational backgrounds. Crockett indicates that beliefs and values which
are appropriate for achievement striving in occupations are more characteristic of the middle class than the working class, but they are found
manifest in people of both classes. In Crockett's study the hypothesis
researched was that "respondents with strong achievement motives will
show greater upward mobility and less downward mobility than respondents weak in achievement motive." [5] The analysis clearly showed that
achievement motive is related to upward mobility among sons of
fathers in low prestige categories but not among the sons of fathers in
high prestige categories. It was further found that the strength of affiliation motive was positively associated with upward mobility. This was
explained by observing that in large-scale bureaucratic work environments as contrasted with the historically small-scale entrepreneurial environments, reward in terms of upward mobility goes to those who participate harmoniously in the work systems. It is also observed that the
experience of upward vertical mobility may in fact increase one's
strength of achievement motivation. In any event, Crockett's data for a
national sample indicate that the strength of achievement motive as revealed by thematic aperception is a relevant personality characteristic
in contributing to occupational mobility.[6]

In a more limited study, Chinoy's investigation of the aspirations of automobile workers revealed a general acceptance of the ideology of getting ahead and the view of America as the land of opportunity. More realistically, the respondents saw very little opportunity for promotion to salaried positions in the automobile industry. They were acutely aware of the changes in the occupational structure which have rendered engineering and management highly selective categories of work into which one is invited only after a period of long and appropriate training. Rather than lose hope and turn to pessimism, the automobile workers whom Chinoy interviewed tended to transfer their goals for getting ahead to their children. For them they were ambitious and expressed a desire for occupational mobility.[7]

The concept "level of occupational aspiration" has come into use.[8] The LOA concept is defined as "the area (a point or limited range of points) of the occupational prestige hierarchy which an individual views as a goal. The range of an individual's LOA is bounded in two general ways: (1) by what he views as realistically probable versus idealistically desirable for him, and (2) by the goals which he has for the near versus the distant future."[9] The LOA is determined by an Occupational Aspiration Scale, OAS, which is a multiple choice instrument. It is designed primarily for male high school students. Its validity for others remains to be demonstrated. Its format is based on both long- and short-range idealistic goals and long- and short-range realistic goals.

High occupational aspirations for both youth and adults are realistically associated with mobility. As one moves up in the occupational hierarchy career achievement is widely facilitated by mobility. It is not implied that upward occupational mobility is achieved only by geographical mobility. The evidence, however, does support the generalization that upward occupational achievement is more probable when one has a high occupational aspiration and a willingness to be horizontally as well as vertically mobile.

In a Utah study of rural youth in 1960 the strong association between educational and occupational aspiration was demonstrated.[10] College training was widely perceived as a prerequisite for much upward vertical occupational mobility. High motivation from both parents and teachers was also associated with high educational and occupational aspirations.

From various perspectives it is always clear that occupation is a thing to be achieved in the ideology of the open-class American society. Informal factors and social organization may limit, indeed in some cases inhibit, occupational mobility, but in the main such mobility is an overt experience of American life. In a nearly naïve way freedom in occupational mobility supports the general ideology of individual freedom in decision-making. A more perceptive examination of the situation reveals that there are few mechanisms in the society for disseminating a widespread knowledge of occupations. In fact, what the majority of people experience is the choosing among a few occupations, usually those closely associated with the parental generation.

Occupational mobility contributes a measure of flexibility to the labor force. This has a positive value for the society to the extent that it enables the labor force to be geographically and technologically located in those places where it is most needed. Occupational mobility has the liability of contributing to unemployment due both to technological displacement and geographical relocation.

VERTICAL AND HORIZONTAL OCCUPATIONAL MOBILITY

The concept of vertical mobility involves movement upward or downward within a given occupation or to a higher or lower ranked occupation. Upward vertical mobility may be exemplified in the case of a junior executive being promoted to a senior executive in the same office, or in the case of a parish clergyman being promoted to the position of bishop or cardinal. Downward vertical mobility is essentially the opposite of upward vertical mobility. In executive and scientific occupations one may achieve a position of top administrator at a middle point in one's career and later be reduced to a less demanding and lower ranking position as one's abilities and/or initiative become less vigorous. And in academic life one may be required to step down from administration, in the direction of retirement, several years before one is required to retire from the teaching activities.

Horizontal occupational mobility involves moving one's place of work from one geographical location to another. The amount of distance is a matter of operational definition. In most research it involves moving across a county boundary at least, and by definition it excludes daily commuting. Horizontal occupational mobility may be illustrated by the transferring of an employee from one location to another, where the job assignment remains the same. It is also job shifting—e.g. from minister to professor or store manager to store manager at the same level. Occupational boundary maintenance minimizes this type of mobility, i.e. the ideology of specialization.

Vertical and horizontal mobility are not contradictory or exclusive concepts. Often a promotion involving upward vertical mobility is also carried out by horizontal mobility. For example, a junior executive may be located for several years at a regional office or plant, and with a promotion may be relocated in the home office in some other region. The two types of occupational mobility are often closely associated.

Intergenerational occupational mobility has been the subject of a considerable amount of empirical investigation. Researchers are concerned with showing the association or disparity between the total occupational experience of the father and that of the son. The methodological complications of this research are many, and they are discussed in some detail later in this chapter. The main thrust of this investigation has been addressed to questions concerning the amount of continued openness or closure of the occupational expression in the nation.

INTERGENERATIONAL MOBILITY

The maintenance of opportunity for occupational mobility is ideologically crucial for the open-class society. The techniques for maintaining such mobility opportunities are far from absolute, and the measures of such mobility are far from thorough. The study of intergenerational mobility is one of the most widely used techniques for measuring the amount of openness or closure.

A study of occupational mobility in San Jose, California, in 1933–34 has been elevated to a near classic position in intergenerational research.[11] This was a study of the regular occupation of 610 fathers compared to the regular occupation of their 1,547 sons. Of 77 sons of professional fathers nearly one-quarter entered professional-level occupations. The professional sons of professional fathers constituted slightly less than 10 per cent of a total number of professional sons. Combining these two findings it was revealed that one-fourth of professional fathers had sons enter the professions, but that only one-tenth of the professionals were their sons. In short, the son of a professional man has a great opportunity for entering the professions, but the professions remained widely open to many sons from nonprofessional backgrounds.

It was concluded from the San Jose study that the majority of occupational men had not moved far. While there was much occupational mobility, most practitioners in the several occupational categories had come from families where the father was in the same category or from a category immediately above or below that of the parental generation.[12]

Another study of occupational mobility, based on data from marriage license applications in Marion County, Indiana, compared trends in 1910 with those in 1940.[13] The findings in this study suggested that the over-all rates of mobility for the 1910 and the 1940 samples were the same. There were variations within the occupational categories, but not in the total movement. For example, the opportunity for movement was less in 1940 for the sons of professionals, proprietors, and clerks. The opportunity for movement in 1940 was greater for the sons of skilled, semi-skilled, and unskilled workers. The Indiana data further revealed that there was greater variation in the amount of movement into the several occupational categories than out of them. In both 1910 and 1940 sons had a higher probability of becoming professionals, semiprofessionals, proprietors, or clerks than of becoming semiskilled and unskilled workers. In both 1910 and 1940 there was a tendency for sons to move more frequently out of proprietary and farming occupations than into them. In both time periods it was discovered that sons had a greater probability of entering their fathers' occupations than for movement into any other single occupational class. Finally, it was discovered that in both 1910 and 1940 there was greatest ease in moving from one white-collar occupation to another. There was a lesser amount of downward mobility, that is movement from white-collar to blue-collar classes, in 1940 than 1910. It was, however, as easy in 1940 as in 1910 to move from a blue-collar occupation to a white-collar occupation.[14]

In the mid 1950's Chinoy summarized mobility trends in the nation.[15] He was concerned with answering questions about the possible continued rate of upward occupational mobility. Following his careful analysis of the several pieces of research, he concluded that no final answer can be given to such questions. The evidence cited is important. In Davidson and Anderson's 1933–34 San Jose study the general tendency for sons to be located in their father's occupational category, more than any others, was reported. In 1945 Centers reported that 35 per cent of his respondents were in occupations which were higher than those of their fathers, but 29 per cent were in occupations which were lower than those of their fathers. In both of these studies it was indicated that most mobility, when it did occur, was to occupational categories adjacent to that of the parental generation.[16]

In 1957 another study of occupational mobility was made from a national sample. These data were analyzed and compared to the earlier studies.[17] The 1957 data were based on an area probability "cluster" sample which was made up of adult Americans living in private households. The sample totaled 1,023 males for whom occupational data for themselves and their fathers were available. The data on which the study is based resulted from the following questions: "What kind of work do you do?" and "What kind of work did your father do for a living while you were growing up?" The occupational categories were arranged into seven ranks: professional, business, white-collar, skilled-manual, semiskilled, unskilled, and farmer. This ranking of occupations was used so that comparisons could be made with the earlier intergenerational studies. The 1957 data are presented in Table III.1. In 1957 for every origin category except unskilled workers the most typical occupational destination was that of the father's occupational category.

From this point of view it might be said that 30 per cent of the men in the sample had inherited their father's occupational category. "Inherited" must be used in a qualified manner, however. The fact that a father and son appear in the same occupational category may be determined by circumstances exterior to their family life. In addition to the tendency to move into the parental occupational category, where there was movement in other directions it was usually to an adjacent or nearly adjacent occupational category. It was also found that the sons of farmers tended to go into manual occupations when they could not enter agriculture.

If one will assume, for the sake of analysis, that the so-called urban occupational categories are ranked hierarchically, then a view of upward and downward occupational mobility may be obtained. Nearly one-fourth of the men in 1957 had moved up from an urban occupa-

TABLE III.1

Occupation of Males, by Father's Occupation, 1957

Occupation of Respondent's Father	Occupation of Male Respondents (in percentages and mobility ratios) [a]							N (100.0%) [b]
	Professional	Business	White Collar	Skilled Manual	Semi-Skilled	Unskilled	Farmer	
Professional	40.4% (4.81)	19.1% (1.45)	12.8% (.91)	19.1% (.72)	2.1% (.12)	4.3% (.47)	2.1% (.18)	47
Business	18.3 (2.18)	25.8 (1.96)	22.5 (1.61)	15.0 (.57)	12.5 (.72)	1.7 (.18)	4.2 (.36)	120
White collar	20.3 (2.41)	17.4 (1.32)	24.6 (1.76)	20.3 (.77)	10.1 (.59)	5.8 (.64)	1.4 (.13)	69
Skilled manual	8.5 (1.02)	13.6 (1.03)	15.6 (1.11)	42.2 (1.59)	14.6 (.84)	4.5 (.50)	1.0 (.09)	199
Semi-skilled	2.3 (.28)	6.3 (.47)	17.2 (1.23)	28.9 (1.09)	32.8 (1.90)	10.2 (1.12)	2.3 (.20)	128

Unskilled	1.5 (.18)	6.1 (.46)	10.6 (.76)	36.4 (1.37)	27.3 (1.58)	15.2 (1.66)	3.0 (.26)	66
Farmer	2.5 (.30)	11.2 (.85)	8.4 (.60)	21.6 (.81)	16.5 (.95)	13.5 (1.48)	26.4 (2.29)	394
All respondents (N's)	86	135	143	271	177	93	118	1023

Summary Mobility Measures: Per cent mobile:

Observed	70.0%
Structural movement	27.0
Circulation	43.0
Full-equality model	84.8
Cramér's V	.246

---

[a] Cell entries in parentheses are mobility ratios, defined as the ratio of the observed cell frequency to the cell frequency expected under conditions of full equality of opportunity.

[b] Some rows do not total to exactly 100.0% because of rounding.

Source: Elton F. Jackson and Harry J. Crockett, Jr., "Occupational Mobility in the United States: A Point Estimate and Trend Comparison," American Sociological Review, 29 (February 1964), 7.

tion to a higher urban occupation. By contrast, about one-sixth had moved downward in the occupational hierarchy.

Maximum stability and equal opportunity models. The maximum stability occupational model is a technique for differentiating occupational circulation from structural movement. The data reveal that the number of sons in the urban occupational categories is greater than the number of fathers preceding them. In farming the opposite is true. This is primarily a function of the expansion of the urban occupations and the contraction of the rural occupations.

Differential birth rate also contributes to the number of sons available for the occupational categories. In some of the lower occupations there has been a high birth rate and in some of the upper occupations a relatively low birth rate. When the birth rate falls below the replacement ratio this in and of itself provides a structure for occupational mobility or precipitates a modification in the organization of the labor force.

The stability or inheritance model suggests that, had it functioned at a maximum, the sons of urban fathers could have inherited their father's occupational level but only about one-fourth of the sons of farmers could have inherited their father's occupation. Analysis of the data using the stability model, therefore, suggests that 73 per cent of the sample could have inherited occupations, while 27 per cent were forced to move due to structural changes in the organization of the labor force over which the respondents had no control. The amount of mobility actually discovered in the data is far greater than that which would have been anticipated by the stability model. In fact, even in the urban occupations where complete inheritance was a possibility there was no case where most of the sons entered or inherited the occupational level of their fathers.

Comparison with the maximum stability model, then, indicates that of the 70 per cent who did in fact move, the movement of 27 per cent can be attributed to structural conditions; the remaining 43 per cent may be counted as circulators. "Circulation" represents mutual exchange among the occupational categories, for example, upward mobility balanced by downward mobility, and (less frequently) movement from the farm balanced by movement from urban to rural employment. The amount of circulation suggests how open the system would be in times of structural stability.[18]

In the equal or full-equality model it is assumed that the occupation of the father has no effect on that of the son.[19] From the analysis using the full-equality model it is concluded that occupational transmission in the U.S. in 1957 was closer to open equality than to maximum inheritance. In other words, in spite of the tendency for sons to enter the occupational categories of their fathers, the parental influence is comparatively slight.

National trends. A set of 1957 data were compared to the 1945 data analyzed by Centers.[20] Centers's study was based on the first national sample of males. In order to make the two studies' data comparable Centers's categories of business were merged into one and his two categories of farmers into one. The 1957 data were reduced to adult white males employed full-time or part-time and/or individuals whose fathers were not farmers. The comparison of the two studies shows similar patterns of movement. Occupational inheritance and movement to adjacent occupational categories is most frequent in both time periods. There were differences, however. In 1957 slightly more mobility was observed than in the preceding period. Moreover, urban sons experienced more upward mobility in 1957 than in 1945. The analysis in terms of the maximum stability model indicated that the proportion of respondents who were "forced" to move by structural conditions was similar in the two time periods.

The differences in mobility between 1945 and 1957 were not great, but more mobility was experienced in 1957. Part of the difference may be a function of the fact that Centers's analysis was made just prior to the end of World War II. The significance of that war on occupation is far from ascertained. It is suggested that the war might have broadened the occupational aspirations of some, precipitated downward mobility for others, and minimized family ties between fathers and sons in terms of occupations. The findings were also interpreted to suggest that they might reflect a reduction in the long-term system of occupational transmission due to increased educational opportunities and also to the decreasing importance of inherited wealth for occupational success.

It is possible to make another comparative analysis in occupational mobility for the years 1947, 1952, and 1957. In this case the samples all consist of adult males, both white and nonwhite, and sons of farmers and non-farmers alike. This second comparison involves a more comprehensive sample than that for 1945 to 1957; however, it is limited to the broad occupational categories: nonmanual, manual, and farm. The most general observation concerning these data is that occupational mobility is strikingly similar for the three time periods. It is to be noted that between 1947 and 1957 the proportion of farmers' sons going into manual occupations increased greatly. Accordingly, a greatly reduced proportion of farmers' sons remained in agricultural occupations. This trend in mobility was primarily due to structural shifts rather than individual aspirations.

The amount of occupational mobility increased slightly between 1947 and 1957. The increased mobility was primarily due to structural shifts, in terms of the maximum stability model. Or put another way, the amount of mobility attributed to circulation decreased slightly while the total mobility increased. The explanation for this structural movement is almost entirely in terms of farmers' sons being forced out of agriculture. When the amount of mobility for the three time periods is limited to comparisons among urban workers these differential trends do not obtain.[21]

In summary, concerning the intergenerational mobility trends it must be asserted again that in 1957 the differential replacement rates contribute to a movement of about one-fourth of American men from farm origins into urban occupations. There was a considerable circulation among occupations beyond this minimum forced by structural changes. Indeed, the amount of movement was closer to that of a full equality of opportunity model than to the minimum precipitated by structural shifts. The comparisons for occupational mobility of the several national samples since World War II by conservative estimate do suggest that the rate of mobility has increased somewhat. Certainly, one must observe that there is scant evidence for asserting an increasing rigidity in occupational mobility.

These several comparisons of occupational mobility at the national level pertain to intergenerational mobility only. There is also a vast amount of mobility within occupations.

JOB SHIFTING AND CAREERS

Other major areas of occupational mobility involve changes from one job to another and movement from one place to another within a given career. These kinds of occupational mobility affect a greater number of workers than does intergenerational mobility. Indeed, intergenerational mobility might be observed as most important from an ideological point of view—that is, from a point of view of the openness or the closedness of the societal organization.

Mobility within an occupation is important for career development. It is an area of mobility over which the various occupational practitioners potentially, and often in fact, have a considerable measure of control. For example, various internal occupational organizational norms like retirement systems, deferred commissions, and a variety of fringe benefits may be organized to deter job changing or to facilitate it. Moreover, job changing may be encouraged or discouraged by governmental organization, often particularly by the policies of the Department of Labor. In times of national emergency many special efforts may be made to help workers change their jobs from one type of operation to another or to "freeze" them to jobs. The retraining act programs are designed to facilitate the change from one job to another. They are designed to reduce unemployment, indeed, to achieve near full employment.

Job shifting. The average working life of an American worker was 46 years in the mid twentieth century.[22] The number of years in the working life varied from a high of 52 for service workers to a low of 40 for professionals and technical workers. How many jobs does a person hold during his working life span? There is no absolute answer to this question, but some considerable measure of evidence is available from a large study of labor force mobility.[23] From data obtained in a study of six cities it is possible to estimate that a worker holds between 11 and 12 jobs in his working lifetime. Put another way, it was reported that an average of 2.6 jobs were held for the 10 year period from 1940 to 1950. In another study, in Oakland, California, Lipset and Bendix reported that an average of 4.8 jobs were held for an average of 25.3 years in the labor force. From such data one should anticipate that the typical worker would hold 9 jobs throughout a working lifetime of some 46 years.[24] From these kinds of data one might observe that the typical American worker probably changes his job once in every 3 to 5 years.

Job mobility is not evenly distributed throughout the several occupations. In some occupations mobility is far more frequent than in others. In the six-cities study it was reported that between 1940 and 1949 laborers held an average of 3.1 jobs for the high and managers and professionals each held an average of 2.4 positions for the low. At the lower end of the occupational continuum there is a greater frequency of job changing. At the upper end of the occupational continuum there appears to be a reduced amount of job changing. This is partly due to the orientation to work as a way of life in the higher occupations. Accordingly, a worker experiences mobility there upward or downward in his career, while he continues to maintain himself in the same occupation or profession.

In the six-cities study it was further revealed that some 55 per cent of the men who changed their employer also changed their occupation and industry. Men more frequently than women change occupations when they change their employers.

Career patterns and mobility. In 1948 an investigation was made of the mobility of scientists.[25] The study was based on a sample of 1122 persons who held Ph.D. degrees in chemistry, physics, or biology. Scientists were said to have changed their jobs when they moved from one field of specialization to another, from one type of activity to another, from one employer to another, or from one state of employment to another.

Long periods of training are required for the kinds of scientists investigated. Nevertheless, three-fourths of the biologists and chemists indicated some experience outside of their specific specialty. One out of four of the scientists in all three disciplines indicated that at some previous time they had worked in an entirely different discipline. For example, about one-third of the men in physics had been employed in some other science; 22 per cent of those in biology and 15 per cent of those in chemistry had similarly been employed in another science. Nevertheless, the point to be understood is that only a minority of the scientists had work histories outside of their major area of occupation. Transfers between fields of specialization were recorded, but they were not characteristic of the occupations.

Most of the scientists had identified at an early point in their higher education (typically by the junior year) the type of speciality in which they desired to work. This point was even more clearly discovered when it was revealed that four out of five had undergraduate majors in the area in which they had taken their Ph.D. and in which they felt themselves to be most occupationally competent. Only 2 per cent reported their field of highest competence to be other than the area of their Ph.D.

The scientists reported more change of employers than changes of job and focus of occupation. Many had started as laboratory or research assistants in universities or lower research offices. As they progressed in their careers and completed their training they worked into higher positions in the several types of research agencies and other agencies which employ scientists.

Professionals are often observed to be among the least mobile of occupational men. In fact, the number of workers who are called professionals are heterogeneous in many respects, one of which is mobility. Within the several categories of professionals a different amount of mobility is reported.[26] Reiss's data come from a national sample of white males aged 25 years and over in the cities of Chicago, Los Angeles, Philadelphia, and San Francisco. Persons who held professional jobs between 1940 and 1950 were included. For analytical purposes the professionals were divided into five categories, four of which were used by Carr-Saunders.[27]

Between 1940 and 1950 varying patterns of occupational mobility were experienced by the several categories of professionals. The highest proportion of professional attachment, and, accordingly, the least mobility, was experienced for those in the established professions. Only 35 per cent of the respondents in the would-be-professions (e.g. personnel directors, sales engineers, business counselors, etc.) were characterized by high stability. More than half of the respondents in the new professions also manifested characteristics of high stability. All other professional categories were characterized by practitioners with very low degrees of stability. Upward mobility was experienced by 16 per cent of all men in the established professions, 31 per cent in the new professions, 34 per cent in the semi-professions (e.g. pharmacists, optometrists, etc.), 30 per cent in the would-be-professions, and only 27 per cent in the marginal professions. It is clear that professionals are characterized by mobility. The difference between them and other occupational men is more a matter of degree than kind.

Intra-occupational mobility within the engineering profession has been studied in some detail.[28] A questionnaire was mailed to a sample of engineers who graduated between 1911 and 1950. Information was collected concerning the specific jobs which the respondents had in the profession of engineering and these in turn were analyzed by the occupation of the father and by the respondent's year of graduation. The data indicate that sons of fathers of high occupations more frequently occupy high positions in engineering. Sons of fathers of low occupations are indeed recruited into engineering, but their occupational place in the engineering profession is typically low. This evidence suggests that while the total occupational structure of the nation might be characterized by a considerable measure of openness, there is closure to a great extent within the respective occupational or professional category. When the era or year of graduation was held constant (i.e. 1911–30, 1931–40, 1941–50), again the findings revealed that the sons of fathers of high status occupations tended to be more represented in the high engineering positions. This condition obtains for all three eras or time periods. The researchers conclude that there is a possible trend toward rigidity for mobility within this occupation.

The occupational mobility experienced by American businessmen has been reported in two major studies.[29] The purposes of these studies were to determine the social classes from which American businessmen were recruited and to contribute some understanding of the influence of heredity and environmental factors on business leadership. Among the most striking findings is the evidence that in 1952 a larger proportion of the businessmen were recruited from laboring categories than in 1928, 15 per cent and 11 per cent, respectively. It is also notable that the farmers' sons enter business positions less frequently in the current period than the earlier one, 9 per cent and 12 per cent, respectively. The significance of this finding is magnified in its importance due to the force of out-migration from agricultural occupations. In the 1950's business leaders were recruited more frequently from the white-collar and professional backgrounds than in the late 1920's. The sons of minor executives entered business leadership more frequently in 1952 than in 1928, but in part this may be a function of the inclusion of foremen with minor executives in the 1952 data.

The occupational origin of business leaders is given considerably more depth of meaning when the distribution of the business leaders' fathers is compared to the distribution of the adult male population (see Table III.2). Here the data indicate that business leaders whose fathers were in laboring occupations have increased proportionately more rapidly than the laboring category in the population. The increase of business leaders whose fathers were in white-collar work has been proportional to the white-collar increase in the total labor force.

In summary, from the comparison of occupational mobility among

TABLE III.2

Occupational Mobility Rates: Percentage of 1928 and 1952 Business Leaders' Fathers Compared with Percentage of Adult Males of 1900 and 1920

Occupation	Comparison for 1928 Group		Comparison for 1952 Group	
	Fathers of Business Leaders	U.S. Adult Males of 1900	Fathers of Business Leaders	U.S. Adult Males of 1920
Laborer	11%	45%	15%	47%
Clerk or salesman	5	7	8	10
Business owner or executive	58	6	52	11
Professional man	13	3	14	4
Farmer	12	38	9	27
Other	1	1	2	1
Total	100	100	100	100

Source: W. Lloyd Warner and James C. Abegglen, *Occupational Mobility in American Business and Industry* (Minneapolis: University of Minnesota Press, 1955), p. 46.

business leaders in 1928 and 1952, it is observed that the underrepresented categories are laborers, farmers, and white-collar workers. In 1928 some 29 per cent of the business leaders came from these three underrepresented occupational categories. The three categories constituted some 91 per cent of the nation's population. In sharp contrast, 71 per cent of the 1928 business leaders were sons of 9 per cent of the population. By 1952 business leaders who were sons of farmers, laborers, or white-collar workers had increased to 34 per cent, while these categories constituted some 84 per cent of the national population. The high status occupational groups in the population had increased from 9 to 16 per cent, while their representation among business elites had decreased from 71 to 66 per cent.[30]

OCCUPATIONAL STRUCTURES AND MOBILITY

Occupational structures influence the amount and direction of mobility in several ways. For example, occupational training and education is rigorously required of those entering many types of work, particularly the professions. Once one has been able to enter the occupation or profession, continued growth and training may be required for each promotion as an avenue for upward vertical mobility. Without such improvement in knowledge and skills one may experience no mobility or be forced to experience downward vertical mobility. With the proliferation of knowledge and skills, education and preparation for work continues to be less complete and less adequate for a life's work at the time of initial entry into the occupation than it has been in the past. Continual preparation for work is of critical importance for upward vertical mobility, and its absence is most determining for downward vertical mobility.

Occupational mobility is directly influenced by age norms. For occupations in general, most upward vertical mobility occurs between the ages of 25 and 45. In most cases it is found that men reach their highest point on the occupational ladder by about age 50.[31] For the last 15 or 20 years of the work life most individuals experience little occupational mobility at all, or a moderate amount of downward mobility. In the lower occupations one typically enters at an earlier age and experiences a maximum of occupational mobility early in the work life. For employees on the lower half of the occupational continuum there is little upward vertical mobility during the second half of their work life. Indeed, most mobility that they experience is horizontal.

Occupational mobility and income. Some specific research has been designed to investigate whether or not the incomes of mobile men are different from the stable men in occupations.[32] The data for the research were taken from surveys by the Detroit Area Study. They were collected between 1952 and 1957 and constitute a total sample of 1570 white male family heads. The respondents were divided into occupational categories as follows: "stratum I includes marginal and professional workers and the like; stratum II, clerical and sales workers; stratum III, craftsmen and foremen; stratum IV, operatives, laborers, and service workers." [33] The findings were clear. Those individuals who experienced stability in their occupation had higher incomes than mobile family heads, regardless of whether the mobility was upward or downward. In 14 of the 20 various combinations of age and stratum the incomes of the stable occupational men are higher than those of their mobile counterparts. Moreover, in those cases where there are exceptions they tend to be among those men who are under age 40, where the highest occupational income is not expected because of youth.

Occupational mobility and family. An analysis of Detroit Area Survey data has indicated that upwardly mobile families tend to take on the characteristics of the stratum of their destination. Among downwardly mobile individuals no such association obtains. Furthermore, it is found that the young upwardly mobile persons are not able to allow themselves to develop close personal contacts. Moreover, even occupational achievement does not necessarily ensure informal social acceptance by the nonmobile members of a social stratum.[34] It is also revealed that upwardly mobile persons gradually adopt new patterns of informal visiting and interaction.

It has been argued that extended family relations are antithetical to occupational mobility.[35] More recently this position has been modified. In a study of 920 white married women in an urban Buffalo area in 1952 Litwak found that occupationally mobile individuals are as likely as others to have family visits. In fact the research data indicated that it was geographical mobility rather than occupational mobility which accounts for differential family contacts. The occupationally mobile groups have a moderate identification with families.

The association between union membership and occupational mobility has been studied both in the San Francisco Bay area and the Detroit area.[36] In the two areas the major findings were highly similar. In the main, it was discovered that most of the downwardly mobile men were union members. The great majority of upwardly mobile men did not belong to unions. Once again this finding presents more evidence for the general conclusion that the effects of mobility on participation in many secondary relationships is relatively minor.

Occupational mobility and church membership have also been studied.[37] This relationship has been researched in the Detroit area data. Whether the movement is upward or downward, the mobile men are little less likely to belong to churches than the stable occupational men, 51.8 per cent and 54.4 per cent, respectively. This small difference is not significant at the 5 per cent level. In terms of church attendance the difference was little greater, and statistically significant. In the total sample 42.6 per cent of the stable men and 55.9 per cent of the mobile occupational men attended church once a week or more.

SUMMARY AND IMPLICATIONS

The findings from intergenerational mobility are conjectural. Certainly there is little or no basis for observing that rigidity has come to characterize the labor force organization. On the other hand, there is very little evidence to warrant the conclusion that occupational mobility has increased in recent years. Job shifting and career achievement are two areas of mobility in which members of the labor force participate frequently. In the highly established occupations and professions there is a minimum amount of mobility between types of work. In these places of work the mobility is characterized most by career achievement.

The occupational structures of education, age, and income make highly forceful and directive impacts on mobility. Education is clearly a prerequisite for entering many occupations. Workers in a very young age category or a very old age category will be sharply limited in their mobility.

The relationship between occupational mobility and general social participation is not great. Union membership, church membership, etc., are only vaguely related to occupational mobility.

Occupational mobility is a widely discussed phenomenon, but it is little understood, though many emotional expressions have been put forth in its defense. Few social mechanisms have been widely established to facilitate such mobility.

Free occupational mobility is a central dimension of the open-class societal ideology. Freedom to choose an occupation has been widely held to be the right of an individual. In a voluntaristic society it is necessary to establish norms of occupational mobility in order to distribute and redistribute the labor force in those areas where it is needed for the ongoing operation of the society. A considerable amount of occupational mobility is accordingly functional for societal organization.

Occupational mobility also serves the individual by constituting a mechanism for achieving success. Theoretically at least, the individual is enabled to participate in an occupation equal to his abilities and motivation.

Viewed from an alternative perspective, occupational mobility is dysfunctional for both society and individuals. A considerable amount of unemployment is related to occupational mobility. While workers are moving between jobs they typically experience loss of time in the labor force. Moreover, frustrations, dysfunctions, and frequently anomie are thrust upon those individuals and their families who experience occupational mobility.

NOTES

1. Pitirim Sorokin, "American Millionaires and Multimillionaires," *Social Forces*, 3 (May 1925), 627–40; P. Sorokin, *Social Mobility* (New York: Harper & Bros., 1927); Percy E. Davidson and H. Dewey Anderson, *Occupational Mobility in an American Community* (Stanford: Stanford University Press, 1937); Alba M. Edwards, *A Socio-Economic Grouping of the Gainful Workers of the United States* (Washington, D.C.: U.S. Department of Commerce, Bureau of the Census, 1938); Louis L. Dublin and Robert J. Vane, Jr., "Shifting of Occupations among Wage Earners as Determined by Occupational History of Industrial Policyholders," *Monthly Labor Review*, 19 (April 1924), 34–42; W. A. Anderson, *The Transmission of Farming as an Occupation* (Cornell: Agriculture Experiment Station, Bulletin 768, 1941); and F. W. Taussig and C. S. Joslyn, *America Business Leaders* (New York: The Macmillan Company, 1932).

2. Davidson and Anderson, *Occupational Mobility*.

3. Edward Gross, *Work and Society* (New York: Thomas Y. Crowell Co., 1958), pp. 168ff.

4. Harry J. Crockett, Jr., "The Achievement Motive and Differential Occupational Mobility in the United States," *American Sociological Review*, 27 (April 1962), 191–204; Leonard Reissman, "Levels of Aspirations and Social Class," *American Sociological Review*, 18 (June 1953), 233–42; and Ely Chinoy, "The Traditional Opportunity and the Aspirations of Automobile Workers," *American Journal of Sociology*, LVII (March 1952), 453–9.
5. Crockett, "Achievement Motive."
6. Ibid. p. 204.
7. Chinoy, "Traditional Opportunity."
8. Archibald O. Haller and Irwin W. Miller, *The Occupational Aspiration Scale: Theory, Structure and Correlates* (Michigan: Agriculture Experiment Station, Technical Bulletin No. 288, 1963); I. W. Miller and A. O. Haller, "A Measure of Level of Occupational Aspiration," *Personnel and Guidance Journal*, 42 (January 1964), 448–55; LaMar T. Empey, "Social Class and Occupational Aspiration," *American Sociological Review*, 21 (December 1956), 703–9; R. G. Holloway and J. V. Berrman, "The Educational and Occupational Aspirations and Plans of Negro and White Male Elementary School Student," *Pacific Sociological Review*, 2 (Fall 1959), 56–60; and Richard M. Stephenson, "Mobility Orientation and Stratification of One Thousand Ninth Graders," *American Sociological Review*, 22 (April 1957), 204–12.
9. Miller and Haller, "Occupational Aspiration," p. 448.
10. John R. Christiansen, *et al.*, *Educational and Occupational Aspirations of High School Seniors in Three Central Utah Counties* (Brigham Young University, Social Science Bulletin No. 1, 1962).
11. Davidson and Anderson, *Occupational Mobility*.
12. Ibid. pp. 164–5.
13. Natalie Rogoff, *Recent Trends in Occupational Mobility* (Glencoe: Free Press, 1953).
14. Ibid. pp. 62–3.
15. Ely Chinoy, "Social Mobility Trends in the United States," *American Sociological Review*, 20 (April 1955), 180–86.
16. Ibid. p. 185.
17. Elton F. Jackson and Harry J. Crockett, Jr., "Occupational Mobility in the United States: A Point Estimate and Trend Comparison," *American Sociological Review*, 29 (February 1964), 5–15. A more complete discussion of the collection of this data is found in Gerald Gurin, *et al.*, *Americans View their Mental Health* (New York: Basic Books, 1960).
18. Jackson and Crockett, "Occupational Mobility in the United States," p. 8.
19. Ibid. p. 8.
20. Richard Centers, "Occupational Mobility of Urban Occupational Strata," *American Sociological Review*, 13 (April 1948), 197–203.
21. Jackson and Crockett, "Occupational Mobility in the United States," p. 15.

22. A. J. Jaffe and R. O. Carleton, *Occupational Mobility in the United States, 1930–1960* (New York: Columbia University, King's Crown Press, 1954), p. 50.
23. Gladys Palmer, *Labor Mobility in Six Cities* (New York: Social Science Research Council, 1954), p. 72.
24. Robert Dubin, *World of Work* (Englewood Cliffs, N.J.: Prentice-Hall, Inc., 1958).
25. *Occupational Mobility of Scientists* (Washington, D.C.: Bureau of Labor Statistics, U.S. Department of Labor, Bulletin No. 1121, 1953).
26. Albert J. Reiss, Jr., "Occupational Mobility of Professional Workers," *American Sociological Review*, 20 (December 1955), 693–700.
27. Alexander Morris Carr-Saunders, "Metropolitan Conditions and Traditional Professional Relationships," in the *Metropolis in Modern Life*, ed. by Robert M. Fisher (Garden City, N.Y.: Doubleday and Co., 1955), pp. 280–81.
28. Robert Perrucci, "The Significance of Intra-Occupational Mobility: Some Methodological and Theoretical Notes, together with a Case Study of Engineers," *American Sociological Review*, 26 (December 1961), 874–83.
29. F. W. Taussig and C. S. Joslyn, *American Business Leaders* (New York: The Macmillan Company, 1932); and W. Lloyd Warner and James C. Abegglen, *Occupational Mobility in American Business and Industry* (Minneapolis: University of Minnesota Press, 1955).
30. Warner and Abegglen, *Occupational Mobility in American Business*, pp. 50–51.
31. Dubin, *World of Work*, p. 270.
32. Richard F. Curtis, "Income and Occupational Mobility," *American Sociological Review*, 25 (October 1960), 727–30.
33. Ibid. p. 729.
34. Richard F. Curtis, "Occupational Mobility and Urban Social Life," *American Journal of Sociology*, LXV (November 1959), 296–8.
35. Eugene Litwak, "Occupational Mobility and Extended Family Cohesion," *American Sociological Review*, 25 (February 1960), 9–21.
36. Richard F. Curtis, "Note on Occupational Mobility and Union Membership in Detroit: A Replication," *Social Forces*, 38 (October 1959), 69–71.
37. Richard F. Curtis, "Occupational Mobility and Church Participation," *Social Forces*, 38 (May 1960), 315–19.

SUPPLEMENTARY READINGS

Ely Chinoy, "The Traditional Opportunity and the Aspirations of Automobile Workers," *American Journal of Sociology*, LVII (March 1952), 453–9.
Harry J. Crockett, Jr., "The Achievement Motive and Differential Occupa-

tional Mobility in the United States," *American Sociological Review*, 27 (April 1962), 191–204.

Richard F. Curtis, "Income and Occupational Mobility," *American Sociological Review*, 25 (October 1960), 727–30.

Elton F. Jackson and Harry J. Crockett, Jr., "Occupational Mobility in the United States: A Point Estimate and Trend Comparison," *American Sociological Review*, 29 (February 1964), 5–15.

Eugene Litwak, "Occupational Mobility and Extended Family Cohesion," *American Sociological Review*, 25 (February 1960), 9–21.

Albert J. Reiss, Jr., "Occupational Mobility of Professional Workers," *American Sociological Review*, 20 (December 1955), 693–700.

W. Lloyd Warner and James C. Abegglen, *Occupational Mobility in American Business and Industry* (Minneapolis: University of Minnesota Press, 1964).

BUREAUCRACY AS AN OCCUPATIONAL ENVIRONMENT IV

Occupational organizations are largely dependent on the social organizational structures of the society of which they are a part. Yet one may observe that, particularly in the urbanized societies, an individual's occupation to a great extent determines his way of life. If one has the opportunity to know only a single fact about the life of an individual in urbanized society, knowledge of his occupation will be the most definitive. The importance of occupation in the life of an individual, however, in no way detracts from the observation that occupations are more determined by the society of which they are a part than they are determining on that society. There is, of course, some degree of reciprocity between societal organization and occupational organization.

In Chapters IV, V, and VI the differential impacts of the societal organizational structures of bureaucracy, professionalization, and unionization will be demonstrated on occupational structures. These three societal structures are not mutually exclusive. Nonetheless, they are sufficiently distinct that they may be studied as dominant types and occupations may be analyzed within their environmental spheres.

In bureaucratic environments one observes that occupational organization is influenced and directed from the top down. In such an environment the integrity of free-standing occupations is sharply limited; their autonomy is reduced to a minimum. Such major occupational norms as recruitment, training, remuneration, and status are all influenced by the rationalistic rule-organized character of the bureaucracy. Work tasks are assigned from the point of view of efficiency more than for the integrity or status of the occupation. There is little room for creativity and imaginative expansion and growth for occupations. Recruitment is objective and impartial, and minimally controlled by occupational practitioners.

Occupations in the environment of professionalization experience a

maximum of autonomy and fullness of expression. In this social organizational environment occupational organizations are more dominating
than in any others. Organization and control emanate primarily from
within the occupational structure itself. Occupational men are theoretically free to establish their own work tasks. Maximum creativity is
achieved in professionalization. In terms of recruitment, the practitioners dominate and control selection of colleagues. In the professionalization environment the greatest delusion of the occupational organization is experienced as professions and way of life become un-
differentiable at many junctures.

In the environment of unionization occupational organization is
characteristically less free-standing than in professionalization. In contrast to the environment of bureaucracy, the impact on occupations is
made from the bottom up. Work space is negotiated. Occupational
practitioners are largely dependent upon the environment the union
negotiates with their employers. As in the case of bureaucracy, but for
different reasons, creativity is reduced to a near minimum. Efforts at
scientific management of workers are particularly repugnant to unions.
Unions are an intermediate occupational authority. Depending on their
negotiations, the magnitude of occupational integrity is precarious; it is
reduced at one time and expanded at another.

From a societal organizational point of view, occupations exist more
for their services to the society than for their independent integrity.
With the expansion of professionalization, societal organization may be
more characterized by contract and status organization. Such conditions
may contribute to high prestige for some occupations while precipitating patterns of social distance and segregation in other aspects of societal organization. In bureaucratic organization a vast multiplicity of
occupations are utilized, but their free-standing integrity is subjugated
to the societal efficiency goals articulated through the bureaucracy.
Unionization represents a negotiated intermediate space between professionalization and bureaucracy. No attempt is made here to defend
any one of these environmental conditions; the focus of this analysis
concerns their differential impact on the integrity of occupations.

BUREAUCRACY AND SOCIAL ORGANIZATION

Bureaucracy is a type of social organization designed to accomplish
large-scale administrative tasks by rationalistic and systematic co-ordina-

tion of masses of individuals in a multiplicity of occupations.[1] Bureaucratic aims in the mass urbanized society are toward a total efficiency through the integration of multiple occupations for the ends of major institutions of the society. By contrast, the proliferation of free-standing occupations invites the vying and jockeying for position, prestige, and status among the several occupations and without their necessarily sustaining any perspective view of the totality of societal organization.

The experience of bureaucracy is not new. Rudimentary examples that existed more than a thousand years ago in Egypt, Rome, and China are cited by Weber.[2] The Weberian analysis of bureaucracy is regarded as classic. Indeed, Weber was the originator of the systematic study of bureaucracy.[3]

According to Weber, the concept of bureaucracy is characterized by six principal conditions:

I. There is the principle of fixed and official jurisdictional areas, which are generally ordered by rules, that is, by laws or administrative regulations.

1. The regular activities required for the purposes of the bureaucratically governed structure are distributed in a fixed way as official duties.

2. The authority to give the commands required for the discharge of these duties is distributed in a stable way and is strictly delimited by rules concerning the coercive means, physical, sacerdotal, or otherwise, which may be placed at the disposal of officials.

3. Methodical provision is made for the regular and continuous fulfilment of these duties and for the execution of the corresponding rights; only persons who have the generally regulated qualifications to serve are employed.

In public and lawful government these three elements constitute "bureaucratic authority." In private economic domination, they constitute bureaucratic "management." Bureaucracy, thus understood, is fully developed in political and ecclesiastical communities only in the modern state, and, in the private economy, only in the most advanced institutions of capitalism. Permanent and public office authority, with fixed jurisdiction, is not the historical rule but rather the exception. This is so even in large political structures such as those of the ancient Orient, the Germanic and Mongolian empires of conquest, or of may feudal structures of state. In all these cases, the ruler executes the most important measures through personal trustees, table-companions, or court-servants. Their commissions and authority are not precisely delimited and are temporarily called into being for each case.

II. The principles of office hierarchy and of levels of graded authority mean a firmly ordered system of super- and subordination in which there is a supervision of the lower offices by the higher ones. Such a system offers the governed the possibility of appealing the decision of a lower office to its higher authority, in a definitely regulated manner. With the full development of the bureaucratic type, the office hierarchy is monocratically organized. The principle of hierarchical office authority is found in all bureaucratic structures: in state and ecclesiastical structures as well as in large party organizations and private enterprises. It does not matter for the character of bureaucracy whether its authority is called "private" or "public."

When the principle of jurisdictional "competency" is fully carried through, hierarchical subordination—at least in public office—does not mean that the "higher" authority is simply authorized to take over the business of the "lower." Indeed, the opposite is the rule. Once established and having fulfilled its task, an office tends to continue in existence and be held by another incumbent.

III. The management of the modern office is based upon written documents ("the files") which are preserved in their original or draught form. There is, therefore, a staff of subaltern officials and scribes of all sorts. The body of officials actively engage in a "public" office, along with the respective apparatus of material implements and the files, make up a "bureau." In private enterprise, "the bureau" is often called "the office."

In principle, the modern organization of the civil service separates the bureau from the private domicile of the official, and, in general, bureaucracy segregates official activity as something distinct from the sphere of private life. Public monies and equipment are divorced from the private property of the official. The condition is everywhere the product of a long development. Nowadays, it is found in public as well as in private enterprises; in the latter, the principle extends even to the leading entrepreneur. In principle, the executive office is separated from the household, business from private correspondence, and business assets from private fortunes. The more consistently the modern type of business management has been carried through the more are these separations the case. The beginnings of this process are to be found as early as the Middle Ages.

It is the peculiarity of the modern entrepreneur that he conducts business himself as the "first official" of his enterprise, in the very same way in which the ruler of a specifically modern bureaucratic state spoke of himself as "the first servant" of the state.* The idea that the bureau activities of the state are intrinsically different in character from the management of private economic offices is a continental European notion and, by way of contrast, is totally foreign to the American way.

IV. Office management, at least all specialized office management—and such management is distinctly modern—usually presupposes thorough and expert training. This increasingly holds for the modern executive and employee of private enterprises, in the same manner as it holds for the state official.

* Frederick II of Prussia.

V. When the office is fully developed, official activity demands the full working capacity of the official, irrespective of the fact that his obligatory time in the bureau may be firmly delimited. In the normal case, this is only the product of a long development, in the public as well as in the private office. Formerly, in all cases, the normal state of affairs was reversed: official business was discharged as a secondary activity.

VI. The management of the office follows general rules, which are more or less stable, more or less exhaustive, and which can be learned. Knowledge of these rules represents a special technical learning which the officials possess. It involves jurisprudence, or administrative or business management.

The reduction of modern office management to rules is deeply embedded in its very nature. The theory of modern public administration, for instance, assumes that the authority to order certain matters by decree— which has been legally granted to public authorities—does not entitle the bureau to regulate the matter by commands given for each case, but only to regulate the matter abstractly. This stands in extreme contrast to the regulation of all relationships through individual privileges and bestowals of favor, which is absolutely dominant in patrimonialism, at least in so far as such relationships are not fixed by sacred tradition.[4]

Formal and informal organization. The concept of bureaucracy as presented by Weber is a matter of formal organization. It ideally involves secondary rather than primary relationships. The excessive emphasis on formal organization has led to much criticism of bureaucracy and dysfunction in its operation. The rules of organization are virtually static, and behavior which is overly adherent to them is rigid. Empirical research in bureaucratic work environment has demonstrated repeatedly that patterns of unofficial and informal organization are juxtaposed with formal structures. In order to facilitate the dynamics of bureaucracy, strong informal primary interaction patterns develop, even though they are subjugated to the formal regulations.

Informal organization is documented in the bureaucracy of the navy. Often it is a facilitating mechanism and intended to support the official bureaucracy. In other cases informal organization is identified as erosive to and contradictory to the official bureaucratic organization. For example, work colleagues in a bureaucratic structure may establish norms which include, "Don't be a rate buster by working too fast!" "Don't be a chiseler by working too slowly!" "Don't act bossy!" and "Don't be a squealer!"[5] The informal norms of the bureaucracy are supported by ostracism, ridicule, and related techniques for practitioner control.

The concept of bureaucracy as modified through empirical research is expanded to include the informal structure in addition to the formal structure.

Bureaucracies in many occupational areas. The concept of bureaucracy is generic. In popular usage bureaucracy is disproportionately associated with governmental organization. It is a correct observation that most modern governments are bureaucratic in structure. Accordingly, the occupational environment for most government civil servants is bureaucratic. The many professionals and specialists who are employed by government necessarily also work in a bureaucratic or pseudo-bureaucratic environment. In addition to the well-established government bureaucracies, that form of rationalistic organization is also widely used in industrial corporations and to a lesser extent in universities, churches, and so forth. Occupational men in all of these various areas of work are influenced by the environment of bureaucracy.

BUREAUCRACY AND OCCUPATIONAL ORGANIZATION

In bureaucracies occupational recruitment, training, remuneration, status, and functions are all influenced by the norms of general work efficiency which are oriented to the total enterprise rather than to individual occupations or individual practitioners. Recruitment norms are fundamental in occupational organization. To the extent that occupational practitioners define and control recruitment the occupation's integrity as a free-standing entity is increased. To the extent that outside definition and determination of recruitment is accepted the boundary maintenance of the occupation is invaded and its free-standing character is reduced. In the formal organization of bureaucracy, recruitment is moved out of the areas of patronage and nepotism. Recruitment is objective rather than subjective. The merit of these systems of recruitment is not in question; the importance of the consideration lies in the fact that the definition of recruitment rests with the bureaucracy rather than the occupational practitioners. The occupation is accordingly influenced by the social organization structure of which it is a part.[6]

The type of occupational men who are recruited into bureaucracies, it is said, are "passively compulsive" personality types, whose interest is in security and the dullness of routine more than in creativity.[7] The occupational man in the bureaucracy is found to gain his prestige and support from his position in the hierarchy.[8]

Career orientations. Rule-oriented individuals find the routine of the bureaucracy an agreeable environment in which to work. Yet in spite of the formality of the bureaucracy all of the details of work are not adequately structured by rule specification. Responsible bureaucratic innovation is encouraged by the conservative balance of conformity and initiative in the effort at professionalization. When professionalization is used as a mechanism of organization it involves development of norms for career service. Accordingly, many occupational men in the bureaucracy make that work location a lifelong experience.[9] The reward for this kind of professionalized conservative service is security in tenure, a regular salary, and, in the contemporary situation, a variety of fringe benefits such as medical protection, vacation, and retirement pensions.

A clear distinction must be made between professionalization as a mechanism and professionals as occupational men. The bureaucracy seeks to establish mechanisms of professionalization to accomplish its end in many situations. It also, in other situations, employs professionals as occupational men. Often it is easy in a bureaucracy to achieve professionalization as a mechanism of control over workers who are not members of professional occupations.

The ends of professionals, even when employed in bureaucratic settings, are often more cosmopolitan than local. The professionals insist in identifying with the subject area of their profession often in a prior order to an identification with their bureaucratic setting. Career professionals in a bureaucracy are often looked upon as having lower occupational status than career professionals whose work is not circumscribed by bureaucratic organization.

In any event, it may be asserted that a career orientation which is consistent with bureaucratic organization involves a commitment to a routinized life plan of work. In Marvick's analysis he identifies three career types: skill-bound specialists, place-bound institutionalists, and free-agent hybrids. The first is a cosmopolitan, the second a local, and the third gives no directional commitment or loyalty.[10]

Work organizational patterns in bureaucracies. Gouldner has identified three patterns of bureaucracy: mock, representative, and punishment-centered.[11] In the case of the mock bureaucratic pattern, rules and regulations are established from sources outside of the work environment. For example, in numerous bureaucratically organized factories there may be a number of rules which are established by insurance

FIGURE IV.1

Summary of factors associated with the three patterns of bureaucracy

MOCK	REPRESENTATIVE	PUNISHMENT-CENTERED
	1. Who Usually Initiates the Rules?	
The rule or rules are imposed on the group by some "outside" agency. *Neither* workers nor management, neither superiors nor subordinates, identify themselves with or participate in the establishment of the rules or view them as their own. e. g.—The "no-smoking" rule was initiated by the insurance company.	*Both* groups initiate the rules and view them as their own. e. g.—Pressure was exerted by union *and* management to initiate and develop the safety program. Workers and supervisors could make modifications of the program at periodic meetings.	The rule arises in response to the pressure of *either* workers or management, but is *not jointly* initiated by them. The group which does not initiate the rule views it as imposed upon it by the other. e. g.—Through their union the workers initiated the bidding system. Supervisors viewed it as something to which the Company was forced to adhere.
	2. Whose Values Legitimate the Rules?	
Neither superiors nor subordinates can, ordinarily, legitimate the rule in terms of their own values.	Usually, *both* workers and management can legitimate the rules in terms of their own key values. e. g.—Management legitimated the safety program by tying it to *production*. Workers legitimized it via their values on personal and bodily welfare, maintenance of income, and cleanliness.	*Either* superiors or subordinates alone consider the rule legitimate; the other may concede on grounds of expediency, but does not define the rule as legitimate. e. g.—Workers considered the bidding system "fair," since they viewed it as minimizing personal favoritism in the distribution of jobs. Supervisors conformed to it largely because they feared the consequences of deviation.

3. Whose Values Are Violated by Enforcement of the Rules?

Enforcement of the rule violates the values of *both groups*.

e. g.—If the no-smoking rule were put into effect, it would violate the value on "personal equality" held by workers and supervisors, since office workers would still be privileged to smoke.

Under most conditions, enforcement of the rules entails violations of *neither* group's values.

e. g.—It is only under comparatively *exceptional* circumstances that enforcement of the safety rules interfered with a value held by management, say, a value on production.

Enforcement of the rules violates the values of only one group, *either* superiors or subordinates.

e. g.—The bidding rules threatened management's value on the use of skill and ability as criteria for occupational recruitment.

4. What Are the Standard Explanations of Deviations from the Rules?

The deviant pattern is viewed as an expression of "uncontrollable" needs or of "human nature."

e. g.—People were held to smoke because of "nervousness."

Deviance is attributed to ignorance or *well-intentioned carelessness*—i. e., it is an unanticipated by-product of behavior oriented to some other end, and thus an "accident." This we call a "utilitarian" conception of deviance.

e. g.—Violation of the safety rule might be seen as motivated by concern for production, rather than by a deliberate intention to have accidents. If for example, a worker got a hernia, this might be attributed to his ignorance of proper lifting technique.

In the main, deviance is attributed to *deliberate* intent. Deviance is thought to be the deviant's *end*. This we call a "voluntaristic" conception of deviance.

e. g.—When a worker was absent without an excuse, this was *not* viewed as an expression of an uncontrollable impulse, or as an unanticipated consequence of other interests. It was believed to be *wilful*.

95

Summary of factors associated with the three patterns of bureaucracy
(*cont.*)

5. What Effects Do the Rules Have Upon the Status of the Participants?

MOCK	REPRESENTATIVE	PUNISHMENT-CENTERED
Ordinarily, deviation from the rule is status-enhancing for workers and management. Conformance to the rule would be status-impairing for both.	Usually, deviation from the rules impairs the status of superiors *and* subordinates, while conformance ordinarily permits both a measure of status improvement.	Conformance to or deviation from the rules leads to status gains *either* for workers or supervisors, but not for both, and to status losses for the other.
e. g.—Violation of the no-smoking rule tended to minimize the visibility of status differentials, by preventing the emergence of a privileged stratum of smokers.	e. g.—The safety program increased the prestige of workers' jobs by improving the cleanliness of the plant (the "good housekeeping" component), as well as enabling workers to initiate action for their superiors through the safety meetings. It also facilitated management's ability to realize its production obligations, and provided it with legitimations for extended control over the worker.	e. g.—Workers' conformance to the bidding system allowed them to escape from tense relations with certain supervisors, or to secure jobs and promotions without dependence upon supervisory favors. It deprived supers of the customary prerogative of recommending workers for promotion or for hiring.

6. Summary of Defining Characteristics or Symptoms

MOCK	REPRESENTATIVE	PUNISHMENT-CENTERED
(a) Rules are neither enforced by management nor obeyed by workers.	(a) Rules are both enforced by management and obeyed by workers.	(a) Rules either enforced by workers or management, and evaded by the other.
(b) Usually entails little conflict between the two groups.	(b) Generates a few tensions, but little overt conflict.	(b) Entails relatively great tension and conflict.
(c) Joint violation and evasion of rules is buttressed by the informal sentiments of the participants.	(c) Joint support for rules buttressed by informal sentiments, mutual participation, initiation, and education of workers and management.	(c) Enforced by punishment and supported by the informal sentiments of *either* workers or management.

Source: Alvin W. Gouldner, *Patterns of Industrial Bureaucracy* (Glencoe: The Free Press, 1964), pp. 216-17.

agencies which serve both the industry and the workers. These rules, often concerning safety and health, in the work situation are sometimes supported by the management, sometimes supported by the workers, but often supported by neither.

In a representative bureaucratic organization the rules are established jointly by the occupational practitioners and by the managers. In this work situation the bureaucratic rules are typically supported by all workers in the environment. They support their mutual advantage and detract from no one's status.

The punishment-centered bureaucratic work environment is characterized by rules that are unilaterally promulgated by pressure from workers or by authority from management. In this work situation the support of the bureaucratic rules is in continual contradiction to the work space and ideology of one or the other category of people in the bureaucracy. The equilibrium balance is always precarious, and a conflict situation is characteristically latent. The major characteristics of these three patterns of bureaucratic work situations are summarized in Figure IV.1.

Inducements and incentives. Bureaucratic organization, like other forms of organization in the work world, must be addressed to the problem of motivation. In the main, the bureaucratic answer to this situation is stability and security. Regular pay, a life career, and retirement benefits constitute the normative rewards for a relatively unimaginative work space. For great masses of occupational men this bureaucratic idiom constitutes an optimum work environment.

Individuals are most willing to accept the goals of an organization when they are at the same time directly or indirectly achieving their personal goals.[12] In the bureaucratic organization of churches there is extreme congruence between the goals of the organization and the personal goals of individuals. Workers in industrial bureaucracies, however, on some occasions experience goal congruence and in other circumstances do not. For example, the goals of the managers may include expansion of the industry and increased profits. The workers may also agree on the expansion and profit increase, but a differential judgment is entered into concerning the proportion of the increased profit for the workers versus the industry. At this point goal congruence may be reduced to a minimum. Indeed, in many cases it may be observed that unionization constitutes for many occupational men a more agreeable occupational environment for negotiating a fair share of the industrial profits.

In some bureaucracies the goals are relatively tangible and the decision-making relative to the goals is largely taken out of the realm of conjecture. For example, in an oil refining industry goals and decisions are concerned with the production of a high quality product for designated markets. In this case there is a minimum of difficulty in assessing the value and contribution which various occupational men make in the refinement and preparation of the product.

In the bureaucracy of a large university the general goal is education, but its achievement is often a point of view, a matter of judgment. The community of scholars may be research-oriented, publication-oriented, devoted to mass teaching, and so forth. The range of the enterprise may extend from a graduate research library with an international collection to a huge football stadium on the campus in a small country town location. Evaluation of the contribution of occupational men whose work is centered in the graduate research library or whose work is central to the athletic program is a matter of much conjecture concerning the goals of the bureaucratic enterprise. The inducement and incentives which attract workers to athletic direction may be far different from those which attract scholars to the dust and labor in a research library. In a bureaucracy it is noted that the incentive techniques may not only be different, but should be hierarchical in their order. The salary and fringe benefits of the distinguished football coach may be far more than the stipend and benefits for the international research scholar, and this is a subject of question—if not disjuncture—in the intellectual bureaucracy.

The most tangible employee incentive in the bureaucracy is monetary remuneration. It is amplified with security and fringe benefits. From the bureaucratic organizational point of view it is most often desirable for the service of the occupational man to be of an undifferentiated type. In reality, most bureaucracies must deal with occupational men who have an image of their work as an entity in and of itself. The status, prestige, and nature of the occupation stand alone, as it were, so that in addition to the incentives for the worker there must be sufficient space for the sustaining of the occupation as well. The associated goals of the organized occupation may or may not be in congruence with the goals of the bureaucracy.

In bureaucracies promotion opportunities often constitute another major incentive for participation. This incentive has the dual advantage of economic gain and prestige bestowal. In the main in the hierarchical organization those positions nearer the top carry greater economic remuneration and more extensive fringe benefits than those beneath them. Moreover, each higher position in the hierarchy typically carries a greater prestige. In the modern operation of bureaucracies in scientific urbanized areas this hierarchical order often does some considerable measure of abuse to the organization of occupations. Particularly those occupations at the professional level are more often organized horizontally than vertically. Scientific researchers, for example, may have higher status than laboratory directors, deans, or other research administrators. In some cases bureaucracies have been modified to recognize the high level contributions of some professionals and scientists and thereby keep them in productive research positions rather than recruit them, as a result of hierarchy, into top administrative positions.[13]

Another incentive for occupational men in bureaucracies, particularly in the urbanized society, is the size and growth of the organization itself. There is a widespread notion that bigness and growth are more desirable than smallness and contraction. These are two judgments made about the nature of society, the nature of bureaucracy, and the nature of occupational organization. Many other judgments could be made, but they seldom are in the urbanized society. For example, emphasis might be placed unilaterally on quality. Depending on the occupational situation, largeness may or may not have a positive impact on quality. The very nature of growth or progress is more a function of definition than of absolute conditions. In any event the bureaucratic environment that is big, and that is increasing, is usually looked upon with more favor than one without these characteristics. In the growing bureaucracy individual occupations may also enjoy a social space for growth prosperity. For example, the emerging occupation of administrative science is to a great extent a function of expansion of bureaucracies in the urbanized society. The newly developing occupation of hospital administrators is another example of a bureaucratic work space contributing to the growth and expansion of a heretofore unknown occupation.

The impact of bureaucratic incentives on occupational men and occupational organizations is readily exemplified.

Succession. In bureaucratic organizations succession is one of the many items of formal specification. The rules and regulations of the office theoretically precede the occupant of the office and succeed the occupant of the office. Regardless of whether the occupational man in the bureaucracy is at the bottom, middle, or top of the hierarchy, his roles are theoretically established in the formal organization. Succession, therefore, is not associated with personality or individualism. All of this is in sharp contrast to the personality cults and charisma of the past and/or non-bureaucratic organizations.

Particularly in the science-oriented occupations, the level of importance and contribution of the practitioner is associated with the body of knowledge he accumulates and manipulates rather than with his personality as such. Theoretically, the occupational competency of one position should be the same as and interchangeable with that of another. Physicians, as such, are certified occupationally because of their ability to understand and use a specified body of knowledge. Similar observations in terms of understanding and succession might be made for attorneys, professors, clergymen, and many other professionals.

In sharp contrast, one can observe other occupations in which the differential role achievement is normative and where succession is a problem which cannot be effectively regulated by a bureaucracy. Occupations that have to do with the arts constitute examples. Within the occupation of painters one does not look for a successor to Rembrandt, El Greco, Dali, or Pollock. In the occupation of the theater one does not expect to find successors to the Barrymores. The nature of the occupation and the order of work are such that individual differences in role manifestation are expected, indeed, even encouraged.

Bureaucracy influences occupational organization, sometimes in a complimentary way, other times in a contradictory way. But always in the mass urbanized society where occupations have proliferated, as indicated by the U.S. Census, to more than 20,000, some specific societal mechanisms must be operative to establish order among the various occupations. Bureaucracy serves society as one such mechanism among many occupations.

EXAMPLES OF BUREAUCRATIC IMPACT ON OCCUPATIONS

Some occupations have had a free-standing organization and they have been invaded only recently by bureaucracies. Medicine, law, and engineering are examples of free-standing occupations, all of which have experienced differential impacts by bureaucracies in recent years. Most excessive is the case of medicine, which has been confronted with socialization in varying degrees of specificity. Law is coming to be related to governmental bureaucracy in a substantively different way. A disproportionate number of policy-making political bureaucrats are attorneys. The relation of the occupation of law to government bureaucracies is to a great extent a matter of boundary deterioration and invasion. In effect, there is a considerable fusion. The historically free-standing occupation of engineering experiences bureaucratization in still another way. In the scientific technological society the services of occupational engineers are of vast importance to governments. Accordingly, they are commissioned and/or employed within the bureaucracy in relatively large numbers, but their employment is far from any form of socialization of the occupation. Finally, one might observe that the neophyte occupation of civil servants has emerged almost entirely from within bureaucratic structures. Indeed, one of the difficulties in the emergence of civil service as an occupation is its patronization by government.

Occupations like public school teaching have been historically socialized. Yet public school teachers do in fact constitute a well-organized occupation. And, unlike civil servants, school teachers may, and in some cases do, seek and obtain viable occupation employment as teachers outside of the governmentally controlled education structures. To this extent public school teaching is more similar to law in its occupational relation to government bureaucracy than to the several other examples cited. It is distinguished from law by the fact that the majority of its practitioners are in some form of government employment. Moreover, the major manifestations of the occupation are articulated within the structure of the government schools bureaucracy. By contrast, the majority of the occupational practitioners in law remain outside of government contractual employment. Similarly, the major body of the occupational experience and knowledge remains exterior to rather than integrated within the government bureaucracy.

This next section of the chapter is devoted to an examination of the specific and differential impacts which various forms of bureaucracies make on occupations.

Professions. Blau and Scott in two separate studies have investigated the impact of professionalization on social workers.[14] In the main this kind of research is directed toward greater understanding of the generally observed notion that professionals tend to be cosmopolitans in their orientation. By this it is meant that they are more committed to the content of their profession than they are to a loyalty to the particular organization which employs them. The result of this kind of situation is that professionals are quite willing to move from one place of employment to another for opportunities which they believe will enable them to serve their discipline better, even though such mobility may not contribute to the goals of the bureaucracy in which they work. In the Blau and Scott studies the hypothesis was tested "That there is an inverse relationship between professional commitment and organizational loyalty." [15]

Two populations of social workers were studied; one in a large metropolitan area, referred to as *city agency*, and the other in a smaller urban area, referred to as *county agency*. Some of the respondents had graduate training in social work and others did not. It was anticipated that those practitioners with graduate training would more frequently choose reference situations external to their bureaucratic agencies than those with the lack of such training. Such a relationship was discovered but it was not as pronounced as anticipated. Ultimately, the researchers analyzed the impact of bureaucracy on four types of respondents: first, those with graduate training and outside reference groups (profession-oriented); second, those with outside reference groups but with no graduate training (reference-group-oriented); third, those with graduate training and no outside reference groups (training-oriented); and finally, those without graduate training and without outside reference groups (bureaucracy-oriented). [16]

To study the relationship between bureaucracy and these four types of respondents questions were asked concerning conference attendance, activity in local welfare groups, beliefs concerning supervisor's training at advanced levels, and notions concerning increased assistance to clients. It was anticipated that the professionally oriented respondents should attend more professional meetings and participate more frequently in local welfare activities than the bureaucratically oriented practitioners. Furthermore, it was anticipated that those with professional orientations would expect supervisors to have a professional level of training and finally that the professionally oriented participants should be most concerned about the amount of assistance rendered to clients. The data confirm the predictions and contribute to the evidence that bureaucracy makes a differential impact on practitioners.

Another test of the relationship between professionalization and bureaucracy concerns the willingness of practitioners to leave their agency positions for private agencies. Again, it is discovered that practitioners with the greatest professional orientation are least loyal to the bureaucratic agency.

The bureaucratization of medical practice is becoming more widely accepted in the second half of the twentieth century. This trend and development, however, has not progressed as far in the United States as in several other countries. Therefore, the evidence for bureaucratic impact on this professional occupation is cited in the research of Ben-David in Israel.[17] The intervention of bureaucracy in the practice of medicine has had a longer history in the Jewish community in Palestine than in many other countries. In a technical sense, however, it must be noted that the government of Israel does not provide medical insurance. Nevertheless, most of the wage and salaried workers have medical insurance service provided by the Sick Fund of the General Federation of Labor. Membership in this federation is virtually required in order to obtain a position. Furthermore, a majority of the self-employed in agriculture have adopted this coverage. A formalized medical coverage is in effect ubiquitous.

In general it was found that the impact of bureaucratization on medical practice was met with dissatisfaction by physicians in Israel. In particular there were complaints concerning administrative lack of efficiency, and, even more professionally frustrating, interference with the practice of medicine itself. The administration of the medical program was directed by laymen. Ben-David points out, however, that it was entirely possible that some of the inefficiency was due to the physicians own unwillingness to co-operate. The doctors also asserted that working with the organization caused them to experience a loss of professional independence. They felt that the Israel Federation of Labor exploited doctors by their excessive direction of work in places of strict supervision. Moreover, in the bureaucratic organization of the medical practice the doctors had lost most of their power in referral to specialists and/or to certain hospitals. Patients are sent to hospitals for examinations and then the disposition of their case is made through bureau-cratic channels. Generally, home visits are made by different doctors. In this system a doctor loses personal contact with "his" patient.[18]

Another form of resentment was the doctors' belief that patients came to them for no particular need, but just because it cost them nothing directly. Accordingly, it was asserted that such patients made unreasonable demands of the physicians, and showed them little or no respect. In juxtaposition patients asserted that the physicians showed them an insufficient attention and that they were impersonal in their treatment. The patients explained this on the basis that the doctor had really nothing to lose financially if his clientele declined.

The National Health Service in England constitutes a form of bureaucratization and socialization of medical practice.[19] Since its inauguration in 1948, the overwhelming majority of both general prac-titioners and specialists are reported to work wholly or partly in the National Health Service. In terms of practice orientation it is found that the family doctor situation has virtually withered away. Under the National Health Service Program doctors tend to treat individuals rather than families. The details of organization in hospitals are greatly complicated by the bureaucratic routines that are demanded by the operation. Yet in the British system it is noted that a doctor-patient relationship is still preserved, at least theoretically. The doctor's fees are based on the number of patients he treats, even when the individual patients are not fee-paying persons. To this extent physicians still have a responsibility for developing the integrity of their practice and profes-sion.

Schoolteaching, according to Lewis and Maude, was the first profes-sion to be socialized, and in effect bureaucratized. The teachers have their professional boundary maintenance greatly invaded, if not de-stroyed, by the periodic visits from government inspectors to determine the satisfactoriness of their work. "One educationalist confided to us his private opinion that the profession will have taken a big step for-ward toward its proper status on the day when a headmaster throws one of H. M. inspectors out of the school room window!" [20] While this assertion may be extreme it illustrates one dimension of bureau-cratization on professional occupations. Decisions concerning the organ-ization of schools are made at a bureaucratic level above the teachers.

The remuneration of teachers is low, and many are leaving the profession, or after their training do not enter it but take some alternative work. The profession becomes continually more dependent on the state. The National Union of Teachers is active in its trade union features, but even that behavior is questionable in terms of strengthening the professional image.

In the United States the profession of public school teaching historically has been subjugated to the governmental bureaucracies of the several states. Although there are some private and some church-related schools, approximately 95 per cent of the school age children and their teachers are in public bureaucratized schools. The general curriculum and organization of the schools are determined at a state level. Locally, boards of education in conjunction with professional school administrators establish policy for and operate the schools. The National Education Association is the professional agency for representing teachers. With an ever-increasing impact of bureaucracy on the profession, the National Education Association has countered by expanding its trade union characteristics in negotiating specifically for higher teacher salaries. Again, it is a matter of question whether this trade union manifestation is functional toward expanding the professional image of public school teachers. In any event it illustrates one of the responses that professional occupational people make as their work environment becomes bureaucratized.

Scientists as occupational men in recent years are finding employment by government bureaucracies in ever greater numbers. From the origin of the federal government to the present time there continually has been some consideration of promotion and development of science with the service of national goals implied. Since the middle of the twentieth century the federal government's support (see Table IV.1) of science has increased by such vast proportions that the bureaucratization of occupational work in this area is more a real issue than ever before. The federal government expenditures for research increased from almost $3 million in 1953 to over $12 million in 1963. Two million dollars in research funds came from other sources in 1953 and $5 million from other sources in 1963. In the cases of industry, colleges, and other nonprofit organizations, the government funds constricted the greatest amount of research support.[21]

With increasing government participation in scientific research support, bills were introduced for several years for the establishment of a

TABLE IV.1

Funds for Research and Development and Basic Research, by Source: 1953, 1957 & 1963 *

(In millions of dollars)

Performance Sector and Source of Funds [a]	1953	1957	1963 [d]
Research & development [b]			
Total funds used	5,160	5,660	17,350
Federal government	1,010	1,280	2,400
Federal funds	1,010	1,280	2,400
Industry	3,630	7,730	12,720
Federal funds	1,430	4,330	7,340
Industry funds	2,200	3,400	5,380
Colleges & universities	420	650	1,700
Federal funds	260	415	1,300
Industry funds	20	25	65
College & university funds [c]	120	180	260
Other nonprofit institutions' funds [c]	20	30	75
Other nonprofit institutions	100	150	530
Federal funds	60	80	300
Industry funds	20	30	120
Other nonprofit institutions' funds [c]	20	40	110
Basic Research			
Total funds used	412	721	1,815
Federal government	45	90	275
Federal funds	45	90	275
Industry	151	271	500
Federal funds	19	41	150
Industry funds	132	230	350
Colleges & universities	190	300	840
Federal funds	110	173	530
Industry funds	10	12	30
College & university funds [c]	57	90	220
Other nonprofit institutions' funds [c]	13	25	60
Other nonprofit institutions	26	60	200
Federal funds	10	30	105
Industry funds	4	5	20
Other nonprofit institutions' funds [c]	12	25	75

* Includes Alaska and Hawaii. The U.S. totals have been revised because of a shift in the time period designation from a hyphenated year (1953–54) to a single year (1953), e.g. data for calendar year 1954 for Industry and Other nonprofit institutions are now combined with data for the Federal and university sectors for their fiscal year 1954 (July 1953 through June 1954). Data refer in general to the natural sci-

National Science Foundation. In 1950 such a foundation was established. The National Science Foundation is charged with the support of basic research. In addition to this foundation the Department of Defense, Atomic Energy Commission, Federal Security Agency, Department of Agriculture, and other agencies contribute funds to both applied and basic research.

In a governmental bureaucracy questions are raised and judgments are made concerning the administration of scientific researchers.[22] It is argued by Polanyi that there are two basic systems of organization, first, corporate order, and second, spontaneous order. Bureaucracy in contemporary society is characterized by corporate order. Basic scientific research is characterized by spontaneous order. To the extent that this bifurcation of order into two systems is valid, and the assignment of science to one and bureaucracy to the other, it is a succinct summarization of the situation.

The impact of bureaucracy on scientific occupations is illustrated in the restriction of communication, the evaluation of products for their commercial importance, and formal assignments to research in given areas reducing freedom of inquiry.[23] It is not so much questioned that secrecy in research may be essential to defense preparedness, but it remains a subversion of the principle of basic inquiry in science. The very notion of science in its intellectual and occupational tradition involves freedom of inquiry without limits to organizations, agencies, bureaucracies, or national boundaries.

The bureaucratic impact on religious organization is seen particularly in the Roman Catholic Church, the Episcopalian Church, and the Methodist Church. One can find additional examples of smaller hierarchically organized churches.[24] By contrast, sects have little formal organization and few, if any, real signs of bureaucracy.

Bureaucracy is not essential to religion, but it is widespread in large-

ences including engineering; however, some funds for psychology and the social sciences could not be eliminated. The major portion of funds excludes capital expenditures for research and development. (Expenditures at Federal contract research centers administered by industry, colleges and universities and other nonprofit institutions are included in the totals of the respective sectors.)
[a] Data on sources of funds are based on reports by the performers.
[b] Includes basic research, applied research, and development.
[e] Includes State and local government funds received by these institutions and used for research and development.
[d] Preliminary.
Source: *Statistical Abstract*, U.S. 1965, p. 545.

scale religious organizations. Bureaucracy is, in fact, contradictory to much of religion in its characteristics of standardization and antipathy for clients. Individual concern and covenant life are important characteristics of much behavior in churches. The interests of the organized church and principles of bureaucracy overlap in the characteristics of self-perpetuation and formalisms. There is some clash between the rationalism of bureaucracy and the supernaturalism of religion. But the church is inevitably program-oriented, and in urbanized societies program efficiency is facilitated by bureaucracy in the church as elsewhere.

Denominational churches have long manifested strong interest in self-perpetuation. Attainment of their goals is aided by specialization. Bureaucracy is a suitable environment for ordering specialists and specialisms. Certainly the open-country and small-town ministers largely remain generalists in an age of specialists. But the character of church organization is dominated from central offices, from large cities (and more recently from suburbs), not from the open country.

Members of churches are themselves becoming accustomed to bureaucracies and accept such organization for the church and the clergy. Religion as an occupation is more and more being carried out in the environment of bureaucracy.

The bureaucratic impact on the military profession is of long standing in the United States. The congruency between the military professionals and bureaucracy is greater than in many occupations. The military itself, as an occupation, is hierarchically organized and internally organized along bureaucratic lines. In spite of all this, congressional investigations of the military establishment have almost become normative as an external impact on the occupation.

Mercenary military men have been identified in earlier centuries. Emerging forms of professionalism among the military practitioners could be discerned in the eighteenth century. But Coates [25] and Janowitz [26] also submit that the military profession did not really emerge until the nineteenth century. The social history of governmental bureaucracy and military professionalism-bureaucratization have taken place simultaneously in the United States. Accordingly, this had led to a less free-standing occupation, and to near-ideological acceptance of integration between the military occupation and the government bureaucracy. Moreover, the American military establishment has its being in the service of the people through the government bureaucracy. It may, therefore, exist as an occupation and a profession to upgrade its efficiency and effectiveness in service to the bureaucracy and the people. It has few if any goals that are outside of and alternative to serving the national bureaucracy. Due to this organizational space, along with numerous other factors, the military occupation has historically experienced a limited prestige. Ideologically, the power of the military has been subjugated to the central governmental bureaucracy as religion has been separated from the central governmental bureaucracy.

The impact of bureaucracy on the internal organization of the military is illustrated in the case of the navy.[27] Informal organizational norms are reported to operate in the navy. Specifically, these are patterns of behavior concerning rules, groups, and sanctions of procedure which are not recorded in the official blueprints but are generated by spontaneity and maintained by the need for flexibility in day-to-day operations. Formally, the new recruit learns the intricacies of the navy's central operation through high pressure instruction. Via participant observation he must also learn the informal structure.

Industrial occupations. The functions of executives have been widely discussed, frequently reported, and occasionally researched.[28] Executive roles are typically carried out in bureaucracies. The occupations of executives are intricately related with bureaucracies. They are expected to assume responsibility, to make decisions, to co-ordinate, and to organize an enterprise. It would be hard indeed to imagine an occupational category where the goals of the participants overlap more with the goals of the organization. Like the military occupation, which essentially serves a bureaucracy, occupational executives exist to serve their agencies. Though their activities exist as a free-standing occupation, there is an articulation of principles of management.

The so-called principles of management remain to a great extent in an area of contradiction. Nevertheless, an increasing body of research suggests that there are some managerial patterns regardless of the bureaucracy in which a particular executive or manager is located. The occupational characteristics of executives are researched to the point that there is some agreement and consistency concerning them. The expansion of private bureaucracies in the form of large corporations, as contrasted with privately owned businesses, has contributed to the growth of the occupation of professional management men. It is sug-

gested by some that the rise of professional managers is of such proportion that they are on the way to becoming a new ruling class.[29]

In the mass organizations there is such extensive separation of ownership and control that the goals of management and the goals of stock
owners may from time to time represent considerable disparity. On the
other hand, the limited tenure of professional managers organizationally reduces their independent power and contributes to the strength of
the bureaucracy in which they operate. The decision-making of professional executives and managers will differ from owner-managers and the
historic captains of industry. Professional managers often come from
middle range backgrounds. They are specifically trained to manage.
They are continually reminded of their middle range position by their
salary rather than their ownership. As managers of a private bureaucracy much of their decision-making is influenced by if not determined
by the co-ordinating of activities and decisions of their subordinates
and superordinates. They are, indeed, decision-making co-ordinators.[30]

In their various forms executive and managerial occupations are implicitly and explicitly integrated with the norms of bureaucratic social
organization.

Government executives. Higher civil servants or government executives are moving in the direction of a free-standing occupational status.
They are the occupational men and women most often referred to as
the bureaucrats. The nomenclature, however, is not altogether correct.
The occupational bureaucrats are typically middle range executives who
make a career of working in government. Occupationally, they are in a
structural space lower than that of political policy-making and above
that of the clerical detail which is associated with the carrying out of
decisions. Their behavioral characteristics are being recorded with increasing frequency as a result of research investigation.[31]

Executives began to emerge in government as a part of the absolute
monarchies in the sixteenth century in Europe. In more recent governments, individuals are appointed for their technical qualifications to
work as officials in carrying out the decisions of their political superiors.
In the contemporary government this body of executive administrators
tend to become professionalized and carry out their work independent
of their personal sentiments. The policies that they administer are determined by legislatures and elected officials. It is characteristic of
these occupational workers to direct and administer the authority that

is the domain of their superiors. In terms of origins the federal executives come disproportionately from the professions, and other executive positions. A more detailed analysis of the professional category reveals that most of them came from an engineering background. Others came from law and science in equal proportion, and the remaining few were distributed almost miscellaneously through the several professions. In 1951, according to the Warner study, the federal executives who were in the highest ranks (above GS-18) had fathers in the following occupations: professions, 33.3 per cent; business executive or owner, 24.3 per cent; white-collar worker, 11.3 per cent; laborer, 11.1 per cent; farmer, 10.5 per cent; and owner of small business, 9.5 per cent.[32] The occupational background of the federal executives themselves and the occupational background of their fathers is far from representative of the distribution of the nation's labor force. These occupational men are specialists, and they come from a background and training of specialties.

Women federal executives are a minority, about 1 in 75. They are important, nevertheless, because they represent a new and increasing occupational type. Women are concentrated in the lower government service rank levels. More than 50 per cent of the workers in the ranks GS-2 to GS-6 are women.[33] From GS-13 to GS-18 women constituted less than 5 per cent in each case. Opportunities for women who are trained in white-collar skills are expanding in the federal executive positions. Nonetheless, at the higher levels women are seldom recruited, and in those exceptional cases they experience their career in a man's world.

SUMMARY AND IMPLICATIONS

Bureaucracy as a major form of social organization is directed toward the integration of many divergent elements of a complex society for a common and widely accepted set of goals. The widespread increase of occupational autonomy and the proliferation of occupations following the Industrial Revolution has not always been consistent with the broader goals of the society of which they are a part. In some cases the various occupations compete for their own free-standing development in such a way that their contribution to the ongoing organization of the society is jeopardized.

Bureaucracy is seen as a particularly effective mechanism for achieving integration among a multiplicity of occupations that are more or less scientific in their origin and in their idiom of contribution. The nature of bureaucracy is rationalistic, systematic, impersonal, and rigorously organized around goals.

In their environment of an ideally organized bureaucracy many of the areas of occupational organization must be modified to a point of consistency with the broader goals of the total bureaucracy. To this extent bureaucracy makes a direct, powerful, and sometimes devastating impact on occupational organization. Recruitment, training, career patterns, and succession are all major areas in which the rule and regulatory capacity of a bureaucracy makes an impact on occupations.

The impact of bureaucracy varies from one type of occupation to another. Professional and scientific occupations are often highly developed and greatly oriented to their propagation and maintenance. Indeed, in some cases the very rule regulation which systematizes a bureaucracy is contradictory to the intellectual content of a scientific occupation or a profession. By contrast, other major occupations are bureaucratic by their own internal nature, as in the case of professional military men. Still more extreme in this direction is the case of federal executives or high civil servants whose occupational organization is hierarchical and bureaucratic. Moreover, the occupation is developed within the framework of the bureaucracy in which the practitioners are typically employed.

It is characteristic, therefore, of the impact of bureaucracy on occupations to permeate the boundary maintenance and to direct the goals of the occupational men to a considerable congruence with the goals of the bureaucracy and the broader national goals.

NOTES

1. Peter M. Blau, *Bureaucracy in Modern Society* (New York: Random House, 1956).
2. H. H. Gerth and C. Wright Mills (eds.), *From Max Weber: Essays in Sociology* (New York: Oxford University Press, 1946), p. 204.
3. Robert K. Merton, *et al.* (eds.), *Reader in Bureaucracy* (New York: The Free Press of Glencoe, 1952), pp. 17ff.
4. Gerth and Mills, *From Max Weber*, pp. 196–8; and Max Weber, *The Theory of Social and Economic Organization*, trans. by A. M. Henderson and Talcott Parsons (New York: Oxford University Press, 1947).

5. Blau, *Bureaucracy*, p. 54.
6. Walter Rice Sharp, *The French Civil Service: Bureaucracy in Transition* (New York: The Macmillan Co., 1931), pp. 75–120.
7. Dwaine Marvick, *Career Perspectives in a Bureaucratic Setting* (Ann Arbor: University of Michigan Press, Michigan Governmental Studies, No. 27, 1954), p. 2; see also Robert K. Merton, *Social Theory and Social Structure* (Glencoe: Free Press, 1949), chap. 5, "Bureaucratic Structure and Personality," and chap. 6, "Role of the Intellectual in Public Bureaucracy."
8. Reinhard Bendix, *Higher Civil Servants in American Society* (Boulder: University of Colorado Press, 1949).
9. Leonard D. White, *Government Career Service* (Chicago: Chicago University Press, 1935), p. 7.
10. Marvick, *Career Perspectives*, pp. 94ff.
11. Alvin W. Gouldner, *Patterns of Industrial Bureaucracy* (Glencoe, Illinois: The Free Press, 1954), pp. 215–28.
12. Herbert A. Simon, *Administrative Behavior* (2nd Ed.; New York: The Free Press, 1945–1965), pp. 110–22.
13. For a further discussion of incentives see Herbert A. Simon, *Administrative Behavior*, esp. pp. 115–17.
14. Peter M. Blau and W. Richard Scott, *Formal Organizations: A Comparative Approach* (San Francisco: Chandler Publishing Co., 1962), pp. 66–71 *et passim*. See also W. Richard Scott, "A Case Study of Professional Workers in a Bureaucratic Setting" (Unpublished Ph.D. Dissertation, Department of Sociology, University of Chicago, 1961).
15. Blau and Scott, *Formal Organizations*, p. 66; see also Barney G. Glaser, *Organizational Scientists* (New York: Bobbs-Merrill Co., Inc., 1964).
16. Ibid. p. 67.
17. J. Ben-David, "The Professional Role of the Physician in Bureaucratized Medicine: a Study in Role Conflict," *Human Relations*, 11 (August 1958), pp. 255–74.
18. Ibid. p. 259.
19. Roy Lewis and Angus Maude, *Professional People* (London: Phoenix House, Ltd., 1952), pp. 173–206; and R. W. Harris, *National Health Insurance in Great Britain, 1911–1946* (London: George Allen and Unwin, Ltd., 1946).
20. Ibid. p. 201.
21. Robert W. Lamson, "The Present Strains between Science and Government," *Social Forces*, 33 (May 1955), 360–67.
22. Michael Polanyi, *The Logic of Liberty* (London: Routledge and Kegan Paul Ltd., 1951), pp. 111–37; Peter F. Drucker, "Management of Professional Employees," *Harvard Business Review*, 30 (May–June 1952), 84–90.
23. Walter Gellhorn, *Security, Loyalty, and Science* (Ithaca: Cornell University Press, 1950), pp. 34–62.

24. C. H. Page, "Bureaucracy and the Liberal Church," *The Review of Religion*, 16 (March 1952), 137–50.
25. Charles H. Coates and Roland J. Pelligrin, *Military Sociology* (University Park, Maryland: Social Science Press, 1965), pp. 199–220.
26. Morris Janowitz, *The Professional Soldier* (Glencoe: The Free Press, 1960).
27. Charles H. Page, "Bureaucracy's Other Face," *Social Forces*, 25 (October 1946), 89–94.
28. Chester I. Barnard, *The Functions of the Executive* (Cambridge: Harvard University Press, 1948); the editors of *Fortune*, *The Executive Life* (New York: Doubleday and Co., Inc., 1956); Walter I. Wardwell, "Social Integration, Bureaucratization, and the Professions," *Social Forces*, 33 (May 1955), 356–9.
29. James Burnham, *The Managerial Revolution* (New York: John Day, 1941); Robert Tannenbaum, *et al.*, *Leadership and Organization* (New York: McGraw-Hill Book Co., Inc., 1961), see esp. chap. 15.
30. Robert A. Gordon, *Business Leadership in the Large Corporation* (Washington, D.C.: The Brookings Institute, 1945), pp. 317–28; Rensis Likert, *New Patterns of Management* (New York: McGraw-Hill Book Co., Inc., 1961); and Garret L. Borgen and William V. Haney, *Organizational Relations and Management Action* (New York: McGraw-Hill Book Co., Inc., 1966).
31. Reinhard Bendix, *Higher Civil Servants in American Society: A Study of the Social Origins, the Careers, and the Power Position of Higher Federal Administration* (Boulder, Colorado: University of Colorado Studies, Series in Sociology, No. 2, 1949); Marvick, *Career Perspectives*; and W. Lloyd Warner, *et al.*, *The American Federal Executive* (New Haven and London: Yale University Press, 1963).
32. Warner, *et al.*, *American Federal Executive*, p. 163.
33. Ibid. p. 179.

SUPPLEMENTARY READINGS

Peter M. Blau and W. Richard Scott, *Formal Organizations: A Comparative Approach* (San Francisco: Chandler Publishing Co., 1962).
II. II. Gerth and C. Wright Mills (eds.), *From Max Weber: Essays in Sociology* (New York: Oxford University Press, 1946).
Barney G. Glaser, *Organizational Scientists* (New York: Bobbs-Merrill Co., Inc., 1964).
Alvin W. Gouldner, *Patterns of Industrial Bureaucracy* (Glencoe: The Free Press, 1954).
Morris Janowitz, *The Professional Soldier* (Glencoe: The Free Press, 1960).

PROFESSIONALIZATION AS AN OCCUPATIONAL ENVIRONMENT V

Professionalization is a second major occupational environment. Professions are not new among the occupations, but they occupy a position of importance in urbanized society that is unique in history.[1] Moreover in addition to the professions themselves the aura of professionalism is persuasive in the urbanized society. Professionalism far exceeds professions, and it becomes a model for occupational aspirations for most workers in commercial and industrial jobs.[2]

The importance of professions and professionalism to the social structure of society centers in their responsibility for the pursuit of science and liberal learning and the practice of practical arts in medicine, technology, law, and teaching. In idea societies these occupational functions are of exceedingly great importance. Their cultivation is complex and their practice to date remains extraordinarily difficult. Professionalization is the occupational structure which provides the nurture, prestige, and remuneration for occupational men which is sufficient for their dedication and sacrifice to the discipline demanded in rendering these high services.

The social space for the environment of professionalization is liberally awarded by society as it seeks to obtain high level idea services. Professions in social organization are mechanisms for achieving specified high level services. In effect, it is apparent that the urbanized society wants an expanding number of idea services, and does not necessarily want professions as such. If the innovative, creative, high level practitioner-ship of professionals could be obtained by alternate mechanisms, there is little reason to believe that society would continue to pay the high price in prestige and remuneration currently awarded to professionals. Indeed, one witnesses from time to time broad efforts to control, if not reduce, the power and authority of professionals. This is recently illustrated by the socialization of medicine in Great Britain, and the pressure for socialized medicine in the United States.

Professionalization as an occupational environment is a system of organization which supports, nurtures, and encourages responsible service oriented creativity. It is a high level occupational environment characterized by maximum autonomy for occupations.

Professionalization as an occupational environment is a part of the larger social organization of society. Accordingly, it is often found in a less than pure form. Frequently professionalization is partly integrated with bureaucratization and/or with unionization as occupational environments. These three major occupational environments range from totally separated to greatly integrated. For example, many salaried professionals, often research scientists, are employed in bureaucratic agencies. The autonomy of the professionalization environment is compromised in cases of integration, but far from destroyed. In other situations it is reported that professionals, for example, some engineers and some nurses, may become unionized. Again, the boundary maintenance of the environment of professionalization is invaded, but not destroyed. In all, professionalization is a viable occupational environment with power to forge much of its ultimate image. In other cases its power may be less, but sufficient to force negotiation.

The environment of professionalization never has been greater than in the contemporary idea urbanized society.

DEVELOPMENT OF PROFESSIONALIZATION

Professions, as known in the second half of the twentieth century in the Western world, emerged gradually following the end of the Middle Ages. The precise details of their genesis are not assembled, nor is their social history written. Moreover, the chronicle of human work activity in religion, medicine, and law is a fascinating tale, leading back to ancient and preliterate times.[3] It is possible that such early practitioners of religion, medicine, and law were among the progenitors of the professions. To say that they were early professionals, however, is to deal in much conjecture.

Professionals of modern times constitute specific categories of workers in the division of labor. They manifest a consciousness of kind, participate in formally structured occupational associations; theoretically view their calling as an altruistic service to mankind; endeavor to maintain a considerable control over their work, style of life, colleagues, and so on. The occupational organization and structure of professional life described above was conspicuously absent during most of the period prior to the early Renaissance. There were specialists among the ancients—priests, medicine men, and a host of others. Yet it is not such individuals but the superstructure of their consciousness of organization and ideology which singles out professionalization of contemporary times. In Greece and Rome lawyers and physicians were not characterized by their special training. The physician in Rome was more like a slave, attached as it were to a rich man's household. Accountants, architects, and engineers similarly were retained by the great Roman estates. Independence, training, and vocational organizations were generally not associated with the occupations.[4]

. During the Middle Ages many activities now performed by professionals were the concern of the clergy. It is an oversimplification, however, to assume that priests, for example, were the medical professionals of the period. Coulton writes, "The belief that monks and friars were the doctors of the Middle Ages is a gigantic delusion." [5] Nevertheless, knowledge and learning for generations was in the custodial care of the Church. No systems of social order or ideas were stronger than those of the Church.[6] Doctrines were specific, and the opposition to the practice of medicine was clear. The Councils of Reims (1125) and Lateran (1139) both discouraged the clergy's interest in medicine. Contempt for the flesh was a general principle. More specifically it was held that men of religion should not touch those parts of the body which cannot honorably be talked about. In 1163 the Council of Tours prohibited surgery, indicating that the Church abhorred bloodshed. Again in 1284 and 1300 the Councils of Nimes and of Bayeux adminished subdeacons, deacons, and priests against surgery and incision.[7]

In spite of all this, a new occupational consciousness was developing between the twelfth and the fourteenth centuries. It was articulated through a wave of association and guild formations. Still, by the seventeenth century only the three professions of divinity, law, and physique were widely identified.

The waning of the Middle Ages was characterized by a contracting of the social space importance of religious institutions. Concomitantly, universities were born with the Renaissance, and they became, among other things, training centers for the professionals. Professionalism as an environment grew with the universities. As universities gradually became secularized, the professions also began to gain freedom. The Royal College of Physicians of London, for example, was founded in 1518. English common law was never under the Church or the universities. Lawyers organized in the Inns of Court in the fifteenth century and were secular from the beginning. The Inns of Court were in fact both a legal guild and a legal university. Surgeons and apothecaries also organized into training guilds.

The first proliferation of professionalization was between the Renaissance and the Industrial Revolution. Guild organization was a first step along the way to professionalization for many occupations. Surgeons, apothecaries, and scriveners were first organized in this manner. These occupations in combination with physicians and lawyers became recognized as a new type of public servant. Unwin indicated that this corporate spirit "had become universal among all classes of dwellers in cities before the end of the fifteenth century. The clergy . . . , the legal, medical, and teaching professions; the merchant, the shopkeeper, and the craftsman . . . were all entrenched behind the bulwarks of professional association." [8] By the end of the eighteenth century (1799) the *Trinnial Directory of London* enumerated professional-type occupational listings, including barristers, attorneys, physicians, surgeons, apothecaries, chemists and druggists, dentists, opticians, architects, surveyors, auctioneers, and accountants.[9]

PROFESSIONALISM IN THE UNITED STATES

In colonial and early national America, intellectual life was characteristically dominated by the clergy. In addition to providing spiritual leadership, the clergy were teachers, compilers of laws, and authors of books. Through dogma and theology the clergy exercised dominion over the minds of laymen.[10]

The legal profession was soon to rival the clergy in America, first as a locus of secular learning and later as a dominating occupation. Lawyers became numerous and powerful. Legislative representatives were lawyers more often than not. They were particularly suited to the challenges of statecraft. Tocqueville believed the profession of law had reached aristocratic proportions. Touring the nation in the 1830's, he noted that there was no official noble class; indeed there were few literary men, and there was a wide distrust of the wealthy. It was his judgment, however, that lawyers constituted a high political class and stood as a cultivated segment in the society. He asserted that the character of an aristocracy rests at the judicial bench and the bar.[11]

Burritt traced the pattern of academic degrees awarded by Harvard, Yale, Pennsylvania, King's College (Columbia), and other schools from 1702, 1756, and 1758, respectively. The pattern was clear and definitive. Training leading to the ministry was most important prior to the Revolutionary War. Training for degrees in law dominated after the 1770's. The ministry, Burritt asserts, was central to the colonial society. It was the profession which required the most advanced education. Accordingly, as one might expect, it was the dominant subject of training at Harvard during the early years. The dominance of the clergy in training continued for about a century, but after the Revolutionary War other professions began to claim more graduates.[12] Formal training was not an absolute prerequisite for practice in the ministry, law, medicine, or other occupations of this type in the colonial and early national period. Yet the training patterns are the best evidence of avant garde trends in professional development.

The power struggle between the clergy and the legal profession continued from the 1770's through the first half of the nineteenth century and up to the Civil War. After the Civil War the character of American social life and social organization was irreversibly modified. Division of labor, specialization, industrialization, and urbanization were all clearly to dominate agrarianisms, and any notions of a manoral system of social organization were destroyed. Social space for professionalism was assured in the new and complex division of labor in the post-Civil War society.

The era of the generalist and/or the subsistence agriculturalist was gone. Factories and assembly lines came into their own as well as ideas like Frederick Taylor's scientific management of workers, union organization in crafts by the American Federation of Labor (1884), and later in industry by the Congress of Industrial Organizations (1935).

Growth trends. The shift of labor has been from field to factory; from physical input to idea creativity. Non-farm occupations have grown more rapidly than farm occupations during each decade since

1820.[13] Since 1870 the white-collar workers have been the most rapidly growing category of non-farm occupations. Professionals are part of this rapidly growing labor force. They are quiet and seldom obtrusive in their ascendency.

From the 1870's to the 1930's professionals were among the trusted guardians of the *laissez-faire* faith. Their model was the fee-taker, an independent entrepreneur, exemplified by physicians and lawyers rather than by ministers and professors. Yet the entrepreneurial image was not encouraged; indeed, it was taboo. Ideologically, professionals were not to be characterized as businessmen. Altruism, service to humanity, welfare of others, were paramount considerations in the expanding environment of professionalism. This image, however, involved considerable stereotype. The ministry, education, medicine, and law are all professions which developed early. The ministry and education are in practically all cases salaried, while medicine and law are more frequently structured by fee-taking. The environment of professionalization is replete with both salary and fee-taking structures from its origin.

The balance of power among professionals is precarious and the top prestige positions in the environment are slippery. The status of professionals probably never has been higher than in twentieth-century America.[14] The complexities of industrial urbanized society have generated more specializations, more esoteric knowledge, and more professionals. Many of the most important aspects of American society depend upon the services of professionals. When complex societies are developed on material knowledge systems through science, the amateur is less than respectable, he is often persecuted as an impostor. Trained competence is required and respected. Indeed, in some cases mistakes at work are paid for by the generalist who employs the professional for that precise purpose.[15] Decisions in government, industry, and organizations are based on the information gathered and prepared by professionals of all sorts. A specific professional person can be dismissed or replaced, but his services will necessarily be provided by another of his tribe of specialists.[16] The professional man is seldom a ranking individual in power structures. Indeed, when he fills a power position he generally gives up his professional services and becomes an administrator—that is, a generalist.[17]

The role of professionals as experts who do not characteristically dominate power structures means that, although their positions are prestigeful, professionalism is not among the most characteristic features of the society. Far more characteristic of the times are: capitalism, free enterprise, the business elite, and social welfare. The small power place of professionals in the greater society can be viewed another way. A comparatively small group of managers, officials, and proprietors, approximately 10 per cent of the labor force, organize and administer the work of the nation. These executive and administrative decision-makers are assisted in their tasks by the professionals, a comparatively silent 9 per cent of the labor force.[18]

Since the trend toward social welfare organizations growing out of the depression years of the 1930's, there has been a marked increase in the number of salaried professionals and neo-professionals. This trend has been even more accentuated since the 1950's, from which time scientific inquiry and research development into new areas has contributed to the proliferation of specialists and would-be professionals. The case of the growing number of professional bodies is illustrated by the engineering societies in America, which include the American Society of Civil Engineers (1852), the American Institute of Mining and Metallurgical Engineers (1871), the American Society of Mechanical Engineers (1880), the American Institute of Electrical Engineers (1884), the American Institute of Chemical Engineers (1908), and the American Institute of Radio Engineers (1912).[19] Higher civil servants in America also have endeavored to establish themselves as a profession. Many of them, however, were trained in other professions prior to their entry into the government service careers. Nevertheless, their striving for professionalization continues unabated.[20]

Statistics recorded in the United States census from the 1870's to the present reveal the upsurge of the professions, and constitute an index of the expanding environment of professionalization. In 1870 professionals numbered less than half a million and constituted less than 3 per cent of the nation's gainful workers (see Table V.1). By 1960 the professionals, semiprofessionals, and kindred workers constituted more than 10 per cent of the labor force.

Between 1900 and 1930 the professionals experienced a dramatic 168 per cent increase in proportion in the labor force. They were only exceeded by the clerical workers' unprecedented 394 per cent increase. During the period the total labor force increased by less than 68 per

TABLE V.1

Professionals in the Labor Force, 1870–1960

Year	Number	Per Cent of the Labor Force
1960	7,232,410	11.8
1950	5,080,528	8.6
1940	3,878,618	7.5
1930	3,253,884	6.8
1920	2,171,251	5.1
1910	1,711,275	4.6
1900	1,180,501	4.1
1890	876,299	3.8
1880	549,822	3.2
1870	342,107	2.6

Source: Alba M. Edwards, *Population: Comparative Occupational Statistics for the United States, 1870 to 1940* (Washington, D.C.: Government Printing Office, 1943), pp. 100–101. The figures in column 3 for 1960, 1950, and 1940 are taken from Max Rutzick and Sol Swerdloff, "The Occupational Structure of U.S. Employment; 1940–1960," *Monthly Labor Review*, 85 (November, 1962), 1209–1213.

cent.[21] Between 1930 and 1950 the total labor force increased over 21 per cent, and the professionals increased nearly 54 per cent, but they were surpassed by greater increases among the service, clerical, and operative workers. Between 1950 and 1960 professional workers increased more rapidly than all others, 47 per cent compared to 15 per cent for the labor force, and compared to 34 per cent for clerical workers, the next highest category.

The rapid quantitative expansion of the professions has brought both advantages and disadvantages to the environment. The first expansion brought advantages in the form of recognition, social space, and prestige. Continual growth has brought saturation, less quality, semi-professionals, and the echoes at least of deprofessionalization. Even though the services of professionals are clearly utilized by society, the occupational integrity of the professionals is highly tenuous. The clergy in particular is in precarious straits. Their educational attainment remains reasonably high, but there is a growing body of evidence which suggests that the masses of people consider their role of little importance.[22]

Ideas of professional service and occupational organization were integral parts of the European culture that was brought by the colonists and early immigrants to America. The United States experienced an occupational metamorphosis between the colonial period and the end of the nineteenth century. A major part of this occupational change is the ascendency of professionalization as an environment. The nature of that environment is complex.

THE PROFESSIONAL OCCUPATIONAL ENVIRONMENT

The environment of professionalism is characterized by the factors of expertise, autonomy, commitment, and responsibility. In the case of expertise it is asserted that the professional environment is one in which an advanced body of specialized knowledge and skills are required. These are usually obtained through long and demanding training, most often academic in nature. In maintaining the expertise of practitioners occupational structures are established for training. In addition, norms for inclusion or exclusion of membership are also established.

The dimension of autonomy in the professional environment is manifested in occupational structures which demand that practitioners be free to make their own decisions. In this way the professionals are set apart from lay restrictions. It is particularly at this point that conflict between the environment of professionalization and that of bureaucracy and unionization occur.

The dimension of commitment in the professional environment often leads to the characterization of altruism as contrasted with individual aggrandizement. Though in fact it is not argued that the professional is completely altruistic as compared to egoistic, it is submitted that the institutional patterns are radically different from those of business.[23] Professionals are concerned with their economic status, and in part motivated by it. But their commitment is also to service for their fellow man as well as to maintaining and expanding the body of knowledge which is their expertise. In short, getting ahead in the environment of professionalism is as much measured by obtaining the esteem of one's colleagues as by advancement in one's place of employment or otherwise by economic measures. Commitment is to the occupational environment more than to what one can get out of it.

The professional dimension of responsibility concerns control over practitioners, self-discipline, codes of ethics, and authority. The environment of professionalism is strongly built on boundary maintenances including the right to select, train, and control practitioners internally. It is argued that, given the nature of a specialized body of knowledge, only colleagues, not external generalists, are really capable of understanding the situation sufficiently to make appropriate decisions for the control of practitioners.

The nature of authority is at once both strong and unique in the professional environment. It is strong because fellow practitioners alone have the basis for making decisions concerning their body of knowledge. Yet collectively professionals have little power in the social organization of the society of which they are a part. Their powerful authority is greatly limited to their specific area of expertise. This is illustrated in the case of the physician who may give orders to a patient concerning health habits, or an attorney who may give advice to a client in terms of his legal rights. In these and other cases of professional authority the client is free to accept or reject the advice. In the case of normative political authority, broad categories or citizens are required to conform to regulations or be subject to penalty for their deviations. The authority of professionals may further be said to be subject-matter-specific. One does not expect the engineer to speak with authority in spiritual matters, or the clergyman to speak with authority concerning civil law, etc. The authority of expertise is limited to a given body of knowledge, and not ideally transferable to general situations.

Codes of ethics are frequently promulgated by professional bodies. These codes enumerate the services to clients, the rights of clients, and the rights of practitioners.

Engineers. In the several professions of engineering are approrpiate examples of occupational behavior in the environment of professionalism. Engineers are often salaried rather than fee-taking professionals. Their manifest sense of professionalism precipitates many clashes between their organizational employers and their occupational organization.[24] In those cases where engineers are professionally oriented they view their work expression largely in the terms of academic scientists. This is a university model, and one which often fits poorly with corporation goals. Engineers more often work in corporations than in universities. The professionally oriented engineer is motivated to do work that is meaningful to his body of knowledge and to the furthering of his reputation in his profession. His professional pride grows on maintaining standards of excellence for engineering. In sharp contrast to the professional idiom, industrial managers may see the primary function of the engineer as the development of products to be sold at a profit. The high standards of engineering from a management point of view are but means to the profit-motivated end. Furthermore, the engineer as a professional prefers to operate in terms of scientific logic. He is unwilling to compromise answers, and to this extent from the point of view of management is an unrealistic prima donna.

In terms of authority the professionally oriented engineer views his research as subject to discussion by colleagues. Closure by external authority through management bureaucracy is unacceptable. The professional engineer looks upon his management superiors as organizational men whose inferior technical knowledge reduces the importance of their judgments concerning the engineering work. In terms of productivity, engineers desire to work directly with other colleagues in the firm, regardless of their place in the hierarchy. The bureaucratic red tape of an industrial laboratory is little respected by the professional engineer, and the best management looks upon such engineers as undisciplined.

Finally, the environment of professionalization in focusing on creativity and service is difficult, if not impossible, to fit into an organizational format of nine to five, Monday through Friday. The idea-oriented professional moves intensively from one creative period to the next, rather than routinely through hours of regulated work. The expression of creativity, the professionals argue, cannot be scheduled into eight-hour periods. When the professional has hit upon a particularly innovative idea he may work on it for long hours, at night, or on weekends. There may be intervening periods during which the professional manifests little creative productivity at all. While the validity of arguments concerning greater or lesser productivity remains undetermined in terms of regulated work periods versus free work periods, the importance of the situation here is to understand the norms of professionalism. Valid or not, at this time the environment of professionalism is characterized by freedom to regulate work periods.

The environment of professionalism is strong, and management must continually make concessions for it.

Management and the professional environment. The professional environment provides an occupational training which develops individual initiative and responsibility. This is not to be misunderstood as individualism for its own sake. Many professionals may from time to time work effectively in research teams. What it does mean is that professionals expect their associates to be colleagues, persons with whom they consult at an idea level, rather than individuals they respect because of superior-inferior relationships.[25] In this regard the professional environment stands in sharp contrast to the organizational bureaucratic environment.

Close observation of professionals by noncolleagues in an organizational structure is resisted. In fact, supervision as such is against the ideal of the professional. It may be asserted that professional people prefer to work as "senior" and "junior" individuals rather than in a "boss" and "subordinate" relationship. The situation is further complicated by the professionals' lack of desire to become administrators, on the one hand, and by their general ineptness, on the other hand, when they do become administrators. Administration in a typical bureaucratic sense is generally inconsistent with the ideal model of the professional environment.

Professional recognition is achieved most by esteem from colleagues. When the professional environment and the bureaucratic environment become integrated, efforts to recognize professionals by promoting them into administrative positions are generally resisted by practitioners. The promotion of a distinguished professional researcher is critically viewed as destroying both a good man and the position. In compromise with the professional environment some promotions are made in the form of calling the individual a "special advisor" or "research consultant," where the pay is equal to the advanced position but where the administrative details are not incumbent upon the promoted individual. The professional environment is becoming increasingly more effective in gaining its forms of recognition in bureaucratic structures. In effect, there is a professionalizing of bureaucratic environments in which many professionals work and have their being. In spite of these gains for the professional environment, it is often found that professionals continue to be more cosmopolitans than locals—more identifying with their subject matter than with the firm where they are employed. Professionalization of the occupational environment is characterized by a tenacious devotion to subject and service, and only a modified and/or compromised identification with the establishment of employment. There may be a continual exposure to business ethics but little acceptance of them by professionals.

Teamwork and interdisciplinary professional behavior is an expanding part of the environment in the second half of the twentieth century. Since World War II the bulk of research in the United States is sponsored increasingly by large administrative units, often governmental. The dilettante bits-and-pieces professional has limited effectiveness in the mass urbanized society. This co-operative teamwork development in no way implies a lesser value on the efforts of an individual practitioner, but recognizes the complexity of the mass society. Team organization is a structural modification of the professional environment to produce more effectively within its own organizational structure. This is far from mass production in scientific inquiry. It is by contrast the organization of scientists by scientists to mount programs of investigation that will be more broad gauged and fundamenal to the demands of the society of which they are a part.

The organization of professional teamwork is further designed to enhance intellectual stimulation among colleagues. It provides a division of labor at a professional level for the sake of idea investigation, rather than for the structure of organization as such.[26] Professional team organization involves some hierarchy. Usually there is a director of a particular project. In most cases the director has final authority for decision-making and for writing the findings. In some other cases attempts may be made for joint decision-making. In either case, in the professional occupational environment the hierarchy and/or decision-making is determined by professionals for professionals rather than by the larger environment.

Productivity and the professional environment. Measurement of professional productivity is precarious. And even if some agreement is reached concerning measures of productivity, then the causes of productivity are still more evasive. It is generally found that the most productive professionals show concrete evidences of production at an early age. Those who are productive at an early age show a slightly greater probability of continuing to be productive later. But there are exceptions. Some great idea breakthroughs have been products of unique experiences. Yet the professional environment, as an environment, is normatively based on those typical patterns of behavior in the environment of creativity and service.

The measures of professional productivity are subjects of question and debate for practitioners, and of consternation for bureaucratic administrators who employ large numbers of professionals in their research and development divisions. As bureaucratic managements have measured efficiency in the production of tangible goods, they have also desired to measure the efficiency of their creative scientific output—and to increase this efficiency.[27] The situation is illustrated by a study of professionals employed in the aeronautical and electronic industries in Southern California. They suggested that their time was being utilized with less than 36 per cent effectiveness. The largest single proportion of their time (26 per cent) was reported as devoted to supervision, and much of this was inefficient in their judgment. The second largest proportion of time was devoted to conferences (14 per cent), and again much of that time was considered to be inefficient. The third largest proportion of time (approximately 12 per cent) was devoted to routine technical work activities, and all of this was considered to be inefficient. The fourth amount of time (12 per cent) was devoted to nonroutine technical work, and all of this considered to be efficient use of their time. It is the fourth item, technical work, which is judged to be of importance by scientists. Their own professional environment, and the several environments in which they are employed, need to increase the amount of time devoted to this productivity, and to continue the high efficiency of time utilized in that manner.

Professional occupational men are also found to be highly mobile. In the study reported above the average scientist had changed his job once in every 3.3 years. With this high proportion of job changing it was estimated that there was a further loss of from 10 to 30 per cent of the potential output.

Norms of efficiency concerning professional production do not yet exist within the environment as such. Instead, the professional environment focuses on stimulation and recognition after productivity is achieved. It is an environment of creativity with few mechanisms for standardization.

Professional memberships. Memberships and participation in professional societies and associations are considered important by practitioners. These associations are forms of presentation, of debate, and of stimulation. Presumably they are part of a rich and stimulating environment of creativity. Accordingly, as professionals are more extensively employed in bureaucratic environments, their employers find it advantageous to facilitate professional memberships. This is another index of the invasion of the professional environment by the bureaucratic environment. Surveys show that many employers of professionals now provide all the cost of membership in their associations and societies. In some cases the employing agencies approve the membership through a department head, appropriate a specified amount of money for memberships and travel to meetings, or otherwise encourage that a few of the company's employees constitute a membership committee for review of the requests for support.[28] But regardless of the technique, recognition is now given to the importance of participating in professional associations as one of the dimensions required for a favorable professional environment.

Finally, the professional environment is characterized at specific times and in specific places by militantcy. Part of the militant manifestation is a matter of boundary maintenance and part of it is an increasing of the domain of the professional environment as such. For example, in the recent efforts made by public school teachers to become more professional it is reported that there is a militant behavior against bureaucratic roles.[29] Those teacher practitioners who are most professional in their orientation demonstrate greater involvement in overt conflicts. In the case of teachers specific organizational steps are increasingly followed to define their roles for participation, their client relationships, and judgments concerning the content of their work by fellow practitioners rather than by outside lay persons.

In sum, the environment of professionalization is internally strong. It is difficult to identify and understand, and accordingly it is difficult to attack directly in power struggles with other occupational environments. The professional environment is evasive in the guise of colleagueship. Its expertise is internal, and few if any effective mechanisms have been achieved for systematic external review of professional behavior.

OVER PROFESSIONALIZATION

With the rise in prestige of professionalization, many occupations in the twentieth century are systematically attempting to gain professional status. By many indexes the number of professionals is accelerating with extraordinary rapidity. Not only are old line professionals increasing their number of practitioners, but new occupations come into existence at a technological level and at a semi- or pseudo-professional level. Moreover, many old occupations are changing their names and some of their images in efforts to become professional-like. This is illustrated in the case of janitors becoming custodial engineers, chimney sweeps becoming decarbonizers, etc.[30]

There is also evidence for arguments that few of the occupations which attempt professionalization achieve it. In an empirical study of managers of real estate firms in the suburbs of Washington, D.C. (Maryland) it is found that they desired professional status, but lacked essential elements of professional behavior. In addition to lacking some of the professional characteristics, it is also found that professionalization is dysfunctional to some occupations.[31] In an empirical study of life insurance salesmen it is discovered that their systematic efforts to become professionals tend to reduce their effectiveness as measured by their reaching a large number of clients. Among the several steps toward professionalization taken by the life insurance men were the establishment of a journal, promulgation of a code of ethics, and the development of high level systematic training. It was in the level of training that the dysfunctionalization became most apparent. The course of training prepared life insurance men to relate themselves effectively to a small number of wealthy clients. In effect the most highly trained life insurance men (Chartered Life Underwriters) became desk men, executive types more than salesmen. In addition, when they did sell their contacts were with those on the upper end of the occupational continuum more than with the typical citizen who also needs protection.

SUMMARY AND IMPLICATIONS

Professionalization is an expanding occupational environment, and one of the most important occupational environments in the urbanized society. It is an environment generated by and for idea people. It is an environment of occupational persons who are devoted to creativity and service norms.

Professionals are old in terms of service but as systematic occupational participants they have come into their own only since the Middle Ages. Professionalization as an occupational environment is still newer, essentially a post-Renaissance development.

In the United States, professionals and professionalism have grown rapidly. In a society where ideas are power, the environment of professionalization carries a high level of importance.

The environment of professionalization is characterized by extreme occupational control on the part of practitioners. This is effected through several factors, including an esoteric body of knowledge, systematic boundary maintenance through recruitment and training, social control by informal colleague relationships, motivation framed in service and altruism, and a dedication to ideas. Through these several mechanisms the professionalized occupational environment is rigorously controlled. Yet professionalization, like the other occupational environments, is a part of the social organization of the society in which it exists. Professionals are engaged in continually negotiating their social space, and their balance of power. Professionals are increasingly employed in bureaucracies. Moreover, in some few cases they are confronted with unionization. In most instances the strength of the professional environment has been sufficient to effectively deter unionization. In resisting unions professional societies and associations have come in many cases to appear more union-like as they deal with their conditions of work in addition to their dealing with the body of professional knowledge.

In the case of bureaucracies, professionals have been more modified and less effective in resistance. Yet it is also found that where professionals enter bureaucratic structures the forces of modification are distinctly reciprocal, and the environment of professionalization precipitates many changes in the environment of bureaucracy.

The power of professionalization is nonpolitical, and the authority of professionals is limited to their technical subject area. Yet on neither of these accounts is the power of professionalization to be underestimated. Considering that as an occupational environment professionalization is small in terms of the number of people controlled by it, its authority, image, and prestige are nearly overwhelming.

Small and growing as professionalism is, concern for over professionalization is increasingly heard since the 1930's. Part of this is due to the attributing of professional nomenclature to many occupations that are in fact far from achieving professional status. It is also found that when some occupations seek professional conditions they dilute their service.

More importantly, it may be observed that the environment of professionalization is expanding rapidly because it is central to idea creativity, and idea power is increasingly more central to the organized society.

Professionalization as an occupational environment is more central to the urbanized industrial society than to other types of society. Its social space and social power are both widely consistent with the configuration of the society at this time.

NOTES

1. Talcott Parsons, "The Professions and Social Structure," *Social Forces*, 17 (May 1939), 457–67.
2. George Strauss, "Professionalism and Occupational Associations," *Industrial Relations*, 2 (May 1963), 7–31; see also T. H. Marshall, "The Recent History of Professionalism in Relation to Social Structure and Social Policy," *The Canadian Journal of Economics and Political Science*, 5 (August 1939), 325–40.
3. A. M. Carr-Saunders and P. A. Wilson, *The Professions* (London: Oxford University Press, 1933); Roy Lewis and Angus Maude, *Professional People* (London: Phoenix House Ltd., 1952); Roscoe Pound, *The Lawyer from Antiquity to Modern Times* (Saint Paul: West Publishing Company, 1953); Henry E. Sigerist, *A History of Medicine* (New York: Oxford University Press, 1951); and Alfred North Whitehead, *Adventures of Ideas* (New York: The Macmillan Company, 1953).
4. Carr-Saunders and Wilson, *Professions*.
5. G. G. Coulton, *Medieval Panorama* (Cambridge: The University Press, 1939), p. 447.
6. William Carroll Bark, *Origins of the Medieval World* (New York: Doubleday and Co., Anchor Books, 1960).
7. Coulton, *Medieval Panorama*, pp. 445–6.
8. George Unwin, *The Guilds and Companies of London* (London: Methuen and Co., 1908), p. 172.
9. Carr-Saunders and Wilson, *Professions*, pp. 295–6.
10. Charles A. Beard and Mary R. Beard, *The Rise of American Civilization* (Rev. and enlarged ed.; New York: The Macmillan Company, 1954), vol. 1, p. 146.
11. Alexis de Tocqueville, *Democracy in America* (New York: Vintage Books, 1958), vol. 1, p. 288.
12. Bailey B. Burritt, *Professional Distribution of College and University Graduates* (Washington, D.C.: U.S. Bureau of Education Bulletin No. 19, 1912), p. 15.
13. Donald J. Bogue, *The Population of the United States* (New York: The Free Press, 1959), p. 478; and Lee Taylor and Arthur R. Jones, Jr.,

Agribusiness and the Labor Force (Louisiana: Agricultural Experiment Station Bulletin, No. 562, 1963).

14. Talcott Parsons, *Professions and Social Structure;* Lewis and Maude, *Professional People,* pp. 1–13; and Lee Taylor and Arthur R. Jones, Jr., *Rural Life and Urbanized Society* (New York: Oxford University Press, 1964), chaps. 12 and 13.

15. Everett Cherrington Hughes, *Men and Their Work* (Glencoe: The Free Press, 1958), pp. 88–101.

16. Arthur J. Vidich and Joseph Bensman, *Small Town in Mass Society* (New York: Doubleday and Company, Anchor Books, 1960).

17. Hughes, *Men and Their Work,* p. 137; and Lee Taylor and Arthur R. Jones, "Professionals and Specialists in Agribusiness: An Analysis of Social Organization and Power," *Sociologia Ruralis,* V, 4 (1965), 339–348.

18. Bogue, *Population,* p. 472.

19. Ralph J. Smith, *Engineering as a Profession* (New York: McGraw-Hill Book Company, 1956), p. 35.

20. Reinhard Bendix, *Higher Civil Servants in American Society* (Boulder, Colorado: University of Colorado Press, 1949).

21. Bogue, *Population,* p. 475.

22. Warren Hagstrom, "The Protestant Clergy as a Profession," *Berkeley Publications in Social Institutions,* 3 (Spring 1957), 1–12; Stanley H. Chapman, "The Minister: Professional Man of the Church," *Social Forces,* 23 (December 1944), 202–6; and Lewis and Maude, *Professional People,* pp. 138–50.

23. Parsons, *Professions and Social Structure.*

24. Strauss, *Professionalism,* pp. 22–31.

25. Peter F. Drucker, "Management and the Professional Employee," *Harvard Business Review,* 30 (May-June 1952), 84–90.

26. Joseph W. Eaton, "Social Processes of Professional Teamwork," *American Sociological Review,* 16 (October 1951), 707–13.

27. Irving Hirsch, William Milwitt, and William J. Oakes, "Increasing the Productivity of Scientists," *Harvard Business Review,* 36 (March-April 1958), 66–76.

28. "Subsidizing Membership in Professional and Technical Societies," *Management Record,* 13 (April 1951), 140–41.

29. Ronald G. Corwin, "Militant Professionalism, Initiative and Compliance in Public Education," *Sociology of Education,* 38 (Summer 1965), 310–31.

30. Lewis and Maude, *Professional People;* and Nelson N. Foote, "The Professionalization of Labor in Detroit," *The American Journal of Sociology,* 58 (January 1953), 371–80.

31. Lee Taylor and Roland J. Pellegrin, "Professionalization: Its Functions and Dysfunctions for the Life Insurance Occupation," *Social Forces,* 38 (December 1959), 110–14.

SUPPLEMENTARY READINGS

Ronald G. Corwin, "Militant Professionalism, Initiative and Compliance in Public Education," *Sociology of Education*, 38 (Summer 1965), 310–31.

Everett Cherrington Hughes, *Men and their Work* (Glencoe: The Free Press, 1958).

Roy Lewis and Angus Maude, *Professional People* (London: Phoenix House Ltd., 1952).

Talcott Parsons, "The Professions and Social Structure," *Social Forces*, 17 (May 1939), 457–67.

Lee Taylor and Roland J. Pellegrin, "Professionalization: Its Functions and Dysfunctions for the Life Insurance Occupation," *Social Forces*, 38 (December 1959), 110–14.

UNIONIZATION AS AN OCCUPATIONAL ENVIRONMENT VI

Unionization is the second of three major occupational environments. In social organizational characteristics it is intermediate as an environment between professionalization and bureaucracy. The social space of the unionized environment is negotiated. It is neither controlled by occupational practitioners nor by their employers. A fluctuating equilibrium is achieved repeatedly by negotiations between these two related forces. By contrast, in the environment of professionalization occupational practitioners experience a maximum of autonomy in their social organization. In the environment of bureaucracy occupational practitioners experience a minimum of autonomy.

In the environment of unionization authority is theoretically from the bottom up. Unionization is a structure in which workers are organized to have a strong voice. By contrast, in the environment of professionalization authority is an internal matter, a matter of colleagueship, or a situation of practitioner equals. In bureaucracy authority is hierarchical and theoretically from the top down.

The environment of unionization is dynamic, often unpredictable, and characterized normatively by conflict. The environment of professionalization, on the other hand, is characterized by creativity, motivation, and strong independent occupational organization. The environment of bureaucracy is typically characterized as static, with a minimum of independent motivation, and practitioners subjected to the rigors of a nearly immobile system.

All of these environments are ideal types. The concrete expressions of them are less pure. Indeed, one finds some hierarchy in professionalization and some informality in the otherwise formally structured environment of bureaucracy. In unionization there is a hierarchy in organization, identifiable creativity, and innovation, and strong measures of systematic stability contribute to occupational systems and to the social organization.

Yet above all else the environment of unionization is characterized by negotiation and conflict. From the point of view of societal organization, the organization of the union environment is a mechanism for articulate worker expression. The power and the dignity of workers are typically increased by this environment. The unionization environment is found in societies that have departed or are departing from a ruralized social organization and moving in the direction of an urbanized industrial social organization. The environment of unionization is more typical of societies with complex systems of social organization than of those with a minimum of complexity. The anatomy of occupations is exposed most broadly in an environment of unionization. The structures of unionized occupations are brought forth to do battle through negotiation and strike. In professionalization the strength of occupations is intensive. But, the anatomy of occupations is obscure, internal, and shrouded from the public view. Professions are strong and exclusive and difficult to control by societies. Occupations in the environment of bureaucracy have a limited free-standing anatomy. They are exposed to society as in unionization, but in their weakness rather than in their strength.

The environment of unionization that is examined in this chapter emerged primarily in the late nineteenth century, as industrialization and urbanization expanded throughout the society. The environment of unionization has expanded and contracted to various degrees from time to time, but it continues to the present date to be viable.

UNIONIZATION AND SOCIAL ORGANIZATION

Ideologies. The trade union movement, Tannenbaum asserts, is conservative in essence although profoundly revolutionary in some of its immediate outcomes.[1] The focus of its conservative thrust is on the achievement of security for individual workers. In the advent of the Industrial Revolution there was a broad societal disruption in the form of tearing workers loose from their former community ties, and a subsequent demise of ruralized society. Thrust from a primary group relationship, workers were ejected to survive as they might on their naked resources or to achieve new forms of collective security. To this collective end the union is central, building on the individualized identity of workers and providing a form for their successful representation.

The landed estate, the manoral organization, and the cottage industry all were gone. The worker stood upright on a new individualistic front expressing himself and defending his expression through actions that in the short run appeared revolutionary, namely, strikes, walk-outs, riots, and so forth. But, all of these in the long run may be seen social organizationally as efforts to provide a new security; a new conservatism.

In this environment of developing unionization there were supporting ideologies for inherent and equal rights, privileges and immunities, and moral and intellectual freedoms. The newness in the unionization environment is not personal insecurity as such. Through the ages, particularly in ruralized organization, men have known the insecurities of nature and its wrath upon them. Natural disasters were accepted and feared. The gods of men have been mobilized to provide security, among other things, in the face of these disasters. The insecurity that is central to the environment of unionization is social rather than natural. It results from being removed from a set of primary social relationships. Indeed, in the days of the captains of industry the individual worker stood alone, occupationally with dignity, but typically with helplessness. Such lonely workers had in common an environment, though originally unarticulated, in the employer, the industry, the physical work space, the amenities of the job, the craft of the tasks, and the production from the work effort. When these various elements of the environment were articulated, unionization was one of the profoundest results—a new environment.

In the new unionization environment there was a commonality in association, in language, in craft and task, in industry and shop. In the environment of unionization the employer stood less big and the employee shrank less diminutively.

Assertions of the newness of the unionization environment as part of the Industrial Revolution in the eighteenth and nineteenth centuries are not without cognizance of earlier related manifestations. Unionization as such was preceded by the guild organizations throughout much of Europe in the Middle Ages. Forerunners of this form of organization in the guild formation are also noted in China, India, Islam and other ancient societies in periods before the time of Christ. It might be observed that the environment of unionization is in part a return to earlier forms of social organization. Partially at least this is valid, although it is modified by new urbanization and a new industrialism. It is old and conservative in those of its norms which provide security for occupational practitioners where work is characterized by high and complex divisions of labor.

While in the main the environment of unionization in America follows the patterns and traditions described above, Marxists and students of comparative labor movement history have described the situations here as "American exceptualism."[2] This exceptualism is cited when comparisons are made between the United States, Great Britain, Scandinavia, The Netherlands, Switzerland, Australia, Canada, and New Zealand. The similarities are legion, while the differences focus on ideology, class solidarity, tactics, organizational structure, and patterns of leadership behavior.[3] In ideology, conservatism is found to be more extensive than is unionism in several of the other countries. In America class solidarity involves more self-interest, tactics are more militant, organization is more decentralized, and there are more full-time salaried leaders.[4] While the differences between the American unionization environment and that in other countries are real they are insufficient to render the American union environment as a qualitatively different phenomenon. More specifically, this point might be made by observing that while American unions are involved in political power struggles, union-supported political parties or labor parties never have been sustained here as they have been in Europe.

Major American societal norms tend to permeate a strong boundary maintenance of the union environment. For example, the dominant cultural themes of success, getting ahead, and equality are in effect structural limitations within which a union environment must be built. Or from the other point of view, practitioner allegiance to unions is seldom so exclusive or extensive as to negate for the individual the possibility of dramatic achievement and basic equality regardless of one's origin in terms of class, creed, or race. In short, Americans support the environment of unionization up to a point; a point at which it continues to be a mechanism for their success but not to a point at which it becomes a totally viable alternative system of social organization.

In sharp contrast to these American societal norms one typically finds in the other Western societies where unionization has developed more traditionalistic or aristocratic social stratification. There, accordingly, it is normative for an individual to behave appropriately within his stratum. In doing this unionization as an environment is relatively free, indeed encouraged, to develop as a total environment offering a viable alternative and in direct competition with environments in other strata of the society. In societies characterized by more rigid rigorous stratification, labor political parties supported by the environment of unions make sense. In the relatively more open-class stratification of America no one wants to identify fully with a labor party as long as there is any implication that by doing so it may either inhibit or deny them the maximum possibility for achievement in mobility to the very apex of the class structure. It is precisely at this juncture that one sees most clearly American unionization as an occupational environment and not as a total configuration for societal organization. The apex of achievement for unionization in America is not an alternative form of societal organization but a mechanism in which occupational practitioners can negotiate for any and all rights that are available to occupational men anywhere in the society.

The boundary maintenance of the unionized environment is also permeated by norms having to do with income and conspicuous consumption. While the statuses of major occupations are found to have great similarity in rank in Western societies, money and consumption appear to be of greater importance in America.[5] In short, a blue-collar skilled worker in America who earns a high wage may conspicuously consume items for food, clothing, and residence in such a manner that away from his job he may be incognito or may even be recognized as a member of the white-collar or professional classes. His identity away from the work environment will in few cases, if at all, involve identification with unionization. More recently, and conversely, as white-collar workers are unionized they live and work in two quite divergent environments. The impact of unionization on their work is persuasive; its impact on their way of life may be negligible. Indeed, where possible they may aspire to professionalization as a way of life. The environment of unionization for occupations must not be confused with a working class ideology.

It is also observed that in America unionization departs from an ideology of socialism and follows more a "bigness" ideology, i.e. it seeks large memberships, big offices, many officers, etc. The executives and leaders in the unions may properly refer to their experience as a career of a business type more than a commitment to a social movement. Furthermore, one may achieve a legitimate success as a labor union official. The union leader who is able to gain results in negotiation is rewarded in terms of high salary and other occupational amenities; indeed, his rewards are similar to those of the successful business executive.[6] It may even be correct to view executive positions in unions as avenues for upward vertical mobility.

In the United States one finds a higher proportion of union leaders to number of members than in other countries. Therefore, not only is working up the union hierarchy an acceptable career, but it is a probable career in terms of a number of opportunities. A ratio of one official to every 300 members in a nation where union membership approaches 20 million renders such positions a fairly large occupational category, 60,000 or more. Some glamorous or high prestige occupations in the sciences may involve a smaller number of practitioners. At the other extreme, in Norway one observes that there are more than 2000 members per officer, and a total of only 240 officers. Yet the proportion of union officers to the Norwegian population is about 0.06 per cent while the proportion of union officers to the American population is about 0.03 per cent.

With such a relatively large number of union officials in the United States, union conventions often are dominated by officials rather than by the rank and file members. This creates an atmosphere that approximates more that of a professional association than of a social movement. The environment of unionization is far from being characterized as an association of equals, and in fact is organized into bodies of leaders and followers. There continues to be extensive lay participation in the organization of unions, but the professional life hierarchy of officials in the nature of the divison of labor in balance of power are strikingly able to dominate the decision-making and direction of action.

Membership trends. Union memberships became significant in the latter part of the nineteenth century. It was in the 1930's, however, that the first great upsurge in union membership obtained. In the 1930's the largest union was estimated to have less than 300,000 members, and only six had 100,000 members or more.[7] By the 1960's the nation's largest union had more than 1,500,000 members, the next six had in excess of 750,000, and the next fourteen had 300,000 members or more.[8] These increases in union memberships are notable. Nonetheless, when compared to the total population one finds that in 1933, 5.2 per cent of the labor force was in unions and in 1960, 21.9 per cent of the labor force was in unions. The high point was reached in 1953, when 25.2 per cent of the labor force was in unions.

Furthermore, it is observed that the concentration of membership in a few unions has in effect diversified.[9] Estey reports: "that concentration in the ranks of the two largest unions, both individually and collectively, has declined substantially, especially since 1935." [10] The nation's two largest unions peaked in membership around 1900. From 1901 to 1962 their combined membership fell from 25.3 per cent to 15.3 per cent of the nation's total union membership. During this same period the absolute number of members increased from 285,000 to 2,450,000. While the Teamsters and United Mine Workers continue to be major unions in number of members and in power and definition of ideology, they now represent a smaller proportion of the nation's organized labor than in earlier points in history. The rank positions of the third, fourth, fifth, and sixth largest unions on an individual and collective basis have increased over the past 60 years. Only in the case of the six largest unions does the record show that the 1962 proportion of membership is greater than in 1903. The largest union represented 13 per cent of the membership in 1903 and only 9 per cent in 1962. This pattern of a lesser proportion of the membership in the 1960's than at the turn of the century obtained for those other unions between the second and fifth largest.

In terms of social organization the data on union membership reveal that particularly since the 1930's the dispersion has subjected organized labor to a greater breadth of decision-making and control. Union membership is becoming relatively more decentralized. This does not in and of itself imply a greater democratization of union organization, even though it documents a dispersion of power. It is consistent with the above observations that the environment of unionization in the United States is relatively conservative and essentially a forum for worker expression in the American success dream.

The expansion of unions has accelerated and decreased at different times in history. The first increase in union membership took place between 1897 and 1904. The next notable expansion in membership was in the 1930's. This expansion and contraction of union membership further illustrates the importance of this environment as a mechanism for achievement more than as an alternative system of social organization.

Union solidarity. The organization and environment of the union is further illustrated by a case study of solidarity. In 1949 Rose and associates studied a sample of the members of Local 688 in St. Louis.[11] The study is based on nearly 400 interviews, a representative sample of the local union. No attempt is made to argue that one can generalize from this specific time and place study to all unionization in the nation, but the case is sufficient to illustrate solidarity as one dimension of the union environment.

It is found that a strong loyalty to the unions is associated with two variables: first, the success of the union in achieving goals for increasing worker income, security, and job satisfaction; and second, the amount of participation by the rank and file members in union events. The attitude of the member's family toward the union is also of significance. Hence, it is suggested that union organizers consider participation on the part of family members in some auxiliary forms.

The strong solidarity that is manifest in such union organization is not in itself to be viewed as antagonism toward employers. Indeed, within the framework of solidarity there is manifest the feeling that the unions' forceful actions should nevertheless be fair to employers. In terms of the notion of fairness, members suggest that there are points beyond which the union could not force issues for wage increases and expect the businesses to remain solvent. The membership does not support union unilateral action to the point of jeopardizing business solvency.

Union members indicate a considerable interest in the new dimensions of focus—i.e. extending fringe benefits and recreational activities.

Union loyalty and solidarity on the part of members tend to be for the local union rather than for the national or international organization. This characteristic of membership has strong implications for understanding the total unionization environment. As previously reported from other indexes, repeatedly one finds that the environment is a mechanism for achievement rather than a way-of-life social movement.

The social organizational characteristics of union in ideology, membership, and solidarity all reveal the importance of this occupational environment as a mechanism for achievement, representation, and dignity of the workers represented.

UNIONIZATION AND OCCUPATIONAL ORGANIZATION

Most occupational practitioners are not union members. Occupational organization as such does not require union membership. In some cases the internal organization of an occupation is weakened if not devastated by the union organization of its members, while in other cases an occupation may reach higher levels of strength by the organization of its members. In either event the boundary maintenance of the occupation is permeated when practitioners are unionized. The free-standing integrity of the occupation is reduced, compromised, as the union negotiates greater or lesser amounts of the occupational space of the workers.

In the case of most blue-collar occupations the expansion of unionization contributes to the strengthening of these types of work, even though they are forced to share the power of their social organization with the union organization. It is much less clear that many so-called white-collar occupations (that recently have been confronted with unionization, and have succumbed to it) are strengthened by this practitioner affiliation. Many of these white-collar occupations have considerable historical experience with a free-standing occupational integrity. It is largely on this basis that they resist unionization until they are no longer able to achieve remunerative benefits sufficient to their status image. In organizing the white-collar workers the tactics of union leaders are often modified to offend less and appeal more to their professionalistic occupational orientations.

Functions and leadership. The functions of the unions are auditory and broad, permeating the boundary of other free-standing occupations. First among their functions is an effort to force management to consider systematically the effects of their policies on the practices and behavior of workers. As a voice for workers, and to a considerable extent as a voice for occupations, the pressure of unions reduces the autonomy of management. A second function of the union is to achieve economic gain for its members. At best, the autonomy of management is compromised with the leadership of the unions in negotiating terms of remuneration. A third function of the union environment is the procurement of security for the organized workers. They establish contracts which specify the conditions for hiring, promoting, firing, and so forth. A fourth function of the union is to aid the individual worker psychologically and emotionally. In part, this is achieved by increasing the status and dignity of the worker by providing collectively for power and force in confrontations with management. A fifth function of the union environment is the direct conferring of status; this is an attempt to develop a class consciousness. A final primary function of the union environment is the provision of social participation ranging broadly from recreation, to banking, to insurance.

To the extent that occupations are extensively organized internally and tend to become a way of life for their practitioners, the above enumerated functions of the union environment stand as forceful negations of the occupational autonomy. Indeed, the environment of unionization for the highly developed and organized occupation is one of opposition and conflict of an order similar to the conflict between unions and managements. It follows, therefore, that unionization of professional workers is by the nature of their case of strong occupational organization more resisted than the unionization of less well organized occupational groups. Much less conflict is involved in the unionization of a new occupational group of a relatively silent or inarticulate occupational group. As occupations become internally well organized, e.g. as in the case of the fee-taking professionals, they develop specific mechanisms for controlling their own practices and conditions of work. They establish norms for their own fees, and to a considerable extent they develop a monopoly in their remuneration structures. They establish security for their practitioners through the mechanisms of colleagueship and through their ability to accept or reject future generations of participants. They confer status on their practitioners largely through the control of their behavior to one another and the ethics of their service to their clientele. When the occupationally well-organized professions' social participation becomes so persuasive that it is nearly impossible to distinguish the way of life from the occupation itself, the major functions of the union are internally provided by the highly organized occupations.

The leaders of unions must have multiple talents to fulfill the several and diverse functions of their organizations. Accordingly, they are reported to be both able and ambitious; often they are individuals who feel trapped in their jobs. An outlet for their frustration is leadership expressed in their unions. In other cases, they may be both aggressive and rebellious. This may be expressed in an emotional personality and with a quickness to resist authority and a willingness to "stick one's neck out."

In still other cases, union leaders are found to be, particularly at the local level, apathetic individuals who in effect got "pushed into the job." During the depression years of the 1930's there were numerous intellectual types who after being graduated from college were unable to find work appropriate to their education. Numerous persons of this type entered union leadership and used their knowledge and talents to achieve new equilibriums and new status quos. Some may be accused of being radicals and communists in their orientation, but such behavior patterns are inconsistent with the essential middle range and conservative orientation of the American union environment.

The traditional impact of the labor union leader is to speak forcefully to management, point out inequities, and demand changes for amelioration. At the local level the shop steward watches for areas of grievance, argues with the foreman or other management officials concerning injustices, seeks to arouse the local membership to defend their rights, advises the membership on what should be expected as a fair deal, and, when all else fails, organizes for strike and does battle until favorable settlements are reached.

When occupations are poorly organized and/or where they are the lower end of the socioeconomic occupational continuum the environment of the labor union as an articulate voice for the workers is both acceptable and largely effective. But where the occupations are of a white-collar and professional type, and where they are highly organized, they are, on the one hand, more capable of speaking for themselves and, on the other hand, less willing to have their occupational organization identified with conflict, bargaining, and negotiating situations. Indeed, the ideology and extensive occupational organization of some professions is such that it is beneath them—a loss of status—to bargain or negotiate with clients or management. Through colleagueship, training, selection, social control, ethics, and so forth they are able to achieve amenities in the work situation at least equal to those grappled for by the unions, and often in excess of those obtained by the unions' tactics.

The environment of unionization is seen to be unnecessary for many highly organized occupations. And in other cases, even when the occupational organization is less extensive or articulate, the techniques utilized in the union environment are objectionable to the occupational practitioners. Therefore, in order for the unionization environment to be effective, particularly for more than the blue-collar occupations, it is incumbent upon the leaders to demonstrate that their bargaining and negotiations are demonstratively more effective than those of personal and professional agreements. It is also essential for the union leaders to modify their techniques of grievance, aggressiveness, conflict and to substitute for these more professional patterns of association with white-collar and professional occupational practitioners and more ethical and less ostentatious means of presenting the white-collar, professional interest to the management.

Union functions and leadership techniques are not designed for the building of strong occupational images. They represent workers more and occupations less in patterns of negotiation. The historic strength of the union environment, particularly in the U.S., developed among blue-collar assembly line workers when these occupations were in their embryonic stages. In the absence of or prior to the development of mechanisms for occupational communication to employers, unions effectively and forcefully fulfilled this role. Accordingly, there is little need for and considerable rejection of the union environment among the more fully developed occupations like the professions. There are differ-

TABLE VI.1
Social Status vs. Per Cent Unionized

	Rank in Social Status [a]	Per cent Unionized [b]
Blue-collar	5	56.4
Railroad clerks, letter carriers, etc.	4	30.0
Office workers	3	9.3
Public school teachers	2	4.6
Engineers	1	3.5

[a] C. C. North and P. K. Hatt, "Jobs and Occupations," in R. Bendix and S. M. Lipset (eds.), *Class, Status and Power* (Glencoe: Free Press, 1953), pp. 411–26.
[b] B. Solomon and R. K. Burns, "Unionization of White-Collar Employees: Extent, Potential and Implications," *The Journal of Business of the University of Chicago*, 36 (April 1963), 141–65.
Source: Bernard P. Indik and Bernard Goldstein, "Professional Engineers Look at Unions" in *Industrial Relations Research Association: Proceedings of the Sixteenth Annual Meeting*, Publication No. 32 (Boston, Mass.: December 27–28, 1963), 211.

ences in the extent to which occupations have their practitioners organized by unions.

Extent of unionization by occupations. Blue-collar skilled worker occupations have been and continue to be more extensively organized by unions than other occupational types (see Table VI.1). In the past 20 years more efforts have been made to organize white-collar and professional workers and some notable gains have been made. Still, the typical white-collar and professional occupational practitioners are not characterized by union membership. Finally, the unskilled and laboring occupational practitioners (including farm laborers) are the least reached by union organization. Union strength is in those occupations that are rather well organized, but where the practitioners, even though understanding the American success dream, are disadvantaged in achievement through the most acceptable means. To these workers the environment of unionization is an acceptable complement to their somewhat floundering and inprecise occupational organizations.

Union organization is least effective among those residual occupational categories at the lower end of the occupational continuum. At the lowest levels, workers are hardly occupationally organized and often too inept as individuals to view their situation as deprived, much less to systematically aspire to upward vertical mobility and success. In such a milieu neither occupational organization nor union organization are easily achieved.

At the upper end of the occupational continuum the professional and many of the white-collar occupational practitioners are a privileged, if not an aristocratic caste. In many instances their occupational self-expression is totally adequate. Accordingly, they are effective in their ability both to negotiate with their clientele and employers and to resist union approaches as superficial and unnecessary.

Differential union membership by occupational category is vast, and the differences are not narrowing much. Historically unions have been associated with blue-collar workers, so any gains among white-collar workers appear to be significant at first. But the proportion of white-collar workers is growing rapidly, and they now outnumber manual workers. Meanwhile union memberships show little expansion. Necessarily their big growth potential is among white-collar workers, where their actual gains are modest.[12]

Membership and occupational mobility. Studies in both San Fran-

cisco and Detroit reveal that the overwhelming majority of downwardly
mobile men are union members while the great majority of upwardly
mobile men resist union membership.[13] Although union membership
is not wholly a matter of voluntarism the downward and upward differential memberships generally support the hypothesis that mobile occupational men tend to identify with the occupational categories toward which they are moving. Downwardly mobile workers may in some
cases be forced to accept union membership in order to obtain a job,
but upwardly mobile workers will seldom face such a requirement.

In the San Francisco area it was found that 76 per cent of the nonmobile manual workers and only 63 per cent of the downwardly mobile
workers were union members. In Detroit the respective percentages
were 71 and 67. The differential trend was in the same direction, but in
Detroit the absolute differences were insufficient for them to be statistically significant at the 5 per cent level.

It is further found that manual workers whose fathers are in managerial and professional occupations tend to be union members more
often than do sons of fathers who are in clerical and sales occupations.
These findings are interpreted to mean that there is greater resistance
to unionization when one is only moderately downwardly mobile than
when excessively downwardly mobile. In short, those who have moved
downward only slightly will continue to aspire to upward vertical mobility and hence prefer to manifest those occupational characteristics of
those above them.

In the main, similar relationships were found in both San Francisco
and Detroit between mobility and union membership. This is further
evidence that the impact of unionization is less where occupational organization is strong and greater where occupational organization is
weak.

EXAMPLES OF UNIONIZATION IMPACT ON OCCUPATIONS

We start in reverse order, as it were, proceeding from professionals, to
other white-collar, through blue-collar, and finally to agricultural occupations. Some of the least extensively organized workers are found in
the professions, but it is in these occupations where some of the most
imaginative efforts are being made by union organizers. Accordingly, it
is in the professions that the interaction between the environment of

unionization and occupational organization is most explicit. White-collar worker organization is generally at an intermediate position on a continuum from minimum to maximum union organization. Blue-collar occupational union organization is characteristically at the maximum end of the continuum. Examples here show normative cases of the impact of unionization on occupations.

The recent attempts to organize the small number of agricultural workers are unique. Until very recently most agricultural work was scarcely occupational and certainly not unionized. The importance of examining the impact of the environment of unionization and the agricultural workers is that it illustrates more the balance of power between total unionization and total occupational organization. This situation raises questions concerning the possibility of the environment of unionization dominating a category of workers in the almost or complete absence of occupational organization.

Professional occupations. Professional engineers were threatened by the depression years of the 1930's and challenged almost beyond tolerance limits during the war years of the 1940's. The juxtaposing of these traumatic decades contributed to a considerable amount of development of professional engineering unions during World War II and the immediate postwar period. In addition to the change in environment for engineers, their rate of growth, and that of their technical associates, has been about two and one-half times that of the nation's labor force in recent decades. Furthermore, the profession of engineering has shifted rapidly from that characterized by independent entrepreneurship to one in which about two-thirds of the practicing engineers are employed by industry. Added to all of this metamorphosis was the passage of the National Labor Relations Act in 1935, which developed the possibility that engineers might be engulfed, as it were, into the union movement as shop workers in their midst were organized. In 1947, with the passage of the Taft-Hartley Act, this threat of the dominant unionization environment was finally effectively eliminated for engineers.

As the engineering environment changed, and as the number of practitioners grew, many of their professional privileges were eroded and fragmented. At the same time the privileges, benefits, and wages of shop employees were improved, largely as a result of union contract negotiations. The gap between the shop workers and the professional engineers narrowed sharply. The stage was set for an expanding and strengthening of the professional organization engineers or for their accepting support from unions.

Between 1945 and 1947 most of the engineering unions were established. Some of this union formulation was encouraged by engineering professional societies. These engineering units were sharply separated from the mainstream of the nation's industrial union organizations. The number of engineers represented by the professional unions has continued to increase. Dissatisfaction among engineers also has continued to a considerable extent. Accordingly, the engineers' joint council subsequently studied the situation and released a statement concerning professional status and employment conditions.[14] The statement was organized under three topics: Professional Treatment, Personal Treatment, and Financial Treatment. Under the professional treatment category were listed the following kinds of items: a feeling that professional engineers were not sufficiently identified with management; need for improved and extended channels of communication between top management and non-supervisory engineers; the importance of more recognition of the engineer as a professional employee; and the avoidance of further assignment of engineers to sub-professional work. Other similar related issues were stated. Under the subject of personal treatment the following items were indicated: inadequate recognition of the engineer as an individual; inadequate criteria for measuring the progress of the engineer's accomplishments; need for more systematic mechanisms for training and rotations; need for improvement in statements concerning promotion policies; developments of techniques for avoidance of insecurity; and so forth. Subsumed under the category of financial treatment were included the following: salary increases commensurate with the technical contribution of the engineers; larger pay differentials between engineers and skilled workers; larger differentials between experienced and starting engineers; and so forth. In all, the grievances and inequities in the occupational environment of engineers were similar to those historically cited by unions in their negotiation with management. Yet, professional engineers resisted, indeed were against, trade unionism as an effective mechanism for redress of their grievances.

The professional engineering unions engaged in negotiations and in some cases even strikes. But the main thrust of their approach was and is to "educate management." In 1952 seventeen engineering unions met in Chicago to establish what has become a National Federation of Engineering Unions known as Engineers and Scientists of America (ESA). The constitution and by-laws of this federation list as their purpose:

. . . to promote the economic, professional, and social welfare of engineering and scientific employees by: (a) Gathering and disseminating to the Member Units, engineering students, and other interested parties, information concerning salaries and working conditions, living costs, bargaining procedures, legislation, and other pertinent information; (b) Assisting in the establishment of collective bargaining units of professional employees, and assisting such units upon their request in bargaining negotiations with employers, and in proceeding under the National Labor Relations Laws; (c) Rendering assistance in the organization of other similar homogeneous groups of professional employees; (d) Acting as spokesmen for all engineering and scientific employees before governmental bodies; (e) Seeking improvement in the quality of engineering and scientific education and promoting, in educational institutions, a better understanding of industrial employment.[15]

In 1958–59 Walton interviewed a sample of most of the professional union leaders. The study focused on the following basic questions: (1) How are management policy practices influenced in companies where professional unions operate? (2) What are the collective bargaining objectives of the engineering unions? (3) Following items one and two, what management changes have taken place as a result of the engineering unions? We are interested primarily in Walton's findings concerning the characteristics of engineering unionism and their impact on the occupations of engineering as a profession.

It is found that engineers are little interested in the typical American trade union "get-tough type" of hard bargaining. Instead, they opt for the education of management approach as their chief strategy. In sum, the operation is to utilize debate rather than give-and-take negotiations.[16]

Another characteristic of the professional engineering movement is the rapid turnover of leadership. There is some tendency for full-time officials, but in the nature of the professional environment most engineers are unwilling to become sufficiently close to a union ideology to desire full-time leadership services. At one point it was asserted that all engineers must take their turn on the grievance committee. Each is expected to be a committee man for two years and a chairman in the third year. Using the membership roster, the rotating assignments are systematically made.[17]

In essence, the enginering union mentality might be put as follows. The engineer manifests a general middle class consciousness. Essentially, he is management-oriented and sees unionization as an obstacle to this orientation and to his class status. Furthermore, the engineer is a traditional professional type. Accordingly, he tends to view the union as a negation of his professional individualism. As a person with a considerable social awareness, in addition to a professional body of knowledge, he sees the union as somewhat legitimized as a means of expression and as a means of influencing one's environment. Finally, in terms of leadership aspirations the engineer is interested in achieving positions of authority in business and politics. Unionization leadership may be utilized as a step toward this end, but not as an end in itself.[18]

The professional engineering units have major impact contributions on salary levels, fringe benefits, and merit systems. Professional unions also have made occupational impacts on procedures for layoffs, hiring, promoting, transfer, and discipline. Finally, the engineering unions have made a contribution in the area of organizational environment concerning jurisdictional issues, management responsibility, and employee relations. In all, the professional unions have used some of the format of the trade union environment, but studiously attempted to modify it to a greater consistency with professional occupational organization. In essence, unionization at the professional level is a technique for sharpening and breaking into greater relevance the occupational organization of the profession, as a profession rather than as a major component in the environment of unionization.

Unionization of professional engineers is from two sources, some being from within professional society organizations and some from within recognized affiliates of trade union associations. In the latter category is the oldest engineers' union, the American Federation of Technical Engineers, an AFL-CIO affiliate dating from 1918. It has experienced several name changes and some different orientations in the composition of membership. Currently, only about 1000 industrial engineers are represented in its membership, and the balance of the organization's approximately 12,000 members are sub-professionals and pre-professionals.[19]

The second early trade union to represent professionals was the Federation of Architects, Engineers, Chemists, and Technicians, a CIO affiliate in 1937. Subsequently it grew, merged with other unions, was accused of communist leanings in the late 1940's, and in the 1950's went out of existence.[20]

The Seattle Professional Engineering Employee Association is an appropriate example of the independent engineering type of unionization that developed during the 1940's. SPEEA was organized to represent engineer employees at the Boeing Airplane Company. SPEEA's purpose was to maintain a strictly professional unit. It was originally hindered by the National Labor Relations Board, but, in 1946, by an 81 per cent vote, it was selected as the bargaining agent for approximately 1000 Boeing engineers.[21]

In SPEEA's efforts to represent only professionals it adhered to a rigorous restriction of membership to those engineers and scientists with a Bachelors degree, or its equivalent, or more. Furthermore, membership in the organization is voluntary, no effort is made to obtain a union-shop agreement. It is also on record as attempting to settle agreements without recourse to strike. It further bargains for minimum and maximum salary scales for categories of worker rather than for specific pay rates for specific jobs. In accomplishing its purpose SPEEA gathers, analyzes, and publishes data on salaries and other conditions of engineers' employment. In most of these characteristics its position is weakened in a traditional trade union sense, but it is given integrity in a professional organization sense.

SPEEA membership has increased from about 600 in 1949 to some 2700 in the 1960's. Its actual membership as a proportion of the potential has varied from 30 per cent at the time of origin to nearly 52 per cent in 1953 and subsequently dropped to only 29 per cent in the 1960's.

In 1953, shortly after the success of SPEEA, a national organization, The Engineers and Scientists of America (ESA) was established as a professional unionization unit. In true professional style ESA went on record as opposing national strikes and supporting nationally directed bargaining. For a short period of time ESA grew, and at its height membership included fourteen major bargaining units. By the mid 1950's ESA had begun to decline in membership and importance.

Determining the number of professionals in union membership and the number of professionals represented by unions is precarious at best. Estimates suggest that approximately 5000 of the 19,000 AFL-CIO so-called professional affiliates are really professionals. It is further esti-mated that approximately 41,000 scientists and engineers are repre-sented by unions. Put another way, in 1959 there were some 1,096,200 engineers and scientists employed in the civilian economy; only 4 per cent of these are estimated to be represented by unions, and only 2 per cent are believed to be union members. Engineers account for most of that membership. Breaking it down further, it is estimated that less than half of one per cent of all engineers and scientists in the civilian economy hold memberships in AFL-CIO affiliated unions.[22] In addi-tion to this already small proportion of membership, the limited avail-able evidence suggests that in recent years both union representation and union membership is declining among these professionals.

It is clear from these limited data that the environment of unioniza-tion among professional engineers and scientists has never been a real-ity for more than a small fraction of these professional practitioners.

When the situation of unionization among professionals is examined more generally, several specific negative and positive factors can be enumerated.[23] Negative factors include (1) the notion that collective action or bargaining is incompatible with professional status. (2) Pro-fessional men have accepted many of the stereotyped and negative be-liefs about trade unions and hence tend to reject them. (3) The soci-eties of professionals tend to work systematically against the develop-ment of unions among their members. (4) Management has in a number of cases joined with professionals in strongly opposing union-ization. (5) The position of professionals in many firms has not been conducive to the development of strong collective bargaining posi-tions.

The factors that have caused professionals to favor unionization are as follows: (1) General changes in the socioeconomic organization of the society have reduced the gap between professional work, and skilled work brought routine to what traditionally was professional work. (2) As professionals become salaried they often lose security, or are sub-jected to a set of conditions which give them no more security than many other workers in the industry. (3) As an apparent loss of some status has accrued for numerous professionals, they have desired group action, less for unionization as such, and more for building a new strength for their professional occupation. In any event, this had led them in some cases to favor group action ultimately in a manner similar to union development. And (4), there are some new orientations of professional societies. In some cases they view moderated forms of negotiation, education, or bargaining as being consistent with basic notions of professionalization.

The case of unionization manifestations among the professionals is further illustrated in public school teaching.[24] Both teachers and the general public have questioned the professional propriety of teachers either to engage in collective bargaining or to strike. As is traditional with other professionals, teachers have questioned such procedures as being basically inconsistent with their occupational image. Other practitioners have examined the situation from an opposing point of view. For example, they indicate that as professionals teachers from time to time have the obligation to strike and/or to negotiate when the conditions of teaching are not acceptable to those of a minimum level professional standing. But, indeed, strikes are not thereby against children, but for them, in the upgrading of the environment in which teaching, learning, and creativity take place.

In any event, teachers have gone on strike. Between 1940 and 1954 the record shows more than 90 work stoppages involving over 20,000 individuals. The average length of these work stoppages is nine days. Slightly over half of the stoppages had to do with wages and hours in the environment; 14 per cent were related to organizational factors, for example, the right for recognition; and another 30 per cent concerned other working conditions, for example, job security, physical and administrative school conditions, and policies related to school organization.

The record shows that while teachers have gone on strike, and for a full range of reasons, they do not favor the use of the strike and believe that when it is used it should be used with extreme restraint. The National Education Association has no official strike policy. Its leaders and its membership have a general image of no-strike or anti-strike. The American Federation of Teachers in fact does have a no-strike policy. But when one examines the affiliation of teachers involved in work stoppages it is clear that 31 per cent have been affiliated with the AFL,

26 per cent with no teachers' organization, 24 per cent with NEA affiliates, 15 per cent with CIO affiliates, and 9 per cent with independent
organizations.[25]

Collective bargaining in the nursing profession illustrates another
case of occupational practitioners on the periphery of the environment
of unionization.[26] The American Nursing Association was organized in
1896. Among its several purposes are included the promotion of usefulness, honor, and promoting of financial and related interests of nursing
as a profession. During the depression years of the 1930's the status of
the nursing profession deteriorated. Indeed, by 1937 the condition had
become so critical that the leaders of the occupation feared that it
might succumb to aggressive unionization. Accordingly in that year the
official journal carried an editorial admonishing nurses against unionization.[27]

By the 1940's and World War II the economic problems of the
nursing profession were compounded. In 1941 the California State
Nurses Association adopted a basic salary schedule, but it was unable to
get hospitals to support it. In 1946 the American Nurses Association
developed an aggressive economic security program. In that year the
California State Nurses Association engaged in collective bargaining
and finally was successful in reaching its first agreement. This success
led to acclaim from nurses in other areas, and in that year the official
journal editorialized distinguishing between collective bargaining and
unionization, supporting the former but not the latter. Other examples
of collective bargaining achieved success. Finally, in 1950, the American
Nurses Association adopted a no-strike policy, in effect reaffirming the
internal strength of the organization of nursing as an occupation.

By 1960 the American Nursing Association records reported some 75
agreements resulting from collective bargaining situations in which 115
institutions covering some 8000 nurses had accepted working conditions
achieved through negotiation. The subjects for collective bargaining included recognition, coverage, salary, shift differential, special services
differential, on-call pay, sick leave, vacations, holidays, seniority, health
programs, and adjudication of grievances.[28]

Other white-collar occupations. Efforts to organize white-collar workers into the environment of unionization come about due to the decreasing proportion of blue-collar workers and the increasing proportion
of white-collar workers, and due to the narrowing of the gap of status

between blue- and white-collar workers. In short, it is in the interest of unions in expanding membership to organize white-collar workers because their numbers and proportions are expanding. It is in the interest of the white-collar workers because the status of the blue-collar workers is increasing to such a place that white-collar workers have few tangible advantages over them. This is not to say that the status of white-collar workers as such has declined but more that it remains stable while that of the blue-collar workers increases.[29]

There were a few office locals organized as early as the 1920's.[30] The first real thrust for organization of office employees occurred in the 1930's. In 1934 the AFL had participated in the organization of some thirty-four local office employee unions. For a variety of organization and tactical reasons the AFL, however, never chartered these local units. In 1937 twenty-three of these locals met in convention, condemning the AFL for insufficient support, and praising the CIO. The CIO responded by chartering them as the United Office and Professional Workers of America (UOPWA). The organization of office workers continued to grow slowly. In 1945 the AFL finally chartered the Office Employees International Union (OEIU). Both of these international white-collar unions prospered for a few years. By the late 1940's, however, the UOPWA showed signs of communist influence. Its officers refused to sign the non-communist affidavits, endorsed Henry Wallace as a presidential candidate, and subsequently, in 1950, the union was expelled from the CIO.

The extent of office worker union organization is still not great. In the 1950's out of approximately 4.3 million non-government office employees only about 13 per cent, or some 500,000 were organized.[31]

The organization of white-collar workers tends to be along industrial union types. In most cases the white-collar workers are not organized until after production workers are organized. This tends to break down resistance for unionization because many of the white-collar workers are daughters, wives, sisters, or friends of the production workers. The industrial unions are frequently able to offer office employees more systematic and effective collective bargaining programs than are separate white-collar union organizations. It is not yet clear whether the white-collar unionization is developing with an ideological commitment to the union environment or if it is a matter of white-collar workers accepting the effectiveness of union negotiations—in fact, in effect, buying it by paying their dues but aside from this offering little ideological commitment. In any event a counter to the acceleration of white-collar unionization has been increased interest in white-collar workers on the part of management.

Blue-collar occupations. The most traditional environment of unionization in the United States is illustrated among blue-collar workers. The United Brotherhood of Carpenters and Joiners is an illustrious example. It was organized in Chicago, in 1881, by a convention of thirty-six delegates from local carpenter unions.[32] In recent years its membership has been in excess of 800,000. This makes it a key social structure in the organization of the building and construction industry, as well as one of the most influential voices traditionally in the AFL and still a strong voice in the AFL-CIO.

The organization of the union is strongly controlled from a national office which has ultimate authority over subordinate local units. Internal democracy is not a strong characteristic of the carpenters' union. From 1915 to 1952 the union was capably directed but with the strong hand of one man as its president. Recently, upon his retirement, his son succeeded him. The individual member has little power in the organization of the union and against the effective authority of the top leadership. Nevertheless, most of the carpenters' union members are satisfied with the way their union is run.

Membership in the union is through apprenticeship and/or training in specific related crafts. While the types of occupations in the union are expanding to some degree, the vast majority of the members are still employed as carpenters in the building and construction industry.

A second important example of viable blue-collar unionism is the International Association of Machinists, organized in 1888. It is the prototype of an old craft union.[33] In name this union is run with considerable internal organizational integrity and characterized by considerable democratic action. Its primary focus is on metal fabrication and on occupations in lathes and mill work. In more recent years its focus has expanded to the point that it has become essentially an industrial union in metal fabricating occupations. Its membership is large and in 1960 was in excess of 820,000.

Its main organizational characteristics were developed in the 1930's. In spite of its efforts to expand in recent years its membership has declined somewhat. Most of its members (70 per cent) continue to be in major metal fabricating work. The importance of workers in the railroad industry has fallen to under 10 per cent. Tool and dye work is less than 2 per cent. Most of the union members, 41 per cent, are in contract work, and the second largest proportion, 23 per cent, are in air frame work.

The skill distribution of the union's members from 1947 and 1952 has been analyzed. Journeymen were the largest category in both periods, but they have dropped from 47 per cent in the earlier period to only 40 per cent at the later period. Production workers has increased from 23 per cent to 35 per cent. Specialists and helpers have remained as rather stable proportions over the time period.

The environment of occupational men in carpentry and machinist occupations has been and is vastly dominated by the structure of unionization. While the occupations continue to be strong and the practitioners manifest articulate identities, they are interrelated with their union organization and not separate or free-standing entities.

Agricultural occupations. Agricultural occupations traditionally have been among the least union organized. Indeed, while remaining almost untouched by unionization until recent decades, the industry of agriculture has similarly organized few free-standing articulated occupations. Labor and way of life, in the so-called family farm organization, hardly have been separated until after World War II.

The most notable exception to lack of unionization among agricultural occupations has long existed in Hawaii. In 1945 the Territorial Legislature enacted the Hawaiian Employment Relations Act. This was locally called the "Little Wagner Act" because it provided a Wagner-like assistance to unions in organizing agricultural workers. The union was quick to show that it represented the majority of the agricultural employees on the 30 sugar plantations. The Act was passed in May and by September collective bargaining agreements were signed.[34] Unionization in the pineapple industry has followed a similar if more difficult pattern.

Numerous attempts have been made to organize agricultural workers on the continental United States, but in general unionization has met with little success in this occupational arena.

SUMMARY AND IMPLICATIONS

The environment of unionization as known in the United States is part of the industrial urbanized social organization. It is ideologically con-

servative. In short, the environment of unionization is less than definitive as a social movement articulating an ideology in and for itself. In
the main, the environment of unionization is a mechanism appended
to many well-organized occupations which serves primarily in relating
these occupations from their internal organization to the societal environment of which they are a part.

Unionization modifies occupational organization, indeed, it perme-
ates the boundary maintenance of occupations. Yet unionization as
such is not ideologically opposed to occupational organizations; it is in
fact generally supportive of occupational organizations.

Unionization has been a most strong adjunct to those middle range
occupations, namely the blue-collar categories of work, where the practitioners have seen opportunity but had limited avenues for successful achievement. Unionization has been used as a mechanism for
representing their point of view, contributing their strength, and maintaining their security. In those occupations that are professional and
white-collar the internal organization of the occupation as such has
been strong. As a result the overt manifestation of the mainline professions and of many white-collar practitioners has been the resistance of
unionization. In many cases this is somewhat myopically viewed as opposition to unionization. In fact, a more discerning analysis warrants a
conclusion that the professions and white-collar occupations rather
than being against unionization have little need of unionization.

In the agricultural occupations one finds the least amount of unionization of all the occupational categories. Again, it is less that there has
been systematic opposition to unionization than it is that the industry
of agriculture has in effect not even generated effective free-standing
occupations. Until the middle of the twentieth century agriculture was
ideologically more a family farm way of life than an industry in which
labor was articulately separated from management and production as
such. In an environment where even occupational organization is nearly inarticulate there is no body of social structures to which the environment of unionization can be effectively related. In a unionization
environment where there is no unilateral ideology the union has little
to offer in the agricultural industry.

Organized occupations have succumbed to the efforts of unionization by reducing its ideological projection and by utilizing its forceful-
ness in negotiation to accomplish internal occupational organizational

ends. In sum, occupations are influenced less by unions than unions by occupations in the United States.

NOTES

1. Frank Tannenbaum, "The Social Function of Trade Unionism," *Political Science Quarterly*, 62 (June 1947), 161–94; see also John Herling, *Labor Unions in America* (Washington, D.C.: Robert B. Luce, Inc., 1964); "The Crisis in the American Trade Union Movement," Entire Issue, *Annals of the American Academy of Political and Social Science*, 350 (November 1963).
2. Seymour Martin Lipset, "Trade Unions and Social Structure: I," *Industrial Relations*, 1 (October 1961), 75–89, see also Part II in *Industrial Relations*, 1 (February 1962), 89–110.
3. Ibid. p. 77.
4. Ibid. p. 77; for a further discussion of these points see also Seymour M. Lipset, "Le Syndicalisme américain et les valeurs de la société americaine," *Sociologie du Travail*, II (avril-jui 1961), 161–81.
5. Alex Inkeles and Peter Rossi, "National Comparisons of Occupational Prestige," *American Journal of Sociology*, 61 (January 1956), 329–39.
6. Lipset, "Trade Unions," Part II, p. 90.
7. Leo Wolman, *Ebb and Flow in Trade Unionism* (New York: National Bureau of Economic Research, 1936).
8. *Directory of National and International Labor Unions in the United States*, 1965 (Washington, D.C.: U.S.D.L., Bureau of Labor Statistics, Bulletin No. 1493, 1965), p. 53.
9. Martin S. Estey, "Trends in Concentration of Union Membership, 1897–1962," *The Quarterly Journal of Economics*, LXXX (August 1961), 343–60.
10. Ibid. p. 348.
11. Arnold M. Rose, *Union Solidarity: The Internal Cohesion of a Labor Union* (Minneapolis: The University of Minnesota Press, 1952).
12. Albert A. Blum, "The Prospects for Office Employee Unionization," *Industrial Relations Research Association: Proceedings 16th Annual Meeting* (Boston, 1963), pp. 182ff.
13. Seymour Martin Lipset and Joan Gordon, "Mobility and Trade Union Membership," in Bendix and Lipset (eds.), *Class Status and Power* (Glencoe, Illinois: The Free Press, 1953), pp. 491–500; and Richard F. Curtis, "Note on Occupational Mobility and Union Membership in Detroit: A Replication," *Social Forces*, 38 (October 1959), 69–71.
14. Engineers Joint Council, *Professional Standards and Employment Conditions* (New York: Report No. 101, May 1956).
15. Richard E. Walton, *The Impact of the Professional Engineering Union: A Study of Collective Bargaining Among Engineers and Scientists*

and Its Significance for Management (Boston: Graduate School of Business Administration, Harvard University, 1961), p. 27.

16. Ibid. p. 37.
17. Ibid. p. 39.
18. Ibid. p. 40.
19. Eldon J. Devorak, "Will Engineers Unionize?," *Industrial Relations,* II (May 1963), 45–65.
20. Vera Shlaknan, "Unionism and Professional Organizations Among Engineers," *Science and Society,* 14 (Fall 1950), 323–4.
21. "Boeing Engineers Choose SPEEA for Bargaining," *The Professional Engineer,* 1 (December 1945), 1.
22. Devorak, "Will Engineers Unionize?," pp. 59–60.
23. Bernard Goldstein, "Unions and the Professional Employee," *The Journal of Business,* 27 (October 1954), 276–84; Bernard Goldstein, "Aspects of the Nature of Unionism Among Salaried Professionals in Industry," *American Sociological Review,* 20 (April 1955), 199–205; and Bernard Goldstein, "The Prospective of Unionized Professionals," *Social Forces,* 37 (May 1959), 323–7.
24. Myron Lieberman, "Teachers Strikes: An Analysis of the Issues," *Harvard Educational Review,* 26 (Winter 1956), 39–70.
25. Ibid. p. 46.
26. Daniel H. Kruger, "Bargaining and the Nursing Profession," *Monthly Labor Review,* 84 (July 1961), 699–705; and Wendell L. French and Richard Robinson, "Collective Bargaining by Nurses and Other Professionals: Anomaly or Trend?," *Labor Law Journal,* 11 (October 1960), 903–10ff.
27. Editorial, "Nurse Membership in Unions," *American Journal of Nursing,* 37 (July 1937), 766–7.
28. Kruger, "Bargaining," p. 703.
29. Everett M. Kassalow, "New Union Frontier: White-Collar Workers," *Harvard Business Review,* 40 (January-February 1962), 41–52; and Everett M. Kassalow, "The Prospects for White-Collar Union Growth," *Industrial Relations,* 5 (October 1965), 37–47; and Everett M. Kassalow, "United States," in Adolf Sturmthal (ed.), *White-Collar Trade Unions* (Urbana: University of Illinois Press, 1966).
30. "A Union for Bank Clerks," *Literary Digest,* 79 (November 17, 1923), 16; and *The Ledger* (Official Journal of the Bookkeepers, Stenographers, and Accountants Union, Local 12646, AFL), 3 (June 1937), 1.
31. Elinor Waters, "Unionization of Office Employees," *The Journal of Business,* 27 (October 1954), 285–92.
32. Morris A. Horowitz, *The Structure and Government of the Carpenters' Union* (New York and London: John Wiley & Sons, Inc., 1962).
33. Mark Perlman, *Democracy in the International Association of Machinists* (New York and London: John Wiley & Sons, Inc., 1962).
34. Philip Brooks, *Multiple-Industry Unionism in Hawaii* (New York: Ea-

gle Enterprises, 1952); see also Edward Johannessen, *The Hawaiian Labor Movement* (Boston: Bruce Humphries, Inc., 1956); and Curtis Aller, *Labor Relations in the Hawaiian Sugar Industry* (Berkeley: University of California Institute of Industrial Relations, 1957).

SUPPLEMENTARY READINGS

"The Crisis in the American Trade Union Movement," Entire Issue, *Annals of the American Academy of Political and Social Science*, 350 (November 1963).

Morris A. Horowitz, *The Structure and Government of the Carpenters' Union* (New York and London: John Wiley & Sons, Inc., 1962).

Everett M. Kassalow, "New Union Frontier: White-Collar Workers," *Harvard Business Review*, 40 (January-February 1962), 41–52.

Daniel H. Kruger, "Bargaining and the Nursing Profession," *Monthly Labor Review*, 84 (July 1961), 699–705.

Adolf Sturmthal (ed.), *White-Collar Trade Unions* (Urbana: University of Illinois Press, 1966).

OCCUPATIONAL STATUS AND PRESTIGE VII

Occupations are everywhere ordered into status hierarchies. Moreover, there is a differential prestige associated with the occupations in a particular stratum as well as between strata. In urbanized societies in general, and in the United States in particular, occupations are differentiated on the basis of income, rights and privileges, and other forms of remuneration that are given to their practitioners. Occupations are differentiated on the basis of cleanness or dirtiness of work. They are differentiated into manual and mental categories. More recently, occupations have been emphatically differentiated by style of dress, into the so-called white-collar and blue-collar categories. This is not an exhaustive list of the bases for ranking occupations hierarchically, but it is sufficient to suggest multiple directions such hierarchical rankings can take.

Occupations constitute one category of statuses utilized in organizing a society. The subject of this chapter concerns the hierarchical ranking of these statuses. At this time there is no clear or final answer concerning the basis for the hierarchical ranking of occupations. Davis and Moore have suggested one of the most provocative possible answers in their assertion that some occupations are functionally more important and others less important.[1] Their position is that a society has a vast range of different tasks to be accomplished in order to assure its survival. These various occupational tasks are different in the amount of training required, the amount of sacrifice necessitated, the amount of education which is appropriate, and the general attractiveness of the work. In a volunteristic society, where the social organization maintains most occupations as achieved rather than ascribed, differential rewards constitute a primary mechanism for enlisting people into the several occupations in the hierarchy. The various occupations have differential

164

importance for the society, and, within limits, they must be fulfilled. The social organization and the occupational organization must, therefore, be integrated in such a way as to induce an appropriate number of persons to enter the several occupations. This in no way suggests that a society must reward an occupation in terms of its intrinsic value, but only that it must arrange for sufficient reward to attract an adequate number of occupational men. This and other positions will be analyzed in more detail in a later section in this chapter.

Occupational prestige is of particular importance in urbanized societies. The merit which is attributed to an occupation is both a challenge and a reward to potential occupational practitioners in a society where achievement is normative. What people believe about the worth and value of an occupation, whether the belief is valid in fact or not, is important in job aspiration and career behavior.

The concern with and study of occupational rank dates at least from the late nineteenth century. William Hunt, in 1897, working for the U.S. Bureau of the Census, arranged gainful workers into four categories: proprietary class, clerical class, skilled worker class, and laboring class. This type of concern was carried forward by Alba Edwards, who in 1917 published an article in the *Journal of the American Statistical Association* in which he arranged gainful workers into nine socioeconomic categories. In 1921 Yerkes and his colleagues studied intelligence test scores which were the results of instruments administered to World War I recruits. The scores were arranged into what was called the Army Alpha Test and given to soldiers coming from some 55 civilian occupations. In 1925 George Counts developed the first occupational prestige scale. In 1933 Alba Edwards revised his 1917 occupational categories in terms of the 1930 Census data. In 1947 the National Opinion Research Center carried out a monumental study on the popular evaluation of jobs and occupations. In 1956 Inkeles and Rossi synthesized data from various studies in the United States, Great Britain, New Zealand, Japan, The Union of Soviet Socialist Republics, and Germany. This gave an international comparison of occupational ranks in various areas of the world. Finally, in the chronology of the study of occupational hierarchy Robert Hodge and associates have made a 1963 re-study of the 1947 N.O.R.C. analysis of occupational prestige.

The content of this chapter is based on a considerable body of empirical evidence, although the subject is far from adequately researched. Yet on the basis of the evidence currently available one observation is relevant, namely, that occupational hierarchy in the industrial urbanized societies is quite similar.

OCCUPATIONS AND SOCIAL STRATIFICATION

Attempts to deal with the relations between occupations and social stratification are discussed in this section. In 1945 Davis and Moore published their article, "Some Principles of Social Stratification." [2] This is a sharply functional statement of stratification theory, and it has been both widely used and heavily criticized. They suggest there are two determinants of positional rank. The first is a matter of function. The greatest rewards and the highest ranks go to those occupations which are of the most importance for society. The second is a matter of means. Occupations which require the most training and talent are awarded the highest ranks.[3] The further explanation of this position makes it clear that it is unnecessary for a society to reward positions in proportion to their functional importance. It is only necessary to make an award which is adequate to secure a sufficient number of people in the required positions. In short, the reward system is negatively aimed at keeping the less essential positions from competing successfully with the more essential positions.

It is further argued by Davis and Moore that there is a differential scarcity of personnel. All positions require some sort of skill or capacity even if at a minimal level. These capacities are either inherent or achieved through training. In most occupations both inherent qualities and training are required. It may be that scarcity will be discovered in one or both of these areas. On the other hand, talent may be abundant and training inadequate. The authors suggest that modern medicine is well within the intellectual capacity of a great number of individuals. Nevertheless, the training required is so long, arduous, and expensive that few people would aspire to such a dirty and difficult occupation unless the differential rewards were great. In cases where either skills or training are limited and the need for such occupational practitioners is great the status and prestige of the occupation must be high as a compensation for recruitment and participation.

The Davis and Moore theory is difficult to put to empirical test, but some such tests have been made. Simpson and Simpson studied correlates of occupational prestige and reported their findings in 1960.[4] In this study, ratings of the 90 occupations used in the National Opinion Research Center study were made by 21 social science graduate student judges on the basis of responsibility, training, education, skill required in the occupation, and personal autonomy. The principal finding was that training-education-skill and responsibility collectively account for the great amount of variance in occupational prestige. This research tends to validate the several theoretical statements concerning the functional rankings of occupations. The authors believe that their data are consistent with the Davis and Moore theory of stratification. They analyze functional responsibility and assert that while it may not be the same as functional importance, it is a close estimate of it.[5] It is argued from this research that an index of occupational prestige could be constructed using training-education-skill and responsibility.

Functional importance for the hierarchy of occupation has been suggestively researched in the two sharply contrasting communities of Las Vegas, Nevada, and Amherst, Massachusetts.[6] Las Vegas may be described as a recreation-tourist community where the economy is primarily built on gambling and commercial entertainment. Amherst might be called an educational town, housing a prestigious liberal arts college and a state university. The notion is that the functional importance of occupations in these two diverse communities should be different. High school students in the two communities were asked to evaluate the following occupations: college president, college professor, philosopher, card dealer, crap dealer, manager of a casino, and roulette dealer. The prestige ranking of these occupations is reported in Table VII.1. The findings show no significant difference in the ranking of the occupations by the students in the two communities. When six occupational categories are ranked, namely, education, profession, business, skilled, gambling, and unskilled, the overwhelming indication of the findings is that there is no significant difference in the average prestige rating of the occupational categories in Amherst and Las Vegas. The students' ranking of these occupational categories was further analyzed by holding constant their vocational plans. Once again it is observed that regardless of whether or not the students aim for professional, business, or blue-collar work, they rank the occupational categories similarly.

TABLE VII. 1

Prestige Rankings of Educational and Gambling Occupations
for Amherst and Las Vegas Samples

| | Samples | |
Occupation	Amherst (N = 90)	Las Vegas (N = 95)
College president	2	3
College professor	6	4
Philosopher	7	7
Card dealer	24	23
Crap dealer	23	15
Manager of a casino	20	14
Roulette dealer	22	22

Source: Lionel S. Lewis and Joseph Lopreato, "Functional Importance and Prestige of Occupations," *The Pacific Sociological Review*, 6 (Fall 1963), 57.

This evidence does not appear to support the functional theory of
occupational hierarchy and social stratification. The authors do correctly point out, however, that the functionalist position is based on
societal analysis while this research is based on comparing two communities within the same society.

Another statement of the relation between occupation and social
stratification is projected by Hatt.[7] The Hatt statement is a modification of the Davis and Moore position cited earlier. Hatt asserts that the
concept of stratification rests upon four postulates:

1. Differential positions occur in many different social structures, e.g., religious, governmental, economic.
2. The rewards of these positions are of various types, e.g., financial gain,
   advantageous working conditions, and honorific value or "psychic income."
3. Some combination of all the rewards attached to any position constitutes
   the invidious value of that position and hence its prestige.
4. Total societal position is a summation of prestige, modified by the esteem bestowed by others as a reward for the manner in which the expectations associated with any given status are fulfilled.[8]

Hatt's theory of the relation between occupation and social stratification is based on both prestige and situs. To test this notion a series of
occupational families or situses was posited. The occupational families
should have related prestige in the public mind if the hypothesis is to
be validated. The evidence from this analysis tends to support the via-

bility of a vertical-horizontal occupational analysis. The vertical analysis is in terms of prestige, while the horizontal analysis is in terms of situs. The importance of this research is its pointing up of another dimension of occupational prestige and social organization.

The weight of evidence still lies in the direction of a functional distribution of occupations in a hierarchy.

PRESTIGE OF OCCUPATIONS

A pioneering empirical analysis of the social status of occupations was made in 1925 by Counts.[9] Forty-five occupations were selected more or less at random from the entire vocational spectrum. The study was opened with an introductory statement to the respondent which suggested that there is a tendency to "look up to" persons engaged in some occupations and "down on" individuals employed in other occupations. It was further suggested that one might even be ashamed or proud of people on the basis of the occupations in which they are engaged. Number one was to be assigned to the occupations most looked up to, number two to the occupation second most looked up to, and so on in descending order through the 45 occupations. Respondents were instructed to first arrange the 45 occupations into nine categories, putting the highest in the first category and the lowest in the ninth category. Then the categories were to be combined into one list of 45 occupations from highest to lowest.

Six categories of persons ranked the occupations, including 82 Minneapolis school teachers; 62 University of Minnesota College of Agriculture freshmen; 60 senior boys in the Milwaukee Trade School; 78 Bridgeport, Connecticut, High School seniors; and 42 Wallingford, Connecticut, High School seniors.[10] The findings demonstrated a high agreement in the ranking of the occupations by the six categories of individuals. The average ranking for the six sets of raters is reported in Table VII.2. The banker ranked highest, followed by the college professor, the physician, the clergyman, the lawyer, and so on, with the ditch digger ranking forty-fifth.

This early study demonstrated the differential occupational status that was perceived by several categories of raters. This clear perception of an occupational hierarchy was firmly documented. Regardless of the equalitarian ideology operative in the national social organization, the reality of occupational life is couched in hierarchy.

TABLE VII.2

Forty-five Occupations Ranked According to Social Status by 450 Persons

	Rank
Army captain	9
Auto manufacturer	6
Banker	1
Barber	36
Blacksmith	38
Bookkeeper	21
Carpenter	28
Chauffeur	35
Civil engineer	8
Clergyman	4
Coal miner	39
College professor	2
Ditch digger	45
Dry goods merchant	14
Electrician	22
Elementary school teacher	13
Factory manager	12
Factory operative	37
Farmer	16
Foreign missionary	11
Grocer	20
High school teacher	10
Hod carrier	43
Insurance agent	24
Janitor	40
Lawyer	5
Locomotive engineer	23
Machinist	17
Mail carrier	26
Man of leisure	15
Motorman	34
Physician	3
Plumber	32
Policeman	25
Railroad conductor	27
Rural school teacher	19
Salesman	29
Soldier	30
Street cleaner	44

	Rank
Superintendent of schools	7
Tailor	33
Teamster	42
Traveling salesman	18
Typesetter	31
Waiter	41

Source: George S. Counts, "The Social Status of Occupations: A Problem in Vocational Guidance," *The Social Review*, 33 (January 1925), pp. 17–18.

Another landmark in the measure of occupational prestige was published by Smith in 1943.[11] This study involved the ranking of 100 occupations. The raters were 45 undergraduate students from Baker University, 175 undergraduates of the University of Kansas; 100 seniors from Abilene, Kansas, High School; and 25 students from Olatag, Kansas, High School. The ratings were taken during the school years 1938–1939, 1939–1940, and 1940–1941.

The entire procedure consisted of two main parts: (1) preliminary ranking of the occupations from high to low prestige status on the basis of the order of rank at a dinner honoring a celebrity, with an average member of each occupational class being seated at a formal dinner nearer to or farther from the celebrity than the average member of another, the distinctions between occupations to be made entirely on the basis of occupational prestige; and (2) rating each occupation on a scale of 100 points, the lower limit of this scale being conceived as reserved for the occupation having the lowest prestige in the United States according to the rater's personal estimation, and the highest as being reserved for the occupation having the highest prestige, regardless of whether the extreme limits were included in the occupations of the study.[12]

The title and definition of each occupation was supplied on a separate sheet of paper. The rater was admonished to go through the occupations quickly and arrange them in several groups from extremely high to extremely low. After a preliminary ranking another ranking was suggested for putting the occupations into a final order. This was a time-consuming instrument, with the average rater taking approximately one hour.

In 1947 a monumental National Opinion Research Center study of jobs and occupations was reported.[13] This was a nationwide cross section sample of Americans. The instrument was designed to produce in-

TABLE VII.3
Distributions of Prestige Ratings, United States, 1947 and 1963

Occupation	1947 NORC Score	Rank	1963 NORC Score	Rank
U.S. Supreme Court Justice	96	1	94	1
Physician	93	2.5	93	2
Nuclear physicist	86	18	92	3.5
Scientist	89	8	92	3.5
Government scientist	88	10.5	91	5.5
State governor	93	2.5	91	5.5
Cabinet member in the federal gov't.	92	4.5	90	8
College professor	89	8	90	8
U.S. representative in Congress	89	8	90	8
Chemist	86	18	89	11
Lawyer	86	18	89	11
Diplomat in the U.S. foreign service	92	4.5	89	11
Dentist	86	18	88	14
Architect	86	18	88	14
County judge	87	13	88	14
Psychologist	85	22	87	17.5
Minister	87	13	87	17.5
Member of the board of directors of a large corporation	86	18	87	17.5
Mayor of a large city	90	6	87	17.5
Priest	86	18	86	21.5
Head of a department in a state government	87	13	86	21.5
Civil engineer	84	23	86	21.5
Airline pilot	83	24.5	86	21.5
Banker	88	10.5	85	24.5
Biologist	81	29	85	24.5
Sociologist	82	26.5	83	26
Instructor in public schools	79	34	82	27.5
Captain in the regular army	80	31.5	82	27.5
Accountant for a large business	81	29	81	29.5
Public school teacher	78	36	81	29.5
Owner of a factory that employs about 100 people	82	26.5	80	31.5
Building contractor	79	34	80	31.5
Artist who paints pictures that are exhibited in galleries	83	24.5	78	34.5
Musician in a symphony orchestra	81	29	78	34.5
Author of novels	80	31.5	78	34.5
Economist	79	34	78	34.5
Official of an international labor union	75	40.5	77	37
Railroad engineer	77	37.5	76	39

Occupation	1947 NORC Score	Rank	1963 NORC Score	Rank
Electrician	73	45	76	39
County agricultural agent	77	37.5	76	39
Owner-operator of a printing shop	74	42.5	75	41.5
Trained machinist	73	45	75	41.5
Farm owner & operator	76	39	74	44
Undertaker	72	47	74	44
Welfare worker for a city gov't	73	45	74	44
Newspaper columnist	74	42.5	73	46
Policeman	67	55	72	47
Reporter on a daily newspaper	71	48	71	48
Radio announcer	75	40.5	70	49.5
Bookkeeper	68	51.5	70	49.5
Tenant farmer	68	51.5	69	51.5
Insurance agent	68	51.5	69	51.5
Carpenter	65	58	68	53
Manager of a small store in a city	69	49	67	54.5
A local official of a labor union	62	62	67	54.5
Mail carrier	66	57	66	57
Railroad conductor	67	55	66	57
Traveling salesman for a wholesale concern	68	51.5	66	57
Plumber	63	59.5	65	59
Automobile repairman	63	59.5	64	60
Playground director	67	55	63	62.5
Barber	59	66	63	62.5
Machine operator in a factory	60	64.5	63	62.5
Owner-operator of a lunch stand	62	62	63	62.5
Corporal in the regular army	60	64.5	62	65.5
Garage mechanic	62	62	62	65.5
Truck driver	54	71	59	67
Fisherman who owns his own boat	58	68	58	68
Clerk in a store	58	68	56	70
Milk route man	54	71	56	70
Streetcar motorman	58	68	56	70
Lumberjack	53	73	55	72.5
Restaurant cook	54	71	55	72.5
Singer in a nightclub	52	74.5	54	74
Filling station attendant	52	74.5	51	75
Dockworker	47	81.5	50	77.5
Railroad section hand	48	79.5	50	77.5
Night watchman	47	81.5	50	77.5
Coal miner	49	77.5	50	77.5
Restaurant waiter	48	79.5	49	80.5
Taxi driver	49	77.5	49	80.5
Farm hand	50	76	48	83
Janitor	44	85.5	48	83

TABLE VII.3 (cont.)

Occupation	1947 NORC Score	Rank	1963 NORC Score	Rank
Bartender	44	85.5	48	83
Clothes presser in a laundry	46	83	45	85
Soda fountain clerk	45	84	44	86
Sharecropper	40	87	42	87
Garbage collector	35	88	39	88
Street sweeper	34	89	36	89
Shoe shiner	33	90	34	90
Average	70		71	

Source: Robert W. Hodge, Paul M. Siegel, and Peter H. Rossi, "Occupational Prestige in the United States, 1925–1963," *American Journal of Sociology*, LXX (November 1964), 290–92.

formation for exploring some of the basic opinions concerning occupations. The instrument included 90 occupations. (See Table VII.3, the 1947 column.) Each respondent was instructed to pick out the statement that best gave his own personal opinion of the general standing of each job. The statements were: excellent standing, good standing, average standing, somewhat below average standing, poor standing, and don't know. Furthermore, the respondents were admonished not to judge a job according to their opinion of one person known in such a job. Some of the major findings in this research are discussed below.

The best jobs. Highly specialized training and excessive responsibility for public welfare were chief factors in contributing to the prestige of jobs. Accordingly, the Supreme Court Justice, physician, state governor, cabinet member in the federal government, and diplomat in the U.S. Foreign Service were the five top ranking occupations. They were followed by mayor of a large city, college professor, scientist, U.S. Representative in Congress, and banker. At the bottom end of the continuum the occupations were shoe shiner, street sweeper, garbage collector, share cropper, and janitor. These extremes in occupational rank clearly illustrate the two major criteria for the ranking.

Rating by geographical location of respondent. For all regions of the country—Northeast, Middle West, West, and South—there was general agreement concerning the hierarchy of occupations. For those differences that did persist it was discovered that non-farm laborers were ranked lower in the Middle West and the South. Professionals and semiprofessionals along with government officials were ranked slightly higher in the Northeast than in other areas.

Size of place. The average ranking given to occupations was somewhat lower in rural areas and small towns than in larger urban areas. Residents of metropolitan areas gave higher ranking to "sophisticated" occupations than did rural and small-town people. This is illustrated by higher ratings for artists, musicians, novelists, night club singers, bartenders, radio announcers, newspaper writers, scientific occupations, and priests. Rural and small-town respondents rated farm owner, railroad conductor, and mail carrier higher than metropolitan respondents did.[14]

Occupation, age, sex, education, and economic level. Respondents tended to rank their own occupation considerably higher than the average evaluation for it. Higher ratings were often given to many of the occupations by unskilled laborers and domestic workers than by those persons in higher occupations. Lower rankings were given to the sophisticated occupations by farmers and non-farm laborers in many cases.

Occupations typically were given slightly lower rankings by young people than by their elders. Men and women, by contrast, differed very little in their rating of occupations. Although the difference was slight, women tended to give a higher rating to many occupations than men. A significantly higher rating was given by women than men to educational occupations, social work, positions associated with the arts, religion, and protective service occupations.

When the educational level of respondents was held constant it was discovered that respondents with a high school education tended to rank occupations in intermediate positions above those with only elementary school education and below those with college education. Respondents with the highest levels of education tended to rank scientific jobs higher than those with a lesser amount of education.

The economic level of respondents was closely related to their educational attainment. Accordingly, those in the higher economic categories tended to rank scientific occupations higher than respondents in lower economic categories. Those with lower economic resources tended to show higher rank for occupations in the service work categories.

Factors conditioning job evaluations. High income was the most frequently mentioned factor for giving jobs an excellent standing. Second only to income was the belief that jobs should contribute to the needs and service of humanity. This is illustrated by the following 11 responses: "The job pays so well, 18 per cent; it serves humanity, it is an essential job, 16 per cent; preparation requires much education, hard work, 14 per cent; the job carries social prestige, 14 per cent; it requires high moral standards, honesty, responsibility, 9 per cent; it requires intelligence and ability, 9 per cent; it provides security, steady work, 5 per cent; the job has a good future, the field is not overcrowded, 3 per cent; the job is pleasant, safe, and easy, 2 per cent; it affords a maximum chance for initiative and freedom, less than 0.5 per cent; and miscellaneous answers, don't know, no answer, 10 per cent." Those individuals who had low incomes tended to be more impressed by the high income occupations. Professional and college-educated people placed less importance on the material returns of occupations.

Job evaluation could be viewed by asking what is most important when a young man is considering a life's work. Thirty-three per cent of the respondents indicated that he should select something in which he will be interested; 16 per cent said that he should have native ability for the task, 14 per cent indicated the financial aspects of the position, 10 per cent reported that he should consider possibilities for advancement. The remaining categories all included less than 10 per cent.

This summarizes the major findings from the NORC study of occupational prestige. The study also gives some insight concerning the basis for the judgments about the several occupations. The additional information collected in the study is less directly related to the subject of hierarchy and prestige.

The NORC study was updated after a period of 16 years.[15] The 1963 study was based again on interviews with a national sample of adults and youth. The major findings of the study is extremely clear. There are very few changes in the occupational prestige rankings over the 16 year period. The findings for 1947 and 1963 are summarized in Table VII.3. In the 1960's there was some slight basis for inferring that blue-collar occupations had slightly higher scores than in the mid 1940's. There was also some evidence that marginal professionals like night club singers were given slightly lower ratings than in the earlier study. The 1963 data were compared, to the extent possible, to earlier occupational prestige studies going all the way back to 1925. In the main, it is observed that for this nearly 40 year period there is no substantial change in the occupational structure in the nation.

The measurement of occupational prestige is far from absolute. Nevertheless, the evidence which is available both nationally and internationally suggests that in the urbanized and industrialized societies the occupational prestige hierarchy has been relatively stable in the mid twentieth century.

OCCUPATIONAL ORGANIZATION AND PRESTIGE

In the preceding sections of this chapter occupational status and prestige are examined in terms of social stratification and on the basis by which they are attributed popularly to occupations. In this section we examine several aspects of occupational prestige from the intra-occupational point of view. Often within a given occupation several career stages are ranked hierarchically. A differential prestige is generated by this very nature of occupational organization.

Intra-occupational prestige. In 1955 a study was reported on the differential prestige among school superintendents; it was the study of hierarchy within a specific occupation.[16] The data were based on a stratified random sample of the superintendents' positions in Massachusetts. The data were collected by a mail questionnaire instrument. The instructions were: "for each of the superintendencies listed in the following pages please indicate, by checking the appropriate column, whether you feel superintendents would consider a move from your present position to this superintendency as a gain or loss in professional standing." [17] There were five check list categories, ranging from a great gain in professional standing to a great loss in professional standing. After they had responded to the questions using these instructions, the respondents were asked to identify the three criteria they believed that most superintendents would use in judging the standing of their occupation. Then they were asked to indicate if they had used such criteria, and if not what criteria had they used.

It was hypothesized in this research that "the prestige of one specific position will be higher than that of another to the extent that the positions allow the incumbent to make a larger contribution to the 'functions.' " [18] Further, it was believed that the function of the position would be determined by the size of the managerial responsibility in relation to the size of school organization. It was believed that the importance of the function would also be measured in terms of the quality of the school system. Finally, it was believed that one could get an image of the function of the position by the facilities available to the incumbent.

The criteria by which the superintendents evaluated their positions were: facilities, professional quality, responsibility, salary, and other. For these several factors it was discovered that the superintendent's salary correlated most with prestige, .89. This was followed closely by the median salary of teachers, showing a correlation of .86 and the number of pupils with a correlation of .78. Very little correlation was demonstrated for the other factors with prestige. It was hypothesized that prestige would be a function of the superintendents' opportunity to contribute to the major function of their enterprise. In fact it was discovered that the single item, salary, was more reliable than the constellation of items which served as a measure of opportunity to contribute. Of summary importance for our concern here, however, is the clear documentation for differential intra-occupational prestige.

Occupational prestige of dentists. In 1962 findings from a broad study of the occupational prestige of dentists were reported.[19] The data on which this report is based were collected in a National Opinion Research Center Survey concerning attitudes and practices toward dental care. The information was collected on a national sample of 1862 adults. As a part of this study the respondents were asked to indicate their notion of the prestige of dentists. To do so they ranked the following seven occupations: owner of a factory employing about 100 people, physician, official of an international labor union, trained machinist, lawyer, dentist, and university professor. The focus of the study, nevertheless, was on dentists rather than the total range of occupations.

It was anticipated that the prestige of dentists would vary with the preconceived importance of the work which they performed, the value of the benefit of dental care, the differential value of the dentist's roles, etc. In fact, it was found that the relationship between these attitudes about dentists and their prestige was not great. Indeed, the findings suggested that dentists were given high prestige in those cases where it was believed that the respondents thought professionals in general were given high prestige, and that dentists were professionals. In short, the overriding finding in this research suggests that occupational prestige may be attributed more by situs of occupational families than by the perception of individual occupational practitioners.

Occupational prestige of male nurses. Male nurses were studied in a psychiatric hospital in Boston which is one of the leading centers for training such personnel.[20] The focus of this study was the contrasting of male nurses with their female colleagues concerning their conceptions of intra-hospital status and their place in the general system of stratification outside of the hospital. It was discovered that the men were concentrated in the wards housing male and often senile patients. Or by contrast there was a general tendency for them to fill higher official positions. It was also found that the male nurses tended to identify with the physicians. They desired to decrease the social distance between the doctors and themselves. The physicians, nevertheless, did not welcome the male nurses into their colleagueship. Accordingly, 50 per cent of the male nurses, compared to only 15 per cent of the female nurses, believed that physicians did not show them an appropriately high status. The relations between the male and female nurses were also highly problematic. One female nurse asserts that nursing could be good for men, but they are not able to accept it—that is, to know who they are socio-psychologically. Their understanding about how other nurses see them is incorrect. At nurses' conventions they identify as laymen rather than professionals. Men fail to support nursing organizations, even when it would be to their advantage to do so. They rationalize that their frustration with nursing is insufficient salaries and too few top jobs. Women nurses feel that men enter the occupation because they lean toward feminine roles, then they are ultimately unable to adjust to the consequences.[21]

The views of men in nursing are reported. Over half of the male respondents believed that the men in the occupation were equal to the women, but far less than half of the women nurses gave a similar response. Of the females, 35 per cent indicated that the men are satisfactory, but primarily in the difficult and psychiatric cases. By contrast, only 2 per cent of the men accepted such an occupational role. Slightly more than one-quarter of the female respondents indicated that male nurses tended to be homosexual. Only 2 per cent of the male nurses themselves accepted such a judgment.

The evidence from this research suggests that male nurses are marginal men; their prestige is precarious. They find it difficult to identify with a normatively female role. Their often higher status in nursing organization brings social distance and colleague frustrations for them. Their attempt to identify with male physicians is thwarted by the general closure of this higher occupation.

Occupational prestige of physicians. It is often implicitly assumed that the high prestige attributed to some occupations is a reflection of the high judgments which raters have about those occupations. A 1960 study based on a probability sample of registered voters in a precinct in Cambridge, Massachusetts, revealed considerable disparity between the prestige given to physicians and the attitudes about their occupation.[22] The respondents were presented with a list of ten occupations and asked to identify the three which they believed to have the highest prestige. The respondents were also given a series of statements and asked to indicate their agreement.

It was discovered that doctors were given the usual high prestige status in spite of the fact that there was a considerable range in judgment concerning the behavior of physicians. In some cases there was a high prestige ranking for physicians even when considerable hostility was manifested toward them. It was suggested that the medical profession may be more important for some people than others, and their judgment about its functioning may vary while its prestige may remain relatively constant. Moreover, high prestige may result from a perception of norms concerning medical roles in general. To this extent the prestige may be attributed more to the normative system than to individual actors in the roles. Finally, it was suggested that respondents may react to differential standards of role performance. In any event, this research points to the differentiation in prestige for a categorical situation vs. prestige attributed to individual occupational practitioners.

Occupational prestige and residence. A study reported in 1956 was designed to investigate the relation between occupational prestige level and type of leisure participation.[23] Data were collected from a sample of urban adult males in Columbus, Ohio. Occupational prestige was divided into five classes: level one, including professionals; level two, managers, officials, and proprietors; level three, sales and clerical workers; level four, skilled craftsmen; and level five, service workers, semi-skilled and unskilled laborers.

Distinct types of leisure and occupational prestige are shown to be associated. The level of significance test is the Chi-square. Persons in the upper prestige occupational levels tended to participate more in theatrical performances, concerts, lectures, gallery attendance, community service work, pleasure reading, etc. In the lower prestige occupations the types of leisure that were most participated in included baseball game attendance, zoo visiting, tavern frequenting, auto theater attendance, and car pleasure riding. In some cases a more careful analysis of the data revealed a curvilinear relationship. For example, the frequency of playing golf increased with prestige rank until the middle status was reached. As one moved beyond that into the upper prestige ranks participation in golf declined somewhat.

Most of the data that have previously been reported in this chapter reveal the prestige of occupations in the judgment or attitudes of the general public and/or the practitioners. The kind of research reported here illustrates the prestige of occupations by showing correlation with other normative factors in human behavior, in this case leisure.

Occupational prestige vs. occupational excellence. Implicit in most of the preceding discussions is the notion that differential occupational prestige is functional to recruitment of individuals into those places where they are most needed in the labor force. A recent and provocative inquiry into the nature of occupational excellence suggests that high motivation more than occupational prestige is the primary ingredient required for moving people into strategic occupations.[24] It is suggested in this research that the excellence demanded for an occupational role plus the prestige which the occupation confers are positively related to the occupation's attractiveness. The data for the research are based on a sample of 116 undergraduates in psychology courses at the University of Texas. Their achievement motivation was measured by responses to four thematic apperception test pictures. Respondents were then asked to evaluate occupations in terms of their prestige, competence required, and attractiveness.

Detailed analysis of the data revealed that both the excellence demanded by the occupational roles and the prestige conferred by the occupation contributed to an increased attractiveness. Still it was argued that the strength of such attractiveness was related to the motivational structure of the members of the role system. In sum, it is reported from these data that the allocation of members to roles depends on the number of individuals available with high achievement motivation and achievement values more than on the prestige of the occupations.

The ranking of occupations in the U.S. Census has a forceful impact on the organization of occupations, regardless of the popular evaluation of their prestige. The Census data constitute the largest single summary of occupational organization. These data are profoundly valuable, but they are collected to service multiple users. Accordingly, the hierarchy in certain instances leaves much to be desired from the point of view of sociological analysis, even when it may be adequate and valuable for other uses.

In 1917 Alba Edwards grouped the gainful workers of the United States into nine socioeconomic categories. Again in 1933, using the 1930 Census data, he up-dated his classification as follows:

1. Professional persons
2. Proprietors, managers, and officials
   a. Farmers (owners and tenants)
   b. Wholesale and retail dealers
   c. Other proprietors, managers, and officials
3. Clerks and kindred workers
4. Skilled workers and foremen
5. Semiskilled workers
   a. Semiskilled workers in manufacturing
   b. Other semiskilled workers
6. Unskilled workers
   a. Farm laborers
   b. Factory and building construction laborers
   c. Other laborers
   d. Servant classes

An attempt was made to differentiate occupations on the basis of skill and more precisely into mental and manual categories. Categories 4, 5, and 6 are primarily differentiated on the basis of skill. Edwards indicates that there is much difficulty in this classifying of occupations. Indeed, he asserts that in the several categories there are doubtlessly some workers who are incorrectly placed, but he believes they are so few in number that they do not invalidate the system. The census data were re-examined for 1920 and 1910 so that a reasonably good trend analysis of occupational organization is available from virtually the beginning of the twentieth century.

The earliest so-called occupational data to appear in the U.S. Census publications really constituted broad inquiries into industrial fields. The 1820 Census was the first to present any occupational data at all. At that time inquiry was made into the number of persons in each family, including slaves, who were engaged in agriculture, commerce, and manufacturing. No such data were collected in 1830. In 1840 the occupational data were expanded slightly, again including slaves, and recorded in the following categories: mining; agriculture; commerce; manufacturers and trades; navigation of the ocean, canals, lakes and rivers; and learned professions and engineers.

In 1850 the first real occupational data were collected. At that time the actual occupations of free males age 16 and over were recorded. The data were analyzed by states and territories and constituted an alphabetical list of some 323 occupations. These occupations were subsumed into 10 main categories: commerce, trade, manufacturing, mechanic arts, and mining; agriculture; labor not agricultural; army, sea, and river navigation; law, medicine, and divinity; other pursuits requiring an education; government, civil service; domestic servants; other occupations.[25] Again in 1860 occupational inquiry was made, and the list was expanded to 584. In 1870 the Census made occupational inquiry for all persons in the population. But prior to 1910 the occupational returns were so indefinite that the only possible classification was largely industrial. Even the industrial classification was deficient. The enumerators were expected to record both the type of work and the place of work, but only a single column was provided on the schedule for this purpose.[26]

By 1960 several special reports were issued by the census concerning occupations. The occupational hierarchy was listed as follows: Professional, technical, and kindred workers; farmers and farm managers; managers, officials, and proprietors except farm; clerical and kindred workers; sales workers; craftsmen, foremen, and kindred workers; operatives and kindred workers; private household workers, except private household; farm laborers and foremen; laborers, except farm and mine. The census occupational hierarchy is extensively detailed in a *Diction-*

ary of Occupational Titles. In this volume nearly 40,000 types of work are summarized into about 20,000 occupations, and these in turn, are categorized into the above occupational hierarchy.

SUMMARY AND IMPLICATIONS

Occupational status and prestige have become an integral part of the nation's social organization and a central element of occupational organization. The matter of ranking of occupations is of vast importance in an open-class society. It implies that in the absence of a general assignment of work there must be competition on the part of individuals to achieve entry into any particular rung on the occupational hierarchy. There must be mechanisms of recruitment on the part of occupations for their own organizational maintenance and on the part of the nation for the effective operation of its several areas of social organization. In short, in a success-oriented society occupations have come to constitute a highly visible demonstration of one's achievement. There is much associated with occupations that has very little to do with the ongoing economic tasks of operating the nation. The status qualities of occupations have come to take on a meaning in and of themselves.

The study of occupational prestige is complex and far from adequately understood. There has developed, however, a great body of empirical data which gives insight into the occupational hierarchies from the point of view of the general public and from the experience of occupational practitioners. Summaries of these various pieces of research must be tentative and qualified. Nevertheless, the general status of knowledge suggests that the occupational hierarchy in the industrial urbanized society is highly stable in the twentieth century. Moreover, the little evidence that is available for international comparisons suggests a great degree of similarity in the occupational hierarchies of the several industrial nations where the subject is researched.

NOTES

1. Kingsley Davis and Wilbert Moore, "Some Principles of Stratification," *American Sociological Review*, 10 (April 1945), 242–9.
2. Ibid.

3. Ibid. p. 243.
4. Richard L. Simpson and Ida Harper Simpson, "Correlates and Estimation of Occupational Prestige," *The American Journal of Sociology*, LXVI (September 1960), 135–40.
5. Ibid. p. 139.
6. Lionel S. Lewis and Joseph Lopreato, "Functional Importance and Prestige of Occupations," *Pacific Sociological Review*, 6 (Spring 1963), 55–9.
7. Paul K. Hatt, "Occupation and Social Stratification," *American Journal of Sociology*, LV (May 1950), 533–43.
8. Ibid. p. 533.
9. George Counts, "The Social Status of Occupations: A Problem in Vocational Guidance," *The School Review*, 33 (January 1925), 16–27.
10. Ibid. p. 19.
11. Mapheus Smith, "An Empirical Scale of Prestige Status of Occupations," *American Sociological Review*, 8 (April 1943), 185–92.
12. Ibid. p. 186.
13. "Jobs and Occupations: A Popular Evaluation," *Opinion News*, 9 (September 1947), 3–13.
14. Ibid. p. 6.
15. Robert W. Hodge, Paul M. Siegel, and Peter H. Rossi, "Occupational Prestige in the United States, 1925 to 1963," *American Journal of Sociology*, LXX (November 1964), 286–302.
16. Ward S. Mason and Neal Gross, "Intra-Occupational Prestige Differentiation: The School Superintendency," *American Sociological Review*, 20 (June 1955), 326–31.
17. Ibid. p. 327.
18. Ibid. p. 328.
19. Louis Kreisbry, "The Basis of Occupational Prestige: The Case of Dentists," *American Sociological Review*, 27 (April 1962), 238–44.
20. Bernard E. Segal, "Male Nurses: A Case Study in Status Contradiction and Prestige Loss," *Social Forces*, 41 (October 1962), 31–8.
21. Ibid. p. 35.
22. William A. Gamson and Howard Schuman, "Some Under-Currents in the Prestige of Physicians," *American Journal of Sociology*, LXIX (January 1963), 463–79.
23. Alfred C. Clarke, "The Use of Leisure and Its Relations to Levels of Occupational Prestige," *American Sociological Review*, 21 (June 1956), 301–7.
24. Eugene Burnstein, Robert Moulton, and Paul Liberty, Jr., "Prestige vs. Excellence as Determinants of Role Attractiveness," *American Sociological Review*, 28 (April 1963), 212–19.
25. Alba M. Edwards, *Comparative Occupational Statistics for the United States, 1870–1940* (Washington, D.C.: U.S. Government Printing Office, 1943), p. 87.

SUPPLEMENTARY READINGS

William A. Gamson and Howard Schuman, "Some Undercurrents in the Prestige of Physicians," *American Journal of Sociology*, LXVIII (January 1963), 463–79.

Robert W. Hodge, *et al.*, "Occupational Prestige in the United States, 1925–1963," *American Sociological Review*, LXX (November 1964), 286–302.

Louis Kreisbry, "The Basis of Occupational Prestige: The Case of Dentists," *American Sociological Review*, 27 (April 1962), 232–44.

Richard L. Simpson and Ida Harper Simpson, "Correlates and Estimation of Occupational Prestige," *American Journal of Sociology*, LXVI (September 1960), 135–40.

OCCUPATIONAL STRUCTURES AND INSTITUTIONS 2

Many occupations in the second half of the twentieth century in urbanized American society have become characterized by extensive internal organization. Several specific structures and institutions combine to constitute the forms of occupational organization. They follow a systematic order from the entering of occupations through the moving out of occupations. In Part Two these structures and institutions are examined.

Chapters VIII, IX, and X concern one's aspirations for different occupations, differential types of occupational preparation, and the procedures for entering occupations.

After one enters an occupation, one's work procedures are institutionalized as career stages. Specific forms of remuneration and control are provided. Associations and societies are major elements of advanced occupations, particularly the professions. Finally, the most recently developed occupational structures have to do with retirement—with getting out of occupations.

Part Two of this book is a systematic analysis of getting into occupations, behavior while in occupations, and getting out of occupations. It is an internal examination of occupations.

OCCUPATIONAL ASPIRATION IN URBANIZED SOCIETY VIII

In open-class urbanized societies ideology and social organization help in the choosing of occupations by individuals. On the other hand, many of the structures of occupations internally tend to negate the individual's opportunity to choose occupations. Indeed, they reserve the right for practitioners to select or recruit each new generation of occupational fellows. In addition, the sheer multiplicity of occupations, even in the freest, most open-class society, tends to negate effective aspiring and choosing of occupations due to the absence of societal or occupational mechanisms for communicating to the potential aspirants the wide range of occupations that are consistent with individual interests and abilities.

One of the most definitive characteristics of the occupational nature of the urbanized society is the conspicuous absence of appropriate mechanisms for communicating occupational knowledge and equating occupations with interests and abilities. Therefore, one does not aspire systematically to 20,000 or more occupations, but perhaps to a dozen or less. Or, put another way, freedom to choose in a structure of ignorance is considerably less than real freedom. Ideologically one can aspire to any occupation, and theoretically one can choose any occupation for which one has the interest and ability. In fact, measures of interests and abilities are only partially understood. Mechanisms for communicating the occupational characteristics and requirements are nearly nonexistent, the U.S. Department of Labor's *Occupational Outlook Handbook* notwithstanding. The *Occupational Outlook Handbooks* are a gigantic step in the direction of the communication of occupations, yet diminutive in view of the complexities of the total situation.

Occupational aspirations in the urbanized society may be viewed as individual dimensions of the recruitment process. This is most clearly articulated by the phrase "occupational choice." The several theories of occupational choosing recognize, more or less, the occupational structures and the social structures which make major impacts or delimitations on choosing.

CONCEPTS OF OCCUPATIONAL ASPIRATION AND CHOOSING

An early attempt to formulate a theory of occupational choice was provided by Ginzberg and his associates.[1] This is an interdisciplinary hypothesis, the thesis of which is that (1) occupational choice is a process, (2) the process is largely irreversible, and (3) it involves compromise as an essential aspect of occupational choices.[2] This notion of occupational choice further asserts that the decision is formulated over a period of years identified as specific stages: fantasy, tentative, and realistic.

The fantasy period is characterized by young children thinking about what they want to be as adults. The fantasy is unrestrained by viable considerations either of one's capacity or of the range of real opportunities. Presumably in fantasy one can become whatever one desires.

The tentative period starts usually between the ages of 10 to 12. Youngsters with advanced intellectual and emotional development enter it at earlier ages and those who are less developed at later ages. In the tentative period the individual refines his choosing in terms of desired future satisfactions rather than immediate satisfactions. Still the variables manipulated are subjective—interests and values.

The realistic period starts between the ages of 16 and 18. Earlier subjective choices must now be compromised with the objective facts of one's environment. Often this period is characterized by narrowing one's choice from, for example, science in general, to a specific scientific occupation, say physics.

In subsequent development and review, deficiencies in the Ginzberg theory will be suggested. Although the Ginzberg team include in their discussion of factors which influence occupational choice reality factors (social and economic environment), educational structures, emotional conditions, and the impact of values, this is from some perspectives an insufficient analysis.[3] The deficiencies include an absence of the values and impact of the reference group members of the so-called chooser. Moreover, considerations from the point of view of role theory are not presented. Psychological conditions concerning the nature, development, and predictive values of interests are largely ignored.[4] Finally, this theory of occupational choice largely fails to present any conceptualization of the decision-making process as such. It is variously asserted that the decision-making process is one of continual compromise, but this is by assertion rather than by description and analysis of the compromises.

The occupational choice theory posited by Ginzberg and his associates is a significant contribution both substantively and in terms of the intellectual attention it brought to focus on the problem.

A theory of vocational development put forth by psychologist Super is one of the viable and constructive responses to the Ginzberg occupational choice theory.[5] The Super formulation is more comprehensive than that of Ginzberg. The following ten propositions constitute the Super theory:

(1) People differ in their abilities, interests, and personalities.
(2) They are qualified, by virtue of their characteristics, each for a number of occupations.
(3) Each of these occupations requires a characteristic pattern of abilities, interests, and personality traits, with tolerances wide enough, however, to allow both some variety of occupations for each individual and some variety of individuals in each occupation.
(4) Vocational preferences and competencies, the situations in which people live and work, and hence their self concepts change with time and experience (although self concepts are generally fairly stable from late adolescence until late maturity), making choice and adjustment a continuous process.
(5) This process may be summed up in a series of life stages characterized as those of growth, exploration, establishment, maintenance, and decline, and these stages may in turn be sub-divided into (a) the fantasy, tentative, and realistic phases of the exploratory stage, and (b) the trial and stable phases of the establishment stage.
(6) The nature of the career pattern (that is, the occupational level attained and the sequence, frequency, and duration of trial and stable jobs) is determined by the individual's parental socio-economic level, mental ability, and personality characteristics, and by the opportunities to which he is exposed.
(7) Development through the life stages can be guided, partly by facilitating the process of maturation of abilities and interests and partly by aiding in reality testing and in the development of the self concept.

(8) The process of vocational development is essentially that of developing and implementing a self concept: it is a compromise process in which the self concept is a product of the interaction of inherited aptitudes, neural and endocrine make-up, opportunity to play various roles, and evaluations of the extent to which the results of role playing meet with the approval of superiors and fellows.

(9) The process of compromise between individual and social factors, between self concept and reality, is one of role playing, whether the role is played in fantasy, in the counseling interview, or in real life activities such as school classes, clubs, part-time work, and entry jobs.

(10) Work satisfactions and life satisfactions depend upon the extent to which the individual finds adequate outlets for his abilities, interests, personality traits, and values; they depend upon his establishment in a type of work, a work situation, and a way of life in which he can play the kind of role which his growth and exploratory experiences have led him to consider congenial and appropriate.[6]

Amid the contributions of Super's theory stand the following principal criticisms: (1) little analysis of decision-making as such, (2) only limited reference to the importance of occupational opportunities as factors in vocational development, and (3) only parental socio-economic level is referred to as a reference group situation determining the nature of the career pattern.[7]

Both the Ginzberg and Super conceptual formulations concerning occupational choice are basic contributions. They both contribute to the delineation of the situation and focus attention for further research and analysis on the importance of the subject.

The next contribution to occupational choice conceptualizations in chronological order was that of Blau and his associates.[8] The Blau conceptual framework consists of the following three major points: (1) an investigation of occupations for (a) their psychological characteristics, (b) their economic structures, and (c) their social structures; (2) social structural influences include (a) the personality development of the chooser and (b) the socio-economic conditions within which selections take place; and (3) the conceptual view of occupational choice as a process of compromise between the preferences for and expectations of being able to get into the various occupations. In the Blau framework more emphasis is placed on the differentiation between preference and expectation, but still little suggestion that both preferences and expectations are built upon a very limited knowledge on the part of individuals concerning the multiplicity of occupations. Aside from this perspective differentiation between preferences and expectations, the Blau theory offers few advances over the criticisms leveled against the Super and Ginzberg theories. Decision-making as such is given little attention. Reference group situations are alluded to but overt analyses are absent.

In sum, Blau and his associates assert that choosing an occupation is sharply restricted by lack of information concerning real opportunities. This is so much the case that choices are seldom viably made between occupations.

A sociological analysis of occupational choice is the next formulation in this intellectual endeavor.[9] The sociological conceptualization focuses specifically on the process of occupational decision-making. Slocum emphasizes "playing-at" roles in occupational decision-making. In this technique, both the novice and experienced occupational person when considering new or alternate occupations imagines the requirements and benefits of the occupation. The process involves the presupposition of approval by significant others. The playing-at occupational roles may be covert. When it becomes overt this more sharply articulated process is referred to as "role-playing."[10] Slocum views the process of playing-at roles as central in the selection of one role from an alternative and, thereby, central in decision-making.

The suggestion of rational decision-making in occupational choosing is found in the early theories. Slocum submits that occupational decision-making may be rationalistic but need not be so. He reasons that it is in fact doubtful if any occupational decisions are made at a fully rational level. The arena of information appropriate to ranges of occupations, interests, and abilities, is not systematically brought together in such a way that is conducive to firm rational occupational decision-making. While the occupational chooser, through vocational counseling, guidance, and other avenues of assistance, may obtain a considerable amount of knowledge about both occupations and his interests and ability, this typically gives the chooser a body of information for little more than a bare minimum of the more than 20,000 occupations. Accordingly, Slocum hypothesizes "A continuum of rationality, with decisions ranging from those made purely on impulse to those which may be regarded as fully rational."[11] Miller and Form assert that rational occupational choosing is rare. By contrast, accident, they submit, is a deciding factor in most cases.[12] Although it may be properly concluded that the majority of occupational choices are considerably less than rational, it is the assertion of the Slocum position that a greater degree of rationality could be achieved in the decision-making process.

The sociological milieu of occupational decision-making includes four major types of influences on the choice decision process: personal variables, impersonal social and cultural factors, perceived interpersonal relationships, and values of reference groups. Examples of the influences of personal variables include chronological age, physical health, mental ability, and sex. In terms of all of these, the decision for or against specific occupations is considerably differentiated. Broadly speaking, some occupations are so frequently selected by women and others by men that they are referred to as women's or men's occupations. Other occupations have specific age entry levels as well as, evermore frequently now, specific age exiting levels.

Occupational decision-making is vastly influenced by socio-cultural factors. In the Renaissance Period of the Western world, for example, a precocious young man was directed by his cultural conditions to select an occupation in the arts for high prestige and recognition. A similar young man in the second half of the twentieth century in an urbanized society would select an occupation in science, technology, or the white-collar professions.

Similarly, the interpersonal relationships which are associated with various kinds of occupations influence their being selected or rejected. The gregarious individual might select an occupation that involves high rates of interaction with people, for example, sales. An individual who is less favorably oriented to dealing with people might in juxtaposition select an occupation like forestry or mining, where intensity and high rates of interaction with people are less characteristic of the occupation. Or, similarly, the impact of interpersonal relationships influences the awareness of occupations and accordingly decisions for or against them. This is illustrated by the empirical findings that many occupational people can identify parents, teachers, counselors, friends, and others as having influenced their choice for or against a designated occupation.

The values of total reference groups are variables which make an impact on the total occupational direction of choosing. For example, members of the professional classes place a sufficiently high importance on education to enable their progeny to be disproportionately prepared to select professional occupations for themselves. By contrast, many members of the middle and lower classes may be insufficiently aware of the relationship between occupation and education, and while emotionally aspiring for high occupational choice they may neglect to develop the valuable high education appropriate to such occupational choices.

Slocum's analysis of sociological aspects of occupational choice include playing-at occupational roles, differential rationality, and types of influence factors. While placing more emphasis on the explanation of decision-making than most of his predecessors, Slocum never really comes to grips with the structural situation which leads to such high degrees of irrationality in choosing. His contribution, nevertheless, is a major refinement to the occupational conceptualization literature in the area of choice decision-making.

The concept of occupational choice is further refined by Kuvlesky and Bealer.[13] These authors specifically observe that occupational choice has to do with psychological preferences and desires of individuals regarding work statuses. Accordingly, choice or aspiration is but one part of the total process of occupational attainment. The notion of aspiration is differentiated into three analytical elements, namely, a person or persons, wanting (orientation), and social object (goal). The individual in his orientation to goal elements typically is concerned with multiple factors simultaneously, for example, occupation, residence, education, and income. The orientation of the individual to the several goals may vary from strong to weak. In sum, this refinement of the occupational choice process illustrates the need to know both whether the goal is high or low and whether the intensity of the orientation is strong or weak.

The several theories of occupational aspiration include elements ranging from an economic domination to a psychological domination. Recognition is given to the organizational and structural elements related to the aspiration situation, but in no cases are the organizational and structural factors analyzed to the point of fully explaining their articulation from the individual to the occupation. In all, it is continuously assumed that the individual will recognize his cultural orientation and make his choice, and that, within the various cultural limitations, relatively more or less rational decision-making will be made. In fact, the individual seldom if ever has sufficient occupational information to approach high degrees of rational choosing.

In 1954 some of the above factors associated with job finding and the theory of occupational choice were empirically studied for workers with actual employment experience.[14] The assumption empirically tested is the "traditional wage and resource allocation theory that workers, like other economic units, possess, or can get, sufficient market information to enable them to make intelligent choices between alternatives. Although this does not imply that perfect knowledge is a prerequisite, it does imply, first, that workers are aware of the availability of alternative jobs; secondly, that they can get specific information on conditions of employment; and thirdly, that workers are free to examine and consider alternatives before making their choices—that they find it possible to actually 'shop' for jobs." [15] The data on which this report is based illustrate that in several labor markets, there is little tendency for factory workers to compare jobs for their greatest advantages or disadvantages. An unemployed worker informally obtains limited information on a very few jobs, and takes the first real job available which meets a minimum number of absolute standards. The social organizational situation is one in which job hunting is costly as well as time-consuming. Moreover, the structural situation is such that failure to take a job when it is available usually means that there is no basis to defer judgment; in effect, the job is lost.

Research shows that, far from rationalistically analyzing a job market, workers typically obtain information about jobs informally through friends or relatives, or they make direct application at places of employment, study job advertisements, or, finally, follow contacts offered by former employers, unions, or employment agencies.

It is also found that, in addition to careful rationalistic analysis of job choices, the minimum standards which job-hunting workers will accept vary in a strong inverse relationship to the amount of time they have been unemployed. In one case it is reported people unemployed less than three months expect a median minimum wage of 90 per cent of their previous wage; people unemployed between three to six months expect only a 60 per cent wage; and people unemployed for six months or more will accept jobs paying only half of their last wage.[16] In occupational choosing, the information is insufficient to allow for high levels of rationality even under the most optimum conditions. As the conditions deteriorate, as in periods of unemployment, the systematic aspiring and choosing of occupations is reduced.

ASPIRATIONS AND REALITIES

Empirical evidence illustrates that most respondents in the study of occupational choice can differentiate rather sharply between aspirations and expectations.[17] Dispersion between aspirations and expectations is found to be multidirectional. In many cases an individual may aspire to a high profession, for example engineering, but in fact overtly indicate that he expects to attain a job in the building industry. This disparity may be explained on a rational basis in terms of the individual's understanding that the profession of engineering will require a college course of training for which the respondent recognizes perhaps an intellectual inability, a condition of insufficient finances, or an inability to defer immediate gratifications for long-range gratifications.

In other directions it is found that disparity between aspiration and expectation may not be lower. Often the son of an entrepreneur may aspire to an alternative occupation, for example, a profession of a salaried type, but as an only heir to his family business he may concede to formal or informal pressures to inherit the business. In still another direction one may aspire to an occupation lower than that actually expected. An individual of great intellectual ability from a distinguished family may aspire to an unillustrious occupation, for example, elementary school teaching, but expect to concede to family pressures and go into an executive occupation.

Ability to differentiate between aspirations and expectations is found at various age levels but is particularly documented among adolescents.[18] This wide manifestation of differentiation between aspirations and expectations illustrates one level of attempted rationality in occupational choosing.

It is typically found that occupational expectations are considerably more realistic or rational than occupational aspirations. When asked about aspirations most respondents will report a high prestige occupation or an illustrious or glamorous one. Or, put another way, occupational expectations tend to reflect more accurately the occupational structure of an area and a time than do occupational aspirations.

Over occupational aspiring is social organizationally consistent with the American success and achievement ideology. In an open-class pyramidal stratification system one who understands the norms of his society will aspire, by the nature of that normative system, to situations that are higher than are realistically expected for achievement. When the disparity between aspiration and expectation becomes too great and persists too long, and when, through the hard knocks of life, one is forced to scale down or otherwise bring to closer congruence the aspirations and expectations, frustration and anomie are experienced. With the widespread and excessive aspiration for high level professions the norms of occupational choosing are more frustrated than facilitated. After considerable pursuit of the specific norms of high level occupations one must identify alternative occupations and then devote time and energy to unlearning, as it were, the norms of the higher occupation and learn a second set of occupational norms that are consistent with the occupations that one can expect with structural realism.

Realities and inconsistencies of occupational choosing are disproportionately influenced by the cultural norms of one's locality groups. In large urban areas there is a disproportionate choosing or aspiring to glamorous occupations. In small rural areas there is a disproportionate aspiring to agricultural and related occupations. There is in neither case evidence that occupational aspirations and/or expectations are made rationalistically in terms of a sound understanding of the distribution of the nation's labor force and/or the projections of the labor force for the specific areas.

Unreal aspirations and misconceptions concerning occupations are partly engendered by the questions asked concerning the nature of one's anticipated goals.[19] Some exaggerated aspiration responses are largely a product of the way the inquiries are put. Grunes submits that it would be helpful in studying students' understanding of occupations to ask them to indicate their "dream job," the occupation they are "really trying for," and the occupation they "really expect to get."[20] Such a possibility for three responses would give the student a more valid range of alternatives consistent with his age and sophistication. More specifically, it is found that some students in the lower socioeconomic levels preferred to avoid firming up real occupational goals. They are less confident in the aspiration situation; indeed, they find it unpleasant. A greater range of acceptable responses would offer them the possibility of more comfortable accuracies.

The wider range of acceptable responses would also reduce some of the apparent frustration from gross occupational misconceptions. For example, students' guesses concerning occupational income are often grossly incorrect. They might aspire more reasonably if indexes for their aspirations were put in terms of a way of life as illustrated by a type of housing rather than by the implication that they should understand the amount of monetary return of an occupation. The wide misconception is found more frequently among lower groups and manifested more often by boys than girls.

Comparison of occupational expectations with the census distribution of the labor force reveals that even the most realistic responses are incongruent with the actual possibilities. The importance, therefore, of reducing fantastic aspirations and giving basis for more realistic expectations is of a vital order.

Grunes studied the perception of a sample of American high school students. The basic assumption was that the student should understand the world which is psychologically "there," because it will determine for the individual what he thinks and does. The purpose was to understand how groups of occupations are seen by students. The procedure was the Grouping Test. It consisted of a list of 51 different occupations which represented all of the major categories in the *Dictionary of Occupational Titles*. The instructions were ". . . group the following occupations as many ways as you can. For example, make groups according to which kinds of people work at the jobs, what kinds of work they do, etc. Give each group a title that tells what kinds of jobs belong under it. . . . At least two jobs must be in each group you make. You may use the same job under as many titles as you wish. For example: people who would probably know how to give first aid: air line stewardesses, doctors, nurses, physical education teachers. . . . The more groups you make within the time limit (15 minutes) the higher your score. You may use any types of groups you can think of. . . ." [21]

The normative occupational clusters were as follows: "A. College professor, minister, doctor, nurse, teacher, and less clearly: engineer, social worker, reporter, businessman (require education, ability, brains, social skill; are paid highly; strength not required). A-B. Businessman and woman (characteristics similar to A, but less stress on education). B. Business woman, office worker, secretary, stenographer, bank clerk, and less clearly: salesperson, store clerk ('business,' verbally skilled). C-1. Carpenter, mechanic, welder (skilled, strong). C-2. Farmer, rancher, hired man on farm, truck driver, and less clearly: ditch digger, garbage collector, janitor (hard work, common labor, strong, require little education or much of anything except strength). B-D. Salesperson, store clerk, waiter, waitress ('business,' require social skill). D. Dish washer, cook, maid, housewife, married woman who stays home and keeps house, cleaning woman, and less clearly: elevator operator, waitress, janitor (common labor, hard work requires little of anything, stupid, not own boss, uneducated)." [22]

This common view of the students in terms of occupational categories is to a considerable extent consistent with the major categories in the *Dictionary of Occupational Titles*. Yet where there is disparity it involves an overemphasis, and ultimately an overaspiration for white-collar occupations and a corresponding underaspiration for many other occupations essential to the social organization of the society. The cluster view of the students provides a basis whereby counselors may in many appropriate cases encourage students to expect more rationally somewhat lower prestige jobs, but ones for which there is a considerable need in the society. The inconsistencies in the students' clustering of occupations from the *Dictionary of Occupational Titles* hierarchy in many cases suggests that in the respondents' perception it is possible to encourage them to aspire more realistically to some of the minor occupations in the categories. This will encourage aspirations that are consistent with their perceptual notions and also which are more consistent with the distribution of the labor force.

Occupational aspirations are differentially influenced by subcultural situations. This is carefully illustrated by a study of Wisconsin senior high school girls.[23] The students were chosen so that their schools would be representative of an urban metropolitan area and of rural and small-town areas. Questionnaires from 188 rural students and 190 urban students were subjected to intensified analysis. Half of these showed a preference for nursing and the other half did not. Within the rural and urban respondents about half of each group selected and rejected nursing.

The content of the study focused on the impact of impressions concerning nursing that were received from individuals and from communication media. The most favorable impressions were obtained from nursing students, peer group persons interested in nursing, hospital nurses, and family doctors. The most favorable impressions for nursing from communication media were bulletins for nursing schools, pamphlets, television programs, radio programs, college and university bulletins, and books.

In further analysis, it was found that those who preferred nursing also had more precise recall of receiving favorable impressions both from persons and from communications. In this respect there were few differences between rural and urban students.

Orzack's interpretation of these findings emphasizes the importance of the individuals participating in various subcultural or specialized areas of the society and as a result becoming acquainted with a limited number of occupations. It is asserted that the notion of differential association, originally specified with reference to criminal behavior, might be appropriate in analyzing preferences for careers.[24] In sum, it is found that in terms of occupational aspiration and realities the various individual and mass communication items in the students' culture furnish widely differing amounts of information regarding careers. The differential cultural elements also provide a full range from favorable to unfavorable images.

No implication is suggested that differential association, although found for nursing, is universal in occupational aspirations. It is suggested, however, that the dispersion between aspirations and realities may be a function of differential association and subcultural impacts.

STRUCTURAL FACTORS

Education and ability.[25] Occupational choosing is closely linked with experience in the educational system. The amount and type of education that an individual obtains are poignantly determining factors on occupational choosing and occupational achieving. Conversely, it can be observed that the educational system effectively functions to bar some individuals from occupations.

The type of educational training offered by institutions varies considerably. Therefore, in terms of occupational choosing it is not only important to participate or not participate in an educational experience, but to participate in a particular kind of educational experience and to achieve in it at a particular level if one is to effectively choose a particular occupational course. The various educational systems typically include vocational courses in agriculture, business, shop, home economics, and others. In addition they include a college preparatory curriculum, or a general course. The selecting and adhering to one of these courses in education is highly directive for subsequent occupational choice and occupational experience. In addition, the educational social system provides motivation for making a choice, information for the chooser in making the choice, and a continuing reality check for the occupational choices.

Although the choosing of an occupation is not required by educational systems it is frequently a significant product. An analysis of the occupational choices of senior male students in four Florida colleges illustrates the situation.[26] Nearly 95 per cent of the college seniors had in fact made an occupational choice. It was recognized that occupational choices and college majors for both men and women could be made before entering college or during the college experience. Over half of the males chose their major subject and selected their occupational aspiration during their college experience. Almost half (46 per cent) of the females also made their major subject choice and occupational choice during their college experience.

The influence of faculty on occupational choosing was highly significant. It was differentiated by student ability, and found to be more important for students with less ability but of considerable importance for all students. Faculty impact on occupational choosing also varied inversely with the high-to-low occupation of the father. Particularly for male students, the faculty influence was less when the father's occupation was professional than when it was blue-collar. For female students, the faculty impact was least where the father's occupation was white-collar.

Finally, the educational environment was directive in its providing a check on the reality of training for vocation. Some occupational curriculum are specifically oriented to vocational training, some pre-professional, and some liberal arts. Accordingly, this environment continues to offer the student and his associates an arena to examine the relevance of the educational course being pursued for the occupational choice indicated.

The vocational importance of a college education is further asserted in a study reporting differential rural-urban meaning.[27] In a study of students at Washington State University it was found that those who had a rural background looked upon their college training as slightly more vocational than those of a non-rural background. For example, 92 per cent of the farm background students, compared to only 90 per cent of those with a non-farm background, viewed their college training as fundamentally a matter of occupational preparation. But more important even than the differential is the excessive meaning of college for occupational choosing and preparation. In choosing majors the farm background students most frequently chose agricultural majors. Moreover, the farm background students were more certain that their choice of major was the correct one for them. Their reasons for satisfaction with the major, however, tended to be for less academic reasons than were those of the respondents with a non-farm background.

Considerably more non-farm background respondents planned to take vocationally oriented graduate work than farm background respondents. The researchers interpret these data to suggest that while the farm background students view college as a matter for occupational preparation, they are less academic in their orientation, and ultimately they view the college degree as being less important in and for itself.

Family influence on occupational aspiration. Much of the empirical literature provides credence for the notion that the family is one of the most important structural elements in the occupational choosing environment. This is generally based on the assumption that children in a family environment become differentially acquainted with occupations, particularly the work of the father. Moreover, it is implied that the images of work and of occupations are considerably established in the family situation.

White-collar occupational families constitute an environment in which progeny will have a more favorable image of the world of work, higher expectancies in terms of occupational rewards, and higher aspirations. Conversely, it is asserted that the environment of blue-collar occupational families presents a less favorable image of work, and somewhat less thrust for high aspirational orientations.

A study in Ames, Iowa, illustrated the impact of family and parental influence on aspirations.[28] The sample was stratified to include both blue-collar and white-collar families. The majority of both types of families reported that there were discussions about occupations. Indeed, slightly more of the blue-collar fathers (76 per cent) than white-collar fathers (63 per cent) reported that they talked specifically with their children about work. But what they said varied. White-collar families expressed higher job satisfaction scores than blue-collar families. In the main both types of families tended not to encourage their children to follow the father's occupations, but this negative orientation was more noticeable among the blue-collar parents. When asked if they would like to see their children follow their type of work, only 24 per cent of the white-collar and only 13 per cent of the blue-collar fathers reported that they would.

Interviews were taken with the children over age 10. These respondents were less proud of their father's work when in blue-collar occupations than white-collar ones. Correspondingly, the blue-collar fathers reported that they believe their children would prefer to see them in higher prestige occupations.

The differential impact of families' occupational position on children's perception is clear. There is more satisfaction with the occupational environment when it is a white-collar one than a blue-collar one.

The impact of family on occupational choosing can be seen from still a different perspective.[29] In addition to documenting the fact that families contribute to differential perceptions of occupations, it is important to know why, within such environments, various degrees of success drives are manifested. One suggestion of an answer for differential success motivation comes from the study of 153 male and 197 female university students. The findings supported the notion that high aspirational levels correlate with unsatisfactory interpersonal relationships in the family of orientation. The "high" aspirers stated that they had experienced feelings of rejection more frequently than did those in the "lower" group. Some 42 per cent of the high aspirers reported the experience of some type of rejection by their fathers. In contrast, only 24 per cent of the low aspirers reported such feelings. Rejections by the mother were reported by 34 per cent of the high aspirers and only 20 per cent of the low aspirers. A similar kind of finding is reported by respondents who suggested that there had been favoritism toward another son or daughter. The same study also reports that more high than low aspirers felt less attachment to their parents. Also during their childhood they had experienced lesser degrees of happiness.

The authors caution that wide generalizations are unwarranted from this particular study because the universe was a relatively homogeneous, predominantly urban, Middle Western, Protestant, middle class population. Nevertheless, the findings add further support to psychoanalytic assumptions that unsatisfactory interpersonal family relationships are significantly related to high aspiration patterns of behavior.

The impact of family on occupational aspirations can be still put another way. It is suggested by Lipset and Bendix that boys from higher social class families have in fact an advantage in that they will know more about the labor market. Still more particularly, it is asserted that those who receive occupational advice from numerous individuals have a greater probability of entering the labor force at higher occupational levels.[30] This same reasoning leads authors to the position that working class parents are less well equipped to provide valid occupational counseling for their children than those in occupational classes above them because of their more limited knowledge of the total range of occupations.

To test the above notions Simpson and Simpson interviewed 380 workers in two cities to investigate their sources of advice concerning occupations and compare that with their occupational experience.[31] They hypothesized ". . . that values indicating positive attraction to work are characteristic of workers entering the labor force at the lower levels." [32] The findings support the hypothesis that the status level of the first job is positively related to the number of advisers. For example, over 57 per cent of the men who had three or more advisers before their first job entered white-collar work, and almost 20 per cent entered upper white-collar jobs. For men with two or less advisers, only 36 per cent entered white-collar jobs at once, and only 11 per cent of these were upper white-collar positions.[33]

In addition to having multiple advisers, those who reported that their primary occupational adviser was a non-family member tended to enter higher level occupations for their first jobs than those who relied on family consultation as the main occupational source. Nearly 70 per cent of the workers whose advice had come from non-family members began their work in white-collar careers, and over 30 per cent of these in the upper white-collar categories. By contrast, family advisers were related to only 41 per cent of white-collar entrants, and, more precisely, to only 14 per cent of those who entered upper white-collar categories.

Simpson and Simpson also report that respondents who had positive values for work more often entered high status jobs than those holding less positive values. This research goes on to examine the proposition that advice and values can be a reflection of father's status and not independent factors affecting occupational choice. When values for work were negative, advice appeared to have an independent effect. Moreover, advice also appeared to be independent among workers from white-collar family backgrounds.[34]

Social status and occupational aspirations. There is a widespread claim in the social science literature that social class is a factor marking a differential impact on occupational aspirations.[35] Examination of the data and findings of the Sewell research illustrate the nature of the case. The hypothesis researched was "that levels of educational and occupational aspirations of youth of both sexes are associated with the social status of their families, when the effects of intelligence are controlled." [36] Sewell and associates studied more than 4000 high school seniors concerning this issue. Respondents who planned to enter a regular four-year college were considered to have high educational aspirations. On the North-Hatt occupational prestige scale those respondents who aspired to positions equal to or higher than public school teachers were assumed to have high occupational aspirations.

The findings in the Sewell research strongly supported the hypothesis of association between social class and aspiration. Specifically, they reported that females from high social status families manifested higher educational aspirations than those from lower status families. For them, however, there was no manifest significant difference in occupational aspirations between their high and low status backgrounds. In terms of plans for entering college, males from high status families aspired to college more frequently than those from low status families. Finally, males from high status families aspired to higher occupational roles than those from low status families. In the main, these findings offer credence to the primary notion that occupational aspiration for both men and women is influenced by the social status of which they are a part.

Structural factors influencing occupational aspirations vary both in type and in intensity. But regardless of their variation their impact is real. The aspiring of individuals is directed, limited, and constrained by the various impacts of structural elements in the social organization of the urbanized society. The individual's freedom to choose an occupation is in fact set within the limitations of the several structural factors.

The realities of structural factors are brought sharply into focus by a broad range of empirical research. The occupational aspirational subject is only partly understood until one has examined the findings of a sample of this diverse research. These studies are reported next.

EMPIRICAL EXAMPLES OF OCCUPATIONAL ASPIRATIONS

Participants in occupations are widely known to be influential models for those who aspire to occupations. This is lucidly illustrated in a study of occupational aspirations of a sample of urban senior Negro male high school students.[37] In fourteen urban high schools 301 students were interviewed. Among the questions asked were the following:

1. Do you know anyone in the occupation you prefer? 2. Have any persons in your preferred occupation(s) influenced your decision directly or indirectly? 3. In what occupation(s) are the persons who have influenced your decisions? 4. If your decision to enter your preferred occupation has not been influenced by anyone, where did you learn about the occupation? [38]

The findings reveal that 70 per cent of the respondents had some acquaintance with persons in the occupations to which they aspired. Moreover, 70 per cent of those who knew someone in the occupation asserted that their decision-making was influenced by the acquaintance.

An acknowledged high influence by occupational models was reported for occupational repairman, teacher, barber, and tailor. In contrast, little influence was reported for the following occupations: engineer, radio technician, player in a dance band, and baseball player. This research reveals a specific relationship between respondents' occupational aspirations and their influence by persons in the given occupation. Such influence factors in terms of social organization should have a conservative impact in sustaining a dominant stability in the status quo of the occupational structure of the labor force. In juxtaposition, such an influence situation reduces the probability of occupational mobility. Finally, this influence situation is inhibiting to occupational changes that are consistent with technological and other structural changes in the organization of the society.

Another type of influence on occupational choice is size of community rather than individuals. In Lipset's early Oakland, California, study, it was found that a large community of orientation contributes to a set of circumstances for more upward occupational mobility more than a small community of orientation does.[39] The essence of such assertions is based on the observation that small communities have little occupational heterogeneity while large communities have maximum occupational heterogeneity. As a result of this differential community occupational nature one becomes acquainted with either a full range or a minimum number of occupations.

A rigorous test of this differential community influence on occupational choice is reported in a Florida statewide study of ninth grade white students.[40] Schedules of respondents were disqualified when they reported housewife or when the questionnaire was incomplete. Ultimately the study was based on a sample of 6775 males and 6475 females, or 13,250 ninth-graders.

The hypothesis tested in this study was: "Variations in occupational aspirations of ninth grade students are independent of differences in size of community when the factors of intelligence and father's occupation are controlled." [41] To determine aspiration the students were asked "In what occupation do you think that you will most likely be working ten years from now?" Responses were divided into high and low occupations with the high being represented as professional and the low as non-professional. The size of the community in which the school attended was located was taken as the independent variable. Accordingly, five community size classifications were established: under 2500; 2500 to 10,000; 10,000 to 50,000; 50,000 to 250,000; and over 250,000. The control variables in the study were intelligence and father's occupation. The latter was divided into five categories: professional, other white-collar, skilled, semiskilled and unskilled, and agricultural.

The findings reveal that for both male and female students there was a significant positive association between high or professional occupational choices and the size of community in which the school was located. In qualifying this finding it was reported that when father's intelligence or occupation was held constant there was no consistent relationship for females' aspirations and their size of community. The findings for males were more conclusive. In this case the aspirations differed sharply with size of community. Specifically, for males from rural communities under 2500 population less than 40 per cent chose professional occupations. For males from communities of 250,000 population, over 65 per cent aspired to professional occupations.

The Florida data support the hypothesis of positive association between size of community in which one's school is located and occupational aspiration for males, but not for females. The differential occupational position was held constant.

In a study of still younger children, age 12, it is found that reasonable tentative occupational choices could be made by most (60 per cent) of the students.[42] This study was in part a test of the Ginzberg theory that fantasy occupational choices are made before 11 years of age and tentative occupational choices are made between the ages of 11 and 17, followed by realistic choices after the age of 17.[43] In addition, this study attempted to investigate whether or not occupational choices were more a function of age or of factors like socio-economic environment, sex, race, intelligence, and reading ability.

The respondents were all sixth-graders in three Michigan schools. One school was in a middle socio-economic neighborhood, another school in a low socio-economic neighborhood, and a third in a low socio-economic neighborhood with all Negro children. In all there were 116 respondents. Their average age was 12—none was below age 11 or over age 16. According to the Ginzberg hypothesis they should be making tentative occupational choices.

To determine the students' occupational orientation they were asked to write a paragraph indicating what they would like to do occupationally when they grew up and to specify why they had made that particular choice. The students' papers were subsequently submitted to judges and classified according to the Ginzberg notions. Occupational choices designated as fantastic were defined as: "translations of simple needs and impulses into occupational goals. Tentative choices indicated those decisions based on capacities, interests, and values of the individual." [44]

In the first school it was found that most girls did in fact make tentative choices, while less than half of the boys were able to do so. In the second school (low income) still most of the girls were able to make tentative choices and half of the boys were able to do so. In the third school (Negro) most girls again made tentative occupational choices, but only approximately half of the boys were able to do so. For the total sample three-fourths of the girls were able to make tentative occupational choices, compared to only 41 per cent of the boys showing a similar level of occupational maturity. The findings also reveal that ability to make tentative rather than fantastic occupational choices was related to intellectual capacity. Those whose I.Q.'s ranged from 100 to 129 typically were able to make tentative occupational choices, while those with I.Q.'s under 90 were seldom able to do so. In a similar way, reading ability was related to occupational choosing. Those who were retarded in their reading more frequently made fantastic occupational aspirations than those with normal reading ability. The authors interpret their data as evidence which basically supports the Ginzberg theory of tentative occupational choosing for twelve-year-olds.

Occupational aspirations were studied by administering a questionnaire to 141 male students in a co-educational parochial high school in the Washington, D.C., area. Most of the respondents were white Catholics. Their ages ranged from 13 to 19 and their grade from 9 to 12.[45] The research was designed to investigate the general hypothesis that students with high socio-economic status will aspire to high occupational levels and that the discrepancy between occupational aspiration and actual expectation will be greater for low status students. A second hypothesis was that students with high status would value work more than students with a low socio-economic status. Finally, a third hypothesis was researched, namely, that students from a high socio-economic status would perceive more occupational opportunities.

The findings reveal that more than 70 per cent of the students in high statuses, that is, those whose fathers were in professions and semi-professions and managerial occupations, did aspire to similar high level occupations. In contrast, only 65 per cent of the students from a low socio-economic background, those whose fathers were engaged in skilled and semiskilled occupations, did choose high status occupations. Moreover, these respondents manifested a high degree of consistency between occupational aspirations and actual expectations. Slightly more than 52 per cent showed a perfect consistancy between aspirations and expectations.

In terms of the second hypothesis, it was found that more than 63 per cent of the students from high socio-economic backgrounds placed a high value on work. And in sharp contrast, only 42 per cent of those students whose fathers were in low occupational categories placed a similarly high value on work. In the case of the third hypothesis it was again found that more than half of those students from high socio-economic backgrounds perceived wide ranges of occupational opportunities.

While the author cautions against overgeneralization from this relatively homogeneous urban selected high school population, in terms of its parameters, the evidence is persuasive that for high school students occupational choosing is greatly influenced by the socio-economic background of the student.

The undergraduate college experience is a great occupational choosing arena. Freshmen enter college with a wide range of occupational aspirations, but usually in the upper half of the occupational continuum. During undergraduate study they both change and sharpen their occupational choices.

In 1961 a National Opinion Research Center study was conducted on a national sample of June graduates.[46] The subject of the study focused on career decisions. The graduating college seniors reported their freshmen career choices were arts and sciences, 18 per cent; professions, 70 per cent; and business, 12 per cent. After four years of college 37 per cent of the students shifted from one occupational choice to another. Eight per cent of the students had no career choice as freshmen, so about half (45 per cent) had experienced some change. Essentially the changes involve gains for education and business and losses for medicine and engineering. The social sciences, the biological sciences, law, and the humanities are traders.

In spite of this shifting the career choices of freshmen and seniors are remarkably the same. This is to say, after four years of college most students are still interested in the same occupational area, if not the same occupation.

Aspirations for graduate study. In the 1960's the aspiration for graduate study has become widespread, and approximately one-third of each new baccalaureate class proceeds to such advanced study. College enrollment has increased at a dramatic rate: for example, 19 per cent of those age 18 to 19 entered college in 1900, compared to 42 per cent in 1960. Similarly, in the 1920's less than 1000 Ph.D.'s were awarded annually, while by the 1960's the number had reached approximately 10,000. Accordingly, a recent study of students' aspirations for postgraduate work reports that a bachelor's degree recipient in the 1960's will be more likely to anticipate graduate study than a high school graduate to anticipate college.[47]

Davis's great aspiration study is based on questionnaires administered in the spring of 1961 to nearly 34,000 June graduates. The graduates constituted a sample of students from 135 colleges and universities.

When queried about their plans for graduate study, nearly three-fourths responded that they had some. Nineteen per cent had already been accepted by a graduate or professional school. Another 12 per cent had specific plans but had not yet been accepted. The largest proportion, 30 per cent, definitely planned to go on for graduate or professional study at a fixed future date. Fifteen per cent anticipated graduate study but did not specify a specific date. The remaining 24 per cent had no specific plans for further advanced study.

When further investigation was made concerning their career plans, the largest proportion, 33 per cent, anticipated that their employer would be an elementary or secondary school system. Another 27 per cent anticipated work with a private company employing more than 100 employees. Employment with the U.S. federal government was anticipated by 14 per cent. The remainder expected that their graduate study would lead them to careers in small private companies, in family businesses, to be self-employed, in research organizations, in colleges and universities, with state or local governments, and so forth.

The subject of their anticipated career, in a rational way, followed closely the type of employment they anticipated. The largest proportion, 33 per cent, expected a career in education. Business careers were anticipated by 18 per cent. Other types of professional careers were anticipated by 15 per cent. Eleven per cent expected that their work would be in the social sciences and humanities. Only 8 per cent anticipated science as such, and only 3 and 4 per cent, respectively, anticipated work in medicine or law.[48]

Field of specialization was studied in some detail. In the main, it was found that for these great aspirers there was a high degree of rationalistic consistency in their career planning from undergraduate study, to graduate training, to career anticipation. In undergraduate study nearly 40 per cent of the respondents majored in the arts and sciences and slightly more than 45 per cent majored in professional fields, mostly education. Another 15 per cent were students in business administration and in a few cases in agriculture. In anticipated graduate study only 30 per cent planned continued work in the arts and sciences, nearly half of these in the humanities and fine arts. Nearly 57 per cent in anticipation of graduate work expected their study to be in professional fields. Almost 30 per cent of these anticipated advanced training in education. Only 12 per cent planned graduate study in business administration and agriculture. Finally, as a result of this pattern of undergraduate and graduate training, approximately 60 per cent anticipated occupational careers in the professions. Eighteen per cent expected their career to be in the arts and sciences and 20 per cent in business administration and agriculture. In all, it might be observed that they aspired to be the high talent manpower of their generation. Perceptively enough, they understand that the high talent manpower constitute the idea people in the professions and the executive ranks. It is for these careers that they systematically seek training.

The occupational aspirations of women. Women historically have been, and continue to be, members of the work force. But never before have occupational aspirations for women been more real. Government publications report that in 1870 only 13 per cent of the women in the United States were occupationally employed.[49] By the 1960's nearly 40 per cent of the American women were actively reported to be engaged in the labor force.

A study of high school and college girls in Washington in 1952 and 1954 illustrates the kinds of occupational choices made by women, and compares their aspirations to the distribution of employed women in the state of Washington for 1950.[50] The predominant occupational aspirations for college women were teacher, 27 per cent; secretary, 15 per cent; other professional occupations, 12 per cent; semi-professional occupations, 10 per cent; and the remainder widely distributed through the full range of other occupations. The aspirations of high school girls were secretary, 22 per cent; teacher, 11 per cent; nurse, 10 per cent; and the others widely distributed. In the state population the census reported as the predominant female occupations secretary, 10 per cent; teacher, 5 per cent; managerial and official, 6 per cent; bookkeeper, 6 per cent; nursing, 4 per cent; and the others widely distributed.

The occupational choices of women showed considerable dispersion from the distribution of those currently in the labor force. Part of this may be explained as irrationality in occupational aspiration, and part of the dispersion may be explained by the rapid increases in proportion of women in the labor force. Due to this high increase it may be expected that particularly those higher trained women will move into new and glamorous occupations.

But most important is the continued finding that women are clearly able to articulate occupational choices. Among the above respondents for the college category more than half, 53 per cent, explained their motivation for occupational choice in terms of continued interest and intellectual challenge. Another 34 per cent responded that money and security contributed to their choice. Others were concerned with service to humanity, public recognition, freedom in behavior, etc. Among the high school aspirants 31 per cent explained that their desire was for continued interest and challenge, 29 per cent for money and security, 20 per cent for service to humanity, and the rest had widely divergent motivations.

Persistence of women in occupational choosing is also empirically identified. In a study of clergywomen it is reported that their occupational entry is frequently blocked. Accordingly, they follow alternative occupations in teaching, welfare, or other aspects of religious work until such a time as they are ultimately able to enter their chosen occupation.[51] Historical structures have precipitated a bias for males in the clerical occupations. As the norms prohibiting women's entry into the clergy have eroded, those for whom this was a first occupational choice have moved quickly if silently and persistently into their most coveted occupation.

Occupational aspirations and fear of failure. The literature on occupational choice is laden with the judgments that in order to achieve any vocation one should have both ability and interest appropriate to the work. Accordingly, it is hypothesized by Mahone that "Persons who are fearful of failure tend to be unrealistic in their vocational choice with respect to both ability and interest."[52] Further it is reasoned that the fearful person, one who is more strongly motivated to avoid failure than to achieve success, will tend to overaspire or underaspire, but in any event to avoid the maximum range of risk. Or put another way, the fear of failure should cause the aspirant to avoid the most realistic occupation in an effort to minimize intermediate risk.

Mahone studied 135 male college students in introductory psychology, French, and mathematics courses at the University of Michigan to test the above notions. Three judges were asked to range the respondents' aspirations in terms of realistic, overaspiring, or underaspiring. It was found that "On each criterion of realistic versus unrealistic vocational aspiration, significantly more subjects who were low in achievement motivation and high in achievement-related anxiety were classified as unrealistic than subjects who were high in achievement motivation and low in achievement-related anxiety. Thus the major hypothesis of the study was supported." [53]

SUMMARY AND IMPLICATIONS

Occupational aspirations in the urbanized society ideologically focus on the choice of individuals in terms of career orientation. They emphasize the freedom of the individual to choose, but close study of social organization and of occupational organization reveals that there are few if any effective mechanisms for supporting the ideological freedom of individual occupational choice.

The several theories of occupational aspiration recognize both individual freedom in choosing and socio-cultural structures which limit the range of choosing. Mechanisms to facilitate occupational aspiration are less recognized and accordingly are almost never explained.

Occupational aspirations and the realities of the choosing show considerable disparity. Even within the structural limits and the limits of information, the poor measures of ability and the questionable measures of interest, aspirants can usually distinguish between their ideological choice at an abstract level and what they anticipate as a concrete occupational reality. Structural factors which contribute to the limiting of occupational choice are education, family, and status, among many others. For most occupations a specific educational and training level is required for entry. Without the proper educational achievement one is structurally limited from further realistic consideration of such an occupation. Families contribute to the motivation and delimiting of occupational choices. Research shows that the most important single persuasive influence of occupational choosers are their families. Yet, given the changes in occupational structures in the urbanized societies, many families, particularly those in the semiskilled and unskilled occupations, have a limited perspective of opportunities in future occupations. Accordingly, their range of influence is limiting to the aspirant. In a somewhat similar manner to family, social status of the aspirant contributes to the environment of his occupational choice. Those in the upper half of the socio-economic continuum receive occupations as an integral part of their class status. They choose to continue in occupations which support their higher or lower statuses.

The many types of empirical studies of occupational choosing reveal the process from elementary school students to the college graduate ranks. They are similarly reported for males and for females and for persons from large urban and small rural ecological areas. The empirical events in occupational choosing are widely recorded. Yet the choosing continues to be a process of considerable ignorance. It is confounded by an urbanized social milieu in which the labor force social organization involves the utilization of more than 20,000 occupations. The occupational organization and the social organization of the society provide few if any mechanistic norms for equating and understanding of the range of occupations with one's abilities and interests. Accordingly, one's occupational aspiration and one's choice are narrowly limited and the multiplicity of the urbanized society affords little freedom consistency with the abstract ideology.

NOTES

1. Eli Ginzberg, *et al., Occupational Choice* (New York: Columbia University Press, 1951).
2. Ibid. pp. 185–98.
3. Ibid. pp. 11, 12.
4. Donald E. Super, "A Theory of Vocational Development," *The American Psychologist*, 8 (May 1953), 185–90.
5. Ibid.
6. Ibid. pp. 189–90.
7. W. L. Slocum, "Some Sociological Aspects of Occupational Choice," *The American Journal of Economics and Sociology*, 18 (January 1959), 141; and P. W. Musgrave, "Towards a Sociological Theory of Occupational Choice," *The Sociological Review*, 15 (March 1967), 33–46.
8. Peter Blau, *et al.*, "Occupational Choice: A Conceptual Framework," *Industrial and Labor Relations Review*, 9 (July 1956), 531–43.
9. Slocum, "Sociological Aspects."
10. Walter Coutu, "Role-Taking Versus Role-Playing," *American Sociological Review*, 16 (April 1951), 181–2; see also Ralph H. Turner, "Role-Taking, Role Standpoint and Reference Group Behavior," *American Journal of Sociology*, 62 (January 1956), 316–28; G. H. Mead, *Mind, Self, and Society* (Chicago: University of Chicago Press, 1934).
11. Slocum, "Sociological Aspects," p. 143.

12. D. C. Miller and W. H. Form, *Industrial Sociology* (New York: Harper and Bros., 1951), p. 651.
13. William P. Kuvlesky and Robert C. Bealer, "A Clarification of the Concept 'Occupational Choice,' " paper read at the Rural Sociological Society Meetings, August 1964, Macdonald College, Province of Quebec, Canada.
14. Abraham Bluestone, "Job Finding and the Theory of Job Choice," *Monthly Labor Review*, 78 (October 1955), 1139–44.
15. Ibid. p. 1139.
16. Lloyd G. Reynolds, *The Structure of Labor Markets* (New York: Harper and Bros., 1951), pp. 109–10.
17. R. N. Stephenson, "Realism of Vocational Choice: A Critique and an Example," *Personnel and Guidance Journal*, 35 (April 1957), 482–8; Joe P. Bail and A. Gordon Nelson, *Choosing an Occupation* (Cornell: Agricultural Extension Miscellaneous Bulletin 45, 1963).
18. Richard M. Stephenson, "Mobility Orientation and Stratification of One Thousand Ninth Graders," *American Sociological Review*, 22 (April 1957), 204–12.
19. Willa Freeman Grunes, "On Perception of Occupations," *The Personnel and Guidance Journal*, 34 (January 1956), 276–9.
20. Ibid. p. 278.
21. Ibid. p. 276.
22. Ibid. pp. 276–7.
23. Louis H. Orzack, "Occupational Impressions, Occupational Preferences, and Residence," *The Personnel and Guidance Journal*, 38 (January 1960), 358–63.
24. Edward H. Southerland and Donald R. Cressey, *Principles of Criminology* (5th Ed.; Philadelphia: J. D. Lippincott Co., 1955).
25. Harry K. Schwarzweller, "Value Orientations in Educational and Occupational Choices," *Rural Sociology*, 24 (September 1959), 246–56.
26. Jerry L. L. Miller, "Occupational Choice and the Educational System," *The Journal of Education and Sociology*, 34 (November 1960), 117–26.
27. Herman M. Case, "College as a Factor in Occupational Choice: A Study of Different Perceptions by Farm and Non-Farm Youth," *The Journal of Educational Sociology*, 30 (December 1956), 191–9.
28. William G. Dyer, "Parental Influence on the Job Attitudes of Children from Two Occupational Strata," *Sociology and Social Research*, 42 (January-February 1958), 203–6.
29. Russell R. Dynes, *et al.*, "Levels of Occupational Aspiration: Some Aspects of Family Experience as a Variable," *American Sociological Review*, 21 (April 1956), 212–15.
30. Seymour Martin Lipset and Reinhard Bendix, *Social Mobility in Industrial Society* (Berkeley and Los Angeles: University of California Press, 1959), pp. 194–6.

31. Richard L. Simpson and Ida Harper Simpson, "Social Origins, Occupational Advice, Occupational Values, and Work Careers," *Social Forces*, 40 (March 1962), 264–71.
32. Ibid. p. 265.
33. Ibid. p. 268.
34. Ibid. p. 269.
35. See Herbert H. Hyman, "The Value Systems of Different Classes: A Social Psychological Contribution to the Analysis of Stratification," in Reinhart Bendix and Seymour Martin Lipset (eds.), *Class, Status, and Power* (Glencoe: The Free Press, 1953); Seymour Martin Lipset, "Social Mobility and Urbanization," *Rural Sociology*, 20 (September-December 1956), 220–28; Leonard Reissman, "Levels of Aspiration and Social Class," *American Sociological Review*, 18 (June 1953), 233–42; and William H. Sewell, *et al.*, "Social Status and Educational and Occupational Aspiration," *American Sociological Review*, 22 (February 1957), 67–73.
36. Ibid. p. 69.
37. Odell Uzzell, "Influencers of Occupational Choice," *The Personnel and Guidance Journal*, 39 (April 1961), 666–9.
38. Ibid. p. 666.
39. Seymour M. Lipset, "Social Mobility and Urbanization," *Rural Sociology*, 20 (September 1955), 220–28.
40. Charles M. Grigg and Russell Middleton, "Community of Orientation and Occupational Aspirations of Ninth Grade Students," *Social Forces*, 38 (May 1960), 303–8.
41. Ibid. p. 304.
42. Donald A. Davis and others, "Occupational Choice of Twelve-Year-Olds," *The Personnel and Guidance Journal*, 40 (March 1962), 628–9.
43. Eli Ginzberg, "Toward a Theory of Occupational Choice," *Occupations*, 30 (April 1952), 491–4.
44. Ibid. pp. 492–3.
45. Wilma Goetz, "Occupational Aspirations of the Male Students in a Selected High School," *The American Catholic Sociological Review*, 23 (Winter 1962), 338–49.
46. James A. Davis, *Undergraduate Career Decisions* (Chicago: Aldine Publishing Co., 1965).
47. James A. Davis, *Great Aspirations: The Graduate School Plans of America's College Seniors* (Chicago: Aldine Publishing Company, 1964), pp. 42–3.
48. Ibid. pp. 12–13.
49. Women's Bureau, *1952 Handbook of Facts on Women Workers* (Washington, D.C.: U.S. Department of Labor, Bulletin 242, 1952).
50. W. L. Slocum and LaMar T. Empey, *Occupational Planning by Young Women: A Study of Occupational Experiences, Aspirations, Attitudes, and Plans of College and High School Girls* (Washington, D.C.: Washington Agricultural Experiment Station, Bulletin 568, 1956).

51. Arthur R. Jones, Jr., and Lee Taylor, "Differential Recruitment of Female Professionals: A Case Study of Clergy Women" (paper presented at the annual meeting of the Southern Sociological Society, Atlanta, Georgia, April 1964).
52. Charles H. Mahone, "Fear of Failure and Unrealistic Vocational Aspirations," *Journal of Abnormal and Social Psychology*, 60 (March 1960), 253–61.
53. Ibid. p. 260.

SUPPLEMENTARY READINGS

James A. Davis, *Great Aspirations: The Graduate School Plans of America's College Seniors* (Chicago: Aldine Publishing Co., 1964).

Eli Ginzberg, *et al., Occupational Choice* (New York: Columbia University Press, 1951).

Charles H. Mahone, "Fear of Failure and Unrealistic Vocational Aspirations," *Journal of Abnormal and Social Psychology*, 60 (March 1960), 253–61.

Jerry L. L. Miller, "Occupational Choice and the Educational System," *Journal of Education and Sociology*, 34 (November 1960), 117–26.

Richard L. Simpson and Ida Harper Simpson, "Social Origins, Occupational Advice, Occupational Values, and Work Careers," *Social Forces*, 40 (March 1962), 264–71.

Odell Uzzell, "Influencers of Occupational Choice," *Personnel and Guidance Journal*, 39 (April 1961), 666–9.

PREPARING FOR AN OCCUPATION IX

Much of America's education is broadly vocational. A considerable amount of it is oriented toward preparation for specific occupations. Education and training as related to job preparation are often overlapping, sometimes nearly indistinguishable. Preparation for an occupation is of vast significance for the social organization and occupational organization of a society. To a great extent the knowledge, skills, and adaptability of a society's workers determine its rate of economic and technological process.[1]

The general education of workers is primarily obtained by study in the elementary and secondary schools of the nation. In recent years an increasing number of workers are continuing their study in junior colleges, technical institutes, special schools, colleges, and universities. Still more occupational training is provided by a diversity of sources. For example, there are programs for apprenticeship, on the job inservice training, training provided by the various branches of the military, and a variety of forms of adult education.

Until recently there has been very little specific information concerning the nature of occupational training of the nation's labor force. Accordingly, in 1963 the U.S. Department of Labor undertook a nation-wide survey to determine how adult workers received their occupational preparation. The specific purposes of the study were to determine: (1) how many workers had received formal occupational training, (2) what kind of training they had had, and (3) how their training was related to their education.[2] This national study included only those workers who had completed less than three years of college. Workers with more education were considered to be in the professions in most cases. In the professions education and training are so interrelated that a different kind of inquiry is necessary for the study of occupational preparation. The findings of the 1963 survey are reported later in the chapter.

With the growth of the Industrial Revolution and the proliferation of the division of labor, occupational preparation has continued to come to the forefront of importance. After 1900 one observes the specific development in Europe of a variety of programs to promote folk education or work education. Worker education movements were soon to develop in the United States as well. In the United States, however, much of the systematic public educational system is perhaps more worker-oriented than that of Europe. In any case, the late nineteenth century and early twentieth century were periods when new norms were specifically established for the occupational preparation of workers.[3] Occupational education is dynamically influenced in the United States by the fundamental speeding up of the rate of accumulation of knowledge. Much of the occupational preparation in the past was effectively oriented toward the learning of a total trade or craft. This learning, by the nature of the case, would typically sustain the worker through the duration of his life's career. Currently one observer reports that about half of what a graduate engineer learns today will be out of date in ten years. Moreover, half of what that same engineer will need to know in the years ahead is not available to him now.[4] The essence of contemporary occupational preparation is process, continual education, renewal, and upgrading of the level of knowledge and skills.

FROM APPRENTICESHIP TO PROFESSIONAL SCHOOLS

The great tradition of occupational preparation is apprenticeship. By definition it is a "combination of education and industry. It is a process of learning by doing, under which a minor is taught the art of a trade by one who is at the moment engaged in it; the minor paying either in whole or in part for his instruction by the work done on objects destined for the master's consumption or sale."[5]

It is often asserted that apprenticeship had its origin in the medieval European town. Certainly it had a central place in the craft guilds of that period. Douglas asserts that the origin of apprenticeship goes back to earliest times. He identifies it in the Babylonian Code of Hammurabi (2100 B.C.) and in the writings of the ancient Greeks and Romans.[6] In any event, apprenticeship was the effective mechanism of occupational preparation until the extensive rise of the industrial production systems.

The decline of the apprenticeship system is illustrated in the following census statistics. The ratio of workers to the number of apprentices clearly declines for the period.

Year	Number of Apprentices	Total Number Employed in Manufacturing and Mining	Ratio
1860	55,326	1,850,034	1 to 33
1880	44,170	3,837,112	1 to 87
1890	82,057	5,091,293	1 to 62
1900	81,603	7,112,987	1 to 88
1910	118,964	11,623,605	1 to 98

Douglas indicates several causes for the decline. First, the need for a large proportion of skilled workers in industry is no longer required in a craft sense. The development of machinery and mass production specialization has made it unnecessary for the great majority of factory workers to know more than a few steps in an operation. Apprenticeship is designed for total learning of a total craft or skill. The new industrialism carries specialization to the ultimate and requires only partial learning and routine repetition.

A second cause for the decline of apprenticeship is the belief that is it unprofitable for the employers, workmen, parents, and youth themselves to train the few all-round workmen who are needed. In short, it is the goal of the apprentice to learn as much about a total situation as is possible. By contrast it is in the employer's interest to produce labor as cheaply as possible, and to have that labor specialized in a specific task rather than a total occupation. It is further asserted that workmen in the shops dislike apprentices. The new workers are potential rivals. The young learner might be more skillful than the master.

A third difficulty which plagues the apprenticeship system is the general inadequacy on the part of masters to be instructors. Often the so-called masters themselves have inadequate training. They seldom have any training in the skills for training others. In short, even when they are excellent craftsmen, it does not follow that they are capable teachers. Parents of apprentices are also raising questions concerning the system. If they are ambitious for their children they are often discouraged by the uncertainty and precariousness of the training itself. In other cases they lack the financial resources required to provide the apprenticeship training. What is more, if they lack financial resources it is often more desirable to encourage the youth to enter remunerative work immediately rather than to experience a period of training.

Finally, apprenticeship faces a difficult hostility from the apprentices themselves. Often the youth do not understand that their wages might be appropriately increased by the experience of the apprenticeship. Moreover, apprenticeship involves a specific discipline which is often contradictory to the notions of independence which the youth wish to express. Youth do not like to bind themselves either legally or verbally for the specific requirements demanded in apprenticeship.[7] With the decline, although not the absence, of apprenticeship American workers have experienced occupational training in a variety of other ways.

Training of American workers. The interrelatedness of training and education already is indicated. High school graduation is now typically required for admission to industrial training programs, to company schools, and to apprenticeship courses. Similarly, in the military services' training programs, higher education experience is related to the more profitable training experiences.

A Department of Labor survey shows that of the 52 million workers between the ages of 22 and 64 who had completed less than three years of college, 32 per cent (16.9 million) had no more than an eighth grade education. Only one-sixth of these had formal training. Twenty-three per cent (12.2 million) had some high school experience but had not graduated. Almost half of these individuals had some occupational training. Thirty-five per cent (18.1 million) of the respondents had graduated from high school and had not experienced any college training. Nevertheless, two-thirds of these individuals had some occupational training. Nine per cent (4.6 million) had attended college for one to two years. Three-fourths of this category of respondents had some occupational training.[8] These findings make it clear that formal education and training for occupations are related. Two-thirds of those with occupational training had graduated from high school; seven-tenths of those who had not experienced occupational training had not graduated from high school.

It was found that women more often than men were high school graduates. It was also found that the women graduates more frequently had experienced some occupational training.

As workers, both men and women, attained higher education, they more frequently had multiple types of occupational training. For example, those workers who had completed some college were about three times as likely to have prepared for two or more occupations as those who had not gone beyond elementary school. It is clear that workers with more education had greater opportunities for occupational training. It might also be that they had more initiative and more ability as well.

TABLE IX.1

Types of Occupational Training

Occupation or field in which training is required	Training programs taken previously	Training programs in progress
All programs: Number (in thousands)	35,428	1,484
Per cent	100	100
White-collar jobs:		
Professional, technical, and kindred occupations	12	23
Clerical occupations	13	4
Business and commercial fields	16	5
Sales occupations	(a)	1
Merchandising field	1	1
Blue-collar jobs:		
Craftsmen, foremen, and kindred occupations	24	26
Operative occupations	2	1
Dressmaking and related fields	1	1
General trades field	3	1
Service jobs:		
Home economics field	3	1
Other service occupations	4	4
Farm jobs:		
Agricultural field	4	2
Occupations and fields not elsewhere classified	15	25
Occupation or field not available	3	4

a Less than 0.5 per cent.
Note: The sums of components may not equal totals because of rounding.
Source: *Formal Occupational Training of Adult Workers* (Washington, D.C.: Manpower/Automation Research, Monograph No. 2, 1964), p. 10.

Occupational preparation of workers is also closely related to age. Of workers age 45 and over, only one-third had completed high school. Of younger workers, one-half had completed high school. The pressure for occupational training, however, is indicated by the finding that, among the older workers, a sizable proportion had started some vocational training after age 35. Indeed, as a result of the occupational training taken later in life by older workers, the disparity in the amount of occupational training between the older and younger workers was slightly less than the disparity between their levels of education.

Nature of job training. About one-fourth of the workers in job training programs were preparing for a second or even third occupational field. Similarly, as many as one-tenth of the training programs represented more intensive training in an occupation where one was already experienced.[9] The specific types of occupational training are listed in Table IX.1. The greatest amount of training was taken by workers in the craft areas. This was followed by the relatively high proportion who took training in business and commercial fields.

The various institutional types of occupational training programs are reported in Table IX.2. Nearly 40 per cent of all the respondents who

TABLE IX.2

Institutional Sources of Occupational Training

Source of training	Training programs taken previously			Training programs in progress		
	Total	Men	Women	Total	Men	Women
All sources	100.0	100.0	100.0	100.0	100.0	100.0
High school	37.7	29.5	55.4	10.5	8.5	17.8
Special school	19.4	15.4	28.0	22.6	18.1	39.5
Armed Forces	11.4	16.2	1.2	2.9	3.0	2.5
Apprenticeship	8.2	11.7	.8	16.6	20.9	.6
Company school	6.2	7.5	4.9	12.6	13.7	8.6
Correspondence school	6.0	7.7	2.4	21.2	24.1	10.5
Technical institute	6.0	8.2	1.3	6.9	8.5	.6
Junior college	4.5	3.8	6.0	6.5	2.9	19.7
Other	.1	.1	(^{a})	.1	.2	—

^{a} Less than 0.05 per cent.
Note: The sums of components may not equal totals because of rounding.
Source: *Formal Occupational Training of Adult Workers* (Washington, D.C.: Manpower/Automation Research, Monograph No. 2, 1964), p. 11.

reported previous training had taken it in high schools. Another nearly 20 per cent had training for occupations in special schools. The armed forces constituted the third numerically most significant source for occupational training. Twenty-nine per cent of the men had occupational training in high school, compared to 55 per cent of the women. Similarly, 15 per cent of the men had occupational training in special schools and 28 per cent of the women had such special school training. As might be expected, 16 per cent of the males had occupational training associated with the armed forces, but only 1.2 per cent of the women had this as a source of occupational training.

Service occupational training for barbers, hairdressers, and cosmotologists, and practical nurses was typically provided in special schools. In 1957 the George-Braden Act Amendment also provided for some special training for practical nurses and medical and dental technicians. Barbers also still obtain their training by apprenticeship in some cases.[10]

The duration of occupational training and the rate of completion of such training varied greatly by the occupation for which study was undertaken. Concerning completion, the rate ranged from about 95 per cent for office machine operators, insurance agents, bakers, and hairdressers, to a low of about 50 per cent for artists and art teachers. In most cases it was discovered that completion rates were higher in those areas where the armed forces and company schools were the primary sources of training and lower where correspondence schools were the primary sources of training. The completion rates were higher for women than for men, regardless of the source of training. The completion rates for non-white men and women were significantly below the average of the other workers.

In general, training was more often used by women than by men. This also varied with age, and ages of 55 and 64 were using their training more directly than those under age 35. Those men who had experienced occupational training later in their life were more likely to use it on a specific job than they were to use training taken at an earlier period.

Specifically, only 44 per cent of the males between the ages of 45 and 54 who had completed their training before age 18 were using it on the job. By contrast, nearly 70 per cent of those who had taken training after age 45 were using it on the job. In effect the training acquired in later life was for specific jobs; that acquired in earlier years was for a general occupational area in which some jobs did not materialize.

Substantially more women than men were using early training. Among 35- to 44-year-old workers, for example, two-fifths of the men and three-fifths of the women whose most recent training had begun before the age of 18 were using it on their current job. This difference reflects the greater prevalence of multiple skill training for men. It may also be associated with the somewhat greater occupational mobility for men; 27 per cent of the men, but only 17 per cent of the women, had used their early training on a previous job. Thus, about one-third of the men but only one-fifth of the women had never used their early training. Undoubtedly, girls, with their traditionally more limited job choices, can make "wiser" training choices than boys. In addition, there are inevitable inconsistencies between mandatory training in the Armed Forces and civilian job choice.[11]

Types of occupational training. A majority of the workers in the national survey were found to have little or no occupational training. Among those who did have training the survey made inquiry into the nature and sources. Most of the respondents indicated that they had "just picked up" the appropriate skills or that they had obtained them informally through on the job training and experience. There were also combinations of on the job training and formal training. No training was needed according to 8 per cent of the respondents. Over half (56 per cent) reported on the job occupational training. This on the job training meant some instruction from supervisors or fellow workers, it meant some company training courses on a part-time basis or for a short number of weeks, and other unique experiences. Apprenticeship, although a type of on the job training, is not included here. Casual learning was reported by nearly half of the respondents. By this they meant that they learned from a friend or relative, "just picked it up," etc. Thirty per cent of the respondents indicated that they learned their current occupation through specific and formal training.

By type of occupation, as expected, those workers in professional and technical occupations had most frequently learned their jobs through formal training. Nearly two-thirds of them reported such training (see Table IX.3). Next to the professionals, clerical workers were the only other category where a majority of the participants indicated that they had experienced formal occupational training. Since this category included the occupations of secretary and stenographer, where formal

TABLE IX.3

Type of Occupational Training

Current occupational group	Total employed in occupation (%)	Per cent [a] reporting job learned by—		
		Formal Training [b]	On the job Training [c]	Casual Methods [d]
All occupational groups	100.0	30.2	56.2	45.4
Professional, technical, and kindred workers	100.0	64.6	66.7	33.2
Managers, officials, and proprietors, except farm	100.0	36.2	57.1	55.7
Clerical and kindred workers	100.0	53.6	71.4	29.5
Sales workers	100.0	23.4	60.2	47.4
Craftsmen, foremen, and kindred workers	100.0	40.6	64.8	47.5
Operatives and kindred workers	100.0	12.9	61.8	42.6
Private household workers	100.0	10.3	9.3	56.4
Service workers, except private household	100.0	24.6	45.5	42.7
Laborers, except farm and mine	100.0	6.9	40.0	50.5
Farmers and farm managers	100.0	20.1	17.6	79.7
Farm laborers and foremen	100.0	11.1	19.2	64.8

[a] Since about one-third of the respondents indicated more than one way, the sums of the percentages exceed 100.0. These figures include all civilian labor force participants aged 22 to 64 with less than three years of college. For the unemployed, data relate to the last job held.
[b] Includes training obtained in schools of all kinds (company training schools as well, where training was full-time and lasted at least six weeks), apprenticeship, and the armed forces.
[c] Includes on the job training by supervisors, company training course (part-time, or full-time for less than six weeks), and "worked way up by promotion."
[d] Includes learning from a relative or friend, "just picked it up," and other such methods.
Source: *Formal Occupational Training of Adult Workers* (Washington, D.C.: Manpower/Automation Research, Monograph No. 2, 1964), p. 18.

training is almost universally required, the discovery of widespread formal training was anticipated.

In the blue-collar work categories—craftsmen, for example—less than half of the cases reported that they had experienced formal occupational training appropriate to their current jobs. Where there was formal training it was most frequently reported by pipe fitters, compositors and type setters, tool and die makers, machinists, airplane mechanics, radio and television mechanics, and utility linemen and servicemen.

Little formal training was obtained by farmers, construction workers, and bakers. Semiskilled factory workers seldom relied on formal occupational training. Similarly, most workers in sales and managerial positions learned their trade through occupational experience rather than formal instruction.

Approximately one-fourth of the service workers had experienced formal occupational training en route to their current jobs. In particular those in barbering and hairdressing jobs, health jobs, and police and firemen jobs had experienced occupational training (see Table IX.3).

In the national survey the role of formal training was possibly underrepresented. Respondents were asked about training for their current job, and little effort was made to determine what training they might have had for earlier jobs. For some workers in supervisory positions no training was reported; they may have had training for the jobs they held prior to their supervisory positions. Finally, it is observed that many of the older women used some of their specific high school training in their early work experience before marriage. In their later work experience many of them moved into sales and clerical occupations for which they experienced little or no occupational training.

As the amount of time invested in occupational training increased, the likelihood that the worker used the occupational training on the job also increased. Specifically, as one examines the professional and technical occupations it is reported that the practitioners disproportionately use the occupational training that they receive.

Finally, for workers who experience formal training, many respond that their current occupation did not make valuable use of that training.

Higher education and occupational training. American society annually invests billions of dollars in the education of professionals and other highly skilled workers. *The National Survey of Formal Occupational Training for Adults* reported that 80 per cent of the 8.7 million workers with three or more years of college utilized the subjects of their major area of study in their work. The proportion using their major college training for occupational work varied from 93 per cent in the health sciences to only 67 per cent in the biological sciences. It is most clear that more than half of the college majors in the full range of subjects used their area of study in their occupational endeavor. Furthermore, college graduates are more likely to be working in their major area of study than those who attended college but were not graduated. There is little difference in the over-all proportions of the younger and older workers using their subject of college training. Even among those college-trained people who are not engaged in the subject of their major, nearly half are employed in some alternative professional, technical, or managerial position.

In the pressure for more education in the occupational experience the most remarkable achievements are made at the high school level. In 1962, 55 per cent of the nation's workers aged 18 to 64 years were graduated from high school, while in 1940 only 32 per cent of the nation's workers were graduated from high school.[12]

College graduates in the nation's labor force have risen very rapidly in recent years. They constituted 8 per cent in 1952 and 11 per cent by 1962 (see Figure IX.1).

FIGURE IX.1

Distribution of the labor force 25 to 64 years old, by educational attainment and age group, 1960

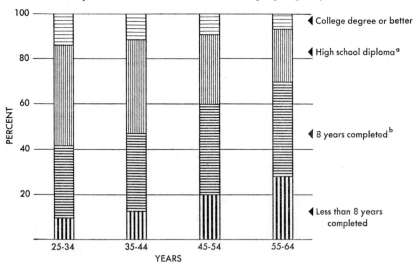

aIncludes those who did not complete college.
bIncludes those who did not complete high school.

Source: *Manpower Report of the President* (Washington, D.C.: U.S. Government Printing Office, 1964), p. 73.

The significance of a highly educated and trained labor force can be underscored by observing that the United States, with only 6 per cent of the world's population, publishes some 27 per cent of the world's newspapers, produces about 40 per cent of all electrical power, and uses nearly 60 per cent of the world's telephones. Its people drive over three-fourths of the world's automobiles.[13] These benefits and many others are primarily the harvest reaped from the creative and imaginative production of a small proportion of the nation's workers. "After all the other credits are properly assigned, the nation still owes much to a small group of able men, men who play critical roles in science, industrial, technological, and cultural developments.[14]

The United States continues to place increasing importance on highly trained specialists as the economy grows. During the first half of the twentieth century schoolteachers increased one and one-fourth times more rapidly than the national population. Health workers increased two and one-half times more rapidly than the nation's population. Engineers grew five times faster and scientists ten times faster than the population. The national population was 76 million in 1900 and 150 million in 1950; the nation's professionals increased four times during that period.[15]

Put another way, it is observed that the nation's economic and social well-being are continually and more intensively dependent upon a small group of occupational practitioners in the scientific and professional fields.[16] The National Manpower Council monograph on scientific and professional manpower indicates that since 1900 the number of workers in the sciences and professions has accelerated at approximately twice the rate of growth of the national population. Shortages of highly trained manpower in several occupations continue to be critical. The future demand for workers in these highly trained occupational categories is anticipated to be great. In all, strengthening and expanding of the mechanisms to move people through courses of training for high level occupations seem to be recommended in terms of social organization.

Schools, universities, and institutes. Colleges and professional schools are the primary training centers for scientists and professionals. There are more than 2000 institutions of higher education in the United States. About one-fourth of these institutions are organized for only two years of study. The other three-quarters of the institutions are classified as four-year schools: universities, 141; liberal arts colleges, 756;

independent professional schools, 543. Of the independent professional schools there are teachers colleges, 198; technical schools, 64; theological and religious schools, 173; schools of art, 46; and other professional schools, 75.[17] The exact number of scientific and professional training centers is unknown, but most of the four-year institutions contribute directly and/or indirectly to scientific and professional occupational preparation. Most of the nation's professional schools are in one way or another related as units in complex university organizations. For example, most teachers' colleges, business schools, library schools, and schools of social work, to name but a few, are associated with larger universities. In juxtaposition one can observe that there are some 25 independent schools of engineering, 12 of law, 10 of medicine, and 7 of pharmacy. Bible, osteopathy, and theology schools are predominantly independent.[18]

In studying 10 professions McGlothlin reports that 7 have some schools which are independent of colleges or universities. In the cases of architecture and nursing only two each of their schools are independent. Six of the 126 law schools are independent. Eleven of 78 medical schools are independent. For engineering, 35 of 210 schools are independent. The number of independent teachers' colleges (125) is the largest, out of 1200 colleges or universities which provide some teacher education. Independent teachers' colleges are declining rapidly, however, as they tend to become general colleges.[19] The independent professional schools face the difficulty of building a basic and substantial course in the humanities and the sciences related to their specific course of study. Those independent professional schools that are successful in achieving the basic course of study in effect approximate the condition of a substantial university in and of themselves. An example is the Massachusetts Institute of Technology.

The importance of professional schools for occupational training is further illustrated by statistics concerning enrollments and degrees granted. The United States Office of Education reports the total doctoral degrees earned by type of institutions as follows: universities, 11,562; liberal arts colleges, 268; teachers colleges, 118; technological schools, 714; theological schools, 103; art schools, 4; and other professional schools, 53.[20] Most of the doctoral degrees are awarded by universities and professional schools, and the importance of those institutions as occupational training centers cannot be overestimated. It has been demonstrated that approximately 600,000 students were enrolled in programs leading to professional degrees in 23 fields in 1953. This is indeed less than half of the total collegiate enrollment for that year, but it must also be understood that many matriculants in non-professional programs are in fact in pre-professional programs. From another point of view, it has been noted that in 1952–53 the number of degrees conferred in professional fields constituted about 64 per cent of all degrees conferred.[21] It is not possible to state with precision the amount of professional occupational training in the nation's colleges and universities. Nevertheless, it seems reasonable to indicate that over half of such institutions, and probably up to three-fourths of them, are engaged in some amount of professional occupational training.

Teachers for professionals.[22] The ideal teacher for professionals is said to be a scholar with practitioner experience. Accordingly, professional schools endeavor to obtain highly knowledgeable faculty members who also have experienced some years as practitioners. McGlothlin reports that medical schools tend to select their faculties on the basis of research, leadership, and teaching ability, plus capacity for growth.

In training professional engineers it is asserted that distinguished faculties are more important than details of curricula or facilities. The ideal for an engineering faculty includes intellectual capacity, study for continuing mastery of the field, inspiration of students for creative intellectual work, interesting enthusiasm for the development of men, and interest in creative writing and teaching.

In social work the characteristics of a faculty are highly similar to those in engineering. Knowledge, experience, and creativity appear to be important characteristics.

In a publication entitled *The Architect Admits Injury*, the ideal teacher for the profession is outlined. The teacher of architects should have wide professional experience and should be a specialist in a specific subject area. The teacher-architect should be able to inspire his students and co-operate with his colleagues. Finally, he should be interested in the whole development of architecture as a profession.

In sum, the teachers of professionals should be dedicated to scholarship, practitioners by experience, and have a distinguished ability to teach.

In most universities the Ph.D. degree is typically required for the full professorship in those subjects where the degree is regularly awarded. In professional schools, by some degree of contrast, the highest degree is sometimes waived as a requirement. For example, one often finds in nursing, architecture, engineering, law, social work, and veterinary medicine that many members of the professional school faculties hold only the first professional degree—but have combined their experience in a distinguished way. Nevertheless, it is often reported that as newer and younger faculty members are added to these professional faculties the final or Ph.D. degree is more prevalently required.

The professions and the sciences are heavily oriented toward research as well as to practitioner experience. Accordingly, the selection of faculties for professional education involves heavy emphasis on demonstrated research experience. Dietrick and Berson report that research ability is a primary consideration in the selection of full-time medical faculty members. Publication is a prime consideration in the selecting of law faculty members. Other professional schools put less emphasis on publication. In architecture, for example, a 1950 faculty survey revealed that only 19 per cent of the faculty had published articles and only 6 per cent had published books.

Status and salaries of professional teachers. McGlothlin used full professorships as one index of the status of professional faculties. He found, for example, that about 60 per cent of the faculty members in law held full professorships and, in contrast, that only 32 per cent in business, 28 per cent in engineering, and 27 per cent in architecture held full professorships.[23] He reasons that, if one uses the full professorship as a measure of status, the law school faculties have a status twice as high as the several others to which they might be compared.

The measure of status of professional school faculties is far from precise. Nevertheless, there is some basis for reasoning that the faculties of the older professions, for example, law and medicine, may equal or exceed the status of liberal arts and science faculties. The faculties of more recently established professions, such as social work, teaching, and nursing, tend to convey a status that is less than the other professional faculties. Often it is less than that of the faculties of that of the liberal arts and sciences.

The study of salaries of professional faculties is a far more tangible matter. At the outset one observes that there is difficulty in recruiting professional faculties because practitioners in the field are often paid more highly than teachers. It already has been observed that professional schools desire to have faculties with practitioner experience. Therefore, they are in direct competition with practitioners. To meet this competition, professional schools, particularly in medicine and law, in many cases allow the faculty to continue some measure of clinical practice and/or consultation for private fees.

In engineering schools the salaries for faculty are typically lower than the income of practicing engineers. On several occasions professional engineering societies have recommended that the pay scales for teachers be upgraded to a place where they are competitive with practitioners.

Studies of remuneration in the professional schools show that medical faculties obtain the highest salaries. The increase in professional salaries in other schools, however, in recent years has been at a greater rate than in medical schools. Professors in professional schools also generally tend to receive higher stipends than professors in other parts of universities and colleges. While the professional schools' faculty stipends may be sufficiently low to make recruitment difficult, they have been higher than other teaching faculty salaries and reflect the esteem and importance of higher occupational training.

The highest school in the United States is the graduate school. In many ways and with much justification it might be referred to as the nation's highest level professional school. An extensive report of graduate education in the United States was made in 1960.[24] It is revealed in this survey that universities are the primary places of undergraduate study for future graduate schools. Indeed as many as two-thirds of the nation's young scholars took their baccalaureate degrees at universities. It is also noted, however, that the rate of production of future Ph.D.'s is sometimes higher at the smaller liberal arts schools, even though the number of such students is greater from the universities.

The social backgrounds of graduate students in several respects tend to be heterogeneous. In terms of father's occupation: 27 per cent were from professional and executive positions; 21 per cent from small businesses; 21 per cent from clerical, sales, service; 11 per cent agriculture; 14 per cent skilled; and 6 per cent unskilled.

The educational background of fathers of graduate students was also reported. Thirteen per cent of them had more than college education, another 13 per cent had only graduated from college, 12 per cent had attended college but had not graduated, 17 per cent had graduated from high school, 9 per cent had attended high school but had not graduated, 32 per cent had not attended high school, and 4 per cent had fallen in miscellaneous educational experiences. The social backgrounds of graduate students tend to be highly similar regardless of professional field. There is, however, some differentiation in terms of the universities at which the students receive their undergaduate degrees. At the top universities there is a tendency for graduate students to come from the upper half of the socio-economic continuum.

The decision to continue graduate study for the doctorate degree was often made late in the educational experience. Only 45 per cent of the in-residence graduate students reported that they had made the decision by the end of their undergraduate college experience. The remaining 65 per cent had made their decision to continue for higher educational study after they had completely terminated their baccalaureate study. This is in sharp contrast to the decision-making on the part of individuals who work toward degrees in medicine and law at the professional level. Typically, potential doctors and lawyers know early in their career that they intend to work systematically in professional schools.

In the pressure for a more highly trained manpower, and in the competition among graduate schools, it is discovered that virtually everyone who wants to enter such a course of training may ultimately find a place in which to enter. Along with the report of relative ease and great possibility for entering the graduate school is the report of high attrition experiences. Standards for entrance are often relatively low, but levels of performance required are high. The result is that in graduate training many students spend long years in the experience, and many others drop out completely. It is reported in this study, for example, that the attrition is 40 per cent among doctoral students, 40 per cent among law students, and under 10 per cent for medical students. Duration for the years of study for doctoral students is on the average eight, for law students three, and for medical students four. Only about 50 per cent of the doctoral students devote their full time to study, about 66 per cent of the law students devote their full time to study, and nearly 100 per cent of the medical students devote their full time to study.[25]

CHANGING TECHNOLOGY AND TRAINING DEMANDS

A highly educated labor force is essential to the operation of an advanced, industrial, urbanized society. The key workers, idea professionals and specialists, are faced with a most critical situation in which the accumulation of knowledge is such that they must continue to renew their understanding or be outdated, by-passed several times in the course of their individual careers. Moreover, as the result of the high level and dynamic idea production which they create, important workers at the lower levels of the labor force experience automation and cybernetics, in such a way that in the course of their working lifetime new occupations come into existence that were not known at the time of their entry into the labor force, and numerous occupations that were important at the time that individuals first entered the labor force are obliterated before they have completed their life work. The character of occupational training for such a dynamic technology must therefore be continual and processual.

One report holds that a tool and die maker will never again possess as much relevant information as the day he completes his apprenticeship. His competence is continually eroded as he has to deal with new and developing technologies.[26]

Our occupational preparation is still oriented, as it were, to the horse and buggy days. But we are in an accelerating age. The operation of occupational training is oriented as if the typical worker can acquire in the first 20 years or so of his life enough formal education and training to meet his needs and establish him on an ascending career line through a remaining 40 years or so during which he will be employed. But far from this situation, what one actually finds is that the worker's knowledge and training starts rapidly on the road to obsolescence at the time of graduation. This worker knowledge characterized by erosion and obsolescence takes place whether the graduation is from the graduate school, the undergraduate college, the high school, or the elementary school. One-shot training for an occupational lifetime is outmoded in a dynamic urbanized society.

While this problem of training erosion strikes at the very heart of the sciences and professions, it is in no way limited there, or even to the white-collar occupations. Among the ranks of blue-collar workers and service workers this skill erosion is also widespread. It is clear that there is no place in the modern world for workers who are untrained and uneducated.

Chamberlain suggests some forms of continuing education which might be articulated into the occupational and social organizational character of the nation. For example, the 40-hour work week might be re-organized so that one is on the job for 32 hours plus an additional subsidized 8 hours for study, on or off the job, as appropriate. This would preserve the notion of a five-day work week while building into it a mechanism for continuing education. The increased training would be an *investment* for the employer, assuring a competent manpower source. The employee, in this system of continuing education, would be as obligated for the last eight hours of training as if he were doing production work.[27]

Another mechanism for continuing education would be to provide for release time every three to five years for a period of full-time vocational study. This system would operate on the principle of time accumulated, similar to that for unemployment or sick benefits. The employee would be allowed to accumulate a number of months of educational benefit time. This program could be made more attractive to employees by creating some form of certificates or degrees to be awarded in recognition of the time spent in the classroom. This type of program would depend on both public and private support.[28]

Chamberlain further raises questions which have a sound basis in social organization. It might be pondered, for example, that even if we were to devise alternative systems of social organization for continual training and renewal of training there remain questions concerning the degree to which the masses of the population will commit themselves to a lifetime of learning. Moreover, for a substantial majority of people there is the possibility that the continual absorption of knowledge is distasteful, repugnant. In short, it might be projected that if programs for continual training and education are established the problem of drop-outs will continue to increase. In other words, where there is a completely voluntary system of education the notion of drop-out has little meaning at all. In systems of highly compulsory education and training, drop-out becomes highly relevant. The question raised concerns the degree to which the human animal will be continually capable of absorbing knowledge and training and at what point high rates of drop-out will reflect his unwillingness and/or inability to continue a life of training.

The cost of such continual educational programs is visualized by some as a matter of investment, which will be offset by the increased productivity of the society's people. From this point of view it is argued that while the cost may be great, it will be self-liquidating. In any event, the ideological cost and commitment appears to be as great or greater than the economic cost.

TRAINING AND RETRAINING

It no longer remains an ideology that an untrained labor force in the urbanized industrial society is dysfunctional. High levels of unemployment which have characterized America in the post World War II years are often explained in terms of the number of untrained and/or inappropriately trained workers.

The problem of unemployment and underemployment is greatest among workers at the lower end of the occupational continuum, and a major federal effort is being made to change and overcome this situation. The Manpower Development and Training Act of 1962 is a significant social structure reflecting a cognizance on the part of the American people of the basic facts of scientific and technological change on the nation's labor force. The Manpower Development and Training Act has three major aspects, or titles. Title I is devoted to manpower requirements, development, and utilization. More specifically, Title I is concerned with research programs. The directions of research concern the identification of occupations for which shortages will be anticipated in the future; the nature of automation and technological changes; job mobility; and obtaining the experience necessary for entering an occupation.

Another phase of Title I concerns the dissemination of information concerning the skill and training requirements for specific types of occupations. Accordingly, the Secretary of Labor is directed to gather and publish information on skill requirements, occupational outlook, job opportunities, labor supply in various skills, and employment trends. Related to this information gathering and dissemination the Secretary of Labor is further directed to make broad surveys and analysis of the manpower requirements of the nation and to study and recommend means for ameliorating the undesirable effects of automation and technological changes.

Finally, Title I requires the President of the United States to transmit to Congress each year a report concerning manpower requirements, resources, utilization and training.

Title II of the Act concerns training and skill development programs. Specific criteria are identified for the selecting of individuals to participate in the training programs. In those cases where it is necessary stipends are paid to the trainees. Training will be conducted in public schools, on the job, and in a variety of other organizational places.

Title III of the Act includes a requirement for the Secretary of Labor to report to Congress each year. This report is to contain an evaluation of programs under the direction of the Act. The report will also indicate the number of persons trained, the types of training activities undertaken, the number of unemployed and underemployed persons who have obtained employment as a result of their training, and so forth.[29]

A review of the progress of the program may be illustrated as follows: specific occupational training in 40 states; over 300 training projects; over 600 courses; 109 occupations; and over 1300 trainees in an individual year.[30] This is a grass roots vocational training program. It includes older workers, younger workers, workers with low educational attainment, and workers from small communities and rural areas. The specific accomplishments of the program are illustrated by examples of former miners in West Virginia who are now trained in up-to-date welding techniques, by migratory farm workers in Texas who are now trained in the latest skills for farm machinery operations, and so forth.[31]

Specific occupational training for women is also being organized. The demand for well-trained stenographers, typists, and other qualified clerical workers is widespread. In order to meet much of this need nearly half of the women who have taken training under the Manpower Development and Training Act have done so in clerical occupational areas.[32]

SUMMARY AND IMPLICATIONS

Preparations for occupations in the urbanized society are never ending and always changing. The dynamics of occupational organization and social organization in the urbanized society are sufficiently great that the first most important characteristic of occupational preparation is that of a continual process. The second most important characteristic of occupational preparation is high level educational training. In an advanced society the proper functioning of a labor force can be achieved best by highly skilled workers.

It is reported that approximately half of the nation's workers currently engaged in the labor force have had little or no specific occupational training. But this is a changing situation. Younger workers in the labor force continually have a greater amount of specific occupational preparation.

In the early days of the colonies and of the nation, apprenticeship constituted the primary mechanism for most specific occupational preparation from the professions to the crafts. Those occupations in lower categories required little or no specific preparation at all. Apprenticeship in the professions soon was replaced by more rigorous training in professional schools. Gradually apprenticeship tended to be replaced for the crafts as machines and automation reduced the amount of total job understanding which the worker needed. As job specification expanded workers more quickly and adequately prepared to do one or two steps in a job and did not need to understand the total operation. As a result there is a general pressure in the society for an across the board up-grading in the preparation for occupations. Accordingly, much of secondary education is occupational, much of the training in colleges and universities is occupational.

As science and technology—indeed, knowledge—continue to proliferate at an accelerated rate the occupational preparation obtained in the school years becomes more and more inadequate as one continues through a career. New notions of occupational training are being suggested. Some of these notions would provide for a continual occupational training by working a 40-hour week, but with the specific provision that a specified number of hours during that week be devoted to continual study and up-to-date occupational preparation.

At the other extreme of the occupational continuum specific mechanisms are being developed for the training and retraining of workers who are being displaced by technological shifts and changes in the greater society. The Manpower Development and Training Act is a specific example of such a developing social mechanism.

NOTES

1. *Manpower Report of the President* (Washington, D.C.: U.S. Government Printing Office, 1964), p. 65.
2. *Formal Occupational Training of Adult Workers: Its Extent, Nature and Use* (Washington, D.C.: Manpower/Automation Research, Monograph No. 2, 1964).
3. Nels Anderson, *Dimensions of Work* (New York: David MacKay Company, Inc., 1964), pp. 65ff.
4. Neil W. Chamberlain, "Retooling the Mind," *Atlantic Monthly*, 214 (September 1964), 48.
5. Paul H. Douglas, *American Apprenticeship and Industrial Education* (New York: Columbia University, 1921), p. 11.
6. Ibid. pp. 12–16.
7. Ibid. pp. 80–84.
8. *Formal Occupational Training of Adult Workers*, p. 5.
9. Ibid. p. 10.
10. Ibid. p. 13.
11. Ibid. p. 15.
12. *Manpower Report of the President*, p. 72.
13. Dale Wolffe, *America's Resources of Specialized Talent* (New York: Harper and Brothers, 1954), p. 1.
14. Ibid.
15. Ibid. p. 2.
16. *National Manpower Council, A Policy of Scientific and Professional Manpower* (New York: Columbia University Press, 1953), p. 7.
17. Nelson B. Henry (ed.), *Education for the Professions* (Chicago: University of Chicago Press, 1962), p. 8.
18. Ibid. p. 10.
19. William J. McGlothlin, *Patterns of Professional Education* (New York: G. P. Putnam's Sons, 1960), pp. 169–70.
20. Lloyd E. Blanch, *Education for the Professions* (Washington, D.C.: U.S. Office of Education, 1955); and Patricia Wright, *Earned Degrees Conferred, 1962–1963* (Washington, D.C.: U.S. Office of Education, Circular No. 777, 1965), pp. 20–21.
21. Blanch, *Education*, p. 15.
22. McGlothlin, *Patterns*.
23. Ibid. p. 10.
24. Bernard Berelson, *Graduate Education in the United States* (New York: McGraw-Hill Book Co., Inc., 1960).
25. Ibid. p. 154.
26. Chamberlain, "Retooling the Mind," p. 49.
27. Ibid. pp. 49–50.
28. Ibid.

29. *An Explanation of the Manpower Development and Training Act* (Washington, D.C.: U.S. Government Printing Office, Revised, December 1962).
30. *Occupational Training: Pathway to Employment* (Washington, D.C.: U.S. Government Printing Office, June 1963).
31. Ibid. p. 14.
32. *Occupational Training of Women under the Manpower Development and Training Act* (Washington, D.C.: U.S. Government Printing Office, No. 3, July 1964), p. 11.

SUPPLEMENTARY READINGS

Neil W. Chamberlain, "Retooling the Mind," *Atlantic Monthly*, 214 (September 1964), 48–50.
An Explanation of the Manpower Development and Training Act (Washington, D.C.: U.S. Government Printing Office, 1962).
Formal Occupational Training of Adult Workers: Its Extent, Nature, and Use (Washington, D.C.: Manpower/Automation Research, Monograph No. 2, 1964).
Nelson B. Henry (ed.), *Education for the Professions* (Chicago: University of Chicago Press, 1962).
Occupational Training of Women under the Manpower Development and Training Act (Washington, D.C.: U.S. Government Printing Office, No. 3, July 1964).

ENTERING AN OCCUPATION X

Entering an occupation is a special normative phenomenon usually sharply differentiated from occupational choosing and from occupational preparation. In the upper, professional-like, or more well-developed occupations the phenomenon of entering is largely centered in the folkways and mores of recruitment. Among the vocationally more well prepared, occupational recruitment is an experience anticipated and often one systematically prepared for. In the lower and often less well organized occupations the norms of recruitment are less precise, indeed sometimes almost nonexistent. For the less well occupationally prepared, the school drop-outs or hard-core unemployed, there is little experience with systematic job recruitment and more acquaintance with job hunting. The job hunt is a normative type of behavior for vast numbers of American workers. Recruitment, as a behavioral phenomenon, is essentially a mechanism of the well-organized occupations. Job hunting is a loosely organized behavioral experience initiated primarily by the potential occupational practitioner left to his own devices and seeking.

Between the behavioral patterns of recruitment and job hunting are the norms of employment services. The most notable of these services is the U.S. Employment Service. It is supplemented by many professional employment services and by many private entrepreneurial employment services.

At different levels of social organization, recruitment, job hunting, and employment services constitute the range of major behavioral patterns for entering occupations.

The experience of entering occupations is multiple for most practitioners in the U.S. labor force. The transition from school to work is an experience known to practically all males, and to an ever-increasing

244

proportion of females. For a smaller proportion of individuals there is an experience of entering an occupation during trial work periods prior to formal departure from schools. For most members of the urbanized society labor force there is movement from one job to another many times, often every three to five years, during the so-called stable work period. In addition to this pattern of job changing and/or job mobility it is normative for many occupational practitioners, particularly in the professions, to enter and re-enter occupations as they progress upward or downward through their work careers. This is illustrated by the case of the medical doctor who moves at mid-career to enter a new occupation as a hospital administrator, the case of the professor who moves at mid-career to become a dean or higher academic administrator, or the case of an engineer who moves at mid-career to become a top level manager. Or it is also normative for one to terminate a career in civil service occupations at an early age and then to enter a less demanding but challenging occupation at a lower level. In short, it must be clearly understood that occupational entry is a multiple experience, and one associated both positively and negatively with moving both upward and downward in career stages.

SCHOOL TO WORK

The school to work occupational entry experience has become an almost universal characteristic in the United States as practically all youngsters are enrolled in schools through age 16 and most through age 18. Yet younger workers have had comparatively higher unemployment rates than those in any other age category.[1]

Leaving school for work is largely a matter of graduation from a secondary school, but it may involve dropping out of school before graduation. And, for an increasing proportion, now approximately one-half, of the high school graduates, leaving school involves some additional education, often college, before formal entry into an occupation. The transition phenomenon has been studied in seven locations by the Bureau of Labor Statistics.[2] Their study areas were cities ranging in population from about 30,000 to 350,000, excluding both rural and large metropolitan communities. The surveys reported sharp differences in intellectual ability as recorded by the Otis Mental Ability group tests for drop-outs and graduates. Those who scored less than 85 were typically drop-outs as compared to the graduates. Numerous drop-outs were found to have high intellectual capacities and to be examples of wastage when they did not go on for higher training and occupational preparation; for most of the drop-outs, however, no such wastage was recorded on the basis of mental ability reported. Most of the drop-outs left school at age 16 (34 per cent) or age 17 (27 per cent). Some left school before age 16, and of course some dropped out before graduation but after age 17. In the study areas it was required by law under most conditions for students to remain in school through age 16. Yet in most areas students age 14 or over could work part-time and go to school part-time under special conditions. This facilitated their entering an occupation and being prepared to drop out of school completely at the earliest possible occasion. Many of the drop-outs have not finished eight grades of school and certainly most of them leave school before they reach the period of maximum occupational training and maximum occupational information, counseling, and guidance.

The criticalness in the transition from school to work is usually seen as a matter of leaving high school with or without adequate occupational preparation or with or without adequate preparation for entering college or more advanced training. Wolfbein suggests, by contrast, that occupational education and guidance might well begin in elementary grades. This would involve the development of attitudes and information orienting youth to environmental forces in the world of work in the grades before presenting him with formal guidance material in high school. In short, occupational information dissemination and guidance would become developmental processes.[3]

The bulk of first entries into an occupation come with the leaving of school. Yet the extent to which it is the school's responsibility to prepare youngsters for entering the world of work is a matter of considerable debate. There is little basis for doubting the empirical observations that few high school graduates or drop-outs are well prepared for occupational entry. First occupational entry may or may not be a traumatic experience, but in most cases it is less than smooth or systematic.

RECRUITMENT

Recruitment for many well-organized occupations is a systematic and formal process. It is often supported by specific recruitment personnel.[4] In the large law firm there is the so-called hiring partner, whose task is essentially that of recruitment. In large industries there are specific personnel officers. In colleges, universities, and other schools with strong occupational preparation there are placement offices.

The formal recruitment process is supported with a body of literature. Some of this is designed to be as objective as possible in every detail, for example, the U.S. Department of Labor's *Occupational Outlook Handbooks* and its associated quarterly magazine. Much of the recruitment literature is specifically designed to be propagandistic and to create a specifically favorable or slanted image for a particular occupation.

Most recruitment is of a positive type—it is designed to bring people with specified characteristics into a given occupation. Some recruitment, however, is negative; it is designed to move people out of an occupational category. This is exemplified in the case of farming and many laboring occupations. Much recruitment material is age-specific, sex-specific, and education-specific. It is the nature of the recruitment mechanism to sift and select, essentially to match the right people with the right jobs. Yet it must be noted that recruitment as a mechanism, often developed by the internal organization of an occupation, is designed to provide a practitioner force for the ends of the occupation. Seldom are recruitment folkways and mores designed to take into account the interests and desires of the individual as such. By contrast, they are designed to enumerate the characteristics of the job and to identify human beings with such skills.

The recruitment process varies considerably from one category of occupations to another.[5] In the professions recruitment is almost completely controlled by the internal organization of the occupation. In the building craft occupations there are numerous formal recruitment mores, but final judgment on the competency of practitioners rests with engineers and/or other professionals above and outside of the occupation. In skilled, often blue-collar, factory work, recruitment is frequently controlled by the employers or unions. Retail occupations have few if any formal norms of recruitment.

The following selected examples illustrate the norms of recruitment into specific types of occupations.

Teacher recruitment. Recruitment of elementary and secondary school teachers involves a number of formalized norms, but none to the extent of constituting a nationwide recruitment or placement agency. This profession has considerable strength of internal organization, modified by two notable weaknesses. The first of these is localized political control of school systems coupled with state certification of teachers. The second is the high proportion of women, and often married women, who systematically move into and out of the occupation at different periods in life. The training of schoolteachers is systematic and professionalistic. But the boundary maintenance of the occupation is permeated by an exterior political control and eroded by the interior practitioner characteristic of women who often move into and out of the occupation. Frequently they are teachers who are second salary earners in a family. Accordingly, it is difficult for this profession to have a more tight and rigorous recruitment mechanism. The National Education Association has not maintained a national level placement service. Neither has the U.S. Office of Education provided such a service.[6] In spite of the absence of a national teacher recruitment mechanism there are well organized university and college placement bureaus, large urban school systems supporting their own placement offices, state departments of education supporting recruitment, private placement agencies, and the services of the U.S. Employment Service.

Much teacher recruitment, similar to the case of other professionals, is handled on an informal rather than formal basis. Frequently the superior candidates are identified during their training period. Their employment is effectively established on an informal basis before they leave college, although formal appointments may be signed only after the completion of certain specified school district tests and interviews. Much teacher recruitment remains at an informal to semiformal level.

Professor recruitment. The marketplace for college professors is a dynamic intrigue which on the surface seems to defy normative recruitment patterns. Yet, imperfect though the system may be, it is a good example of a profession's internal control of its recruitment procedures.[7] In a most recent study, *The Market for College Teachers,* an analysis was made of social scientists in southern universities. The method most frequently reported by the institution in announcing its position was to contact other graduate schools (90 per cent), inform friends (71 per cent), and make contacts at professional meetings (35 per cent). Listing with employment agencies (14 per cent) was the least frequently used technique (see Table X.1). By contrast, faculty

TABLE X.1

Methods Used to Advertise Vacancies

Methods	Department Chairmen [a] (Per cent)
Informed friends	71
Contacted graduate schools	90
Made contacts at professional meetings	35
Listed with an employment agency or used want ads in professional journals	14
Consulted "blind" letters	29

[a] Percentage of 49 department chairmen who responded to the question, "How did you go about locating the names of persons who might fill the vacancy?"
Source: David G. Brown, *The Market for College Teachers* (Chapel Hill: The University of North Carolina Press, 1965), p. 95.

members looking for positions most often inform friends (95 per cent), contact graduate schools (62 per cent), and attend professional meetings (35 per cent). Similar to the institution, they least frequently listed their availability with employment agencies. This informing of friends and rejection of employment agencies on the surface might appear to render recruitment in the academic profession almost a non-system. In effect what it means is that the institution seeking to fill a position has little if any systematic means for evaluating all the potential candidates. Similarly the candidates have little systematic way for comparing all of the available positions. In effect the system operates on a basis of personal knowledge and cliqueism. In such a system the cost of recruitment is frequently high. Or, put another way, the schools that can afford to invest a considerable amount of money and professional time in recruitment are able to identify more high quality candidates and to select from among the best.

Informal factors related to image also influence the recruitment milieu for academics. Some schools, by the nature of their academic reputation and by fact of their geographic location, tend to attract a certain type of candidate and to reject other types. For example, some universities with great graduate schools and rigorous selection of students may also be known as publish or perish systems. To such environments typically only aggressive and brilliant scholars are attracted.

Other schools, some equally as good in educational quality, are known for undergraduate focus and limited emphasis on graduate instruction and research production. A different type of candidate will be attracted to them accordingly.

Another major type of recruitment is illustrated in the academic profession. This is movement into positions of academic administration.[8] A recent study of college presidents in 78 new appointments reveals the following characteristics. Their average age at taking office was 47 to 48 years. Many had changed from one presidency to another and their average age at first appointment was approximately 45 years. The most frequent previous position was that of dean (25 per cent), another presidency (17 per cent), assistant to the president (13 percent), etc. Other positions ranged from professor, to lawyer, minister, army general, industrial manager, and foundation associate. The Ph.D. degree was held by over two-thirds of the new appointees. Often the recruitment is a promotion up from within the particular institution. Whatever the direct line of recruitment, most studies reveal that most presidents and deans were professors at an earlier point in their career. The normal process in recruitment is typically from professor to dean, sometimes by way of department chairmanship, and from dean to the presidency.[9]

Recruitment into academic occupations is in effect informally controlled by practitioners. They establish the characteristics of the occupation and to a considerable extent the conditions of work. Practitioners informally and sometimes formally establish the precise requirements for training and in effect achieve their recruitment as part of the training process. One must complete the course of training in order to be properly considered for further participation in the occupation. After successful completion of the course of training further complex patterns of informal recruitment are operative for higher positions, often administrative, within the occupation.

Dentistry recruitment. As in other occupations, initial recruitment into dentistry is a function of the status and prestige of the occupation, largely as manifested by the practitioners. Specific and rigorous standards of training are established. This is in part a recruitment mechanism, for one is effectively excluded from the occupation if the course of training is not passed. The American College of Dentistry constitutes an organizational form in which the details of training and the characteristics of recruits are considered.[10]

The image syndrome structuring dentistry recruitment includes five major categories: prestige, financial earnings, human service, autonomy, and manual skill.[11] These five syndrome features are central to the considerations manifested by students who seek entry into dentistry schools. The occupation carries the title doctor, and this is a matter of high prestige. The earnings of dentists are above average, indeed only slightly less than those of physicians. It is an occupation which offers the practitioner an opportunity for service to human kind. In the employee mass society, dentistry is an occupation that is still largely a fee-taking free entrepreneurial type of business. The nature of the occupation is such that it requires a high level of manual dexterity, and in a scientific idea-oriented society it is one of the few high occupations that is more manual than intellectual. These combined characteristics constitute a recruitment structure.

In a study of over 3500 entering dentistry students in 1958 a detailed comparison was made with law, teaching, social work, engineering, and medicine.[12] (See Table X.2.) Dentistry students viewed their future profession as essentially equal to medicine in providing human service and much more a field of human service than law and engineering. In terms of the prospects for making money they considered it less propitious than law and less than medicine, but more than engineering, social work, and teaching. Finally, they viewed dentistry as providing more autonomy than any of the other occupations with which they were asked to make comparisons.

In the recruitment structure for dentistry it must be particularly noted that recent studies show their choice of dentistry over medicine is a dominant pattern.[13] It was found that in over 5000 applicants to dental schools only 6 per cent had been refused admission to medical schools. In another study of dental students it was discovered that only 7 per cent had ever applied to medical school, and only half of these had been rejected.[14] In short, the recruitment norms of dentistry attract people positively and directly to the occupation. It does not appear to be a compromise or second-rate choice for those who had desired medical school as such. The image of dentistry is free-standing, and recruitment into it is guided by a positive image of the occupation.

Banker recruitment. Recruitment into banking occupations is greatly structured to identify security-oriented authoritarian personality types.[15] The banking occupation, in the case of the larger banks, is

TABLE X.2

Entering Dental Students' Comparison of Dentistry with Five Other Professions

Profession Compared	Dentistry Provides:	Relative Opportunity for:					
		Human Service		Making Money		Autonomy	
		N	Per Cent	N	Per Cent	N	Per Cent
Law......	More.....	2,468	71.9	1,086	31.0	1,986	58.1
	Less.....	310	9.0	1,861	53.0	658	19.2
	Same.....	657	19.1	563	16.0	777	22.7
	Subtotal	3,435	100.0	3,510	100.0	3,421	100.0
Teaching..	More.....	995	29.1	2,929	85.5	2,922	83.5
	Less.....	1,239	36.2	421	12.3	388	11.1
	Same.....	1,188	34.7	76	2.2	188	5.4
	Subtotal	3,422	100.0	3,426	100.0	3,498	100.0
Social work	More.....	1,316	38.5	2,913	85.1	2,852	83.3
	Less.....	1,016	29.7	437	12.8	443	12.9
	Same.....	1,085	31.8	71	2.1	129	3.8
	Subtotal	3,417	100.0	3,421	100.0	3,424	100.0

TABLE X.2 (cont.)

Profession Compared	Dentistry Provides:	Relative Opportunity for:					
		Human Service		Making Money		Autonomy	
		N	Per Cent	N	Per Cent	N	Per Cent
Engineering	More	2,684	78.1	1,558	46.0	2,634	76.9
	Less	290	8.4	1,204	35.5	504	14.7
	Same	463	13.5	626	18.5	286	8.4
	Subtotal	3,437	100.0	3,388	100.0	3,424	100.0
Medicine	More	141	4.1	426	12.5	1,689	49.4
	Less	1,507	43.9	2,011	59.0	549	16.1
	Same	1,783	52.0	970	28.5	1,178	34.5
	Subtotal	3,431	100.0	3,407	100.0	3,416	100.0

Source: D. M. More and Nathan Kohn, Jr., "Some Motives for Entering Dentistry," American Journal of Sociology, 66 (July 1960), 51.

characterized by the designation of hiring officers. Their specific job is recruitment, and more particularly to identify the "right type" of person for practitionership. One hiring officer's response illustrates the situation,

We always ask who recommends them and usually we know a little about the other person. We also consider the individual—is he sloppy, is he neat, are his fingernails clean, and what sort of poise does he have. His approach, as you know, that's an important thing for me. For example, I had a young kid come in the other day to apply for a job. Without saying anything he pulled out a package of cigarettes and started smoking. Now imagine that —a junior in high school saunters in here and starts smoking without even asking if he could—so I knew he wasn't the type for us and I let him go. I usually like a certain type of youngster—a quiet youngster, slightly on the nervous side. Oh, I don't mean that he or she should be completely upset, but I think that's the kind of person we are looking for. They should have a certain amount of poise and should not do too much talking.[16]

The hiring officer's recruitment orientation is quite specific. The recruitment syndrome includes in the occupation's image: security in position, slow advancement, a minimum opportunity for initiative, and a high emphasis upon status rewards rather than on economic remuneration.

McMurry studied some 900 banking and investment-house employees. Most were given primary mental ability tests, the Kuder Preference Record, and the Allport-Vernon Study of Values as measures of their interests and personality characteristics. It was found in essence that as a function of the recruitment characteristics the occupation brought few people into its practitioner ranks who had high administrative ability and great imagination. Given the comparative routine of many of the stages in the occupation the recruiting system produced a practitioner appropriate to the demands. At the top level, however, there were few who could be promoted from within for imaginative management and direction of large banking firms. It was found that in terms of personality types many who were recruited into banking were never completely emotionally weaned from their parents. Or, by contrast, they had grown up in such loveless environments that they were threatened by the decision-making demands of adult responsibility. Hence the security and routine of highly specified banking operations constituted an occupational environment of tranquility and compatibility.

Management recruitment. Recruitment into management positions is a matter of identifying high talent creative manpower in the urbanized society. The recruitment syndrome for high talent management manpower involves two highly different normative structures, one following executive authority and the other following colleague authority. Firms that can at once effectively identify and differentiate these two authorities and at the same time bring a compatible interaction between the two establish a milieu for effective recruitment.[17] Princeton sociologist Simon Marcson states most fully the need for successfully differentiating executive and colleague authority if highest level recruitment is to be achieved. Creative management people, he submits, require an environment of recognition, participation, self-realization, and predictability. In order to maintain high levels of enthusiasm and motivation it is essential that the work environment include these ingredients. More and more high talent management is recruited from professional ranks. Effective management recruitment must increasingly accommodate for the environment of high level professionalism.

Sales recruitment. Recruitment into sales occupations is characterized more by difficulties in attracting practitioners than by selecting and excluding individuals. Much of the occupational recruitment analyzed to this point has focused on selection, often exclusive. In the urbanized, scientific, idea society, sales occupations hold few attractions. Even the possibility of high earnings is not sufficient to attract many candidates.[18] The occupations of selling are less tightly organized than, for example, many professions. Yet historically in the United States vast numbers of persons have sought opportunities in sales. But in the second half of the twentieth century sales occupations have become typically characterized by middle to low status. Few apply and the recruitment norms are necessarily designed to encourage more candidates. The National Sales Executives Incorporated have mounted intensive programs to stimulate interest in selling occupations, particularly among college students. Still most college graduates do not prefer sales at all. When they do it is reported their interest is greatest in work in a large corporation environment, where sales are of a highly specialized nature, preferably of tangible items like heavy machinery, where the industry will provide them with an extensive specific training course, where there will be little travel involved in their selling, and, above all else, where they will be placed on a salary. The possibility for monetary remuneration in sales being considerably above the average occupational earning is great. Yet the college graduates in particular are little impressed with the possibility of such high earnings at the price of the insecurity and low status often associated with sales. The norms of systematic recruitment involve more than materialism.

Recruitment into other types of occupations, particularly the lower prestige white-collar occupations and most blue-collar occupations, is guided by extensive systems, but typically is more controlled by the management in the place of employment than by the occupation as such. Most of the many thousands of occupations are not sufficiently well organized to dominate and control their own recruitment.

THE JOB HUNT

Most members of the nation's labor force look for jobs in occupations that do not structure their own recruitment. During most of the years since World War II the United States has had in effect fewer jobs than it has had potential employees. Hence organized occupations, by the nature of the society of which they are a part, have tended to be exclusive rather than inclusive in identifying practitioners. The onus of finding occupational employment has rested more on potential employees than on employers and occupations. Both occupations and employers have had the general security of knowing that throughout the society there is a supply of individuals who can be brought into practitionership. Potential employees, by contrast, have been faced with searching for work in a society and among occupations where there are few mechanisms to facilitate their broad acquaintance with the possibilities.

Blue-collar workers. Job seeking is a normative tradition among blue-collar workers.[19] Among the socio-psychological norms in the job seeking structure are achievement motivation or the willingness to persist in the process of hunting work, achievement values which focus on economic success, and anxiety in job interview situations.[20]

In Sheppard and Belitsky's 1965 study of the efforts of unemployed workers to hunt for jobs it was found, first, that those who used the public employment service were in most cases characterized by relatively low achievement values. Second, they manifested a high anxiety in job interview situations. It was also found that the effectiveness of an unemployed worker's search for a new job was frequently impaired by his expectations of being called back to his old job at a future date. Third, it was found that the unemployed workers whose economic achievement values were high were more thorough and successful in seeking new jobs than those who placed less value on success achievement. Fourth, it was found that unemployed workers characterized by a high motivation and a low interview anxiety tended to obtain new jobs more easily than others. Finally, the unemployed workers who found new jobs most quickly started their job search immediately after being laid off. They were aggressive in contacting all kinds of firms regardless of whether or not they had a knowledge that those firms were hiring.

For those who were most successful in finding new jobs the male unemployed workers typically began to look for new places of work within one week after being laid off. The folkways through which these workers sought a new job included friends and relatives, direct company applications, unions, and, finally, the employment service. Among skilled workers, direct company application and union contacts were the most effective in getting new jobs. The assistance of friends and relatives was most helpful for the semiskilled workers. For the unskilled workers the employment service constituted the greatest source of help.

The importance of socio-psychological factors was considerable regardless of educational level. Individuals who held high values on achievement and success started looking for new jobs sooner and found employment faster than those holding alternate values. Unemployed workers who manifested high anxiety about job interviews were slower in obtaining new employment than those for whom the situation constituted a minimum of anxiety.

It was further found by Sheppard and Belitsky that most blue-collar workers had not moved in order to look for employment. Women were more immobile than men, but typically neither changed their place of residence to look for a job. When moves were reported they usually involved many hundreds of miles. Over 40 per cent of the males had considered moving, while only a few women even considered it.

The possibility for blue-collar mobility may be great. It was found that when asked if they would accept a better job 1000 miles from their present location, almost 60 per cent responded affirmatively. Still more would move if their travel and relocation expenses were paid. One cannot overgeneralize from a case study and from hypothetical questions. Nevertheless, there is some suggestion that norms of mobility could be expanded in the job hunting situation. In the absence of national occupational mobility policies the employment services become major structures in job hunting.

EMPLOYMENT SERVICES

Employment services are federal, state, private entrepreneurial, and private professional. The image of employment services in an open-class free enterprise ideology society is less than prestigious. Indeed, the stereotype is widely held that the most able occupational people will be able to enter employment on their own initiative and without the assistance of employment services. But with the increasing multiplicity of jobs over the last century, with the increased mobility of the labor force, and with the increased educational attainment of the population, the rugged individualistic approach to entering occupations is often less than advantageous both for individuals and employers. Accordingly, more systematic norms and structures are being developed both by occupations and by the society for systematic occupational entry. Notable among these growing structures is the federal-state employment service.

Federal-state employment service system. The Wagner-Peysner Act of 1933 created the U.S. Employment Service.[21] The government employment service is charged with the development of a national system of employment offices, the establishment of standards and review plans for operations, the carrying out of statistical and research work, and the development and maintenance of interstate recruitment programs. Approximately 2000 local offices throughout the nation carry out the details of this federal-state employment service. The local offices are federally financed but operated by the respective state employment services.

The federal-state employment service has been primarily a placement operation, that of bringing together workers and jobs. On a national level for the past decade the public employment service has participated in about 15 per cent of all new hirings.[22] The proportion of participation by the government employment service is small, but it is consistent with the historical operation of the free enterprise society.

Traditionally the national employment service has aimed at providing an orderly functioning in the job marketplace and not domination of the entering of occupations. In addition to referring applicants to employers, the employment service provides testing and counseling to applicants. Specialized services are provided for minority groups, handicapped individuals, inexperienced youths, migratory farm workers, veterans, etc.

In the 1960's the services of the national employment organization have increased. Professional offices are being established to provide detailed assistance in the placement of professional workers. Another new direction of service is the establishing of a network of an electronic data processing and telecommunications systems for inter-regional recruitment and placement. This project is known as LINCS (Labor Inventory Communications System).

Developing the employability of workers is a new and fundamentally major different dimension for the employment service. This is supported primarily by the Manpower Development and Training Act of 1962. In addition to counseling and placement, the national employment service is now identifying major categories of individuals who can profit from additional training. Accordingly, they are recommended for special training programs conducted under contractual arrangements with schools. After the training programs the individuals come back to the employment service to be assisted in placement.

In spite of the several changes in new directions of the employment service the greatest proportion of the staff time is still focused on placement work (taking job applications and job orders, selection and referral of workers for jobs, and verification of placement). Counseling is the second most time-consuming activity. The third amount of time is placed on labor market information. The fourth amount of time is on testing, and the remainder is on various services.[23]

The employment service estimated penetration in the placement process is greatest for unskilled workers, 30 per cent; next for clerical and sales workers, 14 per cent; third for service workers, 13 per cent; fourth for semiskilled workers, 11 per cent; fifth for professional and managerial workers, 10 per cent; and least of all for skilled workers, 8 per cent.[24]

The employment service has been since the 1930's and continues to be in the 1960's primarily a job exchange organization.

Private employment services. Private enterprise employment services are increasing in the United States. In 1948 it was estimated that there were some 2231 private agencies employing 4580 workers. By 1958 the number of agencies had increased to nearly 4000 with approximately 16,700 employees. Between 1948 and 1958 their receipts increased from $31 million to $101 million.[25] By 1964 the number of private employment agencies was approximately 4300 with a personnel of 25,000 and an income of $145 million.[26] A high proportion of the users of private employment agencies are women, most of whom seek placement in clerical and secretarial jobs. The average fee paid in recent years for placement is a little more than $30.00. The above figures constitute a structural review of the value of the job exchange process performed by private employment services. It is observed by some that these private agencies constitute a savings in the cost of the job search between jobs for employees. From the point of view of employers it is argued that they reduce the cost of recruitment and the cost of turnover. From the social organizational point of view of the nation it may be argued that private employment agencies are facilitating mechanisms that reduce the cost of unemployment of the nation's workers. It is also observed, however, that private employment agencies reap a profitable business and leave a residue of unemployed at the lower end of the occupational continuum for the public employment service.[27]

No firm body of data exists to record the normative and social history of private employment agencies. Nevertheless they constitute one among several mechanisms for entering and re-entering occupations.

Professional employment services. There is an old and solid tradition that well-qualified professionals enter their employment informally through colleagues, professors, and friends. Indeed, most have in the past, and many still do. The informal market is far from extinct, but in the mass urbanized society, experiencing enormous increases in the number of professionals it is clearly inadequate. Recognizing this vacuum and need, many professional agencies are coming into existence. Virtually every educational and professional association provides some full-time or part-time employment service activities. In many cases the employment services are provided by the professional schools, and this is done systematically, rather than informally. By the mid 1960's more than 2500 different organizations were providing employment service.[28] More than 200 college placement offices are operating. In some cases there may be multiple placement offices at a given college, each operated by a separate professional school. In addition to the colleges, over 200 professional associations are providing employment assistance.[29] Religious groups also maintain employment agencies. All of these are supplemented by a variety of special agencies—the Woodrow Wilson Foundation, the Danforth Foundation, the Northeast College Association, the Council for Émigrés in the Professions, the Association of Emeriti, and numerous others.

The organization and charges for the professional employment services are minimal. This is illustrated in the case of the American Psychological Association. In the early 1960's this association published a monthly employment bulletin with a circulation of approximately 3000. Nominal fees were charged to employers who listed their positions either confidentially or openly. Similarly, nominal fees were charged to available candidates who listed, confidentially, their availability. In subsequent years this kind of employment announcement operation has spread from society to society, but continual efforts are made to accelerate and expedite the employment process.

The entering of professional level occupations is facilitated by the societies and associations of the occupations, even if the mechanisms and processes are of a near-primitive type. The more highly organized occupations continue, even if reluctantly, to recognize the importance of establishing their own mechanisms for providing entry into their occupational employment.

SUMMARY AND IMPLICATIONS

The entry into occupations in its initial process is essentially an experience of leaving school to join the labor force. In the processes of continuing education and of retraining the leaving school for occupational entry may occur many times in the working life of a given individual.

Recruitment into occupations is a major structural phenomenon, particularly in the case of the highly organized occupations of the professional type. The major mechanism for recruitment is the rigorous establishment of training demands. Entry into the occupation or profession is typically restricted to those who have completed the proper course of training.

Recruitment is also found in the case of some occupations which do not specify a particular course of training. This is particularly illustrated in the case of recruitment to sales occupations. The effectiveness of recruitment, however, tends to be greater where the training for the occupation is more rigorous.

The hunting for a job is the most widespread structural experience in the entering of an occupation. This is widely characteristic of the lower white-collar occupations and of most blue-collar occupations. In such cases there is little notion of recruitment and employers generally establish their own personnel offices for selecting workers to enter occupations in their establishment.

Employment services, ranging from federal-state, to private, and to professional associations, are specific mechanisms of the twentieth century which are gaining increasing importance in the process of entering occupations. Employment services are utilized for entering occupations from the highest to the lowest types. In the higher more intensely organized occupations, particularly those of the professional range, the employment services are generally organized and operated by the occupation's internal organization. In the case of workers entering typically semiskilled and unskilled occupations the government employment services are most widely utilized. The private entrepreneurial employment services are used primarily by those practitioners in the intermediate range of occupations.

The implications of the increasing importance of employment and recruitment services are that occupational proliferation, occupational mobility, and geographical mobility are all combining in such a mix that it is necessary from the point of view of both societal organization and occupational organization to specify and formalize processes for systematic entry and re-entry into occupations. In addition to choosing an occupation and preparing for an occupation, it is finally necessary to enter and/or to re-enter specific places of employment in the occupation. In the mass urbanized society with a greater number of occupations and an enormous population, individual employees and individual employers on their own are unable to identify the fullest range of employment opportunities and employee potentials. The development of increasingly formal mechanisms for entering occupations is consistent with the complexities of societal organization and with the multiplicity of occupations.

NOTES

1. Seymour L. Wolfbein, "Transition from School to Work: A Study of the School Leaver," *Personnel and Guidance Journal*, 38 (October 1959), 98–105.
2. Ibid.
3. Ibid. p. 103.
4. E. O. Smigel, "Impact of Recruitment on the Organization of the Large Law Firm," *American Sociological Review*, 25 (February 1960), 56.
5. Theodore Caplow, *The Sociology of Work* (Minneapolis: The University of Minnesota Press, 1954).
6. *Special Memo* (Washington, D.C.: National Education Association, Research Division, February 1957).
7. Theodore Caplow and Reece J. McGee, *The Academic Marketplace* (New York: Basic Books, Inc., 1958); David G. Brown, *The Market for College Teachers* (Chapel Hill: The University of North Carolina Press, 1965); John E. Stecklein and Robert I. Lathrop, *Faculty Attraction and Retention: Factors Affecting Faculty Mobility at the University of Minnesota* (Minneapolis: University of Minnesota Press, 1960); and Logan Wilson, *The Academic Man: A Study in the Sociology of a Profession* (New York: Oxford University Press, 1942).
8. Algo D. Henderson, "Finding and Training Academic Administrators," *Public Administration Review*, 20 (Winter 1960), 17–22.
9. J. E. Gordon, "The President: Has the Pattern of College and University Leadership Changed?" *Journal of Higher Education*, 24 (March 1953), 135–40.
10. D. M. More, "Social Origins of Future Dentists," *Midwest Sociologist*, 21 (July 1959), 69–76; D. M. More and Nathan Kohn, Jr., "Some Motives for Entering Dentistry," *American Journal of Sociology*, 66 (July 1960), 48–53; Enrico Quarantelli, "The Career Choice Patterns of Dentistry Students," *Journal of Health and Human Behavior*, 2 (Summer 1961), 124–32; and Elliott H. Pennell and Marilyn Y. Pennell, *Health Manpower Source Book: Section 7, Dentists* (Washington, D.C.: U.S. Department of Health, Education, and Welfare, 1955), p. 37.
11. More and Kohn, "Motives for Entering Dentistry," p. 48.
12. Ibid. p. 51.
13. William R. Mann and Grace Parkin, "The Dental School Applicant," *Journal of Dental Education*, 24 (March 1960), 33.
14. Quarantelli, "Career Choice Patterns," p. 131.
15. Robert N. McMurry, "Recruitment, Dependency, and Morale in the Banking Industry," *Administrative Science Quarterly*, 3 (June 1958), 87–106; Chris Argyris, "Human Relations in a Bank," *Harvard Busi-*

ness Review, 32 (September–October 1954), 66; and Chris Argyris, "Some Problems of Conceptualizing Organizational Climate: A Case Study of a Bank," *Administrative Science Quarterly*, 2 (March 1958), 501–20.

16. Argyris, "Human Relations in a Bank," p. 64.
17. "New Way to Attract Brain Power," *Nation's Business*, 47 (October 1959), 82–6; and Robert N. McMurry, "Manhunt for Top Executives," *Harvard Business Review*, 32 (January–February 1954), 54.
18. "Help Wanted: Sales," *Fortune*, 45 (May 1952), 100ff.
19. Harold L. Sheppard and Harvey Belitsky, *The Job Hunt: Job Seeking Behavior of Unemployed Workers in a Local Economy* (Washington, D.C.: W. E. Upjohn Institute for Employment Research, 1965).
20. See "The Search for Work," in *Manpower Research Programs* (Washington, D.C.: U.S. Department of Labor, Manpower Administration, 1966), p. 78.
21. *Manpower Report of the President* (Washington, D.C.: U.S. Department of Labor, 1965), pp. 159–69; "The New United States Employment Service," *Employment Security Review*, 29 (April 1962); and Richard A. Lester, *Manpower Planning in a Free Society* (Princeton: Princeton University Press, 1966).
22. *Manpower Report of the President*, p. 159.
23. Lester, *Manpower Planning*, p. 47.
24. "Employment Service Participation in the Labor Market" (Washington, D.C.: U.S. Employment Service, November 23, 1962), mimeo p. 4; see also Lester, *Manpower Planning*, p. 72.
25. L. P. Adams, "The Public Employment Service," in J. M. Becker (ed.), *In Aid of the Unemployed* (Baltimore: The Johns Hopkins Press, 1965), p. 219; see also Lester, *Manpower Planning*, p. 181.
26. Testimony of Jack Skeels in Public Employment Service, Hearings Before the Select Sub-committee on Labor, Committee on Education and Labor, House of Representatives, 88th Cong., 2nd Sess., U.S. Government Printing Office, Washington, D.C., 1964, p. 465.
27. Lester, *Manpower Planning*, p. 180.
28. David G. Brown, *Placement Services for College Teachers* (Chapel Hill: Report to the Office of Manpower, Automation and Training, U.S. Department of Labor, 1965).
29. *National Directory of Employment Services* (1st Ed.; Detroit, Michigan: Gale Research Company, 1962).

SUPPLEMENTARY READINGS

J. M. Becker (ed.), *In Aid of the Unemployed* (Baltimore: The Johns Hopkins Press, 1965).
David G. Brown, *The Market for College Teachers* (Chapel Hill: University of North Carolina Press, 1965).

Theodore Caplow and Reece J. McGee, *The Academic Marketplace* (New York: Basic Books, Inc., 1958).

Harold L. Sheppard and Harvey Belitsky, *The Job Hunt: Job Seeking Behavior of Unemployed Workers in a Local Economy* (Washington, D.C.: W. E. Upjohn Institute for Employment Research, 1965).

E. O. Smigel, "Impact of Recruitment on the Organization of the Large Law Firm," *American Sociological Review*, 25 (February 1960), 56–60.

Seymour L. Wolfbein, "Transition from School to Work," *Personnel and Guidance Journal*, 38 (October 1959), 98–105.

OCCUPATIONAL CAREER PATTERNS XI

Occupational career patterns are experienced by a minority of the workers in urbanized society. Or, put another way, most occupational men and women in the nation's labor force experience only some elements of career patterning, but less than total careers. Career implies norms and structuring, identifiable and discrete stages, through which practitioners pass as they experience a life's work in a given occupation. In numerous viable occupations boundaries are permeated by union and bureaucratic social structures. It is precisely where occupational structures and institutions are strongest and most free-standing that occupational career patterns are most identifiable.

In the balance of social organization and occupational organization both stability and flexibility are achieved by the attainment of strong career patterns in some occupations, weak career patterns in other occupations, and an absence of career patterns in a few occupations. While career patterns bring stability and predictability to many occupational environments, if pushed to an excessive development they render occupations static. When career patterns are sufficiently rigid that they exclude new developments related to the given occupation, those new developments may be organized into alternative, and perhaps competing, occupations, or they might atrophy. Career patterns, therefore, preserve both the character and the precision of an occupation, but in so doing they inhibit the growth of the occupation.

CONCEPTS AND DEFINITIONS

Structurally the concept of career involves a limited focus. By definition career is a succession of related jobs, hierarchical in prestige, with ordered directions for an individual to pass through them in a predictable sequence.[1]

The differences between work and career are great. In work, an individual accepts a job, the primary purpose of which is to obtain the means to non-work ends. A job under such circumstances is a relatively isolated experience, a mechanism for earning a living. The notion of career implies a great number of future expectations. These future expectations extend through the work lifetime of the individual. Indeed, longevity of experience is one of the norms of career. Other norms of career include rights, privileges, status, nonfinancial rewards, and monetary compensation.

Some occupational careers are conspicuously in public view while others are esoteric or private in character. Conspicuous careers are illustrated by most salaried professionals in bureaucratic environments, where by the nature of the case the specifications of the career stages are officially a matter of public record.

Esoteric and private types of careers characterize vast numbers of occupations. Indeed many of the occupational careers in the new and developing sciences and technologies are of this type. Similarly, many of the occupational careers in operative work elude broad public scrutiny, and, although far from new, they remain obscure. Career structure brings stability to occupations whether it is overt or covert, public or private. Where the career patterning is overt, occupational choosing, planning, and organization is facilitated for large numbers of the labor force and potential labor force. Where occupational career patterns are covert they may serve the structure and stability of the internal organization of the occupation well but they contribute little to the public image or recognition of the occupation.

Career organization contributes in several ways to the internal character of occupations. For example, when occupations are broken down into several specialized tasks, and the tasks are associated with career developmental stages, a system of incentives for the individual to move systematically through is established. From a negative point of view, rigid career stages may also justify conditions identified as trained in capacity. The detailed specification of work associated with the career stage limits one's activities to that career stage and justifies a practitioner in his refusal to do those work tasks associated with other career stages. Such rigid boundary maintenance between career stages may appear as incapacity. Rigid demarcation of the characteristics of career stages may also inhibit or limit ambition. When career stages become enforced with bureaucratic ritual the practitioner may become isolated or bypassed in a particular stage of the career and soon have no ambition to progress to stages higher in the hierarchy. Nevertheless in many occupations it is desirable to have practitioners who will fill lower and middle range career stage tasks faithfully and capably. The limiting of ambitions may, therefore, be both an advantage and a disadvantage, depending on the ultimate need for the occupational organization.

Occupational career hierarchies generally lead practitioners to promotion within occupations rather than between occupations. This is another manifestation of the stabiliy which career brings to occupational organization. Careers establish and make known the rules by which the occupational gain is ordered. When one moves between occupational careers the rules of the game are less apparent and one may have to start in the second occupation at a lower career stage than those in the age peer group who have participated longer in that particular occupation. Illustrations of career occupational shifts are seen as one moves from professor to dean, from minister to sociologist, from army officer to civilian executive, from professional practitioner to elected official, etc. The career norms that one has learned and that contributed to one's success in one occupational hierarchy may or may not be of value in the second occupational hierarchy of career norms. Moreover, one's associated style of life may change as one shifts from career to career.[2]

Career patterns of individuals. Occupational career stages are generally marked by three phases: initial, trial, and stable.[3] In discovering these stages and formulating them conceptually Miller and Form sampled 276 individuals in terms of their occupational histories. The sample was selected to match the gainfully employed person in the State of Ohio. An effort was made to record both part-time and full-time work experiences of the respondents. Their occupational work was subsequently classified into the Alba Edwards Census Scale, ranging from professional to domestic occupations. Inspection of these job histories led to the trichotomy of initial, trial, and stable work periods.

By definition the concept initial work period includes all part-time or full-time jobs held by an individual until his formal education is completed. In many instances the initial work period jobs are the before or after school or summer types. In some few cases the initial period jobs are full-time work, but in most cases they are part-time work.

The trial work period by definition includes the shopping around and obtaining of a few full-time jobs before the individual settles on a specific occupation for his life's work. In some situations the trial work period is in effect required by apprenticeship training. Miller and Form further specify that jobs are classified as trial when there is movement from one occupation or place of employment to another within periods of three-years' duration.

Finally, the stable work period is defined as that point in the occupational career when the practitioner remains for a period of 3 years or more in the same occupation. Accordingly, it is recognized that for some practitioners the stable work period is never reached in their entire work history. For others there is some alteration between stable and trial periods throughout their work history.

When studies reveal that the typical occupational practitioner in America changes his job every 3 to 5 years there is considerable evidence that occupational careers are not experienced by huge numbers of practitioners in the labor force. Yet all job changing is not inhibitory to career progression. In some professional and other white-collar occupations it is normative for practitioners to proceed through their occupational career by changing employers. Indeed, this does not necessarily change one's type of work. One may be expected to move up the occupational hierarchy with employer changing and/or geographical mobility as acceptable mechanisms. This career mobility pattern is clearly illustrated in the case of executives and professors.

In the Ohio Career Study data it was reported that the average length of time spent in the initial period was 3 years. This ranged from only 2 years for clerical workers to approximately 4 years for both domestics and professionals. The average number of years in the trial period was 6. The minimum was 4 years in the professions and the maximum was 7.5 years in unskilled laboring occupations. In the stable period the average number of years was 18. This ranged from a maximum of 22 years for proprietors to a minimum of only 8 years for domestics. Figures XI.1 through XI.7 illustrate the career patterns for workers in each occupational level. From Figure XI.1 it can be observed that professional practitioners originate in many occupational categories but move quickly to their professional careers. Once they enter a profession they seldom move to try an alternate occupation. In Figure XI.2 it is clear that proprietors also originate from a wide range of occupations.

They experience considerable upward vertical mobility, and once the stable period is reached they remain there for a relatively long duration. In Figure XI.3 some upward vertical mobility is also recorded for clerical workers as well as a considerable amount of downward vertical mobility. Skilled workers tend to originate in the unskilled and semi-skilled categories. Accordingly, they move up only slightly. Semiskilled workers experience some upward vertical mobility from unskilled and domestic categories. In Figures XI.6 and XI.7 it is clear that little mobility is experienced on the part of either unskilled or domestic workers. They tend to originate in their occupational category and remain there through the whole of their work experience.

In terms of these career pattern analyses the authors conclude that occupational career security is associated with white-collar and skilled work. Occupational career insecurity is more typical for semiskilled, un-skilled, and domestic workers. Furthermore, when a practitioner is once

FIGURE XI.1

Career patterns of professional workers

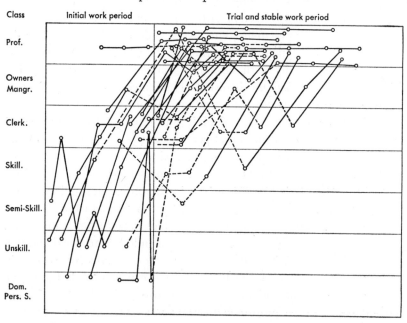

Source: William H. Form and Delbert C. Miller, "Occupational Career Pattern as a Sociological Instrument," *American Journal of Sociology*, 54 (January 1949), 322.

started on a given occupational level, there is a tendency for him to remain on that level.

Career stages within an occupation. Career stages are reported for the internal organization of specific occupations. This is clearly illustrated in the case of medicine.[4] Empirical research in the medical profession reveals four career stages, as follows: (1) the development of ambition for the profession; (2) obtaining admission in a medical institution; (3) developing a clientele; and (4) achieving patterns of informal relationships with one's colleagues.

In the medical profession, and in other highly organized occupations, these stages or covert norms constitute mechanisms for stong internal control on the behavior of practitioners. From the outset the career norm of ambition is a mechanism by which the practitioners tend to socialize and recruit future practitioners from their same occupational stratum or closely related strata. Once in the "fraternity," behavior is

FIGURE XI.2

Career patterns of proprietors and managerial workers

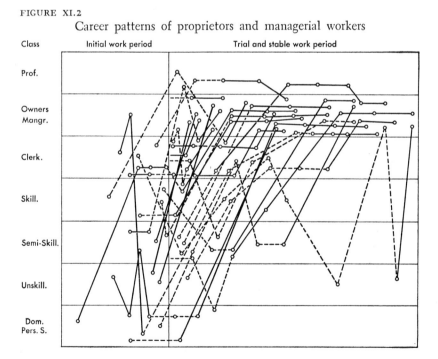

Source: William H. Form and Delbert C. Miller, "Occupational Career Pattern as a Sociological Instrument," *American Journal of Sociology,* 54 (January 1949), 323.

further controlled by career norms which must be met in order to gain full admission to hospitals, clinics, laboratories, nursing homes, dispensaries, and medical associations. In short, in the occupation of medicine becoming a doctor by academic degree is not to become a doctor in occupational fact. One's career is further dependent on following a set of norms for overt participation in the occupation. After admission to the facilities of the occupation, still another set of norms must be negotiated for further career development as it relates to building a clientele. In addition to obtaining patients, one wants to keep a selected clientele. In doing this the relationships between the generalists and the specialists are particularly critical. Definite, although covert, folkways are established to guide the practitioners in relation to each other and with their own patients as well as with the patients of others.

Finally, before the gauntlet is run and the fullness of the career reached a final set of norms must be negotiated to achieve an internal colleagueship. The colleague inner core is characterized by three norms.

FIGURE XI.3

Career patterns of clerical workers

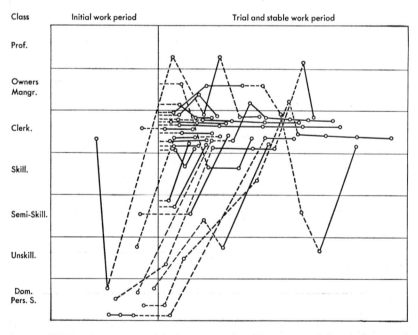

Source: William H. Form and Delbert C. Miller, "Occupational Career Pattern as a Sociological Instrument," *American Journal of Sociology*, 54 (January 1949), 323.

The first has to do with a technical division of labor. The body of knowledge in contemporary medicine is greater than the capacity of a single practitioner. Specialists are the manifestation of this diversity of knowledge, and the inner core colleagues manage the integration of the distinctive lines of specialization. Second, the inner core norms constitute a market control. It is through this organization that they insure that patients will ultimately get to the proper specialists to obtain the type of help that they need. Physical proximity in medical buildings and often adjacency to major hospitals facilitates this organization of their market. The third norm of the inner core colleagues is the secret society impact of a small first name primary group relationship. There is peer groupage, similarity in educational experience, and homogeneity in social and economic backgrounds. From this third stage in the career development the system and balance of the medical occupation is directed and controlled.

It is in this restricted occupational view of career that one asserts

FIGURE XI.4
Career patterns of skilled workers and foremen

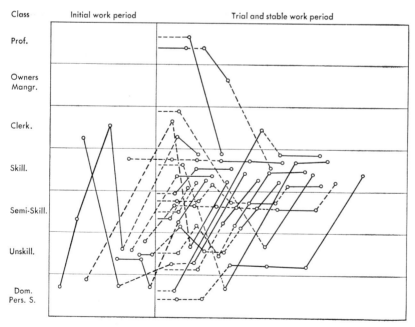

Source: William H. Form and Delbert C. Miller, "Occupational Career Pattern as a Sociological Instrument," *American Journal of Sociology*, 54 (January 1949), 324.

that only a minority of the labor force experiences it. Yet in the industrial urbanized society careers are proliferating both in number and in details. For example, many new white-collar occupations are being organized with considerable longevity and internal organizational stability. The details of career stages are also increasing as there are longer and more specific training periods for many occupations. We move next to an examination of internal career details or dimensions.

CAREER DIMENSIONS

Differential identification with occupational careers. Willingness and ability to identify with careers varies among the several occupations. For some occupations there is discovered an intensive career identification long before actual entry, and for other occupations practitioners never experience a grasp of identity. Degrees of identification are

FIGURE XI.5

Career patterns of semiskilled workers

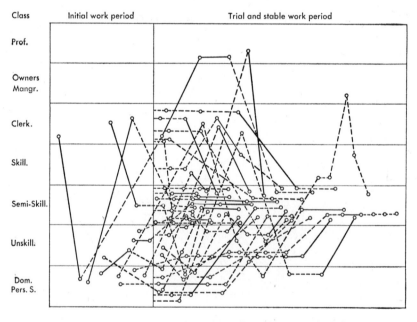

Source: William H. Form and Delbert C. Miller, "Occupational Career Pattern as a Sociological Instrument," *American Journal of Sociology*, 54 (January 1949), 324.

sharply illustrated in a case of interviews taken with male graduate students in physiology, philosophy, and mechanical engineering.[5] The advanced training experience of a graduate or professional school is a more or less intense part of the total occupational career experience. From one point of view, the advanced training school is the environment in which practitioners or trainers of practitioners not only disseminate the technical skills of the respective occupations but select subsequent generations of practitioners. In the graduate school experience the "who am I?" may become focused and precise or remain diffuse as career articulation is precise or diffuse. In the training environment there are socio-psychological mechanisms for the development of interest in problems, pride in skills, the acquisition of ideologies, and the internatization of the motives for the career.

Four major elements for identification are listed: (1) occupational title and its related ideologies, (2) an individual's commitment to spe-

FIGURE XI.6

Career patterns of unskilled workers

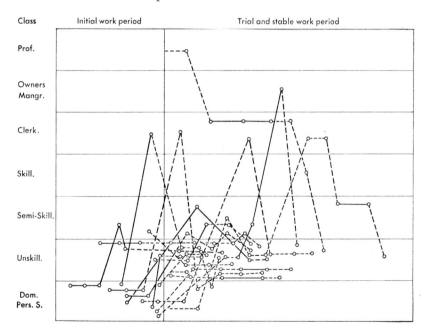

Source: William H. Form and Delbert C. Miller, "Occupational Career Pattern as a Sociological Instrument," *American Journal of Sociology*, 54 (January 1949), 325.

cific tasks, (3) an individual's commitment to particular organizations or positions within institutions, and (4) the importance of one's position for the larger society.

Physiology students manifest strong title identification. They express feelings of commitment to larger groups, devotion to the building of science, and belief in the ultimate value of their work. They view themselves as the knowledge producers on which medical practitioners exist. In short, they are of prior importance to the medical doctors.

Engineers also have a strong identification with the title of their work. But, unlike the physiology students, the engineers identify less with a particular part of their profession.

In sharp contrast, philosophy students reveal little specific identification with their title. Indeed some tend to resist the title. One student, for example, reported that he was hesitant to think of himself as a philosopher and thereby be in the same distinguished company with intellectuals like Plato or Aristotle. Their image is more that of a gen-

FIGURE XI.7
Career patterns of domestic and personal service workers

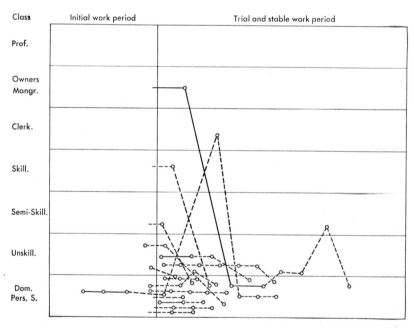

Source: William H. Form and Delbert C. Miller, "Occupational Career Pattern as a Sociological Instrument," *American Journal of Sociology*, 54 (January 1949), 325.

eral intellectual. They desire to be placed in society in such a way that they are free to deal with a broad range of interests, and hence, specific career commitment is difficult to articulate.

In terms of commitment to task the physiology students focused specifically on research and more particularly on a designated methodology for their research. In an opposite manner the engineering students had little focus on specific task. The engineers thought they might work in several specific tasks and in the fullness of their career achieve high positions in management. In effect the engineers had confidence that they would be equal to the several tasks of their profession. Philosophy students continued in their diffuse rather than specific view of their career. As intellectuals they would probably attain the fullness of their career in university life. As a result their specific tasks would be disproportionately teaching. They did not, however, view teaching as a task that is peculiarly that of the philosopher. In short when asked what one would do, the physiologist would respond medical research; the engineer, technical planning of many sorts as well as management; the philosopher, teaching, working with students, but hardly viewing these as integral to the concern of a philosopher and more as a means to the ends of sustenance so that the philosopher can get along about his intellectual work, diffuse and evasive though it might be.

Career perception and social position are related in the views of these graduate students. The physiology students are typically of middle class origins and they view themselves as moving up in society. Similarly, for most of the engineers success in their career would mean moving up in the social hierarchy. The philosophy students by contrast renounce pursuit of social class mobility. By viewing themselves as intellectuals they presume to be different in important respects, among them the matter of social class. They view the position strongly, and do not expect parents or many others to understand their position. They are prepared to break relations with those individuals who do not understand their lack of concern for and devotion to numerous contemporary social values.

The typical graduate student in physiology has not done his undergraduate work in the field. Many of the physiologists originally aspired to careers as physicians. Some felt that they might still switch fields to medicine.[6] But the organization of laboratory and research work in physiology illuminates the importance and fascination of research and discovery. The driving day-and-night devotion to research, research assistanceship work with the in-group, etc., combine to lessen the identification with other occupations and to intensify career identification with physiology.

For engineers the choice of an occupation is made early; certainly in undergraduate school and in some cases even earlier. They are inculcated with the notion that the engineer is a logical thinker, planner and analyzer, one who moves to take opportunities for advancement, and often moves into the higher ranks of management. Advanced study for young engineers is to a greater or lesser degree a matter of improving one's marketability. The advanced study professional engineering student usually also continues his practitioner status; this is to say, he is a professional first and a part-time student second. The career identification is that of professional engineering even when one spends a short part-time or full-time period in advanced study.

Graduate study in philosophy is selected negatively rather than positively, as the least bad among undesirable possibilities. The choice is for the life of the intellectual. They want to be broad-gauged in their intellectual challenge and to range from science through aesthetics to metaphysics and ethics. To maintain the greatest possible range of inquiry and openness of mind involves a career posture that tends to negate the specificities of strong occupational identity and specific occupational organization.

Career identification even in occupations involving such advanced training as college and graduate school varies sharply. In the case of engineering the career identification is strong almost in spite of the school. In the case of physiology career identification is sharply intensified by the course of study. In philosophy the course of study is a mechanism for a way of life and has little to do with career identification other than the sustaining of the way of life. In most occupations that require considerably smaller amounts of training career identification tends to be minimal.

Informal factors. In the absence of regularly identified formal career stages it is widely observed that remarkably clear career experiences are associated with many occupations. In such cases, then, when career is less than clearly a matter of formal stages, it becomes a matter of informal factors supplementing or overriding the formal stages.[7]

Dalton studied the career patterns of 226 individuals as they were selected and promoted through managerial hierarchies. He was concerned with discovering what factors were operative in advancement of individuals in a factory hierarchy. The respondents in the study included all salaried managers in a single plant. They were distributed as 93 first-line foremen, 61 general foremen, 36 superintendents and assistants, and 36 staff heads' assistants and specialists.[8]

The researcher was a participant observer in the plant. Data for the analysis included objective information on age at appointment, years of service, years of education, and current age. In addition specific observations were made on such designated informal factors as member of group organizations, religion, ethnic background, etc.

Dalton found, for example, that most Protestant non-Masons and Catholics agreed that being a Mason was a prerequisite to advancement in the plant. At one point the younger Catholics indicated "ninety-five per cent of management belong to the Masons" and at another point that "Masons are getting too strong in the plant." [9]

Ethnic origin was another informal factor asserted to be a major consideration in career advancement. Analysis of the situation did reveal that a disproportionate number of top positions were given to Anglo-Saxon and German ethnic types. Scandinavian, Italian, Polish, French, Serbo-Croatian, Negro, and Spanish were also found in the sample universe, but seldom in the highest positions.

It was further asserted that membership in the local yacht club provided connections essential to promotion. Analysis of memberships did reveal that 114 officers of the plant were yacht club members. While the proportion of club membership was not high enough to be alarming, interviews and casual comments reveal that efforts to maintain the club's physical plant tended to win favor with higher plant officers.

Political party affiliation was from all suggestions Republican for the top management. The evidence for this included the following: (1) overt statements favoring the Republicans, (2) a practically universal reading of avowedly Republican newspapers, (3) discussion favoring the Democrats was covert and then chiefly among the first-line foremen, and (4) where officers had been political incumbents they were Republicans.[10]

The importance of this study concerning informal factors is to demonstrate their reality; but the author indicates that they in no way mean that natural capacity is considered second to the informal factors.

Implicit prior to the operation of the informal factors are the objective requirements for the various occupational levels. The point of emphasis here is that, given several individuals with nearly equal objective competencies, informal factors will then be used in the final selection. In effect, then, it is found that most formal career stages and informal career factors are universally operative. But the dominance of the formal or the informal varies greatly from one occupation to another. In the urbanized society, with an increasing proportion of white-collar occupations, and with increasing strength of internal occupational organization, the power of formal career stages is expanding. Similarly, both in occupational organization and in societal organization, social norms and social structures are being advanced which inhibit, and in some cases eliminate, informal factors that are overtly discriminatory.

Career success. While career patterns vary from occupation to occupation, definitions of career success also vary. In a study of top level executives and first-line supervisors in industry, business, government, and educational environments it is reported that two sharply differentiated definitions of success operate.[11] For executives success is a matter of change in goals and fluctuations through time. The typical executive responded that when he began his career he was naïve concerning the highest satisfactions and achievements possible. In effect, he played down his original definitions of success and accented new and more ambitious ideas of job satisfaction. As executives started their career they defined success in terms of big money, authority over people, and prestige. They also included in their notion of success conspicuous consumption in the form of a big car, a big house, and a big yacht. As they moved through their careers they shifted their definition to inner satisfactions. They had a feeling of pride and contentment in their accomplishments. They felt a sense of reward when they were capable problem solvers. Their attention turned to satisfactions in the developing of young people, having the courage of their convictions, and realizing that people appreciate their efforts and have confidence in their ability. Indeed, success was more in terms of accomplishment and less in terms of financial security.

Definitions of success for supervisors are considerably more modest and record less change through the course of the career. The American success dream is a part of their ideology. But they soon become aware that their achievements would be of a modest proportion without accelerated social and educational background. The social milieu for them produced a success situation in terms of security, decent wages, liking one's job, being treated well by fellow workers and supervisors, ability to provide educational opportunities for one's children, leading of a happy life away from one's work, employment in a place with physically good working conditions, and having sufficient time away from work for leisure, rest, and recreation.

Executives accepted as part of their career achievement high mobility. Supervisors accepted as a part of their career situation little mobility and the need for achieving in the social space in which they were located.

The breadth of career structures includes a multiplicity of definitions of success. Indeed, as one moves through the career stages of a given occupation the definition of success may change from one stage to the next. In other occupations the definition of career success tends to be stable throughout the entirety of the practitioner experience in the occupation.

Mobility and career. Mobility in occupational career patterns is one of the most basic dimensions. Most of the mobility is movement within categories of occupations, namely, within manual occupations or non-manual occupations. Mobility that involves interchange between manual and non-manual occupations is at a minimum.[12] In the Lipset and Bendix Oakland, California, Labor Market Study it was discovered that for those in manual jobs from 9 to 13 per cent had experienced part of their career in non-manual occupations. On the other hand, those in non-manual work reported a range of 5 to 29 per cent who had spent some of their work period in manual work. The authors caution against broad generalization from the Oakland case study. The area has grown much recently and is characterized by considerable in-migration. Furthermore, the nature of the study design is such that it does not always adequately reveal the number of occupational changes experienced and certainly does not provide an adequate means for estimating the continuing occupational experiences that respondents can anticipate after the study. With these qualifications one may still conclude that most males over age 31 had spent some time in an alternate category. A more detailed study of the data, however, reveal that most of those who cross categories are persons from the non-manual occupations. This is to say, they may experience a period of time as self-employed persons.

There is a less strong tendency for persons who work predominantly in manual occupations to move for short periods of time into non-manual occupations. For example, nearly 70 per cent of business owners spent some proportion of their occupational career in manual work. Eighty-two per cent of the owner white-collar workers have experienced some career time in manual work, etc. Most professionals, on the other hand, have not spent part of their career in manual work. For those occupational persons in manual work less than 50 per cent in any case had experienced part of their career in non-manual occupations.

Mobility between self-employed and employee career experiences has been important in a historic perspective. In the eighteenth century a typical career was a self-employed type. By the second half of the twentieth century the typical career pattern was an employee type. During the nineteenth century and early part of the twentieth century there was a considerable amount of shifting between self-employed and employee career patterns. Still the ideology for self-employment is widely recognized, but the realistic opportunities for self-employment are few indeed. The United States is in fact an employee society.

There is much mobility from one geographical area to another which is related to occupational career patterns. Indeed, career success in many occupations is predicated in part on one's willingness to move geographically. Geographical career mobility patterns are to be widely observed in the salaried professions and in executive occupations.

Career problems. Career problems are noted to vary as one progresses through the several career stages.[13] The situation is illustrated by a study of research scientists in a large government medical organization. Three career stages were held constant: junior investigator, senior investigator, and supervisor. At the junior investigator level of experience career concern primarily focused on job security. At the middle career range of the senior investigator career problems focused on promotion, specifically to supervisor. And at the senior or supervisor investigator level the career problems focused on one's ability to remain in the organization for the duration of one's work experience. In the organization of this occupational environment two types of career orientation were identified. In the first case one could have a professional career orientation. In this situation significant rewards and goals were those of the advancement of science and basic inquiry. The second career orientation was that of organizational focus. In this second situation the practitioner obtained major rewards and goals by climbing up the administrative hierarchy in the government research unit.

This particular occcpational environment is an organization designed for basic research. Most of these practitioners were in careers where professional recognition was of a high order of importance. The criteria for esteem typically included: (1) quality of work, (2) capacity for development, (3) ability to work well with other investigators, (4) general reputation in the field, (5) relative capability in relation to peers, and (6) ability in non-scientific job demands.[14]

In this research environment the variation of career problems at each stage was presumed to be characterized by a different intensity on the basis of felt recognition. Accordingly, respondents were asked about their degree of satisfaction with job security. In the lower ranking positions it was discovered that researchers who felt a high degree of recognition also felt greater job security than those with a lesser degree of recognition. At the top career stage, however, there was no difference between perception of job security and perception of recognition.

The researchers were also asked about their plans to stay on permanently in the government research organization and their high or low felt recognition. At all three career levels those who believed they had a high degree of recognition indicated more frequently that they plan to remain for the duration of their occupation.

A major career problem is related to the practitioner's orientation, namely to his internal focusing on the content of his occupation or to the external focusing on alternative career and occupational opportunities. This differential career orientation was suggested in the above study of researchers in a government organization, when it was asserted that some respondents manifested professional career orientations while others manifested organizational career orientations. Most of the literature focusing on this aspect of career problems refers to the two orientations as being either cosmopolitan or local.[15]

In the cosmopolitan-local career patterns in industry, the cosmopolitans tend to be the kind of experts who find it necessary to "sell" management on their plans. Or put another way, they do not have the power to demand that their ideas be put into effect. They are given recognition, but when promotions come around they do not get the major promotions. In short, the experts prefer to pursue their specialty as an area in and for itself at the expense of becoming company men. As a result they may move from company to company using their expertise and giving little loyalty identification to their organization. The cosmopolitans more often than the locals will tend to be itinerants.

Cosmopolitans in government agencies will again be experts utilizing their technical occupational information in application to particular problems but seeking to maintain the recognition of their fellow experts outside of government employment. To this extent they resist becoming establishment men, and in terms of reference group they seek to secure the high judgment of their professional colleagues in other locations.

In the case of college environments the career problems of cosmopolitans and locals are clear. Cosmopolitans tend to be high publishers. They work for the reduction of teaching loads so that they will have more time for private research, writing, and other personal professional activites. If they have insufficient time for their professional research, they, more than the locals, will tend to find their job less satisfactory. Also they find fewer colleagues in their existing faculty with whom they can share professional interests, show less organizational loyalty, know fewer local faculty members, get more intellectual stimulation from faculty at other colleges, and find salaries at their college less satisfactory than at other colleges. Those manifesting local career patterns will be more interested in participating in tenure decision-making situations, faculty appointments and administration, decisions concerning curricular organization, considerations concerning the college funds, and planning for course and examination scheduling.

Career patterns of cosmopolitans and locals compliment each other and need to be appropriately balanced for any particular organization. The problems associated with these career orientations are most evident when an organization gets an excess of practitioners oriented in either of these directions. A disproportionate number of cosmopolitans in an occupational environment can produce in-fighting and vast disorganization. In juxtaposition, a disproportionate number of locals in an occupational environment can produce excessive stagnation and mediocrity. The challenge, therefore, is to identify the career orientations of practitioners and continually keep them in an appropriate balance. Yet the career orientation of a given occupational practitioner may at one stage in the work life be cosmopolitan, at another stage local. In the work experience of a given practitioner there may from time to time be considerable variation in orientation from cosmopolitan to local. In other cases a given practitioner may go through all of his career stages as either a cosmopolitan or as a local.

Still other variations on the cosmopolitan-local career theme are noted. Particularly in science occupations, research has illustrated that young scientists out of graduate school are often oriented to careers in basic research. They articulate this notion by the belief that men are judged primarily on the basis of their scientific ability rather than on their position. Their ideal is that they are to push back the frontiers of knowledge rather than to make money.[16] Such a career orientation, while recognized as admirable and laudatory from many points of view, is a problem factor in the mundane operation of research and development laboratories. Administrators in scientific research laboratories are faced with communicating the possibility for basic research while solving immediate and practical problems. After a few years on the job, however, researchers develop broader interests. They become more conversant with practical problems and develop an interest in solving them.[17]

In effect, then, it is argued that the problem of career orientation is largely a function of environment. As one experiences more time in practicing research laboratories the problem challenges there become relevant and significant.

Still another variation in the career problem situation is that of the practicing scientist who seeks to move from research investigation work to administration when he feels he is no longer able to compete with young researchers in idea innovation, or when, in some cases, he has exceeded the salary scale for research scientists. In some specific work environments the upper salary scale for research professionals is sharply limited while that of top executives may be double or more than that of the research professionals. In such cases traditional career orientations may become a problem for practitioners who reach the apex of one orientation at any early age. They may then seek to move from the investigator career into the administrator career and move up in a new type of career hierarchy.

Career dimensions focus primarily on the internal aspects of intensely organized occupations. Some of their manifestations are overt and reasonably conspicuous to the ordinary observer, but most career dimensions are covert and only become clearly apparent to the initiated, to those who have gained entry into the social organization of the occupation as such.

PERSONALITY AND LIFE STYLES

The frame of reference in which careers are studied is also a frame of reference for studying personality identity. Identity, even for adults, is not a once gained and continually maintained unchanging matter. By contrast, as one moves through the several stages of a career the adult identity changes with the social position. Personality is shaped by the experiencing of and the movement through careers. And from another point of view changes in careers are illuminations of changes in personalities. For those major categories of occupational practitioners in careers the study of their changes is also a study of personality.[18]

The personality manifestations of individuals in the training socialization career stages are influenced by the nature of their occupation. Professional engineer trainees manifest confident personalities for rational decision-making and managerial enterprises. Professional trainees in philosophy manifest a near-normlessness and considerable rejection of major norms of the urbanized society. The personality manifestation of students in the new sciences is greatly oriented to basic inquiry, while their mature occupational experiences will in most cases demand a more practical orientation.

The personality of individual practitioners is modified as they participate in the recruitment entry phases of their career. Some may manifest the protege personality. Others may manifest the role of the fair-haired boy. Some may be second-bests and keenly aware that in the recruitment process they were accepted only after several more sought after candidates were found to be unavailable.

Then the personality continues to be modified as the practitioner moves into promotion, stagnation, or downgrading. Some by perception and acceptance of formal and informal factors will move up the occupational hierarchy. Accordingly, as previously reported, particularly for executives, one's goals and success ideas—indeed one's personality— must be flexible and accept new orientations commensurate with the promotions. Others may be "frozen" in their particular position, by-passed, promoted "up" to a second-rate position, to be gotten rid of gracefully. One may be removed to a remote location, and even eventually brought back into the hierarchy at a higher position. As the individual is moved through the avenues of a career his personality is manipulated, as it were, by structural shifts. Participating in occupational careers demands a personality posture consistent with mobility.

At the end of moving through occupational careers a final personality adjustment for retirement is pressed upon the actor. Retirement may be abrupt and involve considerable downgrading, as in the case of a taxi dancer who starts at the top when she is young, pretty and shapely. At the end of her career there is little left, and she may be dumped into the category of streetwalker. In other occupations abrupt changes may be thrust upon the practitioner when great physical skill is required, and when, because of chronological aging, that skill is no longer operative. Or there may be in the case of many fee-taking professionals gradual retirement as the practice is transferred over a period of time to a younger protege.

Personality and occupational career patterns are integrally related from the earliest stages of training through the practitioner years and into the finality of retirement.

Life styles. It has been long presumed, and supported by various evidence, that the career life styles of individuals are influenced by religious orientation. The "Protestant ethic" has held widespread currency in Europe and America. Studies of family planning, voting, and more recently Lenski's *The Religious Factor* [19] have all pointed to religion as a significant variable.

More recently a study based on a national cluster sample throws considerable doubt on the continuing differential impact of the Roman Catholic religion on career plans in the United States.[20] The National Opinion Research Center Study was designed to test the following kinds of propositions: (1) There will be a lesser probability of Catholics going to college; (2) There will be a lower probability of Catholic graduates entering graduate school; (3) Catholic graduates will probably choose the arts and sciences with low frequencies when entering graduate school; (4) When Catholics go into the sciences, there will be a lower probability of their entering the physical sciences; (5) Catholics who go into academic fields will opt for research careers with a low frequency; (6) Those Catholics who enter academic fields will be less religious than other Catholics; (7) A disproportionate number of Catholics will tend to choose work in large corporations, desiring security and avoidance of great pressure.[21] The findings generally did not support these hypotheses. In general Catholics were found to proceed in career behavior in a manner similar to those adhering to other religions. Only in the case of over-choice of large corporations was the hypothesis sustained in the Protestant ethic complex, and only in the case of the over-choice of business as a career in the anti-intellectualism complex was the hypothesis sustained. In effect, there was little evidence of anti-intellectualism among Catholic college graduates in career planning. This study showed the main lines of difference to be on a continuum from Jew to Gentile rather than from Protestant to Catholic.

Personality and career are closely related. Style of life and career traditionally have been closely related, but as measured by the factor of religion there is little identifiable influence.

Career patterns, dimensions, and styles of life are found in the most intensely organized occupations. Their particular empirical content varies, however, with the nature of the occupation. In the pages that follow selected examples of occupational career types are reported.

Management career development. Internship as a specific career stage is expanding in importance and utility. By definition internship is a post-college-university level practical experience training program. It is widely known in medicine, and since the mid 1930's management internships for business have been expanding under the efforts of the National Institute of Public Affairs.[22]

The management internship career program reported here is the Junior Management Assistant Program. It was developed in 1948 for government employees in GS-7 through GS-12 ranks.[23] Selection of interns for the program follows a criterion as follows: (1) high general intelligence, (2) resourceful drive for solving problems, (3) objectivity in problem-solving, (4) keen ability to organize one's own affairs and those of others, (5) an expansive and alert mind, (6) objectivity in view of one's self, and (7) firm ideas concerning one's career goals.

The internship training program is designed to facilitate one's progression through the career ladder. It is also designed to expedite shifting from technical skills and abilities to an overview of the big picture in efforts for long-range planning and organization. The program lasts for many months and makes it possible for interns to become understudies to successful executives. The intern is expected to prepare a project thesis in which he argues a plan for formulating and developing management improvements or for carrying out a management improvement plan already formulated. Study of the federal government's intern management program has revealed a wide success on the part of trainees to move upward in their career development and to become effective broad-gauge administrators.[24]

Public health careers. Movement into public health work is particularly instructive in the understanding of careers. The stages in private practice medical careers are widely documented. Movement into public health careers are more deviant than normative. Yet the public health physicians must have generally the same training as the fee-taking practitioners. Their practice is more for community service than handling individual patients on an individual basis. The entry norms into medical training do not move one in the direction of selecting public health as a career. Moreover, if a student entering medical school manifests considerable interest in public health problems, the environment will do little to stimulate and further that interest. In the dominant medical training public health tends to be a marginal field. The pressures in the training environment are against its selection.

A study of career commitment among medical students supports the hypothesis that the public health orientation is a deviant choice, one often resulting from a medical school socialization that is incomplete.[25] In fact the public health choice is so secondary and unencouraged in the medical schools that it is often made as a career commitment after leaving medical school. It is found that the public health choice is most frequently made by physicians who manifest less specific career commitment. Or put another way, the choice for a public health career is frequently the result of receptivity to accidental influences.

In the mainstream of medicine, three major career types are identified.[26] The first career type is colleagueship. This is characterized by practitioners identifying closely with the medical institutions, indeed, with medicine as a community. In this career line success is achieved by moving up in the hospital structure, by close acceptance in the intra-fraternity, and by approval or recognition from one's peers. The second major career pattern is individualistic. For practitioners with this orientation the occupation is essentially a business, and one in which there is strong competition for patients and fees. The ambitions of such doctors are for high income and high status. The third career pattern for medical doctors is a friendship orientation. In this case the practitioner has a primary loyalty to persons rather than to institutions. Such individuals are more altruistic. They are more interested in serving others than in their own aggrandizement. There are many slight variations on these medical careers. They are all broadly condoned in the occupational organization.

Music careers. Career manifestations of professional musicians vary widely from those in the nation's top symphony orchestras to those in jazz. In the study of career it is sufficient to illustrate norms in music as reported from empirical investigation of symphony musicians.[27] The occupation of music is one of several which focuses on aesthetic experiences. In urbanized America these are given a precarious economic reward. In addition, music is much influenced by a dominating management, an apathetic public, a union, and, finally, a recording industry. The occupation is sharply permeated at many points by external forces. Yet the career commitments of many musical artists is of considerable strength.

Career aspirations of symphony musicians focus on achieving positions in one of the nation's fifteen or twenty major symphonies, or indeed, even in one of the top three. Achieving career success to this end is accomplished early if at all. Top orchestras generally accept the norm of hiring new men who are under age 35. Once within the orchestra system the career stages focus on moving up to a position like that of the first violin player. The career stage is to focus on section principles. Finally the ultimate career success involves becoming a self-employed soloist. Opportunities for success in any of these career stages are sharply limited by the very few positions available. As one progresses through the career stages there are some precise distinctions made between the older and the younger members of the orchestras. The younger musicians tend to live in a quasi-Bohemian style and are looked upon as "characters" and "queers" by the older men, who frequently want little or no interaction with them. In the eyes of the younger men their older associates are viewed as defectors from the artistic and professional values. Accordingly, they are of little interest as significant others to the younger men who still aspire to upward mobility.

Teaching careers. Career patterns in public school teaching often follow a more horizontal than vertical line.[28] The young public school teacher entering the first school position is often relegated to the less prestigeful neighborhoods or the smaller communities. Career success in this situation involves movement to major school systems, to larger cities, to the advanced and/or accelerated schools in the systems, and finally to schools that service selected highly homogeneous middle and upper class students.

Vertical career mobility is also a part of the structural system. It usually involves moving out of the teaching positions as such and moving into administrative positions, however. Otherwise the organization of the occupation is established in such a way that one is trained and certified for the primary grades in the elementary system, for the upper elementary grades, for the junior high school specialized subjects, and for the senior high school specialized subjects. The nature of that system involves very little upward or downward mobility from one certification level to another.

Career patterns of college teachers, and in particular Negro college teachers, are set apart from those in the public school system.[29] The career characteristics are clearly illustrated by a study of Negro college teachers in 53 of the 72 Negro colleges. The careers of the Negro college teachers typically start as they work their way through college. They are graduated at the secondary level in most cases from segregated schools that are more poorly equipped and have lower standards than the counterpart white schools. More than half of the Negro teachers have lower social class origins, while only about one-third of their white colleagues have similar origins. Their college education is taken both in Negro and white universities. The Negro colleges recruit their faculty from all parts of the nation, and the Negro practitioners have much higher status in the Negro community than do their white counterparts in the white community. Typically the Negro college instructor is in the upper class of the Negro community.

Moving through the career stages in the Negro college environment involves a considerable amount of informal relations or "pull" with the administration. Moreover administrative functions tend to be given higher value than either research or teaching. Hence moving up the career hierarchy often means moving into administration.

Journalism careers. Occupational careers may be understood from the responses of potential practitioners as is illustrated in the following case concerning journalism. High school students hosted by the Graduate School of Journalism at Columbia University were asked about their views of careers in journalism. Less than 30 per cent of the respondents indicated that they anticipated professional careers in journalism, 60 per cent did not anticipate such an occupation, and a residue of 10 per cent were undecided. Their view of journalism was that it is a low-paying occupation, lacking in prestige, and less than conducive to a good family life. When the responses were limited to those who anticipated careers in journalism the work was viewed as exciting and useful to society. Still it was considered to be a difficult occupation; one compounded with much competition in the avenues of success. The type of journalism careers most desired, for those who anticipated such an occupation, were newspaper work (28 per cent), free-lance writing (21 per cent), magazine journalism (19 per cent), radio and television (9 per cent) and the remainder in a list of miscellaneous related aspects of the occupation.

The stereotyped image of occupational careers, as illustrated in the case of journalism, with difficult family life, relatively low income, and relatively low prestige, have negative impacts on recruitment, and do little to support the internal strength of the occupational organization. Where the image of careers in an occupation is strong the occupational organization is strengthened.

SUMMARY AND IMPLICATIONS

Career patterns are characteristic of many occupations, but far from all of them. As occupational organization increases in strength and dynamics, career patterns are intensified and more precisely articulated.

The conceptual notion of career patterns involves longevity, commitment, specificity of function, and hierarchy. The nature of career involves stages or steps or degrees that are often, but not necessarily, arranged in a hierarchy.

The dimensions of a career range from the process of identification through informal factors, factors of success, mobility, and, finally, problems of perception and organization. Dimensions of career are reciprocally related to personality and to life styles.

The implications of career patterns for occupational structures and institutions are internal strength of organization and external viability. Those occupations for which broadly identifiable career patterns are reported are more powerful and more free-standing than those occupations for which career patterns are fleeting, esoteric, or nonexistent. Career patterns are, in effect, major forms of occupational structures. Many occupational folkways, mores, and, ultimately, institutions are derived from the concrete internal career patterns.

NOTES

1. Harold L. Wilensky, "Work, Careers, and Social Integration," *International Social Science Journal*, 12 (Fall 1960), 543–60; and Robert Dubin, *World of Work* (Englewood Cliffs, N.J.: Prentice-Hall, Inc., 1958), pp. 276ff.
2. William H. Form and Delbert C. Miller, "Occupational Career Pattern as a Sociological Instrument," *American Journal of Sociology*, 54 (January 1949), 317–29; and Harold L. Wilensky, "Sociological Aspects of Leisure," *The International Social Science Journal*, 12 (Fall 1960), 555–8.
3. Form and Miller, "Occupational Career Pattern."
4. Oswald Hall, "The Stages of a Medical Career," *American Journal of Sociology*, 53 (March 1948), 327–36.
5. Howard S. Becker and James W. Carper, "The Development of Identification with an Occupation," *American Journal of Sociology*, LXI (January 1956), 289–98; and Howard S. Becker and James Carper, "The Elements of Identification with an Occupation," *American Sociological Review*, 21 (June 1956), 341–8.
6. Becker and Carper, "The Development of Identification," p. 291.
7. Melville Dalton, "Informal Factors in Career Achievement," *American Journal of Sociology*, LVI (March 1951), 407–15.
8. Ibid. p. 407.
9. Ibid. p. 411.
10. Ibid. p. 414.
11. Roland J. Pellegrin and Charles H. Coates, "Executives and Supervisors: Contrasting Definitions of Career Success," *Administrative Science Quarterly*, 1 (March 1957), 506–17.
12. Seymour M. Lipset and Reinhard Bendix, "Social Mobility and Occupational Career Patterns," *American Journal of Sociology*, LVII (March 1952), 494–504.

13. Barney G. Glaser, "Variations in the Importance of Recognition in Scientists' Careers," *Social Problems*, 10 (Winter 1963), 268–76.
14. Ibid. p. 272.
15. Alvan W. Gouldner, "Cosmopolitans and Locals: Toward an Analysis of Latent Social Roles," *Administrative Science Quarterly*, 2 (December 1957), 281–306; see also Peter M. Blau and W. Richard Scott, *Formal Organization* (San Francisco: Chandler Publishing Co., 1962); Alvan W. Gouldner, *Patterns of Industrial Bureaucracy* (Glencoe: The Free Press, 1954); Leonard Reissman, "A Study of Role Conceptions in Bureaucracy," *Social Forces*, 27 (March 1949), 305–10; and Vernon J. Bentz, "A Study of Leadership in a Liberal Arts College" (Columbus, Ohio: Ohio State University, 1950, mimeo).
16. Simon Marcson, *The Scientist in American Industry* (New York: Harper and Bros., 1960), pp. 65–70.
17. Ibid. p. 66.
18. Howard S. Becker and Anselm L. Strauss, "Careers, Personalities, and Adult Socialization," *American Journal of Sociology*, LXII (November 1956), 253–63.
19. Gerhard Lenski, *The Religious Factor* (Rev. Ed.; New York: Doubleday Anchor Books, Inc., 1963).
20. Andrew M. Greeley, "Influence of the 'Religious Factor' on Career Plans and Occupational Values of College Graduates," *American Journal of Sociology*, 68 (May 1963), 658–71.
21. Ibid. p. 659.
22. Karl E. Stromsem, *The Work of the National Institute of Public Affairs* (Washington, D.C.: National Institute of Public Affairs, 1949); and Mitchell Dreese and Karl E. Stromsem, "Factors Related to Rapidity of Rise of Interns in Federal Service," *Public Personnel Review*, 12 (No. 1, 1951), 31–7.
23. Charles A. Ullmann, "Management Internships in the Federal Government," *Personnel and Guidance Journal*, 36 (May 1958), 612–22.
24. E. Grant Youmans, "Federal Management Intern Career Programs," *Public Personnel Review*, 17 (No. 2, 1956), 71–8.
25. Kurt W. Black, *et al.*, "Public Health as a Career of Medicine: Secondary Choice Within a Profession," *American Sociological Review*, 23 (October 1958), 533–41.
26. Oswald Hall, "Types of Medical Careers," *American Journal of Sociology*, LV (November 1949), 243–53.
27. David L. Westby, "The Career Experience of the Symphony Musician," *Social Forces*, 38 (March 1960), 223–30.
28. Howard S. Becker, "The Career of the Chicago Public School Teacher," *American Journal of Sociology*, LVII (March 1952), 470–77.
29. Daniel C. Thompson, "Career Patterns of Teachers in Negro Colleges," *Social Forces*, 36 (March 1958), 270–76.

SUPPLEMENTARY READINGS

Howard S. Becker and Anselm L. Strauss, "Careers, Personalities, and Adult Socialization," *American Journal of Sociology*, LXII (November 1956), 253–63.

William H. Form and Delbert C. Miller, "Occupational Career Pattern as a Sociological Instrument," *American Journal of Sociology*, 54 (January 1949), 317–29.

Barney G. Glaser, "Variations in the Importance of Recognition in Scientists' Careers," *Social Problems*, 10 (Winter 1963), 268–76.

Andrew M. Greenley, "Influence of the 'Religious Factor' on Career Plans and Occupational Values of College Graduates," *American Journal of Sociology*, 68 (May 1963), 658–71.

Simon Marcson, *The Scientist in American Industry* (New York: Harper and Bros., 1960).

Roland J. Pellegrin and Charles H. Coates, "Executives and Supervisors: Contrasting Definitions of Career Success," *Administrative Science Quarterly*, 1 (March 1957), 506–17.

David L. Westby, "The Career Experience of the Symphony Musician," *Social Forces*, 38 (March 1960), 223–30.

OCCUPATIONAL REMUNERATION AND REWARDS XII

Occupations are engaged in by individuals for multiple types of remuneration. In contemporary Western society occupational men engage in their work for monetary return. Indeed, it is most often observed that the occupation in which one is employed is a means of obtaining money for sustenance. There is also much evidence from the research on the meaning of work which suggests that men are not motivated in their occupations by money alone. Accordingly, in addition to monetary compensation the subject of fringe benefits is treated in this chapter. Occupational rewards are also discovered in the work environment where colleagueship, status, assistants, and other accouterments are meaningful to occupational men in urbanized society. The remuneration for professional, executive, and the union-represented occupations are sufficiently divergent that separate sections in this chapter are devoted to the normative patterns in each of these occupational categories.

MONETARY COMPENSATION

Types of monetary compensation. In the urbanized employee society most occupational men receive wages as their primary type of monetary compensation. In most industrial occupations workers are referred to as wage earners. In these cases they earn a specified amount per hour, the sum total of which is typically paid to them on a weekly basis. Wages are characteristic, therefore, among blue-collar workers. They are the result of rigorously controlled and recorded amount of time worked. With the specifications of contract conditions the amount of the weekly wage will vary directly with the number of hours worked, being less if one does not report for work and being more if one works overtime.

Two major theories are advanced for determining the level of wages. One concerns the classical or Marxian economics point of view, and the second is derived by theorists from Marshall to Keynes. In the Marxian point of view it is held that wages are determined by the cost of subsistence and represent the minimum that is possible for the survival of the workers. From the second point of view it is asserted that wages are determined by the margin of net productivity.

Wages are variously used as incentives in motivating occupational workers. The notion of wage incentive refers to the remuneration of workers in terms of their output on a predetermined formula basis. With standards of performance specified, workers can compete against their own earlier records as well as with fellow workers. The two essentials in wage incentive systems are first, a standard of performance specifications, and second, earnings directly and promptly paid on a formula basis.[1] Wage incentive plans are typically opposed by unions. There is a widespread notion that the wage incentive plans are declining in the United States, but the evidence negates the notion.[2]

The rate of wage becomes the subject of much worker-union negotiation regardless of the difficulty in determining the appropriate level.

The second major type of monetary compensation is salary. Salary is greatly similar to wage, but there are significant subtle differences. Salary is generally paid to the occupational man bi-weekly or monthly. Salary is based on periods of work that are typically longer than the hour. Accordingly, the salaried worker is not accustomed to computing his rate of pay by the hour. This is important from the point of view of status and prestige. The prestige of salary is greater than that of wage. The status of the salary earner is such that normatively he does not punch a time clock; instead he is expected to order his own work time in accordance with the task to which he is assigned or accepted for himself. In most cases those occupations which award their members with salaries are on the upper half of the occupational continuum. They may be professional and executive occupations; certainly they are white-collar occupations.

Salaries, like wages, are arrived at by negotiation and often assured by contract. In some cases salaries are even the subject of union negotiation and contract. Often salaries are a matter of individual negotiation between the employee and the employer.

The commission is another type of monetary compensation. It is characteristically found among many sales workers. Often is it used for opportunity and the stimulation of initiative. Frequently in an occupation where the workers are paid by commission, no minimum amount of money is guaranteed and the maximum earning is limited primarily only by the individual's capacity and initiative. During prime occupational years commissioned remuneration is frequently high. Modified forms of commission often are used to reduce the high and low extremes. In these cases a minimum wage or salary is guaranteed and the commission is only paid on work productivity which exceeds the minimum.

The bonus is another type of monetary compensation. Like the commission it is awarded for extra work and initiative. But unlike commission, the bonus is not necessarily systematically and regularly planned. The enterprising occupational person has no assurance that he will receive a bonus for his extra effort.

Honorariums are specific cash awards given to participants in the idea occupations when their services are requested for some sort of specific consultation or lecture. The honorarium is awarded for the utilization of one's special talent in addition to the undertakings for which one is awarded a salary. Put another way, the honorarium is an honorary payment for professional service for which custom and ideology prohibits the establishing of any set price.

Finally, the stipend may be referred to as a generic monetary compensation. Originally it referred to a small gift or donation. In urbanized society the stipend has become genteel, an aristocratic manner, if you will, of referring to the monetary compensation received by persons in the idea occupations. In a most specific and tangible way the stipend is currently used to refer to the small payments which are made to students of the professions.

In sum, while occupational men work both for money and other rewards it is clear that even the manner by which they receive their monetary compensation is related to the prestige and status systems of which they are a part.

Occupation and income: census statistics. The most recent census (1960) reveals that the median annual earnings of men in the United States ranges from $14,561 for physicians to $550 for newsboys. Between these extremes, or for the 80 per cent of occupations between the tenth and ninetieth percentiles, the median income for males ranges from $7,780 to $2,857.[3]

As generally anticipated, professional occupations tend to be rewarded with the highest monetary incomes. Of the 32 top paid occupations listed by Rutzick, some 26 were in the professional category. It must not be overlooked, however, that some professional occupations are awarded considerably less monetary income—for example, teachers, religious workers, and librarians. Religious workers are listed below paper hangers, librarians below bus drivers, teachers below clerks, and so on.

The low paid professionals typically have a high educational attainment. Much of the reduced monetary income is explained by the high proportion of women in such occupations. Moreover, the work in such occupations is often part-time rather than full-time.

Workers in managerial occupations are often among the highly paid members of the labor force. For example, the self-employed in banking, insurance and real estate, and the salaried in manufacturing are all located among the 10 highest paying occupations. The education of these workers in managerial occupations is typically considerably lower than that of the professionals.

The money income of workers in sales and clerical occupations varies greatly. Those in stock and bond sales and in manufacturing sales are often highly remunerated. Similarly, their educational attainment is high. Other sales and most of the clerical workers are generally found on the lower half of the occupational earnings continuum.

Workers in craft occupations receive high hourly remuneration. On the other hand, their annual income is often middle to low. This is primarily explained by the seasonality of the work experience, or, in any event, by the low number of weeks worked per year. The educational attainment of the craftsmen is, like their earnings, from average to low. With greater education they typically earn more, but their income range is low regardless of their education.

Among workers in operative occupations the income is typically in the lower half of the occupational continuum. The skill requirements are less than those in the crafts, and the educational attainment is not great. The number of weeks worked by operatives is considerably less than 50 per year, and this contributes to their somewhat lower income.

Service workers as a total category are low on the income continuum. Nevertheless, there is a considerable division with protective service workers—firemen, policemen, and sheriffs—considerably above a second category which includes ushers, recreation attendants, and boot-blacks.

Workers in laboring occupations are typically the lowest paid indi-viduals in the labor force. Their job skills are low and ephemeral. Their education is at a minimum level. Among the several types of laborers, those in farm work are at the extreme lower end of the continuum. This is contributed to by the seasonality of the experience in addition to the low skills and low education.

Table XII.1 shows the occupations and earnings of males in the civil-ian labor force for the nation and by regions. For all workers between the ages of 25 and 64 the median annual income was $5,083, and the mean was $5,847. The considerably higher income figure for the mean reflects the extreme in compensation for individual cases. For both me-dian and mean it is clear that the occupational participant receives ad-ditional money for each increment of education, ranging from $4,000 at the elementary level to $5,000 to $6,000 at the high school level, to $7,000 to $9,000 for four years of college and to approximately $8,000 to $11,000 for five years of college or more. In the North and West and in the Southern regions the national pattern also obtains: more education equals more income at all levels. Moreover, at all levels it is reported that the North and West regions award workers higher monetary compensations than does the South.

In Table XII.1 the highest mean income is recorded for managers, officials, and proprietors, at the national level. Regionally, however, professionals in the South receive higher compensation than managers in the South. Among managers and officials more education means more income at all levels and in all regions. The highest monetary re-turn accrues to managers and officials between the ages of 45 and 54, or at an approximate midpoint in their career.

Professionals are the second highest paid occupational category in the nation, and the highest occupational category in the South. Indeed, among professionals more education means more income in all cases. Their highest period of remuneration is between the ages of 45 and 54, or again at approximately the middle point in their career.

Sales workers are the third highest paid occupational category in the nation. In this occupation more education up to college experience contributes to higher earnings. There is some doubt, however, that education beyond four years of college systematically contributes to

TABLE XII.1 Occupation and Earning of Males in the Civilian Labor Force with Earnings in 1959 for the U.S., North and West, and South: 1960

Occupational Categories	U.S.		North and West		South	
	Median	Mean	Median	Mean	Median	Mean
Total						
Total 25 to 64 years old	$5,083	$5,847	$5,372	$6,215	$4,080	$4,905
Elementary	4,474	4,725	4,673	4,930	3,606	3,979
High School	5,541	6,132	5,652	6,266	5,097	5,675
College: 4 years	7,428	9,255	7,634	9,518	6,844	8,503
5 or more	7,968	11,136	8,076	11,205	7,578	10,944
Professional						
Total 25 to 64 years old	6,978	8,762	7,180	8,906	6,492	8,336
Elementary	5,443	5,991	5,735	6,356	4,431	4,881
High School	6,481	7,104	6,597	7,240	6,056	6,636
College: 4 years	7,387	8,309	7,606	8,543	6,746	7,628
5 or more	7,968	11,361	8,088	11,360	7,528	11,485
45 to 54 years old	8,056	10,905	8,295	11,122	7,128	10,321
College: 5 or more years	9,598	16,167	9,776	16,173	8,933	16,548
Managers, officials, and proprietors, except farm						
Total 25 to 64 years old	6,855	9,387	7,190	9,835	6,100	8,269
Elementary	5,525	7,151	5,739	7,486	4,750	6,128
High School	6,750	8,742	6,937	9,004	6,191	8,047
College: 4 years	9,361	13,217	9,537	13,734	8,837	11,801
5 years or more	9,777	13,842	9,881	14,343	9,418	12,372
45 to 54 years old	7,232	10,304	6,976	11,105	6,304	8,936
College: 5 years or more	11,993	18,605	11,050	21,546	11,352	15,018

TABLE XII.1 (cont.)

Occupational Categories	U.S.		North and West		South	
	Median	Mean	Median	Mean	Median	Mean
Sales workers						
Total 25 to 64 years old	$5,747	$6,990	$5,981	$7,329	$5,047	$6,079
Elementary	4,580	5,397	4,817	5,708	3,850	4,509
High School	5,766	6,797	5,955	7,057	5,199	6,047
College: 4 years	7,358	9,324	7,563	9,625	6,818	8,403
5 or more years	7,661	9,450	7,815	9,478	7,141	9,560
55 to 64 years old	5,111	6,612	6,144	7,881	5,512	6,594
College: 5 years or more	7,167	13,210	8,818	11,745	8,125	11,116
Clerical and kindred workers						
Total 25 to 64 years old	5,216	5,372	5,292	5,466	4,923	5,077
Elementary	4,824	4,843	4,930	4,934	4,292	4,456
High School	5,311	5,451	5,378	5,544	5,052	5,145
College: 4 years	5,792	6,323	5,848	6,401	5,668	6,139
5 or more	6,094	6,743	6,025	6,642	6,326	7,028
45 to 54 years old	5,369	5,632	5,185	5,429	5,079	5,310
College: 5 or more	6,876	7,693	6,075	7,689	7,257	8,041
Craftsmen, foremen and kindred workers						
Total 25 to 64 years old	5,444	5,585	5,694	5,898	4,590	4,735
Elementary	5,157	5,245	5,342	5,460	4,350	4,490
High School	5,903	6,091	6,034	6,250	5,399	5,505
College: 4 years	7,421	7,941	7,639	8,133	6,787	7,406
5 or more	8,037	8,688	8,177	8,807	7,367	8,261
45 to 54 years old	5,450	5,615	5,977	6,228	4,905	5,039
College: 5 years or more	8,383	9,380	8,974	9,535	8,002	8,560

TABLE XII.1 (cont.)

Occupational Categories	U.S. Median	U.S. Mean	North and West Median	North and West Mean	South Median	South Mean
Operatives and kindred workers						
Total 25 to 64 years old	$4,465	$4,702	$4,966	$5,040	$3,573	$3,811
Elementary	4,612	4,667	4,801	4,872	3,685	3,880
High School	5,198	5,271	5,316	5,423	4,549	4,669
College: 4 years	5,428	5,852	5,510	5,873	5,116	6,002
5 or more	5,210	5,799	5,350	5,891	4,548	5,326
35 to 44 years old	4,902	4,954	5,210	5,309	3,807	4,031
College: 5 or more	6,006	7,206	6,047	6,984	5,525	5,972
Farmers and farm managers						
Total 25 to 64 years old	2,447	3,348	2,891	3,830	1,655	2,758
Elementary	2,414	3,199	2,612	3,373	1,720	2,583
High School	3,832	5,427	3,804	5,117	2,963	4,217
College: 4 years	4,406	6,988	4,318	6,142	4,635	9,309
5 or more	4,517	6,330	4,382	5,942	—	—
45 to 54 years old	2,381	3,417	2,817	3,854	1,642	2,771
College	4,386	7,642	4,442	7,249	3,982	6,476
Service workers, including private household						
Total 25 to 64 years old	3,799	3,974	4,104	4,251	2,901	3,194
Elementary	3,624	3,757	3,780	3,917	2,910	3,107
High School	4,618	4,689	4,821	4,886	3,782	3,946
College: 4 years	4,873	5,184	5,172	5,499	3,687	4,255
5 or more	4,591	5,399	4,676	5,315	—	—
35 to 44 years old	4,220	4,375	4,550	4,692	2,842	3,204
College: 5 years or more	6,344	7,010	6,389	6,807	3,915	4,786

TABLE XII.1 (cont.)

Occupational Categories	U.S.		North and West		South	
	Median	Mean	Median	Mean	Median	Mean
Laborers, except farm and mine						
Total 25 to 64 years old	$3,504	$3,578	$4,107	$4,092	$2,387	$2,601
Elementary	3,760	3,775	4,054	4,027	2,677	2,842
High School	4,335	4,393	4,534	4,598	3,291	3,537
College: 4 years	4,406	4,990	4,648	5,050	3,787	5,104
5 or more	4,109	4,589	4,157	4,557	—	—
35 to 44 years old	3,690	3,765	4,277	4,294	2,520	2,762
College: 4 years	4,914	5,353	5,213	5,549	4,173	4,262
Farm laborers and foremen						
Total 25 to 64 years old	1,577	1,976	2,226	2,494	1,061	1,424
Elementary	1,986	2,258	2,258	2,461	1,349	1,661
High School	2,772	3,161	2,946	3,303	2,075	2,698
College: 4 years	3,944	4,348	3,886	4,287	2,724	3,725
5 or more	—	—	—	—	—	—
35 to 44 years old	1,673	2,090	2,387	2,667	1,069	1,417
College: 1 to 3 years	4,142	4,647	3,149	3,643	2,247	3,052

Source: U.S. Bureau of the Census, U.S. Census of Population: 1960. Subject Reports. Occupation by Earnings and Education. Final Report PC (2) 7B U.S. Government Printing Office, Washington, D.C., 1963, Tables 1, 2, and 3.

sales workers' high incomes. Unlike the previous two occupational categories reported, sales workers achieved their highest remuneration late in their career, between the ages of 55 and 64.

Completing the white-collar categories, the clerical and kindred workers have a peak average income of some $7,693. The apex of their earning comes in the middle career period of ages 45 to 54. In clerical work more education means more income, but the total range of the income is greatly limited. Indeed, the income of craft workers typically exceeds that of clerical workers.

Craftsmen, foremen, and kindred workers are the most highly compensated category of occupation in the so-called blue-collar ranks. Nationally their highest wage is $9,380. Extensive education contributes to greater earnings for craft workers. Nevertheless, regionally, their highest earning is reached between the ages of 35 and 44.

Operative and kindred workers have a high income slightly less than that of the clerical workers, or approximately $7,000. Extensive education—that is, more than four years of college, does not contribute to continued higher earnings for operative workers. Their skills are often more manual than mental. Accordingly, their highest earning period is reached earlier in their career, between the ages of 35 and 44.

Farmers and farm managers are generalists in an occupational world of specialists. Accordingly, their maximum income is low in comparison to their societal contribution. Nationally their high income is less than $8,000 annually for those who have completed a college education. The peak earnings for farmers and farm managers come in the middle of their career, between the ages of 45 and 54. Few of the farmers and farm managers are college-educated, but those who are receive the top earnings. In sharp contrast to the rest of the nation, college-educated farmers in the Southern region have a peak income annually of more than $9,000. The high income is reached early in their career, between the ages of 30 to 44.

Service workers, laborers except farm, and farm laborers have low mean incomes, ranging from $7,000 to $5,000 to $4,600, respectively. Their high earning periods are early in their careers, between ages 35 and 44. College education is limited among workers in these occupations, but even here the higher education contributes to higher income.

Differential occupational earning by sex has become a major consideration with the increase of women in the labor force. Table XII.2 reports the median earnings by occupation by male and female. For all males the median income is $4,621 and for all females $2,257. On the surface this is a striking difference, but a more penetrating study of Table XII.2 indicates that approximately 70 per cent of the men work between 50 and 52 weeks in the year, while only 50 per cent of the women work so continuously. In short, one of the major explanations for the differential male and female earnings by occupation is the number of weeks worked. Women earn less because they work less. The highest median income is reported for males in the managerial occupations. This is also the occupational category in which the highest proportion of males work between 50 and 52 weeks. Among females those employed in managerial occupations have the second highest earning, and the highest proportion of full-time employment. Male professionals have the second highest median earning and the third highest proportion of male workers employed 50 to 52 weeks. Female professionals have the highest median earning, but one of the lowest proportions of full-time workers.

The highest earnings among males in the labor force are awarded to managers, professionals, craftsmen, and sales workers, in descending order. The highest earnings for females in the labor force are awarded to professionals, managerials, clerical workers, and craft workers.

FRINGE BENEFITS

Fringe benefits have become a dynamic part of American occupational life during the post-World War II years. The notion of "fringe," as it is called, is related to that part of remuneration which does not directly affect wages and hours. From modest beginnings fringe benefits have mushroomed rapidly; currently they constitute a major item in the total labor cost of America's workers.

Fringe benefits may be grouped into several categories. For example, there are those benefits which may be referred to as legally acquired— namely, old age, survivors, and disability insurance, unemployment compensation, workmen's compensation, and related contributions that are now established by law. A second category concerns primarily the area of pensions and related matters. This includes pension plan premiums, life insurance premiums, death benefits, sickness, accident and

TABLE XII.2

Earnings in 1959 of Persons in the Experienced Civilian Labor Force by Occupation and Sex for the United States: 1960

Occupational Categories	Male		Female	
	Median	Per Cent Worked 50 to 52 weeks	Median	Per Cent Worked 50 to 52 weeks
Professional	$6,619	77.4	$3,625	38.0
Managers, officials and proprietors, except farm	6,664	87.4	3,335	75.2
Sales workers	4,987	75.4	1,498	45.4
Craftsmen, foremen and kindred workers	5,204	67.9	2,927	60.6
Clerical and kindred workers	4,785	76.4	3,017	64.4
Operatives and kindred workers	4,299	62.5	2,319	45.1
Farmers and farm managers	2,169	79.4	836	65.0
Service workers	3,310	66.1	1,385	43.4
Private household	1,078	47.0	684	37.7
Laborers, except farm and mine	2,948	44.7	1,872	41.1
Farm laborers and foremen	1,066	42.2	602	19.0
Total	$4,621	68.8	$2,257	50.5

Source: U.S. Bureau of the Census, *U.S. Census of Population: 1960. Detailed Characteristics. U.S. Summary.* Final Report PC (D-11). U.S. Government Printing Office, Washington, D.C., 1963, Table 208.

medical insurance, hospitalization insurance, and a variety of similarly related compensations. A third category of fringe benefits includes payment for time not worked. Examples are paid rest periods, lunch periods, wash-up time, travel time, clothes-change time, get-ready time, paid vacations, and bonuses in lieu of vacations, payments for holidays not worked, and others of a similar nature. Finally, a fourth category of fringe benefits include profit-sharing payments, contributions to employees' thrift plans, Christmas or other special bonuses, employee education expenditures, and related remunerations.[4]

Complete and exact statistics concerning fringe benefits do not exist. This is partly due to the qualitative nature of the subject, which includes such matters as coffee breaks in fringe benefits. Nevertheless, an overview of the fringe benefit situation is provided by U.S. Department of Commerce statistics and by selected studies of the Chamber of Commerce of the United States. In 1965 the Chamber of Commerce completed its tenth study based on reports from 1181 companies. The summary of findings reveal the following profile. Fringe payments range from under 7 per cent to over 70 per cent of company pay rolls. The average 1965 fringe benefit payments constituted approximately 25 per cent of the company's payroll, or $1,502 per year per employee. Fringe benefit payments varied by regions. They were highest in the Northeast, followed by the East North Central, Western, and Southern states. The big companies were noted for paying higher fringe benefits than the smaller firms.[5]

The proportion of fringe benefit payments by type of fringe benefits is reported in Table XII.3. Approximately 8 per cent of the fringe benefit payments went for time not worked, and another 8 per cent for pensions and related conditions; 5 per cent of the fringe benefit payments were taken out by the legally required items, 2.5 per cent of the payments went for lunch and rest periods, and a final nearly 2 per cent were related to profit-sharing plans.

Table XII.4 reports the continual rise in the cost of fringe benefits from 1947 to 1965 for some 84 companies that have continually participated in the Chamber of Commerce surveys. The increase was from 16.1 per cent of the total payroll in 1947 to 28.1 per cent in 1965, or an increase of 75 per cent in 18 years. The data in this table reveal that the two major classes of fringe benefits are first, pension and other agreed-upon payments, and, second, payments for time not worked. In

TABLE XII.3

Fringe Payments by Type of Payment, 1965

Type of Payment	Total, All Companies	Total, All Manufacturing	Total, All Nonmanufacturing
Total fringe payments as per cent of payroll	24.7%	23.6%	26.9%
1. Legally required payments (employer's share only)	4.9	5.3	4.4
a. Old Age, Survivors and Disability Insurance	2.7	2.8	2.6
b. Unemployment Compensation	1.4	1.5	1.0
c. Workmen's Compensation (including estimated cost for self-insured)	0.7	0.9	0.5
d. Railroad Retirement Tax, Railroad Unemployment Insurance, state sickness benefits insurance, etc.[b]	0.1	0.1	0.3
2. Pension and other agreed-upon payments (employer's share only)	7.7	6.7	9.2
a. Pension plan premiums and pension payments not covered by insurance type plan (net)	3.7	2.8	5.5
b. Life insurance premiums, death benefits, sickness, accident and medical-care insurance premiums, hospitalization insurance, etc. (net)	3.0	3.3	2.4
c. Contributions to privately financed unemployment benefit funds	0.1	0.1	(a)
d. Separation or termination pay allowance	0.1	0.1	0.1
e. Discounts on goods and services purchased from company by employees	0.2	0.1	0.3
f. Employee meals furnished by company	0.3	0.1	0.5
g. Miscellaneous payments (compensation payments in excess of legal requirements, payments to needy employees, etc.)	0.3	0.2	0.4

TABLE XII.3 (cont.)

Type of Payment	Total, All Companies	Total, All Manufacturing	Total, All Nonmanufacturing
3. Paid rest periods, lunch periods, wash-up time, travel time, clothes-change time, get-ready time, etc.	2.5	2.7	2.2
4. Payments for time not worked	7.7	7.2	8.7
a. Paid vacations and bonuses in lieu of vacation	4.1	4.2	4.1
b. Payments for holidays not worked	2.6	2.4	2.7
c. Paid sick leave	0.7	0.4	1.4
d. Payments for State or National Guard duty, jury, witness, and voting pay allowances, payments for time lost due to death in family or other personal reasons, etc.	0.3	0.2	0.5
5. Other items	1.9	1.7	2.4
a. Profit-sharing payments	1.1	1.0	1.3
b. Contributions to employee thrift plans	0.1	0.1	0.2
c. Christmas or other special bonuses, service awards, suggestion awards, etc.	0.4	0.4	0.6
d. Employee education expenditures (tuition refunds, etc.)	0.1	(a)	0.1
e. Special wage payments ordered by courts, payments to union stewards, etc.	0.2	0.2	0.2
Total fringe payments as cents per payroll hour	71.5¢	67.6¢	79.0¢
Total fringe payments as dollars per year per employee	$1502	$1437	$1618
Number of companies	1181	775	406

a Less than 0.05%
b Figure shown is considerably less than legal rate, as most reporting companies had only a small proportion of employees covered by tax.
Source: *Fringe Benefits, 1965* (Washington, D.C.: Chamber of Commerce of the United States of America, 1966), p. 9.

TABLE XII.4

Comparison of 1947 and 1965 Fringe Payments for 84 Companies

Item	1947	1949	1951	1953	1955	1957	1959	1961	1963	1965
All Industries (84 Companies)										
1. As per cent of payroll, total	16.1	17.9	19.7	21.2	22.4	24.0	25.2	27.1	28.8	28.1
a. Legally required payments (employer's share only)	2.6	2.5	2.9	2.7	2.9	3.1	3.6	4.2	4.8	4.2
b. Pension and other agreed-upon payments (employer's share only)	5.0	5.9	6.1	7.0	7.5	8.2	8.8	9.3	9.8	9.9
c. Paid rest periods, lunch periods, etc.	1.6	1.8	1.8	2.2	2.4	2.5	2.3	2.5	2.6	2.4
d. Payments for time not worked	5.6	6.3	7.2	7.6	7.7	8.4	8.7	9.2	9.4	9.6
e. Profit-sharing payments, bonuses, etc.	1.3	1.4	1.7	1.7	1.9	1.8	1.8	1.9	2.2	2.0
2. As cents per payroll hour	22.1	27.7	35.5	43.6	48.5	54.4	63.6	73.9	85.8	88.8
3. As dollars per year per employee	450	564	729	901	1004	1147	1292	1530	1806	1874

Source: *Fringe Benefits, 1965* (Washington, D.C.: Chamber of Commerce of the United States of America, 1966), p. 27.

the pension category the increase was from 5.0 per cent of the payroll to 9.9 per cent, and in the payments for time not worked the increase was from 5.6 per cent to 9.6 per cent.

The Bureau of Labor Statistics findings also substantiate the widespread existence and the increasing importance of fringe benefits. In a survey of establishments employing 96 per cent of the nation's production workers in manufacturing, the Bureau found that over 90 per cent reported expenditures for paid leave and welfare plans.[6] The Bureau's survey indicates further that vacations, holidays, group insurance, health and welfare plans, and pensions are now well-established social norms in the occupational world.

The significance of fringe benefits in occupational organization is great, indeed, revolutionary. Traditionally the concept of remuneration has been contingent upon time and condition of work. The recent widespread adoption of fringe benefits now precipitates a condition where few occupational men are not paid for some time when they do not work. As a result of this dramatic change it now becomes necessary to report statistics concerning earnings per hour and, in addition, earnings per hours paid for.

In the organization of industrial compensation it is observed that most fringe benefits are attached to individual employees rather than to the system. In short, this means that the occupational man receives vacations, holidays, pensions, health insurance, etc., with little regard to whether or not he works a 48-hour week, a 40-hour week, or a shorter week. Such a condition in the organization of work contributes to a situation which often makes it cheaper to pay individuals for overtime work than to employ additional workers who will qualify for costly fringe benefits.

HEALTH AND INSURANCE BENEFITS FOR SALARIED EMPLOYEES

The various forms of remuneration of salaried employees reflect both status and material advantage over other types of employees. Anderson and Hahn report that salaried employees, for example, have greater health and insurance coverage fringe benefits than production workers. Nonetheless, unlike production workers, the salaried employees typically pay part of their fringe benefit cost.[7] The basic coverage concerning health benefits, hospital, surgical, and medical are typically the same for both production and salaried workers. The difference comes in the greater comprehensiveness of the fringe benefits for the salaried workers.

Typically, the health insurance programs for the salaried workers provide multiple protection for active and retired employees and their dependents. The cost of this extended comprehensive coverage is considerable. Only one out of seven employers paid the entire cost for active workers. In the case of retired workers the employer more frequently paid the entire cost.

Salaried employees typically have life insurance benefits that are considerably higher than those awarded to production workers. As in the other additional coverages for salaried workers, the employee is generally expected to make some partial contribution to the life insurance coverage.

This pattern for more comprehensive than average extended coverages for the salaried employee is also reported for surgical benefits, basic medical benefits, major medical benefits, maternity benefits, and the entire range of such benefits for the retired employees.

PAID VACATIONS AND HOLIDAYS

Vacations with pay began to become a subject for collective bargaining agreement in the 1940's, but the experience was not widespread. Where it did occur the typical vacation period was one week. By 1957 the paid vacation was typical in collective bargaining, and 91 per cent of the workers had such a benefit. Often the time of vacation was increased from one to three weeks. The trend for increasing paid vacations has continued. By the 1960's it was widespread both for production and office workers, with office workers typically having a longer period of vacation than plant workers. It was estimated, indeed, that in 1960 the total vacation time amounted to between 96 and 100 million vacation weeks.[8] In sum this meant that approximately 85 per cent of all nonagricultural wage and salary workers had a paid vacation as a fringe benefit.

The widespread acceptance of paid holidays is of even more recent origin than of paid vacations. Typically, hourly rated employees were not given paid vacations prior to World War II. The National War Labor Board allowed six paid holidays to be recognized in wage stabilization agreements. Nevertheless, the Bureau of Labor Statistics reported that in 1943 a majority of workers in manufacturing, construction, and mining were given time off without pay for holidays. This situation has changed sharply. In 1958 a survey showed that over 12 per cent of employees were without paid holiday fringe benefits.[9]

The number of paid holidays is increasing along with the increasing number of workers with such coverage. In the 1940's six holidays were recognized, and by the 1960's the average among office workers was 7.8 and among production employees 7.0.[10]

PROFIT-SHARING

Profit-sharing is another form of benefit which some workers receive. It is usually defined as an arrangement whereby employees receive a share, often fixed in advance, of the profits, or, from another point of view, a procedure whereby an employer makes payments to employees, at a specified rate, in monetary sums based on the profits of the business.[11]

The experience of profit-sharing is not of recent origin. It has been in existence for approximately a century and a half. Profit-sharing is often intended to be an incentive for workers. It is, however, not without its complications. At any time when there must be a reduction in the profit-shared bonuses the possibility of employee discontent is greatly increased. In the 1960's more than 30,000 profit-sharing plans were reported. The number of workers actually covered in such plans, however, is often limited to high ranking or key employees.[12] It is traditional for profit-sharing to be more widespread among salaried employees than among wage earners. Most profit-sharing is observed to take place in those industries where the return on investment is consistently high. Profit-sharing plans also are found dispropotionately among those businesses with high labor turnover costs. In these cases the plan often it used as a mechanism for retaining key personnel. Profit-sharing plans are generally not widely found where there is seasonal instability in the labor force, nor are they found in those places where labor unionization is strongest. Unions have typically offered opposition to profit-sharing schemes. In effect, it is argued that employers often used profit-sharing devices as a means of detouring unionization. It is further pointed out by union officials that profit-sharing plans enable management to manipulate the level of profit in the favor of top management and at the expense of the wage worker.[13]

Profit-sharing plans are also questioned by stockholders. The assertion is that such profits would ordinarily go to the stockholders rather than be distributed to the employees.[14] The evidence is far from complete concerning this type of question. There is, however, some considerable suggestion that the result of profit-sharing motivation is sufficient to increase the total return without loss to shareholders.

Profit-sharing continues to be a significant fringe benefit to occupational men regardless of its relative advantages and disadvantages to the total systems of production.

WORK ENVIRONMENTAL REWARDS

Environmental rewards are in most cases of a relatively intangible character. Yet in the urbanized society they are significant in terms of status and prestige. The types of environmental rewards range from colleague relationships, scientific equipment, status and prestige, assistants and accouterments, and general physical conditions.

Colleague relationships as remuneration. Relationships among colleagues may constitute one of the most important conditions of work among idea people. Key occupational men may be attracted to particular centers as places of work on the basis of the production and reputation of related workers already located at that center. The possibility of a stimulating colleagueship with individuals who are concerned with an area of inquiry related to one's own may well exceed the importance of a physical environment and of monetary remunerations. In short, an employer may be able to offer the most favorable monetary compensation and the most satisfactory physical environment. But the lone or solitary worker in such a favorable environment might still seek the interactional benefit of a high level colleagueship. The working conditions which men seek, particularly those at the innovative level, are often more nonmaterial than material. Greater importance may be placed on colleagueship or potential colleagueship than on other more tangible and immediate material rewards.

Technical equipment. In a technological and scientific age the equipment with which many laboratories are supplied constitute significant fringe benefits for workers. Workers may move horizontally from one position to another at what appears to be the same rank and status, but the workers' move in such a case is motivated primarily by a desire for better tools and equipment to facilitate work, production, and creativity. Research and development laboratories have come to constitute vitally important places of work for many high level occupations. In such occupations, vast amounts of equipment, money for acquisition of new equipment, and special laboratories and assistants especially provided for creating and assembling new equipment may constitute a sufficient fringe benefit to move workers from one location and one position to another. For example, some historically famous research laboratories and universities may be unable to provide their staffs with the most advanced research equipment because of physical building limitations or budgets. New and more well-equipped commercial laboratories and/or government laboratories, which have a reputation for giving their personnel a lesser amount of freedom concerning research directions, may be able to recruit some of the most capable personnel from those positions which are less adequately provided for in terms of technical equipment. The type, quality, and extent of technological equipment—even that essential to the successful performance of many occupations—often remains in effect a fringe benefit.

Status and prestige rewards. Hierarchical ranking of positions within occupations is widespread in the urbanized societies. Each of the hierarchical positions constitutes a status which is superior or inferior to other statuses. The signs and symbols of the various statuses may be rigorously specified and highly tangible. Informally the difference and/or respect which may be accorded the signs and symbols of status may vary considerably.

Status among wage workers is indicated by their respective hourly wages, dirtiness or cleanliness of the job, seniority in the position, etc. Status ranks are specified in state and civil service jobs. Salary, duration, and proficiency are among the key factors utilized as the status distinctions. In libraries, hospitals, and law firms, one finds status symbols from assistants to senior librarians, from interns to general practitioners to specialists; from nurse's aids to registered nurses to graduate nurses; from junior partner to full partner. Similarly in universities, military establishments, and religious bodies hierarchies are typically established. Among faculties the ranks are clear, ranging from instructor to assistant professor to associate professor and to professor, and, in recent cases, to research professor and/or distinguished professor. The military ranks from the enlisted individual to the commissioned officer and to the higher ranking generals and admirals are clear. In some religious bodies the rankings from parish priest to bishops, archbishops, and higher orders are organizationally established.

Associated with the achievement of each higher status in the occupation is a differential treatment that is a special occupational reward. The status rewards in occupations become of more intense significance in a society where the middle class is broad and where the monetary remuneration among the many occupations is extremely narrow. With reduction in number of captains of industry and systematic efforts for the raising of workers from the bare subsistence level, historically important major differential rewards for occupations are being eradicated. Along with the shift in social organization the importance of status rewards is greatly increased. Subtle variations in the prestige of occupations also become of increasing importance when other more tangible differential occupational rewards are reduced. For example, the prestige of white-collar work over blue-collar work is greatly magnified in the tendency to reduce the differential monetary reward for these categories of workers. The prestige of salaried workers over wage earners is similarly magnified. The prestige of innovative work over assembly-line work is extended in an urbanized society where many traditional mechanisms of individualism are contracted, if not eliminated. These and many other dimensions of prestige in occupations are increasing in their magnitude as reward mechanisms.

Assistants and accouterments as rewards. For many occupational men to function at the highest level of efficiency and creativity the work environment requires many assistants in addition to a favorable set of circumstances for themselves. In most executive and professional occupations the holders of senior positions are as effective or as limited as the range and service of their assistants are effective. Assistants in executive and managerial occupations may include technical experts, secretarial and clerical personnel, and personal servants. In a professional research laboratory the assistants may be students, or they may be less trained semiprofessionals whose time is available for the services required by senior reseachers. In the research environment assistants may work in technical areas, in supporting areas—for example, libraries and other data collection centers—or they may work in publication production ranging from stenographic services to manuscript editing.

Some assistants may be lower ranking occupational workers whose job is regular and service-oriented. In such cases the assistant typically works for the general management or the research laboratory rather than for individual superiors. A more prestigeful fringe benefit is found in those cases where individual assistants are assigned for major portions of their time to work for specific occupational superiors in a range of tasks which are organizationally at the discretion of the superiors.

Among the special accouterments are the provision of facilities, practitioner time, and recognition for the senior administrator or researcher to engage in basic or pioneering inquiry of his own choosing which may or may not have any considerable relation to the general hours managerial or research enterprise. In some scientific research laboratories, for example, high level researchers are attracted in part on the basis that a certain proportion of their time will be free for using the resources and facilities of the laboratory in their own esoteric investigations without question or direction from administrators.

Team research is growing in its importance and facilitated in its operation by assistance from both junior and senior professionals in different but related areas of inquiry. The possibility of such assistance as an organized and recognized part of the work environment contributes greatly to the attractiveness of a situation.

Physical facilities as a reward. Physical facilities of the place of work have become widespread subjects of negotiation from salaried employees to wage workers. At the salaried level physical facilities in the work place are often matters of status. The importance of top executives, junior executives, and lower supporting personnel may be made overtly visible by their physical offices. The senior executive's office may be large, expensively furnished, thickly carpeted, decorated with planters, and supplied with silver drinking urns, etc.[15] The size of the office space and the quality of the furnishings for each lower rank may be sufficiently reduced to remind the worker of his status, and to announce to those who call in the different offices the status of their place of call.

Physical surroundings may include such technical items as the amount of light, the color of walls in offices and factories, the presence or absence of music, the provision of abundant washrooms and water closets, the maintenance of adequate lunchroom and dining facilities, or the support of appropriate recreation facilities. The precise meaning of such physical conditions continues to be the subject of a considerable amount of research.

PROFESSIONAL REMUNERATION

The monetary pay of professionals is generally either by fee-taking or by salary. Physicians and attorneys are typically paid by the charge of individual fees for their individual services. Professors, teachers, clergymen, librarians, indeed, most professionals, are paid by salary. The monetary compensation of the professionals is the second highest in the nation; it is exceeded only by those in the managerial and proprietor category. In spite of this second highest statistical ranking the compensation of most professionals is sufficiently low to position them firmly within the middle class to the extent that income is a determinant of social class position. Moreover, it already has been pointed out that the compensation of professionals ranges greatly. Some have an income which considerably exceeds the typical income of individuals in the managerial proprietor category. Others have incomes sufficiently low as to place them beneath many craft and operative workers.

Nonmonetary remuneration and rewards are probably more important for most professionals than their money earning power. This is not intended to overemphasize the altruism often attributed to professionals. Regardless of the presence or absence of an altruistic motivation, the status of professional and its many associated conditions constitute an immeasurable remuneration for such an occupation in an urbanized society. The importance of this remuneration is clearly evident by the striving of many lesser occupations for the achievement of professional status. In a middle class society where monetary return is widely leveled the more intangible designation of "professional" takes on an enhanced, often exaggerated significance.

The remuneration of professionals involves several special situations. The notion of professional implies at least a generalized commitment to altruism. The professional is concerned with his occupation as a means for contributing to the condition of society as well as providing him with the means for subsistence. The professional views his service as a high calling. Related to both of these is an orientation away from, if not against, unionization and conflict negotiation of salary stipend compensations. Accordingly, as wage workers have negotiated and gone on strike for higher salaries, along with a multitude of other benefits, the monetary compensation of professionals is often comparatively reduced.

The money compensation of professionals, furthermore, is often curiously, indeed, inequitably, distributed among the fellow practitioners. In part this is related to, if not justified by, changes in technology and the body of knowledge upon which practitioners must be prepared to draw. This is dramatically illustrated by observing that engineers fifteen years ago were designing piston engines, about a decade ago were designing jet planes, a half a dozen years ago were concerned with missile construction, and now most recently are directing the design of space satellites.[16] With these great changes in the demands on engineers the body of knowledge and the retooling of practitioners cannot be overestimated. The younger and more recently trained engineers are frequently more capable of achieving and learning the new bodies of knowledge prerequisite for the contemporary demands. Such situations often result in the deterioration of the older engineers' salaries in comparison to their younger colleagues. Nowhere is the body of knowledge of occupational workers more critical than in the professions. In a society that supports professionals only because of the special services they render rather than by ideological commitment, the younger, more avant garde, trained practitioners are at a disproportionate advantage in salary competition.

EXECUTIVE COMPENSATION

Workers in the managerial-proprietory category are awarded with the highest median remuneration in the nation. Executives, within the broader category, are among the highest paid salaried employees. In addition to their salary, which constitutes a major dimension of their remuneration, executives are found to be among the recipients of the most lavish fringe benefits.[17] In addition, executives receive deferred compensation. They may receive stock options, or qualified options as special remunerative incentives. The deferred benefits have real advantages for older executives whose day-to-day living costs are reduced. For younger executives, often the junior executives, the deferred rewards offer little positive incentive. The young junior executive is often at the peak of his child-raising family experience, and immediate income rather than deferred remuneration is most attractive.

The compensation of executives is further complicated by promotion situations. In some cases policies of promotion from within are followed and in other firms the policy of bringing in outsiders for top positions is followed. In either event the new executive is most often paid more than his predecessors.[18] In short, the condition is that executive costs continually increase due to social structural and occupational expectations which may or may not be consistent with their occupational functions.

The criteria for executive pay is often observed to be far from systematic. Generally speaking, executives are assumed to have more responsibility and more weighty decisions to make. Accordingly, their several kinds of remuneration are greater than those of the workers beneath them. Moreover, executives are often ranked hierarchically and the organizational plan calls for clearly demarcated differences in salary within the several ranks. The consideration for differential executive pay seldom takes in an adequate appreciation of their differential social organizational space. In short, some executives may have their work environment greatly supplemented by far more extensive use of assistants and specialists than others. In some cases, then, the total cost of the executive operation for the assistants and specialists may be far greater than for the executive himself. Nevertheless the ideology prevails that the executive should be the recipient of a high and differential reward. The high cost of executive sustainment in recent years is leading to new and penetrating inquiry into possible criteria for their remuneration.[19]

UNION AND BARGAINING

Union representation of workers constitutes a third and in several ways most distinctive set of norms in the whole arena of occupational remuneration and rewards. In the main union representation applies to wage workers, production workers, or blue-collar workers. Important exceptions, however, exist, and in some cases white-collar and professional workers are represented by unions as well.

Collective bargaining is one of the major functions of unions.[20] Collective bargaining is a mechanism or tactic which labor uses in its negotiation with management. The intent of bargaining negotiations is to increase wages, reduce hours worked, and expand and intensify a full range of fringe benefits. About half of the nation's employed workers are covered by some type of agreements which result from collective bargaining. In some specific industries the number of workers covered by collective bargaining negotiation reaches approximately 90 per cent.[21] Although the specific intent of collective bargaining is multifocused, the primary goal is most frequently to increase the level of wages. Union bargaining is most frequently oriented to hourly wage rate increases, but in some cases support is also given to incentive systems.

Details of collective bargaining, after hourly wage rates are accepted, turn to the number of hours worked, job tenure, and policies of seniority. A guaranteed annual wage is another goal toward which the union bargaining teams work. Efforts are also made to specify the number of workers to be employed in various kinds of units in the industrial operation. Matters concerning the conditions of work are related to safety provisions, clean laboratories, adequate lighting and ventilation, sufficient washrooms and dressing rooms, and a variety of related fringe benefits.

The norms of collective bargaining are largely established by government acts. Even such legislation as the Taft-Hartley Act, which outlawed practices like the closed shop, in effect assured the right of unions to bargain.

SUMMARY AND IMPLICATIONS

Occupational remunerations and rewards include monetary compensation, multiple fringe benefits, and a variety of work environments. The most widely recognized remuneration is monetary. Historically money has been by far the most significant aspect of gain in occupational work. With the ubiquity of urbanized society, differential monetary rewards in occupations are greatly leveled. In such a condition of social organization and occupational organization fringe benefits and work environments become most distinguishing and significant as occupational remunerations and rewards. The great and abiding difference in occupations are the status and prestige differential rewards.

Social benefits are increasingly provided by governments. Governments, particularly the Federal Government, devote more policy and funds to the provision of basic subsistence income for all the people. Occupations continue to be the major mechanism by which individuals earn a living. From the professions to the unskilled jobs, people work to make money. But with societally leveled incomes, the subtleties of remuneration are more important for understanding occupations than their cash rewards. The remuneration in differential work environments, differential status, differential fringe benefits are all of major importance for occupational organization. These subtle occupational rewards go beyond the boundary of the work. The remunerative-reward occupational norms have important impacts on the society as a whole.

NOTES

1. William B. Wolf, *Wage Incentives as a Marginal Tool* (New York: Columbia University Press, 1957), p. 5. See also Garth L. Mangum, "Are Wage Incentives becoming Obsolete?" *Industrial Relations*, 2 (October 1962), 73–96.
2. Myron W. Lewis, "Conservation of Manpower by the Use of Wage Incentives," paper presented before Spring Mechanical Engineering Conference, American Society of Engineers—Engineers Society of Western Pennsylvania, March 19, 1952; Joseph M. Sherman, "Incentives Pay in American Industry, 1945–46," *Monthly Labor Review*, LXV (November 1947), 335–8; and L. Earl Lewis, "Extent of Incentive Pay in Manufacturing," *Monthly Labor Review*, LXXXIII (May 1960), 461–3.
3. Max A. Rutzick, "A Ranking of U.S. Occupations by Earnings," *Monthly Labor Review*, 88 (March 1965), 249–55.
4. Gordon F. Bloom and Herbert R. Northrup, *Economics of Labor Relations* (5th Ed.; Homewood, Ill.: Richard D. Irwin, Inc., 1965), pp. 209–10; and *Fringe Benefits*, 1963 (Washington, D.C.: Chamber of Commerce of the United States of America, 1964), pp. 4–32.
5. *Fringe Benefits*, 1963, p. 5.
6. Enzo A. Puglisi, "Supplementary Remuneration for Factory Workers, 1959," *Monthly Labor Review*, 85 (January 1962), 31.
7. Arne H. Anderson and William F. Hahn, "Health and Insurance Benefits for Salaried Employees," *Monthly Labor Review*, 86 (November 1963), 1266–74.
8. Peter Henle, "Recent Growth of Paid Leisure for U.S. Workers," *Monthly Labor Review*, 85 (March 1962), 249–57.
9. "Vacations and Holiday Provisions in Union Agreements," *Monthly Labor Review*, 66 (May 1943), 929; and "Paid Holidays in Major Contracts, 1958," *Monthly Labor Review*, 82 (January 1959), 26–32.
10. Henle, "Recent Growth of Paid Leisure," p. 254.
11. J. J. Jehring and B. L. Metzger, *The Stockholder and Employee Profit Sharing* (Evanston, Ill.: Profit Sharing Research Foundation, 1960), pp. 12–13.
12. Bloom and Northrup, *Economics of Labor Relations*, p. 201; and B. L. Metzger, *Profit Sharing and Perspective* (Evanston, Ill.: Profit Sharing Research Foundation, 1964).

13. Bloom and Northrup, *Economics of Labor Relations*, p. 202.
14. Jehring and Metzger, *Stockholder and Employee Profit Sharing*, p. 12.
15. Eric Larrabee, "The Wreck of the Status System," *Horizon*, 2 (November 1959), 21–5.
16. W. Lee Hansen, "Professional Engineers: Salary Structure Problems," *Industrial Relations*, 2 (May 1963), 33–44.
17. Arch Patton, "Executive Compensation by 1970," *Harvard Business Review*, 42 (September–October 1964), 137–46.
18. Ibid. p. 139.
19. Elliott Jacques, "Objective Measures for Paid Differentials," *Harvard Business Review*, 40 (January–February 1962), 133–8; and Herbert A. Simon, "The Compensation of Executives," *Sociometry*, 20 (March 1957), 32–5.
20. Eugene V. Schneider, *Industrial Sociology* (New York: McGraw-Hill Book Co., Inc., 1957), chap. 13.
21. Florence Patterson, *American Labor Unions* (New York: Harper and Bros., 1952), pp. 164–5.

SUPPLEMENTARY READINGS

Arne H. Anderson and William F. Hahn, "Health and Insurance Benefits for Salaried Employees," *Monthly Labor Review*, 86 (November 1963), 1266–74.
W. Lee Hansen, "Professional Engineers: Salary Structure Problems," *Industrial Relations*, 2 (May 1963), 33–44.
Peter Henle, "Recent Growth of Paid Leisure for U.S. Workers," *Monthly Labor Review*, 85 (March 1962), 249–57.
Elliott Jacques, "Objective Measures for Paid Differentials," *Harvard Business Review*, 40 (January–February 1962), 133–8.
L. Earl Lewis, "Extent of Incentive Pay in Manufacturing," *Monthly Labor Review*, 83 (May 1960), 461–3.

OCCUPATIONAL CONTROLS OF WORK BEHAVIOR XIII

There are major occupational structures and institutions which have to do with the control of practitioners in their respective occupations. Occupational institutions guide one in aspiring to an occupation, in preparing for an occupation, in entering an occupation, in progressing through the career stages, in obtaining remuneration, and in both overt and covert practitioner behavior. Much of the strength and viability of occupations are revealed in their organizational ability to control practitioner behavior. Some occupations, in great displays of strength, are able to exercise extensive control over the manner in which practitioners relate to one another and over the manner in which they relate to clientele. The military hierarchy is a widely recognized example of an occupation controlling the interactional relationships between and among its members. Occupational hierarchies in the academic profession are more for external relation to clients, while practitioners, almost regardless of their position in the hierarchy, relate to each other as equals, if not as colleagues. The legal profession is a convenient example of control of practitioners in relation to clients. Matters of advertising, referral, and fees as related to clients are all more rather than less regulated by the internal organization of the occupation.

Occupational controls are essentially of two types: direct and indirect. The direct are the most obvious, easily discernible by both practitioners and the general public. The indirect are less easily identifiable by the general public, and frequently less than precise for practitioners. In the social organizational nature of the case, however, the indirect controls are often more persuasive than the direct ones.

There are many types of direct occupational controls on worker behavior. Major among them are rules, licensing, seniority, and unionization.

Rules: positive and negative. Rules are widespread in the occupational organization of workers in urbanized industrial societies. Their organizational significance is to render complex work situations predictable. Workers know what is expected of them, and those who order their work environment know what they can expect from the workers. This reference is made in terms of formal more than informal rules. Moreover, rules are specific constructs of the occupation itself or precipitated by the environment in which the occupation is located. Put another way, rules must be established, articulated, communicated, and ultimately enforced.[1] Rules, in short, are formal, establishing rights, privileges, and expectancies.

Positive rules are extremely numerous. They are partly a function of the rapid job of changing of workers and partly a function of the changing demands of work situations. As workers move from job to job and as older technologies expire and new ones replace them rules provide order and stability in occupations.

Dubin cites several specific reasons for the enumeration of rules in the control of workers. First is the high turnover of practitioners. As workers change jobs on the average every 3 to 5 years, it becomes more orderly both in the process of production and in the integration of workers to establish their procedures by rules. Accordingly, in many middle range and lower level occupational roles the expected behavior of workers varies little from one practitioner to another. Even in advanced professional and executive work roles, rules establish the periphery within which innovation and creativity are acceptable. To innovate, create, or direct may be major rule demands, but ethical limits may be implied or specifically specified. Therefore as top management changes from practitioner to practitioner the rules still establish broadly the rightful limit of such innovation.

A second reason for the promulgation of rules is the high degree of internal occupational mobility.[2] For example, occupational rules specify and govern the change from apprenticeship to master craftsman. Occupational rules differentiate less precisely the roles of teachers and administrators in elementary and secondary schools. Accordingly, in this occupation the administrator may be in an office part of the time and in a classroom part of the time. Or, by contrast, a classroom teacher may be freed from some instructional duties and be given specific administrative responsibilities. With such a fragmented rule structure it is difficult for teachers and administrators to know precisely who they are.

A third reason for rule proliferation is the bureaucratic environment in which many occupations are located. In the contractual, secondary, bureaucratic society, an occupational man is theoretically judged a success or a failure in terms of an objective evaluation of his performance. In order to assure the operation of such impartial judging it is necessary to have minute rule specification recognized in advance by all workers and agreed to by them if they are to be effective competitors and producers in their occupational situations.

A fourth reason for positive rule structures in occupations is that they free administrators from being forced to make decisions of favoritism and partiality. In short, the rules not only enable the workers to know who they are, but they establish rights and privileges for the hierarchy in the occupation as well. Compliance with occupational rules is more easily enforceable and administration made more equitable when most extenuating circumstances are by definition eliminated in advance. The avoidance of personal discrimination and the increasing of individual respect is maximized with a widely understood rule structure.

Negative rules establish prohibitions of various types. Their impact is frequently direct, if not dramatic, on occupational behavior. Often, however, they are external to the occupational organization, being more frequently precipitated by the environment in which the occupation is located. Many ordinances by local or regional governments providing health standards, safety standards, physical appearance standards, etc., infringe upon occupational behavior, and are beyond the direct control of practitioners. Many operative and unskilled occupations experience such loose internal organization that their workers are from time to time taken advantage of until negative rules are established from outside the occupation. The sweat-shop situations, poor physical working conditions, and long hours of work often have been more abruptly controlled by negative rules from outside of the occupation than by positive rules established internally. In the more advanced and professional types of occupations the posture of internal organization is more offensive than defensive. Accordingly, these strong occupations promulgate many positive rules which make demands on their employers and modify their work environments to their advantage, and often to some short-range disadvantage for the environment.

Licensing. Licensing is one of the most tangible occupational control devices.[3] It is formalized in ordinances that are direct and contractual. By the nature of the case licenses are provided and/or required by governments or agencies. But further, in the nature of the case, the criteria for establishing licensing and for evaluating practitioners is usually organized by fellow practitioners and then given the legal approval of government agencies. In some few cases government agencies tend to assess practitioner proficiencies, but in most cases governments call boards of practitioners to advise and direct in the functions of licensing.[4] Norms of licensing are old; they originally grew out of medieval guild organization. Although guilds as such never were widely established in the United States their pattern of having been chartered, certified, and assured the right of practice by political authorities has become a part of the social milieu of occupational organization in the urbanized society. This is illustrated by the certification of law in more than half of the colonial governments in what is now the United States. With the establishing of the nation, licensing continued, expanded some, and then contracted to reach an all-time low in the early part of the nineteenth century. Following the Civil War, urbanization structures in the society were accelerated. They were accompanied by secondary contractual relations, and as a part of this general social configuration a renewal and a revitalizing of licensing for occupations were developed.

By the middle of the twentieth century some 75 occupations carried licensing certification by one or more states.[5] In the 1870's attorneys and teachers were the occupations most frequently licensed. The range of occupations licensed tends to show a concentration in the professions with a few skilled and service occupations also being included.

Often it is possible to distinguish licensing as imposed or induced. Imposed licensing usually brings government pressure on irregular practices. Frequently it is in response to unfair or criminal behavior, and is an attempt to protect clients from occupational practitioners. But imposed licensing from time to time has had recognizable advantages for the occupation internally. To the extent that it avoids doubt in the mind of the public and casts esteem, if not prestige, on the behavior of practitioners, it is a desirable social structure in the developing of strength in the occupation as such. Accordingly, most occupations in recent years have induced licensing as a part of their internal organization and aggrandizement. Indeed, in the case of some occupational practitioners licensing is viewed as one of the effective steps in the direction of increasing professionalization. To be a licensed practitioner is almost universally a mark of acceptability, if not of distinction.

Seniority. Many specific occupational structures have been developed as practitioners have attempted to protect themselves against arbitrary policies of management.[6] Developing norms of seniority has constituted one of the most powerful elements in the limitation of managerial authority and the protecting of rights of occupational workers.

The importance of seniority is revealed in a study of 326,000 employees in 8 organizations in the Western states. The workers were in federal employment, manufacturing, unionized and nonunionized firms, etc.[7]

Seniority was initially developed and used as a strong weapon for defending the rights of workers. In the initial days of industrialization and strong occupational development this was a most effective defensive structure. But in the second half of the twentieth century, with many stronger occupations, and with a rapidly accelerating and changing technology, many of the implications of seniority are less than essential in occupational control. As modern occupational practitioners have multiple forms of liability in representing themselves to management they tend in most cases not to favor the use of seniority in promotions. Disciplinary discharge and special privileges both constituted situations in which approximately half of the respondents tended to favor seniority as an effective mechanism for dealing with the situation.

In a more detailed analysis of male employees concerning lay-offs, promotions, and disciplinary discharge it is generally found that those with higher occupations and higher education tend to favor seniority least. By contrast, those who are older and those who have experienced longer periods of employment tend more frequently to favor the use of seniority rules. For example, 41 per cent of the unskilled manual workers favored the use of seniority in lay-off, compared to only 19 per cent of the professionals favoring such occupational organization. Ten per cent of the skilled manual workers favored the use of seniority in promotions, compared to only 1 per cent of the professionals. Finally, and by contrast, more professionals than unskilled manual workers, 53 per cent and 43 per cent, respectively, favored the use of seniority in discharge disciplinary actions. Similar patterns were discovered when workers with less than an eighth-grade education were compared to those with a college education.

Employee attitude toward seniority is varied, but it suggests an origin in history which is less than updated to the work situations in the second half of the twentieth century. The occupational respondents surveyed desire in general to work in rule-governed environments. Nevertheless, they favor rules stressing evaluation of qualification and performance rather than rules established on length of service, namely seniority. In the absence of the apparent possibility for fair evaluation of performance strong normative support for seniority is reported.

Unionization. Unionization is a powerful and aggressive mechanism of control on occupational behavior. It is almost always an external control, coming from outside the occupational organization as such. This is to say that most unions are national or international organizations which negotiate and bargain or otherwise represent broad categories of occupational men. To this extent they constitute an external force directing and controlling occupational behavior. There are some unions, few in number, that are known as professional unions. These unions are internal parts of the occupational organization, and as such when they constitute mechanisms of control they are internal control structures.

Unionization structures developed in the United States in the last quarter of the nineteenth century. Unionization expanded at a time when industrialization was expanding, when many thousands of workers were shifting rapidly from rural to urban life, and when they felt disenfranchisement and anomie. The vast and expanding numbers of blue-collar workers submitted a considerable measure of their occupational control to the domain of unions in return for collective bargaining and other forceful techniques whereby they could be represented to powerful managements. The control directions of unions for the largely inarticulate blue-collar workers were essentially the provision of security, identification, and increased rewards.

Union control of occupational men demands their support for collective action. When bargaining and negotiation break off, unions control occupational men to the extent of demanding their participation in strikes, picketing, and other forms of collective resistance. Unions discipline their members to ensure support, and they control members by asking for financial support, participation in meetings, etc.

Unions exercise many other forms of control. They seek to regulate hours of work, conditions of work, and qualifications for employment. Furthermore, unions attempt to exclude from occupational participation those who are not their members. They attempt to regulate apprenticeship and training for occupational membership. Finally, unions bring disciplinary action against their members in demand for support of union regulations.

In the second half of the twentieth century the labor force of the nation has continued to shift, this time from blue-collar to white-collar, rather than from agricultural to industrial. White-collar workers now outnumber manual workers. Unionization to date is less than effective in achieving widespread bargaining rights for white-collar workers. To this extent the mechanism of unionization as a technique for occupational control is much less extensive among white-collar than blue-collar workers. White-collar workers tend to have stronger internal occupational organization. Often where negotiation is needed they represent themselves collectively, rather than deferring the right of representation and negotiation to a union. Even more, the white-collar occupations strive to achieve professionalization, and thereby aspire to public approval without direct negotiation. As more and more workers become white-collar participants, and more white-collar occupational people become professionals, the esteem and respect accorded to such occupations is being diluted. Accordingly, such occupational persons are increasingly finding it necessary to bargain and negotiate for their behavioral space. Some notable advances are being made in white-collar unionization, as unions bid to represent the new white-collar workers. The white-collar workers are less interested in obtaining occupational control through bargaining, conflict, and strife, than they are in obtaining control through prestige and status—through wide public approval.

Indeed, such occupational personnel will attempt to control the behavior of their practitioners by codes of ethics and professional behavioral standards. After all of these mechanisms fail, and public respect and remuneration reach minimal levels, the new white-collar occupational men will succumb to control of their space by direct negotiational practices.

It is not yet clear in the relations between societal organization and occupational organization if white-collar and professional people will be awarded such high status in the urbanized society that unionization control of behavior will be rendered essentially irrelevant, or if the increase of the white-collar workers will so reduce their general prestige that direct negotiation will be required. It is at this point of analysis that one observes the power struggle between societal organization and occupational organization. To the extent that occupational organization becomes dominant both in the life of human beings and over the society as a whole, control of workers will not be negotiated for. To the extent that societal organization tends to dominate occupational organization the more viable occupations will be forced to continually negotiate for their social space. In this latter case the control of practitioners will be shared with the occupation's internal organization, with social mechanisms such as unions, and with the societal organization. Where occupations control the lives of men and mark the configuration of societies practitioner control will be by definition an integral part of the respective occupational structures.

INDIRECT CONTROLS

Indirect controls of occupational practitioner behavior are fewer in number than the direct controls, and far more subtle. Yet in their subtle and covert character the indirect controls are often more persuasive than the direct ones. Moreover, they are more perplexing in this balance of power struggle between occupational organization and societal organization. Direct controls are visible, and regulations (for instance, legislation) can be designed to counter the formal controls directly. The uninitiated or nonparticipants in the occupations find the informal controls difficult to understand. It is difficult to order the norms of society in such a way as to relate to the informal occupational controls effectively. In a structural sense these internal controls can, although they do not necessarily, act in subversive and devisive ways as the occupation relates to the society of which it is a part.

Codes of ethics. One of the most notable examples of an indirect occupational control is a code of ethics. Many of the highly organized occupations, particularly the professions, have from time to time promulgated specific codes of ethics. In some cases the code of ethics is intended for public knowledge and public consumption. In most cases the code of ethics is only known to exist in the most general terms by the public, and may or may not be known in its specific details by occupational practitioners. In any event it is the essence rather than the letter of the code of ethics that is important. Its strength lies more in the aura and ideology associated with it than in its specific documented and/or regulatory detail. The code of ethics for control is more a mood, an occupational posture, than a document of rules and regulations, of rights and privileges. Although it is typically printed, and frequently specific in many details, the absolute enforcement of a code of ethics is frequently difficult and sometimes impossible. Yet its importance as a control mechanism over the behavior of occupational practitioners is in no way to be underestimated.

Codes of ethics are widely considered to be one of the indexes of a profession. Therefore, occupations which seek professional status may specifically adopt a code of ethics. The code of ethics is a formal statement of the functions and responsibilities of a category of occupational men. It sets forth the relationships of the occupational practitioners to their multiple publics, and to other occupations. It is typical for the code of ethics to state the pattern of interaction that is most condoned among members of the occupations. The ethics will usually indicate the type of training recognized for the occupation, the form, character, and amount of remuneration, and the standards of practice.[8]

The expansion of occupational codes of ethics following the Civil War have been generally highly differentiated from the broad notions of ethical behavior associated with general entrepreneurial business practices. Or, put another way, the ethics of the marketplace are not to be misinterpreted as a code of ethics for occupational practitioners. The ethics in occupations tend to express a consciousness of the freestanding nature of the occupation in and of itself. Ethical standards in business practice, by contrast, involve an image of a social order and a humane morality, rather than a consciousness of kind on the part of businessmen.[9] Tawney asserted, in 1920, that the difference between industry and the professions was unmistakable. The major criterion of industry is to make profit for the shareholders. Professionals do enter their work as a means to a livelihood, but their success is measured in their service to mankind and not by their profits.[10] Yet some of these distinctions between general ethical practices in social organization and special ethical practices in occupational organization are diminishing in this second half of the twentieth century.

The code of ethics on the surface appears to have some of the characteristics of a licensing ordinance, yet it remains sharply distinct. The major part within the jurisdiction of the occupation as such. Even licensing ordinance is partially or totally external to the occupation. The code of ethics is generated from within and remains wholly or in a when it is printed and made public the behavioral and interactional nature of the code of ethics is shrouded from the view of the general public. In short, the public has little direct access to the way, for example, medical practitioners enforce their code of ethics on their fellow members. It may be announced from time to time that a formal hearing or investigation is being held concerning the practice of an individual occupational man. But the details of the case involve the competencies of specialists in such a way that the general public is incapable of evaluating the full nature of the case. The code of ethics, therefore, is at once both public and private, overt and covert, announced and secretive. The essence of the code of ethics is most fully understood in the nature of colleagueship.

Colleagueship. Colleagueship is a most powerful mechanism of indirect occupational control. It is seldom clearly seen by persons outside of the occupation, and only dimly illuminated among the fellow practitioners. As a mechanism of control, colleagueship operates almost exclusively in the upper occupational and professional categories. It may contribute endorsement and deep validation of one's ideas where their innovativeness is new and where general practitioners, to say nothing of the general public, have little basis for evaluating their validity or falsity. The high judgment of colleagues in such early stages of development and creativity constitutes a strong mechanism of support or a forceful condemnation.

Colleagueship as a mechanism of control may also be manifested in the form of a cult or intellectual trust.[11] Such colleagueship is false or a deterrent for basic innovativeness. It encourages, on the other hand, the refinement of ideas associated with an already articulated position or situation. The great man is the originator of the idea area or subject, and the cultists or trustists are those who follow in a colleagueal relationship risking little in terms of a great innovation and knowing who they are in the shadow of an already accepted great idea area. Accordingly, such cultists are controlled or perametered in their scope of inquiry.

One may experience professional colleagueship and/or idea colleagueship. Professional colleagueship is a little more visible or tangible. Its control may be more specifically directive. Acts of professional colleagueship, for example, would be those of an older professional quietly, unobtrusively, and sometimes secretively, recommending that a young professional, known to him, be named to a prestigious committee, awarded a significant research grant, be made known to publishers, etc. Indirectly the behavior of occupational practitioners is vastly modified by such acts of indirect professional colleagueship. These are among the informal factors which operate in internal occupational organization. They may lead in their control to the development of "establishments" and ultimately to factions and devisiveness in the organization of an occupation. The warmth of colleagueship is central to the nurturing of new ideas, and the exclusiveness of colleagueship to the nurturing of factions.

Colleague control of occupational behavior is well illustrated in the area of basic research.[12] The phenomenon of basic research is so complex and esoteric, so evasive of formal systems of organization, that colleague relationships tend to produce a social system, a way of life, in which basic research is shrouded with protection and with stimulation. In this arena of occupational behavior colleagues have the power to give rewards in the form of applause, respect, footnoting, titles, prizes, and other honors.[13] The occupational behavior demanded of the scientist in basic inquiry is to be humble, industrious, and rigorous; motivated for the mission of science, and devoted in work to an inspired curiosity. General occupational practitioners and formal systems of organization are in most cases inadequate for recognition in these situations. The control of colleagues is, therefore, pertinent and important to this end. The formal role of the occupational research administrator is made difficult and also more challenging where the indirect impact of colleague relationships are most validating to practitioners.

Social distance. Boundary maintenance is a phenomenon which is central to strong occupational organization. Maintaining it becomes a matter of aggrandizement in defending the frontiers. Accordingly, social distance is often developed between occupations as they attempt to defend their own practice in a subject area by excluding other occupations from work in the same area.[14] In the complex division of labor of urbanized societies it is the nature of the situation that occupations are frequently faced with contact and interaction with other occupations. Each has a competency area, the central focus of which is on a particular and separate subject. But at the periphery of the several occupations there is often much lack of precision concerning the boundary between them. Indeed, there is so much overlapping in some cases that new occupations have developed in a hyphenated manner, drawing substance and content from two related occupations, as illustrated in chemical engineering or social psychology.

The domain of lawyers and social workers frequently brings them in contact and disagreement. The social worker's counsel with a client over many years may involve the rendering of advice which lawyers may view as legal advice. In contrast the social worker may view the lawyer's decisions and directives to a client as counseling. From one concrete case to the next there is a possibility of considerable variation in judgment in the finding of the proper role for the legal occupation and the proper role for professional social workers. Further social distance may develop among lawyers and social workers in terms of the differential resources available to them. For example, the legal fraternity has through long years of aggrandizement developed the structures for subpoenas and warrants whereby they may force individuals to act. Social work as a considerably newer profession must in many cases continue to rely on persuasion, education, and conciliation in working with clients. In short, one occupation may be at a disadvantage compared to another occupation because of differential internal organization.

The social distance between and among occupations is further illustrated by power struggles. This is still a matter of definition of territorial domain and the maintenance of jurisdictional rights. It is illustrated in the case of the clergy in the Western world where since the late Middle Ages observers have often noted a decline in the occupation. In effect such an observation is that the clergy through the years have lost in the power struggle against first one and then another of the learned occupations. In the second half of the twentieth century the clerical occupation has been reduced back to where it started, namely to a social space having to do primarily with the spiritual realm of man. In effect, its control over the occupations of medicine, education, law, etc., has declined as these occupations have grown and established their own organizational identity.

The power struggle among occupations is further illustrated in the proliferation of specialists, technicians, and pseudo-technicians.[15] In the medical occupation there is the continual threat of developing new specialities. The parent occupations may at a particular time reject these new developments, and thereby enhance their probability of becoming free-standing occupations. If the parent occupations take this course by default they are giving encouragement to the development of new occupations and they may in effect be encouraging new power struggles. This situation is illustrated with the rise of psychiatrists, psychologists, dental surgeons, optical surgeons, and many others. The services of these occupations are desired and accepted by the larger society. Whether or not they are recognized as members of the American Medical Association as an occupation is of little consequence to the general public.

In still another example, the social space of the legal occupation is being invaded by the presumptuous aggrandizement of the life insurance occupation, as its practitioners attempt to become professionals.[16] In this case the Chartered Life Underwriters have rapidly gained professional-like characteristics. Their mental agility and professional aspirations are virtually without end. Consequently, representatives of the legal occupation named a committee and sat in conference with members of the new and aggressive life insurance occupation. Their aim is the reformulation and reaffirming of boundaries between the two occupations. In the balance of power and the control over occupational practitioners, the life insurance occupation gained recognition in the mere forcing of the legal occupation representatives to sit in conference with it.

The balance of power among and between occupations is fluid, continually changing. Indirectly, occupational practitioners are controlled in much of their behavior depending on the particular power position their occupation holds in the hierarchy at a given time.

Discrimination is still another specific form of social distance in the occupational environment. It may, indeed, be along ethnic, religious, education, or sex lines. White and Negro professional occupations have been, until recently, separately organized in the United States. White and Negro clergymen, white and Negro medical doctors, and white and Negro attorneys were, in the nineteenth century and the first half of the twentieth century, often separated into different occupational organizations even though the content and subject of their work was the same. Control of occupational practitioners is further influenced by sex. For example, the nursing occupation is dominated by women. By contrast the practice of medicine is male-dominated. In both occupations one finds examples of the opposite sex, and their status and roles are usually disadvantaged accordingly.[17]

Blalock asserts a number of theoretical propositions concerning occupational discrimination, as follows:

1. The greater the importance of high individual performance to the productivity of the work group, the lower the degree of minority discrimination by employers. 2. The greater the competition among employers for persons with high performance levels, the lower the degree of minority discrimination by employers. 3. The easier it is accurately to evaluate an individual's performance level, the lower the degree of minority discrimination by employers. 4. To the degree that high individual performance works to an advantage of other members of the work group who share rewards of high performance, the higher the positive correlation between performance and status within the group, and the lower the degree of minority discrimination by group members. 5. The fewer the restrictions placed on performance by members of the work group, the lower the degree of minority discrimination. 6. To the degree that a work group consists of a number of specialists interacting as a team and that there is little or no serious competition among these members, the lower the degree of minority discrimination by group members. 7. To the degree that a group member's position is threatened by anonymous outsiders rather than other members of his own group, the lower the degree of minority discrimination by group members. 8. To the extent that an individual's success depends primarily on his own performance, rather than on limiting or restricting the performance of specific other individuals, the lower the degree of minority discrimination by group members. 9. To the degree that high performance does not lead to power over other members of the work group, the lower the degree of minority discrimination by group members. 10. To the degree that group members find it difficult or disadvantageous to change jobs in order to avoid minority members, the lower the degree of minority discrimination by employers. 11. To the extent that it is difficult to prevent the minority from acquiring the necessary skills for high performance, the lower the degree of discrimination. That is especially likely when: (a) skill depends

primarily on innate abilities, (b) skill can be developed without prolonged or expensive training, or (c) it is difficult to maintain a monopoly of skills through secrecy or the control of facilities. 12. To the extent that performance level is relatively independent of skill in interpersonal relationships, the lower the degree of discrimination. 13. The lower the degree of purely social interaction on the job, the lower the degree of discrimination.[18]

The subtleties of social distance in indirect occupational practitioner control are compounded by their generation both from within occupational organization and from without through the general societal organization.

Superordination-subordination. Occupational superior and subordinate situations are widely found as a part of a hierarchical division of labor and as a part of a hierarchical system of social organization. Nowhere is superordination and subordination more vividly illustrated than in the organization of the military occupation. The military's superordinate-subordinate hierarchy is indeed a matter of technological differentiation and of functional differentiation. But superordinate-subordinate differentiation at the technical and organizational level is found in many occupations. In the military this type of differentiation takes on a different configuration, a meaning in and for itself. A part of the very fabric of the organization of professional military occupations in the urbanized societies involves a deference to authority and a discipline in authority for its own sake. Indeed, superordination-subordination is a major internal characteristic of this occupation. The behavior of practitioners is sharply controlled by the nature of this hierarchy. Its form as well as its content are central to one's career success.[19]

A superordinate-subordinate hierarchy is also found in the academic occupations. In the organization of academia the practitioners are ranked full professor, associate professor, assistant professor, and instructor. With shifting pressures on this occupation the instructor position has gone out of fashion, and it exists more as a historic phenomenon than as a contemporary reality. The full professor is often not "full" enough, and new ranks seem to be developing above him in the form of titled distinguished professorships and research professorships. Yet while the exact position in the hierarchy remains to be determined for the distinguished and research professorships, and, at the other end, for the instructorships, the importance of hierarchy for the occupational organization is only partly perceived in terms of these ranks. In sharpest contrast to the military the superordinate-subordinate ranks in the academic occupation are more organizational than behavioral controls on individual practitioners. Indeed, most practitioners look upon one another as a community of equals in carrying out the internal technology of their idea work. Organizationally only full professors may vote on certain matters, while instructors and assistant professors may be specifically excluded from certain inner sanctums of counsel and voting. But in the work of ideas and in the brilliance of insight and the prodigiousness of scholarship the full or associate professor may not by the nature of the system be either subordinate or superordinate to others in the system.

In scientific occupations theories of traditional organization and scientific ideals are at odds on almost every issue.[20] In the scientific establishments superior-subordinate social organization takes on the following characteristics as meaning: (1) decision-making involves wide participation rather than centralized control, (2) small face-to-face group interaction rather than individualism is the basic pattern of social organization, (3) instead of individual authority there is a norm of mutual confidence, (4) superiors are agents for maintaining intra- and inter-group relations, and (5) members develop greater internal responsibility, rather than having greater external control imposed on their tasks.[21]

This is not to argue that in scientific occupations superordinate authority is of little importance or virtually nonexistent. Quite the contrary, there is supervisory authority, but it is "soft" in nature rather than authoritarian. The superior in such a system is challenged by the need to have a complicated set of leadership skills. And the subordinate must accept more responsibility than in an authoritarian system. Management positions in such occupations are made more complex because they must be aware of multiple variables in the decision-making processes. In such an occupational environment the role of the supervisor is a vital and complex one in developing high morale. The role of the supervisor is further important and complex in developing inter-group relationships, indeed in becoming a colleague in the process of idea pursuit.

Alienation is a fundamental dimension in the control of occupational practitioner behavior.[22] By alienation is meant the subjectively experienced powerlessness to control one's own work activities. In Pearlin's study of nurses in a large mental hospital, alienation was found to be intensified where authority relationships limited reciprocal influence of subordinates. Alienation in occupational organization may be physical, social, or hierarchical. In all events, the individual practitioner becomes powerless to direct or to negotiate his occupational space and relation with fellow workers. Alienation is a more damning control on occupational practitioners than an articulated hierarchy such as that found in the military. In the military hierarchy one knows precisely what one's status is expected to be in each situation. But in alienation one's role definitions and self-identity are extracted and frustrated.

Superordination and subordination as dimensions of occupational control are multidirectional, one in the form of excessive specification and the other direction in the form of power and identity loss.

SUMMARY AND IMPLICATIONS

The control of occupations and of occupational practitioners is of importance to occupations and to societies. Occupations are concerned with the control of their own practitioners in terms of aggrandizement and negotiation of social space in the total world of work. Societies are concerned with the control of occupational behavior in the interest of client protection and in the balancing of power between occupational organization and societal organization.

Social control in societies in general is a matter achieved by folkways, mores, and laws. Societal control over occupations and over individual occupational practitioners is more difficult. Direct controls in the form of rules and licensing are overt and negotiable. Indirect controls are more influenced by worker relationships and by the intrigue of colleagueships. It is at this point that occupations have a potential strength in control of their organization and of their practitioners which is greater than that of the society to control them. Yet it is seldom that colleagueship is ever sufficiently articulated in an organizational manner to maximize; its potential for control. In short, if occupational colleagues were to organize they could become viable factions for societal organization. In the nature of the case, colleagueship is most often an internal structure focused on stimulating and rewarding practitioners rather than on the achievement of power in and for itself.

In sum, occupational controls remain largely free from societal controls
but constitute little threat to societal organization.

NOTES

1. Robert Dubin, *World of Work* (Englewood Cliffs, N.J.: Prentice-Hall,
   Inc., 1958), pp. 352ff.
2. Ibid. pp. 264–86.
3. Sidney Spector and William Frederick, *Occupational Licensing Legislation in the States* (Chicago: The Council of State Governors, 1952).
4. J. A. C. Grant, "The Guild Returns to America: Part I," *Journal of
   Politics*, 4 (August 1942), 303–36, and "Part II," 4 (November 1942),
   458–77.
5. Spector and Frederick, *Occupational Licensing Legislation*, p. 16.
6. Howard M. Vollmer, *Employee Rights and the Employment Relationship* (Berkeley and Los Angeles: University of California Press, 1960);
   and Philip Selznick and Howard Vollmer, "Rule of Law in Industry:
   Seniority Rights," *Industrial Relations*, 1 (May 1962), 97–116.
7. Selznick and Vollmer, *Rule of Law*, pp. 99, 100.
8. For an extensive treatment of ethics see the entire issue of the *Annals
   of the American Academy of Political and Social Science*, 297 (January
   1955), 118–24.
9. R. H. Tawney, *The Acquisitive Society* (New York: Harcourt, Brace &
   Co., 1920), pp. 91–122; William Miller (ed.), *Men in Business* (Cambridge: Harvard University Press, 1952); and Louis D. Brandeis, *Business: A Profession* (Boston: Small, Maynard, 1914).
10. Tawney, *Acquisitive Society*, p. 94.
11. Logan Wilson, *The Academic Man* (New York: Oxford University
    Press, 1942).
12. Herbert A. Shepard, "Basic Research and the Social System of Pure
    Science," *Philosophy of Science*, 23 (January 1956), 48–57.
13. Ibid. p. 53.
14. John S. Bradway, "Social Distance between Lawyers and Social Work-
    ers," *Sociology and Social Research*, 14 (July–August 1930), 516–23;
    and Arthur E. Briggs, "Social Distance between Lawyers and Doctors,"
    Sociology and Social Research, 13 (November–December 1928), 156–
    63.
15. Oswald Hall, "The Informal Organization of the Medical Profession,"
    Canadian Journal of Economics and Political Science, 12 (February
    1946), 30–44; and William A. Glaser, "Doctors and Politics," *Amer-
    ican Journal of Sociology*, LXVI (November 1960), 230–45.
16. Deane C. Davis, "Are You Practicing Law?," *Journal of the American
    Academy of Chartered Life Underwriters*, 4 (December 1949), 18–25;
    N. Baxter Maddox, "The Life Underwriter-Trustman Team," *Journal*

of the American Society of Chartered Life Underwriters, 3 (September 1949), 329–35; and Jack N. Lott and Robert H. Coray, *Law in Medical and Dental Practice* (Chicago: Foundation Press, 1942).

17. H. M. Blalock, Jr., "Occupational Discrimination: Some Theoretical Positions," *Social Problems,* 9 (Winter 1962), 240–47.
18. Ibid. pp. 245–6.
19. Charles H. Coates and Roland J. Pellegrin, *Military Sociology* (University Park: The Social Science Press, 1965); and Morris Janowitz, *The Professional Soldier* (Glencoe, Ill.: The Free Press, 1960).
20. Herbert A. Shepard, "Superiors and Subordinates in Research," *The Journal of Business,* 29 (October 1956,) 261–7.
21. Ibid. p. 261.
22. Leonard I. Pearlin, "Alienation from Work: A Study of Nursing Personnel," *American Sociological Review,* 27 (June 1962), 314–26.

SUPPLEMENTARY READINGS

John S. Bradway, "Social Distance between Lawyers and Social Workers," *Sociology and Social Research,* 14 (July–August 1930), 516–23.

Deane C. Davis, "Are You Practicing Law?," *Journal of the American Academy of Chartered Life Underwriters,* 4 (December 1949), 18–25.

Leonard I. Pearlin, "Alienation from Work: A Study of Nursing Personnel," *American Sociological Review,* 27 (June 1962), 314–26.

Herbert A. Shepard, "Superiors and Subordinates in Research," *Journal of Business,* 29 (October 1956), 261–7.

Sidney Spector and William Frederick, *Occupational Licensing Legislation in the States* (Chicago: The Council of State Governors, 1952).

ASSOCIATIONS AND SOCIETIES XIV

Occupational associations serve many functions. They may be categorized for two areas: first, the safeguarding of the traditional rights and privileges of the occupation against competing areas of the society, and second, a concern with the internal organization of the occupation and control over its practitioners. More specifically, the functions of occupational associations include the establishing of the work area of identification. The actual job description and job title may from time to time be a subject of the occupational association's consideration. The image of an occupation may be examined for improvement, for example. Development committees within occupational associations may be established and assigned the task of defining and expanding the domain of an occupation. In all, occupational identification is a matter of some considerable complexity, and associations may be concerned with its details.

Occupational associations may devote specific attention to the status of the work of their practitioners. The status of an occupation involves more than its title and image. Indeed, status is influenced by external social structures in the society over which the occupational associations may have little or no direct control. In any event, to the extent that occupational associations are able to direct and control the status of the area of work, efforts may be identified in their organizations for this end.

The objectives of an occupation from time to time become the subject of consideration at its associational meetings. A decision may be reached and an effort made to expand the objectives of a particular occupation, to include additional or alternative functions. For example, the orientation may be shifted from a national to an international arena. Or the focus of an occupation might be expanded from the study of preliterate societies to include the study of contemporary society. By contrast, through the force of licensing or some other directive an occupation may be excluded from some area of endeavor. An occupational association's members may address themselves to the problem of closure or exclusion and attempt to negotiate or ameliorate the conditions.

Achieving more extensive remuneration for workers is one of the most widely publicized functions of occupational associations. Trade union associations are most notable in this.

Fraternalism is another function often served by occupational associations. Agendas of associational meetings may include economic interests, control of practitioners, boundary maintenance, etc. But often associated throughout or in summary of a meeting there is a colleagueship and fraternalistic experience engendered by the interactional situation in and of itself. In other cases, specific examples might be identified where occupational associations address themselves to the function of fraternalism. Some specific social occasions may be planned.

Occupational associations bring about, in many cases, such viable and nearly independent occupational conditions of existence that practitioners may identify more with the occupation and its associational aspects than with the specific environment in which they carry out their work tasks. The manifestation of this situation is the supporting of occupational cosmopolitans as contrasted with occupational locals. Occupational cosmopolitans identify more with the subject matter of their occupation than with the place of work.

One might be prone to assert that, historically, occupational associations are as old as occupations themselves. In a more specific and formal sense, however, one might prefer to identify guilds as an early and highly articulate example of occupational associations. They exemplify clear efforts on the part of occupational practitioners to protect their traditional rights and privileges, in many cases before a free market economy was established. The guilds were influenced from external social structures in such a way that they contributed to support for the estate stratification system.

Labor unions have constituted the next vast movement in occupational associational developments. The impact of organized labor has tended to overshadow most other types of occupational associations of the late nineteenth century and the first half of the twentieth. Trade unions have become widely recognized as the common form of employee representation. They constitute the occupational associations for a vast number of production workers. In the main, their effort has been a representational counterbalance against the driving expansion of capitalists. Somewhat adjacent to the main stream of the labor movement is the organization of the Foreman's Association of America. This relatively recent development of foremen organizations is an important example of collective occupational representation.

The American Management Association is fundamentally an occupational association. Much of its nature is to be sharply differentiated from the trade unionism previously cited, but its viability for occupational representation is not to be underestimated. Numerous aspects of its programs have facilitated the occupational identification of managers. In this respect it must be clearly differentiated from the National Association of Manufacturers, which represents company interests rather than the human or personal interests of managers themselves. The latter is not an occupational association, while the former is.

Professional societies in much of their undertaking represent their practitioners' occupational interests. Indeed, they have more in common with trade unions than most of their members care to recognize. They are frequently concerned with the boundary maintenance of their area of work. Examples of specific concern with licensing are not difficult to discover. They specifically address themselves to the broad area of remuneration, and a focus on salary is often the central interest. Their concern over the manifest behavior of their practitioners is widely known. And the image of the professions is considered so sacrosanct that its review by the societies become a standard purification rite. A more subtle or careful occupational association could hardly be imagined than the professional societies. White-collar unionism, including both professionals and nonprofessionals, is coming to constitute an even more important dimension in the area of occupational associations.

One might observe that learned societies constitute an ultimate in occupational organizations. They are few in number and aloof in nature. The limited view which one can gain of them suggests that they are above the earthiness of the labor details that are so central to much occupational organization. Indeed when one can find a formal spokesman for such societies the nature of the statement is usually a negation of their occupational associational character.

By way of introduction the multiple functions of occupational associations are illustrated. The range of occupational associations is suggested as a continuum from the learned societies at one end to the trade unions at the other. Both the functions and the forms of the associations which are the subject of this chapter are many and intriguing.

GUILDS

Guild associations constituted one of the earliest forms of occupational organizations. Guilds were a widespread part of medieval society in Europe. Their breadth was sufficient to include both craftsmen and merchants. To a great extent the purpose of the guilds was supervision and quality control in the production of goods and the transaction of services. The occupational character of the guild associations is clear. They established entrance fees and other entrance conditions. The course of training in the form of apprenticeship was under their direction and specifications.

The strength of the guilds was often excessive. Membership was compulsory if one was to be a practitioner in an area represented. This was clearly illustrated in the length of apprenticeship, which was often sharply criticized.[1] In addition to specifying the nature of the apprenticeship the guilds were often able to limit the number of apprenticeships that would be available. Furthermore from time to time it came to be their practice to let out apprentices prior to the termination of their period of training. The occupational strength of the guild associations is illustrated by these few examples.

The guild system was operative in the American colonies, but it was unable to become securely established.[2] On the American side of the Atlantic court decisions were often rendered against the guilds. They were a deteriorating type from the outset in the colonies. With the establishment of the new nation, legislation soon gave occupational control to agencies other than guilds.

What the guilds did bring to colonial and early national America was a system and precedence for occupational awareness and association. While the guilds failed to become firmly established their legacy is widespread in the form of contemporary occupational associations and societies. The occupational association that is known currently in the United States is therefore less than an American invention and more of American adaptation of the guild systems of an earlier era in Europe.

The following sections of this chapter deal with several of the contemporary manifestations of occupational associations and societies.

TRADE UNIONS

Trade unions have been traditionally a form of occupational association by which blue-collar workers gained representation. Indeed, on the American scene, trade union worker representation dominates other forms of occupational associations. The number of workers represented by the trade unions seldom exceeds one-fourth of the nation's labor force.[3] The domination of trade unions is by drama and emotion rather than by numbers. The vociferousness of trade union leaders is in effect part of their stock in trade.

Trade unionism most clearly dates from 1881 with founding of the American Federation of Labor, but the growth has been sporadic. Indeed, some commentators on the situation, among them Daniel Bell, submit that the future for trade unions in the United States is dim. The data suggest that the growth in trade union membership in recent years is only approximately equal to the growth of the labor force. Moreover, the great movement of workers is into the white-collar categories and an exodus from the blue-collar categories. White-collar workers have traditionally been difficult to organize into unions.

Trade unions are traditionally a blue-collar phenomenon. They are often shunned by the white-collar workers in general and the professionals in particular. Their loud representation of the blue-collar workers is in sharp contrast to the almost quiet association and society representation of white-collar and professional workers. The latter's occupational organizations are often exceedingly strong, but they desire less publicity and project a more dignified and rationalistic overt behavior.

In the face of some decline among blue-collar workers, labor unions are moving forthrightly and systematically in the direction of organizing white-collar and professional workers. By the end of the first half of the twentieth century some remarkable strides had been made in the organization of white-collar and professional workers, even though their representation was far from typical. The subject of trade unions as a form of occupational association must now properly include blue-collar workers, white-collar workers, and professional workers.

Blue-collar workers. The experience of unions as a blue-collar association of workers is everywhere understood. In the following paragraphs attention will be specifically focused, however, on the occupational and associational character of unions for blue-collar workers. In the main, and beyond all else, union occupational associations exist to achieve the goals of their member workers. They are member-oriented rather than thing-oriented. Theoretically, at least, these union occupational associations are democratic in their nature. A direct measure of their effectiveness in representing their members is the number of agreements or contracts which specify conditions in the work environment. In recent years these contracts have totaled well over 100,000.[4] The occupational interest in individuals in the union associations is illustrated in the printing of agreements in small booklet forms that are designed to fit into the pockets of foremen, stewards, and other individual members. The goal is personnel representation, and workers are continually reminded of the implementation of it through forms prepared for them.

The goals of unions for their members are many. Wage increases are fundamental. It is said that the employees feel they need more money, and moreover, that they merit it. The union as an occupational association is engaged forthrightly in an effort to achieve a higher and more equitable share of the profits for their members. Put another way, one of the basic provisions in the contract is the stipulation of wages and their many subcharacteristics. In addition to the basic pay rates, there are usually stipulations for bonuses, increases, merit, apprentices, and many other specific conditions which bear upon the amount of money which should accrue to the members.

Fringe benefits are a second major area of contract negotiation. In the second half of the twentieth century they have come to constitute one of the basic and important forms of remuneration. Included in fringe benefits are the numbers of hours worked per week, paid vacations, paid holidays, severance pay, sickness benefits, accident benefits, disability benefits, and a host of others. The spread of fringe benefits continues to expand. The number of workers covered is continually being increased. Accordingly, the cost of fringe benefits is coming to be a major item in goods production. Fringe benefits per worker are so high that it is often more feasible for management to pay workers overtime than to expand the number of employees. In short, from an occupational point of view the weight of fringe benefits is sufficiently excessive that it deters the employment of new workers, and to that end defeats part of the occupational goals of unions. The trend for several years has been to ask employers to expand the fringe benefits and to assume a larger proportion of the cost for these provisions. In some cases, notably in retirement and health, the employer is increasingly being asked to pay the total provision.[5]

A specific wage-fringe benefit goal toward which unions have worked is the so called "guaranteed annual wage" or, more precisely, a supplemental unemployment benefit. In 1955 the negotiations with Ford Motor Company and General Motors Corporation achieved a new breakthrough for blue-collar workers. The principle was at last established that management might assume some responsibility for wages to its unemployed workers under a variety of specified conditions. The United Automobile Workers Union did not achieve in full a guaranteed annual wage, but it did unquestionably gain its principle and materially achieve a monetary contribution from the companies which was a supplemental income for unemployment.[6]

Good working conditions are another area of major occupational consideration on the part of labor unions for their blue-collar members. They are concerned with the hours worked, the safety of the work environment, the cleanliness of the place of work, the attractiveness of the place of work, and a full range of facilities to be provided in the place of work for the employees.[7]

The conditions of employment, discharge, and discipline of workers are all occupationally substantive areas to which union negotiators address themselves. The employee, for example, must not be discharged without "cause" or "just cause." The worker must not be disciplined without a proper hearing to present the facts of the situation from the several relevant points of view. The adjustment of individual grievances is a matter to be rigorously regulated and accordingly removed from the area of personality and individual abuse.

The activities which union members believe their leaders should participate in have been studied.[8] There is a high degree of consistency ranging from the top concerning wage negotiation down to community welfare and other miscellaneous activities. This array of activities that are desired by union members is illustrated in Table XIV.1. Rose's study of a local union in St. Louis in terms of the data presented in Table XIV.1 is sufficiently typical to be used as an illustration of the

TABLE XIV.1

Attitudes of 392 Union Members Regarding the Union's Main Functions

Question: "What do you think are the main things your union should work for right now, either through collective bargaining or through social action in the community?"

Answer	Percentage of Members [a]
Higher wages and/or collective bargaining	33.7
Better working conditions in the shop	18.4
Benefits outside the shop, such as LHI [b]	9.4
Job security and seniority	8.4
Political action	5.4
Organizing the unorganized	5.1
Better employer-employee relationships	3.8
General and community welfare	3.1
Miscellaneous	6.1
Nothing	4.9
No answer	7.7
Don't know	19.1

[a] The percentages total more than 100 because some people gave more than one answer.
[b] The LHI is the Labor Health Institute, the free medical service organization which the union secured for most of its members through collective bargaining with the employers.
Source: Arnold M. Rose, Union Solidarity (Minneapolis: University of Minnesota, 1952), p. 142.

occupational direction union members prefer their leaders to take.

The trends and directions of American labor unions are expanding from the traditional wage negotiation to include a full range of social and domestic questions for workers and the nation. The social and liberal directions which are ever more coming to characterize union activities both directly and indirectly make their programs more attractive and central to white-collar and professional workers. Part of this direction is a response to the general shift of social organization and occupational organization in the nation. Part of the shift is a premeditated effort on the part of blue-collar unionism to broaden its scope and appeal to white-collar workers.

The Foreman's Association of America was founded in 1941.[9] This occupational association was a union from the outset. The marginality of the foremen makes the example of extraordinary importance. Higher management had long accepted the notion that foremen are a part of management. The majority of foremen also tend to identify with management. Nevertheless, during the pressure of the World War II years foremen were required to work longer hours and more days per week and yet were not given the occupational benefits of the men under their supervision. In the face of such a hard reality they turned to the establishment of their own occupational association for purposes of negotiation. Under the Wagner Act the National Labor Relations Board handed down a decision requiring employers to bargain with organized foremen. The Packard Motor Company was the test case. The foremen's right to negotiate was sustained by the Supreme Court. Their advantages, however, were ephemeral. Indeed, little more than four months had elapsed when the Supreme Court decision favoring foremen was overruled by Congress in the form of the Taft-Hartley Act.

The history and content of the foremen's union experience is of less importance here than the social organizational dynamics it illustrates. The role of an occupational association to represent its practitioners as determined by structural changes in the organization of society (World War II) and the organization of occupations (tradition of contract bargaining) can hardly be more clearly illustrated. The ability of occupational men to view the nature of their work in perspective and abstractly is clear. The details and contents of occupational organizations are designed to present the occupations favorably and to represent their interests.

White-collar unionism. The goals and ideologies of white-collar workers are so traditionally different from those of blue-collar workers that their respective occupational organizational representation vary significantly. Indeed, it is asserted that white-collar unions are different.[10] Strauss's report is based on field investigation of some 9 unions, 4 typically industrial internationals; 3 white-collar unions only; and 2 unaffiliated. The workers represented by these unions were primarily in clerical, typist, bookkeeping, and professional engineering occupations. It was found that the white-collar workers were oriented to management, in some cases partly in it and partly out of it. They were oriented to salaries rather than to wages. Moreover, they continued to operate firmly within the American dream of rags to riches. Their view of unions was largely dirty, noisy, and lower class. Given such an ideological view, no matter how unwarranted, traditional unionism has a poor record for offering much to the white-collar workers.

Nevertheless, the American labor movement is making an all-out effort to organize white-collar workers. From several points of view it has to expand in this direction or wither away.[11] The white-collar workers now outnumber the blue-collar workers at a national level. In bold recognition of this shift in balance in the labor force the AFL-CIO has held a major conference on "problems of the white-collar worker." There is some precedence for white-collar organization. Most particularly, the postal workers have been organized for more than 60 years. Other examples of long periods of organization are found among such specialized professions as musicians, actors, and newspapermen. Nevertheless, the major categories of white-collar workers remain virgin territory for union organization.

One of the major difficulties in organizing white-collar workers is the amount of dignity and prestige which they already have by the very nature of their title and other details of occupational work. In addition to higher wages, workers in the United States often have been willing to accept and utilize union representation to gain dignity and status. In most cases this is a condition already attained by the white-collar workers. It is evident from some of the studies of job satisfaction, however, that with mass production and automation there is a considerable amount of routinization which is rapidly coming to characterize white-collar positions. In short, the dignity and meaning of work that has historically characterized these positions is being diluted in certain cases.

It is difficult to organize many white-collar workers because of their high rate of job shifting and their low intensity of identification with their labor force activity. Many white-collar workers are part-time and/or seasonal. A substantial number are married women who work more on a supplementary basis than on a basis of need and necessity. The gains that unions have sought to achieve are more acceptable to the full-time regular worker who by desire or by necessity identifies firmly with the labor force.

The white-collar worker's psychology is most characterized by the

American Dream and an image of the success mechanism. The challenge of unionism, therefore, is to operate within this ideology of the worker and to demonstrate the union's facility in contributing to the achievement of this ideological end. The challenge of union organizers for this new category in the labor force might be listed as follows:

One, convince the white-collar man that he is not getting the dignified treatment he deserves and that unions can get it for him; two, persuade him to think in less selfless "professional" terms and more about his own wages, working conditions, and security; three, show him that he can gain more by staying with one employer and doing collective battle than by carrying his job with him to another employer when he becomes dissatisfied; four, find a "professional standards" approach broad enough to appeal to dozens of occupational groups in a single unit; five, convert the white-collar man's private dream of upward mobility into a conviction that his hope lies in uniting with fellow workers; six, persuade him that it is sometimes more important to fight the boss than to get along with him; seven, show him that long-range security is worth the sacrifice of a short-range strike; and, eight, finally, make him believe that all those high-living labor leaders are really working for his interest ("and anyway, they're not officers in *our* union").[12]

The new middle class approach to union organization involves several gimmicks for up-grading the image of unions. For example, newspapermen are represented by a Newspaper Guild (rather than union), and another group of workers are represented by Office Employees (not workers) International Union. Grievance committees have become "office relations committees" and international bargaining committees have become "Presidents Committees." In the new trend there is a de-emphasis of the class struggle and a replacement by themes which suggest protection for rather than fighting with the boss.[13]

Where there is an increasing interest on the part of white-collar workers to participate in unions there is usually an accompanying loss of prestige, heavy pressure from management in the work environment, or a greater contact with production workers who are already unionized. Nevertheless, even in the face of these changing conditions white-collar union members often participate less in meetings than their blue-collar counterparts. The white-collar workers want to preserve recognition of their individual merit rather than to be treated in mass.

The strength of white-collar unions is often sapped because a strike on their part frequently does not bring to a halt the production operation of the place where they are employed. Striking white-collar workers may frustrate and complicate office operations, but usually at some level of efficiency production may continue for a considerable amount of time. What is more, many of the white-collar workers are so relatively unskilled or possess such a general skill that their replacement is relatively easy. It repeatedly becomes clear that white-collar workers are not interested in giving up their middle class aspirations and ideologies, so when they lower themselves, as it were, to union representation it is only on the basis that the unions are able to demonstrate a contribution in facilitating their original goals.

In spite of all the arguments that white-collar workers are difficult to organize Mills points out the fact that most of them have had no choice at all. For the typical white-collar worker there is no union available for him to choose.[14] What is more, white-collar workers typically have little personal knowledge or contact with union situations. Their friends and relatives are typically neither unionized nor ideologically favorably disposed to unionization. In terms of political party orientation the white-collar workers tend to be Independents or Republicans and accordingly have little basis or a negative basis for identifying with unions. The whole situation is confounded by the white-collar worker's degree of job satisfaction, which is often high. He may be far from an altruist, but still he may approach much of his work situation by asking what he can give it at least as intensely as what he can take from it. In short, white-collar work is frequently as much an end in itself as a means to an end. What service is objectively left for unions to render to workers in an environment of this type?

Yet in the mass urbanized society basic structural changes are being made manifest in the organization of work. The differential prestige between white-collar and blue-collar work worlds is being reduced. The working environment of the blue-collar employee is rapidly being upgraded to a position which competes favorably with that of white-collar workers and, in some cases, surpasses it. The white-collar workers are coming to recognize these fundamental changes in the world of work. Examples can be given from professional societies, where their activities are more intensively directed to the securing of those advantages that have historically been the domain of unions. The American Nurses Association since 1946 has supported an economic security program which is based on collective bargaining. The American Association of University Professors supports an aggressive committee for the study and analysis of salary and other remuneration benefits awarded to its members. The line between these activities of occupational associations and guilds, for differentiating them from unions, is more spurious than real. Mills argues that indeed the common denominators of unionism are not divided according to the style of dress or the pay period of workers.[15] Unionism is clearly an expedient and hard-driving mechanism for achieving an immediate goal more than it is a matter of value or ideology. In many cases white-collar unions are a matter of necessity and survival in the employee urbanized society. From another point of view, organization of white-collar workers is an example of the formulation of a new ideology.

Professionals and unionization. Professional associations and societies traditionally are the antithesis of labor unions in their overt characteristics and pronouncements. Certainly, professional codes of ethics are more oriented to altruism and service for clients and society than toward aggrandizement for practitioners. Covertly, however, many activities of the professional societies in recent years are hard to distinguish from those of unions in their content, even though the form of expression may vary considerably. Part of the trade unionist activity of professional societies has been no doubt stimulated as a mechanism to detour the outreach of unions to such professionals and semiprofessionals as nurses, teachers, social workers, librarians, engineers, chemists, and others. Indeed, in the post-World War II years the confrontation of professions with labor unionism has been frequent, even if affiliation has been slow.[16]

Engineering is an important starting place for the examination of the impact of unionization on a profession. During the depression years of the 1930's engineers were faced with severe unemployment, salary reductions, demotions, and various threats to their security. Indeed, the American Society of Civil Engineers admonished its chapters to establish committees on economic conditions and provided a field staff to facilitate the accomplishment of their works.[17] Regardless of the negative orientation which engineers ideologically hold concerning unions, the crisis of an economic depression and its reverberations throughout their work environment necessitated their consideration of union bargaining techniques.

In 1942 the National Labor Relations Board declared that professionals were not eligible to be included in bargaining units unless a majority of them expressed the desire to do so. To this extent professionals were protected from the encroaching efforts of the AFL and the CIO.[18]

By the mid-1950's some 25 unaffiliated groups were representing engineers and scientists. In the main they were stopgap organizations, designed to offer the advantages of unions for professionals while remaining outside of them. Ultimately some of these organizations were unable to resist affiliation with the established unions. The Engineers and Scientists of America Organization was established in 1953 as a loose confederation of certified collective bargaining organizations still outside of union domination. The policies of this kind of negotiation clearly reflect the professional characteristics of the persons represented. There is every effort made to achieve high salaries, but the bargaining design is to establish a minimum salary and leave a range for merit increases. This is in sharp contrast to the fixed hourly rate or piece rates that are so characteristic of traditional union bargaining.[19]

Another example of the professional orientation in bargaining is the preservation of the value for individual worth over the principle of seniority. Still another example is the retaining of the notion of freedom to work and the voluntary character of the professional union as opposed to the required condition in many trade unions.

The professional negotiation is pitched at a relatively high and dignified level. The aim is that of acting like gentlemen rather than pounding the table. The intent is to place the facts rationally and squarely before management and to avoid emotionalism. The ideal is to educate management and by hard reasoning together to win management to the professional point of view.

The accomplishments of the professional unions are notable in their own right. Their power nonetheless is limited, but they gain a measure of pseudo-strength by continuing to remind their membership of the terrible alternative in the form of AFL-CIO affiliation.

The condition of professional engineering has both advantages and disadvantages. One of the most important occupational facts that results from its precarious history is a wide variety of occupational associations. They include: (1) knowledge-advancing learned societies; (2) technical societies, which intend to both advance knowledge and the interests of knowledge users; (3) organizations concerned only with professional advancement; (4) non-collective bargaining organizations which meet with management to discuss professional problems; (5) unions not affiliated with AFL-CIO, which admit only professional engineers; (6) unions which admit both engineers and technicians; and (7) AFL-CIO unions.[20]

Unionization among the nation's public school teachers has a colorful, vehement, and emotional history. Teachers in general and the National Education Association in particular struggle so desperately for professional attainment that they consider most aspects of unionization to be excessively repulsive. This value is combined with a highly purist notion that a teachers' strike is against children—an intolerable and perhaps immoral behavior. Recently questions concerning these extreme views of the nature of the teaching profession have been raised.[21] Lieberman argues that to hold the view that teachers' strikes are against children is a misrepresentation of the issues. By contrast, one might argue that teaching under unfavorable conditions does more harm to children in the long run than a strike would be in the short run. From this position it might be defended that some strikes could be *for* children.

In spite of the general position against teachers' strikes and teachers' unions, some teachers are unionized and they do go on strikes.[22] In 1961 the New York City teachers voted to let the American Federation of Teachers, an AFL-CIO affiliate, represent them, rather than the Teachers Bargaining Organization, a nonunion teacher group which nominally represented the National Education Association. In a provocative analysis Fred Smith argues that teachers in New York City in contrast to teachers in small areas might be expected to cast their votes in favor of unionization.[23] While the New York teachers may be better trained and receive higher salaries than many teachers in smaller areas of the nation, their rank and prestige in New York's professional community and its general labor force places them lower than they would be in many smaller communities. In a small town the public school teacher may have the best education, receive the highest salary, and enjoy the most favorable working conditions to be found there. Indeed, they may be ranked with physicians, attorneys, clergymen, and other professionals of a like type. In the community of which they are a part their professional standing may be favorable indeed. In the New York community the professional standing of the teachers is unillustrious, unglamorous, and often almost obscure. In the latter situation the profession is ripe for union invasion while in the former the profession is prepared to do battle in resistance.

Nurses constitute another important example of collective bargaining on the part of a profession. The American Nursing Association has sought recognition as a collective bargaining agent.[24] In a manner similar to that of engineers and teachers, nurses are oriented to professional altruism for their clients and the good of man. This selflessness may assure them of reward elsewhere, but it has hardly gained them high remuneration in the here and now. By 1946 nursing had reached such a low level that the association established an economic security program. This was a collective design within a professional association which aimed at achieving much of the function of a labor union. Kruger submits that this is, in effect, labor union development within professional organizations. Nevertheless in the articulation of nurses there was some considerable inconsistency.[25] Without facing this contradiction the nursing association moved in the direction of collective bargaining nearly 20 years later. The American Nursing Association has established its bargaining organization in such a way that its state units do the negotiating and thereby officially leave the national organization free from this so-called labor union stigma. In the states and nationally, the picture is quite clear. Some 48 of the 54 units are reported to have adopted an economic security program for bargaining. Each state association under the direction of its executive secretary negotiates with the employers. Their accomplishments are notable. A 1960 report in the American Nursing Association records reveal that 75 agreements affecting 115 institutions and protecting nearly 8000 professional nurses were in effect.

The content of the agreements include "recognition, coverage, salary, shift differential, special services differential, on-call pay, sick leave, vacations, holidays, seniority, health programs, and adjudication of grievances." [26] In the nursing negotiations some of the agreements required that all nurses become members of the association within 30 days of the contract or be subject to dismissal.

Numerous special conditions were included in the negotiated contracts. For example, those employed in operating and delivery rooms typically received additional pay. The 40-hour, five-day week was standard. Overtime compensation was specified. Paid holidays and vacations were included. Health programs for the nurses were virtually universal. Pension plans were, by contrast, most conspicuous by their absence. And, finally, as a standard part of the agreements a procedure was established for grievance reporting and resolution.

Since 1946 the economic security program supported by the American Nursing Association has brought a continual advancement for the profession, even if the rate of improvement has been slow. A major deterrent to further progress for nurses is that many are outside of the places of employment which are guaranteed the right of negotiation by the National Labor Relations Act. This Act exempts in coverage those who work in nonprofit hospitals and publicly owned hospitals, both federal and nonfederal. The law does not prevent their engaging in bargaining, but it gives them a minimum strength for requiring recognition of their negotiators.

Professionals and semiprofessionals alike are increasingly faced with work in the environment of unionization. Professionals are ideologically and emotionally opposed to union membership. They believe, somewhat naïvely, that their high prestige is in return for their altruism. The hard reality of the labor organization in the urbanized society makes it ever more clear that the social prestige and the social space for professionals is won by default, and not by esteem. Their high position is accorded because of their performance of a service that heretofore was either unperformed or less capably performed by other members of the labor force. As technology and labor organization change, many services once rendered by professionals can now be rendered by nonprofessionals or semiprofessionals. To this extent the professionals are once again faced with negotiation for and defense of both their occupational space and social prestige. The alternatives seem to be the expansion of unionist characteristics within the professional associations or the succumbing to affiliated unionization.

The professional association and/or society is at the opposite end of the continuum from unions. Lewis and Maude submit that the professional association is a framework within which sanctions and controls are structured for directing practitioners in meeting their complex responsibilities to their colleagues and clients.[27] In the main they argue that professional organizations are primarily disciplinary, even in their educational dimensions. Their aim is directed toward facilitating and controlling a high level of service to society. The client theoretically is unable to evaluate the proficiency of many professionals. The professional organizations therefore play a major role in maintaining standards and protecting the public.

In the United States the growth of professional associations has been extensive in recent years. In addition to occupational control and protection of the public, many of the professional associations have taken on distinct unionistic roles. The proliferation and nature of professional associations may be illustrated in the case of hospitals, where one finds such organizations for everyone: physicians, hospital administrators, housekeepers, medical records librarians, and laboratory technicians. These associations work for the economic and social welfare of their members. Moreover, they fight for full professional status, including certification, training, codes of ethics, and so forth.[28]

A still more unusual example of an occupational association is the learned society. Its differentiation from the professional association is not always clear, but where an effort is made to distinguish it, the point is made that it is the scientists' occupational association. In other words, if it is warranted to distinguish scientists from applied professionals, then the learned society is the occupational association with more scientists than professionals. It is held here that this distinction is more one of degree than of kind.

The behavior of professionals in occupational associations has not been widely researched. Nevertheless, a careful and insightful piece of empirical evidence is available for chemists.[29] A national study was made of the chemists in the American Chemical Society. In 1962 the membership totaled approximately 93,000, about 60 per cent of the 150,000 chemists and chemical engineers in the country. Some evidence was also collected for the occupational associational views of nonmembers of the American Chemical Society. The nonmembers of the professional association were discovered to typically view themselves as something less than genuine scientists. In this case the locals identify more with the industry in which they work than with the subject of chemistry. Another category of nonmembers are those who tend to think of themselves as insufficiently advanced or learned to deserve membership in the American Chemical Society. Some of these individuals are young and their career patterns are not yet established. For example, should they enter business their professional association with chemistry will be of little value. There is a variety of other miscel-

TABLE XIV.2

Participation in American Chemical Society Activities

	Academicians (N = 398)	Research Administrators (N = 329)	Industrial Ph.D.'s (N = 500)	Industrial Non-Ph.D.'s (N = 500)	Bench Chemists (N = 294)	Chemical Engr's (N = 490)	Administrators & others (N = 278)	Total (N = 2789)
At home participation								
Read an ACS technical journal regularly	86	85	91	81	82	82	80	84
Vote regularly for officers	77	80	78	68	61	68	74	72
Contributed to building fund	49	63	56	57	51	45	53	51
Discussed ACS meetings with others frequently	46	40	42	34	37	23	29	36
Organizational participation								
Attended a local section meeting in last two years	76	73	77	68	64	55	57	68
Attended a national meeting in past two years	49	56	68	43	30	30	31	45
Made use of employment clearing house at some time	27	45	38	26	19	20	29	29

TABLE XIV.2 (cont.)

Scientific contribution								
Published a paper in an ACS journal in past five years	43	29	53	17	13	5	10	24
Read a paper at a local, regional, divisional, or national meeting at any time	50	49	47	18	15	14	22	31
Leadership participation								
Had been a local section officer	28	27	14	7	8	10	16	15
Had been a national officer	4	3	1	1	—	—	3	2

Source: Anselm L. Strauss and Lee Rainwater, *The Professional Scientist* (Chicago: Aldine Publishing Co., 1962), p. 176.

laneous notions concerning the American Chemical Society on the part of its nonmembers.

The focus of the study was on membership participation in the society. Reading of the technical journal was the most frequent form of participation, and 84 per cent of the members indicated such participation. Seventy-two per cent of the members indicated that they voted with some regularity for officers in the society. Slightly more than half contributed to the society's building fund. Thirty-six per cent reported frequently discussing the Amercian Chemical Society's affairs with other persons. Local section meetings were attended with considerable frequency, 68 per cent going at least twice a year. Slightly less than half of the members had attended a national meeting in the last two years. Nearly 30 per cent had used the employment clearing house at one time or another in their career. Reading and publishing of papers at the meetings or in the journal were far less frequent forms of participation (see Table XIV. 2).

The forms of participation in the professional society varied considerably on the basis of whether the individual was an academician, research administrator, industrial worker with a Ph.D., industrial worker without a Ph.D., etc. In the main the industrial Ph.D.'s seemed to manifest the highest rates of participation in the various society activities. They were closely followed by the academicians and in some few cases exceeded by them. It is clear from these data that the American Chemical Society is greatly looked up to and utilized for its learned characteristics.

Respondents were asked if their society was sufficiently professional. Approximately 30 per cent felt the society standards were too low. Others felt that all chemists should be eligible for membership, but that there should be a greater range of ranks within the membership. Over half of the members responded that the primary function of the society was the publication of journals. Very little importance was placed on the society's participation in unionization conditions and the establishment of salary standards.

Questions were asked concerning the society's responsibility for sustaining and/or improving the status of chemistry. Nearly two-thirds of the respondents indicated that the society should do more to publicize the important contributions which chemists are making. Over half of the respondents reported that a professional code of ethics is desirable.

At the other end of the continuum, nearly 40 per cent of the respondents indicated that the society should avoid establishing a professional board of examination. Four per cent also indicated that the society should avoid legal licensing or certification.

The running of the society was divided between the academicians and the Ph.D.'s in industry. Some indication of antagonism between these two categories of members was reported, but it did not characterize the society.

To the extent that the American Chemical Society is at all an equitable example, such an organization is greatly oriented to technical and academic matters, but it does not wholly exclude the more mundane economic and boundary maintenance details of the practitioners.

SUMMARY AND IMPLICATIONS

Occupational associations are numerous in the urbanized society. Their proliferation is greatly related to the proliferation of occupations themselves. In the urbanized society there is a distinct tendency for occupations to take on a meaning in and for themselves, and in such a situation occupational associations become more significant.

The associations are implicitly and/or explicitly concerned with improvements and training of practitioners. As occupations are more free and independent, their associations fulfill deeper and broader roles in the occupational maintenance. Occupational associations from unions to societies constitute major structures in the control of occupational practitioners. The directives for control vary greatly from the negotiated contract to the subtlety of a code of ethics.

In one form or another occupational associations are typically concerned with the remuneration of their practitioners. The unions come directly to the center of this situation and negotiate for minimum wages and maximum fringe benefits. Many professional societies are less forceful in wage or salary representation. Indeed, many of them have not yet been given the right by law to negotiate in behalf of their membership. Furthermore, many of the professional societies prefer to collect salary information, analyze it, and present their findings in an educational form. This is a quieter and more dignified technique for presenting the case of remuneration, albeit subject to question for its effectiveness. In the urbanized employee society the union aspects of wage and remuneration negotiations are coming to be widespread throughout the occupational world.

Occupational associations are broadly concerned with ideology. Their statements may range from the esoteric, through the pontifical, to the declaratory. The ideology of occupational men ranges from the human relations approach to the conflict approach.

In sum, it might be observed that the occupational associations are the public forms for a highly articulate occupational world.

NOTES

1. Adam Smith, *An Inquiry into the Nature and Causes of the Wealth of Nations* (New York: The Modern Library, 1937), pp. 101–2.
2. J. A. C. Grant, "The Guild Returns to America, I," *The Journal of Politics*, 4 (August 1942), 303–36.
3. Walter Galenson and Seymour Martin Lipset, *Labor and Trade Unionism: An Interdisciplinary Reader* (New York: John Wiley & Sons, Inc., 1960), pp. 69–71.
4. Charles B. Spaulding, *An Introduction to Industrial Sociology* (San Francisco: Chandler Publishing Co., 1961), p. 377.
5. Evan Keith Rowe, "Health, Insurance and Pension in Union Contracts," *Monthly Labor Review*, 78 (September 1955), 993–1000.
6. *Agreements between Ford Motor Company and the UAW-AFL-CIO* (Industrial Relations Staff, Ford Motor Co., December 1958), p. 199ff; see also *The Guaranteed Annual Wage* (Washington, D.C.: Bureau of National Affairs, 1955).
7. Spaulding, *Industrial Sociology*, p. 385.
8. Morris S. Viteles, *Motivation and Morale in Industry* (New York: W. W. Norton & Co., 1953), pp. 352–3.
9. Charles P. Larrowe, "A Meteor on the Industrial Relations Horizon: The Foreman's Association of America," *Labor History*, 2 (Fall 1961), 259–95; Ernest Dale, "The American Foreman Unionizes," *Journal of Business* (Chicago) 19 (January 1946), 25–30; Ira B. Cross, Jr., "When Foremen Join the CIO," *Personnel Journal*, 18 (February 1940), 274–83; Robert H. Keys, "Union Membership and Collective Bargaining by Foremen," *Mechanical Engineering*, 66 (April 1944), 251–6; Herman E. Cooper, "The Status of Foremen as 'employees' under the National Labor Relations Act," *Fordham Law Review*, 15 (December 1946), 191–221.
10. George Strauss, "White-Collar Unions are Different!," *Harvard Business Review*, 32 (September 1954), 73–82.
11. Dick Bruner, "Why White-Collar Workers Can't be Organized," in

Sigmund Nosow and William H. Form (eds.), *Man, Work, and Society* (New York: Basic Books, Inc., 1962), pp. 188-96.

12. Bruner, "White-Collar Workers," pp. 195-6.

13. Strauss, "White-Collar Unions," 75-6.

14. C. Wright Mills, *White-Collar* (New York: Oxford University Press, Galaxy Edition, 1956), pp. 304-6.

15. Ibid. p. 317.

16. Bernard Goldstein, "Some Aspects of the Nature of Unionism among Salaried Professionals in Industry," *American Sociological Review*, 20 (April 1955), 199-205.

17. See "Special Committee on Unionization Report," *Civil Engineering*, 8 (March 1938), 216-17; ASCE Committee on Employment Conditions, "Collective Bargaining—A Historical Review," *Civil Engineering*, 14 (July 1944), 311-14; and American Institute of Electrical Engineers Committee on Collective Bargaining and Related Matters, "AIEE Report on Collective Bargaining," *Electrical Engineering*, 6 (July 1945), 239-45.

18. William N. Carey, "Collective Bargaining by Engineers in Los Angeles, California," *Civil Engineering*, 16 (March 1946), 130-31; and Murlan S. Corrington, "How One Group of Engineers Avoided a National Union," *Civil Engineering*, 16 (June 1946), 282-3; Herbert R. Northrup, "Unionization of Professional Engineers and Chemists" (New York: Industrial Relations Councilors, Inc., Industrial Relations Monograph No. 12, 1946).

19. Z. G. Deutsch, "Collective Bargaining: Does it Conflict with Engineering Ethics?," *Chemical and Metallurgical Engineering*, 51 (August 1944), 96-9.

20. George Strauss, "Professionalism and Occupational Associations," *Industrial Relations*, 2 (May 1963), 7-31.

21. Myron Lieberman, "Teachers Strikes: An Analysis of the Issue," *Harvard Educational Review*, 26 (Winter 1956), 46-70.

22. Myron Lieberman, "The Battle for New York City Teachers," *Phi Delta Kappan*, 43 (October 1961), 2-8; and Myron Lieberman, "Teachers Choose a Union," *Nation*, 193 (December 2, 1961), 443-7.

23. Fred M. Smith, "The Teacher's Union vs. the Professional Association," *School and Society*, 90 (December 15, 1962), 439-40.

24. Daniel H. Kruger, "Bargaining and the Nursing Profession," *Monthly Labor Review*, LXXXIV (July 1961), 699-705.

25. Editorial, "Nurse Membership in Unions," *American Journal of Nursing*, 37 (July 1937), 766-7.

26. Ibid. p. 703.

27. Roy Lewis and Angus Maude, *Professional People* (London: Phoenix House Ltd., 1952), pp. 64-5.

28. George Strauss, "Professionalism," p. 9.

29. Anselm L. Strauss and Lee Rainwater, *The Professional Scientist* (Chicago: Aldine Publishing Co., 1962), pp. 172–93.

SUPPLEMENTARY READING

J. A. C. Grant, "The Guild Returns to America," I, *Journal of Politics*, 4 (August 1942), 303–36.
Charles P. Larrowe, "A Meteor on the Industrial Relations Horizon: The Foreman's Association of America," *Labor History*, 2 (Fall 1961), 259–95.
Myron Leiberman, "Teachers Choose a Union," *Nation*, 193 (December 2, 1961), 443–7.
Fred M. Smith, "The Teacher's Union vs. the Professional Association," *School and Society*, 90 (December 15, 1962), 439–40.
George Strauss, "Professionalism and Occupational Associations," *Industrial Relations*, 2 (May 1963), 7–31.

RETIREMENT FROM OCCUPATIONS XV

In this section we have examined the norms and structures of occupational choosing, occupational preparation, occupational entry, and career development. We will close with a chapter concerned with the process of getting out of an occupation. The normative analysis of getting out of occupations is of recent origin. Throughout most of the occupational history of mankind the worker has worked from the period of biological and social maturity essentially to the end of his life. But by the second half of the twentieth century the age-specific norm for entering occupations has advanced to the late teens and early twenties and the skill-specific norm includes both advanced education and vocational training.

Longevity has increased to such a point that the worker now normatively leaves an occupation many years before the end of life. This establishes a new social stage of retirement which is becoming age-specific at approximately 60 years. To an extent retirement is also skill-specific and health-specific as well. In numerous manual occupations the worker's physical strength and dexterity deteriorates to such an extent that by the time he has reached his late fifties and early sixties movement out of the occupation is required, even though, because of advances in medicine and other technologies of living, he may live on for a number of years in a more sedentary way of life. In the case of many mentally oriented occupations the decline of physical ability may be little hindrance to the continued practice of the work. Also in the case of some of the mental-idea occupations one may partly retire while continuing on in the intellectual endeavor at a reduced rate.

In any event, the importance of this chapter lies in the fact that vast numbers of citizens in the urbanized United States live beyond those years when they are fully and completely occupational participants.

GETTING OUT OF AN OCCUPATION

Donald Super suggests that moving out of an occupation can be divided into two stages, namely, change of pace and retirement.[1] The first stage, the pace change, comes in the late fifties, during the sixties, or, sometimes, only in the seventies. Both physical and mental abilities begin to decline, and the individual, by degrees, is unable to keep up a high quantity of work. Sometimes the quality also begins to suffer. In many occupations the career experience can be shifted in this stage so that for the last few participant years in the occupation the individual may continue to make a contribution but in a less quantitatively and 'qualitatively demanding way. This is an experience of tapering off and selection of specific types of work that will be continued. This change of pace phenomenon is most possible in those occupations at the upper end of the continuum, particularly in the professions.

Retirement, as a normative experience, is the complete terminal breaking from one's work. In fact as one examines the world of work more and more the notion of partial retirement is encountered. Partial retirement may or may not be essentially the same phenomenon as change of pace. In some cases one may completely retire from a particular occupation and then enter, on a minimum or part-time basis, another occupation, even while receiving retirement benefits. Retirement plans, often including pensions and annuities, make it increasingly more possible for workers to remove themselves totally from occupations. With no regular job responsibilities and few or no dependents, they are able to lead a life of considerable leisure.

Concomitantly, with the need for getting out of an occupation several years before the end of one's life, and with later years in leisure as a reward of the industrial, materialistic, urbanized society, both occupations and government in their organizational systems are increasing their provisions for remuneration beyond the occupational years.

Pension plans. By mid-century the emergence of national and private retirement systems had expanded vastly, to cover about 9 out of every 10 persons in the civilian labor force.[2] Nearly 8 out of 10 workers are covered by the federal program of Old Age and Survivors Insurance. Many of these have additional industrial pension coverage which supplements the federal retirement program.

Unionization has contributed to the expansion of pension and retirement programs. Since mid-century approximately 80 per cent of the industrial pension plans have been jointly negotiated under collective bargaining conditions.

By the mid-1960's it was reported that some 16,000 private pension plans provided coverage for more than 15.5 million active workers and paid benefits to 1.2 million retired workers.[3] Some of these private pension plans date back to the late nineteenth century, and only 2 per cent of those operative in 1960 were established since 1920. Some of the early plans, exemplified by telephone company plans, are large and cover about 15 per cent of the workers.

Most of the current private pension plans are small. Ninety per cent of the plans, or 14,000, have fewer than 1000 members each. More than half of the plans, 60 per cent, are in manufacturing industries. In all, however, private pension plans continue to grow and it is suggested that they may double between 1960 and 1980. [4]

Social Security retirement benefits. The Social Security Act was passed in 1935. The programs have expanded rapidly and public acceptance is now widespread. Amendments in 1965 marked major additions to the programs in the form of a comprehensive health insurance support for the aged. The basic national program is now old age, survivors, disability, and health insurance (OASDHI). Consideration here will focus only on the retirement aspects of the programs.[5]

Old age insurance was central to the original program. It is a basic government mechanism for providing income to retired workers and their families. By the mid-1960's virtually all gainfully employed persons were covered. Over 90 per cent of the individuals now becoming 65 are covered.

The basic elements of the retirement benefits are (1) earned benefits rather than a means test, (2) workers contribute to finance the program, (3) participation and coverage are compulsory, and (4) rights to benefits are defined by law. To be covered one must have worked and contributed for a minimum of six calendar quarters.

The law provides for a "retirement test" which one must meet in order to qualify for payments. By 1966, after being liberalized several times, the test required that the beneficiary receive no more than $1,500 in annual earnings up to age 72. After age 72 a beneficiary can earn any amount and still receive Social Security payments.

REASONS FOR RETIREMENT

Major reasons for retirement include poor health, compulsory, preference for leisure, and laid off.[6] Retirement decisions may be divided
into two categories, worker decision or employer decision. Differential
reasons for retirement are also recorded when the decision is made for
individuals between age 62 and 64 and after age 65. At the earlier age,
42 per cent of the retirees left their occupation because of poor health.
Eighteen per cent had their work terminated involuntarily by their
employer. By age 65 some 35 per cent who willingly retired gave poor
health as their reason. Nineteen per cent at the upper age responded
that they preferred leisure as a reason for retirement. When the decision
was made by the employer, 20 per cent of the reasons for retirement
were listed as a compulsory age (see Table XV.1).

TABLE XV.1

Reasons for Retirement

Reason	Percentage of men receiving OASDI benefits in 1963 who retired at [a]	
	Age 62 to 64	Age 65 or over
All reasons	100	100
Own decision	59	62
Poor health	42	35
Preferred leisure	11	19
Other reasons	5	8
Employer's decision	41	38
Compulsory retirement age	3	20
Poor health	11	5
Laid off or job discontinued	18	8
Other reasons	8	4

[a] Includes wage and salary workers who retired between 1957 and 1962. "Retire-
ment" means not working at a regular full-time job.
Note: Sums of items may not equal totals because of roundings.
Source: *The Older American Worker* (Washington, D.C.: U.S. Department of
Labor, Research Materials, 1965), p. 74.

Comparative data reveal clearly that the preference for leisure is increasingly becoming a respectable reason for retirement. At mid-century

TABLE XV.2

Retirement by Occupation

Occupation	Percentage Retiring [a]
All men	54
Professional and technical workers	31
Farmers and farm managers	49
Managers, officials, and proprietors	43
Clerical workers	53
Sales workers	54
Craftsmen and foremen	65
Operatives	60
Private household workers	(b)
Service workers	59
Farm laborers and foremen	55
Other laborers	61

[a] Percentage of men age 65 and over who held regular full-time jobs in the designated occupation between 1957 and 1962 but who were not working at such a job in 1962.
[b] Percentage not shown where base is less than 50,000.
Source: *The Older American Worker* (Washington, D.C.: U.S. Department of Labor, Research Materials, 1965), p. 74.

only 1 person in 25 acknowledged stopping work in pursuit of leisure, and by 1963 1 in 5 retirees reported leisure as a reason.[7]

Reasons for retirement are also related to type of occupation. Specifically, blue-collar workers retire in greater proportion than professional and technical occupational workers (see Table XV.2). The data reported reveal that 54 per cent of all occupational men age 65 and over were retired.[8] But 65 per cent of the craftsmen and foremen and 60 per cent of the operatives, compared to only 31 per cent of the professional and technical occupational workers, were retired.

Retirement due to total disability is a special situation, and one for which there is little systematic provision. The economic burden of total disability retirement is often increased when it occurs in earlier years when family responsibilities are extensive. Societal organization for disability retirement is minimal. Individual provision for such retirement benefits is excessively costly. Some industrial retirement plans provide for disability, but usually only after a considerable number of years of service, often still requiring a minimum age, and frequently at an actuarily discounted benefit.

Unless injured on the job or in line of one's occupational duties, disability reasons for retirement are often outside the social organization of an occupation as such. When this disability retirement is caused by extenuating circumstances the organization of occupations is poorly designed to deal with it. When occupations are faced with making disability provisions they are more in the area of social control than of normative provision for retirement.

Compulsory retirement is normative, and involves specific plans for workers at various skill levels to leave the occupation at announced and designated ages. Compulsory retirement may evolve as a part of the occupational organization, or it may be an external force from an environment such as unionization or bureaucracy. In any event, compulsory retirement is systematic rather than idiosyncratic.

Forced retirement, in contrast to compulsory retirement, involves unique circumstances and often traumatic experiences. This is illustrated in the case of an entire division or plant being shut down.[9] In 1956 Packard Motor Company permanently shut down its plants. Eighty-five per cent of the workers were 45 years old or over. Almost 90 per cent had 16 years of seniority and two-thirds had over 23 years of seniority. With this characteristic of middle to advanced age combined with long years of experience with the same company, retirement due to plant shutdown was a traumatic experience for many. Due to the nature of occupational organization it is difficult to enter a new occupational experience at advanced ages and to shift one's pattern of work skills after so many years' experience in a common endeavor.

In other cases forced retirement may appear a little more negotiable. An employer may not shut down a plant completely, but to facilitate its move to automation or other forms of new technology, it may offer to retire some older workers at a pre-normative retirement age. In such cases some additional phasing-out remuneration may be awarded. Still the real choice for the worker in the occupation is minimal.

In the employee society reasons for retirement are increasingly a function of occupational organization and of societal organization. They are decreasingly a function of individual choice. In social organizational terms retirement structures are significant components in balancing dependency ratios and in the provision of planned distribution of the wealth. During most of the twentieth century occupational structural norms have been operative in determining the age at entry and the training at entry. As occupations increase their internal organization they demand more training and accept entry at later ages. Much of the change in age of entry and education in occupations has directly resulted from occupational ideologies. Leaving occupations, however, is a more recent experience. It appears to be considerably more influenced by extra-occupational changes, specifically by increased longevity and by human values for more leisure. In other words, there is less occupational pushing out of practitioners from occupations. Indeed, as practitioners reach advanced age their physical and mental abilities may deteriorate so that they have reduced capacity for occupational performance. But in most cases the retirement ages are already set sufficiently early for most practitioners to be forced to leave the occupation before their contribution to it has reached a point of diminishing return.

PREPARING FOR RETIREMENT

Structures for retirement preparation are of recent origin. It is important that adequate normative preparation be developed to facilitate psychological, financial, and occupational adjustment. The absence of such adjustments result in the need for public and private services. Psychologically, retirement involves a complex adjustment to moving from a familiar set of interactional occupational patterns to an unfamiliar and often uncharted set of leisure interactional patterns. Financially, preparation for retirement needs to start several years before the experience of retirement in order both to arrange for equitable annuity programs and to arrange for meeting responsibilities with reduced income. Occupationally, preparation for retirement is desirable in the interest of removing easily older practitioners whose mental and physical abilities are declining. The desire to remain on in an occupation when one's contribution is marginal creates problems both for the total occupation and for the individuals involved.[10]

Pre-retirement counseling is increasing by dramatic proportions in the second half of the twentieth century. Still much remains to be done before firm normative patterns are achieved. A 1963 study shows, for example, that less than 12 per cent of some 1600 survey firms have pre-retirement programs that are more than the simple explanation of the financial benefits which the employees will receive.[11] In 1964 a study of 974 large companies revealed that 30 per cent did more than "benefit counseling." [12] In 1950 the Equitable Life Assurance Society research revealed that only 13 per cent of 355 companies studied had retirement preparation counseling programs. Currently their counseling program development reached 65 per cent. Similarly in 1964 the National Industrial Conference Board reported that 50 per cent of its 700 manufacturing members had retirement counseling programs that went beyond the simple explaining of financial benefits to be received from the company.[13]

Developing structures for preparation for retirement are being organized by individual companies, by unions, and by universities. The norms that constitute these structures include, first, age for counseling. Many of the programs begin to provide counseling for workers in their fifties, a second program of counseling in the early sixties, and a third program of counseling in the middle sixties or immediately prior to actual retirement. Another set of developing norms have to do with the types of counseling. Essentially these are three, namely, individual counseling, group counseling, and self-study.

Most of the individual counseling is provided by employers. In some cases this starts at age 55 with personal interviews, the content of which focuses on the financial status of the employee and the benefits which he will receive from his company. At age 60 and 64 the employee has succeeding counseling sessions. At the last counseling session the wife is frequently encouraged to participate also. Reading material may be provided to supplement the counseling sessions, and in some companies at the last session a free subscription to the senior citizen magazine *Harvest Years* is provided. Less firmly established is the possible developing norm for the employee to receive letters or other forms of contact from his company after retirement.

Group counseling is being provided in many cases. Often the group counseling situations involve a company using university-prepared courses. The University of Chicago and the University of Wisconsin have prepared extensive materials for this purpose. The University of

Chicago retirement course materials consist of the following types of discussion subjects: (1) older people in American society; (2) why people work; (3) time: in your mind and on your hands; (4) what about money?; (5) making money in retirement; (6) good eating—good health; (7) your body grows older; (8) personal and social relations; mental health; (9) family, friends, and living arrangements; (10) where to live in retirement; (11) the union, the community, and the retired worker; (12) where do you stand? [14] In the Chicago counseling material, discussion guides are provided for participants, and a manual is provided for discussion leaders. The sessions for each topic are intended to be three hours in length.

A third procedure which is developing for pre-retirement preparation involves self-study courses. In this situation companies may begin to provide printed and published materials starting at about the middle fifties. Subsequent materials may be provided in the early sixties and the middle sixties. This self-study type of preparation is easier to manage from the employers' point of view. Yet materials must be continually updated due to changes in Social Security regulations, changes in medical programs, etc.

Occupations as such have done little with preparing specific retirement materials to date. Voluntary groups, employers, unions, and government have provided most of the retirement programs.

Retirement may be viewed as an individual and/or societal achievement. It may also be viewed as an individual trauma and as a social problem. For the organization of occupations, retirement is more a matter of negative than positive concern. That occupations are much concerned with preparation and training is defensible in terms of their organization, because the quality of their practitioners is greatly related to it. The quality of occupational practice is indeed influenced when a significant proportion of practitioners continue on to such an age that their abilities are materially reduced. But in most cases this proportion of practitioners has not become sufficiently great to become a major occupational problem. Retirement that removes individuals completely from their occupation essentially removes them outside of the boundary of the occupation. Occupations are, therefore, more concerned with the age of retirement and the reasons associated with retirement than with the experience in the years after retirement.

AGE NORMS FOR RETIREMENT

The normative age of retirement in the second half of the twentieth century is clearly between the years of 60 and 65.[15] The implications of an increasingly specified retirement age are reported in Dorfman's study of a national sample of 3000 households in which one or more persons were age 65 or over in 1952. It was found that only 41 per cent of the males age 65 or over were in the labor force. Eighty per cent of those out of the labor force had departed because of ill health or because they had reached the conventional retirement age. Little possibility was found for assisting these older retired workers in re-employment. Most of those who were able to assume additional employment had not fully entered the retirement category at all. Finally, it was found that as occupational men moved into their advanced years they were more likely to be demoted than promoted. In effect, with the rapid changes in occupational nature older workers tend to find their skills out of tune with the contemporary labor force needs. It is typically only in the agricultural service and laboring occupations that the last occupation, or the occupation at an age over 65, exceeds the proportion of workers in that occupation between ages 14 and 64. In the idea-professional occupations the proportion of practitioners at age 65 and over is generally less than for all men between ages 14 and 64.

The proportion of men who are still occupational practitioners at age 65 and over varies by occupation. Over two-thirds of the professional and technical practitioners continue on in their occupation. Approximately one-third of the practitioners in each of the clerical, craftsmen, operative, service, farm labor, and other laboring occupations are still in the labor force.

In the main Dorfman finds that the occupational life of those not in the labor force is in a very real sense over. In a significant proportion of the cases their health is not adequate for continued occupational participation, or they do not desire continued participation. Their social lives, however, may be far from terminated, and, hence, their position in society must be systematically dealt with even if their position in occupations is terminated. And if the situation is complex for those who retire by age 65, it is confounded more by those who retire earlier.

Early retirement. Reasons for early retirement are many and complex. But in the main they suggest a disenchantment with the routine of mass society, a general affluence, and a new ethic which expresses retirement in leisure as greatly acceptable in and for itself. Among the most suggestive answers concerning the early retirement situation are found in a 1963 study of individuals who left their occupations in the federal service.[16] About 3000 questionnaires were returned, 91 per cent of the sample. Their essence is characterized as follows: "Thirty-eight years is a plenty." "If you work to the day you die, you're missing something good—like never being a boy." Or another put it this way, "I live alone and am as happy as two bugs in a rug. I have my flowers, and camera, and hi-fi, and I do not have to answer to anyone. I am in hog heaven. I am healthy and ornery as they come, do my own cooking . . . sleep as late as I want . . . give my housework a lick and a promise when it gets too bad . . . watch any TV program I desire, cuss the TV commercials—who would want more?" [17] This in capsule form is the new retirement ethic.

Early retirement in this study was defined as leaving one's occupation between the ages of 55 and 60, or after 30 years of work in the federal service. There are economic penalties for retiring early. Most of those who left their occupations early were in an income bracket between $4,000 and $5,000. Many had been in post office clerk or carrier occupations. The civil service annuities range from less than $100 a month to as much as $1,000 a month. Typical annuities, for 6 out of 10 individuals, range between $200 and $299 a month. For most of these people, therefore, the notion that they wanted to retire while they could still enjoy it was economically a reasonable one. Some put it this way: "I was spending all of my time making a living, so that I had no time to live. When I found myself going to sleep over the newspaper, I decided it was time to quit." Or in another case "I wanted to travel more, I had never been abroad and I knew that if I waited too long I would never make it." [18] At the professional end of the continuum one respondent said: "Believed I had reached the end of the road at GS-16, wanted a new challenge." [19]

In most cases those who retire early from government occupations have worked some since their retirement. In general their work is part-time rather than full-time; they work fewer hours in retirement than they did at their full-time job (see Figures XV.1 and XV.2).

For those who continued to work the most frequent reason given was economic. Often they wanted to qualify for Social Security benefits. The expression by one respondent was: "The retirement income is sufficient if I stay home and putter around and die in a chair of old

FIGURE XV.1

AMOUNT WORKED SINCE RETIREMENT

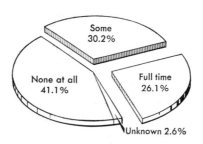

age. But for travel, hobbies, etc., which unfortunately cost money, I find it desirable to work for a while and then spend the money. . . ." [20] Another respondent put it this way, "I found myself depressed. . . . I sought temporary or part-time work and then still enjoyed doing

FIGURE XV.2

HOURS WORKED
(as compared with Government job)

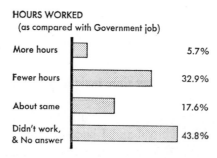

Source: Elizabeth F. Messer, "Thirty-Eight Years is a Plenty," *Civil Service Journal*, 5 (October–December 1964), p. 20.

what I like with the happy thought of being in circulation." [21]

Those who did not seek employment and whose income is sufficient respond favorably to their retirement with challenge in hobbies and other activities. For example, "I like to hunt, fish, golf, play bridge, garden, care for my yard. I love music, good literature, sports, and just plain loafing, which is an art in itself. . . . Work just took up too much of my time." Another affluent and contented retiree said "I wanted to travel some before I died, and I also wanted the time to do just as I please. Now I spend my summers on a nice northern Michigan lake and my winters in Florida, and between times I just travel around and visit my children and friends. I play golf about twice a week and fish all summer." Or another said "I read from five to six hours a day. I studied German for two years at the university. Tomorrow I begin a course in 'Introduction to the New Testament.' I do not have to do anything under tension." [22]

When asked about their over-all financial condition, more than 83 per cent responded that they were getting along satisfactorily. In some cases their remuneration was from annuities, savings, and investments, while most had worked some to supplement their income. In many cases a spouse was also working or receiving an annuity or Social Security benefits.

These respondents felt good about their early retirement experience. Most indicated that they would do it again if they had the opportunity. Many reported a belief that after one had worked for 35 to 40 years they should remove themselves from their occupational responsibility to make room for younger individuals to work up the hierarchy. Some felt that early retirement made it easier for them to adjust to the change. Or it was said that those who work after age 55 or 60 essentially mark their time and pick up their pay checks but make little contribution. Some were equally affirmative in asserting that early retirement is a waste of manpower.

Retirement at an advanced age of between 60 and 65 has become firmly normative. Retirement at an earlier age is experienced by many. It is widely endorsed by those who experience it. It is too soon yet, however, to discern whether both occupationally and social organizationally it will be feasible and/or desirable for an earlier retirement norm to be developed.

RETIREMENT AND LABOR FORCE PARTICIPATION

Retirement is not only increasing in general but it is increasing at earlier ages. For most retirees on old age survival and disability insurance benefits, retirement means leaving one's occupation completely. Nevertheless a substantial and increasing proportion of both men and women in retirement participate to some extent in occupations (see Table XV.3). Among male beneficiaries between the ages of 62 and 64 slightly more than one-quarter had some occupational experience. Moreover, of those between the ages of 65 and 72, 32 per cent had some work experience. The vast majority of those who were non-beneficiaries had some work experience in their retirement. Indeed it is reported, "Thus persons eligible for OASDI working at full-time jobs paying more than allowed under OASDI may postpone the becoming beneficiaries until 72 and on the other hand some beneficiaries who work part-time to meet the retirement test may take a full-time job at 72." [23] In effect it is still too soon to discern fully the impact of early retirement on occupational participation. Individual case studies variously show that the early retirees do engage in some kind of occupational endeavor as a matter of typical pattern for supplementing their income. This is particularly illustrated in the case of retired army officers who leave the service after 20 to 22 years of active duty.[24] In the mid 1960's it was discovered that 90 per cent of the military officers who retired early anticipated occupational employment in their retirement years. In fact within six months after retirement nearly 70 per cent of the officers and over 74 per cent of the enlisted men were working. Some of the remainder were in school, in preparation for further occupational work.

A study of company-initiated early retirement reveals that slightly less than half of the workers looked for permanent positions, and about half of those who looked for work found it, but typically on a part-time basis.[25] In another study it is reported that early retirement is looked upon more favorably when the prospective retiree has what is presumed to be an adequate income.[26] Sixty-three per cent of those who anticipated more than $200 a month in retirement income viewed retirement favorably. By contrast only 38 per cent viewed retirement favorably when they anticipated less than $100 in monthly income. In a comparative international study it is also found that there is a high correlation between favorable viewing of retirement and adequate income.[27]

National data reveal that between the ages of 45 and 59 over 90 per cent of the American males participate in the labor force. Between the ages of 60 and 64 the rate of participation drops to slightly more than 80 per cent. Between the ages of 65 and 69 the participation rate drops

TABLE XV.3

Work Experience by Age and OASDI Beneficiary Status for Persons Aged 62 and Over: Per Cent with Specified Extent of Work Experience, 1962 [a]

Extent of work experience and age	Men Total (a)	Men OASDI full-year benefi- ciaries	Men Non- benefi- ciaries	Women Total (a)	Women OASDI full-year benefi- ciaries	Women Non- benefi- ciaries
Number reporting work experience (in thousands):						
62–64	2,006	233	1,527	2,254	664	1,093
65–72	4,314	2,497	1,230	5,127	3,463	1,289
73 and over	3,391	2,507	802	4,535	2,463	1,916
Percentage with work experience in 1962:						
With some work:						
62–64	79.8	26.6	90.0	33.1	21.7	41.0
65–72	47.0	32.5	65.3	19.6	18.0	21.2
73 and over	22.9	27.4	7.9	5.8	8.2	2.8
Usually at full-time jobs: [b]						
62–64	69.6	6.9	83.6	22.2	8.6	33.0
65–72	30.9	13.7	57.7	9.9	6.6	16.1
73 and over	10.4	12.6	3.1	2.8	4.0	1.1
Full-time, year-round jobs: [c]						
62–64	47.4	2.6	60.1	11.3	2.7	20.1
65–72	17.8	6.3	44.1	4.6	2.3	10.6
73 and over	6.0	7.1	2.4	1.3	2.0	.5
Usually at part time jobs:						
62–64	10.0	20.2	6.4	10.8	13.1	8.0
65–72	15.9	18.9	7.2	9.7	11.3	5.0
73 and over	12.5	14.7	4.7	3.1	4.1	1.7

[a] Total columns include two groups not shown separately—beneficiaries whose benefits were first received during 1962 and a small number who had entitled children or whose own entitlement was as the parent of a deceased worker.

[b] 35 or more hours a week.

[c] 50 or more weeks of work in the year.

Source: Erdman Palmore, "Work Experience and Earnings of the Aged in 1962: Findings of the 1963 Survey of the Aged," *Social Security Bulletin,* 27 (June 1964), 5.

still further, to slightly less than 50 per cent. Finally, after age 70 only one-quarter of the males are found to participate in the labor force. The pattern of female participation in the labor force is similar to that for males, but with a lower rate of participation at all ages. Between the ages of 45 and 59 approximately 50 per cent of the females are in the labor force. Between the ages of 60 and 64 their rate of occupational work drops to slightly more than 30 per cent, then to 17 per cent and finally to 6 per cent in the later years.[28]

One of the most salient reasons for a chapter on retirement in a treatise on occupations is that more systematic efforts are being made to prepare for jobs after retirement.[29] Entering occupations after age 40 has been for some time more than ordinarily precarious. Yet with an increasing proportion of the population falling in the age category of 40 and above it becomes a matter of considerable attention to note the occupational assets of older workers. The fact of these assets may be a subject of much conjecture, but the vociferousness of their articulation is a reason for their being recorded here. Assets for older workers are listed as competence, dependability, results, judgment, and economy.[30] To herald the importance of the older worker, Forty Plus Clubs have made a considerable contribution since their founding in the late 1930's. Their memberships are constituted of males in the upper income brackets, with distinguished occupation record, and a report of good health.

In other places specific organizations for older workers print long lists of occupations suitable to retirees and attempt to facilitate their obtaining employment. In addition to employment opportunities agencies representing older workers attempt to encourage their development of home industries and small businesses for their golden years.

While the details may be conjectural, the abiding evidence is clear —older workers in retirement frequently participate in occupational activities.

Gradual retirement. Well-established norms for gradual retirement programs do not yet exist, but numerous examples of such programs may be identified.[31] In some cases it is clear that the gradual retirement systems are designed to prepare workers for full retirement. Or from the opposite point of view, that of the employer, the gradual retirement system may facilitate the training of a new employee by the retiring one.

In some cases the reduction of work during the work years before 65 may take the form of extended leaves. In other cases the partial retirement may involve a work reduction on a week-to-week basis. Where there is a reduction in the amount of work expected there is also typically a proportionate reduction in remuneration. In one company it is reported that remuneration in work is decreased to the point where remuneration in retirement would exceed that in employment.

A different type of gradual retirement is a form whereby employees are allowed to transfer from one type of work to an alternate type, usually less demanding and sometimes on a part-time basis. The U.S. Department of Health, Education, and Welfare encourages its employees to participate in such job transferral to gradual retirement programs.[32] Still another alternative in gradual retirement, one more widely found in executive occupations, is the complete retirement of an employee in one position followed by the rehiring of the individual in the same or an alternate position. The advantage both to the employee and the employer is that on the rehired basis the continued employment may be terminated for appropriate grounds, on a short notice.

The techniques for gradual retirement are several. They remain at present, however, more at an experimental level than at a normative or structured level.

Differential retirement patterns by occupational groups. It is hypothesized that workers who view their jobs primarily in terms of financial means of survival will accept retirement at a normative age more favorably than those occupational men for whom the meaning of work is bound by extrafinancial perceptions.[33] Impressionistic though the data may be, most conclusions support the hypothesis. For example, a study of male worker retirement plans reveals that relatively more of those in the less skilled jobs indicate that they really expect to retire at the normative age.[34] The less skilled workers, regardless of their age category, reported that in retirement they expected to pursue hobbies, participate in community work, putter around their home and garden, travel, and participate in other leisure-oriented and civic-oriented activities. The more skilled workers expressed a desire, by contrast, to continue work as long as possible. Their response varied little from one age category to another.

When white-collar and blue-collar workers are contrasted at various age categories it is discovered that white-collar workers persist more

tenaciously in their occupation in advanced years than do their counterparts in blue-collar work. Between the ages of 45 and 54, some 34
per cent of the white-collar workers are employed. At age 70 or over, 36
per cent are reported to be employed. For professionals the drop in
proportion is from 10 to 9 per cent. For proprietors it is from 18 to 17
per cent. Clerical workers shift in proportion from 6 per cent to 4 per
cent. Finally, sales workers increased slightly, from 5 per cent at ages 45
to 54 to 6 per cent at age 70 or above. In sharp contrast, the proportion
of blue-collar workers declines from 45 per cent at ages 45 to 54 to only
22 per cent at age 70 or older. Service workers and farm workers also
show an increased proportion in the advanced ages over the middle
ages.

The pattern of women workers varies from one age category to another in a manner that is similar to that for their male counterparts,
but it is more variant for any one age or any one specific occupation.

In some particular occupations the age and nature of retirement is
strongly contested. This is perhaps no more forcefully illustrated than
in the case of airline pilots. For approximately 30 years the Federal
Aviation Agency has attempted to force retirement of pilots at age
60.[35] In the organization of this occupation it has been structurally required for many years that pilots pass a rigorous physical examination
twice in each year. If at any time a pilot is unable to pass the physical
examination, retirement is forced at that point. Accordingly, it is argued
by some that with such rigorous physical examinations it should be acceptable for those pilots in good health to continue in their occupation
for a period of time after age 60. The importance of the case here is
not the validity of the arguments, but the illustration of factors which
influence retirement and the rigorousness with which some occupational men attempt to define their own retirement structures. The Airline Pilot Association has negotiated, debated, and legally contested the
retirement pressures on the occupation. This occupational behavior
again illustrates the validity of the hpothesis that as workers' skills increase and as the view of work includes more than monetary reward,
retirement will be accepted with reluctance.

The differential rate and acceptance of retirement by the various occupational participants leads to the next level of inquiry, namely differential adjustment.

RETIREMENT ADJUSTMENT

Retirement from occupations has many adjustment complications. In general, individuals retire from occupations, but the adjustments associated with retirement are typically of a family proportion. Or, put another way, individuals engage in occupations, but families are typically dependent upon the occupational condition. Adjustment to retirement, therefore, is generally a family adjustment.[36]

The first order of adjustment in retirement has to do with establishing new views of one's usefulness in a condition typically outside of gainful employment. In a culture that long has placed a value on work over that of leisure, being thrust into retirement-leisure time may be difficult until new indices are internalized for evaluating one's worth and usefulness. As the norms of leisure become more respectable full retirement at an early age becomes more compatible.

The second major factor in the retirement adjustment has to do with income. Most occupations are organized in such a way that remuneration is provided almost exclusively for productive contribution. More recently some occupations, particularly those at the upper half of the occupational continuum, are beginning to provide for a systematic annuity program as a part of the normative remuneration system. This is illustrated in the expanding Teacher's Insurance and Annuity Association. Similarly, many clergymen are now covered by at least some minimal annuity program. Most occupations, however, still have no structure for providing retirement annuities. Moreover, most individuals who are now in the retirement experience entered it from a period in occupational organization and social organization which provided little for retirement. The income of many retirees is grossly inadequate. Often the income that is provided is eroded by an inflationary economy. When annuities are based on absolute dollars rather than tied to the fluctuations of the economy those provisions that were made in earlier years tend to be less adequate than when they were being provided.

It is found in case study evidence that retirement is more easily accepted by rural people, particularly farmers, than by their non-rural counterparts. But adjustment problems are also recorded for those in rural life. Part of the differential in retirement adjustment has been until recently due to the gradual retirement of farmers as contrasted with the non-farm workers.

SUMMARY AND IMPLICATIONS

Retirement is a relatively new societal and occupational condition. It is caused by an increase in longevity and by an increase of nonhuman energy input into production and distribution of goods and services. These two conditions, supported by several others, combine to sustain many people for many years in relatively good health beyond that period when they are needed, and when there is room for them, in the ordinary course of participation in occupations.

The experience of retirement often comes about because it is forced by employee policies or poor health. Gradually and increasingly retirement comes about, even at earlier ages, because new values in ethics for leisure are being accepted. From this point of view retirement becomes one of the several achievements of the urbanized industrial society.

The structures of retirement are becoming more precise. The age for retirement is now in the early to middle sixties. In addition, specific norms for retirement preparation are being established and accepted.

Retirement is implicitly, and sometimes explicitly, an occupational phenomenon. Particularly as individuals continue to participate in occupational roles on a part-time or alternate basis the nature and condition of the total occupation are influenced by the capacity, or lack of capacity, of these part-time and alternate participators. As more people move into the age category of life where they will have an opportunity for part-time retirement this condition becomes more critical for the organization of occupations as such. As a boundary maintenance of occupations has been specifically modified to focus on training and recruitment, it may be expected that the boundaries of occupations will come to focus more fully on the mechanisms of retirement.

NOTES

1. Donald E. Super, "Getting Out of an Occupation," *Personnel and Guidance Journal*, 34 (April 1956), 491–3.
2. Robert K. Burns, "Some Unsettled Issues of Retirement Policy," *The Journal of Business*, 27 (April 1954), 137–45.

3. *Labor Mobility and Private Pension Plans* (Washington, D.C.: U.S. Department of Labor, Bureau of Labor Statistics Bulletin No. 1407, 1964), p. 4.

4. Ibid. p. 51.

5. *Social Security Programs in the United States* (Washington, D.C.: U.S. Department of Health, Education, and Welfare, 1966).

6. *The Older American Worker* (Washington, D.C.: U.S. Department of Labor Research Materials, June 1965), p. 74; Harold L. Sheppard, *Too Old to Work, Too Young to Retire: Case Study of a Permanent Plant Shut-Down* (Ann Arbor: Institute of Labor and Industrial Relations, 1959); and Burns, "Issues of Retirement Policy," pp. 138–9.

7. Margaret Stecker, "Why do Beneficiaries Retire? Who Among Them Return to Work?," *Social Security Bulletin*, 18 (May 1955), 3–12.

8. Erdman Palmore, "Retirement Patterns among Aged Men: Findings of the 1963 Survey of the Aged," *Social Security Bulletin*, 27 (August 1964), 3–10.

9. Sheppard, *Too Old to Work*.

10. *The Older American Worker*, pp. 75–6.

11. Edwin B. Shultz, *A Study of Programs of Preparation for Retirement in Industry* (Ithaca, N.Y.: Cornell University Press, 1963).

12. *Corporate Retirement Policies and Practices, Studies in Personnel Policy No. 190* (New York: National Industrial Conference Board, 1964).

13. "How to Prepare Your Employees for Retirement," *Business Management* (August 1966), 53–66.

14. Alastair Heron, "Preparation for Retirement: A New Phase in Occupational Development," *Occupational Psychology*, 36 (January–April 1962), 1–9.

15. Burns, "Issues of Retirement Policy," p. 137; and Robert Dorfman, "The Labor Force Status of Persons Age 65 and Over," *American Economic Review*, 44 (May 1954), 634–44.

16. Elizabeth F. Messer, "Thirty-Eight Years Is a Plenty," *Civil Service Journal*, 5 (October–December 1964), 6–8ff.

17. Ibid. p. 6.

18. Ibid. p. 7.

19. Ibid.

20. Ibid. p. 21.

21. Ibid.

22. Ibid.

23. *The Older American Worker*, p. 72; see also Juvenal Angel, *Occupations for Men and Women after 45* (New York: World Trade Academy Press, 1964).

24. Ibid. p. 73.

25. Theron J. Fields, *Company Initiated Early Retirement as a Means of Work Force Control* (Ithaca, N.Y.: Cornell University, New York State School of Industrial and Labor Relations, 1963).

26. Wayne E. Thompson, "The Impact of Retirement" (Unpublished Ph.D. Thesis, Cornell University, June 1956).
27. Margaret S. Gordon, "Income Security Programs and the Propensity to Retire," in Richard H. Williams, et al. (eds.), Process of Aging, vol. 2 (New York: Atherton Press, 1963).
28. Seymour L. Wolfbein, "Work Patterns of Older People," in Williams, et al., Process of Aging.
29. Maxwell Lehman and Morton Yarmon, Jobs After Retirement (New York: Henry Holt and Co., 1954).
30. Ibid. p. 2.
31. The Older American Worker, pp. 76–7; see also Paul Roman and Philip Taietz, "Organizational Structure and Disengagement: The Emeritus Professor," The Gerontologist, 7 (September 1967), 147–52.
32. Gradual Retirement in the Department of Health, Education, and Welfare (Washington, D.C.: U.S. Department of Health, Education, and Welfare, 1964).
33. Eugene A. Friedmann and Robert J. Havighurst, et al., The Meaning of Work and Retirement (Chicago: University of Chicago Press, 1954).
34. G. Hamilton Crook and Martin Heinstein, The Older Worker in Industry: A Study of the Attitudes of Industrial Workers toward Aging and Retirement (Berkeley: University of California, Institute of Industrial Relations, 1958).
35. Carl M. Ruppenthal, "Compulsory Retirement of Airline Pilots," Industrial and Labor Relations Review, 14 (July 1961), 528–47.
36. Howard E. Bracey, In Retirement (Baton Rouge: Louisiana State University Press, 1967); Philip Taietz, et al., Adjustment to Retirement in Rural New York State (New York: Cornell University Agricultural Experiment Station, Bulletin 919, 1956); and Jacob Tuckman and Irving Lorge, Retirement and the Industrial Worker (New York: Columbia University, Bureau of Publications, Teachers College, 1953).

SUPPLEMENTARY READINGS

Alastair Heron, "Preparation for Retirement: A New Phase in Occupational Development," Occupational Psychology, 36 (January–April 1962), 1–9.
"How to Prepare Your Employees for Retirement," Business Management (August 1966), 53–66.
Labor Mobility and Private Pension Plans (Washington, D.C.: U.S. Department of Labor, Bureau of Labor Statistics Bulletin No. 1407, 1964).
Elizabeth F. Messer, "Thirty-Eight Years is a Plenty," Civil Service Journal, 5 (October–December 1964), 6–8ff.
Erdman Palmore, "Retirement Patterns among Aged Men: Findings of the

1963 Survey of the Aged," *Social Security Bulletin*, 27 (August 1964), 3–10.

Margaret Stecker, "Why do Beneficiaries Retire? Who Among Them Return to Work?," *Social Security Bulletin*, 18 (May 1955), 3–12.

Donald E. Super, "Getting Out of an Occupation," *Personnel and Guidance Journal*, 34 (April 1956), 491–3.

MEANING OF OCCUPATIONS FOR INDIVIDUALS AND SOCIETY 3

The subjects of consideration in Part 3 are the impacts of occupations on the lives of individuals and on society. There are diverse impacts on individuals and many of them have been quite broadly documented. Types of occupational impacts are traced in chapters dealing with meaning of work, colleagues, and family life. A chapter on ideologies illustrates much of occupational impact on society.

The remaining chapters in Part 3 deal with specific categories of occupations, ranging from those which make the most definitive impacts on individuals and society, e.g. the professions, to those which make the least impact, e.g. service jobs. Some of the professional and executive occupations are so extensively organized that they appear from time to time to be independent rather than dependent structures in society. Service work, on the other hand, in some cases is so loosely organized that it is scarcely occupational at all. Characteristics are more imputed to it than generated by it.

Part 3 illustrates the differential impacts of these various occupations.

MEANING OF WORK XVI

Work has had many meanings through the ages. It continues to have many meanings in the urbanized societies of the twentieth century, but now the focus is more on nonmonetary than on monetary meanings. For example, some of the hardest working persons in American society are individuals who are free from the need of money to acquire the essentials of life. Some of these are wealthy industrialists or executives. The number of people for whom work has more than an ordinary monetary meaning also includes scientists, inventors, teachers, ministers, nurses, social workers—indeed, men and women with a "mission." For most of these and for many others, work is more than making a living. They work hard and get a sense of nonmonetary gratification for their toils. In contrast, and in some paradox, the vast numbers of men who must work to obtain money to acquire the basic necessities of life do not work regularly, effectively, or with gratification.[1]

In our contemporary urbanized society, we sell our work in the form of thousands of specialized occupations. Accordingly, we find that the meanings of work and job satisfactions are related to a long list of items: advancement, age, ambition, aspirations, attitudes, colleagues, communication, earnings, emotional adjustment, employee benefits, freedom, friends, health, hours of work, intellectual stimulation, job enlargement, job involvement, length of service, longevity, loyalty, management, marital status, monotony, morale, personality, recognition, repetitive work, responsibility, rules, security, self-concept, seniority, sex, skill, status, supervision, tenure, type of work, working conditions, and work situation.[2]

In this chapter we examine the meanings of work generically. In the succeeding chapters in this section, an examination is made of the nature and meaning of work in the major occupational categories. The subject of examination is the meaning of work in an affluent society where men are characteristically above the elements of subsistence, and, therefore, are challenged and frustrated in their work by diverse, ultimate, and new directions in meaning. When in ages past masses of men in the major societies worked for basic subsistence, their meaning of work ranged essentially from a privilege or blessing by God to a curse from the gods, but in either event, the day-to-day struggle for survival brought a commonness to the meaning of work. In the urbanized and relatively affluent American society, there are few assurances in the meaning of work. Some men are greatly challenged by their work opportunities for innovation, imagination, creativity, freedom, and contribution. Others are deeply frustrated, and often experience anomie, as they lose an ability to know who they are in a work frame of reference. This is nowhere better illustrated than in the case of American women, who enter the labor force each year in greater proportion, but who suffer from a gross lack of meaning for their work endeavor.

THE SIGNIFICANCE OF WORK IN URBANIZED SOCIETY

In ruralized America, the meaning of work was established in the Protestant ethic. Toil with the hands and by the sweat of the brow was honored, considered good discipline, and ennobling to the soul. But the product of this work combined with a scientific mentality and an industrial technology has given men more leisure than their historical Protestant ethic has enabled them to accept gracefully. The very meaning of hard physical work has in effect displaced individual physical energy input with mechanization and more particularly automation and possibly cybernation. Man's hard work in this frame of reference has achieved him a new leisure which must be rationalized. The character of work is shifting in its meaning from the physical to the idea. The shift is from blue-collar to white-collar work.

In capitalist societies, particularly in the nineteenth and twentieth centuries, an effort is made to view the motivation of workers in terms of monetary rewards. Money was and continues to be a significant meaning of work, but of similar importance are security, status, and pleasant working conditions. For increasing numbers of workers these latter meanings are more important than monetary remuneration.

In the 1950's interviews were taken with a national sample of men concerning the meaning of work.[3] In this study, it is found that: (1) work is more than a means to an end for the great majority of employed men; (2) that non-working or unemployment is threatening to men, even before the retirement age; and (3) work serves more than a monetary end for both middle class and working class occupational people, but the nonmonetary significance varies from occupation to occupation.

In this national study respondents were asked, "If by some chance you inherited enough money to live comfortably without working, do you think you would work anyway or not?" [4] The answer affirmed a continuation of work, with 80 per cent favoring it. Respondents were asked about their reasons for continuing work (see Table XVI.1). Thirty-two per cent of the respondents said they would work in order to keep occupied. Another 9 per cent reported that they would continue to work because they enjoy the kind of activity. Ten per cent responded that they would work because it contributes to health and self-respect. Commenting on the same phenomenon from the negative point of view, 14 per cent said they would continue to work to avoid feeling idle.

When the respondents were asked what they would miss if they did not work, 25 per cent reported a feeling of restlessness would occur. Nine per cent said they would miss a feeling of doing something worthwhile. Thirty-one per cent indicated that they would miss the contact with friends.

Reasons for continuing work were analyzed by occupation. Professionals would continue to work primarily because of the interest or the accomplishment of their tasks. In sharp contrast, over 40 per cent of the trade and operative workers reported that they would continue to work in order to be occupied. In addition to continuance of work in general, professionals reported (68 per cent) that they would continue to work in their same kind of endeavor. Similarly, over half of the persons in sales and managerial occupations reported that they too would continue to work in their same or related jobs. On the other hand, more than half of all the workers in the trades, operative, unskilled, and service occupations manifested no such tenaciousness for their occupation even though they desired to continue working.

The significance of such findings is sharply relevant as the work day, the work week, and the work year continue to be shortened with ad-

TABLE XVI.1

Reasons for Continuing Working

Question: "Why do you feel that you would work?"

	Number	Per cent
Positive Reasons		
Enjoy the kind of work	27	9
To be associated with people	4	1
To keep occupied (interested)	93	32
Justifies my existence	14	5
Gives feeling of self-respect	13	5
Keeps individual healthy, good for person	30	10
Other	4	1
Total Positive Reasons	185	63
Negative Reasons		
Without work, would:		
Feel lost, go crazy	42	14
Feel useless	5	2
Feel bored	11	4
Not know what to do with my time, can't be idle	29	10
Habit, inertia	17	6
To keep out of trouble	3	1
Other	2	0
Total negative reasons	109	37
Total responding	294	100
Not ascertained	20	
Total would work	314	
Total would not work	79	
Not ascertained	8	
Total sample	401	

Source: Nancy C. Morse and Robert S. Weiss, "The Function and Meaning of Work and the Job," *American Sociological Review*, 20 (April 1955), p. 192.

vancements in technology. Work is apparently not just a matter of producing and distributing the nation's goods and services, because this is rapidly being rendered more efficient by increased mechanization. But the meaning of work is to be occupied, contributing, creative, and so forth. Freedom from economic work, by machine displacement, is bound to be frustrating for the large numbers of people who report such meanings of work. Reynolds and Shister similarly report that the most important meanings of work are human relations on the job, relations with one's fellow workers, physical characteristics of the work including variety and interest, and finally, wages in terms of a standard of living.[5]

While there is a widespread impression that contemporary workers are losing the incentive to work, the evidence suggests more that old meanings or significance of work are being frustrated and displaced by technology. New meanings are not yet widely identified and accepted. In the social organization of society and the social organization of occupations this transition and fleeting meaning in work is a serious problem. It is less that man is losing his incentive for work and more that the nature of his society and of his occupations are increasingly the handmaidens of his own invention. And while his social engineering is far from complete—indeed, it is essentially a process—the elements of occupational meaning do not fit well the articulation of social organization as a whole. Accordingly, one observer noted, "That is why Picasso is more characteristic of our times than Rubens." [6]

Work and way of life. For professionals it is generally found that work is something of a nearly total way of life. For industrial workers, by contrast, work is little valued as an end in itself and is more important as a mechanism for achieving a means to other goals desired.[7] Indeed, many professionals value their work as central in their life. For some it is an end in itself. Orzack compared the interests of work as a way of life for professional nurses with the Dubin findings for industrial workers (see Table XVI.2). The pattern for professionals, as represented by nurses, is almost the direct opposite of the pattern reported for industrial workers. Nearly 80 per cent of the nurses reported work as their central life interest while slightly less than one-quarter of the industrial workers reported such a high importance for work. Similarly, over 90 per cent of the industrial workers indicated that their informal relations were in non-work frames of reference while 45 per cent of the nurses reported work centered in formal relations. For 67 per cent of the nurses their personal satisfactions were found in work circumstances, compared to only 15 per cent for the industrial workers. Formal organizational relations were work-centered for 91 per cent of the nurses and only 61 per cent were for the industrial workers. Similarly, the technological relations were more work-centered for nurses than for industrial workers. This and similar evidence supports the premise that work as a way of life is measurably different by occupational categories.

The impact of work on a way of life is well illustrated in the case of

TABLE XVI.2

Total "Central Life Interests" and Subordinate Experience
Patterns, for Professional Nurses (Orzack) and Industrial
Workers (Dubin)

Pattern	Professional Nurses (Orzack) Per Cent	Industrial Workers (Dubin) Per Cent
Total "Central Life Interest"		
Work	79	24
Non-work	21	76
Informal Relations		
Work	45	9
Non-work	55	91
General Relations (personal satisfactions)		
Work	67	15
Non-work	33	85
Formal Organization Relations		
Work	91	61
Non-work	9	39
Technological Relations		
Work	87	63
Non-work	13	37
N	150	491

Source: Louis H. Orzack, "Work as a 'Central Life Interest' of Professionals," Social Problems, 7 (Fall 1959), 127.

a 27-year longitudinal study.[8] Forty individuals were originally studied
in 1932–33 concerning their occupations and job satisfactions. In 1959,
they were again studied concerning job satisfactions. The recent study
is based on the responses of 27 persons available from the original
study. The author does not argue that it is possible to generalize to a
larger population from a basis of so few cases. The importance of the
evidence lies in the longitudinality of the study.

After 27 years of following careers of selected respondents, it is
clearly found that older persons are more occupationally satisfied than

younger ones. More particularly, it is found that the greatest increases in job satisfaction are achieved by individuals who have made great changes in their jobs. This finding is in some considerable contrast to a widely held belief that individuals who achieve low job satisfaction should change their personality through therapy more than change their jobs. The respondents in this longitudinal study, with the exception of one individual, had experienced no psychotherapy or counseling psychology. Their adjustments and advancements were achieved through job changing.

The impact of work on the way of life may be summarized as aspiration and achievement in the early years and gratification and satisfaction in the later years. This varies with the particular occupation in which one participates, but in the achievement-oriented urbanized society maximum satisfactions are normatively deferred to the later years. Yet it may indeed be conjectured that this increased satisfaction is less a function of wrestling with achievement than it is of accepting of one's status, regardless of what it is.

The meaning of work in the urbanized mass society is increasingly an experience of creativity and self-expression. Hence, the idea occupations of professionals and executives are more prestigeful and sought after than the relatively more routinized machine-tending occupations. Even in the face of the shortening of the work day, the work week, and the work year there remains an absence of effective alternatives for significant meanings in life other than occupations. In short, for many occupations work continues to be the way of life. And where work is not the way of life, no alternative life expression appears to have comparable viability.

Work and status. Occupation continues to contribute more to an individual's social status than most other factors of life existence. Accordingly, a high degree of constancy is found for occupational prestige from one national area to another and between Oriental and Occidental cultures. The meaning of work and occupation is everywhere such that professionals and idea people are found at the upper end of the occupational continuum while unskilled workers are found at the lower end of the continuum.

Working up the occupational hierarchy is a well-established mechanism for social climbing. When social stratification becomes more rigid and occupational organizations more strong, individuals may have to transfer their aspiration from their own experience to that of their progeny. A recent empirical study of the job satisfactions and statuses of metal tradesmen and carpenters revealed that occupational security is the most singularly important meaning of work factor.[9] Other factors emphasized in illustrating job satisfaction are, in order of importance: good pay, the sort of work liked, pleasant and/or comfortable working circumstances, opportunity to move up into a more highly paying job, possibility of promotion, having a good boss, and working with the people one likes. The meaning of work in these middle status occupations is inevitably job security rather than innovation and creativity. Concern with upward mobility is widely reported, and when the worker is blocked in this effort transfer of his aspirations to his children is generally reported.[10] Other occupations are entered precisely because of the status remuneration which they confer.[11] Danielson interviewed engineers and scientists in ten companies, employed as executives (44), supervisors (91), and nonsupervisory professional employees (277).

Most engineers and scientists were able to isolate specific reasons for their satisfactions (see Table XVI.3). The lack of anything near a

TABLE XVI.3
Employees' Reasons for Satisfaction with Job Activities

Reasons [a]	Times Each Reason was Given
I. Visible Results	
a. I can point to results of *my* effort	42
b. I can see progress toward a goal	9
c. I obtain results that pay off to the company	8
II. Task Completion	
a. I see an idea through from inception to completion	27
b. My predictions or hypotheses work out	10
c. I eliminate problems or "bugs"	7
III. New, Nonroutine, Challenging Work	
a. My work is new, it's pioneering, it requires imagination .	38
b. It's nonroutine, there is variety and balance	33
c. It's a challenge, it taxes my ingenuity	35
IV. Personal Satisfaction	
a. My work gives me creative experiences	41

	Times Each Reason was
Reasons [a]	Given

b. I can take personal pride in my job. (not related to reward) 20
c. My work satisfies my personal curiosity 10
d. It gives me personal satisfaction and it satisfies the company goals 5

V. Recognition from Others
  a. My supervisor trusts me, lets me work on my own 19
  b. As a result of my work, others recognize me as an expert . 15
  c. My supervisor and/or higher management recognizes me for my work 9
  d. I perform a service or help others and gain their respect . 7

VI. Self-Realization (utilization and extension of abilities)
  a. I am extending my college training (broadening) 29
  b. My talents, training and interests are utilized 28
  c. I consider my present work training for the future 4

VII. Relations with People
  a. I have contacts with others within and outside the company 31
  b. There is teamwork in my work group 9

VIII. Miscellaneous
  a. I have an opportunity to contribute to fundamental knowledge 11
  b. I have an opportunity to work on something immediately useful 9
  c. I have an opportunity to work on something I consider important 5

[a] Given by 277 nonsupervisory engineers and scientists.
Source: Lee E. Danielson, *Characteristics of Engineers and Scientists Significant for their Utilization and Motivation* (Ann Arbor: The University of Michigan, 1960), p. 38.

unanimous agreement was anticipated because this type of occupational person is socialized to be an individualist. Nevertheless, some common patterns did obtain. They want their talents and results to be utilized. They, personally, want to be recognized. They want the supervisors to accept engineers' and scientists' individual differences.

From another point of view Danielson's data suggest that supervisors should know that their idea people will want visible results and pride in their work. Scientists emphasize satisfaction in creativity requiring imagination. They want a variety of purposeful tasks. Contact with others, as colleagues, both within and outside of the company is highly important. Support and trust from the supervisor is central to their job satisfaction.

Dissatisfying job activities were also articulated with considerable firmness. Performing routine work was most often cited as a source of dissatisfaction. Preparing and presenting reports, both written and oral, were disliked. Clerical tasks were also cited as burdensome. Experiment testing was not viewed as rewarding. Teaching, supervising, drafting, and a variety of other activities were generally disliked.

Work meanings by occupation and social class. Clear differences are reported for meaning of work by occupation.[12] When questioned about the interest of their occupations a favorable response was reported by nearly 72 per cent of salaried employees and over 92 per cent of professionals and executives. By contrast, only some 54 per cent of all factory workers reported that their jobs were interesting. The differences continue to be reported when workers were asked about hard work as a mechanism for achievement. Only 40 per cent of the factory workers indicated that this was a means for advancement; 49 per cent of the salaried workers believed that harder work would enable them to get ahead; and finally, more than 59 per cent of the professionals and executives respond that hard work would enable them to move up in their occupations. Union membership in the case of factory workers contributed little to differential responses in the meaning of work.

In another study, it is reported that white-collar workers place little importance on the character of work itself, while blue-collar workers are most concerned with the physical conditions in the work situations, with monetary rewards, and with cleanliness in the work environment.[13] In similarly related studies office workers are found to place the highest meaning of work on an interesting situation, while factory workers emphasized security.[14] In still another study of 1300 sales, clerical, and mechanical workers at the Minneapolis Gas Light Company, it was found that the mechanical workers place the highest meaning of work on security and the lowest meaning on type of job, while the sales and clerical workers place the highest importance on type of job and the lowest importance on job security.[15]

The meaning of work in job satisfaction is important both to occupational organization and to societal organization. In a substantial empirical study of more than 700 employees doing clerical work in a company, it is reported that when workers are content with their situations, their pay, and their status, their identification with the company as an organization and their favorable feeling toward supervisors is increased. In juxtaposition, their interest in leaving the company is decreased.[16] The degree of satisfaction which these workers manifest was directly related to the degree of skill required in the job. Even in this case the challenge in the work situation, for job satisfaction, varied among individuals. The degree of satisfaction in meaning which the worker receives for his level of pay and job status is related to his work cycle and his aspirations. In sum, the degree of satisfaction is a function of level of aspiration, need-tension level, and amount of return for the involvement.[17]

Work satisfaction and meaning varies with occupational category. The many case studies of work situations and of occupations confirm this generalization. Accordingly, it is of more than ordinary significance that the white-collar occupations in general, and the professional-executive occupations in particular, are expanding most rapidly in the second half of the twentieth century. It is precisely in these occupations that practitioners report the most intense meaning of work and the most satisfactions. Work continues to contribute to status and meaning for individuals even in the urbanized society where the individual's contribution to work in many areas is being replaced by machines and automation. For many increased meaninglessness of work is overcome by an increasing search for leisure as an end in itself.[18] And so it is that the significance of work in the urbanized society is both changing and challenged for continually vital meaning. It is changing from physical energy input to idea production. It is challenged in that workers spend a lesser number of hours in work and a greater number of hours in leisure. Its vitality is demonstrated by the trend for idea occupations to accelerate much more rapidly than blue-collar occupations.

The meaning of work in its saliency in the urbanized American society of the twentieth century may be far less than the historical Protestant ethic used to be, but by default that ethic which places the meaning of work in a superior position over other meanings for human existence continues almost unabated. The measure of work meaning by the physical input and the sweat of one's brow continues to some extent in the absence of an effective social organization of society based on leisure.

Morale and work. Morale is a long-standing central focus of concern in the meaning of work subject. Psychologists are engaging in extensive research on the subject, and little more than documentation of the phenomenon is achieved to date. The nature of morale remains largely an enigma, a subject of question. Two examples suffice to illustrate the importance of this dimension.

In the first case the study of morale is based on the empirical investigation of a Detroit department store sales unit, staffed by 18 persons—14 men and 1 woman in a sales force, a manager, an assistant manager, and a stock boy.[19] The proposition is widely put forth that morale and high production show no direct correlation.[20] It is frequently found that relatively high rates of production are recorded where there is an extensive degree of poor or low morale. In other cases high morale and high production are reported together. The Detroit study findings again gave support to the observation that high morale and high production are independent variables. Particular focus in this study is on the impact of small work groups. It is found that such small work units are able to establish and maintain pressures for individual conformity. There is evidence in this study that self-determination of the work situation contributes to a high degree of morale. Yet the researchers themselves make no broad claim that self-determination is the variable on which morale depends.

A more recent empirical study was designed to investigate the relations between salary and morale of school teachers.[21] In this study, the research is designed to test the hypothesis that high teacher morale and merit salary schedules are to a considerable degree mutually exclusive. Accordingly, it would follow that high, medium, and low morale should be found in school systems that use a seniority type or single salary schedule. It was indeed the proposition of this research that a statistically different morale relationship would be found among teachers in schools using a merit type of salary schedule from those in schools using a non-merit type of salary schedule. The morale inventory was constructed to examine attitudes in five areas: self, school, community, administration, and policy. Ten statements were constructed as an index for each of the five areas. An example of the instrument is as follows: "Policy—attitudes concerning the policies and policy-making functions relative to the school system. Sample item: Policies under which pay raises are granted are: Very unsatisfactory, Sound and fair, Unfair in many instances, Reasonably satisfactory." [22]

The universe for this study was constituted of teachers in 10 suburban schools. The type of school ranged from large senior high schools to smaller high schools and ultimately included 6 elementary schools. Six hundred and fourteen inventories were administered and collected. Some 336 were in merit salary schools and 278 were in single salary schools. The findings revealed a lack of significant difference between merit and non-merit school salary systems on the morale level of teachers. There were indeed absolute differences reported, but they were insufficient to have occurred more frequently than by chance. A more detailed analysis revealed no significant differences in morale within the five areas of the inventory. This suggests that the nature of morale has a total rather than fragmented meaning for occupational practitioners.

These studies suggest the nature of viable recognition of morale and at the same time reveal the evasiveness of the subject in general. From sales to the professions morale is a widely known and easily identifiable phenomenon. It makes a decisive impact on work; it is a significant meaning of work.

PERSONAL ADJUSTMENT

The meaning of work is illustrated in the diverse personal adjustments which individuals make to their situations. Some of the clearest examples are illustrated in piecework conditions and in situations where output is arbitrarily restricted.

Eleven months of participant observation experience on the drill line in a machine shop enabled Donald Roy to closely examine the norms of piece work behavior.[23] He found that even where piecework was presumably an incentive for individual operator achievement there were many group norms established, and enforced, which indicated the amount of production that would be acceptable under various sets of circumstances. This resulted in quota failings, goldbricking, and so forth. In short, from an occupational organizational point of view such findings signify that the meaning of work is social rather than individual. That even in a work environment which is organizationally structured for piece or individual behavior group norms are rigid and maintained.

In another empirical investigation of semiskilled machine workers restriction on output was reported.[24] This investigation involved 18 men divided among 3 shifts of 6 each. It was found that there were group norms which called for restrictive outputs even when the organization's system provided for financial reward for individual high rates of production. The normative system of production as defined by the employing organization was established by the work study office analysis of time necessary for specific work operations. The findings of this study reveal a social satisfaction gained for the workers in their norm of restrictiveness. At the outset this satisfaction can be articulated as limiting individual competition and increasing group cohesiveness by mutual co-operation. In effect, the men were bargaining both against machines and against management. In the face of a variety of organizational and occupational uncertainties, norms for restricted output, it was revealed, constituted systems of real social support for individuals.

Featherbedding is still another broad example of intense personal adjustment being manifested in cohesive group action. Collective group behavior and high rates of social interaction among occupational practitioners are variously illustrated as strong if not primary meanings of work for individuals.[25]

CONDITIONS OF WORK

An important dimension of meaning in work is clearly identified in repetitive task situations.[26] The widespread assumption is that repetitive work is monotonous, boring, and unchallenging. When performed effectively at all, it is performed by people of low intellectual ability. More careful examination of the meaning of work in repetitive situations reveals that the above generalization is far from valid. In a study of a large assembly department of a factory producing high quality electronic products, it is reported that with careful personnel management and the development of pride in product there is also produced a high order of meaning or significance in work. The details of this assembly situation involve the bringing together in proper order some ten or more quite small delicate parts, often under a magnifying glass, and at a work pace where the time for the job cycle is typically one minute or less. Samples of the output are subject to extreme scrutiny in a quality control department. The research investigating this situation lasted over a period of two years and involved 115 interviews with operators, personnel observation, and both formal and informal inquiry with all levels of the supervisory staff.

The findings reveal that a majority of the operators report their job to be fairly interesting to very interesting. Indeed, less than 20 per cent responded that their job is monotonous or boring. When intelligence level is held constant it is discovered that the high order of satisfaction is not correlated with low intelligence.

In part, the repetitiveness of the job enabled the worker to find significance and meaning by freedom to think about many other situations unrelated to their work. But more important, the work was revealed to be meaningful because the operators were proud of the high quality items which they produced. There was a sense of pride in seeing the parts nicely fitted together. More particularly, there was a high meaning placed on work because the operators believed they were doing something which most people were unable to do.

For efficiency in this repetitive work there was indeed an official method for assembling the several parts. Nonetheless, observation and interviewing revealed that many operators followed different techniques in the effective assembling of the parts. The possibility of this amount of deviation in the techniques contributed to their initiative and job satisfaction.

Such research reveals that a careful analysis of work situations, even repetitive ones, can provide for attractiveness in pride of production and challenge in achievement of techniques. The authors conclude that repetitiveness by itself is an insufficient basis for predicting the quality of meaning in work.

SUMMARY AND IMPLICATIONS

Meaning of work norms in occupational organization range from the precise to the elusive. In the main, norms for articulating meaning of work are greater now in the vastly occupational character of the urbanized society than in previous periods of history. As occupations become more free-standing and make major impacts on social behavior the importance of meaning and significance in work is intensified.

More particularly, as the amount of physical toil required for human subsistence is reduced and machine energy input is increased the diverse meanings of work are punctuated. The meaning of work in way of life occupations is considerably different from the meaning of work in jobs that have scarcely reached an occupational level.

The literature on the meaning of work may be summarized in the assertion that occupational organization has become more free-standing, and symbols for expressing human meaning in work are more clearly articulated. Accordingly in this chapter we have examined the meaning of work as expressed in status, as it is differentiated by occupation and social class. Analysis is made of the dimensions of morale, personal adjustment, and conditions in the work situation as each of these contribute to the meaning or significance of work.

As occupation constitutes one of the most significant elements in determining social status in the urbanized society, the fullness of the expression of the social status is manifested in the meaning and significance of work as perceived by occupational participants. People are characteristically occupational participants in the urbanized society. Their satisfactions or dissatisfactions with life are disproportionately the function of their perceived meaning in work. The next chapters in this section follow a common thesis of reporting the meaning of work in the major occupational categories.

NOTES

1. Alexander R. Heron, *Why Men Work* (Stanford: Stanford University Press, 1948), pp. 12–14.
2. H. Allan Robinson and Ralph P. Conners, "Job Satisfaction Researches of 1960," *Personnel and Guidance Journal*, 40 (December 1961), 373–7; see esp. the bibliography.
3. Nancy C. Morse and Robert S. Weiss, "The Function and Meaning of Work and the Job," *American Sociological Review*, 20 (April 1955), 191–8.
4. Ibid. p. 192.
5. Lloyd G. Reynolds and Joseph Shister, *Job Horizons: A Study of Job Satisfaction and Labor Mobility* (New York: Harper and Bros., 1949), p. 34.
6. Aaron Levenstein, *Why People Work* (New York: Crowell-Collier Publishing Co., 1962), p. 8.
7. Louis H. Orzack, "Work as a 'Central Life Interest' of Professionals," *Social Problems*, 7 (Fall 1959), 125–32; Robert Dubin, "Industrial

Workers' Worlds: A Study of the 'Central Life Interests' of Industrial Workers," *Social Problems*, 3 (January 1956), 131–42; and A. M. Carr-Saunders and P. A. Wilson, *The Professions* (Oxford: Clarendon Press, 1933).

8. Robert Hoppock, "A Twenty-Seven Year Follow-Up on Job Satisfaction of Employed Adults," *Personnel and Guidance Journal*, 38 (February 1960), 489–92.

9. N. S. Dufty, "Occupational Status, Job Satisfaction, and Levels of Aspiration," *The British Journal of Sociology*, 11 (December 1960), 348–55.

10. Ely Chinoy, *Automobile Workers and the American Dream* (Garden City, N.Y.: Doubleday, 1955).

11. Lee E. Danielson, *Characteristics of Engineers and Scientists Significant for their Utilization and Motivation* (Ann Arbor: Bureau of Industrial Relations, University of Michigan, 1960), pp. 36ff.

12. Heron, *Why Men Work*.

13. Elizabeth L. Lyman, "Occupational Differences in the Value Attached to Work," *American Journal of Sociology*, LXI (September 1955), 138–44.

14. Lawrence G. Lindahl, "What Makes a Good Job," *Personnel*, XXV (January 1949), 263–6.

15. Clifford E. Jurgensen, "Selected Factors Which Influence Job Preferences," *Journal of Applied Psychology*, XXXI (December 1947), 553–64.

16. Nancy C. Morse, *Satisfactions in the Work-Job* (Ann Arbor: Survey Research Center, University of Michigan, 1953).

17. Ibid. p. 112.

18. Frederick Hurzberg, *et al.*, *The Motivation to Work* (New York: John Wiley & Sons, Inc., 1964), pp. 138–9.

19. Nicholas Babchuk and William J. Goode, "Work Incentives in a Self-Determined Group," *American Sociological Review*, 18 (October 1951), 679–87.

20. Daniel Katz, "Morale and Motivations in Industry," in *Current Trends in Industrial Psychology* (Pittsburgh: University of Pittsburgh Press, 1949), pp. 145–71.

21. Claude Mathis, "The Relationship Between Salary Policies and Teacher Morale," *Journal of Educational Psychology*, 50 (December 1959), 275–9.

22. Ibid. p. 276.

23. Donald E. Roy, "Work Satisfaction and Social Reward in Quota Achievement: An Analysis of Piece Work Incentive," *American Sociological Review*, 18 (October 1953), 507–14.

24. D. J. Hickson, "Motives of Work of People Who Restrict Their Output," *Occupational Psychology*, 35 (July 1961), 111–21.

25. Heron, *Why Men Work*, pp. 111–18.

26. Arthur N. Turner and Amelia L. Miclette, "Sources of Satisfaction in Repetitive Work," *Occupational Psychology,* 36 (October 1962), 215–31.

SUPPLEMENTARY READING

D. J. Hickson, "Motives of Work of People Who Restrict Their Output," *Occupational Psychology,* 35 (July 1961), 111–21.

Robert Hoppock, "A Twenty-Seven Year Follow-Up on Satisfaction of Employed Adults," *Personnel and Guidance Journal,* 38 (February 1960), 489–92.

Nancy C. Morse and Robert S. Weiss, "The Function and Meaning of Work and the Job," *American Sociological Review,* 20 (April 1955), 191–8.

Louis H. Orzack, "Work as a 'Central Life Interest' of Professionals," *Social Problems,* 7 (Fall 1959), 125–32.

H. Allen Robinson and Ralph P. Conners, "Job Satisfaction Researches of 1960," *Personnel and Guidance Journal,* 40 (December 1961), 373–7.

COLLEAGUESHIP XVII

Colleagueship is a special occupational situation involving deep intellectual stimulation plus an integrity of meaning seldom found in the urbanized society. The word colleague is frequently used by occupational men in the professions and creative areas of work. No specific definition is agreed upon for it. It is a complex phenomenon in sociological conceptualization. In spite of its evasiveness, one suspects that the experience of colleagueship stands at the very core of creative occupational endeavor.

Colleagueship involves intimacy and closeness in a work situation. It is important, therefore, to distinguish carefully between work groups and colleagues.[1] In a typical work group one may have deep intensity and high rates of interaction with a number of people, some of whom are colleagues, others peers, and still others superordinates and subordinates. The work group of an executive might include a few colleagues, namely, fellow executives in the same firm or a complementary firm; superiors and subordinates in the executive hierarchy; aids and assistants from technicians to secretaries to a custodial staff. Colleagues, by contrast to those in the work group, will be limited to individuals whose occupational work is idea production or idea utilization. Colleagues may be individuals in the same subject area, for example, other physicians if the situation is that of a hospital. Or colleagues may be extended to include for the physicians a variety of other professionals whose idea interests and professional competencies may be brought to bear on a common problem. A commonality of colleagueship may from time to time be experienced between clergymen and physicians; or between professors and engineers, etc. There is by contrast no structural basis for the experiencing of colleagueship between professionals and the custodians in their offices.

In this chapter we will consider the nature of colleagueship at a conceptual level and some of its concrete manifestations.

NATURE OF COLLEAGUESHIP

Concept. Colleagueship is an interactional situation, the central focus of which is the facilitation of intellectual stimulation. The structure of colleagueship is vague and esoteric, indeed, an idiom that is difficult to communicate in the urbanized society. The structure of colleagueship is diffuse rather than specific; qualitative rather than quantitative; more characterized by the informal than the formal. All of this seems to negate the idea of structure. There is a structure of colleagueship, but one cannot overstress its minimum rather than maximum detail. The minimum structure is not accidental but purposeful. The vagueness of the structure encourages maximum innovation.

The intellectuality of colleagueship must be viewed broadly. It includes but far exceeds that kind of intellectual expression found among scholars, professionals, and artists. There is an intellectual colleagueship which is a vital part of the endeavors of certain businessmen and executives. Executives may participate in intellectual curiosity and expression when they support basic research or when they view their firm's contribution to the welfare of a society.

Several factors may be identified which contribute to the sense of colleagueship.[2] First is the vital freedom to control membership in colleagueship groups. Colleagueship is voluntary and extremely unofficial. In some cases official entry into an occupation or profession may be both regulated by law and by licensing. Colleagueship groups are more internal and exclusive than the occupation itself. One may have the full rights and certification to function as an occupational practitioner, and yet be excluded from numerous or all colleagueship groups. Moreover, one may desire entry into an occupation, but not aspire to certain kinds of colleague relationships.

A second factor which contributes to the sense of colleagueship is occupational consciousness. Practitioners in a given occupation may enter colleague relationships in deference to their occupation and/or in its expansion. Artists may participate, for example, in colleagueship and thereby occupationally defend themselves against the societal "squares" who so often constitute their clients or patrons. Support by such clients is made more tolerable through colleagueship.

Colleagueship is further supported by formal and informal occupational structures which facilitate interaction. Professional society meetings and the publication of learned journals are two examples of structural interactional mechanisms which contribute to colleagueship.

Special dimensions. Included in colleagueship dimensions are norms of duration, location, friendship, professionalism, cultism, etc. In most cases the duration of colleagueship is for a relatively short period of time. One's area of focus and interests change, one's knowledge accumulates, and, accordingly, what was once an effective colleague experience deteriorates and goes out of existence. Colleagueship between individuals exists as long as both parties to the situation experience intellectual stimulation and growth in knowledge. When their growth through mutual interrogation reaches a point of saturation, their colleagueship on that subject is terminated. It must be noted that the termination of colleagueship in no way implies the deterioration or obliteration of interaction among the individuals. A high rate and intensity of interaction that has come into existence as a result of colleagueship may long endure beyond it in the form of friendship or to some alternative end.

Location of colleagues in proximity or considerable separation may have little impact on the relationship. For example, some physical separation may facilitate colleagues having greater professional association. A professor and his students, who are experiencing a common colleagueship, may participate on each other's programs, in each other's research, and in each other's publications while they are physically separated and experiencing different professional associations. Indeed, the accusation of nepotism or patronage is often avoided in such situations because the colleagueship experience is disguised or unobservable to great numbers of people. On the other hand, physical separation reduces the frequency of contact among colleagues. The opportunity for mutual interrogation is reduced and the areas of mutual interest change.

In the main, the environment of professionalism is conducive to colleagueship. A more careful examination, however, of professional environments reveals that there is much contradiction of colleagueship. There is a public and an official character about professional structures. Much of the structure of professionalism involves a boundary maintenance and occupational aggrandizement which is in excess of or exterior to intellectual stimulation. The time associated with these mundane affairs of professionalism necessarily competes with the time available to be utilized in colleagueship.

A special dimension of colleagueship is importantly illustrated in what some have referred to as cultism.[3] The colleague cult is in effect an intellectual protection agency. It is particularly significant for those individuals who lack an excessive amount of original intellectual creativity. They in fact become satellites to already established idea schools. They refine, specify, proliferate, and generally propagate the work of a "great" scholar from another period or place. Wilson writes that "the so-called 'halo effect' not only gives renown to the mediocre works of a great savant, but also sheds some rays upon his followers." [4] Attaching one's self to a school of thought is often a matter of necessity in a highly ritualized field, however, for the subject matter may be monopolized by networks of "academic cartels" similar to the "Chaucer trusts" and others in literary scholarship.[5] In this kind of cult colleagueship one finds in-group favoritism. There are complimentary book reviews accompanied by patriotism for those in the in-group and exclusion or neglect of the work of those in the out-group.

A careful distinction between colleagueship and friendship is necessary. Colleagues may be friends and friends may be colleagues, but the one circumstance is not prerequisite for the other. Friendship may well be more long enduring than colleagueship. And, moreover, there is no central core of meaning in friendship which involved the depth of intellectual stimulation.

The relation between colleagueship and friendship has been empirically researched for admen, dentists, and professors.[6] It was hypothesized that where there is a high occupational commitment there will be a greater tendency to develop occupational communities. Or by contrast, for individuals who look upon their job as a means to alternative ends, an effective way of making money, there was less tendency to seek out colleagues for leisure and alternative forms of stimulation. It was discovered that dentists had the lowest level of commitment to their work and professors the highest level of commitment, with admen between these two. The empirical findings supported the notion accordingly, with 88 per cent of the professors including colleagues in their friendship groups, 64 per cent of the admen including colleagues in their friendship groups, and only 20 per cent of the dentists including colleagues in their friendship groups. The respondents were asked to list their ten best friends and then colleagues were identified as being enumerated within them or not. The analysis was also carried out on the basis of one's three best friends. Similar results obtained: 84 per cent of the professors, 48 per cent of the admen, and only 16 per cent of the dentists reported that two out of three of their best friends are also occupational colleagues. Even among the dentists it was discovered that when they had a high commitment to their occupation they also had a high proportion of colleagues in their friendship groups. The professors were least able to differentiate their work from their total way of life. They were, however, members of a faculty of a small residential college. The data give little basis for asserting the probability of similar friendship-colleagueship patterns at a large urban idea-factory type university.

The above is sufficient illustration of the evasive and esoteric nature of colleagueship. The character of colleagueship is best understood by accepting its fleeting nature.

OVERT MANIFESTATIONS OF COLLEAGUESHIP

In spite of the covert nature of colleagueship, there are some overt manifestations which are readily seen, including recruitment, obligations, evaluation, and strained relationships. These and others are indeed all aspects of colleagueship, but to study and summarize these characteristics and thereby believe that one has a knowledge of colleagueship is grossly misleading.

Recruitment. An impressive study of some aspects of colleagueship and recruitment is reported for academic men.[7] The information is based on an empirical analysis of interviews with members of academic departments in which vacancies and replacements had occurred. Their consideration of recruitment was, therefore, real rather than hypothetical. The point of view is that of the departmental colleagues. The actors who participate in the recruitment are many, including deans, assistant deans, administrative committees, provosts, vice presidents, presidents or chancellors, and finally, regents or trustees. Some of these administrators associate themselves rather closely with the matter of recruitment and/or dismissal; indeed, more closely than the academic colleagues care to admit. Nevertheless, the nature of the situation is such that the initial advantage in recruitment lies with colleagues rather than administrators.

The rates of participation in recruitment vary by academic position. It is noted that the search for candidates, the evaluation of their credentials, and the initial selection of candidates are all primarily controlled by the chairman and senior colleagues in academic departments. The deans and their committees are the next most frequent participators in this search-evaluation-selection process. Also, all of the departmental members and, finally, the higher administration officials, participate in this stage of recruitment. After the basic selection is made, the colleagues most frequently consult the deans, after which the details of making the offer and closing the contracts are often returned to the colleague level. The official and visible details of recruitment in academic life are extensively handled by colleagues. The strength of colleagues in their own recruitment is further illustrated by the absence of any reports of the failure on the part of trustees to turn down any candidate recommended to them. Indeed, there are few situations in which the trustees are asked to approve a candidate before an official offer may be made. Their role is more official and documentary than directive or evaluative in a colleagueship sense. The roles played by top administrative officials are similarly passive from the colleague's point of view. They may in some cases make the final offers and even interview some candidates before the offers are made. Nonetheless, their actions are primarily in reference to those candidates who are presented to them so that the strength of colleagues in selecting colleagues is still vastly preserved. Respondents reported the recruiting situation as follows:

We consulted other men in the area, and the man who was leaving himself. The Dean was called when we wanted to invite a man up at our expense, and we sent him a dossier at the same time. The Dean's office is primarily a vetoing office, since *he is not a biologist*. [italics added] He only passes on what we initiate.[8]

Another respondent, who viewed the creative and in-depth part of recruitment to be a matter controlled by the colleagues, initiated the details and took the accomplished report to the dean:

I took the credentials to the Dean. He looked at them and said all right, whereupon I wrote to the man that I was asking for his appointment. He accepted, then a formal letter was sent. He was approved by the Dean.[9]

Theoretically, there is an organizational chart or plan at a university within which the recruitment process is stipulated. Between the formal and informal procedures there is often, nevertheless, a considerable gap and obscurity. The balance of power is frequently more determined by the aggressiveness of the parties involved than by the formal organizational chart. In this situation colleagues have the opportunity for strong directiveness, but they are often little organized and by default allow much of their potential power to revert to deans.

It might be expected that in the somewhat obscure, but not clandestine, nature of colleagueship the details of recruitment are not fully known, but are variously surmised. The following quotations are from several individuals at the same college concerning the same appointment. "There was no screening committee; it was all between the Dean and me." "I had to carry the department's choice to the Dean. The Dean has never been known to turn down a departmental selection." "On an appointment like this, an instructor or assistant professor, we just put it on the budget." "We got the approval of the Dean and various members of the co-operating department. There was co-operation on the part of other departments too." "We consulted the Provost." [10]

It remains clear through all of this analysis that the chairman and the senior colleagues have the power and often exercise it to control the recruitment process effectively and intellectually.

There are several more subtle dimensions to colleague recruitment. Much of the dynamics of colleagueship occur in the search and evaluation stages of recruitment. The statistics reporting who participates in these stages are grossly inadequate for revealing the nature of the participation. In the labyrinth of colleagueship, with some intent, there is little overt reporting of what kind of colleague is being searched for. In terms of the cultism referred to earlier one must suspect that there is a category of potential for any recruitment situation, and a great number of other individuals who are hardly considered, if considered at all. This informality and subjectivity is a positive and integral part of colleagueship.

Obligations. The notion of colleague obligation is fairly widespread. It is secondary in nature and only partly related to the inner core of intellectual stimulation. A report by Borenstein of physicians' views of colleague obligations illustrates the situation.[11] In Borenstein's study of physicians the overwhelming majority of the respondents were able to articulately specify their notion of colleague obligations. The remaining few generally dismissed the idea of obligation as no more than the "Golden Rule." The specification of the colleague obligation was put this way, "the physician owes his colleagues a consideration of the aims of the medical profession." Or put another way, the physician is obligated to "keep himself above reproach from a moral standpoint." [12] The idea of obligation was also expanded to include bringing credit to the medical profession in general, avoiding malpractice, and sharing knowledge with one's colleagues. One physician expounded on the obligation to communicate ideas as follows:

The one thing that's particularly true of the medical profession is that there are no secrets in the practice of medicine. In trades, if someone invents something, he wants to get personal benefit from it. In medicine something new is given to the profession.[13]

In another case it was asserted that the colleague obligation is really exemplified in service to the patient.

Honesty. My friend and I quarrel on that. He has a lot of inferiority feelings, so he's always afraid he'll tread on someone's toes. I'd rather lose a referral than go along with a lot of nonsense. You owe them impeccable honesty.[14]

The colleague obligations were stated in still other ways.

A doctor should not criticize another doctor because, after all, one might ask, "why did he do such and such to this patient?" A doctor should not criticize until he knows what went on. *And,* he should evaluate the other doctors *in the times of the day!* I was just talking about that the other day. This woman said, "Doctor ——— took my uterus out, but he didn't take my ——— out. Now, why not?" I said that he did a good operation for the times! If he'd done that today, I would say, "well, that boob!" I try to look at the doctors by these age groups. Oh, these younger ones—I envy them. They have so much better training.[15]

In still another way colleague obligation was expressed for consultation and intellectual proficiency.

The physician should maintain a helpful attitude with his younger colleagues, and an open mind for discussion with any of his colleagues. When called into consultation by any other physician, he should give a straight-forward opinion to that physician and return his patient to him.[16]

Medical etiquette in the area of referral was also cited in terms of colleague obligation. Still another direction of colleague obligation referred to the work situation in general. It was specified that a physician should not take off too many nights a week because in doing so he would not be carrying his share of the medical load.

In all of these statements concerning colleague obligations the general welfare of the occupation or the patient was considered as much if not more than the intellectual stimulation.

Evaluation. Colleague evaluation in several respects is much related to colleague obligations. Colleague evaluations on the part of physicians was examined by Borenstein.[17] In general the evaluation of colleagues centered on their technical knowledge and skill, their personality, and, lastly, on their financial and political stature.

Physicians are largely controlled by their colleagues. Nevertheless in an interview situation one learns that some doctors evaluate others as quacks, but feel they do not have sufficient evidence to go before their local societies and make such charges. The controls are more informal than by direct accusation. Certainly within the hospital structure there may be evaluation and discipline of physicians without public announcement of the cases.

The general evaluation by practitioners of surgery are often critical. It was stated that a certain portion of the organism "flies around this town too much." Another general practitioner evaluator put it this way:

We need so many psychiatrists, but all we get are more carpenters. Surgeons are nothing but carpenters. *Anyone* can be a surgeon. A woman comes in; she has emotional disturbances, and she goes to a man. Because she has a pain in the pelvic region, he says she has an ovarian tumor. He doesn't see a tumor in there; he sees $200! That goes on a lot. We cracked down on them, but doctors are still doing too much of that.[18]

In another expression of evaluation great emphasis was placed on the intellectual practitioner level. In making referrals one physician put it this way:

Think(s) about his skill, of course, and his evaluation of humanity. That's what *I* think about in calling in a consultant—his understanding of people.

Some doctors think only of his manner. But I tell people, "So what if he's gruff and hard; he can help people and that's what counts. He's good at his skill." [19]

Other expressions of evaluation in terms of technical skill were juxtaposed with avoidance of cliques. Certainly the evaluation is both technical and nontechnical.

True colleagues—presence and absence. The poignancy of colleagueship is perhaps no more adequately illustrated than in the search for true colleagues. "Officially" one's colleagues might be those in his immediate work group who share the same discipline or intellectual function. But one's fellow executives, engineers, chemists, artists, etc., may or may not be one's true colleagues. They may in fact be at best only pseudo-colleagues. Germane in the work of the intellectual is the excitement and, at once, the misery of establishing one's own goals. Intellectually, creative work is both satisfying and frustrating, complete and never complete to one's satisfaction. To avoid the frustration of this intellectual milieu colleagues are sought as much for assurance as for intellectual interrogation.[20]

The seeking of colleague assurance is in effect a mechanism for avoiding, or at least diluting, the responsibility of setting one's own goals. It is indeed the seeking for a community of fate that is highly and deeply integrated in intellectual curiosity. The very nature of intellectual production is the creating of something new, something untried, giving birth, as it were, to an idea which may make one a culture hero, or damn one to the irrelevant incorrect, or unwanted. There is a community of comfort.

The highest essence of true colleagueship involves a group or interactional judgment in the establishing and sustaining of goals. The judgment of one's colleagues is often considered to be more relevant than even a highly ostentatious award by generalists who understand less adequately the complexities of the ideas. To provide the maximum degree of stimulation in such a limited goal-colleague space, Riesman asserts, one's true colleagues may be less in one's own discipline and more in adjacent intellectual areas. At any given time the sociologists may find more stimulation and security in colleagueship with a historian or an economist than with a fellow sociologist. Their related approach to a problem provides both stimulation and security in the area of intellectual inquiry.

The presence, or, more correctly, the absence, of colleagueship is clearly illustrated in a report of the relation between engineers and scientists.[21] It is asserted that the prestige of engineers has fallen in comparison to the rising prestige of scientists. The implication is that engineering and science have become bitter rivals, and the author suggests that they in fact are natural allies—that indeed many scientists become important engineers. All the while it is argued that it is erroneous to believe that engineering schools are populated by second-rate individuals who are not able to achieve as scientists.

The fact remains that in occupational organization pure scientists are primarily concerned with the exploration of ideas and the verification of knowledge. Engineers by contrast accept goals for achieving practical results. The idea base on which engineers operate is primarily produced by scientists. Given this differential orientation between the basic and the applied, the condition of competition between engineers and scientists is structurally unwarranted. In fact, they are mutually dependent. The intellectual relation between scientists and engineers is further strengthened by the new devices which engineers have built for supporting basic scientific research. This involves a reciprocity between scientists and engineers which provides a milieu for colleagueship rather than conflict. The ideas and service of both scientists and engineers are indispensable for the progressive development of technology. Their contributions, however, are so sufficiently differentiated that there is little probability of their becoming totally integrated.[22]

The presence of true colleagues is illustrated in medicine by the differential types of medical careers.[23] Hall distinguishes three types of medical careers. Within these careers differential colleague relationships are experienced. A nomenclature given these careers is friendly, individualistic, and colleague.

The colleague career is most characterized by a high identification with the medical institutions in one's area. The informal organization of the medical combine is important for the colleague career. The aim is the successful climbing of the hospital hierarchy, and ultimate acceptance into the inter-fraternity.[24] The following medical doctor's response is an illustration of the colleague career commitment:

There are two distinct types of success in medicine. A lot of young men come out of medical school who either need to start earning money, or are inclined that way. They go into general practice and take on any kind of work they think they can handle. On the other hand, there are men who start off by getting attached to a hospital, spend long hours in the clinics where the older men can see what they are interested in, climb very gradually, but contribute something to the world of medicine.

Let me contrast Dr. F. and Dr. N. The former was the more brilliant. Then they came here to practice. Dr. F. was head and shoulders above his fellow practitioners, but he drifted into a general practice. It is a very lucrative practice, yielding more than mine. Dr. N., on the other hand, stuck around the hospital and paid more and more attention to heart troubles. Now he is an authority in that field and I consider him one of the top men. I waited for five years to associate him with myself; that's how good he is.[25]

In the colleague career milieu, idea contributions are more important than financial success. The colleague career is orderly and follows a succession through intern, extern, active staff member, perhaps department head, and ultimately consulting staff status. There are various folkways and norms which delimit each of these stages in the colleague career. The amount of ambition is informally specified. The length of time that one should remain at each rung in the hierarchy is informally specified.

In the medical colleague career the fellow practitioners exercise maximum control over the work situation. In effect there is an informal sponsorship for many of the young medics in the colleague career. The sponsorship reduces the waiting period en route to active-staff appointment and ultimately facilitates entry into the inter-fraternity. The senior colleagues are continually judging the recruit's devotion to his institutional obligations and his regard for the etiquette of colleague relationships.

The colleague interaction varies at the different stages of the career. In the early stages of the career the junior colleague is faced with treating many charity cases. Later he will be given many important referral patients. Still later in his career he may become the protégé of an older physician and ultimately may take over his practice. This practice-patient transfer is the ultimate colleague career pattern. It is the reward, as it were, for subservience to the system and its propagation.

One of the most insightful situations in the analysis of true colleague situations is found in the relationships between traditional commercial artists.[26] The traditional-role artists or those widely considered to be

the fine artists, are at the top of the prestige hierarchy in the occupation. Commercial-role artists are clearly beneath them. Yet the amount
of support which society gives to the traditional artist is greatly limited.
In the short run the amount of economic and/or other tangible support given the commercial artist is greater. In the society's total organization of the labor force, the experience of shifting from traditional to
commercial artists is widespread. The retaining of one's original colleagues, the attaining of new colleagues, or the frustration between the
two sets of colleagues are all difficult interactional situations. The rationalization given for participation in commercial art to one's original
colleagues is recorded as follows: "Commercial art is used to beautify
the industrial world," "Commercial art is getting better all the time,"
"We raise the standard of living of people." [27] These rationalizations
suggest guilt feelings that one experiences in moving from traditional
to commercial art. It is, as it were, like moving into the enemy's camp.

The justification to the former colleagues is somehow unsatisfying.
The newcomer to commercial art is frustrated with a feeling of having
deserted or betrayed his traditional colleagues. Griff asserts that the
commercial artist has two alternatives. He can move to a different geographical location and thereby avoid most, if not all, interation with his
former colleagues, or he can escape the former colleagues symbolically.
In any event, adapting an escape route seems to be the course most
often taken but least desired. The preference is to retain one's original
colleagues, but the opportunity for doing so is not great.

The social distance between traditional and commercial art in a colleague sense is often extended because of intense feelings of opposition
which are often expressed against commercial art before one actually
enters it. It is common for traditional artists to hold the point of view
that their work is a gift, a talent of some supernatural origin. The colleagues operate in a social milieu in which there is a belief that they are
endowed with a special vision, and, accordingly, obligated to use their
talent for its intended purpose and to the glory of both God and man.
To depart from this ideological space of occupational sacredness into
the commercial art realm of occupational secularness is considered a
prostitution.

For commercial artists to attempt retention of their original colleagues is to try simultaneously to belong to two social systems for
which there is little congruence. Indeed, there is more latent conflict

and competition than co-operation between the social systems. The probability of loss of one's original colleagues is induced by the nature of the social systems.

Traditional artists gain their greatest support from the judgment of their colleagues. Society's general support is meager for them, and hence the judgment of colleagues is even intensified over that for many other occupations. When one becomes a commercial artist the judgment of the colleagues that was so important now becomes a matter of condemnation and criticism. This is a harsh situation indeed in occupational organization. Compartmentalization may be attempted, but withdrawal from one's former colleagues is more structurally probable.

The situation of colleagueship among artists indicates that, in addition to seeking one's true colleagues, one is chosen by or excluded from true colleagueship. Pseudo-colleagueship may be experienced widely and in many ways. True colleagueship by contrast is a condition which one may seek, but a situation into which one is more probably invited.

Colleagueship is further structured by the general social organization of society in addition to the social organization of occupations as such. In the practice of many occupations a worker may be remotely located from other occupational men of a like type. In such a situation the opportunity for colleagueship with one's occupational and intellectual peers is social organizationally obliterated. One may or may not have a viable opportunity for colleagueship with related occupational practitioners.

The above situation of colleague isolation is illustrated in the case of social workers.[28] In the case of the social worker one is often appointed to a small local area where there are no other social workers with whom one might have colleagueship and contact. Usually, however, in this relatively remote environment there is a variety of other occupational men with whom, potentially at least, the social worker might experience colleagueship. Typically in the environment one finds a medical officer, a children's officer, and a variety of other occupational individuals who at least in a broad and general way might be expected to have some concern for social welfare situations. In fact, it is discovered that some social distance rather than colleagueship tends to exist between the social worker and the other peripherally related occupational people. Often the social worker desires to consult the medical officer but finds him inaccessible.

Due in large part to social work's struggle for professionalization there is a great reluctance to seek colleagueship and consultation with occupational personnel in children's work, education, or police protection. All of these various people could be expected to have some general competency in the social welfare area, but are rigorously resisted for professional reasons. The social worker's own judgments about her potential colleagues greatly structure the satisfaction or frustration that the contacts yielded. Indeed, colleagueship and co-operation in this situation are greatly related to personality, more than to the specification of rules.

This situation illustrates the impact of physical proximity on colleagueship, and the impact of professionalization on colleagueship. In this particular situation most physical isolation and professionalization tend to reduce the amount of colleagueship for social workers.

Strained colleague relationships. Strained colleague relationships are revealed from time to time. A careful study records some of their nature and details in academic life.[29] Incidences developing from public pronouncements are fairly common in such innovative occupations as academia. The proper role for academic colleagues in situations of dispute over public pronouncements is far from clear. The concrete experience shows a varied reaction. A report of colleague reactions to the dismissal of a professor of political science by a school board illustrates the complexity.

The reaction was that it divided the faculty, with a few members outraged by the trustees' actions, others who felt one ought to be more careful in what one said, others who felt it was the duty of the faculty members to be sure that what was printed or published was what he had actually said. Others felt that you were a damned fool to get involved in much controversy, others felt that the views allegedly expressed were so outrageous that the university should make no effort to retain such members on the faculty. The over-all effect was that everyone ought to be more cautious.[30]

Attempts at false colleagueship are reported in other cases. For example, a professor may be invited to speak and discover that the audience is politically slanted or questionable. To avoid exposing himself he engages a so-called colleague to speak in his place. Verification of such incidences of false colleagueship is nearly impossible. The importance of the matter, however, rests not on verification, but on the belief that it does in fact exist. The colleagueship strain in such a situation is greater when the facts are limited and the fiction is extended. The torture and agony of stress is more effective in the general absence of a great number of facts.

Lazarsfield and Thielens found a general hesitancy for supporting colleagues under criticism. Sixty-six per cent of their respondents believed that most of their colleagues would support them if they were accused of being in leftist activities. Nonetheless, 28 per cent did not anticipate such support and a residual 6 per cent were uncertain. Furthermore, a tendency to follow the middle of the road was found. Colleagues who deviated from such middle ground were looked upon with some degree of suspicion. For example, one professor who admitted that he was an outspoken liberal complained as follows:

I am an expert on labor matters. I am advisor to labor arbitrations quite often, and employers think I am too liberal. I have not been elected to a school senate committee because my colleagues are afraid that I would make trouble for it. I know I have been put up for that committee, but they always elect some timid fellow who will go along with the crowd.[31]

The irony of much of the strained relations among colleagues lies in the reluctance to support innovation and difference even though the intellectual environment demands creative difference on the part of its participants. The tendency in colleagueships seems to be a straining to support middle of the road positions, while in juxtaposition the great creative intellectual breakthroughs are by nature a matter of independent thinking.

SUMMARY AND IMPLICATIONS

Colleague relationships are central for the meaning of occupations in the lives of many professionals and intellectuals. The meaning of work in the American urbanized society is not fully understood until one examines in some detail the nature of colleagueship. As the labor force becomes more white-collar in nature and more professional in its direction, the environment of colleagueship becomes ever larger and more persuasive in the meaning of work despite its esoteric nature.

Colleagueship has an important significance in the meaning of work organization for the society as well as for the participants. In the main it must be recognized that colleague organization is beyond the control and detailed direction of most formalized structures in the society's organization of the labor force. This is not to imply that colleagueship is a subversive aspect of labor organization. It does have, however, a most peculiar and compatible relationship with scientific and creative inquiry and, to that extent, tends to go beyond loyalty to national or other ethnocentric boundaries. Colleague organization is not ideological in nature. It is neither against nor for a particular national social organization. In such a situation in the mass urbanized society it is suggested that as more workers move into a colleague type of environment it is possible that society will have less control over them or that they will be frustrated by societal attempts to control their occupational behavior.

In an idea-oriented society, colleagueship provides a fruitful environment for maximum idea production. In a bureaucratic and controlled society, colleagueship is an area of frustration; it defies control more because of its evasive and esoteric nature than because of its systematic alternative approach to labor organization and idea production.

NOTES

1. Edward Gross, *Work and Society* (New York: Thomas Y. Crowell Co., 1958), chap. 6.
2. Gross, *Work and Society*, pp. 225–35.
3. Logan Wilson, *The Academic Man* (New York: Oxford University Press, 1942), pp. 208–10.
4. Ibid.
5. Ibid.
6. Joel E. Gerstl, "Determinants of Occupational Community in High Status Occupations," *The Sociological Quarterly*, 2 (January 1961), 37–49.
7. Theodore Caplow and Reece J. McGee, *The Academic Marketplace* (New York: Doubleday, Anchor Book, 1965).
8. Caplow and McGee, *Academic Marketplace*, p. 158.
9. Ibid.
10. Ibid. p. 159.
11. Audrey Farrell Borenstein, "The Ethical Ideal of the Professions: A Sociological Analysis of the Academic and Medical Professions" (Unpublished Ph.D. Thesis, Louisiana State University, Baton Rouge, 1958), pp. 359–79.
12. Ibid. p. 359.
13. Ibid. p. 360.
14. Ibid.

15. Ibid.
16. Ibid.
17. Ibid. pp. 375ff.
18. Ibid. p. 378.
19. Ibid. p. 379.
20. David Riesman, "The Academic Career: Notes on Recruitment and Colleagueship," *Daedalus*, 88 (Winter 1959), 159–61.
21. C. S. Draper, "Engineers and Scientists—Colleagues Not Rivals," *American Engineer*, 32 (August 1962), 42–63.
22. Ibid.
23. Oswald Hall, "Types of Medical Careers," *American Journal of Sociology*, LV (November 1949), 243–53.
24. Oswald Hall, "The Informal Organization of the Medical Profession," *Canadian Journal of Economics and Political Science*, 12 (February 1946), 30–44.
25. Hall, "Types of Medical Careers," p. 246.
26. Mason Griff, "The Commercial Artist," paper read at the American Sociological Association Meeting, New York City, 1960.
27. Ibid.
28. Barbara N. Rogers and Julia Dixon, *Portrait of Social Work* (London: Oxford University Press, 1960), pp. 171–2.
29. Paul F. Lazarsfield and Wagner Thielens, Jr., *The Academic Mind* (Glencoe: Free Press, 1958), pp. 229–35.
30. Ibid. p. 230.
31. Ibid. pp. 234–5.

SUPPLEMENTARY READING

C. S. Draper, "Engineers and Scientists—Colleagues Not Rivals," *American Engineer*, 32 (August 1962), 42–63.

Joel E. Gerstl, "Determinants of Occupational Community in High Status Occupations," *The Sociological Quarterly*, 2 (January 1961), 37–49.

Paul F. Lazarsfield and Wagner Thielens, Jr., *The Academic Mind* (Glencoe: Free Press, 1958), 229–35.

OCCUPATIONAL IDEOLOGIES XVIII

The ideas which men have about occupations and about their own work are among the most important forces in the direction of the totality of living. Occupations may be divided largely into two categories, namely those that constitute a way of life, and those that are means to ends which are not a way of life. In either event, the ideas which occupational men hold about their work are influential upon much of their individual life, and on much of the lives of the dependent individuals around them. This chapter is devoted to a description and analysis of the major dimensions of occupational ideologies.

NATURE AND DIMENSIONS OF OCCUPATIONAL IDEOLOGIES

Occupational ideologies are for all practical purposes ubiquitous. They have vast consequences for political behavior, social creeds, and stereotyped attitudes concerning certain types of work. Occupational ideologies may be so extensively developed and so widely held that in those way-of-life work situations the occupation in effect influences much more than work itself. Indeed, some occupational ideologies are disseminated far beyond the occupational groups from which they emerge. Other occupational ideologies have such limited dissemination within the occupation itself that their existence is precarious.[1]

Parochial and ecumenic ideas. The proposition is projected by Dibble that occupational ideologies which are parochial in nature will seldom if at all be diffused to other occupations and/or beyond the occupational realm. By contrast those occupational ideologies that are ecumenic may be disseminated widely among multiple occupations and beyond the occupational world into other areas relevant for social behavior. Dibble asserts first, that relevant ideas will become accepted

431

more quickly; second, that different problems, obstacles, and goals are associated with different occupations—for example, the daily concerns of bankers and bootblacks are sharply different, and, third, that different lines of work give people different views of life and different occupational ideologies.[2]

An example of parochial occupational ideology with limited dissemination experience and potential is illustrated in the case of janitors whose ideas are considered of little weight and relevance concerning major questions of sanitation. Another example of a parochial ideology is the case of the research professor who is a Chaucer specialist and whose judgments, therefore, concerning comparative systems of economical organization are seldom sought. These two examples of parochial occupation ideology are purposely drawn from opposite ends of the occupational continuum. The intent is to illustrate that occupational ideologies in and of themselves are not barred or limited on the basis of occupational rank or prestige alone.

Examples of ecumenic occupational ideas include the work of actuarial scientists whose meticulous and often almost esoteric mathematical calculations concerning the longevity of a population are nevertheless relevant and highly significant of broad areas of social planning. Similarly, the work of an agricultural scientist concerning the radioactive preservation of food may be highly esoteric, but the ideas generated by such research far exceed the occupations of agricultural scientists, indeed of the occupational world. The work and judgment of such esoteric scientists may determine whether a huge population is appropriately fed, underfed, or overfed. The work and judgments of these scientists may contribute to an agricultural organization that is economically self-sufficient, to one that is experiencing depression, or to one that is experiencing prosperity.

The ideologies of occupations that have to do with the internal organization of work in most cases are not disseminated widely. The ideas generated by an occupation that are concerned with the nature of the contribution the occupation makes to society will often be widely disseminated, particularly in those situations where the occupation deals with specialized and abstract thought.

Ideologies and stratification. Occupations at the upper end of the continuum frequently have more highly developed ideologies than occupations at the lower end of the continuum. Moreover, it is found that the ideologies of the higher ranking occupations are more ecumenic and less parochial than those of the lower occupations.[3] People in high ranking occupations are less concerned with the value of their job for its salary than for its many other forms of remuneration. As a result of this concern for occupation, a great many ideologies are articulated and communicated among the practitioners. Occupational men at the lower end of the continuum are less concerned with their work in and of itself. Any occupation that is an acceptable means to the end they desire will be adequate. As a result of this low concern for occupation, occupational ideologies are not elaborately developed.

Occupational ideologies developed by workers in high ranking positions are often by their nature addressed to individuals both within and beyond the occupation itself. The broad overriding altruistic nature of many high ranking occupations leads the practitioners to wide ideological considerations. The occupational ideologies of workers in operative and craft occupations in most cases are concerned with internal aspects of the work situations. They may be directed to the nature of wages, security of employment, the physical comfort in the work situation, or some related consideration. In these types of ideological expression there is much parochialism and little need or interest on the part of the general public to be concerned.

In short, it is observed that ideologies are directly related to occupational stratification. They are found at all levels, but they are more ecumenic at the upper ranking occupations and more parochial at the lower levels.

Ideologies and boundary maintenance. The expansive ideologies of high ranking occupations contribute to the increased importance of the occupation while decreasing its boundary maintenance. Among those occupations where ideologies characteristically exceed the internal organization of the work, the boundary of the occupation is diffused. For example, in the legal occupation the ideologies of the profession extend beyond the technical considerations of the law and contribute to a social space wherein lawyers participate regularly in political activities such as election to legislatures. Ideologically it is acceptable, indeed encouraged, that members of the legal profession should participate in elected political work. Due to such an ideology the boundary of the legal profession is diffused at several points into general practice in the political arena. Similarly, the ideologies associated with the occupation of the clergy break down boundary maintenance in such a way that the practitioners are expected, from time to time, to make general pronouncements concerning social problems that go far beyond theology and church organization. By contrast to the occupational ideologies in the professions of law and the clergy, the ideologies of such highly trained experts as research professors in ionizing radiation or experts in Chaucer do not encourage pronouncements of their judgments on generalized subjects beyond their technical areas. Ideologies of occupational work are strong among such technical experts but they are oriented to the internal organization of the occupation rather than to the generalized public. Such occupational ideologies contribute to a strong boundary maintenance around the area of work.

INDUSTRIAL REVOLUTION AND IDEOLOGIES

The Industrial Revolution, particularly in England during the eighteenth century, precipitated a major change in occupational ideology. Work in industry required a new discipline of employees. The infant factory system required the worker to put in long hours at regular and recurring intervals. Variety and irregularity of performance were not compatible with machine production. Peasants were accustomed to long hours of work with seasonal variation. During the summer season toil was from sunrise to sunset. But in the winter season the hours were short. Moreover, there were other opportunities for irregularity in work performance when the peasant was his own master.[4]

The occupational ideology of the new industrialism was, in short, workers obey and managers exercise authority. The place of the worker was clearly that of a lower estate, at best to be machine-like and at worst to be a functionary to support the machine operation.

Workers obey—managers exercise authority. By the late eighteenth century the traditional work patterns were disrupted. Industrialism was clearly growing, and a labor force for its support was demanded. While workers were not anxious to change their traditional way of life the poverty of the time made it a virtual necessity. But the new industrial work provided few comforts. The ideology placed the burden of the lower classes on their own idleness and sin. They were second-class citizens without a doubt. In the past the plight of the lower classes was considered beyond control. Now in a manner hardly improved, their plight was considered ideologically to be the result of their own deficiencies, their own responsibility.[5]

The new occupational ideology was aristocratic. The "higher classes" assumed for themselves the responsibility for thinking and decision-making. They assumed some small and vague responsibility for those classes beneath them, but were clear in their assertions that the low classes of workers should be submissive and dependent.

The new industrial leaders were not an altogether admirable class. They too were struggling for recognition. Often they had a conspicuous lack of education and of new ideas. Their motivation was more in a faith in progress than in a systematic inquiry.

Regardless of the less systematic ideologies and the shabby consideration given the lower classes by the managing occupational class, managerial superiority typically prevailed. It was supported indirectly by the increasing population. High birth rates were a tradition in the agrarian era preceding the rise of industrialism. Large numbers of children were an economic advantage where agrarian social organization dominated. Moreover, with high death rates, high birth rates contributed to the sustaining of the total population. Neither of these factors continued to contribute as much to the justification for an increasing population with industrialism. Death rates were gradually being reduced. More specifically, children were a burden rather than an advantage in the congested areas that were proliferating around plant locations.[6]

The main ideas of the new occupational ideologies were clear. Workers were "things" and to be treated virtually like machines. In essence they were really less than human. The tools of production were to be denied workers. A voice in management decision-making was unthinkable. Such firm and autocratic ideologies, at a time of ferment, migration, and change, were subjected to compensating currents of criticism, as might be expected. Alternative ideologies began to be projected by workers and their representatives. Demands for improvement in the work situation were raised. Cries for ownership of the tools of production were echoed. If the upper occupational categories were to assert that the workers' plight was largely his responsibility, then the workers began to assume their responsibilities. And in the new industrialism there developed multiple ideologies associated with the lower categories of workers. These ideologies all generated from among the occupational participants themselves as well as being attributed to them by the occupational superiors and from other sources in the society of which they are a part.

Unions and ideologies. Unions are the megaphones for expressing occupational ideologies which represent workers in primarily middle and low ranking occupations. Internal occupational ideologies are less developed in many skilled and unskilled types of work. Nevertheless, from several areas in society ideologies are generated by and attributed to such workers. Presumably unions constitute a substitute mouthpiece expressing a collective occupational ideology for these categories of workers in the absence of widely articulated ideologies by the occupational men themselves.

Crosser suggests that there are three distinct types of American unionism which one can identify at different periods of history.[7] The types are paternalistic, liberalistic, and revolutionary unions. Each type of union is an outgrowth of an occupational ideology. For example, the paternalistic union was propagated by an ideology of harmony. The liberalistic union was supported by an ideology for balance in marketing. Revolutionary unionism was nourished by the class-struggle ideology.[8]

Following the end of the American Civil War industrial development was accelerated both intensively and extensively. There was some kindling and rekindling of notions of master artisanship which led journeymen to suspect that their social position of prominence would not only be restored but would be continued. Such occupational groups, nevertheless, were threatened by the new systems of production. This was exemplified in the case of shoemakers; they were master craftsmen threatened by the industrial production of their product. To such individuals strikes were unwelcome. They were viewed as beneath the dignity of the master journeymen. Moreover, such elitist occupational men had an ideological orientation which rejected social conflict as an acceptable weapon for achieving their end. The boycott rather than the strike was considered more acceptable and somehow maintained the preservation of dignity appropriate to their occupational status. In short, Crosser asserts that such master artisans in the 1880's still believed that they were members of a harmonious community, rather that a community of conflict.[9]

The ideology of harmony, which supported paternalistic unionism was illustrated by the Order of St. Crispin. This Order believed that journeymen were destined to become independent master craftsmen. Similarly, the Knights of Labor held the belief that when industrial organization was perfected each man would be his own master, indeed, his own employer.[10]

Such a simple ideology of co-operation in a growing, massive, and burgeoning society was ephemeral. The ideology of co-operation was heralded in many quarters, but the complex division of labor in the new industrial order was unable, if not unwilling, to provide sufficient social mechanisms for asserting the empirical dominance of ideologies of co-operation. It is not implied that ideologies of conflict were, in a systematic way, substituted for, superior to, or dominant over ideologies of co-operation. The social history of the period reveals that no unidirectional ideology dominated.

Within the diffuse framework of a cooperative ideology the master craftsman was downgraded and succeeded by the industrial entrepreneurs. The entrepreneurs held an ideology of managers exercising authority. At the outset the authority was paternalistic and benevolent. Workers were considered as machine-like subjects; they were to obey. The ideological view within which workers should be managed was nowhere more articulately stated than in Taylor's theory of scientific management.[11]

Taylorism and benevolent ideologies for workers are exemplified in such industrial organization as the Ford Motor Car production. Efforts were made at job specialization and time and motion efficiency. Premiums were introduced to stimulate workers to increase efficiency. Furthermore, the ideology was carried by Ford to the point that a more efficiently produced car would be cheaper for the market, would render more return for the worker, and indeed, it was implied, would render more reward for managerial organization. In all this paternalism the worker's benefits were determined from above. There was no ideological space for workers to participate in decision-making concerning organization.[12]

The second ideological phase of the American unionism Crosser characterizes as liberalistic.[13] The genesis of liberalistic unionism dates from the end of the nineteenth century, but its articulation is fundamentally a twentieth-century experience. At the end of the nineteenth century and in the first part of the twentieth century the American Federation of Labor, as a major occupational spokesman for various bodies of skilled workers, was implicitly if not explicitly committed to medieval artisan trade union concepts. American Federation of Labor president, Samuel Gompers, did state, however, at an 1899 hearing, that the workers must recognize they were living under a wages system.[14]

Spokesmen for labor believed that the function of the union was primarily bargaining for wages. The AFL understood that in spite of its heritage and ideologies it must adjust to technological innovations. The fate of craftsmanship seemed clear; it was finished. The AFL continued onward with some vigor but apparently also with blinders. Stubborn and persistent, at its 1934 convention the AFL tradition was reasserted, namely, "we considered it our duty to formulate principles which fully protect the jurisdictional rights, of all trade unions organized upon craft lines." [15] It also recognized, however, the so-called "mass-production employees" and asserted that they should be given special charters.

By the middle of the 1930's it was everywhere apparent that millions of workers were not craftsmen: indeed they were unskilled. The Congress of Industrial Organizations had its origin in such an environment. The CIO projected a different ideology for labor. It was liberalistic unionism not based upon craftsmanship but upon the machine age. If not willingly, of necessity it accepted the lower state of the unskilled workers. This acceptance implied a challenge and ideology of negotiation the goal of which would be the up-grading of the dignity of workers as workers rather than as craftsmen or managers. The period of the 1930's was characterized by economic depression. Many workers in addition to these skilled and unskilled were operating under faltering ideologies, if ideologies at all. The possibility of a new liberalistic union representation for vast bodies of workers was at once ever so close and ever so distant. The possibility loomed for union representation of white-collar workers, technical and semiprofessional workers. The social heritage of hierarchical feudalism was dead, and the elevated estate of the higher ranking workers was sufficiently strong to precipitate major resistance to unionism.[16]

Specific dimensions of liberalistic unionism included such claims as the right to work. Further assertions were made on behalf of unemployment insurance, old age pensions, special grants to youth, and so forth. These ideologies of liberalistic unionism have come to be recognized as the wage earners' right to an ever-expanding array of fringe benefits. But in times of economic crisis and unrest among occupational men of a working class such gains seemed slow and often unsure. Techniques of more dramatic action were often accepted.

A third phase of American unionism was revolutionary. It was oriented toward dramatic action. Its ideologies never have been formulated in or carried on by a labor political party. A new surge of revolutionary action in labor organization, which followed World War I and reached a high tempo in the late 1930's, was no exception. Revolutionary unionism was the articulation of occupational ideologies more than political ideologies.[17] Revolutionary unionism made no apologies for playing on the drama of the general strike. It was action-oriented, conflict-oriented, and at times influenced by the communist parties. Revolutionary unionism reached a high point in conflict in the IWW movement.[18]

The success of revolutionary unionism was less than remarkable. The viability of the liberal American democratic tradition coupled with the nearly incomprehensibly great technological and economic resources of the nation are such that these essentially foreign movements are absorbed into the American way of life. The vast and variable complex American society is able to demonstrate much integration by the absorption of individual differences. Some normative space is possible for factions, movements, and derogatory positions. Rendering them normative is a cruel fate; but it is the strength and tool of the liberal democracy to ameliorate differences by integrations.

American unionism was thwarted in its many directions by such passive acceptance that the power of its articulated ideologies was deflated. Unionism fails to maintain a viable set of authority ideologies. Its workers are continually absorbed into the social organization of the greater society. Among the latest seductions are the notions of human relations in industry.

HUMAN RELATIONS IN INDUSTRY AND OCCUPATIONAL IDEOLOGIES

From the 1930's a new set of ideologies gained momentum concerning the rank of middle and lower ranging occupational men. This is the human relations approach to the worker which in many instances is being widely accepted by management. The norms of the human relations approach to workers are not yet ubiquitously accepted by management, but their acceptance at all is a significant new trend.

The quintessence of the new occupational ideologies is aimed at creating a work environment in which individuals and groups will desire to achieve effective production. Favorable attitudes among workers are encouraged by the human relations school. The underlying assumptions are that while gratifications of the workers will be rewarded the goals of the industry will also be furthered. The human relations approach which is being espoused by management is considerably less than altruism or humanitarianism. Indeed the situation which led to the ideology was serendipitous, almost the direct result of scientific management research which largely failed. While the origin of any ideology is multiple, complex, and diffuse, the human relations ideology has an origin that can be very clearly illustrated by specific research, namely the Hawthorne studies.[19]

Among the most famous of the Hawthorne Western Electric Company Studies was the relay assembly test room investigation. In the study the following questions were researched: "Do employees on the 48 hour week really get tired out physically? Are rest periods desirable? Is a shorter work day desirable? What is the effect of changing the type of work equipment? Why does production fall off in the afternoon? What is the attitude of the workers toward their work and toward the company?" In researching these questions six girls who were working on the assembly of telephone relays were selected out of a large work room area to be transferred to a test room where they knew that researchers would be studying and observing all of their work operations. The experimental research with these workers in the test room was predicated on several assumptions concerning cause and effect. Time and again the research scientists' assumptions were not supported. The manifest behavior was in most cases that of catastrophic rejection.

The research was organized into twelve phases or periods. Each phase lasted for a different number of weeks. The time and conditions for various work activities were varied and measured in each phase. Rest periods were, for example, increased and decreased to determine their possible impact on production. Hot snacks were provided, by the company, at one phase and taken away at another. The work day was shortened, and the work week was shortened. Ultimately all work conditions were returned to the original state in another phase. In general, production tended to increase with all manipulations of the work situation, and certainly it did not vary with increasing and decreasing the amenities.[20]

At long last, after the researchers studied and evaluated their observations, it was concluded that production was not determined by physical conditions of work alone. When the attitude of the workers was enthusiastic and favorable to the total situation production was increased and increased dramatically. In this case some workers were singled out for research. This recognition alone gave them a new sense of value and upgraded their attitude and motivation toward work. The major finding of the research was simple; but previously it had been overlooked and the importance of human attitude had been underestimated. The impact of such simple findings is great. The early research findings are primary resources for the origin of the human relation ideology projected by management and attributed to production employees.

Full amplification of human relational ideology, however, was not simple. It would involve any extensive understanding of the nature of human relations. Scientific management and engineering technology had not provided executives with the skills appropriate for the new ideology. Achievement of human relations in the occupational environment of workers was of necessity gradual. Counseling systems for workers were established. Research into the area of human relations continues. Emphasis on the belongingness of workers to small groups is further asserted.[21]

The continued efforts of Roethlisberger and Dickson contributed to the more precise view of work as a system of interacting human beings. In all the notion of personnel divisions and personnel departments became acceptable. Over the years they have established favorable reputations.[22]

The upshot of the ideology was to view the work environment as a social system. Specifically it was argued that the task of management was to keep the work social system in equilibrium.[23]

In maintaining an operative social system continual investigation into the satisfaction achieved by individual workers is required. The human relational ideology is confounded in many ways. Research shows that there are multiple deficiencies in many of the incentive plans which attempt to motivate workers. Conflicts between line and staff workers sabotage the ideology. Inadequacy of roles and bureaucratic rigidities reduce and dilute the impact of the human relation of ideologies. These few examples illustrate that the human relational ideology is characterized by disadvantages as well as advantages.[24]

IDEOLOGIES AND OCCUPATIONAL STEREOTYPES

Ideologies are attributed to a vast number of occupations with great precision in some cases and broad diffuseness in others. The range of worker roles is in part determined by the differential precision of ideologies.

Indeterminate and determinate ideologies. Mack has developed the notion of an occupational continuum of determinateness.[25] The concept of determinate occupational states is characterized by elaborately prescribed conditions for entry and minutely detailed rights and duties which direct the roles of occupational practitioners. The notion of the indeterminate occupational state is characterized by few qualifications for entering the occupation and by a minimum of directives to guide the worker in the specific details of the job.

An indeterminate occupational status is illustrated by garbage collecting. There is a conspicuous absence in the amount of training, education, licensing, or ethical codes which structure the right to enter the occupation. Moreover, after entering the occupation the details and directives of work are few. Most of them are related to the immediate work situation rather than to a broad ideology of work. Immediate and day-to-day directions are given by a supervisor. Interactions with fellow workers constitute other sources of role direction. Congestion by pedestrians and traffic will further structure the details of work. In practically every case the specificity of the work situation is more determined by immediate contingencies than by occupational ideology.

Moving toward the center of the continuum of occupational determinateness, a hotel desk clerk is an example of an intermediate position. In order to enter the occupation, ability to read accurately, write legibly, and speak audibly is broadly required. The work roles are further nominally specified. The clerk must serve clients amiably, suggesting their more superior status whether it is in fact theirs or not. The norms require dispatch in interaction with managers and bellhops accordingly. The ideologies attributed to the hotel desk clerk occupation determine to a considerable degree the acceptable latitude in occupational behavior.

The occupational status of the electrical engineer exemplifies the determinate end of the continuum. The training required is at the professional level. It involves a specified course of study in an accredited engineering school. As engineering is a profession, the behavior of the practitioner is further specified by a code of ethics plus the formal and informal judgment of colleagues. Entrance into the profession is further characterized by rigorous control over the level of competency of the works production.

The following is hypothesized for the relationship between occupational determinateness and occupational ideology:

People in relatively determinate occupational roles have achieved a major goal upon the licensing which permits them to enter the labor force and practice their professions or crafts. Those in less determinate occupations, such as unskilled labor or the nonprofessional white-collar jobs, seem more likely to be pursuing monetary rewards or an occupational status of higher prestige than the one in which they enter the labor force. We shall hypothesize, then, that the person in a determinate occupational status will view his work as an end in itself, and will define future goals in terms of his job, while a person in an indeterminate occupational status will view his work as instrumental, and will define life goals primarily as money. He will more often, then, view his present job as a means of gaining entry into some other occupational status.[26]

Mack's research findings led to a clear acceptance of his hypotheses.

Stereotypes. The occupational stereotype is as essential to an understanding of the work situation as a description of the details of training, remuneration, mobility, and prestige of an occupation.[27] The attributes of an occupation which are illustrated by stereotypes influence the practitioners as well as their general publics. These stereotypes constitute an integral part of occupational ideologies.

When occupations are well known, for example, mail carriers, typists, bakers, carpenters, etc., the range of stereotypes may be great and contribute to the total definition and meaning of the occupation. When occupations are relatively unknown, for example, actuaries, radiologists, group dynamists, etc., there are fewer stereotypes which can be effectively associated with them.

Occupational stereotypes function to condition the roles of workers.

In the complex society where many occupations are not widely known to the total population it is difficult to exchange achievement in the occupation for general prestige in the society.

Often, therefore, one is faced with role definitions at a level of stereotypes. For example, such expressions as shyster, quack, butcher, sissy, etc., contribute to an ideology within which such esteemed professionals as lawyers, physicians, clergy, and others manifest their occupational role behavior. In juxtaposition, stereotypes like humanitarian, defender of morals, and upholder of dignity are alternate stereotypes within which the role manifestations of well-known professionals are carried on. While the stereotypes, both positive and negative, are deviations from the facts of the situation, they are part of the real ideological culture within which occupational practitioners must behave.

The popular literature also reports stereotypes for other occupations, namely, cynical plumbers, stoically gay painters, reckless electricians, etc. Workers may be referred to as militant members of the toiling masses or the backbone of the nation. In any event, as one examines the occupational stereotypes on the lower half of the occupational continuum it is found that they are less coherent and less systematic.

Special ideologies. It is probable that the most widely accepted occupational ideology in American society is the dichotomous white-collar/blue-collar distinction. This differential idea about occupations has been heard with increasing intensity during most of the twentieth century. While the ideology lacks precision in terms of a scientific classificatory system it is sufficiently determinant to attribute prestige, influence recruitment, and direct a style of life. Never before in a democratic society was the social significance of clothing more important for occupation and labor. The ideology lacks precision, however, in that the uniform collar of many occupational men from bus drivers to bellhops may literally be white. The collar color of a scientist or of many professionals may range greatly from the prestigious white. The name given to this important occupational ideology is an abbreviation, but far too precise and determinant to be dismissed as a mere stereotype. The uniformed white-coated physician can easily be confused with the uniformed white-coated barber. The ideological difference for the two occupations is clearly based on more than the color of the collar, or the color of the uniform.

The ideological significance of dress among occupations is of great importance. Among occupational workers at the blue-collar end of the continuum it is observed that the uniform is typically more prestigeful than the lack of uniform. The dearth of research concerning this subject, however, makes it impossible to be certain of the reason for such differential meanings. It might be that the uniformed worker gains most prestige because he or she is able to wear non-occupational identifying street clothing to the place of employment. The uniform may also be a remuneration to the extent that the worker is not required to provide his own occupational clothing. Or it may be that the uniform offers a precise status identification among and between workers in a particular occupation.

The ideological significance of white-collar and blue-collar situations exceeds the matter of clothing itself. A total, if nonetheless diffuse, occupational way of life is associated with the image of dress. For example, some workers in the white-collar categories may be so prestigious that they seldom need to be concerned with the color of their collar. Research scientists are a case in point. In contrast, the top executive or banker more often than not is the prototype of the white-collar worker to the ultimate detail of the actual color of the collar. The way of life of such occupational men may, in effect, vary little by their actual manner of dress.

The helping professions and the service workers constitute another example of widespread dichotomous occupational ideologies. The helping professions include, typically, all of the occupations in the medical combine, along with welfare work. The service workers include such well-known occupations as policemen, firemen, and postmen. The operation of urbanized society is critically dependent upon such categories of occupations. The ideological expectation, nevertheless, of the helping professions is that of altruism. They are expected to contribute to the society over and above a return for their own gratification and/or aggrandizement. The service workers by contrast contribute vitally to the ongoing operation of the society but are not expected to have an abstract notion of their society nor to contribute to it beyond their day-to-day work roles. In short, the work experience of those in the service occupations is one of extreme congruence between the material goals of the workers and the absolute contribution of the work to society. In the helping professions it is accepted that the practitioners should utilize their occupation as a means to the subsistence ends for themselves and those for whom they are responsible. Such a goal is expected of the service workers also. But in the helping professions the practitioners are ideologically expected to have an image and responsibility for their society which exceeds individual accomplishments of individual practitioners.

Other broad occupational ideologies which refer to categories of workers are less widely disseminated. For example, the notion "idea people" in the urbanized society, refers to persons in such occupations from creative arts, to scientific research, through managerial positions. The guardian-of-the-faith ideology refers to the multiple types of religious workers ranging from the pulpit clergy to directors of religious music.

In addition to these ideologies which are associated with categories of occupational research, many individual occupations demonstrate specific ideologies. Examples of these occupational ideologies are examined below.

The professional dance musician is characterized by a special occupational ideology.[28] This occupational practitioner works in an environment which provides for considerable interaction between him and his audience. The relationship is often less than cordial; frequently a matter of conflict. The professional dance musician views his customer-client as beneath him in terms of a capacity for evaluating his occupation. The performance is a technical matter to be judged by peers and fellow practitioners who are considered to be colleagues. The audience is looked upon as different. It is characterized by a lack of understanding. The result is that musicians feel themselves to be isolated. They compound this situation by their own ideology which involves a process of self-segregation. Professional musicians constitute an in-group, and almost all outsiders are considered "squares." The professional musician sees little hope or possibility for educating the "squares" to understand the nature of their talent. "You either have the beat or you can't be trained for it," is their feeling.

The occupational ideology of professional dance musicians is specific and important for the internal organization of practitioner roles. The professional subject of music is volatile and communicated and understood only within. The audience to a great extent is the opposition. The significant others are occupational colleagues. They recognized that they are largely dependent upon the customer-client relationship, but the internal meaning of the occupation is forcefully directed by an ideology which excludes the "squares" and provides for self-segregation among the musicians.

The internal occupational ideology of janitors involves a status dilemma.[29] The occupational rank of janitors is everywhere low. Gold's study of janitors in Chicago reveals an influence of unionization in a manner that tends to increase professionalization among them. Nevertheless, the stereotype of the occupations is that the practitioner is foreign-born, wears dirty clothes, lives in a basement, and removes garbage. In contrast to such a stereotype, empirical reporting of the facts indicates that some janitors have more income than their tenants. When janitors achieve the status symbols of new cars, televisions, and other material objects that are of higher quality than those of the tenants in the buildings where they work, jealousy and aggravation is increased. Jealous tenants, it is reported, are virtually impossible to accommodate. They develop a pattern of always complaining. In fact, to be accommodated is to give recognition to the janitors which they are unwilling to concede.

On the positive side, and in spite of the imputation of the low status ideology, it is found that tenants frequently reveal their problems and secrets to janitorial staffs in their buildings. In many respects the janitors come to be the general confidants of the persons whom they serve.

The occupational ideology that is imputed to low status work is supported by many norms over which the workers have few if any controls. Contractually in the case of unionization the occupation may gain considerable tangible recognition but the prestige in status is awarded less by the union and more by the tenants in the work environment.

The occupational ideology associated with the boxer is primarily generated from within the occupation. The norms of the ideology control and direct the nature of work. The status of the occupation is low, but the general public attributes a diffuse rather than a specific ideology to the occupation. The service rendered by the boxer may be used or not used and hence the exterior ideology associated with the occupation has little specificity.

Professional boxers are recruited from youth in the lower socioeconomic levels.[30] The youth enter boxing in most cases to increase their social status. They come from the culture of local gangs where ring fighting and street fighting is widely known and accepted. Their decision to go into boxing is made early, often at age 10 or 12. Moreover, they are encouraged to enter this occupational experience by managers of local gyms who seek out youth who show ability of this type.

The organization of boxing involves a specific training, managers to support the work, and promoters for image development. The culture of boxing involves protecting the body, in some cases physical cultism, the having of a "fighting heart," widespread concern for various kinds of superstitions, and, above all else, self-confidence. The occupation is highly stratified. Particular weight categories, one's position in a match, the status with the manager, etc., all contribute to the stratification.

In all of these cases the occupational ideology of boxing is more directed to the internal organization of the work than to its external manifestations. The ideology is more generated within the occupation than attributed to it by the general public.

SUMMARY AND IMPLICATIONS

The ideologies we hold about occupations and the whole nature of work greatly influence the lives of men in urbanized society—whether correct or not. With mass literacy and vast communication systems occupational ideologies have a ubiquitous nature in urbanized society.

Some ideologies are parochial while others tend to be ecumenic. Parochial ideologies usually do not go beyond the boundary of a specific occupation. They may influence practitioners greatly, but have little impact on other occupations or society at large. Ecumenic occupational ideologies are generated from within an occupation, influence its practitioners, influence other occupations, and influence the society at large.

In terms of stratification, those occupations in the upper half of the socio-economic continuum, often exemplified by the professions, have completely developed and well-articulated ideologies. Workers at the lower end of the stratification continuum have less a sense of occupation. Accordingly, their occupational ideologies are often more attributed from exterior forces rather than generated internally.

The ideologies of some occupations contribute to rigid boundary maintenance; others are elements which permeate boundaries.

The Industrial Revolution constituted a major structural turning point for occupations in social organization. It was a prime moving force which led to independent free-standing occupations. This was less than intended, however. The first industrial ideologies held the early occupational men to be a subservient class. Workers were to obey. They were to function as nearly as possible as machines. This ideology of subservience was countered with the development of strong unions. They propagated occupational ideologies for the defense of workers. The union ideologies were countered by management with the fostering of human relations in industry ideologies.

Finally, stereotype occupational ideologies are of considerable significance. Stereotypes are typically attributed exteriorly to occupations. They are only partly valid, but they serve to characterize a body of work. And regardless of their exact validity they influence the image of occupations and indirectly make an impact on the structure and organization of occupation.

The most special stereotype ideologies in the United States are white collar and blue-collar. They have some basis in fact. But more important than the factualism of the situation is the aura—indeed, the "total" way of life which these occupational ideologies imply, and often effect.

The implication clearly is that an examination of ideologies is essential for a complete understanding of occupational organization and for the social organization of which the occupations are a part. Occupations are more than formal organizations. They generate an ideological structure and are surrounded by ideological structures. The overt manifestation of occupations at any particular time is both internally and externally influenced by ideologies.

NOTES

1. Vernon K. Dibble, "Occupations and Ideologies," *American Journal of Sociology*, LXVIII (September 1962), 229–41.
2. Ibid. p. 230.
3. Ibid. p. 231.
4. Rhinehart Bendix, *Work and Authority in Industry: Ideologies of Management in the Course of Industrialization* (New York: John Wiley & Sons, Inc., 1956), pp. 38ff.
5. Ibid. p. 16.
6. Ibid. p. 40.

7. Paul K. Crosser, *Ideologies and American Labor* (New York: Oxford University Press, 1941), pp. 111ff.

8. Ibid. p. 111.

9. Ibid. pp. 115–16.

10. Ibid. p. 117.

11. Frederick Winslow Taylor, *The Principles of Scientific Management* (New York: Harper and Bros., 1911).

12. Crosser, *Ideologies*, pp. 123ff.

13. Ibid. pp. 137ff.

14. *U.S. Industrial Commission, Reports of the Industrial Commission,* Vol. 7 (Washington, D.C.: U.S. Government Printing Office, 1901), pp. 596–674, see esp. p. 645.

15. American Federation of Labor, Report of the Proceedings of the 55th Annual Convention, October 7–19, 1935, p. 522.

16. Crosser, *Ideologies*, pp. 156–9.

17. Ibid. p. 179.

18. Paul F. Brissenden, *The First World War, A Study of the American Syndicalism* (New York: Columbia University, 1919).

19. Stuart Chase, *Men at Work* (New York: Harcourt, Brace and Co., 1945), pp. 14–20; and F. J. Roethlisberger and William J. Dickson, *Management and the Worker* (Cambridge: Harvard University Press, 1939).

20. Roethlisberger and Dickson, *Management and the Worker.*

21. Elton Mayo, *The Social Problems of an Industrial Civilization* (Boston: Research Division, Graduate School of Business Administration, Harvard University, 1945), *passim*, esp. p. 118.

22. Jeanne L. Wilensky and Harold L. Wilensky, "Personal Counseling: The Hawthorne Case," *American Journal of Sociology*, 57 (November 1951), 265–80.

23. Roethlisberger and Dickson, *Management and the Worker*, p. 551.

24. Charles B. Spaulding, *An Introduction to Industrial Sociology* (San Francisco: Chandler Publishing Co., 1961), chap. 8.

25. Raymond Mack, "Occupation Ideology and the Determinate Role," *Social Forces*, 36 (October 1957), 37–50.

26. Ibid. p. 39.

27. Theodore Caplow, *The Sociology of Work* (Minneapolis: University of Minnesota Press, 1954), pp. 134–7.

28. Howard S. Becker, "The Professional Dance Musician and His Audience," *American Journal of Sociology*, LVII (September 1951), 136–44.

29. Ray Gold, "Janitors vs. Tenants: A Status-Income Dilemma," *American Journal of Sociology*, LVII (March 1952), 486–93.

30. S. Kirson Weinberg and Henry Arond, "The Occupational Culture of the Boxer," *American Journal of Sociology*, LVII (March 1952), 460–69.

SUPPLEMENTARY READING

Paul K. Crosser, *Ideologies and American Labor* (New York: Oxford University Press, 1941).

Vernon K. Dibble, "Occupations and Ideologies," *American Journal of Sociology*, LXVIII (September 1962), 229–41.

Ray Gold, "Janitors vs. Tenants: A Status-Income Dilemma," *American Journal of Sociology*, LVII (March 1952), 486–93.

Raymond Mack, "Occupational Ideology and the Determinate Role," *Social Forces*, 36 (October 1957), 37–50.

OCCUPATIONS AND FAMILY LIFE $\underset{\longleftarrow}{XIX}$

Man's occupation and his way of life have been integrated throughout much of the long course of history. Indeed ways of life have dominated occupations more often than occupations have dominated ways of life. Moreover, man's ways of life in the main have been family centered. It follows, therefore, that occupations have been historically family centered when and where they have been diffusely articulated. All of this is to observe that much of man's family life has been a subsistence way of survival in which the division of labor was, more often than not, a provisional directive for work. Occupations as such were scarce, but the family center productive tradition was in the main adequate for human survival. With the modern era and the specific articulation of multiple thousands of occupations which are integral parts of the urbanized technological societies there is much incompatibility among work and family situations.[1]

The traditions of work in family environments vary greatly from country to country, culture to culture, and time to time. Family work roles have varied significantly from Africa, to Oceania, to preliterate America, and to colonial America. In virtually all of these situations the roles of work were determined more by family organization than by their own articulated integrity.

When occupations become sufficiently articulated and organized, for example in industrialized and urbanized societies, the nature of work from office, to factory, to shop, varies little from one national area to another. The norms of occupations under the industrial system are directed toward individuals and work groups and not oriented to accommodating family life as such. Men may be employed, women may be employed, or children may be employed, but in the main, the employment is individual rather than family related. Under the industrial and

452

urbanized system the family is forced to adjust to work patterns that are outside the home, to the regulation of occupation by trade unions, to the meaningful definition of work by professional associations, and so forth.

With the advent of human relations in industry one may observe that there is some slight effort to integrate family and occupation. For example the human relations accommodation to occupations may be such that plant picnics, plant newspapers, family birthdates and so forth may be recognized—even if artificially—in an effort to bring family identification with the breadwinner's occupation. Such human relations traditions are widespread but still less than typical. Even where they exist they are at the pleasure of the occupation and the controllers of the work environment and nowhere controlled by the family organization and specification.

The family as a work group which operated for centuries in many parts of the world, including the colonial and early national period in America, is a vanishing type. In the United States the family farm continues in a museum-like culture lag manner. The family impact on scientific commercial farming, although little indeed, is greater than on any other major occupational category for the nation. To be sure, one can still identify numerous family commercial businesses. Individually they are in most cases small. Their duration is typically brief, usually less than one generation. Their systematic impact on the economy of the nation is less vital than their ideological significance. From all perspectives one must conclude that in the urbanized United States family centered occupations are things of the past rather than present.

Cross-cultural studies of urbanization, industrialization, and modernization with relation to family work reveal a rapid decline of family occupations. Specifically, it is reported by Dore that with industrialization younger sons leave the rural family and move to cities to take industrial occupations. There is geographical separation, economic separation, and occupational separation from the stem family.

In the pre-industrial condition the family occupation often remained unchanged for generations. With industrialization and urbanization occupation becomes an individual rather than family matter. Occupationally going beyond one's father is an ideal that has replaced the ideal of following in the father's footsteps.

With industrialization new jobs and occupations are created. They are individual more than family occupations. Accordingly, occupations become dominant over family life.[2]

Occupations in homes. Family occupational work in the home tradition is clearly illustrated and documented in the American family farm and the early cottage industry.[3] Similarly, the family occupation tradition is found in Europe.[4]

In eighteenth-century England industrialization was beginning to develop. Wool manufacture was first important, followed by the production of iron, the production of cotton, and so forth. In spite of the development of industrial notions. Toynbee asserts that in the early 1700's a large part of the English goods were being produced in a domestic system. The concentration of manufacturing in towns, involving their distinct separation from agriculture, was still not a widespread practice. The manufacturer was a man working in his own cottage. Most of the cloth production was still cottage industry at the beginning of the century.[5] A further account of early occupational family endeavor was reported by DeFoe when he wrote of the land near Halifax:

[It was] divided into small enclosures, from two acres to six or seven each, seldom more, every three or four pieces of land had a house belonging to them . . . hardly an house standing out of a speaking-distance from another; . . . we could see at every house a tenter, and on almost every tenter a piece of cloth, kersie or shallon; . . . every clothier must necessarily keep one horse, at least, . . . to carry . . . his manufactures to the market; . . . everyone, generally, keeps a cow or two for his family. By this means, the small pieces of enclosed land about each house are occupied; . . . as for corn they scarce hold corn enough to feed their poultry. . . . yet within we saw the houses full of lusty fellows, some at the dye-vat, some at the loom, others dressing the cloths; the women and children carding, or spinning; all employed from the youngest to the oldest. . . . Not a beggar to be seen, nor an idle person.[6]

Occupations move out of homes. In a general way it is possible to date the period in history when occupations were moved out of the home and into a productive order where they became means in and of themselves. For most of the United States the shift from home to shop and to factory was completed by the third decade of the nineteenth century.[7] The first half of the nineteenth century was a period of rapid industrial expansion characterized by an acceleration of an increasing number of specific occupations. Agriculture as a way of life and a family enterprise persisted until well after the Civil War.

Occupation was first recorded in the 1820 Census. The early recording of occupations was far from precise, but it served as an index of their growing independence. Between 1830 and 1860 the family system of manufacturing was superseded by the factory system. By the 1860's family-made goods were the exception and factory production was making great strides. In newly settled areas there was still family production of goods and services, but this situation changed rapidly. The social organization and ideology provided for systematically produced goods.[8]

The importance of the removal of occupations from homes to their free-standing state lies in the struggle between the family as a total way of life and occupations as the determinants of the way of life. Note that many occupations may determine much of one's way of life while they are a means to an end rather than an end in themselves.[9] Many blue-collar types of occupations are means to an end rather than a free standing way of life. Nonetheless, they are most determinant factors on the practitioners' ways of life. Other occupations, most often exemplified by the professions, constitute both a means to an end and a way of life. In any event, whether the occupation is a way of life or means to an end, in nearly all cases the family way of life is vastly influenced by the occupations of its members. In juxtaposition families continue to make an impact on occupations.

FAMILY AND OCCUPATIONAL DECISION-MAKING

Occupational perception and choosing is very greatly influenced by families. The family gives children an opportunity to observe many adult roles some of which are occupational. Even though much occupational activity is greatly separated from families, the family style of life is influenced by the occupation, and in turn young people perceive the occupational conditions to that extent. Families in many cases provide specific occupational information, or are influential in giving occupational directives. In some few cases they still provide a demonstration of occupational skills. It is clear that families either exert pressure on young people for certain kinds of occupational choices, or the absence of such pressure contributes to the general disorganization in occupational aspiration. Notions of occupational training, success, and satisfaction are in the main influenced by families.[10]

Learning occupational attitudes and values is part of one's early life experience. It is greatly influenced by friends, peer groups, schools, and neighborhoods. Those young people who identify with the occupational subculture of their parental generation are thereby directed, limited, and/or advantaged by their family experience.[11] Given the character of occupational change and social class mobility, it is found that many young people whose families are in the lower half of the socioeconomic continuum have few suitable occupational role models to direct their aspirations. In these cases where there is occupational aspiration above that of the parent, the cues and directives must come from schools and other occupational sources.

The family is further influenced in its occupational directives for its young people by its religious orientation. A Calvinistic influence leads to a socialization for individual responsibility and achievement in the area of executive and professional types of occupations. A Roman Catholic influence, which places importance on authority, leads to occupations which are less idea and imaginative types. In like manner those families that follow Quaker teaching will more often than not direct their young people to occupations like social work and teaching rather than to professional military careers.[12]

The family impact on occupational choosing becomes even more directive and critical later in the youth's life when he or she is faced with actual occupational entry. In this case it is found that children who have early training in independence and decision-making are able to evaluate various possible occupations and make decisions concerning them with greater facility and ease than those young people who have a lesser amount of similar experience. It is found, similarly, that the young person who comes from an upwardly mobile middle class family perceives and has access to more types of occupations than others.[13]

The colleagues and associates of the managerial, professional, and semiprofessional families will by both informal and formal processes prepare the young person to have a wide experience and knowledge of occupations. By sharp contrast, the family experience in the lower class circumstance is sharply limited in terms of youth's understanding of differential occupational opportunities.[14]

The family contribution to occupational experience is further contributed to by specific tangible items like capital and credit, or the ability to finance the education and training of a young person.

Occupational inheritance. Occupations are often passed on from generation to generation within a family.[15] This is particularly illustrated in the case of farming. The professions in general are also noted for occupational inheritance. Precise data concerning occupational inheritance are difficult to obtain, and consequently only general conclusions are warranted. For example, many people change their occupation during the course of their working years, and the studies of occupational inheritance are limited to a given point in time. The distinction between occupational transmission and inheritance is not universally maintained. It may be that high level occupations are more often transmitted and low level occupations characterized by inheritance.

The family structure contributes occupational role models and values in still other ways. The work and play habits of individuals in their families specify the significance of occupation in many instances. For example, when children grow up in the homes of scientists and intellectuals, where they observe the parents frequently engaged in study and intellectual work, value patterns for careers are established. When children grow up in homes where evenings and weekends are spent in television viewing, card playing, and participant games, a lesser number of specific occupational values are developed.

The occupational work of family men in the professions is seldom clearly distinguished from their total way of life.[16] Some report their work is their play or recreation. Intellectuals and scientists report that their work continues well into evenings, holidays, and so forth. The 40-hour week is little known to men in such occupations.

Family organization influences occupational mobility. Parsons suggests that there is a basic disharmony between modern extended families and modern industrial societies. In essence he argues that the extended family is antithetical to occupational mobility.[17] Recent investigation has added refinement and some contradiction to this early notion of Parsons'. Litwak has argued "that a modified extended relation is consonant with occupational mobility and more functional than the isolated nuclear family."[18] Litwak, in 1952, studied the relation between occupation and mobility in a Buffalo, New York, housing survey, which consisted of a sample of 920 white married women. Occupational mobility was measured by comparisons between the job of the husband and that of his father. The findings of this study suggest that the Parsons' hypothesis probably had its greatest validity in the early stages of industrialization when the family farm experience was extremely widespread. In such a case occupational and geographical closeness were great. "In contemporary society, however, extended family relations develop from different institutional sources and as a result do not rely on geographic and occupational proximity for their viability. It is suggested that these modified extended family relations are more consonant with occupational mobility than the isolated nuclear family." [19]

WIVES OF OCCUPATIONAL MEN

In an urbanized status-oriented society the multiple roles of wives of occupational men can be hardly overemphasized. Wives are sometimes presumed to be the driving force behind the occupational males. Their drive may contribute to both challenge and frustration. Wives may contribute to their husbands' occupational roles and identify with them, or they may be introverted bystanders who contribute to the deterioration of their husband's occupation. Wives of executives, military men, ministers, and so forth have been insufficiently studied. The following pages report some of the salient findings.

Executive wives. In White's study of management wives it is revealed that a woman may identify with her husband's occupation but can seldom systematically help in the occupational roles. A bad wife can do much damage to occupational achievement.[20] Such wives are "meddlers," "climbers," "fixers," or "pushers and shovers."

Among the positive roles of the executive wife is stabilization for the executive and family. Research findings reveal that top management personnel are typically lonely, isolated persons. There are few in the immediate work environment to whom they may reveal confidences. Consequently, the wife of such an individual provides stability by being the person to whom he can express his concerns, confidences, and generally unburden himself. The wife is a humanizing influence. One executive reports: "About the time I get fed up with the bastard here I am, going over to dinner at his house. And she's so nice—she jokes about him, kids him to his face—I figure he can't be so bad after all." [21]

Sociability is another positive role for the management wife. She finds it necessary to be an amiable mixer. She must be able to change quickly from identifying with a company community, to being the wife of the branch manager on another occasion, and still in other situations becoming a civic leader or reverting back to quick and gracious entertainment for the touring top executives. The rules of the executive wife's game are often stated as follows:

Don't talk shop gossip with the Girls, particularly those who have husbands in same department.
Don't invite superiors in rank; let them make the first bid.
Don't turn up at the office unless you absolutely have to.
Don't get too chummy with the wives of associates your husband might soon pass on the way up.
Don't be disagreeable to any company people you meet. You never know.
. . .
Be attractive. There is a strong correlation between executive success and the wife's appearance.
Be a phone pal of your husband's secretary.
Never—repeat, never—get tight at a company party (it may go down in a dossier).[22]

Executive life is extensively controlled in many details by the establishment of its image making. The wife must be prepared to accept these directives graciously. For example, as an executive is being moved up in the corporation it might be arranged for him to attain a membership in one of the better local clubs. For the wife's role this is to be the club to which she quietly aspired. Or in another case, the executive who is being moved up may have a specific home singled out to him in a status subdivision where the establishment would like to have its top officials reside. For the executive wife such a neighborhood is the one to which she has quietly aspired.

In the many changes and shifts that accompany manager area occupations there is friction which results between inferiors and superiors, between those who succeed and those who do not. Promotions often constitute many interpersonal and friendship difficulties for the executive wife. Ultimately most of them adjust. They eventually accept a kind of social professionalism for their interperson friendships. Their world is expressed like this: "It's tough. You have got to leave behind your old friends. You have to weigh the people you invite to parties. You have to be careful of who you send Christmas cards to and who you don't. It sounds like snobbery but it's just something you have to do. You have to be a boss's wife." [23]

White finally observes, "Theirs is a sort of First Lady ideal, a woman who takes things as they come with grace and poise, and a measure of *noblesse oblige*; in short, the perfect boss's wife." [24]

The person the executive has selected for a wife is of great significance. In a success-oriented society a man is likely to marry his hometown sweetheart or his college girlfriend. The wife-mother role which is typical for such a woman—and there are many such women—involves a considerable amount of experiences, values, and ideologies which they have known from early life. By contrast, the husband whom she married fifteen years earlier becomes in many cases a very different occupational man as he experiences a success unknown to him at the time of marriage. The occupational success involves a different kind of clothing, speaking with a different accent, and even thinking differently. Many wives find much frustration in keeping up, as it were, with the changing values and manifest behaviors of their occupationally successful husbands. The executive establishment often suggests, therefore, that it is wise for the man to "out marry." The probability of the husband's growing in his occupation to the level of the wife is greater than the lower status wife's chances are of accepting the successful husband's new roles. The college graduate wife is considered most acceptable for the future executive. It is not so much that the education is important to her, but that she will not be subject to a feeling of inferiority as the occupational husband achieves higher rank.

The roles of the executive wife are many. The specific details are far from precise in the broad ranges of the executive space. There is, however, no question that the roles of the executive wife are significant in the impact on the occupational husbands.

Military wives. Janowitz reports that the roles of the army and navy wives became articulated and precise prior to those of the organizational men executives.[25] One military wife has expressed the relation to her husband's occupation as follows:

Life on an Army post in peacetime gives the Army wife far more opportunity, and probably more obligation, to help her husband in his career than most wives find in civilian life. The reasons are fairly obvious. An Army post is something like a company town. Everybody is working for the same outfit. Everybody goes to the same post clubs and chapels and movies and buys their food at the same commissary and miscellaneous articles at the same post exchange. Living on the post, the husband is never far from either his home or work. The people the wife sees at night, at parties or in her home, are the people her husband works with or for. Army protocol requires that the wife get to know the commanding officer and his wife socially. And it is quite common in Army life for the wife to call the ranking officer by his first name while her husband must address him by rank, as "Colonel" or "General." [26]

Military wives contribute to professional solidarity in a very real way by informally breaking down the barriers of the rigid hierarchical system within which their husbands operate. Along with this, nevertheless, the wife and family participate respectfully in the transmission of military traditions.

Family strains are known to be great in military careers. Special personnel have been assigned in personnel service divisions to contribute analysis and facilitate understanding in family life and organization. In short, the establishment seeks to facilitate the family adjustment to the military communities. Special efforts are made, particularly in the Air Force, to enlist the wife as an assistant in the husband's career. In spite of such an ideology, research reports that wives find few ways in which they are able to actually relate themselves to the career.[27] Even informal communication is seldom possible on the part of wives due to the complexity of the service, the often great physical separation, and the frequent security of the operations.

Ministers' wives. In some areas the celibate clergy is widespread, but in the United States it is typically expected that the clergy should be married. The role of the wife should in many cases approximate that of an assistant minister.[28] Among the first of the roles of the clergyman's wife is the operation of the place of residence. In many cases the wife and family are subjected to housing conditions which they consider to be undesirable. Church officers are reported to express concern about ministers' wives being too parsonage-conscious. Furthermore, the women of the church take some pride in the furnishing and decorating of their parsonage. Not infrequently there is some conflict between the taste of the minister's wife and that of the wives of the congregation in terms of the decoration of the parsonage. Nonetheless, one minister's wife has expressed the situation as follows:

Ministers and their wives are too parsonage-conscious. I came near "losing my religion" at the annual conference sessions in June because I heard so many wives scheming for a nice parsonage as if such was the primary goal in life. One wife related in informal conversation how she had personally prompted a certain church for her husband largely because it had the ideal parsonage in a community with fine schools for the children. Not only did she maneuver the appointment by talking to the "right" people in the "right" way, but before she moved into the parsonage she and her husband had engineered a complete redecoration job and could scarcely talk about anything else.[29]

Salaried employment for the minister's wife is another area of difficulty. Without much regard for her talent, the congregation often expects her to be able and available when needed. She may play the piano, teach a Sunday School class, and of course attend all meetings of the women of the church. The clergy wife who is employed is unable to fulfill many of these kinds of tasks. A bishop has expressed the situation as follows:

The wife who can least afford to work outside the home is the minister's wife. This is because the church expects more of her than of other women in the church. When she works, her schedule conflicts with church affairs and she becomes engrossed in interests apart from the church. She is no longer a part of the husband-wife team; she lives with her husband playing "singles." The minister's wife is more important to his work than the wife of any other professional man. Laymen consistently ask about the wife when considering a new minister.[30]

It is also observed that some lay church leaders believe that when the wife works this indicates they are paying an inadequate salary. Or, conversely, it may be argued by the officers of the church that the husband minister needs no increase in salary because of the contribution made by the working wife. Finally, it is observed that in some cases a minister may hesitate to move from one church to another because of the wife's good position in the place where they are located.

Another area of complication for the minister's wife is the feeling of neglect. The husband-father who is a minister is often taken from the family when there is felt need for his presence. The mobility of ministers further complicates the life for his wife and family. In sum, the roles for the wife of a minister are complex. They are gratifying, prestigeful, invaded, and frustrated.

FAMILY AND OCCUPATIONAL WOMEN

In this section we are concerned with what family life does to the occupational women. Does the family experience make the employed woman a more satisfactory occupational individual, or does it make her a higher risk and a less reliable worker? This section is not addressed to the impact that the employed woman makes on her family relationships. The focus of consideration is on occupation, not family. This distinction is important because of the vast and often emotional literature which often concerns the working mother and the deterioration of family organization. The subject of occupational women and their family life is a separate question and one of great importance in the study of occupations.

In the world of work, wife and mother roles constitute complications for women. If she puts the wife-mother role first she will be in many cases excluded from, or at least handicapped in, participation and/or advancement in many types of occupations. Moreover, the work as a housewife and mother is not viewed as an occupation, except possibly in those cases where it is done for hire. Anderson observes, therefore, that the women in the contemporary urbanized society are to a great extent meaningfully excluded from community participation and greatly frustrated in the occupational world. In part her roles are primarily ornamental.[31] Caplow similarly observes that the whole range of housewifely duties are in opposition to the occupational system.[32]

In spite of these contingencies women differentially engage in the occupational world. In times of excessive unemployment women are strongly reminded that their place is in the home. In times of national crises women are encouraged to enter occupations. Over the years women's participation in occupations has increased significantly. In the 1890's approximately 18 per cent of the females aged 14 and over were employed in the American labor market. By the 1960's more than 35 per cent of the American women were similarly employed. Indeed, one-third of the married women living with their husbands are employed. Thirty-five per cent of the women with no children under age 18 are employed. Women with more education are more frequently employed—for example, 23 per cent of those with an eighth-grade education or less were employed, compared to 34 per cent of those with some college education. A similar pattern obtained for wives with no children under age 18; more education meant more employment. There is some tendency, however, for wives to stop working when the husband's income increases.[33]

In the United States it is normative for women to dominate several occupations. A Department of Labor study of the occupations of women between 1870 and 1940 revealed the following: [34]

		Per cent
1.	housekeepers in private families	99.2
2.	dressmakers and seamstresses (not in factory)	98.3
3.	laundresses in private families	98.2
4.	trained nurses and student nurses	97.9
5.	practical nurses and midwives	95.7
6.	attendants in offices of physicians and dentists	95.3
7.	telephone operators	94.6
8.	milliners (not in factory)	94.2
9.	stenographers, typists, secretaries	93.5
10.	servants in private families	91.3
11.	librarians	89.5
12.	office machine operators	86.1
13.	dancers, dancing teachers, chorus girls	80.6
14.	teachers	75.7
15.	religious workers	74.6

Housekeeping, dressmaking, and laundering are for all practical purposes exclusively female occupations, at a service level. Similarly, nursing and medical attendant work is primarily a woman's domain. Office work is dominated by women. The professional area of teaching and library science are disproportionately female occupations.

Some women workers are found in almost all other occupations, but most women work in occupations that are associated with homemaking or the new clerical areas.

Norms and structures affecting occupational women. Several specific and tangible social norms are being developed to facilitate and/or accommodate occupational women.[35] Specific norms include arrangements for taking care of young children in the form of babysitting, nurseries, and a variety of pre-school arrangements. Another norm which influences the supply of occupational women is early marriage, combined with a lesser number of children, shorter hours in the work week, improved working conditions, more freedom from household duties because of improved technology, and finally changing attitude toward occupational women. Education is a social structure which also facilitates the occupational endeavor of women. There is a positive correlation between more education and the probability of occupational work.

Modification in the attitudes concerning occupational women have been greater among men than women. Women have long and tenaciously held to the ideology of their right to work. But prior to World War II Pearl Buck asserted that men believed it was their responsibility to provide for their families, and a working wife suggested their inability or lack of manly accomplishment.[36] With the postwar shift in male ideology the women's right to enter the labor force has become a virtual responsibility. She is expected in the early years of marriage to contribute to the family's economic welfare.

A social structure which facilitates occupational women is the increased demand for clerical, service, professional, and technical occupations. These are occupations for which women can obtain training and effectively compete with men.

The female age structure is related to their occupational participation. Occupational women are typically characterized by a two-phase working cycle. After completing their basic education they generally enter the labor force until married, and/or through the early family years. With the arrival of children and the increasing family responsibilities occupational women often remove themselves temporarily from the labor market. The second working phase for occupational women comes after their children reach school age and when family responsibilities are, accordingly, somewhat contracted. They re-enter the labor force and often remain until their middle or late fifties (see Table XIX.1). Specifically between the ages 45 and 54 the female occupational participation reaches a peak. After age 55 there is a gradual decline in the number of occupational women.

Marital status is a historical question mark for occupational women. By the second half of the twentieth century it is clear that a growing number of married women are also occupational women. In the 1960's, of the approximately 24 million working women, over 60 per cent were married.[37] What is more, 91 per cent of the married women had husbands who were also active in the labor force.

TABLE XIX.1

Labor Force Participation Rates for Women in U.S. by Age, 1963, 1960, and 1950

Age	1963 [a]	1960	1950
All ages	37.4	34	29
14–17 years	18.6	14	11
18–24 years	47.4	45	43
25–34 years	38.4	35	32
35–44 years	45.6	43	35
45–64 years	46.9	42	29
65 years and over	9.7	10	8

[a] May 1963.
Source: Daniel H. Kruger, "Women at Work," *The Personnel Administrator*, 9 (July–August 1964), 8.

Mothers who work are also normatively acceptable. In 1962, of the 18.5 million married women in the labor force, approximately 52 per cent had no children under age 18, but 30 per cent had children between the ages of 6 and 17, and 18 per cent had children under age 6. In any event, the social space for working mothers is normatively established.

By 1960 the census data showed five major employment categories for occupational women: training and care of young, provision for the sick, clothes making, food preparing, and household care (see Table XIX.2). In the main it is noted that these occupations have included

TABLE XIX.2

Women in Occupations Which Have Been Traditional Functions Performed by Women, 1960

Training and caring of young		1,737,079
Teachers, elementary and secondary	1,205,681	
College professors and instructors	39,168	
Musicians and music teachers	111,235	
Artists and art teachers	37,187	
Baby sitters	341,808	
Caring of the sick		1,311,865
Nurses, professional	577,038	

TABLE XIX.2 (cont.)

Student nurses, professional	56,745	
Practical nurses	207,490	
Attendants in hospital and other institutions	300,979	
Medical and dental technicians	87,977	
Social workers	61,465	
Therapists	20,204	
Making and caring of clothing		1,510,111
Sewers and stitchers	579,364	
Dressmakers and seamstresses	119,510	
Textile mill product workers	112,862	
Spinners	41,350	
Apparel workers in manufacturing	319,984	
Laundry and dry cleaning workers	296,294	
Laundresses in private households	40,747	
Preparing and serving of food		1,642,727
Dieticians and nutritionists	24,757	
Cooks	381,078	
Kitchen workers	195,628	
Counter and fountain workers	119,158	
Waitresses	777,362	
Workers in firms manufacturing food products	144,744	
Taking care of the home		1,805,684
Chambermaids and maids	176,619	
Charwomen and cleaners	130,005	
Housekeepers-private	148,983	
Housekeepers and stewards	121,811	
Private household workers	1,228,266	
Total		8,005,466

Source: Daniel H. Kruger, "Women at Work," *The Personnel Administrator*, 9 (July–August 1964), 9.

most of the traditional functions of women. In recent years, however, these functions are organized into articulated and distinct occupational roles. The 8 million women in these five occupational categories constituted slightly more than one-third of all women in the labor force in 1960. Other occupations that show an increasing female participation include business, industry, government, secretary-typists, and bookkeepers.

Occupational women's jobs affected by marital status. Most women workers (30.9 per cent) are in clerical occupations (see Table XIX.3). They are followed by work in service jobs (14.5 per cent), operative work (13.8 per cent), and professional occupations (13.6 per cent). Other large numbers of women are found in private household and sales occupations. Marital status makes little differential impact on the category of occupations in which women work. Nearly 40 per cent of the single women are in clerical work, 31 per cent for married and 24 per cent for other marital statuses (see Table XIX.3)—but this is the largest proportion of women for any occupational type for each marital status. There are only two sharp exceptions to occupational pattern by marital status. Few single women are in operative work, and few married women are private household workers.

The occupations of women are also influenced by the occupations of their husbands. Kruger's study reveals that some 44 per cent of the professional women have husbands who are also professionals. More specifically it is found that half of the married female teachers have husbands who are also educators. In the clerical occupations, over two-fifths of the women workers have husbands in the same occupational category. A similar situation is reported for occupational men and women who are in sales employment. At the other end of the continuum approximately one-fourth of the working women in service work have husbands who are similarly employed. This is not to observe that the occupational structure of wives is most identical with their husbands. For example, wives of clerical workers are found in the professions, and wives of operative workers are found in clerical jobs, etc.

Training for occuptional women. It is already noted that women with more education and training participate more frequently in the work world. The Women's Bureau of the Labor Department makes special efforts to stimulate the creation of training opportunities for women and girls. In 1959–60 the Bureau reviewed a variety of training programs.[38] The study was limited to formal types of training which prepared individuals for initial entry into occupations. By definition, therefore, company orientation programs were largely excluded. The training study program varied in length from a few weeks to just short of the time period required to obtain a college degree. The exact number of participants in such formal occupational training for women is unknown, but it is in the millions.

TABLE XIX.3
Major Occupation Group of Employed Women, Marital Status, March 1962

Major occupation group	Marital Status			
	Total	Single	Married, Husband Present	Other marital status [a]
All occupation groups: Number (thousands)	22,493	5,096	12,716	4,681
Per cent	100.0	100.0	100.0	100.0
Professional, technical, and kindred workers	13.6	16.7	14.2	8.7
Farmers and farm managers	.6	.4	.4	1.3
Managers, officials, and proprietors, except farm	5.1	2.6	5.7	6.2
Clerical and kindred workers	30.9	38.1	30.6	23.8
Sales workers	7.3	5.5	8.7	5.6
Craftsmen, foremen, and kindred workers	1.1	.7	1.2	1.5
Operatives and kindred workers	13.8	7.8	15.6	15.7
Private household workers	10.6	16.8	6.0	16.5
Service workers, except private household	14.5	10.0	14.4	19.6
Farm laborers and foremen	1.9	1.0	2.7	.6
Laborers, except farm and mine	.5	.3	.5	.5

[a] Includes widowed, divorced, and married, spouse absent.
Source: Washington, D.C., United States Department of Labor, 1962.

Nearly 2 million women and girls were engaged in public trade and high school training in 1958–59. Such training programs are supported by both federal and state funds. They are conducted in some 14,000 of the nation's public secondary schools. In these schools the primary subjects of training include practical nursing, needle trades, cosmetology, food trades, and dental and medical assistants. New directions for female training include such occupations as mechanics or repairmen, electronics technicians, textile workers, policewomen, and commercial drivers.

Junior colleges now constitute another major area in which women may obtain special occupational training. Recently their enrollments have totaled approximately 225,000 women students for such purposes. Vocational training in this environment often involves secretarial studies, nursing, dental hygiene, medical technology, etc. These training courses are both full-time and part-time, and are held both in day school and in evening school classes.

About 500,000 women and girls are being trained in private and technical schools and business colleges. This kind of training is typically of a short-term, intensive, and highly practical type. The subjects studied are often stenography, typing, office machine operation, and bookkeeping. In addition, there are special schools for beauty culture, nursing, fashion design, commercial arts, photography, real estate, and a variety of other occupations.

Employment in service training, apprenticeship, and correspondence schools are other major sources of occupational training for women workers. The importance of these various forms of training is that they provide a usable information in such quantity and at such times that the irregularity of the occupational women's labor force participation is accommodated. It is concluded from the survey of occupational training opportunities that training should be broadened to include many of the new and developing work directions. Moreover, within the traditional areas of women's work more intensive training should be provided. Finally, training should be more adapted to the specific work requirements of regions.

Commitment to work on the part of married women was studied in 1955. The study was based on a random sample of some 2713 respondents who were white married women in the childbearing ages.[39] Respondents were asked if they planned to work permanently or temporarily. How long did they expect to work? Did they anticipate leaving and re-entering the work market? The findings of the research revealed that nearly half of the young married women anticipated future extensive work careers. Factors which influenced the sampled wives concerning their future work are primarily of three categories: one, enabling conditions; two, facilitating conditions; and three, precipitating conditions. The enabling conditions include the number of children, the age of children, future child expectations, and current pregnancy. In short, the enabling conditions constitute an analysis of the family status. The facilitating conditions concerned ease in obtaining work. They include the wife's education, work experience prior to marriage, and work experience since marriage. The third category, called precipitating conditons, is concerned with the relative dissatisfaction of the female. Two categories were reported. The first, financial category, including the husband's income and the wife's income. The second category for dissatisfaction was a general attitudinal area including life satisfaction and need for accomplishment.[40]

This kind of research finding suggests that women will continue to make a greater quantitative impact on occupations. It is probable that many will be more highly trained. Their reasons for work are many, including several highly significant factors other than money. Their commitment to work is wide and general. Their commitment to occupation is far more spurious and fleeting.

OCCUPATIONAL UNEMPLOYMENT AND FAMILIES

In 1962 it was reported that more than three out of five persons who were enrolled in the Manpower Development and Training programs were heads of families. Most of the occupational men in managerial, official, and proprietory positions are also family heads. Similarly, in the professional and technical types of occupations married men hold slightly more than half of the positions. As one moves down into the less skilled, semiskilled, and service occupations the number of family heads is reduced. Nevertheless, there is a high proportion of family heads there, particularly among the non-white category of the population.

This condition is significant for the study of occupation and family life because occupation is found to make such a dramatic impact on the way of life of people. The lack of occupation similarly makes an impact. The resulting unemployment contributes to families' reducing their expenditures, often below a satisfactory level for food, medicine, education, and housing. Persons in this negative occupational arena are in most cases individuals who have not completed high school. It is discovered that many of the jobless family heads have an insufficient basic education, inappropriate occupational training, and, in many cases, also lack of motivation. Their impact on occupational image making and recruiting is by necessity, and at best, less than systematic. Their lack of contribution of occupational socialization and recruiting is confounding.[41]

SUMMARY AND IMPLICATIONS

Family life has been historically more determinant on occupations than occupations on family life. The specific and precise articulation of occupations never has been greater than in the contemporary urbanized society.

Occupations began to be moved out of family life in the eighteenth century in both Europe and America. By the nineteenth century the trend for separating family and occupational life was widespread. After the Civil War in the nineteenth century the pendulum swung so that occupational life came to dominate family life.

Family organization continues to provide many formal and informal mechanisms for occupational values and ideologies. The meaning of work and notions of occupational significance are most precise and facilitating when they grow out of family environments. Moreover, the informal socialization for occupations which families contribute bring about much of the phenomenon of occupational inheritance.

Wives of occupational men constitute a separate and important dimension in the occupational arena. It is highly questionable whether the wives of occupational men make a positive contribution to their work or not. There appears to be no question, however, that the "bad" occupational wife is a sharply negative burden. In any event, the roles of wives of occupational men come to be of greater importance for those occupations that are well on the upper end of the occupational continuum.

The influence of family life on occupational women is in several respects being greatly reduced. Or put another way, several changes in the general social organization tend to accommodate working women. These include the reduced number of children, improved home technology, relatively high educational achievement of women, and the increased life span which makes it feasible for many women to re-enter the labor force after the childbearing period. Research findings show that married women anticipate long and systematic work experience before, in some cases during, and after their childraising experience.

Finally in a negative way, unemployment makes a significant impact on families and occupations as well. Much occupational socialization and orientation is still both formally and informally generated from the family experience. Occupational employment virtually negates a positive informal socialization for occupational images in the occupational structure. Unemployment in a family gives the young people few opportunities to perceive positive and alternative occupational roles.

NOTES

1. Theodore Caplow, *The Sociology of Work* (Minneapolis: University of Minnesota Press, 1954); and Nels Anderson, *Dimensions of Work: The Sociology of a Work Culture* (New York: David McKay Co., Inc., 1964), pp. 136-8.
2. R. P. Dore, *City Life in Japan* (London: Routledge and Kegan Paul, 1958), pp. 111-15.
3. Mary Meek Atkeson, *The Women on the Farm* (New York: The Century Co., 1924); Rowla Milton Tryon, *Household Manufacturers in the U.S., 1640 to 1860* (Chicago: The University of Chicago Press, 1917).
4. Arnold Toynbee, *The Industrial Revolution* (Boston: The Beacon Press, 1884, 1957); P. Kropotkin, *Fields, Factories and Workshops* (New York: G. P. Putnam's Sons, 1913).
5. Toynbee, *The Industrial Revolution*, p. 25.
6. Daniel DeFoe, *A Tour Through the Whole Island of Great Britain*, Vol. III, 7th Ed. with additions, improvements, and corrections (London: J. Rivington *et al.*, 1769), pp. 144-6.
7. Tryon, *Household Manufacturers*, p. 268.
8. Ibid. p. 303.
9. Alba M. Edwards, *Comparative Occupational Statistics for the U.S., 1870-1940* (Washington, D.C.: U.S. Bureau of Census, 1940), p. xi.
10. Donald E. Super, *The Psychology of Careers: An Introduction to Vocational Development* (New York: Harper and Bros., 1957), chap. 17.
11. Eugene A. Weinstein, "Children's Conceptions of Occupational Stratification," *Sociology and Social Research*, 4 (March-April 1958), 278-

84; J. R. Porter, "Predicting the Vocational Plans of High School Senior Boys," *Personnel Guidance Journal*, 33 (December 1954), 215–18.

12. Anne Roe, "A Psychological Study of Eminent Biologists," *Psychological Monograph*, 1951, No. 331; R. H. Knapp and H. D. Goodrich, *The Origins of American Scientists* (Chicago: University of Chicago Press, 1952).

13. Super, *Psychology of Careers*, p. 245.

14. August B. Hollingshead, *Elmtown's Youth* (New York: John Wiley & Sons, Inc., 1949).

15. W. A. Anderson, *The Transmission of Farming as an Occupation* (New York: Cornell Agricultural Experiment Station Bulletin No. 768, 1941); Caplow, *Sociology of Work*, see esp. p. 76; Edward Gross, *Work and Society* (New York: Thomas Y. Crowell Co., 1958), pp. 148ff; Don Kanel, *Opportunities for Beginning Farmers, Why Are They Limited?* (Nebraska: Agricultural Experiment Station Bulletin 452, 1960); N. Rogoff, *Recent Trends in Occupational Mobility* (Glencoe: The Free Press, 1953); Elbridge Sibley, *The Recruitment, Selection, and Training of Social Scientists* (New York: Social Science Research Council, Bulletin No. 58, 1948); and Murray A. Straus, "Personal Characteristics and Functional Needs in the Choice of Farming as an Occupation," *Rural Sociology*, 21 (September–December 1956), 257–66.

16. W. W. Charters, "How Much Do College Professors Work?" *Journal of Higher Education*, 13 (June 1942), 298–301; and Anne Roe, *Psychological Study*.

17. Talcott Parsons, "A Revised Analytical Approach to the Theory of Social Stratification," in Reinhard Bendix and Seymour Martin Lipset (eds.), *Class, Status and Power* (Glencoe: Free Press, 1953), pp. 92–128; and Talcott Parsons, "The Social Structure of the Family," in Ruth Nanda Anshen (ed.), *The Family: Its Function and Destiny* (New York: Harper and Bros., 1949), 173–201.

18. Eugene Litwak, "Occupational Mobility and Extended Family Cohesion," *American Sociological Review*, 25 (February 1960), 9–20.

19. Ibid. p. 20.

20. William H. Whyte, Jr., "The Wives of Management," *Fortune*, 44 (October 1951), 86–8ff.

21. Ibid. p. 87.

22. Ibid. p. 88.

23. Ibid. p. 204.

24. Whyte, "Wives of Management."

25. Morris Janowitz, *The Professional Soldier* (Glencoe: The Free Press, 1960), pp. 187–95. See also Nancy Shea, *The Army Wife* (New York: Harper and Bros., 1954); Maurine Clark, *Captain's Bride: General's Lady* (New York: McGraw-Hill Book Co., Inc., 1956).

26. Clark, *Captain's Bride*, p. 33.

27. Clark, *Captain's Bride*.

28. Robert Parks Rankin, "The Ministerial Calling and the Minister's

Wife," *Pastoral Psychology*, 11 (September 1960), 16–22. See also Charles Merrill Smith, *How to Become a Bishop without Being Religious* (New York: Doubleday and Co., Inc., 1965), chap. 2, "Selecting the Clerical Wife."

29. Rankin, "Ministerial Calling," p. 17.
30. Ibid. p. 19.
31. Nels Anderson, *Dimensions of Work*, p. 139.
32. Caplow, *Sociology of Work*, p. 266.
33. Jacob Schiffman, "Family Characteristics of Workers, 1959," *Monthly Labor Review*, 83 (August 1960), 833.
34. Janet M. Hooks, *Women's Occupations through Seven Decades* (Washington, D.C.: U.S. Department of Labor, Women's Bulletin No. 218, 1947), p. 30.
35. Daniel H. Kruger, "Women at Work," *The Personnel Administrator*, 9 (July–August 1964), 11–13; and Richard C. Wilcock, "Women in the American Labor Force: Employment and Unemployment," *Studies in Unemployment*, prepared for the special committee on unemployment problems, United States Senate, U.S. Government Printing Office, 1960.
36. Pearl S. Buck, "Changing Relationships Between Men and Women," *American Women: The Changing Image*, edited by Beverly Benner Cassara (Boston: Beacon Press, 1962), pp. 5, 6.
37. Kruger, "Women at Work," p. 8ff.
38. Jean A. Wells, "Training Women and Girls for Work," *Occupational Outlook Quarterly*, 4 (December 1960), 9–16.
39. F. Ivan Nye and Lewis Waldis Hoffman (eds.), *The Employed Mother in America* (Chicago: Rand, McNally and Company, 1963), pp. 40–63.
40. Ibid. p. 47.
41. *Family Breadwinners: Their Special Training Needs* (Washington, D.C.: U.S. Department of Labor, Manpower Research Bulletin No. 5, January 1964).

SUPPLEMENTARY READING

Maurine Clark, *Captain's Bride: General's Lady* (New York: McGraw-Hill Book Co., Inc., 1956).

Family Breadwinners: Their Special Training Needs (Washington, D.C.: U.S. Department of Labor, Manpower Research Bulletin No. 5, 1964).

Eugene Litwak, "Occupational Mobility and Extended Family Cohesion," *American Sociological Review*, 25 (February 1960), 9–20.

Jacob Schiffman, "Family Characteristics of Workers, 1959," *Monthly Labor Review*, 83 (August 1960), 828–36.

Eugene A. Weinstein, "Children's Conceptions of Occupational Stratification," *Sociology and Social Research*, 4 (March–April 1958), 278–84.

INNOVATIVE OCCUPATIONS: PROFESSIONS AND EXECUTIVES XX

Idea or innovative occupations hold a central place in the social organization of an urbanized and industrial society. Ideas are power in such societies, and professionals, executives, and artists are the primary generators and custodians of ideas.

Some of the idea occupations are traditional, even ancient of origin. Artistic expression is found in all societies and most of them have developed normative structures for identifying artists as occupational types. Administrators and executives are also of ancient origin. They were not always captains of industry; often they were political or religious administrators. But administrative-executive occupations have held illustrious positions in societies through the ages. Professional occupations are also identified, at least in small numbers, from the Middle Ages to the present.

Tremendous proliferation characterizes the innovative occupations in the twentieth century. Dominant among the three major innovative occupational categories are the professionals. It may, in fact, be nearly correct to characterize this middle of the twentieth century in the urbanized society as the age of the professionals. They wield enormous power with their ideas, both creatively and in practitionerships. The professionals, in some considerable contrast to the executives, tend to be silent, unobtrusive workers. But unlike the silent white-collar workers beneath them, their idea power creates for them deference and respect in an aura setting them, as it were, apart from lay people.

In spite of all their great power, professionals tend to be middle class of origin, purpose, and destination. In the United States in the 1950's and 1960's studies show that professionals come disproportionately from the Middle West, are educated disproportionately in church-related colleges, and obtain their doctorates from the nation's big universities.

476

The social behavior of professionals is stereotypically characterized as colleagueship-directed. By this it is implied that colleague authority is more sought after and more respected than bureaucratic or hierarchical authority. It is further implicit that the technical expertise nature of professional work is such that only colleagues are adequately competent to judge one's production.

The professional occupational milieu is dominated by a service orientation. The service may be in fundamental research or other basic creative activity or skilled practitionership. But whatever the specific role of a tribe of professionals they are characterized as both in and of their society. Their innovative and creative occupational roles may cause them at any time to manifest sharp exceptions with a given set of societal norms or structures, but still it is their major idiom to understand and serve their fellow men. In this they are ultimately societally directed even if they are political neutrals.

Professionals are occupationally oriented. They seek to control their own work and work environments. It is the nature of professionalization to construct rigorous occupational norms and to build strong boundary maintenances. Accordingly, they are career-oriented more than family-oriented. And professionals are more society-oriented rather than community-oriented.

These characteristics of professionals overshadow executive and art innovative occupations. So much is this the case that administrators and artists increasingly seek professional occupational forms. There are documented accounts of attempts by hospital administrators to become professionals. Business executives from time to time seek to establish a professional image and professional ethics. Government administrators and civil servants also join in the game of professionalization.

Art occupations in music, painting, theater, etc., also make specific efforts in building professional structures. Artists develop specific professional associations. They attempt to regulate the training and the entry of persons into their creative occupations. They may also unionize or otherwise attempt to regulate their remunerative systems. There is considerable question concerning the occupational appropriateness, the advantages or disadvantages, of professional structures for many occupations, including executive and artist occupations. As the idea-innovative occupational practitioners interact with increasing frequency in a highly common social space with their dramatic professional occupational colleagues, their other-directed effectiveness is often increased with professionalization. Members of the greater society, and members of the many thousands of other occupations, have come to understand and even pay homage to the professional occupational practitioners. Accordingly, some idea-occupational practitioners may be mistaken for professionals and even have attributed to them professional status by persons outside of and beneath the innovative occupational category.

The social space of innovative occupations. Idea-occupational practitioners are often practice-oriented, but their practice or work is based on innovation, research, and systematic or rational analysis. But whether abstract intellectuals or day-to-day practitioners, compared to other occupational men they stand at the vanguard of knowledge. They produce knowledge, their work is the consumption and utilization of knowledge, and their occupational life is determined by knowledge systems and structures.

Societal norms give innovative occupational persons social space for creativity, privilege, and practice. Such occupational men are expected to be different and at the same time to be responsible. They are expected to have knowledge and to impart it dispassionately to all whom it may serve. The social space of innovative occupations is illustrated in Figure XX.1.

FIGURE XX.1

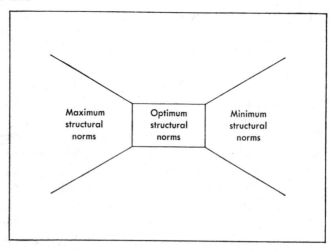

Creativity Continuum

At the left side of the social space creativity continuum one finds maximum structural norms and folkways. In this social space the practitioner professionals find security and definition of occupational roles. Here the general medical practitioners, the civil engineers, the solo attorneys, etc., carry out their model professional practices. They are the users of knowledge and the prescribers of knowledge to individual or corporate clients. They are in every sense practitioner idea people. At this end of the social space continuum the practitioners will create very little indeed. Their sharpness in judgment, however, is critically called for in being able to survey vast bodies of professional knowledge, diagnose a complex situation of a client, and prescribe the proper subject and amount of idea power to the client's question. In carrying out this complex occupational role the professional practitioner must devote himself to the understanding of ideas with the highest integrity and consider the service of clients as his highest calling.

In the middle or rectilinear space in Figure XX.1 there is an optimum environment for innovation and creativity. It is in this space that occupational professionals are confronted with sufficient structure from the internal organization of their occupation to know who they are in a socio-psychological sense. It is in this social space that these same practitioners are confronted with an appropriate mix of societal structures to know what is expected of them, and to know the range of limits within which they may operate to fulfill the expectations. In this social space the urbanized industrial society gives its mandates to its research and development people, to its artistic creators, and to its intellectuals. They are expected to be different, indeed licensed, if you will, to be deviant and at the same time to be respectable in their deviance. Universities and research laboratories are concrete examples of this social space. Their greatness is achieved by their courage for differential examination of phenomenon and by the discipline of their practitioners to the missions or goals of the society of which they are a part. There is both freedom and expectation in this social space. Opportunity is combined with awards in prestige.

At the right side of this social space creativity continuum there is a minimum of social structured norms and a minimum of occupational structure. In this space random and undisciplined innovation and creativity are rampant. Innovation in any area or direction imaginable is structurally possible but few or no rewards are attributed to the creative accomplishments. Such idea production is beyond both the occupational and the societal organization. Such idea innovation is related to few references, or none at all. It is from innovation in this social space that the expression "He was a man before his time" might be generated. It is here that ideas are out of context. Free and undisciplined expression produces little of utilitarian value.

The idea power that makes professionals famous is generated in the transitional space near the intersection of the minimum structure area with the optimum structure area. It is in this middle area that pioneering development laboratories flourish. In this space artists and executives reach dramatic accomplishments—build schools of painting or managerial empires. It is at the intersection of the optimum structure and the maximum structure that dynamic innovations are reduced to routines. In this area ideas continue to have an integrity of form and identity, but more refinement of their character than innovative production is generated. A new, rough, raw, or crude idea may be exciting and potentially powerful, but refinement, specification, elucidation, etc., render the fullest productivity and power of the idea. The three areas of social space on the continuum of innovation are complementary. The interaction patterns between and among these areas of social space are the mechanisms by which the idea people have become of major occupational importance.

PROFESSIONAL IDEA AGE

There are in the 1960's nearly 7 million professional and technical persons (excluding artists), more than 5 million executive persons, and approximately 460,000 artists.[1] Among these the rate of growth of the professionals is the greatest. Indeed, during the first half of the twentieth century professionals tripled in number. Yet such traditional occupations as law and medicine have experienced only a one-quarter increase. The greatest increase has been among engineers—a rate four times faster than other professionals. The rate of increase for accountants and auditors has closely approximated that of the engineers. The expansion in these two occupational areas confirms the importance of technology and record keeping in the urbanized industrial society.[2]

Professionals. There are several notable characteristics which dominate among the occupational professionals. First there is a deep personal investment in the form of many years in education and training. Accordingly, the work of the professional is a dominating life interest. This is different from most clerical and production workers who seek in their occupations remuneration to provide themselves with leisure and other off the job commodities. It is not that the professionals as occupational types oppose leisure, but that the highest fulfillment of their expectations is in excellence and dedication to work.

A second major characteristic of the professional occupational practitioners is high mobility. The intellectual boundary of the professional as an idea person is not set by geographic limits. As technical experts they tend to be interested in ideas, and the application of ideas with little regard for locality. They are willing to move where they can achieve the most excellence, work in the most superior laboratories, and experience the most stimulating colleagueship. They are often cosmopolitans rather than locals. A concomitant of their high mobility is their high rate of employment. In recent years when relatively high unemployment rates have been experienced by the nation's labor force, there has been almost no unemployment of professionals beyond that which can be explained as frictional—the essence of which is normal job changing.[3]

A third overriding characteristic of professional occupational practitioners is their self-regulation or self-direction. In an efficiency-oriented quantifying type of society, questions are continually raised about the effective utilization of the various segments of the nation's manpower. Yet the measures of professional utilization and productivity frustrate if they do not defy the normal standards of judgment. The real measure of professional production in expertise is controlled internally by their occupational practitioner colleagueship. The management of scientific talent [4] is a subject of much consideration but of little real regulation. Professionals may be confronted from time to time by bureaucratic environments which push them to some degree of conformity—for example, to planned program budgeting. Yet effective colonies of professionals as creative idea people may still produce irregularly within such systems. In short, in the systematic society professionals continue to be the most accepted deviants.

The importance of professionals in the societal organization of the labor force is further illustrated by the per capita investment for them. Rosow asserts that professionals are a significant manpower investment in that on a per capita basis they cost 2 to 3 times as much as production or office workers. Their cost is significantly increased due in part to the supporting staffs which they require. Moreover, they require specific and expensive facilities over a long period of time. The professional proportion of the total labor cost is increasing, and it now ranges from one-third to two-thirds of the total. In the 1960's hiring a new college graduate is estimated to be a potential $500,000 investment. In the next 20 years it is anticipated that college graduates will represent a $1 million investment each. Another 25 per cent must be added to cover benefits.[5]

Yet in spite of this high investment in professionals, manpower as an asset appreciates over time. In contrast, machines tend to depreciate. Particularly among professionals, and particularly with continuing education, the human resource manpower investment is one which can be continually changed, modified, enlarged, and grow to the needs as they develop. The investment in idea brainpower is great yet the future of most industries depends increasingly on the engagement of the best minds. Idea power, particularly as manifested among professionals, is the energy—the dynamite—of the urbanized industrial society. Professional occupations have come of age, and the idiom of their age dominates American society.

Executives. Executives are idea people too. Their imagination and creativity is an expertise in management, production, distribution, and competition. And as professionalism comes of age, executives and managers are increasingly influenced by professional occupational norms. The prestige of the captain of industry is surpassed by the scientist professional. Accordingly, executives are seeking now to utilize professional norms, first because of their systematic discipline in inquiry and problem-solving, and secondly to achieve some of the high prestige attributed to professionals as such.

Questions are now more frequently and more forcefully asked about management as a profession.[6] We submit that executives as a category are idea people, that they are tending to be professional-like but that they are in fact not professionals. In the economic system of this nation businesses clearly exist to make money via the mechanism of providing goods and services for the populace. Their means may be more or less regulated by government. The captains of industry are largely gone, a matter of history—ignoble because of their reputation as robber barons. The new managers of the nation's businesses are employees more normatively than they are owners. Herein lies the quest for professionalism and the manifest professional like characteristics.

In 1921 Harvard first awarded the degree of master in business administration. At that time the university president noted that business administration was "the oldest of the arts and the newest of the professions." [7] The record has never let this utterance be dropped even though it was then and now more literary than a statement of fact. By the 1960's the idea that business administration might become a profession is understandably a matter of hope, if not aspiration, on the part of many salaried managers who will have little opportunity ever to be owners, much less robber barons. The greatest probability of high prestige lies more in professionalism than in the power of ownership.

As the prestige of business as an occupation shrinks in the elegance and aura of professionalism, there are increasing attempts to systematize managerial behavior along professional lines. Yet professions are characterized by systematic bodies of knowledge, by service of an altruistic type, by codes of ethics, by long and rigorous training, by associations, and by control over practitioner behavior. Assertions are made that since the depression years of the 1930's business education has acquired a professional status. [8] And more recently reported in a Ford Foundation Study is the assertion that professional education at the university level can be planned for careers in business. [9]

In spite of the above assertions many critics have questioned the notion that there is in fact a scientific body of knowledge for administrative education. It is asserted that review of undergraduate and graduate curriculums in business show wide divergences and disagreements concerning the content of knowledge required. There is an absence of effective control of executives at a colleagueship level in the frantic competition of an economic market. There is an absence of professional associations, and, by contrast, a proliferation of trade associations.

Artists. Artists are idea people at an aesthetic level, and often at a level of social criticism. Literary, visual, and musical artists may all create expressions which subtly, poignantly, cryptically illustrate the issues of the future or review and revitalize the issues of the past. The ideas of artists may be sharply psychological, political, or religious. A high validity of art is vested in its ability to communicate. The aesthetics of art may range from beauty to ugliness, and these conditions themselves are relative to time and place.

Artists as both idea and professional types are controlled more by internal occupational colleagueship than they are by societal structures. Yet there are well-known cases where the arts have been dramatically influenced by societal structures of government, religion, and economics. Within this influence on art the deviancy of professional colleagueship is manifested.

The idea power of professionals, executives, and artists may reach different categories of people in the society in different proportions. The idea thrust from these occupational persons dramatically influences the nature and direction of other occupational men and the configuration of the society as a whole.

OCCUPATIONAL MEANING AND WAY OF LIFE

The meaning of work is known to vary in history from the repulsive, something to be avoided, to a respectable expectancy of men, supported with considerable religious fervor in the Protestant ethic. By the second half of the twentieth century in urbanized America multiple ethics appear to provide reasonable alternatives for the meaning of work in a pluralistic society. For many occupational practitioners work is an acceptable means for achieving nonwork ends and gratifications. For the idea occupational practitioners work normatively becomes a central life interest.[10]

Specific evidence of the central importance of work in the life of professionals is reported in a case study of registered nurses by Orzack. The study of nurses was in the main a replication of Dubin's study of industrial workers on the same subject.[11] The same questionnaire on central life interests items was administered to industrial workers and nurses. In Table XVI.2 (p. 400) the findings are reported. Nearly 80 per cent of the nurses reported work as their central life interest, while approximately the same per cent of industrial workers reported nonwork activities as their central life interest. General personal satisfactions were reported primarily in the work environment by 67 per cent of the nurses compared to only 15 per cent of the industrial workers. Formal organizational relations were more frequently reported in the work environment by professionals than by industrial workers, 91 per cent to 61 per cent, respectively, although both reported the same general pattern of a work relationship. Similarly, both reported that the greatest proportion of their technological relationships involved the work environment, but the intensity was greater for the professional workers than the industrial workers. Both professional and industrial workers reported that informal relationships occurred most frequently in nonwork situations. But the proportion was strikingly different for the two categories of workers, 55 per cent for the professionals compared to 91 per cent for the industrial workers. In short, even the informal relationships of professionals are much more closely related to work than they are for their counterparts in industry.

These case study findings are suggestive for the total occupational structure, but they provide far from sufficient evidence for hard conclusions. At a suggested level it can be implied that work as a central life interest in the second half of the twentieth century will become increasingly more persuasive because professionals are increasing and it is among them that work is a central interest. Yet such a suggestion is tempered by the observation that much of the professional expansion is also in bureaucratic environments. It remains yet to be determined whether the intensity of occupational work as a central life interest for professionals will be, or can be, maintained in an environment of bureaucracy. Such bureaucratic environments by the nature of their case define sharp boundaries within the work structure and between work and the larger society. In a bureaucracy even professionals, idea people, may be pressured, for example, to report to work at a specific hour in the morning and to depart from work at a specific hour in the evening. There may be attempts to limit their access to offices and laboratories after hours, at night, and on weekends. Or the bureaucracy in pressing for mechanisms like planned programmed budgeting may artificially inhibit the essence of professionalism by forcing distinctions to be made between informal life interest in one's work and specific, formal, budgetary measures of one's work.

It is clear, however, that in the professions, executive occupations, and art occupations, work and total life are vastly integrated. The continued effectiveness and efficiency of such work-life integration remains in doubt as increasing millions of workers enter less rigorously defined professional occupations. It is possible that the ideal of professional occupations can be diluted, their service contribution to society reduced, and their high prestige compromised accordingly.

The occupational meaning and way of life of the innovative occupational practitioners is more altruistic than self-aggrandizing. This is not to observe that professionals are solely motivated by altruism, but only to observe that they are more altruistic than aggrandizing.

COMMUNITY NATURE OF INNOVATIVE OCCUPATIONS

When occupations develop highly organized internal structures their boundary maintenance enables them to become in effect communities within the society of which they are a part.[12] The idea occupations all more rather than less exemplify the situation of communities within communities. In the absence of geographical locality they manifest these major community characteristics: (1) practitioners are bounded by a sense of occupational identity; (2) with the admission to practitionership there is little out-mobility; (3) common values, both occupational and social, are widely shared; (4) appropriate roles for both members and non-members are widely agreed upon; (5) an occupational language or jargon is commonly understood by practitioners; (6) collective control over practitioners is maintained; (7) the boundary maintenance of the occupational community is social rather than physical or geographical; and (8) through recruitment and training selection is made of subsequent generations.[13] This community-like strength of the innovative occupations is one of the prime organizational ingredients in their achievement and prestige. As new innovative occupations grow to a point of maturity their community-like characteristics become more fully manifest.

The morphology of professional occupational communities, executive occupational communities, and artist occupational communities is in many ways substantively different. Yet the organizational integration which leads to a community-like identification is universally strong among them. In many respects the community character of artist occupations is insular, removing and protecting them from any dominant society expressions. This is particularly illustrated in research among jazz musicians which reveals their references to members of the larger society as "squares" who do not understand the nature and integrity of music.[14]

In quite sharp contrast the community of executives sustains them in a hyper-extrovertiveness. They are dynamic and other-directed, demanding and forceful in their confrontations with a larger society.

Their rising and falling, their successes and failures, their nobleness and ignobleness, are greatly sustained by the community of their occupational organization. The rounding criticisms heaped upon their ostentatiousness have little devastating effect because their significant others are ultimately more in their occupational community than outside of it. The professionals, in their community character, stand somewhere in a middle ground between the reclusive occupational artists and the extrovertive occupational executives. Professional occupational communities are able to manifest a character through devotion to service having to do with more important things than outward display or a turning inward. These descriptions are at a broad ideal type level. Within the several innovative occupations specific community manifestations may vary. Yet the abiding character of these community occupational manifestations is illustrated by these types.

The occupational community image is held to most tenaciously by those professional practitioners who have been isolated, as it were, for relatively long periods of time during their recruitment and training. This is clearly illustrated in the case of the clergy, the military, and the medical combine.[15] The intensity of community in the executive occupations is less, and, accordingly, the rigor and specification of training is also less.

As many of the innovative occupational practitioners are also members of bureaucracies, their community manifestation and identification is permeated by bureaucratic structures. Where the innovative occupational communities are free from bureaucracy the control over their practitioners is intensified. The public has few valid indexes for measuring the quality of competence in the idea occupations. Members of the idea occupations are greatly accustomed to being ranked and compared by their fellow practitioners, but the rankings are seldom made public. Even in those cases where such rankings are made available the general public is usually incompetent in the specialty area to utilize the rankings adequately. In effect, therefore, the internal power structure of the idea occupational communities is a labyrinth of colleagueship relations.[16]

SOCIAL ORIGINS

Innovative occupations in American society have come to the forefront since the 1860's. They have come to occupational and societal dominance only in the twentieth century. Their origins have been rather widely researched, and some reasonably definitive conclusions are reached.[17] In the main, America's idea occupational practitioners come from modest circumstances. They are disproportionately from the lower middle class, from non-urbanized regions of the nation, and from the small church-related colleges of the Middle West.

Knapp and Goodrich, in their study of American scientists, report that most originated in communities characterized by relatively high social mobility, by little class consciousness, and by a minimum of traditionalism. Form such an environment youth are prepared to leave the occupations of the parental generation and move with courage, initiative, and ambition into new occupational pursuits, often finding challenge in the idea occupations. Further, these authors submit that a disproportionate number of the nation's scientists come from those communities which offer limited vocational opportunities. Where there is a restricted range of occupations in rural or relatively rural areas, combined with a Protestant ethic of striving, there is mobility into the new science idea occupations. Coming from meager backgrounds, these still modest occupations offer both attractive economic remuneration and satisfying prestige. It is also submitted by these authors that at the outset scientists were not for the most part produced by the great universities of the East. There the environment was richer in expressing a fuller range of occupational opportunities. There the universities trained students whose families came from long-standing traditions and considerable social prominence. Accordingly, their matriculants graduated and returned to those occupations that were traditional in their families.

In more recent generations research findings suggest that the practitioners in idea occupations are tending to reproduce themselves from their own progeny, although there is still considerable in-migration. The idea occupations have themselves reached a considerable degree of maturity and stability. While the earlier idea practitioners originated largely in the lower middle class, the new practitioners more often come from the upper middle class.

It remains to be determined whether the great contribution and expansion of the innovative occupations have been motivated by the striving of class mobility or not. It is too soon yet to know if a class leveling and stability of origin will reduce the ferment that historically has contributed to this category of occupations.

SUMMARY AND IMPLICATIONS

Innovative occupations are the keystone to the urbanized industrial society. They are at the top of the occupational hierarchy in power, control, and direction of the other occupational practitioners of the nation's labor force. They are also attributed the highest occupational prestige of the society. Their posture is nonideological and nonpolitical. Their contributions are characteristically those of service, organization, and commentary.

Idea occupational practitioners are disciplined by a devotion to knowledge, and limited by specialist rather than generalist technical expertise. Collectively, their ideas and management control the society. Individually, the innovative occupations are marooned, helpless. In the mass urbanized society where routine and ritual are widespread, creativity and innovation still dominate in the lives of the idea practitioners.

The life and work of idea people tend to be total and integrated. In an affluent society where leisure seems to be a commodity within the reach of most people, idea practitioners find it difficult indeed to differentiate their work and their leisure.

The idea occupational practitioners are servants of their fellow men. Yet, aside from interacting with their clients in rendering service, the innovative practitioners are essentially removed from the whole of their society by a strong, if often elusive, boundary maintenance. The internal organization of their powerful occupations takes on a community-like characteristic.

The genesis of the innovative practitioners has been modest. They have come from environments of limited opportunity and are ideolog-ically motivated by the stimulus or curse of a Protestant ethic. From this origin they are motivated to achieve, and accept reward in service. More recently, the origins of the innovative practitioners has tended to stabilize. The implication of origin stability on motivation and striving is yet unknown. The demand for ideas never has been greater in the society. The application of much idea service is being surrendered to mechanization.

The social organizational space for innovative occupations is increasing by dramatice proportions. Yet there are societal structural suggestions that very real limits exist for the expansion of idea occupations.

NOTES

1. Note that artists are listed in the census as professionals and only separated out here to illustrate the thesis of this chapter. The total artist category includes artists and art teachers, actors, authors, musicians, and music teachers. See U.S. Bureau of the Census, *U.S. Census of Population: 1960. Detailed Characteristics, U.S. Summary* (Washington, D.C.: U.S. Government Printing Office, 1963), pp. 544–6.
2. Jerome M. Rosow, "The Growing Role of Professional and Scientific Personnel," *Management Record*, 24 (February 1962), 19–23.
3. Ibid. p. 19.
4. Jerome W. Blood, *The Management of Scientific Talent* (New York: American Management Association, 1963).
5. Ibid. pp. 20, 21.
6. Paul Donham, "Is Management a Profession?," *Harvard Business Review*, 40 (September–October 1962), 60–68.
7. Ibid. p. 61.
8. *Education for Professional Responsibility* (Pittsburgh: Carnegie Press, 1948), p. 47.
9. *Higher Education for Business* (New York: Columbia University Press, 1959), p. 11.
10. Louis H. Orzack, "Work As a 'Central Life Interest' of Professionals," *Social Problems*, 7 (Fall 1959), 125–32.
11. Robert Dubin, "Industrial Workers Worlds: A Study of the 'Central Life Interests' of Industrial Workers," *Social Problems*, 3 (January 1956), 131–42.
12. William J. Goode, "Community Within A Community: The Professions," *The American Sociological Review*, 22 (April 1957), 194–200.
13. Ibid. p. 194.
14. Howard S. Becker, "Contingencies of the Professional Dance Musician's 'Career,'" *Human Organization*, 12 (Spring 1953), 22–6; John H. Mueller, *The American Symphony Orchestra* (Bloomington: Indiana University Press, 1951); Dennison J. Nash, "Challenge and Response in the American Composer's Career," *Journal of Aesthetics and Art Criticism*, 14 (September 1955), 116–22.
15. Mary Jean Huntington, "The Development of a Professional Self-Image Among Medical Students," in *The Student Physician* (Cambridge:

Harvard University Press, 1957); Robert K. Merton, Howard S. Becker, and James W. Carper, "The Development of Identification with an Occupation," *American Journal of Sociology*, 61 (January 1956), 291, 292.
16. Everett C. Hughes, "Mistakes at Work," *Canadian Journal of Economics and Political Science*, 17 (August 1951), 320–27; and Oswald Hall, "The Informal Organization of the Medical Profession," *Canadian Journal of Economics and Political Science*, 12 (February 1946), 30–44.
17. Robert H. Knapp and H. D. Goodrich, *Origins of American Scientists* (Chicago: University of Chicago Press, 1952); and Joel E. Gerstl, "Social Origins of Engineers," *New Society*, 1 (June 1963), 19, 20.

SUPPLEMENTARY READING

Paul Donham, "Is Management a Profession?," *Harvard Business Review*, 40 (September–October 1962), 60–68.
William J. Goode, "Community within A Community: The Professions," *American Sociological Review*, 22 (April 1957), 194–200.
John H. Mueller, *The American Symphony Orchestra* (Bloomington: Indiana University Press, 1951).
Jerome M. Rosow, "The Growing Role of Professional and Scientific Personnel," *Management Record*, 24 (February 1962), 19–23.

CLERICAL AND SALES OCCUPATIONS

Occupationally and social organizationally, people in clerical and sales work are in middle occupations.[1] The "middleness" of these occupations is determined largely by their location between professionals and managers: the idea occupational people are on one side of them and the farmers, craftsmen, and operatives as production occupational people are on the other side of them. In urbanized industrial society, these middle occupational people fulfill highly essential occupations in transmitting the details of ideas to the producers and in distributing the products of producers to all others.

Both clerical and sales people are typically white-collar workers, yet aside from the white collar and the central position of their occupations, there are many fundamental differences between them. The stereotype of clerical workers is quietness, unobtrusiveness, and devotion to routine. Mills has referred to their environment as that of the great file.[2] While they do more than file, a disproportionate number of them are office workers. They keep vast quantities of records in minute detail. They manipulate data, record information, and report statistics. Where simple routine characterizes their work details, they face displacement by automation. Their identification and ideology have been typically upward, that is, to an association with management. Their lack of initiative and idea expression precipitates a vast gap, however, between them and the professionals and management. Their proximity to the people above them is great, but the social distance between them is also great. Viewed from the top down professionals and managerial people have loosely accepted the identification of clerical workers with them. And although management has done little to strengthen this identification, they have appeared shocked when clerical workers accept union organization. This is viewed as a defiance, a separation, a loss in prestige. Structurally, both occupationally and social organizationally, there has been little basis for integration between the middle occupational people and the idea occupational people. Unionization is structurally to be anticipated.

The potential and ever more frequently actualized power of clerical occupational workers is considerable in urbanized society. Such a society is increasingly more devoted to record keeping and data processing. Clerical workers fulfill these functions.

Sales occupational people fill middle and white-collar positions. They are anything but silent and routine—they are dynamic and persuasive. Individualism characterizes their occupational nature. From the mid-1930's to the present, much research effort has been invested in attempting to predict sales success and to identify the sales personality. The results are extremely disappointing. What makes a salesman, and what makes for sales success, remain an enigma in the industry, and these questions are prime characteristics of the occupation.

Selling occupations range from the near professional in the form of manufacturers representatives to the near laborer in the form of some retail clerks who take orders. With the rapidly increasing quantity and quality of goods and services in the urbanized society, the distributive work of salesmen is an expanding occupational category.

Clerical and sales occupations are also middle categories because they are dependent on the idea occupations as well. Their own definition of their occupational space is eroded from these two perspectives. Nevertheless, their increasing occupational vitality is a function of the buffer or residual space between ideas and production. In the absence of alternative societal and occupational mechanisms, clerical and sales occupations facilitate the increasingly needed interaction between idea and production occupations.

CLERICAL OCCUPATIONS

Some clerical work, particularly in the form of bookkeeping, dates from ancient times. Normatively speaking, however, clerical occupations are a product of the industrial urbanized social organization. In the main, they are a contemporary type of occupation. By the mid-1960's clerical workers constituted the largest single white-collar group.[3] They numbered more than 11 million people. In spite of automation, their rate of increase continues to exceed that of all occupational types in the nation.

In the 1890's all clerical workers were males; in the 1960's clerical workers are for the most part females.[4] Women nearly saturate the clerical occupations of receptionists, attendants, secretaries, telephone operators, and typists (see Figure XXI.1). Women constitute more

FIGURE XXI.1

Clerical occupations in which women comprised a majority of all workers, 1960

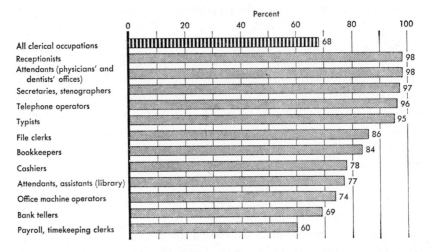

Source: *Clerical Occupations for Women: Today and Tomorrow* (Washington, D.C.: U.S. Department of Labor, Women's Bureau, Bulletin 289, 1964), p. 52.

than three-fourths of the workers in file clerk, bookkeeper, cashier, attendant, and office machine operator positions. Considerably more than half of the bank tellers and payroll time clerks are also women.

Over 2 million of the 11 million clerical workers are in secretary and stenographer occupations (see Figure XXI.2). Bookkeepers constitute almost another million clerical workers. Cashiers and typists combined total more than 1 million. The modal type of clerical occupations are illustrated in these four categories. Office machine operators, telephone operators, receptionists, and others are illustrious and often sensate examples of clerical occupations, but their numbers are relatively few.

In spite of mechanization and automation in the office, clerical occu-

FIGURE XXI.2

The majority of clerical workers are employed in these occupations

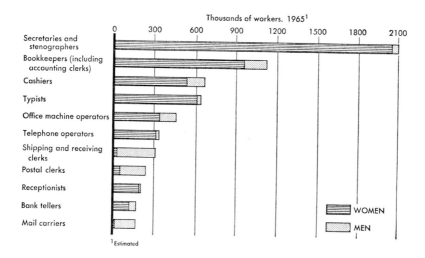

Thousands of workers. 1965[1]

0	300	600	900	1200	1500	1800	2100

Secretaries and stenographers

Bookkeepers (including accounting clerks)

Cashiers

Typists

Office machine operators

Telephone operators

Shipping and receiving clerks

Postal clerks

Receptionists

Bank tellers

Mail carriers

WOMEN

MEN

[1] Estimated

Source: *Occupational Outlook Handbook* (Washington, D.C.: U.S. Department of Labor, Bulletin No. 1450, 1966), p. 279.

pations are expected to increase dramatically in the years ahead. This is largely a function of the type of urbanized social organization which contributes to an ever-increasing volume of paper work. Automation will be used in large offices to reduce, and in some cases to eliminate, routine work. It will contribute to a reducing of the rate of increase in some clerical occupations, but far from eliminating the category, it will often create new clerical types of jobs.

The number of clerical occupations, to repeat, is more a function of urbanized social organization than of occupational aggrandizement. In the division of labor in the twentieth century, clerical occupations are predominantly female occupations. Again the character of the occupations in this case is influenced by social structures more than by internal definition. There is no occupational basis for differentiating the participation by sex.

Occupational norms. The National Office Management Association has made several surveys of the normative trends in the occupation.[5] NOMA surveys show that throughout the 1950's less than 10 per cent of the nation's office workers were covered by collective bargaining agreements. The normative work week for clerical occupations is clearly 40 hours. Pay for overtime is variant, though paid holidays are almost universally provided. The norms for health and life insurance benefits are increasing. Hospitalization and related benefits are provided to 95 per cent of the NOMA respondents, and group life insurance is provided to 90 per cent. The norm for retirement benefits is less extensive, but rapidly increasing; the most recent NOMA survey found three-quarters of the firms studied reporting retirement provisions for clerical workers.

A high rate of turnover is one of the characteristic norms of clerical occupations.[6] Part of the high rate of turnover can be explained by poor selection and poor recruitment processes. But the norm of high turnover is more complex than recruitment alone. Much of it is explained by the high proportion of women participants in the occupational category. For example, it is found in some research that men clerical workers are more interested in security, advancement, and benefits, while women are more interested in type of work, co-workers, supervisor, hours, and working conditions. The interests of men contribute to the building of occupational structures for low rates of turnover, while the interests of women contribute to the weakness of occupational structures for long duration of experience. Due to the overwhelming proportion of women in this occupational category, internal structures for high rates of turnover are indigenous to the occupation.

As a middle type of occupation, supervision is central to the nature of clerical work. It is not a decision-making category of work, but a directed one. The type of supervision is shown to contribute significantly to rate of productivity.[7] These research findings reveal that supervision associated with high rates of production is characterized as follows: (1) the provision of general rather than close supervision, (2) the allowing of maximum authority and responsibility for individuals, (3) maximum time spent in supervision, and (4) employee-oriented rather than production-oriented supervision.[8]

The status hierarchy is a well-established norm in the United States, however democratic the nation may be. More specifically, the status hierarchy is a part of the very fiber of occupational organization. There is, however, some evidence that the indexes of status are sufficiently elusive as to constitute a considerable problem in the ranking of positions.[9] For example, Homans studied clerical workers in one division of a larger company. Their environment was characterized by working in one large room, and by a recent shift from a company union to the CIO. The researcher first spent several weeks observing the interaction patterns of the respondents in their work room. This was followed by interviews in a separate room on company time. The interviews lasted from one to two hours. After the interviews another period of a few weeks was spent in observing the interaction of the respondents. In general the overt behavior and the appraisal of the respondents of their jobs was favorable.

The work of the respondents involved two kinds of posting. In one type of work, the employees were called ledger clerks, and in the other type, cash posters. By the informal standards of the workers themselves the ledger clerk's job was one of higher status than that of the cash posters. There was, nevertheless, no differential pay for the two jobs. The Homans analysis argues that to the extent the workers themselves perceive hierarchical task importance, the rank is real for their behavior even if it is not in the eyes of the supervisors and management. The implications from this analysis suggest that both management and unions could minimize dissatisfaction by letting pay assignment reflect job differentials, partly at least, in a manner consistent with worker evaluations.

It was further suggested from this study of status among clerical workers that when it is necessary to arrange for one worker to fill in for another on the job, dissatisfaction would be minimized if the lower status job holders filled in for higher status job holders. The implementation of this recommendation conflicts, however, with union notions of hierarchy. The union's position is that if the worker is competent to carry out the tasks of the higher position, then the worker should be paid at the rank of that position. This fleeting and evasive nature of status in clerical work is widely recognized.

Clerical workers are white-collar workers. Their ideology is an upward one, looking more toward management above them than to production workers beneath them. Even though a generally silent and unaggressive type of occupational people, the clerical workers are a sharply and subtly status-conscious people. The need to develop especially sensitive norms and structures for recognizing and dealing with status hierarchies is of more critical importance in the occupational organization of clerical jobs than for many others. White-collar workers in general, and certainly clerical workers among them, have tended to identify passively with management. By default they have shown little interest in unionization. It is this generally passive and inarticulate occupational character which has rendered clerical workers so unreceptive to unionization. Their white-collar status, more than negotiated power, is important to them. But their position is eroded, even in status and respect, as unionized blue-collar workers gain in their demands. White-collar workers have demanded little and received little.

In juxtaposition, unions are forced to attempt to appeal more to white-collar workers as their blue-collar worker memberships decline and the number of white-collar workers increases.

In the 1960's the Bureau of Labor Statistics indicates that more than 2.5 million white-collar workers are union members.[10] The number of white-collar union members is increasing in the 1960's. During the same time period, the number of blue-collar workers decreased slightly. The proportion of white-collar union members remains small in terms of the potential, however. In the 1960's less than 15 per cent of the potential white-collar union members were in fact members. Clerical workers in particular continue to manifest an aversion to union membership.[11]

The opportunity for management to deter white-collar unionization of clerical workers is potentially great. But in fact management's affinity for clerical workers is considerably less than the reverse pattern. Accordingly, there is little evidence of management's systematic effort to court the loyalty of clerical workers. As a result, the clerical workers are forced to accept unionization largely through management disinterest.[12]

The National Office Management Association conducts studies to ascertain the impact of unionization on the attitudes and efficiency of office workers.[13] In a NOMA survey conducted in 2002 companies employing 500,000 workers in the United States and Canada only 6 per cent of the companies reported unionization. Most of the respondents reported no unions, no attempts at unionization, and no interest in unionization. There were some attempts at unionization reported, and 3 per cent of the respondents indicated that their employees were in fact interested in joining unions. Respondents listed reasons for lack of union interest as follows: "(1) Loss of prestige and status. (2) Loss of employer-employee relationship. (3) Office workers received the same or more benefits and pay increases as union workers. (4) Opposition to paying dues. (5) Fear of strikes and lockouts." [14] Respondents were also asked the opposite question: what are the reasons for white-collar workers accepting unionization? The answers were unfair administration of pay details, inadequate fringe benefits, lack of systematic promotion policies, and inadequate training of supervisors.[15]

Where unionization has taken place, the attitude of employees is typically favorable to the union. Indeed, only 7 per cent of the respondents reported hostility to their unions. Nevertheless, an overwhelming majority of respondents indicated that unionization had not improved management-employee relations. Sixty-four per cent of the companies reported that office efficiency remained the same after unionization as it was before. Fifty per cent of the respondent companies reported that unionization had made the handling of discharges less favorable than before; 43 per cent indicated no change, and 7 per cent reported improvements. Two-thirds of the responding companies did report that unionization precipitated positive influences on structures for promotion.

In sum, while it was found that companies reported few positive changes resulting from unionization, they were beginning to become alert to the possibilities. They were, in fact, making amendments in their organizations to improve clerical worker jobs and to deter somewhat the advances of union organization.

A specific case study of the organization of clerical workers reveals their confrontation and disintegration in the face of blue-collar unionization advances.[16] The case study is in a plant referred to as No. 37 of The National Corporation. It is located in a large Midwestern city. Four labor unions are involved in the total organization of workers in the plant. The office workers in Plant 37 were organized in 1956. Union's accomplishment there was almost the direct response of salary and fringe benefit advantages awarded to blue-collar workers via contract negotiation and refused to office workers in the absence of union affiliation. The clerical workers found management to be indifferent to their demands. Management viewed the clerical workers' requests as a bluff, and believed they would not unionize.

The study of Plant 37 revealed that management viewed white-collar unionization as a threat. The unionized office workers were reported to have a reduced respect for management. Protected by the unions, they

were willing to work less. Management reported that they were unable
to drive the workers as before due to the threat of union reprisals. Indeed, it was asserted that the workers, particularly the younger ones,
had lost their ambition as unions achieved increased salary and security
for them.

Nowhere is it more clear than in the case of unionization of clerical
workers that occupational men can be molded and made by the social
organizational environment of which they are a part. Repeatedly one observes that the white-collar workers are nonviolent unobtrusive types.
Their occupations are less defined and forged by practitioners and more
molded by a set of external circumstances. And so they unionized less
by decisiveness and more by default.

Automation. The occupational environment of clerical workers is everywhere influenced by automation. Contemporary observers may make
conjectures concerning the recent development of automation or its
gradual evolvement out of the Industrial Revolution. Nonetheless, such
questions remain in an academic realm. Automation is real in fact and
it is real in its consequences for clerical workers.

A leading pioneer architect in automation is John Diebold.[17] This
designer of intensified systematization of work situations asserts that
there are both economic and social advantages in automation. Economically, his argument is that it will lower production costs, increase
output, and reduce waste. Socially, Diebold asserts that automation will
increase the development of new tasks, transform the labor force to
higher skills, and expand the labor requirements. All of these propositions are stated in terms of the long-run development.

Union officials and many workers view their situation in the short
run rather than the long run. Their sentiments echo those of Lord
Keynes, who observed that in the long run we are all dead. Labor's position is not that of a categoric negative against automation, but one of
facilitating the change to avoid short-run disruption.[18] And so it is that
much of the concern with automation is in terms of short-run disruption.[19]

The spread of automation, nevertheless, accelerates. By the mid-
1950's it was still possible to list the large-scale computer installations
briefly in an illustration of their diverse uses. A decade later their accelerated use and acceptance made a straight listing almost unintelligi-

ble. Some form of systematic presentation is required in order to grasp the breadth of their impact.

Some of the increases in automation are offset by the normal turnover and natural attrition in the labor force. Some categories of white-collar workers are characteristically ephemeral, seeking little tenure or seniority. Yet the enormous increase in automation creates the possibility of large-scale displacement of office workers in the second half of the twentieth century.[20] On the other hand, automation increases the direction of data analysis, the intensity of data analysis, and the demand for data analysis. In short, masses of data, their analysis, and retrieval are made possible by this new form of technology. It calls for an upgrading in the type of machine tenders, while at the same time vastly increases the total amount of data analysis. In this respect, automation contributes to the growth and expansion of the office labor force.

Offices with large-scale computers have numerous people in new or specialized occupations for their operation. Some of the new occupations are of a considerably higher level than those for which average workers can be retrained. Other computer-related office occupations are anything but high level—indeed they involve some downgrading. High level or upgraded occupations are illustrated by project planners, programmers, and systems analysis. Among the middle range to lower level occupations are coders, console operators, peripheral equipment operators, key-punch operators, and tape librarians.[21]

In the case of job shifting that is related to computers in offices, the distribution of occupational talent varies little from what it would be without the computer. Those individuals who are upgraded to the level of programmers are the type who have such intellectual and discipline characteristics that they would have achieved higher level occupations even outside of the computer technology. In effect, the introduction of computers may constitute a mechanism for moving some people up more quickly and moving others down more quickly, but it still requires a substantial range in occupations. Programmers stand at the apex of the occupational hierarchy in computer work. Key-punch operators are at the nadir of the occupational continuum. In the first case, college training in mathematics is an essential requirement; in the second case, a high school education with an ability to type is sufficient.

Both occupational extremes are of vital importance in office automation.[22] The summary generalization that is often made asserts that automation in offices and factories does little to upgrade occupations categorically. More typically, there is a full range of occupational changes from high level, through middle level, to low level jobs.

Stimulation, satisfaction, monotony, and routine vary with the level of computer-related occupations.[23] At the key-punch operator occupational level, there is much tedious work with little opportunity for creative thought or innovation. As in earlier studies, it is again reported that in this routine and monotonous work there are excessively high rates of turnover.[24] In one farm equipment company an empirical investigation of key-punch operators showed the annual rate of turnover to range from 55 to 75 per cent. Respondents in this case reported that their work was no different from ordinary factory jobs except that they were paid less.[25] There were few recognizable opportunities for advancement. This was coupled with a minimum of merit or incentive increases.

In other examples of automation, particulary in factories, the pendulum is seen to swing from the direction of monotony and specialization in the direction of job integration or job enlargement. Yet the situation of job enlargement is frequently confounded with that of worker isolation. In the automated situation when one worker, for example, in the Detroit automobile plant, is responsible for several steps in the operation, he is frequently removed by considerable distance from fellow workers. The lack of opportunity for social interaction with other workers leads to job dissatisfaction.[26] While the impact of office automation is still sufficiently new that occupational patterns remain to some degree in doubt, the overriding implication is that physical jobs will remain at about the same level or be slightly downgraded.[27]

A recent president of the Office Employers International Union has viewed automation as a multidirectional monster threatening workers at several levels.[28] From all points of view, the occupational and organizational strength of clerical positions is weak. The workers in clerical occupations are female. Accordingly, their responsibilites and interests in life are divided among occupation, family, and other external situations. Unionization as an external structural impact is less than massively effective as white-collar workers continue to identify tenaciously, at least emotionally, with management rather than with blue-collar workers. Finally, and most recently, automation in the office is remaking the very character of the clerical occupations. The new occupations are determined more by the machine than the nature of the machine is determined by the occupational practitioners.

SALES OCCUPATIONS

Sales occupations, like clerical occupations, are middle types of work. But they are characterized as active rather than passive, as articulate

FIGURE XXI.3
Among the 4.5 million workers in sales occupations in 1965 [1] . . . . about one-half were retail salespeople

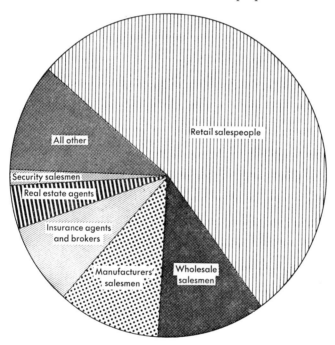

Source: *Occupational Outlook Handbook* (Washington, D.C.: U.S. Department of Labor, Bulletin No. 1450, 1966), p. 305.

rather than silent. Sales occupations are characterized by extreme public visibility. In general the personality type of the practitioners is viewed as extroverted rather than introverted. A more close and careful analysis, however, reveals that the true personality of the successful salesman remains an enigma.

Number and characteristics. In the mid-1960's there were approximately 4.5 million persons employed in sales occupations.[29] About one-quarter of the sales workers are part-time individuals who work 35 hours a week or less. In the retail sales occupations, 2 out of every 5 participants are women. In insurance, real estate, and related types of sales work, the overwhelming majority of the occupational participants are males. Slightly more than one-half of the sales personnel are in retail occupations (see Figure XXI.3). Wholesale, manufacturing, and insurance sales types make up another quarter of the participants in the occupation.

The characteristics of persons in sales occupations range from those with less than high school education to those with more than a baccalaureate degree. There is indeed a vast disparity between over-the-counter retail selling and security brokerage or manufacturer representative sales. About all they have in common is a relatively clean work and a high frequency of interaction with people. Yet selling appears to remain in defiance of science, and by default is in the category of an art. Accordingly, even in those highest sales occupations, there is a considerable basis for differentiation from the professions. The drug sales representative to the medical professional is a widely separated occupational type. Selling in all of its extremes is profoundly a middle occupation.

Sales workers are in middle occupations from another perspective. Their increased social space in the industrial urbanized societies is a function of the make and trade character of the societal organization. In agrarian hoe and dig societies sales occupations are conspicuous by their absence. They are, then, middle in that their amount of social space is dependent on the configuration of societal organization.

Work environment norms. A major dichotomy in the work environment of sales practitioners is traveling vs. sedentary. In some cases this dichotomy is so deep it is characterized by hostility. Frequently one hears sedentary sales persons referred to as being little more than order takers. Normatively such workers wait on people who have already made their major selections in terms of merchandise or service. Such middle sales transacting personnel stand precariously on the precipice of obliteration by means of automation.

But there are no normative occupational structures which make it necessary for sedentary sales persons to be only order takers and to retreat from efforts to influence the decision-making and choosing of persons with whom they come in contact. Their range of contact and areas of control over their customer are necessarily limited by their sedentariness and by the customer's mobility.

The traveling sales persons create more of the norms of their occupation. They move to identify, follow, and influence customers and clients. They may be employee salesmen or independent agents. In both cases their normative structure for relations with customer-clients are determined primarily by their individual behavior or by their occupational norms.[30]

The work environment of sales people is a customer-oriented one, particularly when it is above the "wait on" level.[31] The customer-oriented work environment by the nature of the case contributes to considerable occupational boundary permeation. Basic structural components of the occupation must allow for—indeed facilitate—high and intense rates of social interaction with external situations, namely customer-clients. While some occupations are characterized by near closure, sales occupations are characteristically open. They are structurally constituted to be extremely sensitive to the interests, demands, position, and posture of customer-clients. In all cases, the social organization of sales occupations is influenced by customer-clients.

Norms of the work environment are illustrated by an empirical investigation in 1956 of sales personnel in a large Midwestern retail furniture store.[32] This case study was carried out over a four-year period. A major conclusion was that sales success, as measured by volume and money earned, depends largely on the individual.

The norms for the work environment, namely traveling and sedentary, contribute to a considerable duality within the sales occupation. But when one holds constant this factor of mobility, the commonality of middleness of the occupation is universal.

Personality. The personality of the salesman has been and continues to be a major enigma—yet it is a primary characteristic of the occupation. In Cleveland's review of literature concerning sales personalities for the decade 1935 to 1945, he estimates that more than 350 companies were employing sales aptitude tests.[33] This review of literature involved the citing of over 150 pieces of evidence. The characteristics of successful salesmen most often cited are (1) social contact (locating customer), (2) persuasion, (3) trade knowledge, and (4) clerical knowledge. But this tells very little that is useful in predicting sales success. Indeed, one of the sources cited reports an author observing that "more nonsense has been written about the qualifications necessary for selling than in connection with any other topic in the field." [34] Yet in the face of the vast concern, and in view of the few hard principles, it is anticipated that more psychological investigation will be made of the personality of sales persons.

After some 35 years of inquiry into the nature of sales personalities, several contemporary but still less than conclusive factors may be listed. In the 1960's, reporting from an empirical investigation of dealer salesmen employed by a major oil company, the Wechsler Adult Intelligence Scale Arithmetic and the Tomkins-Horn Picture Arrangement tests yielded correlations with sales success or low performance. The picture arrangement test illustrated dependence, sociophilia, self-confidence, and happiness. Yet as in the past, no broad principle of sales personality is validated by such research. Such findings remain to be validated in many other types of sales situations.

In a more recent study of life insurance sales persons, some fundamental differences were discovered between the well-trained practitioners and those who were not so well trained.[35] The assumption in this research is that the unique contribution of the mobile salesman is his willingness and ability to deliberately intrude upon the privacy of his prospect. This is to say his role is less to deliver goods, for the mails and other delivery persons can do that. He is to intrude and persuade, indeed, to lead to decision-making. In the case of one insurance company employing approximately 1500 underwriters, nearly one-third of whom are full-time, the training ranged considerably. Before any salesmen are hired they are given 20 hours of training. Then before actually going into the field they receive another 8 days of office training. But the training can continue and for some it does. After 2 years of experience nearly 10 per cent went on for advanced training leading to the certified life underwriter diploma.

Questionnaires were sent to all of the underwriters, and 67 per cent were returned. Twenty selected interviews were taken with successful underwriters, and another 20 with unsuccessful ones. When asked about obstacles to success, the reports were as follows: poor territories, poor work habits, and fear of making contacts. It is concluded from the evidence in this study that the most successful salesmen do not work harder than the unsuccessful, but they are more efficient in their work. It is also concluded that indeterminant occupational commitment is more a deterrent for sales success among the underwriters who were less well trained, while anxiety concerning intrusion on personal privacy is more the bane of those who were well trained. This research identifies another dimension in the personality structure of participants in the sales occupations, but its universality remains to be demonstrated.

In still another case, sales success and job satisfaction were studied by sending a mailed questionnaire to the personnel of a large candy company. A total of 1123 questionnaires were returned from a sales force of approximately 1600. It was found that those persons who were most successful as route salesmen were slightly more satisfied with their work situation than their less successful counterparts.[36] The variable of satisfaction vs. some degree of frustration continues to be recognized as a significant component of the sales situation, and it continues to be less than adequately understood.

Still another theory of the ingredients of good salesmanship proposes that the primary components are empathy and ego drive.[37] The first variable, empathy, is the ability to feel as the customer or client does and thereby be able to sell him in terms of his own needs. The second variable is that of ego drive. In this case, the salesman has a desire, indeed, a need, to make the sale, not only because of the money gained, but to achieve. In such an ego situation the customer-client is viewed as a subject who is there to help the salesman fulfill his personal needs. In short, the ego is involved in the drama of conquest. The predictive results of the empathy-ego theory is illustrated for the retail automobile industry, the insurance industry, and the mutual funds industry in Table XXI.1. Seven years of research contributed to the development of a battery of tests with the predictive power illustrated in this table. Still this evidence is based on a limited number of specific types in the broad sales occupational category.

The personality of salesmen continues to be a focal point of importance, but identification of the personality dimensions, much less their control, remains in question.

Social status hierarchy. In the urbanized society it is of more than ordinary significance that salesmen and entertainers are numbered

TABLE XXI.1
Three Examples of Predictive Results from Selection Instrument
Based on Empathy and Ego Drive

IN THE RETAIL AUTOMOBILE INDUSTRY

Number of Men Predicted for Each Group[a]	Data at End of (Months)	Actual Sales Performance (number of men who reached each quarter of sales force)				Quit or Fired
		Top Half		Bottom Half		
		Top/quarter	2nd/quarter	3rd/quarter	Bottom/quarter	
A 34	6 mos.	17	13	1	0	3
	18	19	9	0	0	6
B 49	6	9	23	8	2	7
	18	10	19	8	0	12
C 60	6	0	9	20	14	17
	18	0	2	21	8	29
D 52	6	0	0	10	18	24
	18	0	0	9	7	36

TABLE XXI.1 (cont.)

IN THE INSURANCE INDUSTRY

		6 mos.					
A	22	6 mos.	13	4	1	0	4
		14	13	4	0	0	5
B	55	6	7	23	11	2	12
		14	11	20	7	1	16
C	56	6	1	5	19	12	19
		14	1	4	11	5	35
D	48	6	0	0	4	10	34
		14	0	0	3	4	41

IN THE MUTUAL FUNDS INDUSTRY

		6 mos.					
A	11	6 mos.	5	4	1	0	1
B	20	6	4	9	3	0	4
C	49	6	0	4	15	12	18
D	34	6	0	1	7	10	16

a Predictions made on basis of test, without seeing men or any records:

A means outstanding, top potential as a salesman, almost certain to succeed with high productivity.

B means recommended, good productivity, and can sometimes be designated as developable into an A.

C means not recommended, even though a C can under the right circumstances edge into becoming a low B.

D means absolutely not recommended; the applicant concerned has virtually no possibility of success.

Source: David Mayer and Herbert M. Greenberg, "What Makes a Good Salesman," *Harvard Business Review*, 42 (July–August 1964), 120.

among those with the highest occupational earnings. On the surface it might be observed that such high earnings would lead to high status. But in fact the high earnings are marred by periods of low earning, and high status is not achieved categorically. Indeed the status of sales occupations is less than laudatory. This is illustrated by an article entitled, "I Didn't Raise My Boy to Be a Salesman!"[38] At the time that journal article was printed the national sales executives reported that they were seeking more than 405,000 men for their occupation. Their image is tarnished and the American salesmen have a selling job to do for their own occupation.

In a survey of more than 3000 undergraduate students in 31 colleges and universities the image of the salesman was found to be less than illustrious (see Table XXI.2). The image ranged from travel to money

TABLE XXI.2

Write Down the First 5 Words That Come Into Your Mind in Connection with the Word "Salesman"

Order	All Students (Mentions)	Sales Students	Non-Sales Students
1	Travel (1003)	Money	Fast Talker
2	Money (561)	Appearance	High-Pressure
3	Personality (511)	Personality	Door-to-Door
4	Sales, Sell, Selling (484)	Work (Hard)	Car (Auto)
5	Fast Talker (476)	People	Pressure (Work)
6	Commission (445)	Service	Buy
7	Appearance (409)	Knowledge	Speech
8	Products (399)	Professional	Hours
9	High-Pressure (328)	Help, Helpful	Extrovert
10	Aggressive (246)	Customer	Insurance

Lists are in order of the frequency of mention. Words ranking about the same with both sales and non-sales students were eliminated in the sales and non-sales lists to point up the differences between those two groups.
Source: J. Donald Staunton, "I Didn't Raise My Boy to Be a Salesman!," *The Management Review*, 47 (March 1958), 11.

to fast talker at the upper end of the continuum to aggressive, customer, insurance at the lower end of the continuum. This is in sharp contrast to the prestigeful occupational characteristics of professional, white-collar, ethical, and service-oriented.

In another empirical study of salesmen, the discussion of the occupation centered around the subject of being humiliated.[39] In this study of 66 salesmen in the New York metropolitan area, interviews were taken with individuals in service lines, hard goods, soft goods, automative and industrial products, pharmaceuticals, insurance, and advertising. Their ages ranged from the thirties to the sixties and their incomes from the middle to the upper middle bracket for their area. These respondents were occupational men, committed to their occupation and representing neither beginners nor the elite, but the more typical sales persons for their area. The status of the occupation was found to be less than humiliating. It was put this way, "When I was young and inexperienced, I got into a few humiliating situations . . . (but) I find selling less humiliating as I get older." [40] In spite of this, the respondents reported that the status of the sales occupation is going up; indeed it is becoming more professionalized.

The occupational character of professionalization is an ideal which many salesmen seek, but one which is reported to be dysfunctional for their success.[41] In this interview study with life insurance salesmen, it is reported that the advanced Charter Life Underwriter course of training does in fact lead to a professional-like behavior. But in the sales occupational arena this removes many men from a highly mobile position to a desk- or office-oriented type of position. In short, the Chartered Life Underwriter training reduces the drive for breadth of contact with many clients and increases the capacity for depth of relationships with a few clients.

The social status of the sales occupation is typically on the upper half of the occupational continuum, though it is still near the middle. It is white-collar rather than blue-collar. It remains less than professional, and its occupational organization is not conducive to professionalization. Its income is marked by great variation and is subject to sharp and sudden changes.

SUMMARY AND IMPLICATIONS

Clerical occupations constitute a large proportion of the nation's labor force and they are increasing. Their occupational norms contribute to their being a relatively silent type. They are the meticulous keepers of details. In many cases the great majority of clerical workers are female. This norm further contributes to the weakness of internal occupational structures. Clerical occupations are frequently faced with unionization. Ideologically, clerical workers identify with the people above them, but as their salaries and other work conditions are frequently surpassed by the blue-collar employees beneath them, they become vulnerable to unionization, and frequently accept.

Sales workers are diverse in number and separated in proximity. They are divided into the traveling and sedentary types. But whether sedentary order takers or traveling social, persuasive, invaders of privacy, they are par excellence distributors of goods and services.

The personality type of such occupational individuals remains an enigma. Their social status is as middle range as their total occupational position. The meaning of clerical and sales occupations is clearly that of relevance to the urbanized industrial society. To a large extent, these occupations are products of such societies and their breadth and nature dependent on it.

White-collar middle-range occupations are conspicuously dependent on societal organization. Their status is similarly circumscribed, generally in a middle ground. In societies characterized by industrial urbanized social organization the positions of clerical and sales occupations are reasonably assured and comfortable. Such societies in their configuration are committed to vast amounts of record keeping detail and to the distribution of enormous quantities of goods and services. Persons in the clerical and sales occupations are the functionaries who implement these societal conditions.

When there are attempts at strengthening the internal organization of clerical occupations they are faced with an acceleration of mechanization and automation. And when there are attempts at status aggrandizement, particularly in the sales occupations, the technical achievement of success is eroded. Society gives high prestige to idea people and lesser amounts of prestige to those directly and indirectly controlled by the ideas generated above them.

NOTES

1. Pierre Bideau, "The Status of Traveling Salesmen," *International Labor Review*, 74 (December 1956), 552–67.
2. C. Wright Mills, *White-Collar* (New York: Oxford University Press, Galaxy Ed., 1956).
3. *Clerical Occupations for Women: Today and Tomorrow* (Washington, D.C.: Women's Bureau, U.S. Department of Labor, 1964).

4. Ibid. p. 5.
5. Nicholas L. A. Martucci, "Trends in Personnel Practices for Office Workers," *Management Record*, 21 (June 1959), 186–90.
6. Milton M. Mandell, *Recruiting and Selecting Office Employees* (New York: American Management Association, 1956), pp. 12–13.
7. Daniel Katz, et al., *Productivity, Supervision, and Morale in Office Situations* (Ann Arbor: University of Michigan, 1950); and Nancy C. Morse, *Satisfactions in White-Collar Jobs* (Ann Arbor: University of Michigan, 1953).
8. Katz, *Productivity, Supervision, and Morale*, p. 62.
9. George C. Homans, "Status Among Clerical Workers," *Human Organization*, 12 (Spring 1953), 5–10.
10. U.S. Bureau of Labor Statistics, *Union Membership, 1962* (Washington, D.C.: U.S. Department of Labor, 1964).
11. Benjamin Solomon and Robert K. Burns, "Unionization of White-Collar Employees: Extent, Potential, and Implications," *Journal of Business*, 36 (April 1963), 141–65.
12. John H. Metzler, "Management's Losing Struggle Against Union Organization," *Personnel Administration*, 24 (January–February 1961), 27.
13. Charles E. Ginder, "Unionization in the Office," *Office Executive*, 36 (January 1961), 11–14.
14. Ibid. p. 12.
15. Ibid.
16. Raymond L. Hilgert, "When an Office is Unionized: Its Meaning for Management Policy," *Personnel Administration*, 28 (March–April 1965), 33–8.
17. John Diebold, *Automation: Its Impact on Human Relations* (New York: National Association of Manufacturers, Congress of American Industry, 1954).
18. Edgar Weinberg, "Experiences with the Introduction of Office Automation," *Monthly Labor Review*, 83 (April 1960), 376–80; James R. Bright, "How to Evaluate Automation," *Harvard Business Review*, 33 (July–August 1955), 101–11.
19. Ida Russakoff Hoos, *Automation in the Office* (Washington, D.C.: Public Affairs Press, 1961).
20. Peter Drucker, *America's Next Twenty Years* (New York: Harper and Bros., 1957), p. 28.
21. Ibid. pp. 40ff.
22. James R. Bright, "Does Automation Raise Skill Requirements?," *Harvard Business Review*, 36 (July–August 1958), 85–98.
23. James R. Bright, *Automation and Management* (Boston: Harvard University Press, 1958).
24. American Management Association, *Establishing an Integrated Data-Processing System*, Special Report No. 11, 1956.
25. Ibid.
26. William A. Faunce, "Automation in the Automobile Industry: Some

Conscquences for In-Plant Social Structure," *American Sociological Review*, 23 (August 1958), 401–7.
27. Bright, "Does Automation Raise Skill Requirements?"; Jack Stieber, "Automation and the White-Collar Worker," *Personnel*, 34 (November–December 1957), 11–14; and C. Edward Weber, "Impact of Electronic Data Processing on Clerical Skills," *Personnel Administration*, 22 (January–February 1959), 20–6.
28. Howard Coughlin, "Office Workers Are Changing," *American Federationist*, 63 (July 1956), 22–4.
29. *Occupational Outlook Handbook* (Washington, D.C.: U.S. Department of Labor, Bureau of Labor Statistics, Bulletin No. 1450, 1966), pp. 305ff.
30. Pierre Bideau, "Status of Traveling Salesmen"; see also Frances R. Donovan, *The Sales Lady* (Chicago: The University of Chicago Press, 1929).
31. Lewis Kriesberg, "The Retail Furrier: Concepts of Security and Success," *American Journal of Sociology*, LVII (March 1952), 478–85.
32. Cecil L. French, "Correlates of Success in Retail Selling," *American Journal of Sociology*, LXVI (September 1960), 128–34.
33. Earle A. Cleveland, "Sales Personnel Research, 1935–1945: A Review," *Personnel Psychology*, 1 (Summer 1948), 211–55.
34. H. D. Nixon, *Principles of Selling* (New York: McGraw-Hill Book Co., Inc., 1942), p. 361.
35. Herbert E. Krugman, "Salesmen in Conflict: A Challenge to Marketing," *The Forum*, 23 (July 1958), 59–61.
36. Judson B. Pearson, *et al.*, "Sales Success and Job Satisfaction," *American Sociological Review*, 22 (August 1957), 424–7.
37. David Mayer and Herbert M. Greenberg, "What Makes a Good Salesman," *Harvard Business Review*, 42 (July–August 1964), 119–25.
38. J. Donald Staunton, "I Didn't Raise My Boy to Be a Salesman!: A Survey of Public Attitudes Toward Selling as a Career," *The Management Review*, 47 (March 1958), 9–13ff.
39. F. William Howton and Bernard Rosenberg, "The Salesman: Ideology and Self Image in a Prototypic Occupation," *Social Research*, 32 (Autumn 1965), 277–98.
40. Ibid. pp. 287–8.
41. Lee Taylor and Roland J. Pellegrin, "Professionalization: Its Functions and Dysfunctions for the Life Insurance Occupation," *Social Forces*, 38 (December 1959), 110–14.

SUPPLEMENTARY READING

Clerical Occupations for Women: Today and Tomorrow (Washington, D.C.: Women's Bureau, U.S. Department of Labor, 1964).

David Mayer and Herbert M. Greenberg, "What Makes a Good Salesman," *Harvard Business Review*, 42 (July–August 1964), 119–25.

Judson B. Pearson, *et al.*, "Sales Success and Job Satisfaction," *American Sociological Review*, 22 (August 1957), 424–7.

Benjamin Solomon and Robert K. Burns, "Unionization of White-Collar Employees: Extent, Potential, and Implications," *Journal of Business*, 36 (April 1963), 141–65.

Lee Taylor and Roland J. Pellegrin, "Professionalization: Its Functions and Dysfunctions for the Life Insurance Occupation," *Social Forces*, 38 (December 1959), 110–14.

Edgar Weinberg, "Experiences with the Introduction of Office Automation," *Monthly Labor Review*, 83 (April 1960), 376–80.

AGRIBUSINESS OCCUPATIONS $\underset{\textstyle\diagup\!\diagdown}{\text{XXII}}$

America's classic rural occupation is farming. During the colonial and early national period it dominated the way of life. Statistically it is recorded that more than half the nation's labor force was employed in agriculture until 1880.[1] Since then most of the nation's workers have departed from farming. In spite of the departure the occupation whose responsibility it is to feed the nation's people is sustained by an aura of grandeur and importance greatly in excess of the number of farmer practitioners.[2] Indeed, the idea of the family farm is for all practical purposes as central to the American ideology of life as are the Christian ethic and the monogamous marriage.

But traditional farming has gone out of fashion, and along with it its occupational character. Abundance and overabundance characterize the contemporary American food and fiber industry. Technological innovations, vertical integration, IBM down on the farm, and a variety of other changes force farming into limbo while reducing the farm occupational practitioners to a minimum. In the mid-1930's the nation had approximately 7 million farmers. By the 1960's the number had reduced to approximately 3.5 million. It is predicted that by the 1980's occupational farmers will number less than 1 million.[3]

Ironically, farming, as a specifically articulated occupation, is stronger than before and continues to increase in importance. For example, one may observe that the top 3 per cent of farmers produce more than the 78 per cent at the bottom. Between these two extremes is a transitional category, 19 per cent, the farmers who are occupationally successful but whose future is uncertain.

The 1959 Census of Agriculture reports that the big farmers, constituting under 4 per cent of all farmers, have domain over approximately 50 per cent of the nation's farm land. Their average land holdings reach more than 4000 acres, or more than 6 square miles. This occupational elite in the farming occupation produces over 30 per cent of the nation's crops and livestock. The future is for continued bigness in the occupation. The subsistence farmer is not an occupational man at all —he is a social problem.

The development of farming from a way of life into a bona fide occupation was arduous. The way of life of subsistency and family farming situations which were widespread in colonial and early America were more forced by a peculiar mix of circumstances than sought after as an ideological expression.[4] Notions of systematic farming are identified from colonial times to the present. The way of life situation was produced by the wilderness area and sparsity of population. Industry, urbanity, and commercial farming became firmly established in America at the earliest opportunity. With each advance in technology, industry, urbanization, etc., farming as an occupation pushed forward with greater specificity. In the 1800's farming was at the sickle level. Nearly 60 hours of labor were required to produce an acre of wheat. By the 1880's, with the technology of the horse drawn reaper, only 20 man-hours were invested in the growing and production of an acre of wheat. By the middle of the twentieth century, with a still more advanced technology and a keenly articulated occupation of wheat farmers, only 2 hours or less of labor are required to do the job—and in a more efficient manner than in any previous time in history. In the 1960's the occupation of farming in the irrigated lands of Southern California is characterized by mobile factories in the field.[5]

Science and mechanization have come to farming. Their impact is a forceful redirecting and rebuilding of farming as an occupation. It is often asserted that we are experiencing the decline and fall of agriculture. A less myopic view shows such a position is erroneous. Farming as a free-standing occupation is just coming into its own. Associated with it are a multitude of specialty occupations which are an integral part of the food and fiber industry of the nation. Occupational mobilization in the industry of agriculture never has been greater than in the second half of the twentieth century.

AN OCCUPATIONAL CONCEPT OF AGRIBUSINESS

The proliferation of occupations in the food and fiber industry is subsumed under the generic category of agribusiness. Within the broad concept of agribusiness there are three major components: (1) producing, (2) supplying, and (3) processing-distribution. Subsumed under each of these components are many highly specific and viable occupations.

The concept of agribusiness is of recent origin.[6] The word "agribusiness" was created by Davis and presented in 1955. Since then an abundant amount of research and writing has demonstrated its importance.

The initial agribusiness concept was an economic notion. It treated the occupational element and went so far as to specify an estimated number of workers in agribusiness positions. More recent attempts are made to clarify argibusiness as an occupational concept.[7] The occupational notion of agribusiness includes only those workers in occupations who deal with primary agricultural products. Occupational agribusiness, therefore, includes workers in the distribution of agricultural materials directly related to farm operators, workers in the transportation of rural agricultural products to storage and processing centers, and so forth. The central concern of such workers is bound up in a food and fiber idiom which is inextricably a part of the agribusiness whole. Occupational commercial farmers are vastly important, but they constitute only one occupational tribe among many in the urbanized food and fiber industry. Contemporary occupational farmers are supported in their endeavor by many other closely related occupational men.

TYPES OF AGRIBUSINESS OCCUPATIONS

The major agribusiness occupations include classic farming and its many subtypes; professionals and specialists engaged primarily in food and fiber production research; foresters and their related assistants; wildlife and recreation specialists; farm service occupations; food and fiber sales occupations; food and fiber supplying occupations; plus many other more specific occupations in the industry.[8]

Among these several categories of agribusiness occupations the food and fiber producers are central. For practical purposes they are composed of several types of occupational farmers.

Farming. There is not one type of farming occupation, there are several. For example, commercial farming specialty occupations include livestock ranchers, grain farmers, cotton farmers, tobacco farmers, vegetable farmers, fruit and nut farmers, poultry farmers, and dairy farmers, to name but a few. In the main, such categories of farmers are statistically defined by 50 per cent or more of their gross sales in one commodity area of specialization. Farming occupations are, therefore, being confronted with the mass urbanized society's specializations, but the occupational organization to the several types of farming continues to be characterized by more generalization than specialization. The occupational organization of the reasonably large-scale livestock ranchers or cotton plantation owners continues to be that of a generalist within the area of food or fiber production. The occupational man in such cases is at once an entrepreneur, an owner of the tools of production, a decision-maker, a pseudo-technologist in the area of production, a makeshift cost accountant and market analyst, and a neophyte user of modern banking and insurance facilities. This occupational generalist may utilize some consultation and advice from technical specialists in agricultural extension, supply house experts, or co-op service information centers. Even the large enterprises in food and fiber production are usually sufficiently small to be operated more by occupational generalists than by occupational specialists.

In spite of the vast amount of rural sociological research, much of which is broadly occupational, the precise occupational characteristics of the four largest economic categories of farmers are far from known. The census reports the median age of farmers to be forty-nine years. But such statistics include not only the large commercial farmers but also the smaller subsistence farmers in the lower commercial classes.

Wilcox characterizes some typical types of American farmers at about mid-century in a way which includes some of their occupational nature.[9] Livestock farmers were reported to own their own land in amounts of about 200 acres. With the help of unpaid members of their families the livestock farmers work the equivalent of some 313 ten-hour days a year. They raise 30 to 35 cattle and 60 to 70 pigs annually. Such an investment typically ranges between $40,000 and $50,000, depending primarily on the amount of mechanization. Their gross sales range between $6,000 and $7,000, and their net family income between approximately $3,000 and $4,000. Such an occupational milieu is characteristic of the livestock farmers who were in business for nearly two decades.

Wheat farmers operate large land areas, often about 700 acres. The wheat farmer works about 260 ten-hour days. In addition to his own work he hires some 64 days of labor in the harvest season. His total investment ranges between approximately $40,000 and $50,000. The gross sales are from $6,000 to $7,000, and after expenses the net income is in the range of $2,000.

The occupation of dairy farming is the most persistent in its daily rhythm. The ten-hour day is typical for 364 days in the year. In addition to the work of the owner-operator another 70 days of hired labor in spring and fall seasons is common. The investment is a little less than that of the livestock and wheat farmer; it ranges between approximately $30,000 and $40,000. Sales from such an enterprise typically range between $7,000 and $8,000, with an ultimate income to the family in cash of between $1,500 and $2,000.

In addition to these medium-sized farmers, the nation has over 100,000 so-called large farmers. The large farmers are often incorporated, and operate on a modified factory basis. Hired labor and the latest in technological equipment are combined with a maximum of scientific input.

There are many kinds of both generalist and specialist occupational organizations associated with the several types of farming.[10] The major farm organizations include the Farm Bureau, the Farmers Union, and the Grange. These are generalist occupational organizations. Farmers of many different kinds of specialties can and do belong to these organizations. They are similar in their purposes and functions, with varying strength in different regions of the nation.

Specialty farming occupational organizations include groups like the American Angus Association, American Guernsey Cattle Club, U.S. Trout Farmers Association, National Turkey Federation, American Sheep Producers Council, American Soybean Association, Vegetable Growers Association of America, Forest Farmers Association Cooperative, National Dairy Council, etc.

It should also be noted that organizations like the National Flying Farmers Association and the several agricultural co-operatives influence farming occupations in specific ways. These are not technically occupational organizations, but they make an impact in terms of marketing, purchasing, and general farming ideologies.

Appended to the several types of farming occupations are farm managers and farm laborers. Farm managers indeed constitute an occupation category, but almost no empirical studies exist to report the occupational nature of their work. On the large Economic Class I farms, managers are often highly educated, sometimes college-trained technical specialists. In the chain farming operations, farm managers have a lesser amount of education; indeed they possess characteristics which make them occupationally indistinguishable from the several types of farm owner-operators.

Hired farm workers are an occupational type more by default than by ideology. In most cases they are laborers at the lowest end of the occupational continuum. There is little to suggest that they perceive of themselves as occupational men at all. They are in a seasonal and migratory work experience which involves a minimum of skill and training, as well as a minimum of responsibility to the job.[11] With low training and little responsibility there is the reciprocal relation of absence of tenure, security of income, or any significant amount of fringe benefits. Their characteristics as an occupational category are thrust upon them from a set of social organization and ideological conditions exterior to the work. There is little or no organization of these workers from an occupational point of view. There is no central mechanism which represents them or which speaks in behalf of their interest.

Forestry occupations. Forestry is a professional agribusiness occupation. The contribution of the occupation is of major consequence in the food and fiber production of the nation. The number of practitioners is small, approximately 20,000 in the 1960's, but they have tripled since the 1940's. The outlook for the occupation suggests that there will be a gradual and continual increase in the need for foresters in the foreseeable future.[12] The largest single category of foresters is employed by the U.S. Forest Service. Professionals in the Forest Service total approximately 7500. Another 7000 professionals are employed by private industry where they work in pulp paper, lumber, logging, and milling operations. In all of these cases they are professional advisors and consultants. The various state forest services employ approximately 3000 professional foresters. For the states they work in all phases of forest management and administrative consultation. Approximately 1000 foresters are employed by colleges and universities. In this environment they are primarily engaged in teaching and research. Another nearly 1000 professional foresters manage their own land or work as fee-taking consultants.

The various specialty areas in which foresters work include timber management, wildlife protection, fire control, soil conservation, forest economic planning, range management, and recreation. Timber and range management along with fire control are old and traditional specialties within the professional forest service occupation. Specialization in areas like recreation are of more recent origin.

The curriculum for professional forestry training includes silva-culture, forest protection, forest management, and forest economics. There are over 40 colleges which offer higher education in forestry. The minimum professional degree in forestry is the bachelor of science with a major in the forestry subjects. Advanced degrees, often including the doctorate of philosophy, are required for most high level research and teaching positions. The level of monetary remuneration for professional foresters with the baccalaureate degree is commensurate with that of the average college student. Similarly, the average starting salary for holders of the Ph.D. approximates that for other white-collar research professionals and teachers.

Appended to the professional occupations of forestry are the several types of semiprofessional and subprofessional workers. These include forester aids who facilitate the professional work and carry out its multitude of details.

Professional and specialist occupations. Agribusiness professionals and specialists are an essential category of workers in the urbanized food and fiber industry.[13] An estimate of the number of these workers suggests that they total less than half a million. In any event, they are few compared to the number of farmers. Nevertheless, similar to foresters, their importance far exceeds their numbers. As the proportion of farmers declines the proportion of scientific professionals and specialists increases. Their work and contribution makes it possible for a smaller number of occupational farmers to produce a greater quantity and higher quality of food and fiber products. In the contemporary society these scientific idea people are reciprocally as important as the food and fiber producers themselves. They are powerful, but their power does not rest in a political movement or pressure situation. They propound no major ideology. By sharp contrast, they are a quiet, unobtrusive category of workers.[14]

Agribusiness professional and specialist occupations include workers primarily in the areas of research, education, communication, conservation, and services. Research professionals work in marketing, agricultural economics, engineering, reclamation, and rural sociology. Educational professionals are in vocational teaching, agricultural extension, and university instruction, and serve as consultants to government agencies and in international technical aid. Professional and specialist communications workers are engaged in farm reporting, newspaper work, market reporting, magazines and other publications, motion picture production, radio and television production, and advertising. Professionals in conservation work in soil and water research and action programs, forestry and range research and managerial programs, and in fish and wildlife research, managerial, and recreational programs. Professionals and specialists in service work are engaged in food and fiber inspection and regulation, quality control investigation, statistical work, and veterinarian medicine. This list of types of work in professional specialty agribusiness is suggestive rather than exhaustive.

By the nature of professional work the typical education and training required is at the college level, often at the graduate level. Colleges of agriculture in the land grant universities are the primary training centers.

The places of employment are governmental, agricultural, and related agencies, private manufacturing and supply houses, co-operatives, universities, and a number of state and local government agencies.

Agribusiness professionals and specialists are among the prestigious white-collar category of workers. Their monetary reward is average among professional white-collar workers. In addition to their monetary reward the intangible remunerations include the title professional, research laboratories staffed with equipment and technical assistants, opportunities for publication and communication, and a paternalistic colleagueship which in several respects approximates the *Gemeinschaft* environment of the now passing family farm tradition.

The need for agribusiness professionals and specialists is great and continues to increase. Land grant universities in recent years have graduated approximately 7000 students annually in the agricultural sciences, and they report that the placement needs run approximately double the number of graduates. In sharp contrast to the decline in the numbers of scientific commercial farm operators, there is a growing need for agribusiness professionals and specialists.

Traditionally these agribusiness occupational positions have been filled by persons from farm and rural backgrounds. In some cases in the past there were requirements that one have practical experience on a farm in order to enter these occupations. By the second half of the twentieth century the requirement for farm experience no longer existed. The basic nature of the scientific research investigation in many of these specialty areas is such that there is little or no need for, and certainly no advantage in, a rural or farm experience.

Horticulture, wildlife, and recreation occupations. Many of the horticulture, wildlife, and recreation occupations are rapidly increasing in recent years. They are related to expanding interest in home and garden beautification, landscaping along superhighways, more time and leisure for participation in out-of-door recreation, and so forth.[15]

Occupations at this level typically require only high school graduation. The curriculum of study almost always includes vocational agriculture at one point. After high school graduation and some initial job employment additional specific training may be taken in short courses that are frequently offered by the agricultural colleges of the land grant universities.

Types of work in this occupational category includes city, state, or national park employees; florists; game bird propagators; golf course employees; greenhouse employees; landscape gardeners; nursery employees; tree surgeons; and so forth.

Park work is primarily in an out-of-door environment and involves technical and general maintenance of plants, animals, and waterways. Some of the jobs in park work involve direct social interaction with a vacationing clientele.

Florist occupational positions are primarily of an indoor type. They combine a technical producing, processing, and arranging of flowers for many purposes along with regular customer interaction and general business management skills. In addition to the vocational training programs in agriculture, special short courses are available from time to time in florist management.

Game management and bird propagator workers combine indoor and out-of-door work. These workers are engaged in the technical reproduction of game and fowl. Other aspects of the occupation often involve wildlife protection and regulatory work. Many persons in this occupation are employed by the U.S. Fish and Wildlife Service.

The integration of urban and agribusiness occupations is no more clearly illustrated than in golf course employee jobs. Here the work is primarily in an aesthetic out-of-door environment. The details of the occupation involve the careful production and maintenance of lawns and plants for both recreational utilization and aesthetic gratification.

The range of work in these occupational categories is primarily within the semiskilled and skilled blue-collar end of the occupational continuum. Internal occupational organization is at a minimum level. The characteristics of the several occupations are attributed more by external factors than generated from within by the practitioners.

Farm service occupations. There are many kinds of jobs in this occupational category. In most cases a high school education is required. One should have taken special training in vocational agriculture. After some specific experience it is often desirable for the practitioner to take some specialized short courses at a college of agriculture. Farm service occupations include artificial inseminator, auctioneer, crop duster, crop pollinator, custom farm machine worker, farm building painter, feed and hammer mill operator, fruit caretaker, fruit sprayer, lime spreader, mobile blacksmith shop operator, sheep dipper, and sheep shearer. This is far from an exhaustive list but it illustrates the range of specific jobs.

Artificial inseminators are widely used in the major dairy regions of the nation. The practice is also gradually being extended to beef cattle reproduction. The inseminators are employed by the breeding cooperatives and commercial services. Semen is mailed to the inseminators or picked up from a central location. The inseminators in turn work on an individual basis and must build their own trade. Local farm owner-operators call them when cows are to be bred. The monetary remuneration for this service is usually based on the number of cows inseminated.[16]

With increasing scientific agriculture, crop dusters, pollinators, and sprayers have more frequent demands made for their services. Cotton, truck crop, and fruit regions are increasingly using airplane dusting. The practitioner in this kind of position must have a considerable knowledge about the life cycle of plants and the insects and diseases which attack them. His work is designed to control and direct these phenomena.

Crop pollination is widely used in seed and fruit production. The worker in such a position must have information concerning the flower and blossoming stages of crops and be able to introduce honey bees into the orchards at the proper time. In addition to pollination such a job often involves the individual in honey and beeswax production and sales.

Crop spraying and crop dusting operations are related. Spraying is the application of liquid insecticides and fungicides for the controlling of insects and diseases. It may also involve spraying for weed control.

Feed grinding is a year around job of considerable importance in dairy and livestock regions. The equipment is usually mounted on a truck and taken from farm to farm on regular days following a regular schedule. Farmers will have their grain ready for grinding. The grinding operators are responsible for mixing the grains to the proper balance, and to the farmer's instructions. Protein concentrate may be carried by the feed grinding operator as an additional aspect of his service.[17]

Many of the farm service occupations are of recent origin and related to scientific and technological developments in agribusiness. Other farm service jobs are old and traditional. They have only recently been singled out as separate occupations as a part of the continuing division of labor and specialization which is finally reaching into the food and fiber production operations. The nineteenth-century generalist farmer provided many of the services in his own operation. Now they are becoming specialty jobs. For example, the new scientific type of jobs are artificial inseminator, crop duster, fruit sprayer, lime spreader, and so forth. Traditional jobs include the auctioneer, butcher, building painter, blacksmith worker, and sheep shearer. Indeed, the number of farm operators is sharply decreasing due in part to the reciprocal proliferation of many service jobs.

Farm sales occupations. In modern mechanized agriculture major occupations center around machinery sales and servicing. These jobs are of primary importance in the systematic operation of the nation's food and fiber industry. They are part of the broader specialization in the general social organization of the economic institution. The number of farmers are reduced partially in relation to the number of machines which they own and operate and partially in proportion to the number of service personnel who assist in the sales and maintenance of the production machines. A selected list of major types of work in this occupational category includes farm machinery salesmen, farm machinery fieldmen, farm machinery parts managers, farm tire service operators, and farm machinery mechanics.[18]

The organization of farm machinery sales starts with the field man.

He works primarily to represent manufacturers to farm machinery dealers. He may also be viewed as a service manager or area service man. He demonstrates the operations of new machinery, is a salesman of new machinery, is a sales supervisor, and whenever necessary, a troubleshooter. He represents the home office for the machinery manufacturer. He may in some cases be dressed in a white-collar attire. On the other hand, it must be noted that he must be a capable mechanic and must have an intimate knowledge of the crop and animal production which is related to the equipment that he represents. In addition to working with local sales firms and with farmers, the field man will represent his company at fairs, shows, and a variety of other places where farm machinery will be displayed. He will give talks and lectures to emphasize the importance and value of his equipment. In short, he is involved in a variety of educational services to illustrate the importance and advantages of new machinery.

The work environment of the machinery field man involves a considerable travel over a large area. He works with a great range of people from highly knowledgeable technical experts to individual farm owner-operators. He must relate himself to vocational teachers and vocational classes as well as farm operator practitioners. High school education is a minimum requirement for the farm machinery field man. In more instances the college graduate in agriculture is filling this kind of position.

The farm machinery salesman is the next category in the system of distributing mechanical products to the user. The machinery salesman is a local businessman handling new and used equipment. He travels intensively over a fairly limited region. He must visit and re-visit farmers who are potential buyers of machinery and equipment. His working time is considerably divided between a traveling sales operation and servicing customers who come to his place of business. It is in effect a combination sales and service business. In addition to sales and service there is an educational dimension to the job. Demonstrations, displays, and lectures must frequently be given to local farm groups and youth groups as well. Like the field man, the machinery salesman must have an extensive understanding of the machinery which he handles and the crop and animal production to which it is related. Both major levels of sales occupations combine a knowledge of farming, of technology, and of human relations.

Farm machinery parts managers, their clerks and helpers, and service center foremen together constitute important workers in the farm sales service occupations. High school vocational training along with a considerable amount of mechanical shop training constitute an appropriate educational experience. In these kinds of jobs the worker must have a maximum knowledge of machinery technology. The challenge and significance of the work is enhanced when there is some understanding of the application to which the machines are placed. Proficiency in performance also may be increased where knowledge of application is extended. This technical agricultural knowledge, however, is far less essential to these jobs than it is to the sales positions.

Farm tire service is a highly specialized sales and service local business operation. An extensive knowledge of the product is required for the effective sales. Some knowledge of the technical agricultural operations in which the tire products will be used is also valuable, more for its contribution in establishing rapport for sales than for the application of the product.

The work environment for the tire sales people is both in the shop and on the farm. They sell new products as well as inspect, remove, and repair used products. They work from five to five and one-half days a week, normally on an eight-hour basis.

High school education which involved an emphasis in vocational agriculture, mechanical skills, and business techniques provides the most appropriate core training. Related to these several sales occupations are the jobs of machinery mechanics, mechanics helpers, machine operators, blacksmiths, welders, and general repairmen. High school mechanics training is essential to such jobs. Neither a conceptual knowledge of mechanics nor a scientific knowledge of food and fiber production are central requirements to such jobs.[19]

Farm supply occupations. Commercial scientific farmers provide few of their own supplies. Consequently, there are a number of specific jobs which have developed in the capacity of farm supplying. These jobs include handling, hauling, and selling seed, feeds, fertilizers, farm chemicals, and animal medicines.[20] Most of these jobs fall into the semiskilled and unskilled categories. Some are entrepreneurial, involving managerial skills and sales ability. Typically, however, the occupational category is constituted of employees who work for co-ops and large private enterprises.

In practically all cases the supply types of jobs require high school education only. The interest in the work may be greatly enhanced if one's training includes vocational agriculture. In some cases one's job proficiency may also be facilitated by technical agricultural training courses at the high school level. Nevertheless, in most cases the knowledge and skills required in these jobs may be readily learned by a minimum of on the job participation.

The actual work in most of these kinds of jobs involves mixed skills. For example, a feedmill employee may mix and grind feeds, handle retail sales, and make credit transactions, along with performing his own maintenance and cleanup. A farm equipment supplier may sell new equipment, install the equipment, and service it. He may, for example, handle bulk milk tanks, milkers, gutter cleaners, milk coolers, along with garden tractors, lawn mowers, feeders, water fountains, and brooders. The work situation has in common the provision of supplies for farmers, but aside from that condition it is generalist in nature rather than a specialist position.

Supplying of gas and oils to farmers is a somewhat more specialized job than many other forms of supplying. This usually involves the sales and distribution of gas, oil, grease, and related products for farm equipment. In this case the supplier usually delivers products, and transacts the sales. To a large extent the job involves delivery and sales.

Farm supplying is primarily engaged in by men. In most cases the practitioners are from a rural farm or small-town background. Often they are individuals who have not had the economic resources and/or other means necessary to enter farming as a commercial operation. This is a kind of agribusiness occupation in which the participants are close to food and fiber work while not engaged in farming as such.

Livestock industry occupations. In the past 20 years livestock production has become a highly specialized aspect of the food and fiber industry. Like all other specialization in the economic institutions of the nation, it is supported by a vast number of highly specific occupations. For example, the related jobs include animal industry laboratory assistant or technician, apiary inspector, dairy herd supervisor, egg grader, livestock buyer, livestock disease control worker, livestock truck driver, milk sanitarian or inspector, poultry and egg buyer, and veterinarian's assistant. These jobs are all typically subprofessional. In many cases they are even unskilled. But in any event they are highly specific.

Animal industry technicians work in livestock diagnostic laboratories, agricultural colleges, agricultural research centers, for state departments of agriculture, with large dairies and hatcheries. The specific jobs may include cleaning and sterilizing of equipment, preparing animals for diagnosis, and making a variety of reports. The work may also involve checking blood samples from chickens to test for pullorum disease or from cattle to test for Bang's disease.

The working conditions for these technicians vary, but in most cases they are in laboratories. They are usually clean and well-appointed places to work. Little heavy manual labor is associated with the jobs. High school education is required for such positions. One should have taken a considerable amount of chemistry and biology. Vocational agriculture courses also contribute a basic knowledge needed for this kind of job.

Apiary inspectors are a highly specific category of workers. Primarily they are concerned with detection and eradication of contagious diseases from bee colonies. They visit bee keepers to check methods of production and compliance with laws and regulations. They issue certificates of inspection, and make reports concerning irregularities. Persons in this type of work are typically employed by state governments. High school education is in most cases required for the work.

Dairy plant employees fulfill many specialized tasks in milk processing. At the unskilled level they unload cans, empty and wash them, pump out trucks, weigh milk, and so forth. They may be employed in the maintenance of plant equipment. With more specialized experience and training these workers may pasteurize milk and carry out jobs in the production of ice cream, cheese, and butter. Other related workers may be employed in the packaging and wrapping of the products in preparation for retail sales. The working conditions for this category of occupations involve indoor locations. Sanitary conditions in the place of work are the high order of importance. Much of the work detail will be carried out in cool storage areas. The educational requirement for such employment is at the high school level. Most of the specific knowledge and skill utilized in such work will inevitably be learned by participant experience.

In the urbanized status-conscious society quality and standardization of products is of ever-increasing importance. At the specific operational level in agribusiness work this is illustrated by egg graders and egg inspectors. One starts his experience as an egg grader and with proficiency progresses upward to the higher ranking position of egg inspector. Persons in these jobs are employed by buyers, marketing cooperatives, and specific egg marketing agencies. The working environment is indoors, often in darkened rooms. The work is routinized into the typical eight-hour day. In the larger operations it is often highly specialized. The egg inspector weighs and candles in accordance with specialized methods and local laws. Packages must be checked for proper labeling. In sum, the work involves the preparation of a quality controlled product for a mass retail market.

Livestock buying continues to be an ever-specializing occupation. Buyers purchase stock at auctions, in stock yards, or directly from producers. They resell the animals to butchers, slaughterhouses, or packing companies. Buyers may also buy stock for resale to farmers and ranchers. Their work involves traveling from producer to producer, and from auction house or stock yard to stock yard. It involves bidding and bargaining, extensive record keeping concerning weights, registration papers, health certificates, and bills of sales. These illustrate the many details of the work. High school education with vocational agriculture training is essential.

Livestock disease control is of major importance in quality production of food. The workers involved in disease control usually assist animal inspectors who are typically veterinarians. The job involves identification, tagging, appraising, and branding livestock that range from live, to diseased, to dead. The disinfecting of buildings where diseased animals were kept is an important aspect of the work. Inspection takes place in feeding yards, at farms, at livestock auctions, and in other places where diseases can be produced and spread. The work involves extensive travel to specific places of location. It is typically under the direction and supervision of a professional or technical specialist. High school vocational agriculture training is valuable for work in such positions.

Milk sanitarians or inspectors constitute another degree of specialization in an occupation which is similar to livestock disease control. Inspection takes place on the dairy farms and in accordance with the municipal, state, and federal regulations. Regular visits are made to those dairy farms that ship milk to processing centers. The milking barns and related places are checked for appropriate sanitation control.

The place of work is on location, involving travel from producer to producer. High school training with emphasis on vocational agriculture is important.

Poultry and egg buying is rapidly becoming a new speciality. The buyers contact producers in some cases. In others they are employed by large vertically integrated firms. Their work involves traveling from farms to auctions. Detailed record keeping concerning quantity and quality is central to the occupation. The skills and techniques required for the work are typically those which can be learned by participant observation.

Agriculture extension agents. County extension demonstration work is among the most important of the agribusiness occupational specialties. Its official origin can be dated from the passage of the Smith-Lever Act, in 1914. This Act provided co-operative extension work in agriculture and home economics. This work is developed at both the federal and state-county levels. The occupation is part of a teaching enterprise, aimed at bringing scientific information concerning agriculture and home management to rural and small-town families.

By the second half of the twentieth century county agents were located in most of the nation's more than 3000 counties. In large agricultural counties there may be a number of agents and technical experts. In the smaller counties one agent is typical.

Training for the occupation is at the college level, requiring a baccalaureate degree in agriculture or home economics. The 1960 Census reports some 15,000 agricultural agents. Demand for their service is expected to increase.

In the local county office the agent is the top person in a hierarchical organization. In some states this individual will also hold professional rank in the land grant university. Assisting him are assistant agents, and a number of specialists as they are appropriate for the types of agriculture in the local area.

Also in the local office is the home demonstration agent, along with her associate and assistant agents. Like the county agent, home demonstration agents also may have academic rank. Home demonstration agents are required to have a college degree in home economics.[21]

Several specific county agent's roles have been studied in some depth. A national study has indicated that county agents, and, more particularly, home demonstration agents, need more training in the human relational aspects of their work.[22] Regardless of the type of agriculture which is typical in their county, the agents' educational mission is the dissemination of new information. Their work, therefore, is firmly centered in human relations regardless of the subject matter.

County agents obtain information which they disseminate from extension specialists, experiment station bulletins, farm magazines, direct personal contact with agricultural scientists, key farmers, and extension news releases.[23] Their educational task is to synthesize the information that is appropriate for the agricultural enterprises of their area. In individual contacts and group meetings of many types the agents then attempt to disseminate the new research findings.

The teaching roles of the county agents also have been researched.[24] Thirty-two Michigan and Minnesota county agents maintained extensive records of their daily work activities for one year. Twenty-four per cent of their time was spent in consulting activity, and another 24 per cent in program administration. Selling ideas and organizing events took 17 and 16 per cent of their time, respectively. The remaining 19 per cent of their time went for miscellaneous activities.

While the county agents utilize multiple mechanisms in their teaching and dissemination attempts, findings from research indicate that the greatest recipients and users of the agents' technical assistance are those farmers who least need their assistance from the point of view of economic competition.[25] Theoretically the extension service should have an equal contact with all farmers in their county, or have a greater contact with those farmers who need their service most.

Home demonstration agents, in contrast to county agents, have been the subject of very little research. In a Louisiana study Coxe [26] found professionalization to be one of their most important occupational characteristics. This was demonstrated in their effort to require not only the baccalaureate degree, but to encourage the master's degree as a requirement for advanced positions. The training they expected was rigorous, and it was argued that this training would contribute to the high level proficiency of their contribution to constituents.

Their body of technical knowledge is primarily that of home economics. In this discipline most of the practitioners are highly trained. In addition to a specialized body of knowledge they subscribe to a professional journal. They respond that the journal provides them with information which is of considerable utility in their work. They participate in an association of home demonstration agents. It is believed that this association makes a direct contribution in raising the educational requirements for their profession.

Of the several special occupations in agribusiness that of the home demonstration agent offers one of the most challenging careers for college-educated women.

SUMMARY AND IMPLICATIONS

Farming as an occupational category is characterized by extreme decline. It is a myopic view, however, to assume that agriculturally related occupations are similarly declining or do not exist. Reciprocally related to the decline in the number of farmers is the increase in the number of agribusiness technical specialists who work in a vast range of occupations that supply many materials and types of equipment and services to farm owner-operators. In addition, the processing operation in the food and fiber industry has largely been removed from the domain of the farmer owner-operator. As a consequence, a great number of specific jobs have developed in the area of food and fiber processing and distributing to the mass urbanized market.

The concept of the agribusiness occupation embraces not only food and fiber production (farming), but also the supplying and processing-distributing occupations associated with the industry. In the broad spectrum of agribusiness occupations in addition to farming, one finds the several forestry occupations, occupations concerned with wildlife and recreation, farm service occupations, farm sales occupations, a broad range of livestock industry occupations, and, most significant of all, a ramification of professional specialist occupations. In short, the number of occupational men and women who are engaged in the food and fiber industry continues to constitute a substantial proportion of all the occupational personnel of the nation.

NOTES

1. U.S. Bureau of the Census, *U.S. Census of Agriculture: 1954*, vol. 2, *General Report*, chap. 4, Farm Labor . . . (Washington, D.C.: U.S. Government Printing Office, 1956), p. 237.
2. Lee Taylor and Arthur R. Jones, Jr., *Agribusiness and Labor Force* (Louisiana: Agricultural Experiment Station Bulletin No. 562, 1963), p. 14;

and Joseph Ackerman and Harris Marshall (eds.), *Family Farm Policy* (Chicago: University of Chicago Press, 1947); Arthur J. Vidich and Joseph Bensman, *Small Town in Mass Society* (New York: Doubleday Anchor Books, 1960); Joe R. Motheral, "The Family Farm and the Three Traditions," *Journal of Farm Economics*, 33 (November 1951), 514–29; and Carle C. Zimmerman, "The Family Farm," *Rural Sociology*, 15 (September 1950), 216.

3. Edward Higbee, *Farms and Farmers in an Urban Age* (New York: The Twentieth Century Fund, 1963), p. 3.

4. Lee Taylor and Arthur R. Jones, Jr., *Rural Life and Urbanized Society* (New York: Oxford University Press, 1964).

5. Higbee, *Farms and Farmers*, pp. 8–10.

6. John H. Davis and Ray A. Goldberg, *A Concept of Agribusiness* (Boston: Harvard Business School, Division of Research, 1957); John H. Davis and Kenneth Hinshaw, *Farmer in a Business Suit* (New York: Simon and Schuster, 1957).

7. Taylor and Jones, *Agribusiness and the Labor Force*, pp. 17–20; Lee Taylor and Arthur R. Jones, Jr., "Toward an Occupation Concept of Agribusiness," paper presented at the annual meeting of the Rural Sociological Society, Los Angeles, Calif., August 26, 1963; and Lee Taylor and Arthur R. Jones, Jr., "Professionals and Specialists in Agribusiness," *Sociologia Ruralis*, vol. 5, No. 4 (1965), 339–48.

8. *I've Found My Future in Agriculture* (American Association of Land-Grant Colleges and State Universities, 1958); and Norman K. Hoover, *Handbook of Agricultural Occupations* (Danville, Ill.: The Interstate Printers and Publishers, Inc., 1963).

9. Walter W. Wilcox, "The American Farmers in a Changing World," in *United States Agriculture: Perspectives and Prospects* (New York: Columbia University, Graduate School of Business American Assembly, 1955), pp. 11–14.

10. Taylor and Jones, *Rural Life and Urbanized Society*, pp. 296–8.

11. Olaf F. Larson and Emmit F. Sharp, *Migratory Farm Workers in the Atlantic Coast Stream I* (New York: Cornell Agriculture Experiment Station Bulletin, 948, 1960); and Emmit F. Sharp and Olaf F. Larson, *Migratory Farm Workers in the Atlantic Coast Stream II* (New York: Cornell Agriculture Experiment Station Bulletin, 949, 1960).

12. *Occupational Outlook Handbook* (Washington, D.C.: U.S. Department of Labor, Bulletin No. 1450, 1966), p. 222; *I've Found My Future in Agriculture*; H. Kaufmann, *Forest Ranger* (Baltimore: The Johns Hopkins University Press, 1960); and Hoover, *Handbook of Agricultural Occupations*.

13. Lee Taylor and Arthur R. Jones, *Rural Life and Urbanized Society*, pp. 267–87.

14. Lee Taylor and Arthur R. Jones, Jr., "Professionals and Specialists in Agribusiness."

15. Hoover, *Handbook of Agricultural Occupations*, chap. 10.
16. Hoover, *Handbook of Agricultural Occupations*, p. 82.
17. Ibid. p. 87.
18. Ibid. pp. 95–114.
19. Ibid.
20. Ibid. pp. 117–31.
21. Margery N. Coxe, "The Home Demonstration Agent in Louisiana: an Occupational Study in Stratification, Professionalization, and Recruitment" (Unpublished Master's Thesis, Louisiana State University, 1964).
22. M. C. Wilson and Lucinda Kryle, *Preparation and Training of Extension Workers* (Washington, D.C.: Federal Extension Service, Circular 295, 1938).
23. Everette M. Rogers and Dwayne Yost, "Communication Behavior of County Extension Agents" (Ohio: Agriculture Experiment Station Research Bulletin, 850, 1960).
24. John T. Stone, *How County Agricultural Agents Teach* (East Lansing: Michigan Extension Service, mimeo-bulletin, 1952).
25. A. Lee Coleman, "Diffusion Contact with Extension Work in a New York Rural Community," *Rural Sociology*, 16 (September 1951), 207–16; D. L. Gibson, "The Clientele of the Agricultural Extension Service," *Quarterly Bulletin: Michigan Agricultural Experiment Station*, 26 (May 1944), 237–46; E. J. Niederfrank, *New Hampshire Extension Service Looks at Itself* (Durham, N.H.: Agricultural Extension Service Circular 294, 1949); and Walter L. Slocum, *et al.*, *Extension Contacts, Selected Characteristics, Practices and Attitudes of Washington Farm Families* (Pullman, Washington Agriculture Experiment Station Bulletin, 584, 1958).
26. Coxe, "Home Demonstration Agent."

SUPPLEMENTARY READING

John H. Davis and Kenneth Hinshaw, *Farmer in a Business Suit* (New York: Simon and Schuster, 1957).

Norman K. Hoover, *Handbook of Agricultural Occupations* (Danville, Ill.: The Interstate Printers and Publishers, Inc., 1963).

H. Kaufmann, *Forest Ranger* (Baltimore: The Johns Hopkins University Press, 1960).

Lee Taylor and Arthur R. Jones, *Rural Life and Urbanized Society* (New York: Oxford University Press, 1964), chaps. 12 and 13.

CRAFT AND OPERATIVE OCCUPATIONS XXIII

Craft and operative occupations are manual types of work. Workers in these categories make a massive contribution to urbanized society. Craftsmen work in construction as carpenters, brick masons, electricians, plumbers, and so forth. They produce specific goods as bakers, furriers, tailors, etc. Their numbers include foremen who directly manage most of their production.

Operatives are to a great extent machine tenders in manufacturing enterprises, distributors of goods and services, packers and checkers in the preparation of goods and services, and apprentices—often to the craft occupations.

The approximately 12 million operatives and nearly 9 million craftsmen, or 20 million workers in these categories, constituted 33 per cent of the labor force in 1960. Indeed, the 12 million operatives constitute the largest single census category of occupational workers in the nation's labor force. Craftsmen constitute the second largest occupational category. The growth of craft and operative occupations, however, is slower than that of the total labor force. Between 1950 and 1960, the nation's labor force increased by 14.5 per cent. The operative occupational category experienced an increase of only 6.4 per cent and the craft category only 11.8 per cent. In a society experiencing considerable automation, and facing cybernation, many of those who perform routinized skilled and semiskilled types of work, particularly in the operative occupations, and to a considerable extent in the craft occupations, are vulnerable to displacement by machines.

The defining of occupational categories is not easy. The lack of precision in occupational definition reflects the limited degree to which workers are occupationally organized from within. Indeed, many of their occupational characteristics are imputed to them by the larger society rather than generalized through their own occupational articulation. In short, the meaning of their work is determined more by societal pressures than by practitioner expression.

For the craft or skilled occupations, three criteria are typically designated: first, the individual craftsman possesses distinctive abilities in producing his product: second, the skilled craftsman must achieve a particular high level of competence in order to be designated as a master rather than as an apprentice; third, the skilled worker acquires the ability by pursuing the course of training beyond the limits of simple observation and reading. There is a specific instructional program, often an apprenticeship program.[1] In the *Dictionary of Occupational Titles*, further specifications for the identification of those in skilled or craft occupations include their capacity to exercise a considerable degree of independent judgment, broad manual dexterity, and often a basic responsibility for valuable equipment.[2]

Operative or semiskilled occupations are defined by the *Dictionary of Occupational Titles* as follows:

Manual occupations that are characterized by one, or a combination of parts, of the following requirements: the exercise of manipulative ability of a high order, but limited to a fairly well-defined work routine; major reliance, not so much upon the worker's judgment or dexterity, but upon vigilance and alertness, in situations in which lapses in performance would cause extensive damage to product or equipment; and the exercise or independent judgment to meet variables in the work situation, which is not based on wide knowledge of a work field, and with the nature and extent of the judgments limited either (a) by application over a relatively narrow task situation or (b) by having important decisions made by others.[3]

The primary characteristics, then, of the semiskilled occupations involve a limited routine, a narrow type of knowledge, responsibility for the specific task, and the making of important decisions by others—supervisors or higher idea people. All of these characteristics of the semiskilled tend to minimize strong independent occupational development. The jobs of most workers in the operative category are so integrally related to a larger manufacturing process or other production or distribution process that it is difficult for the practitioners to develop free-standing occupational organizations. Taxi drivers and truck drivers are probably able, social organizationally, to exercise more control over occupational organization than most others in the operative category.

Until well into the twentieth century, America's skilled workers were generally European-born. Part of the difficulties in definition and occupational organization can be accounted for by the annual in-migration of skilled and semiskilled workers from abroad. In the nation's system of social organization, these immigrants started on the lower half of the occupational continuum. Their aspirations were high, nevertheless, and they hoped that America would be that proverbial land of opportunity. Accordingly, they were less interested in developing their craft or operative occupation as a thing in and for itself, and more interested in upward, vertical mobility. In juxtaposition in the social organization of occupation and of the nation's labor force few or inadequate mechanisms were developed for producing an indigenous supply of occupational men in these categories. Berthoff asserts, for example, that in the 1820's and 1830's American employers provided calico printers passage from England to induce them to come to the New World.[4] They came by the shiploads from England to America. In coal and other ore-mining occupations, there was a similar out-migration from Europe across the Atlantic to new jobs. The situation was similar for foreign immigrants in the iron and steel industry. America's rapidly expanding industrialization in the nineteenth century drew heavily on a skilled and semiskilled European labor force. Presumably they came for higher pay and better working conditions, although social legislation assuring worker benefits was passed much earlier in Europe than in America.

Work in craft and operative occupations is old and of long-standing tradition, and the structure and ideological position has long been disproportionately influenced by European migration. But the indigenous organization in America in the mid-twentieth century is now sharply and abruptly being faced by erosion through automation, cybernation, and the more rapid proliferation of idea occupations.

CRAFT AND OPERATIVE MANPOWER AND SOCIAL ORGANIZATION

Skilled manpower and its accompanying occupational organization dates from the Middle Ages in Europe, particularly with the craft guilds. Its origin precedes the Industrial Revolution. Operative or semiskilled manpower has come into existence as an accompanying by-product of the Industrial Revolution. To a great extent, operative workers are machine tenders in large factories or distributors of factory-produced goods.

The number and distribution of skilled and semiskilled workers is intricately related to the social organization of the society of which they are a part. Accordingly, their numbers are extensive in urbanized industrial United States in the 1960's. They are still increasing, but at a less rapid rate than the total labor force. Indeed, there are shortages, some critical, for some specific occupations in these categories. Yet the total craft and operative categories are characterized more by stability than by rapid growth. There are many factors which contribute to the lack of rapid increase. Central among them is the character of social organization of the society. Specifically, this means there is an expansion of idea occupational men in the society disproportionate to that of the other occupational types. The ideas and technologies of the society are being combined in such a way that goods and services are produced more and more by machines and less and less by manual labor. The ideology and social organization of the society are oriented to more free or leisure time for the labor force. Physical labor is being reduced by idea production and technical energy input.

Between 1965 and 1975, more than 4 million skilled jobs alone will have to be filled. This need for skilled workers is due both to an expanding economy and to the replacement of retired workers.[5]

A highly trained labor force, including skilled craftsmen; continues to play a strategic role in the complex organized economy. Shortages in the skilled manpower ranks will still greatly retard the economic progress of the nation. The National Manpower Council has recommended that steps be taken to increase the number of skilled workers. Specifically, the Council has suggested: (1) a strengthening of the input of secondary education for skilled preparation, (2) the development of a more effective vocational guidance, (3) the assuring of equal opportunities for all members of the labor force to acquire skill training, (4) an improvement of the facilities for skill training, and (5) an expansion of the knowledge about manpower needs and resources.[6]

Within the skilled occupational categories, there is a vast difference in growth caused by death and retirement and net increase in the occupation (see Figure XXIII.1). All of the new positions in the printing craft occupations are anticipated to result from deaths and retirements. Only 25 per cent of the new positions for carpenters are anticipated to result from a net growth in the occupation. Bricklayers and electricians will experience almost 50 per cent of their growth as the result of occupational expansion and the remainder will be due to death and retirement. Foremen, television and radio servicemen, and business machine servicemen will all experience more than 50 per cent of their oc-

FIGURE XXIII.1

Estimated Job Openings for Skilled Workmen in
Selected Occupations 1965–75

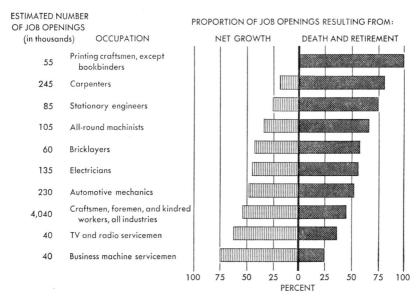

Source: Allan F. Salt, "Estimated Need for Skilled Workers, 1965–75," *Monthly Labor Review*, 89 (April 1966), 366.

cupational growth due to net increases in the occupational categories.

The number of workers in the skilled occupations cannot be increased rapidly due to the many years typically required for their training.[7] The recruitment and training of workers for skilled occupations is further inhibited by the negative image of manual-blue-collar work in the idea-white-collar society. The nature of the tasks in certain occupations may change more rapidly than the image of the occupation. This is illustrated in the case of mining, where the general image of the work is that of unskilled labor, a notion which has no real relevance to the current high skill requirements for the occupation. Similarly, the technological knowledge and skill of the scientific farmer currently far exceeds that of the subsistence way of life operations of earlier centuries.

Automation is sharply reducing the growth of operative or semi-skilled occupations. In the case of societal organization and of occupational organization, automation, it is argued, ideally liberates the worker from toil at unpleasant tasks. It is a stage of advancement in humanizing the work associated with the assembly lines which has recently dehumanized man, often by Taylorism, to a nearly complete animal functioning.[8]

But the complications of man's undertaking to eliminate himself from redundant and boring tasks of work are many. Man should be able to reduce his manual effort while increasing his intellectual effort. The accomplishment should be higher rates of production, more systematic production, high quality products, and free time for the worker. And so it is that the operative occupations are experiencing more automation. This is exemplified in the case of modern glassworks, the textile industry, much of the garment industry, the cigarette industry, motor industry, food processing industries, and many others.

In the transition, much of the labor force has experienced anything but elevation to a greater human dignity. Much short-range and some long-range unemployment is associated with automation. From automation the labor force and the economy benefit broadly, but in the short run, able-bodied workers are displaced. Some will be retrained for higher, more rewarding occupations, and some will not. Some will re-enter the labor force, while others will remain unemployed and/or retired.

The experience of automation is not limited to the operative occupations. It is increasingly known, particularly in clerical occupations, as well as many others in limited situations.

Craft and operative workers are influenced more by the social organization of their society than are many occupational types. They are essentially key functionaries who carry out the details of producing most of the nation's goods and services. They respond to the guidance and direction of managers and superiors more than they direct their own work. They are the prototype workers of the industrial society. But in the shadow of the possible advent of an affluent leisure society, the continued growth and expansion of craft and operative work roles are precarious.

In the short run, the meaning for society of the craft and operative workers is such that there is a greater concern for high quality training than in the past. It is the quantity of their work roles that stands in jeopardy in the near future by new forms of social organization. The quality of highly specialized roles continues to be a matter of concern. There are many calls for more highly trained skilled and semiskilled workers.

APPRENTICESHIP TRAINING

Apprenticeship training is the image widely held for skilled and semi-skilled workers. It is, in fact, a stereotype based only partially on fact. A 1963 survey of the formal training of the nation's workers who had less than three years of college revealed that only 40.6 per cent of the craftsmen and only 12.9 per cent of the operative workers had experienced formal training.[9] Nearly 65 per cent of the craft workers and 62 per cent of the operative workers indicated that they had experienced some on the job training. Forty-seven per cent of the craft workers and 43 per cent of the operative workers reported casual methods of learning their work skills. Respondents were allowed to indicate more than one source of training; therefore, their answers total more than 100 per cent. It is clear, however, that most of the occupational preparation for the skilled and semiskilled workers is acquired outside of formal training programs. Their skill acquisition is typically a product of chance more than of direction and planning.

In another recent survey of training, it is reported that only one out of five industrial establishments sponsors some type of formal instruction.[10] Moreover, of the 37 million workers who were employed by those industries offering training, only 2.7 million enrolled in training programs. Training programs were supported more frequently by larger industries than smaller ones. But where smaller establishments did offer training, the focus tended to be on skilled crafts, namely, in tool or machine operations, in mathematics, and in sales, office, and other white-collar skills. The training of the larger establishments emphasized engineering, technology, and management.

The type of training ranged from safety courses to short, "quickie" courses and finally to basic skill courses. Only 1.5 million of the trainees, however, were engaged in basic substantive skill courses. This survey of the effectiveness of the nation's industries in providing training shows, first, that there is little sponsorship, and, second, that much of the training is less than basic skill development.

In the absence of mass immigration of skilled and semiskilled workers from Europe throughout most of the twentieth century it appears that the nation would rather have a skilled and semiskilled worker problem than skilled and semiskilled worker classes. Most of the workers at these occupational levels are clearly not systematically prepared for them. There is neither a social structural mechanism for systematically servicing the labor force at these levels nor are there strong occupational structures for training and controlling practitioners in these occupations. The occupational experiences at these levels are primarily defined by union-management negotiations.

Apprenticeship. Little viability is achieved by apprenticeship programs in the United States. Little public interest is manifested for them. Indeed, more than a few thoughtful students of the organization of the nation's labor force have taken the position that apprenticeship is obsolete.[11] Desirability or obsolescence of apprenticeship is difficult to demonstrate. Measuring the success of apprenticeship is complicated. Its arena involves both employers and organized labor. Their interests in apprenticeship are different and at times far from compatible. The employer may want more highly skilled workers while the union wants a more regular basis for limiting the number of practitioners, for increasing wages, and specifying other working conditions. The workers themselves give little solace to either employers or unions. Where they work most effectively to express themselves, their motivation is toward upward vertical mobility, typically in moving out of blue-collar and into white-collar positions. Where failure results in this mobility, their interest by default is focused on their own occupational development.

Management's answer to the lack of a free-standing and viable occupational expression, and to the conflict environment of the union, is to invest in the development of machines rather than men. This results in more mechanization, more automation, and most recently, in an interest in cybernation. In a generally affluent society, and one with a small labor market, management is most successful in improving machine efficiency. The most articulate workers are in agreement with this trend because they too want to move up to higher positions. The downwardly mobile and/or less capable workers are left as a residue, a buffer category if you will, for industry and a most inert membership for unions.

Union support for the craft and operative workers in general, and for apprenticeship in particular, is strong because these constitute major components in union survival. Unions represent men, not machines. They gain social space by conflicts and negotiations that grew out of historical ideological commitments. Continually at union conventions there are resolutions supporting apprenticeship. The union's endorsements are for the national apprenticeship program and their prodding is for Congress to provide more adequate funds for the Bureau of Apprenticeship.[12] Along with their call to Congress for more apprenticeship support, unions berate industry for neglecting their training responsibility to employees. Far from believing that apprenticeship programs are moribund, unions assert that if the meager federal support were discontinued, they themselves would continue the development of such programs.

Federal apprenticeship support. The federal apprenticeship program is basically voluntary. Its responsibility is to encourage the establishment of programs and to help improve existing ones. It does not conduct apprenticeship training programs as such. The legislative support for the National Apprenticeship Program came in 1937 with the passage of the Fitzgerald Act.[13] The federally supported Bureau of Apprenticeship and Training works closely with employers, labor, vocational schools, and others concerned with the quality of skilled and semiskilled labor.[14] The fundamentals of the federal Co-ordinated Apprenticeship Program contain the following provisions:

1. The starting age of an apprentice as not less than sixteen years;
2. An established schedule of work processes in which the apprentice will receive instruction and experience on the job;
3. Organized instruction to provide the apprentice with knowledge in technical subjects related to his trade with 144 hours annually normally considered necessary;
4. A progressively increasing schedule of wages;
5. Proper supervision upon the job experience with adequate facilities to train apprentices;
6. Periodic evaluation of the apprentice's progress both in job performance and related knowledge and the maintenance of appropriate records;

7. Employee-employer co-operation;
8. Recognition for successful completions;
9. Selection of men and women for apprenticeship without regard to race, creed, color, national origin, or physical handicap.[15]

The Bureau of Apprenticeship offers technical assistance both to employers and unions in the development or the conduct of apprenticeship programs. It also disseminates information concerning apprenticeship through publications and conferences. The carrying out of the apprenticeship programs is supported by some 9000 apprenticeship committees. They make specific agreements with apprentices (see Figure XXIII.2). Currently, approximately 300 skilled occupations are considered apprenticeable. See Table XXIII.1 for a selected sample of

TABLE XXIII.1

Selected Apprenticeable Occupations

Aircraft Fabricator, 3–4 years	Mailer, 4–5 years
Arborist, 3 years	Miller, 4 years
Automotive Mechanic, 3–4 years	Musical-Instrument Mechanic, 3–4 years
Blacksmith, 4 years	
Bricklayer, 3 years	Orthopedic-Prosthetic Technician, 3–4 years
Canvas Worker, 3 years	
Cement Mason, 3 years	Photoengraver, 5–6 years
Cosmetician, 2 years	Plate Printer, 4 years
Dry Cleaner, Spotter, and Presser, 3–4 years	Printer, 5–6 years
	Roofer, 2–3 years
Electrotyper, 5–6 years	Sign, Scene-and-Pictorial Artist, 3–4 years
Farm-Equipment Mechanic, 3–4 years	
	Stereotyper, 5–6 years
Heat Treater, 4 years	Tailor, 4 years
Leather Worker, 3–4 years	Tile Setter, 3 years
	Wood Carver, 3–5 years

Source: *National Apprenticeship Program* (Washington, D.C.: U.S. Department of Labor, 1965), pp. 9–27.

these occupations. To be considered an apprenticeable occupation, the Bureau specifies the following: (1) that the skills are customarily learned through practical training and experience on the job; (2) that the skills are clearly identified and widely accepted throughout the industry; (3) that the skills be applicable in similar occupations through-

FIGURE XXIII.2

Apprenticeship Agreement

1962 Carpenter Apprenticeship Agreement. Apprentices in the building trades today are indentured to an area joint apprenticeship committee, which transfers them from one employer to another and one construction job to another, so that they may have experience in all kinds of work performed by journeymen.

The undersigned agrees to provide employment and training in accordance with standards named herein.

R. T. Smith Construction Company
(Employer)

Newark, New Jersey
(Address)

(Employer)

APPRENTICESHIP AGREEMENT
Between Apprentice and Joint Apprenticeship Committee

THIS AGREEMENT, entered into this ___2nd___ day of ___February___, 19__62__

between the parties to ___Newark Carpenter Joint Apprenticeship Committee___
(Name of local apprenticeship standards)

represented by the Joint Apprenticeship Committee, hereinafter referred to as the COMMITTEE, and

___Thomas M. Curtis___, born ___April___ ___1___ ___1942___, hereinafter
(Name of apprentice)   (Month) (Day) (Year)

referred to as the APPRENTICE, and (if a minor) _____, hereinafter
(Name of parent or guardian)

referred to as his GUARDIAN.

WITNESSETH THAT:

The Committee agrees to be responsible for the placement and training of said apprentice in the

trade of ___Carpentry___ as work is available, and in consideration said apprentice agrees diligently and faithfully to perform the work incidental to the said trade during the period of apprenticeship, in accordance with the regulations of the Committee. The Apprenticeship Standards referred to herein are hereby incorporated in and made a part of this agreement.

Credit for previous experience at trade, if any ___500___ | Hours. | Apprenticeship remaining ___7500___ | Hours.

Other conditions _____

In witness whereof the parties hereunto set their hands and seals:

___/s/ Thomas M. Curtis___ [SEAL]   ___/s/ John P. White___ [SEAL]
(Apprentice)   (Representative of Joint Apprenticeship Committee)

___2216 Grant Road, Newark, N.J.___   ___Secretary___
(Address)   (Title)

_____ [SEAL]   _____ [SEAL]
(Parent or guardian)   (Representative of Joint Apprenticeship Committee)

_____
(Title)

Registered by the ___Bureau of Apprenticeship and Training, U. S. Department of Labor___
(Name of registration agency)

By _____ Title _____ Date ___February 9___, 1962

Available through Bureau of Apprenticeship and Training,
U. S. Department of Labor, Washington, D. C.

Source: *Apprenticeship: Past and Present* (Washington, D.C.: U.S. Department of Labor, 1962), p. 18.

547

out the entire industry; (4) that the type of training requires at least 2 years of experience to learn; (5) that 144 hours of instruction be the minimum training each year; (6) that the training is not part but the whole of a skill; (7) that the training must not be in the selling, retailing, distributive, managerial, clerical, professional, semi-professional, or agricultural occupations.[16]

Nearly 90 per cent of all registered apprentices in the 1960's are in three trade groups: 65 per cent of the apprentices were in the building trades, 15 per cent in metal trades, and 8 per cent in printing. The remaining 12 per cent were scattered widely through other occupations.[17] This strong apprenticeship in the several trades is to a considerable extent a function of the long history of craft unions which encourage apprenticeship training. In spite of this, the number of apprentices dropped from 120,000 to 87,000 between 1950 and 1960, a drop of 27 per cent (see Table XXIII.2). Brick masons, carpenters, plumbers,

TABLE XXIII.2

Apprentices in Selected Occupations of the Experienced Civilian Labor Force, 1950 and 1960

Occupation	Number 1960	Number 1950	Per cent Change
Total	87,615	120,171	−27.1
Construction and Maintenance Craftsmen:			
Brickmasons, Stonemasons, and Tile Setters	3,199	6,475	−50.6
Carpenters	6,084	10,779	−43.6
Electricians	9,519	9,235	3.1
Plumbers and Pipefitters	8,314	12,395	−32.9
Metal Craftsmen, Except Mechanics:			
Boilermakers	—	—	—
Machinists } Toolmakers }	15,598	15,734	−.9
Molders	—	—	—
Automobile Mechanics and Repairmen	1,908	3,916	−51.3
Printing Trades	11,667	15,600	−25.2

Source: Phyllis Groom, "Statistics on Apprenticeship and Their Limitations," *Monthly Labor Review*, 87 (April 1964), 393.

machinists, automobile repairmen, and printing trade occupations all experienced a decrease in apprentices. Only electricians, with a 3.1 per cent increase, constituted a reversal of the trend. The trend for decline in apprenticeship is clear by statistics of this order. But students of apprenticeship, and of these data, argue that more and expanded apprenticeship is needed in the immediate future. Due to the increasing number of youths entering the labor force and the intensified need for skilled and semiskilled workers in some specified occupations, the contributions of apprenticeship, it is asserted, continue to be of vital importance.

Apprenticeship, like other forms of training, is greatly plagued with a drop-out problem.[18] A 1960 Bureau of Apprenticeship study revealed that approximately one-half of the workers in registered construction industry programs failed to complete their apprenticeship.[19] The range of drop-outs tends to be from about 30 per cent in bricklaying to a high of 80 per cent for roofer apprentices. Over three-quarters of those who drop out do so voluntarily. In most of the other cases, the drop-outs were laid off or discharged, and in a few cases they were forced to discontinue because of the termination of a training program. Reasons for dropping out of the apprentice program are varied. Often it is asserted that the low differential in wages between the apprentice and the journeyman contribute to the drop-out situation. More important, it is argued that the low status of the craft worker in the urbanized idea white-collar society contributes to dropping out.

The great tendency for workers trained in apprenticeship to continue in their craft provides strong evidence in support for apprentice programs. The Bureau of Apprenticeship and Training surveyed workers 6 years after their 1950 apprentice experience.[20] Ninety-three per cent of the workers were still in the crafts for which they had received apprenticeship training. Respondents asserted that their apprenticeship training had enabled them in many cases to qualify for higher positions and more responsibility. Indeed more than one-quarter had already advanced beyond the journeyman category and were working as supervisors or private contractors. Respondents were characteristically enthusiastic about their apprenticeship training, yet often they reported that the training could have been improved. Most frequently, they indicated a need for better instruction in their learning experience.

CRAFTSMEN, FOREMEN, AND KINDRED WORKERS

The census does not delineate skilled workers, blue-collar workers, or manual workers as such. Yet its craftsman category constitutes the most extensive and continuous body of data for workers in these kinds of occupations. The 2.2 million mechanics and repairmen constitute the largest single occupational type in the craftsman category. Most of them, over 600,000, are automobile mechanics. Yet the number of automobile mechanics is decreasing. The second largest occupational category is that of airplane mechanics. They experienced a 45 per cent increase between 1950 and 1960. The 1,175,000 foremen are the second largest occupational type in the craftsman category. Most of these foremen, over 700,000, are in manufacturing work. Foremen experienced a nearly 40 per cent increase between 1950 and 1960, compared to an only 12 per cent increase for the craftsman category. Carpenters are the third largest occupational group, composed of over 800,000 practitioners. Their numbers are decreasing, however, and they experienced an 11 per cent decline in the past decade (see Table XXIII.3).

The profile of skilled workers is as follows: typically a white male, slightly older than other males in the labor force, and possessing about an average amount of education.[21] In 1960, out of the more than 8 million craft workers, only 250,000 were female. Women in craft occupations were most frequently foremen, 78,000; mechanics, 26,000; decorators and window dressers, 23,000; and bakers, 17,000; the remainder were quite widely distributed through the full range of craft occupations. While women have been increasing rapidly in the labor force, their increase in craft occupations was slightly less than 7 per cent between 1950 and 1960.

In spite of the shift in occupations from farm to non-farm types in rural areas, the craft workers continued to be predominantly urban. Over 73 per cent were in urban areas. Only craft workers listed as millers were found with any considerable frequency in rural farm areas, and in this case only 16 per cent. Over half of the inspectors (52 per cent) were located in rural non-farm areas; they were scalers, graders, loggers, and lumbermen. Forty-five per cent of the skilled workers in excavating, grading, and load machinery jobs were located in rural non-farm areas. Blacksmiths, loom fixers, and millers all reported more than 40 per cent of the occupational participants in rural non-farm areas. Finally, the 1960 Census reported about 400,000, or 5 per cent, of the craft workers to be non-white.

Craft workers are a massively important but ideologically and occupationally depressed category of workers in the United States social or-

TABLE XXIII.3
Craft and Operative Employed Workers for 1950 and 1960
(In Thousands)

	1960 Total	1950 Total	% Increase
Craftsmen, foremen, and kindred workers	8,741.3	7,820.6	11.8
Bakers	108.4	120.2	−9.9
Blacksmiths	20.0	43.7	−54.2
Boilermakers	23.7	35.6	−33.4
Bookbinders	27.0	31.2	−13.5
Brickmasons, stonemasons, and tile setters	185.9	165.9	12.2
Cabinetmakers	65.7	73.4	−10.6
Carpenters	818.8	918.8	−10.9
Cement and concrete finishers	40.8	29.6	37.9
Compositors and typesetters	179.6	175.9	2.1
Cranemen, derrickmen, and hoistmen	123.9	103.7	19.6
Decorators and window dressers	50.9	43.4	17.3
Electricians	337.1	311.3	8.3
Electrotypers and stereotypers	9.2	11.8	−22.0
Engravers, except photoengravers	11.3	9.7	15.6
Excavating, grading, and road machine operators	198.8	105.4	88.6
Foremen	1,175.1	845.5	39.0
Construction	96.5	59.0	63.4
Manufacturing	744.0	513.5	44.9
Railroads and railway express service	35.9	54.1	−33.6
Transportation, except railroad	27.1	19.9	36.0
Communications, & utilities, & sanitary service	57.6	40.4	42.7
Other industries (including not reported)	214.1	158.6	35.0
Forgemen and hammermen	11.7	13.1	−10.9
Furriers	3.3	11.0	−70.2
Glaziers	14.9	10.3	45.4
Heat treaters, annealers, and temperers	19.6	17.8	10.2
Inspectors, scalers, and graders, log and lumber	19.7	19.2	2.3
Inspectors (n.e.c.)	98.2	96.1	2.2
Construction	14.9	8.1	83.2
Railroads and railway express service	29.4	36.8	−20.2
Trans., exc. R.R., commun., and other pub. util.	14.5	12.5	15.4
Other industries (including not reported)	39.5	38.6	2.3
Jewelers, watchmakers, goldsmiths, and silversmiths	36.8	45.9	−19.8
Job setters, metal	39.7	24.4	62.5
Linemen and servicemen, telegraph, telephone, power	274.6	213.5	28.6
Locomotive engineers	56.6	73.0	−22.4

TABLE XXIII.3 (cont.)

	1960 Total	1950 Total	% Increase
Craftsmen, foremen, and kindred workers (cont.)			
Locomotive firemen	37.1	54.3	−31.7
Loom fixers	23.9	30.3	−21.2
Machinists	498.7	514.7	−3.1
Mechanics and repairmen	2,223.4	1,729.8	28.5
Air conditioning, heating, and refrigeration	61.9	43.6	42.1
Airplane	114.2	71.4	60.0
Automobile	682.1	654.4	4.2
Office machine	29.3	31.0	−5.7
Radio and television	102.8	75.4	36.5
Railroad and car shop	39.0	47.5	−17.9
Not elsewhere classified	1,193.9	806.6	48.0
Millers, grain, flour, feed, etc.	9.1	9.6	−5.7
Millwrights	64.3	57.9	11.0
Molders, metal	48.9	60.6	−19.2
Motion picture projectionists	17.6	26.2	−33.0
Opticians, and lens grinders and polishers	20.3	19.2	6.0
Painters, construction and maintenance	370.7	391.8	−5.4
Paperhangers	10.2	20.9	−51.4
Pattern and model makers, except paper	38.9	35.9	8.2
Photoengravers and lithographers	25.0	28.5	−12.4
Piano and organ tuners and repairmen	6.0	7.8	−22.6
Plasterers	46.2	60.4	−23.6
Plumbers and pipe fitters	304.5	279.5	8.9
Pressmen and plate printers, printing	73.9	49.3	50.0
Rollers and roll hands, metal	29.7	30.4	−2.3
Roofers and slaters	47.9	44.5	7.9
Shoemakers and repairers, except factory	36.2	57.2	−36.8
Stationary engineers	269.7	214.9	25.5
Stone cutters and stone carvers	6.1	8.7	−29.9
Structural metal workers	58.2	49.5	17.7
Tailors	41.0	82.9	−50.5
Tinsmiths, coppersmiths, and sheet metal workers	135.3	123.2	9.8
Toolmakers, and die makers and setters	182.3	152.7	19.4
Upholsterers	59.4	61.3	−3.1
Craftsmen and kindred workers (n.e.c.)	105.3	68.9	52.6
Former members of the Armed Forces	—	—	—
Operatives and kindred workers	11,897.6	11,180.3	6.4
Apprentices	82.5	115.5	−28.5
Asbestos and insulation workers	18.1	14.2	27.1
Assemblers	614.3	377.9	62.6
Attendants, auto service and parking	351.8	236.8	48.6

	Total 1960	Total 1950	Increase %
Operatives and kindred workers (cont.)			
Blasters and powdermen	6.4	10.9	−41.9
Boatmen, canalmen, and lock keepers	6.8	8.1	−16.8
Brakemen, railroad	61.7	78.6	−21.6
Bus drivers	181.8	155.7	16.8
Chainmen, rodmen, and axmen, surveying	9.6	7.1	36.0
Checkers, examiners, and inspectors, manufacturing	480.1	331.8	44.7
Conductors, bus and street railway	4.2	11.3	−62.4
Deliverymen and routemen	419.7	239.6	75.1
Dressmakers and seamstresses, except factory	119.2	142.3	−16.2
Dyers	18.4	24.2	−24.0
Filers, grinders, and polishers, metal	148.4	147.8	0.4
Fruit, nut, and vegetable graders and packers, except factory	22.1	28.8	−23.3
Furnacemen, smeltermen, and pourers	53.3	55.4	−3.7
Graders and sorters, mfg.	34.4	41.8	−17.5
Heaters, metal	7.7	9.3	−17.4
Knitters, loopers, and toppers, textile	44.0	80.6	−45.4
Laundry and dry cleaning operatives	386.9	430.3	−10.1
Meat cutters, exc. slaughter and packing houses	180.8	171.2	5.6
Milliners	3.8	12.3	−69.0
Mine operatives and laborers (n.e.c.)	290.1	574.3	−49.5
Coal mining	116.3	362.3	−67.9
Crude petroleum and natural gas extraction	91.5	102.6	−10.9
Mining and quarrying, except fuel	82.4	109.4	−24.6
Motormen, mine, factory, logging camp, etc.	12.7	23.9	−46.6
Motormen, street, subway, and elevated railway	7.4	26.5	−72.0
Oilers and greasers, except auto	51.4	59.3	−13.3
Packers and wrappers (n.e.c.)	438.1	326.6	34.1
Painters, except construction and maintenance	138.1	116.9	18.1
Photographic process workers	41.3	28.2	46.4
Power station operators	26.7	21.6	23.4
Sailors and deck hands	32.7	40.8	−19.8
Sawyers	86.7	94.8	−8.5
Sewers and stitchers, mfg.	568.5	471.9	20.5
Spinners, textile	48.8	80.8	−39.7
Stationary firemen	87.9	122.6	−28.3
Switchmen, railroad	57.8	61.3	−5.8
Taxicab drivers and chauffeurs	162.5	203.4	−20.1
Truck and tractor drivers	1,556.8	1,328.6	17.2
Weavers, textile	62.7	97.9	−36.0
Welders and flame-cutters	360.6	261.4	38.0
Operatives and kindred workers (n.e.c.)	4,610.6	4,507.6	2.3
Manufacturing	3,977.9	3,872.8	2.7
Durable goods	1,890.9	1,762.9	7.3
Nondurable goods	2,077.7	2,094.1	−0.8

TABLE XXIII.3 (cont.)

	1960 Total	1950 Total	% Increase
Operatives and kindred workers (cont.)			
Nonmanufacturing ind. (incl. not reported)	632.7	634.9	−0.3
Construction	89.5	66.3	34.9
Railroads and railway express service	52.5	90.9	−42.3
Transportation, except railroad	33.4	29.7	16.2
Communications, & utilities & sanitary service	48.7	50.9	−4.6
Wholesale and retail trade	202.1	212.5	−4.9
Business and repair services	67.1	46.9	42.9
Personal services	13.9	18.9	−26.3
Public administration	43.7	48.2	−9.4
All other industries (incl. not reported)	81.9	71.3	14.8

Source: *U.S. Bureau of the Census, U.S. Census of Population: 1960. Detailed Characteristics, U.S. Summary,* Final Report, PC (1)-1D, Washington, D.C., pp. 530–32.

ganization in the second half of the twentieth century. Occupationally, they are in the doldrums, drifting and inarticulate. The art of craftsmanship has been downgraded by the drama of science, which has captivated the interest and imagination of the nation's people. Accordingly, idea men in occupations are accelerated to high positions. Craftsmanship is more a matter of history than of contemporary importance. Craftsmanship by its nature is based on quality for long duration. The idea scientific society operates with maximum change and short duration. Accordingly, a limited duration of utility for both goods and services is built into their plan of fabrication. In such a societal configuration, the importance of craftsmen is real but at a secondary rather than a primary level. Their value tends to be more for maintenance and repair than for high quality productivity.

OPERATIVE AND KINDRED WORKERS

Operative workers are the nation's largest single occupational category in the labor force. The 1960 Census reported nearly 12 million operative and kindred workers. This was a 6 per cent increase over 1950, but a less dynamic increase than for the nation's total labor force. Much of the increase for operatives came in the expansion of use of trucks for the movement of goods. A much smaller increase among the skilled workers was recorded for those who are machine operators or machine tenders. In part this was a response to automation in factories, but also there was a considerable enlargement in total productive enterprise, which required some new workers.[22] Nearly 4 million of the nation's operative workers are employed in manufacturing. The number of males increased slightly in this kind of employment while the number of females declined slightly. The second largest operative category—1.5 million—is that of truck and tractor drivers. A 17 per cent increase was experienced in the number of drivers, but there was a slight decrease in the number of females. Assemblers, packers and wrappers, checkers and examiners, and deliverymen and routemen, in descending order, are the next largest occupations in the operative category. Some of the largest increases were in these occupations, namely, 75 per cent for delivery-men, 63 per cent for assemblers, 49 per cent for attendants, 45 per cent for checkers, and so forth.[23]

The median age of operative workers is 38 years. This is slightly younger than the median age of 41 for all male employees. Only 1.2 million, or 14 per cent, of the operative workers are reported as non-white. The educational attainment of operative workers is also typically low.

Operative workers constitute a residual category in the labor force. Occupational characteristics are more attributed to them than generated through their own initiative. The manufacturing jobs in the category are continually threatened by automation. Due to the idea emphasis of the society, the routineness of the manufacturing operative jobs renders a low prestige for them. There is little elegance in their work and little to be gained by a vigorous occupational organization.

Many of the operative occupations that have to do with more free-standing work environments are being rapidly displaced by broad shifts in technology. This is exemplified in the case of boatmen, canalmen, and lock keepers; transportation advancements are now being made in airways, not in waterways. In other new and developing operative areas having to do with assembling, packaging, and checking, there is again the ultimate threat of automation. As the steps and stages of the work are new, they are entrusted to individuals. When they become formalized and routinized, the individuals must compete with machines, and, in the nature of the case, usually surrender to them. The durability of a repetitive job is weak compared to that of jobs having to do with ideas or direct services to people.

The characteristics of the work environments of skilled and semi-skilled workers have been reported in numerous studies.

SELECTED STUDIES OF OCCUPATIONAL EXPRESSION IN SKILLED AND SEMISKILLED WORK

The empirical study of men and machines is seldom more clearly seen than in the environment of skilled and semiskilled workers. The following selected case studies illustrate the invaded and dependent nature of occupations in the machine environment.

Workers' dreams and aspirations.[24] Chinoy's study of automobile workers was specifically selected because of the continuing possibility for career mobility from floor sweeper to production boss. Yet in spite of this possibility for achievement most workers did not achieve. They substituted for success in their occupation achievement in a general style of life at home or otherwise away from the job. Getting ahead for them became the acquisition of a new and modern home, job security, time for leisure, and other fringe situations related to work but not to occupation in and for itself. The automobile workers began their careers with limited aspirations, modified their aspirations in terms of work experiences, and, by their mid-thirties, had transferred their aspirations from work to nonwork situations.

For children in their environment there tended to be an aspiration for immediate gratification in a job, car, girl, spending money, etc.[25] The point of their experience is that decisions for occupation, generally white-collar or professional, are made early in one's life and tenaciously held to, or occupation becomes subjugated to an alternative way of life outside of the work arena.

Most of the automobile workers in Chinoy's study had at some time considered leaving the factory for alternative work. Their main motivation was to be their own boss, own a store or farm, make their own decisions and their own directness. Few of the workers, however, had made any specific efforts to move from the factory. Some who did, in fact, had failed and returned. In light of these experiences, the typical worker viewed his toil at the machine as security for himself and his family. He continued to gripe about the routine and monotony of work, to be motivated to some degree in seeking increased wages and expanded fringe benefits, but essentially to be deflated as an occupational man. In the face of the machines, occupational men were reduced in stature. Their self-gratification came more beyond the frame of work than within it.

Restrictions on production.[26] Donald Roy spent eleven months working as a radial-drill operator in the machine shop of a steel processing plant in 1944 and 1945. He became "one of the boys" in the work environment. After his working hours, he systematically recorded notes concerning the behavior of his work associates and his own work experiences.

Quota restriction and goldbricking were two major patterns of behavior manifest against management by workers whose companions were impersonal machines. Quota restriction was reported as a widespread response among workers to the time and motion expectancies of management. In effect, the workers agreed, in opposition to management, on an optimum output for the rate of pay offered in certain machine operations. The expression was typically, "If this is all they're going to pay me for such a job, I will only produce the following amount of work." [27]

Goldbricking is manifest most in piecework. On the "gravy jobs," or desired work, machine operators earn their normative quota quickly and then knock off and take it easy. On the less desirable jobs, they put forth only a minimum effort.

Again the implication in relation of workers to machines is that if a full free-standing organization of occupational integrity is impossible, then human efficiency will be reduced as a matter of principle and freely regulated to illustrate vividly the differentiation between men and machines where occupational identification is absent.

Interpersonal relations and the building industry.[28] The environment of this industry is typically mobile and outside. It is an on-location environment and involves, therefore, moving from site to site as one construction job is completed and another undertaken. The industry involves considerable individual skill and an increasing mechanical input. But it is characterized less by factory organization and mass production and more by the quality of interpersonal relationships.

The foreman of the work crew plays a primary role. The forming of a labor force for any particular job is largely controlled by foremen who select their own crews in response to unions and in negotiation with employers. The importance of the foreman is so rigid that informal selection factors, if not discrimination, cause work crews to be differentiated on the basis of ethnic background and religion. The individual worker must be personally acceptable to the foreman or his potential high quality of production may never be utilized.

The job foreman's strength is largely limited because of the fluidity of his position. A man may be a foreman for several jobs and then be employed at a later time as a worker by another foreman on still another job. In this work environmental situation, the idiosyncratic integrity of both foremen and workers must be dealt with. The frequent organization and disbanding of work crews as one construction job comes into existence and then goes out of existence brings workers together for intense co-operation for brief periods of time and then forces their separation. This situation is not conducive to total occupational building. Workers are less challenged by machines but still occupationally largely unable to stabilize and build a continuity in their work situation.

Foremen and the assembly line.[29] The foreman is a skilled worker in the techniques of management of men. "Officially," he is the front-line representative of the management team. His position is critical to that of the industrial operation and to the men whom he supervises. The foreman is a middleman, as it were, related to management but physically separated from it in his work. The foreman's proximity is in relation to the workers whom he must supervise and to whom he is closer in technical skill and behavioral experience. It is to the foreman that much effort is entrusted for the humanization of industry.

Yet the occupation of the foreman is precarious in its free-standing organization because of the widespread diversity of the content areas they supervise and the minimum of the occupational type in each particular work situation. The foreman is separated from his fellow foremen by the nature of the work situation which involves his close interaction with a large number of subordinates and his line service to a few immediate superiors. The work environment as such offers few natural opportunities for foremen to relate to other foremen. The strength of the foreman occupation comes from their articulateness, the work environment need for their survival, and their individual need for reducing frustration and pressures that come from their middleman situations.

SUMMARY AND IMPLICATIONS

Craft and operative workers are the largest occupational categories reported by the census. They have been the largest categories for a long period of time. Their occupational dynamics, however, are minimal. Typically, their growth is less than that of the labor force as a whole. As the major representative of the blue-collar occupations, their role dynamics are now being exceeded by white-collar occupations.

The position of the skilled and semiskilled workers in the social organization of the nation is a dependent one. Specifically, they are dependent upon the idea people of the society. While their work continues to be of some critical importance, it is work directed by idea people, rather than by the practitioners.

The stereotyped image of training for the skilled and semiskilled workers is apprenticeship. Yet the evidence for the nation reveals that typically these workers learn their work more by informal processes than by any formal training, including apprenticeship.

The craft workers of the nation historically have been European immigrants. In the social and occupational organization of the United States there has been to date no effective mechanism for an adequate production of craft or guild workers. It is as if the nation would rather have a skilled worker problem than a skilled worker occupational class.

Workers in operative occupations constitute a residue for the nation's social organization. Those who are not able to enter and/or achieve in higher occupations can learn quickly the skills and demands for operative work. Their rewards are few, but their expectancies are also few. The society needs their jobs to be done by men until machines can be designed to accomplish the tasks. In the social change of the nation, the weak occupational organization, or its absence, in the operative positions is functional to the workers' frequent displacement from jobs. The increasing occupational status of the operative workers reduces the flexibility with which their positions can be terminated for replacement by machines. To the extent that their work is of a minimum technological level, their skills can be transferred quickly from one place of work to another. Operative occupations are in effect a societal abrasive for the facing of machines by men. Indeed, the meaning of their work is a means to achievement of life's rewards outside of employment.

In the whole of Part Three of this book, we are concerned with the meaning of occupations for individuals and societies. The meaning of craft work for individuals historically has been of a high and specialized order. Indeed, craftsmen have been at the apex or near it in the occupational hierarchy until recently. In the contemporary urbanized society, craftsmen have been displaced by professionals and specialists at the top of the occupational hierarchy. The ego gratification in craft work is reduced for the individual because professionals and specialists are the prototype of the era.

The meaning of craft occupations for society is still vastly important, even though they are overshadowed by professional and managerial occupations. Society needs craftsmen, but the particular kind of social organization of the twentieth century is based on a priority of ideas and men in idea occupations. It is less that the crafts are unimportant and more that a new category of occupations has become of even greater importance in the urbanized society.

The operative or semiskilled occupations are of more recent origin, indeed, they are products or residues of the Industrial Revolution. These occupations are molded almost exclusively by the structures and forces of society rather than by the initiative of individual practitioners. For individuals in these occupations, work is at that functionary level beyond which man's capacity for machine development is not yet reached. In short, there is much that is not occupational about this work.

When it is found that operative workers seek the meaning of their experience outside of occupation, this can be most readily understood from the point of view of the societal organization which creates their social space. Their job is a means to something else, namely, the obtaining of monetary remuneration to provide the goods of life.

The importance of operative workers for society is essential. But their positions are always vulnerable to automation and further technological development. It is their work which is important and not their occupation in and of itself. Accordingly, when new machines are developed, the operative worker social space is replaced.

NOTES

1. A *Policy for Skilled Manpower* (New York: Columbia University Press, 1954), p. 10.

2. *The Skilled Labor Force* (Washington, D.C.: Bureau of Apprenticeship, Technical Bulletin, No. T-140, 1954), p. 4.

3. Ibid. p. 5.

4. Rowland Tappan Berthoff, *British Immigrants in Industrial America* (Cambridge: Harvard University Press, 1963), pp. 31ff.

5. Allen F. Salt, "Estimated Need for Skilled Workers, 1965–75," *Monthly Labor Review*, 89 (April 1966), 365–71.

6. *A Policy for Skilled Manpower*, pp. 19–20.

7. *Skilled and Professional Manpower in Canada, 1945–1965* (Ottawa: Royal Commission on Canada's Economic Prospects, 1957), p. 4.

8. Georges Friedmann, *Industrial Sociology* (Glencoe: The Free Press, 1955), pp. 173–90.

9. *Formal Occupational Training of Adult Workers* (Washington, D.C.: Manpower Administration, U.S. Department of Labor, Research Monograph No. 2, 1964), p. 18.

10. *Training of Workers in American Industry* (Washington, D.C.: Manpower Administration, Research Division Report No. 1, 1962).

11. Felician F. Foltman, "Apprenticeship and Skilled Training: A Trial Balance," *Monthly Labor Review*, 87 (January 1964), 28–35.

12. Ibid. p. 30.

13. Martha F. Riche, "Public Policies and Programs," *Monthly Labor Review*, 87 (February 1964), 143–8.

14. *Apprenticeship: Past and Present* (Washington, D.C.: Bureau of Apprenticeship and Training, revised, 1962).

15. Ibid. p. 31.

16. National Manpower Council, *A Policy for Skilled Manpower* (New York: Columbia University Press, 1954), p. 224.

17. Phyllis Groom, "Statistics on Apprenticeship and Their Limitations," *Monthly Labor Review*, 87 (April 1964), 391–5.

18. Foltman, "Apprenticeship and Skilled Training," pp. 32–3.

19. See *Apprentice Dropouts in the Construction Industry* (Washington, D.C.: U.S. Department of Labor, Bureau of Apprenticeship and Training, 1960), p. 1.

20. *Career Patterns of Former Apprentices* (Washington, D.C.: U.S. Department of Labor, Bureau of Apprenticeship and Training, Bulletin T-147, 1959).

21. *A Policy for Skilled Manpower*, p. 71.

22. Max Rutzick and Sol Swerdloff, "The Occupational Structure in the U.S. Employment, 1940–1960," *Monthly Labor Review*, 85 (November 1962), 1209–13.

23. U.S. Bureau of the Census, U.S. *Census of Population: 1960*, Detailed Characteristics, U.S. Summary, Final Report PC (1)-1D (Washington, D.C.: 1963), p. 531.

24. Ely Chinoy, *Automobile Workers and the American Dream* (New York: Doubleday and Co., Inc., 1955).

25. Joseph A. Kahl, "Educational and Occupational Aspirations of 'Common Man' Boys," *Harvard Educational Review*, 23 (Summer 1953), 186–203.
26. Donald Roy, "Quota Restriction and Gold Bricking in a Machine Shop," *American Journal of Sociology*, LVII (March 1952), 427–42.
27. Ibid.
28. Richard R. Myers, "Interpersonal Relations in the Building Industry," *Applied Anthropology*, 5 (Spring 1946), 1–7.
29. Charles R. Walker, *The Foreman on the Assemblyline* (Cambridge: Harvard University Press, 1956).

SUPPLEMENTARY READING

Ely Chinoy, *Automobile Workers and the American Dream* (New York: Doubleday and Co., Inc., 1955).
Felician F. Foltman, "Apprenticeship and Skilled Training: A Trial Balance," *Monthly Labor Review*, 87 (January 1964), 28–35.
Phyllis Groom, "Statistics on Apprenticeship and Their Limitations," *Monthly Labor Review*, 87 (April 1964), 391–5.
Allen F. Salt, "Estimated Need for Skilled Workers, 1965–75," *Monthly Labor Review*, 89 (April 1966), 365–71.

SERVICE OCCUPATIONS XXIV

Service workers may be defined as those occupational people whose functions focus on rendering comfort, enjoyment, and protection to life and property of other members of the society.

The several occupations that the census lists in the service category are typically of the blue-collar variety. Most of the individuals in them work at the direction of supervisors. They experience a high rate of job turnover. Many service workers engage in part-time jobs. Their educational level is typically low, and the training required for their jobs is often most conspicuous by its absence.

At the other extreme one finds some service workers who are highly educated and who have advanced training. Indeed, the relatively small number of FBI men may be more appropriately included with professionals than with protective service workers. In a similar unhomogeneous way, some chefs are highly skilled people who from many points of view engage in a most creative occupation.

By the mid 1960's census estimates indicated that about 1 out of every 8 workers, or approximately 9 million people, were engaged in service jobs. Service workers are divided into those employed outside of private households and those employed in private households. Approximately three-fourths of the service workers are in jobs outside of individual homes; the remaining one-quarter are employed as private domestics.

Among the nearly 6.5 million service workers employed outside of homes, about three-fourths are working on a full-time basis and the remaining quarter on a part-time basis. One-third of the service workers have jobs as cooks, waiters, and other related workers in restaurants, hotels, and other eating places. Firemen and policemen constitute a special category. Their primary purpose is the protection of

life and property. Service workers in buildings include elevator operators, janitors, and a vast array of other custodial people. Many other
service workers are engaged in activities which render individual services
for individual people. These are the barbers, beauty operators, practical
nurses, and a host of other individual attendants.

The distribution of the major types of service workers employed outside of homes is shown in Figure XXIV.1. There are 11 major cate-

FIGURE XXIV.1

Three-fourths of all service workers employed outside private homes
are in these occupations

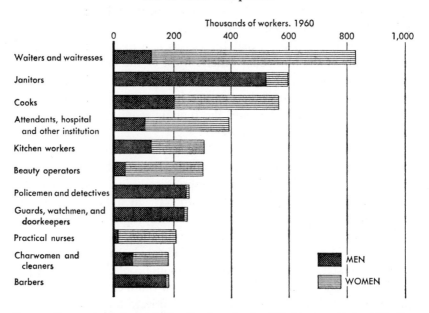

Source: *Occupational Outlook Handbook*: 1963–64 (Washington, D.C.: U.S. Department of Labor, Bulletin No. 1375, 1964), p. 304.

gories. Female workers constitute the majority of waiters, cooks, attendants, kitchen workers, beauty operators, practical nurses, and charwomen. By contrast men constitute the majority of janitors, policemen,
guards, and barbers.

Among the approximately 2.5 million private household workers, the
proportion of women far exceeds that of men; 97 out of every 100.
Moreover, the number of part-time workers is exceedingly high in this

category. Most of these workers are "live outs" rather than "live ins." A dramatically increasing type of work in this category is baby-sitting.[1]

The training required for jobs in the service occupations is typically minimal. For example, in the case of bellmen there is usually no specific training requirement at all. In the cases of barbers, beauticians, practical nurses, and so forth, some specific vocational training is usually required. Workers in the protective service occupations, namely firemen and policemen, often have more training than most of the others in service occupations. The greatest extreme is found in the case of FBI men, where a college degree is required. Comparatively, the FBI workers are a minority group in the service occupations. Many of their characteristics tend to be more atypical than typical. There is some tendency for other police officers and protective workers to prepare for their positions with a college level course of training. This norm, however, is far from universal among the protective workers.

An important characteristic of service workers is the possibility for entrepreneurship. Food workers may develop their own restaurants or catering service operations. Many barbers and beauticians will eventually operate their own shops as small businesses. A few other service workers may eventually ascend in their career to a place where they have minor administrative and/or managerial positions. The chief housekeeper in a large hotel may well be engaged primarily in management and administration.

In the equalitarianly organized urbanized society it is something of an irony that the number of service workers has increased far more rapidly than the total labor force in the 50-year period from 1910 to 1960. The overwhelming proportion of the increase, however, was recorded among workers engaged in jobs outside of private homes. In Figure XXIV.2 one observes that in 1960 the proportion of people in nonprivate household work was three times greater than in 1910. In sharp contrast, the number of private household employees had declined slightly. Service workers have experienced a continual 50-year period of increase in employment outside of private family positions. Domestic workers decreased in 1920 and then increased through 1940. They decreased in proportion sharply between 1940 and 1950, particularly during the World War II years, and have experienced a slight increase in the decade 1950–1960.

Labor Department predictions suggest that the number of service workers will continue to increase by dramatic proportions well into the second half of the twentieth century. It is anticipated, nevertheless, that there will be a considerable difference in increase among the several service occupations. The protective service types of jobs will experience rapid increases. Great increases are also expected in practical

FIGURE XXIV.2

Source: *Occupational Outlook Handbook: 1963–64* (Washington, D.C.: U.S. Department of Labor, Bulletin No. 1375, 1964), p. 305.

nursing, beauty operation, and food preparation and service. Janitors and building caretakers are also expected to be job categories in which increases will be recorded. No significant changes in number of job opportunities are anticipated among domestic workers.

The opportunity trends anticipated for service workers suggest that while the total category will show tremendous increases, some considerable measure of democratic equalitarianism is to be anticipated in the amount of employment increase outside of homes rather than within private family employment. Moreover, the level of training and general status attributed to these service workers may well be expected to increase during the second half of the twentieth century.

Pseudo-occupational nature. The vocabulary phrase—service occupations—requires some qualification in order to sustain its suitability in a conceptual treatise on occupations. At the outset we argued that the concept of occupation is characterized by a variety of norms and folkways. In order for a category of work, or a number of job practitioners, to be called an occupation it is necessary for the work to be characterized by the various norms and folkways and for the practitioners to manifest a consciousness of their fellow workers and to articulate a destiny for their occupation. It is asserted that the characteristics of an occupation are both generated from within the occupation by the practitioners and attributed to the occupation by members of the greater society of which it is a part. In the case of the many so-called service occupations it remains to be demonstrated by empirical research that the practitioners understand a body of norms and folkways and view their occupation at an abstract level with a consciousness of kind. It is clear, however, that many of the occupational characteristics associated with service jobs are attributed, indeed, ascribed to them, by the greater society which utilizes and demands the several services. To the extent that these several jobs have their characteristics assigned to them rather than generated by the practitioners, one might observe that the jobs are only pseudo-occupational.

DOMESTIC SERVICE OCCUPATIONS

A social structural dimension of servitude is widely and historically found in human societies in most geographical areas. The abstract viewing of domestic service at an occupational level is of relatively recent origin. For example, it is observed that in Norway the free servant displaced the role of the serf at the end of the twelfth century.[2] In the Americas indentured white servants were briefly known, but they never became a normative part of the social organization. Negro servitude, however, was widely experienced in both North and South America. The social organization of free servants dates primarily from the nineteenth century in the Americas.

Domestics—servants, maids, helps. The United States long has had a potentially favorable environment for the development of a servant occupation. The dominant ideology in the nation is for freedom of individuals and integrity of individuals. Servants, therefore, have experienced more social space within which to view themselves and their fellow workers as participants in an occupation. For a variety of reasons, which are explained below, participants in this type of work seldom have been able to view their experience occupationally.

To put it succinctly, America has preferred a servant problem to a servant class.[3] In the early national period the thrust of republican spirit and emotion was so great that one human being bitterly opposed being the servant of another. The very notion, servant, was repugnant. To be beholden to individuals for service was viewed as demeaning in the infant democracy.

The social space and labor demand for individual assistance, nevertheless, persisted. The mechanism of accommodation was seen in the attempt that was made to drop the word and replace it by the notion "helps." The idea of help as opposed to service seemed to obliterate a master-servant relationship. One could help another individual while maintaining personal dignity; indeed, in some cases while being social equals. In any event, by the nineteenth century the concept of help appeared to be dominant in domestic service jobs.

The change of title was, nevertheless, insufficient to provide an adequate supply of domestics. In the expanding new nation, rural girls, for a period of time, constituted the best source of help for the new and expanding middle classes. No sooner than this source of supply had become well identified than it was diverted to factory jobs. Factory positions often paid poorly, and the work situations were frequently depressed in other ways as well. Yet the potential employees in the factory were able to maintain a dignity by working with their peers rather than as inferior laborers in a domestic environment.

After the Civil War American class consciousness became more rigid and the supply of national domestics diminished. Accordingly, Irish and German immigrants were recruited into domestic service in the second half of the nineteenth century. Their tenure was short. They too quickly joined the American workers in mills, factories, and shops, and emancipated themselves from the domestic environment.

The Negro long has been a unique case in domestic service in the United States. He experienced a period of indentured servitude, followed well into the middle of the twentieth century by a "voluntary" servitude supported by resistance to his assimilation and as a crutch or escape function for those unwilling to take part in the mainstream of social economic systems.[4] For several reasons, then, social structures and social space, along with ideologies, have combined in an environmental force for sustaining Negroes as a steady supply of domestic workers.[5]

In the second half of the twentieth century the Negro domestic is at last becoming a vanishing type. Following the many domestics who have preceded them, the Negroes are now entering jobs in the factories, shops, etc.

Norms of the domestic occupation. Originally, the strongest norm of the domestic work was the "living in" tradition. Historically, the servant and the help were provided housing and maintenance in their place of work. Often these provisions were shabby and inadequate, in any event substandard, in terms of their contemporary society's standard of living patterns. The joking pattern poignantly illustrates this situation. "Maid: Please, mum, could I have one o' yer red geraniums to kape in me bedroom? Mistress: Oh, no, Bridget, your room is too dark. It would die. Plants must have sunlight and fresh air." [6] The living conditions for domestics improved over the years as their supply became more critical. Over-all the norm of living in, however, has become virtually obliterated. Replacing this norm is the "live out" tradition for domestics in the twentieth century. The live out domestic may work full-time in a home, part-time in a home, or part-time in several homes. As a function of living out the occupation becomes more contractual. The live out maid is in an environment wihch is said to be more dignified and less servile.

The employer-employee relationship in domestic service is ill defined. Indeed, at the end of the nineteenth century the relationship was referred to as that of master and servant.[7] Yet what little there is that is normative about the relationship seems to be the nearly universal definition of the situation as a problem from the point of view of the employer. There is a literature which purports to instruct the parties involved concerning the properness of their respective relationships.

In *The Complete Bachelor* the author wrote:

In the treatment of servants a man must exercise an iron will. He can be kind and considerate, but he must never descend to dispute with one, and certainly not swear at him. To be on familiar terms with one's servants shows the cloven foot of vulgarity. . . . Encourage your servants now and then by a kind word, and see that they have good and wholesome food, clean and comfortable quarters. Once in a while give them a holiday, or an evening off, a cash remembrance at Christmas, and from time to time some part of your wardrobe or cast-off clothing. They are just like children, and must be treated with the rigor and milk discipline which a schoolmaster uses toward his pupils. In all their movements they should be noiseless and as automatic as possible in their actions.[8]

There have been sporadic attempts on the part of domestics and others to systematize the employer-employee relationship. But in the main all efforts at organization among domestics have failed. Haynes reports a domestic workers alliance in 1919. There was also an effort to establish a domestic workers' union in Mobile, Alabama, Fort Worth, Texas, Lawton, Oklahoma, and so forth.[9] In Oslo there has been some recent legislation aimed at structuring the relationships between the housemaid and her employer.[10] In spite of these several efforts, the situation shows a lack of organization. The fact is that the domestic servant's work is functionally diffuse and the several efforts to bring specificity to the job and task details have failed.

Another norm of the occupational circumstance for domestics concerns the employer's expectations. Chaplin argues that employers have with some intent resisted the rationalization of domestic service by not allowing specialization. The obligations of employers to their domestics are limited and arbitrary. In contrast the domestic is expected to give broad and diffuse loyalty to the persons served. In the absence of collective action the response of domestics to their employers' nearly unilateral demands is a high rate of turnover and mobility. Obstacles to the unionization of domestics include (1) excessive transitory and casual workers, (2) separation and isolation of workers, (3) paternalism of some employers, (4) high proportion of women, (5) the impracticability of the strike and other union techniques in domestic work, etc.[11]

Several norms of the domestic's situation are enumerated. There is the absence of fellowship. In the middle class urbanized societies the domestic typically works single handed in the home doing all of those various and generalized tasks that are assigned. The work situation involves few opportunities for interaction with fellow workers.

Another dimension of the worker's situation is the absence of objective criteria for evaluating the performance of duties. In general the purpose of the domestic is to satisfy someone more than to perform certain tangible duties in a specified manner. The plurality of the tasks reduces the possibility for professionalization and makes a systematic training for domestics nearly irrelevant. In effect the job requires the worker more to understand his individual employer than to understand his duties.

Still another perplexing norm of the occupation concerns the invasion of privacy. When the tradition was dominated by living in, privacy was more frequently invaded than it is with the tradition of living out. In spite of the tradition of living out, privacy continues to be a matter little respected by the employer. "Female domestics were subject to a sort of verbal voyeurism on the part of their mistresses." [12]

It is most clear that the several norms of the work situation are more specified by the employers than they are generated by the occupational practitioners. This illustrates the pseudo-occupational aspects of the work.

On into the twentieth century the domestic problem continues to intensify. After World War I the exodus of the maid increased until the 1920's.[13] With the depression years of the 1930's the exodus was somewhat halted; in fact, the number of domestics slightly increased. With the advent of World War II once again a labor force structure was developed which increased the opportunities for domestics to leave the homes and obtain employment in factories. Since World War II the domestic occupation has been in a perpetual limbo. Technology, along with the reduction in the size of families reduces the need for the domestic. The status orientation of the urbanized society, however, increases the demand for domestics. If in the past the primary function of the domestic was to please the master more than to do a job with proficiency, now, in the status years, this is even more the case. Nonetheless, the traditional domestic continues to be a diminishing type of occupation.

The increases that have taken place in domestic service are essentially caused by baby-sitters. The individual is often the daughter of a neighboring family, or an older lady, but in any case she is hardly a candidate for an occupational domestic. Another change in social organization which precipitates a reduction in domestics is the contribution which husbands are making in carrying out the domestic details of the home. Some have said "One definition of the suburban husband is 'a groundsman with sex privileges' ".[14]

Baby-sitters. Baby-sitting is a rapidly expanding domestic occupation. Among the service work occupations, baby-sitting represents over 1 million practitioners. They typically work in the home on a part-time basis.

The National Association for Baby-sitter Registries is providing professional leadership for the occupation. It publishes a *Babysitters Guide,* which is something of a combination of a code of ethics and an instruction manual. It admonishes sitters to be neat and clean, not to wear jewelry that may hurt children, not to drink before or during employment, etc. Instructions are also offered for the care of children.

The National Association holds annual meetings, provides a manual for new agencies, and maintains a roster of certified baby-sitters. As a professional association it promotes baby-sitting in public relations and builds the occupation by educational media. For example, the *Sitter Service Roundtable,* the association newsletter, calls attention to the Maryland Health Department film, "A Babysitter's Guide to Baby Care," and baby care notes from medical science experts.[15]

PERSONAL SERVICE OCCUPATIONS

Personal service occupations may be illustrated in the case of cooks, waiters, bellboys, barbers, and practical nurses. The number of specific service jobs constitutes a long list, but most of them may be subsumed into the general categories of food, public housing, and the health services.

Chefs and cooks. The position of chef is marginal, indeed precarious. In the mass urbanized society the occupational roles and the occupational space of chefs seem to be nearly contradictory. On the one hand it is asserted that the chef is an artist, a creative technician in the preparation of food. Although he works in the kitchen, his status is far from the bottom. In fact in some cases he is viewed as part of the management, salaried at the level of a junior executive, and in much demand.

Chefs occupy the colorful and in several respects artistically unique positions that are central to food preparation. Occupationally, however, chefs and skilled cooks are generally combined. In 1964 the *Occupa-*

tional Outlook Quarterly reported over 500,000 cooks and chefs in the United States.[16]

The occupational characteristics of this work involve a period of participant learning and little specific training. Some informal "chef schools" are operated. They focus on the various techniques for preparing sauces, decorating cakes, and many other culinary skills. Nevertheless, the vocational education program is limited and far from systematic. Vocational courses include care of food equipment, food standards, sanitation, along with cooking methods. After a period of some 15 to 20 years a cook may be promoted to the position of chef or head cook. In large restaurants they will be assisted by several specialists, whose tasks may include the preparing of salads, preparing of pastries, and so forth. There is a considerable specialization and division of labor in the total food preparation enterprises.

Slightly over one-half of the persons employed in this occupation are women. The occupation currently has a considerable shortage of personnel. The U.S. Department of Labor projections report that there is a strong possibility that more practitioners will be needed. This is partly explained by the general expansion of the food services industry. The demand for such practitioners is further increased due to the difficulty which large hotels and restaurants face in recruiting highly skilled cooks and chefs from Europe. This occupation has long been attributed a greater prestige in Europe than in the United States. In recent years the occupation enjoys greater remuneration in Europe, and the exodus is reduced accordingly. The shortage of chefs and cooks is further increased by the failure of young people to select this as a suitable occupation.

Waiters and waitresses. The 1960 Census reports approximately 600,000 waiters and waitresses in the United States. These people are employed primarily in restaurants and other food establishments that are devoted to the retailing of food. Many thousands are employed in railroad dining cars, hotels, department stores, and similar establishments.

Women far outnumber men in this occupation. Waitress jobs constitute a particular opportunity for women. In the hierarchial organization they may often be encouraged to work up into supervisory positions. This pattern of career development is observed even when restaurants are owned by men.

The employment outlook is strong, showing anticipated increased needs. This is a function partly of the expanding population and partly of the increased affluency of the population. No specific training is required for the occupation, but since World War II some training programs have been developed, and they are expanding.[17]

The human structure of the restaurant is complex. The division of labor involves a manager at the top who makes decisions for the organization and who oversees the entire operation. Various echelons of supervisory personnel occupy middle positions between the management and the service workers. In the large restaurant the checker occupies a particularly important and at the same time precarious position. Ideally, one might observe that the checker occupies a quality control position. It is a point at which a judgment is passed concerning the size of portions that are being served, the neatness and artistic arrangement of the servings, and the readiness of the food to be presented to the customer. The waitress identifies with her customer and wants to serve in whatever manner will be most attractive there. The food preparing personnel feel they are the only adequate judges of their production. The role of the checker is often viewed by the personnel on either side as an imposition, an intrusion of management in an area where the judgment is unwarranted. Bartenders and pantry workers are middle people, standing in front of those in the preparation areas and behind the waiters and waitresses who service the customers. Judgment of their proficiency is rendered often by people on opposite sides of them whose goals may or may not involve a considerable measure of congruency. Large-scale restaurant organization was researched by Whyte in a Chicago Loop establishment.[18] He characterizes the social organization as having time clock precision, a considerable division of labor, and a practical routine—all orchestrated, as it were, in competition, conflict, and service to customer desires.

For example, in preparation for an 11:00 a.m. opening, work starts in the kitchen between 5:00 and 6:00 a.m. Baking is usually started first, and the other food preparation follows in order. When the food is ready a team of service-pantry workers have the task of moving it to the steam tables, cold storage cabinets, etc., as appropriate. The pantries are supplied about 30 minutes before the restaurant is opened to the public.

About an hour in advance of opening, the waitresses check all tables in the dining room to see that they are ready. Then the dining room manager reviews the menu of the day with the waitresses so that they can explain the attractiveness of offerings to customers with dispatch and accuracy. This is followed by a review of the waitresses' dress and personal appearance. After all of these many details are checked, the waitresses deploy to their appropriate stations. The general manager makes one last quick check and opens the doors to admit the early luncheon customers at precisely 11:00 a.m.

At opening time social interactions is typically orderly and courteous among customers, waitresses, and other restaurant workers. As the time nears 12:00 noon the pace quickens throughout the entire restaurant social organization. Customers are crowded, hostesses rush the waitresses, orders are filled faster, waitresses try to hurry the work of the pantry staff, the pantry staff presses the kitchen workers, and so on through the hierarchy to the dishwashers.

Precise timing and a well planned system of organization are central to the restaurant operation. Elements of co-operation, competition, and conflict are all found in the restaurant organization. In broad outlines the restaurant is a social system. But its boundaries, almost by definition, are permeated by the idiosyncratic whims of customers. Some accommodation is built into the system for customer irregularity, yet some extenuating circumstances are unanticipated. Waitresses are part of the restaurant establishment, but at times in their direct interaction with customers it is to their advantage to identify with the people they serve. In doing so they may develop a pseudo-clientele. This may produce competition for service and gratuities in the interest of customers and waitresses but to the detriment of the restaurant as an organization and as a business enterprise.

Checkers are appointed in some large restaurants to exercise establishment-oriented surveillance over size of portions of food served in the pantry and over the arrangement of meals served by the waitresses.[19] In the quickened pace and pressure of the peak periods overt conflict erupts from time to time among the waitresses, the checkers, and the pantry workers. Their goals are not always those common to the restaurant organization. Sometimes the goals of the waitresses and of the customers constitute a competing social system.

The relations between the waiters and waitresses and their customers are both rewarding and frustrating. Often it happens that in high quality restaurants the waitresses receive higher earnings than some of their middle range white-collar customers. Indeed, out of the restaurant uniform some waitresses may be as prosperous or more prosperous than the persons they serve. Nevertheless, the status differential favors the customers. The demands of the middle range customers are frequently excessive, presumably a mechanism for announcing and asserting their status. Serving such people may be more frustrating than rewarding. They don't want to be pleased. They announce themselves by moderate complaint rather than by satisfaction.

The role of the waiter or waitress is further reduced in its creative and artistic importance. In the past in Europe, and to a lesser extent in the United States, the waiter or waitress gained renown and status for ability to serve with style and artistry. He or she was required and expected to mix dishes at the table in a grand manner. With the mass production of the urbanized society there is little social space and time for such individuality of service. In effect the waiter or waitress becomes something of a second-rate machine in a routinized position.

When some discretion and artistry is allowed the waiter or waitress the distinguished performance might bring a higher tip. But this system gives little comfort in an equalitarian society. The tip also means that the tipper is superior; the receiver inferior. The dignity of the worker might be less servile and more upgraded by higher wages, more systematization of the work roles, and less tipping. In short, there is some question whether the tipping is needed more by the tipper or by the receiver. It is somewhat myopically viewed as required by the service worker. From a social organizational view it may be more a catharsis for the person being served.

The status hierarchy is further ruptured by the cashiers, who usually receive lower total earnings than the waitresses, but who have higher status, particularly as symbolized by their attractive street dress rather than uniforms. To add more difficulty to an already complex status system, in the distinguished restaurants the chefs have the highest status. The apex of the total restaurant social organization depends, ultimately, on the distinguished quality of food which they prepare. The status of all others is increased or decreased as the reputation of the chef varies. To be a waitress or cashier in a restaurant served by a famous chef is higher status than to work in a lesser restaurant.

Finally, runners and dishwashers are typically at the lower end of the restaurant hierarchy. Their jobs require the least skill, and are rewarded with a minimum of prestige and monetary compensation. Few occupational characteristics operate here that are not attributed by superiors or outsiders to the area of work.

Bellmen and bell captains. The hotel industry is of considerable importance in a mobile urbanized society. The *Census of Business* reports nearly 20,000 hotels in the nation. Currently, they accommodate over 2 million guests per night. Their number of employees will approximate 400,000.[20]

Service workers in the hotel industry are a heterogeneous lot. They range from the housekeepers, engineers, elevator operators, food service workers, to bellmen. Some of these people are more occupationally organized than others. In the 1880's, soon after the American Federation of Labor was established, some hotel workers were organized and granted union charters. There has continued to be some image of the several types of work and attempts at union negotiation for position.

At the lower end of the service work occupations in the hotel industry no particular educational requirement is prerequisite. Some vocational education schools are beginning to offer a limited course of training for these workers. There is some semblance of hierarchy in the organization of these jobs. One often starts as an elevator operator, is promoted to bellman, to bell captain, and ultimately to superintendent of services. The occupational outlook for bellman jobs is for some slight increase.

The norms of the occupation appear to be very few, at least as they are manifested from the practitioners themselves. Again, the bellman occupation is more a pseudo-occupation than a real one, a category of work to which occupational characteristics are attributed by supervisors and clients more than by the practitioners.

The norm of tipping is widely established as a relationship between clients and bellmen.[21] The hourly wages for bellmen are typically less than $1.00 per hour. Indeed, in some cases their wage is even below $0.50 per hour. The Department of Labor issued a report of findings of a 1962 study which indicated the value of tips received by bellmen on an hourly basis. In most cases it was found that the value of tips exceeded that of their wages. In the survey 43 per cent of the bellmen were employed in establishments where their tips averaged at least $1.25 per hour. Bellmen in transient hotels typically receive more tips

than those who are employed in hotels which have a large proportion
of permanent guests.

Barbers and beauticians. From the time of the Barber of Seville to
the present hairdressers have always been a servile class. During some
times in history these workers also have been a colorful and lively category of people. In other places and at other times their characteristics
have been much influenced by their sophisticated clientele. In the mass
urbanized society their station is clearly affirmed at the lower end of
the occupational continuum. In the status-conscious society styles and
forms of hairdressing are of exceeding great importance. The styles,
nonetheless, are established by the clients rather than by the hairdressers. Their practice, by contrast, is related greatly to their proficiency in producing the styles in vogue.

In 1960 the census reported approximately 200,000 barbers, mostly
men. Some occupational characteristics are developed to a fairly high
level by barbers. Training, for example, is highly specified and rigorously required. In most cases one attends a barber school for between 6
and 9 months. After the successful completion of a course of training
the barber must be licensed by state boards.

Another norm which is widely established is that of barbers providing their own equipment, their tools of production. A barber's equipment typically costs from $75 to $100. This tradition of occupational
training and responsibility in equipment ownership leads to some measure of dignity and respectability in the occupation. The tenure in the
occupation is for lengthy duration. Entrepreneurship is another characteristic in this occupation. Approximately one-half of the nation's barbers own their shops. Unionization has become an important aspect of
the occupational organization. The days and hours worked along with
the price for the several services are sharply regulated by union agreements.

Beauticians outnumber barbers. In 1960 they totaled 300,000. Approximately 10 per cent of the beauty operators were men. Occupationally it is important to note that a high proportion of the beauty
operators are part-time workers. Similar to the case for barbers, beauty
operators are subject to 6 to 9 months of special training. In 1961 there
were 2000 beauty schools. After the proper course of training beauty
operators are subject to licensing by states. Their remuneration ranges
greatly. The 1960 statistics show the range from $55 to as high as $300
per week.

PROTECTIVE SERVICE OCCUPATIONS

The main occupations in this category are policemen and firemen. Most of them are in private or municipal employment. There is a substantial number of full-time workers in both of these occupations. They are also both supplemented by auxiliary part-time workers. Within the police category there are many types of specialists ranging from private detectives, to sheriffs, and to FBI agents.

Federal Bureau of Investigation agents. FBI agents constitute a unique category of protective workers. Occupationally, from several points of view, they might more appropriately be included with professionals than with service occupations. Their training and characteristics are professional in type. Their role functions are service-oriented.

FBI agents are a part of the U.S. Department of Justice. In 1963 their number totaled 6000. Most of them were dispersed to some more than 50 field offices. Their training is at a college level, usually in law. The outlook for expansion is poor. Their roles are limited in a nation that abhors a police state.

There is very little than can be said occupationally about this specialized corps of investigators. The most abiding characteristic of their occupation is confidentiality, secretiveness, and the formalized restriction on the divulgence of information concerning their work or its nature.

Policemen and detectives. The number of full-time policemen in 1961 was 175,000. This is primarily a male occupation, and only 3000 of the total full-time practitioners were women. One of the important trends, however, is the tendency for women to be more frequently employed in this kind of work. The outlook for the occupation is strong. Their salary remuneration is of a middle class proportion—ranging typically from $3,000 to as high as $20,000 annually.[22]

There is a dearth of information on the occupational behavior of policemen.[23] From Westley's study of the police in Chicago some considerable insight is gained concerning the role of secrecy. The norm is established as an unwritten law, for example, that policemen should never testify against their fellow officers. For example:

You and your partner pick up a drunk who is breaking up a bar. While you are patting him down you discover that he has five hundred dollars on him. You take him back to the station in a car and your partner sits in the back with him to keep him quiet. When you check him in with the turnkey the money is gone. You realize that your partner has clipped him. What would you do? [24]

Seventy-four per cent of the respondents indicated they would not report their partner in such a case; however, this finding is based on a small number of respondents. Indeed, so many of them resisted the question that it had to be dropped before the study was terminated in order to continue the study. The sanctions supporting secrecy are articulated on the basis that the successful policeman must be able to command the full support of his partners. The work is hazardous, and some of its most important aspects can never be recorded as a paper record but must exist by word of mouth. A breach of secrecy precipitates a loss of confidence among one's colleagues. The function of secrecy is partly determined by the general public. This is to say, the police are viewed as corrupt and often less than law-abiding themselves. This condition causes policemen to identify with other policemen and in effect through secrecy to precipitate something of a subculture. The code of secrecy is an informal but forceful part of the "rookie's" indoctrination into his police work. ". . . the norm of secrecy emerges from common occupational needs, is collectively supported, and is considered of such importance that policemen will break the law to support it." [25]

In another report from the same research Westley indicates that violence as used by policemen is a consequence of their occupational experience.[26] The behavior of the police, even when deviant in the form of violence, has the group sanctions of their fellow workers. In terms of the hazards which the occupation involves in the achievement of its goals, policemen informally legitimize violence as an acceptable form of behavior. Use of violence is viewed as an occupational prerogative, if not a requirement. For example, the club and the gun are the policeman's means of persuasion. The policeman often achieves prestige and career success on the basis of his handling roles of violence. Policemen argue that they gain more prestige from a beat where there is opportunity for violence than from a "clean" beat. Moreover, violence adds some drama to their solution of crimes and the control of the situation. The police in the study further report that they believe the use of violence as a form of punishment is legitimate. If the courts failed to issue punishment they would do so. The belief is that you must act tough and show strength. Moreover, if there is resistance then you go all out in violence to control the individual. More specifically it was reported "if a fellow called a policeman a filthy name, a slap in the mouth would be a good thing, especially if it were out in the public where calling a policeman a bad name would look bad for the police." [27] The police are aware of sanctions that might be brought against them in the use of illegal violence. They nevertheless experience much protection in the secrecy of their colleagueship.

Firemen. In 1960 there were approximately 139,000 full-time firemen in the nation. They are organized in a systematic hierarchical manner. A specified course of training and retraining characterizes the occupation. For many of the practitioners the occupation is a lifetime career.

The technology of fire fighting and of fire protection are not clearly differentiated from the occupation. The fire protection industry supports numerous associations and publications, but they are not occupational in their primary purpose.[28]

Fire chiefs and others in the industry have regular conventions. The Fire Newsletter carries announcements concerning positions available. The following selected titles illustrate the specialization in the occupation: fire prevention technical co-ordinator, safety-fire protection engineer, fire protection supervisor, fire protection specialist, sprinkler engineer, fire safety inspection specialist, etc.

There are numerous indexes of the occupational character of fire prevention, but there is little systematic occupational evidence.

BUILDING SERVICE OCCUPATIONS

The several types of jobs included in building service work are janitors, charwomen, elevator operators, pullman porters, and baggage porters. Among these the janitors and charwomen are the most universal. All types of buildings utilized by all types of people must in one way or another be kept relatively clean and sanitary by the standards of judgment of the mass urbanized society. The occupational implication of this universality of the workers is that regardless of their low status their demand is great. Their absence from work is confounding to the antiseptic society and the minimum necessary changes are quickly made to assure their return to work.

The various kinds of porters are, by contrast, in more limited demand. Their services, nonetheless, are requested by those who are willing and able to pay. Porters are virtually the bottom end of the occupational and societal continuum, but they experience a high rate of interaction with individuals at the upper end of the occupational continuum and in the upper portion of the status hierarchy of society. In short, their service to the total society is not great. Their occupation is, accordingly, more precarious and more degrading. Empirical studies of these workers are unknown, but their organizational and occupational space is readily identifiable.

Janitors. The occupation of janitors or sanitary engineers is more attributed than generated, more pseudo than real. In recent years, however, the occupational space of janitors has become more formalized, principally through the mechanism of unionization. In those places where these workers are unionized they no longer must cater to every whim of their superiors. Unionization brings job specification and role delineation in many ways. Their wages are increased. Their housing location, often free, is an established requirement. The occupational stereotype of the janitor is foreign-born, stupid, lazy, dressed in dirty clothes, basement quartered, and a garbage carrier. In juxtaposition, the practitioner sees himself as the cleaner of the grounds, caretaker and handyman, and finally, after proficiency is achieved in these roles, the manager of the building who is a virtual entrepreneur for tenants' needs. Unlike the housemaid there are some standards and objective judgments by which the work of the building janitor is evaluated. Yet it is reported in a Chicago study that janitors believe one of their most important tasks is to know how to deal with the tenants in their building.[29]

As the janitor's position is upgraded by unionization and more occupational formalization, jealous tenants become virtually impossible to satisfy. They squawk and gripe due to jealousy because of the janitor's new Buick, his color television, and his other symbols of material success.

For those less jealous the pattern of interaction between the janitor and tenant is a matter of confidant. Like the bartender, the barber, and the housemaid, the janitor is expected to hear and keep the several secrets and problems of the tenants.

SUMMARY AND IMPLICATIONS

The service occupations are strong and enduring in number because of the great demand for their contribution to many members of the society. The personal and occupational characteristics of the individual practitioners are such that occupational solidarity is limited and elusive. The occupational space for service jobs is assured by this high rate of demand more than by the aggrandizement of the practitioners. Indeed, many of the service workers are so dispersed, so poorly educated, and so incapable or unwilling to view their occupation and the work world in sufficient perspective that they are unable to contribute much to the internal organizational growth of their occupations.

Nevertheless, the occupational potential of service workers is increasing. They are no longer typically domestics. Three-fourths of them are employed outside of homes. Generally they work in small groups, and sometimes in larger numbers for big businesses. Most nondomestic service workers are employed as waiters or waitresses, janitors, cooks, hospital attendants, etc. Since the beginning of this second half of the twentieth century the nondomestic service occupations have expanded rapidly while private household work has remained nearly stable.

Baby-sitting as a special kind of domestic service work is expanding greatly. There is some trend for its systematic occupational organization, but it remains a special case. In spite of its organization its practitioners are typically older ladies or young girls working only part-time.

The protective service occupations, namely, FBI agents, policemen, and firemen, constitute another unique occupational situation. The FBI agents are the most highly trained of the so-called service workers. They are college graduates. In much of their occupational character they appear to be among the new professionals. Policemen and firemen also have special skill training, but college work is not normative for them. The protective service workers, unlike others in this category, have a low frequency of interaction with the public. Certainly they have little or no customer or client relationships. They are more free-standing occupational men and less depressed into servile relationships. Yet they do not "control" their service as the professionals do. Their occupational organization must accommodate crisis circumstances as normative.

Service occupational practitioners in varying degrees typically respond to the demands of people above them in the work hierarchy. They may have more or less special knowledge or skill, but it is called into service at the request of others.

NOTES

1. *Occupational Outlook Handbook: 1963–64* (Washington, D.C.: U.S. Department of Labor, Bulletin No. 1375, 1964), pp. 304–5.
2. Vilhelm Aubert, "The Housemaid—An Occupational Role in Crisis," *Acta Sociologica*, 1 (1956), 149–58.
3. Russell Lynes, "How America 'Solved' the Servant Problem," *Harpers Magazine*, 227 (July 1963), 46–54; Jane Addams, "A Belated Industry," *American Journal of Sociology*, 1 (March 1896), 536–50; and I. M. Rubinow, "Household Service Labor Problem," *Journal of Home Economics*, 3 (April 1911), 131–40.
4. David Chaplin, "Domestic Service and the Negro," in Arthur B. Shostak and William Gomberg (eds.), *Blue-Collar World: Studies of the American Worker* (Englewood Cliffs, N.J.: Prentice Hall Inc., 1964), pp. 527–36.
5. David Chaplin, *The Amherst Negro* (Unpublished Honors Thesis, Amherst College, 1953); and Elizabeth Ross Haynes, "Negroes in Domestic Service in the United States," *Journal of Negro History*, 8 (October 1923), 384–442.
6. Russell Lynes, *The Domesticated Americans* (New York: Harper and Row Publishers, 1963), p. 167.
7. *The Complete Bachelor* (New York: D. Appleton and Company, 1897), p. 101.
8. Ibid. pp. 95–6.
9. "Plans for Improvement of Domestic Service," *Monthly Labor Review*, 10 (May 1920), 112–16; and Mary T. Waggaman, "Efforts to Standardize the Working Day for Domestic Service," *Monthly Labor Review*, 9 (August 1919), 206–213.
10. Aubert, "The Housemaid."
11. Chaplin, "Domestic Service and the Negro," p. 530.
12. Ibid. p. 532.
13. Paul W. Brown, *America at Work* (1922).
14. Lynes, "How America 'Solved' the Servant Problem," p. 53.
15. *Sitter Service Roundtable*, 8 (May 1965), total issue; and "What Counts Most in Hiring a Baby Sitter," *Good Housekeeping*, 160 (January 1965), 131.
16. *Occupational Outlook Quarterly*, 8 (February 1964), pp. 27, 28; see also *Occupational Outlook Handbook, 1963–64*, pp. 709–11.

17. Matthew Josephson, *Union House, Union Bar* (New York: Random House, 1956), pp. 336 ff.
18. William Foote Whyte, *Human Relations in the Restaurant Industry* (New York: McGraw-Hill Book Co., Inc., 1948); see also Frances Donovan, *The Woman Who Waits* (Boston: Richard G. Badger, 1920).
19. *Restaurants and Other Food Service Enterprises* (Washington, D.C.: U.S. Department of Labor, Bureau of Labor Statistics, 1964).
20. Morris A. Horowitz, *The New Hotel Industry: A Labor Relations Study* (Cambridge: Harvard University Press, 1960); and David J. Jacobson, "What's Ahead for the Hotel Industry," *Harvard Business Review*, 24 (Spring 1946), 344.
21. Fred W. Mohr, "Wages in Hotels and Motels in Twenty-Three Areas, June, 1961," *Monthly Labor Review*, 85 (April 1962), 396–7.
22. Helene T. Lesansky, "Salaries of Firemen and Policemen, 1958–61," *Monthly Labor Review*, 85 (March 1962), 282–6.
23. William A. Westley, "The Police: A Sociological Study of Law, Custom, and Morality" (Unpublished Ph.D. Dissertation, Department of Sociology, University of Chicago, 1951).
24. William A. Westley, "Secrecy and the Police," *Social Forces*, 34 (March 1956), 254–7.
25. Ibid. p. 257.
26. William A. Westley, "Violence and the Police," *American Journal of Sociology*, 59 (July 1953), 34–41.
27. Ibid. p. 39.
28. See the National Fire Prevention Association *Fireman* monthly magazine; *Fire Engineering* (journal of the fire protection profession); *Fire Research Abstracts and Reviews; Fire News*, etc.
29. Ray Gold, "Janitors Versus Tenants: A Status-Income Dilemma," *American Journal of Sociology*, 57 (March 1952), 486–93.

SUPPLEMENTARY READING

Ray Gold, "Janitors vs. Tenants: A Status-Income Dilemma," *American Journal of Sociology*, 57 (March 1952), 486–93.

Morris A. Horowitz, *The New Hotel Industry: A Labor Relations Study* (Cambridge: Harvard University Press, 1960).

Helene T. Lesansky, "Salaries of Firemen and Policemen, 1958–61," *Monthly Labor Review*, 85 (March 1962), 282–6.

Russell Lynes, "How America 'Solved' the Servant Problem," *Harpers Magazine*, 227 (July 1963), 46–54.

William A. Westley, "Secrecy and the Police," *Social Forces*, 34 (March 1956), 254–7.

William Foote Whyte, *Human Relations in the Restaurant Industry* (New York: McGraw-Hill Book Co., Inc., 1948).

INDEX

Ackerman, Joseph, 535
Adams, L. P., 264
Anderson, Nels, 242, 463
Anderson, W. A., 474
Apprenticeship, 221, 544, 549
  Bureau of Apprenticeship and Training, 545, 549
  occupations, 546
  training, 543
  union support, 545
Argyris, Chris, 263
aspirations, 64, 189, 190, 197, 206, 210, 214, 556
  empirical examples of, 207
  family influence on, 203
  for graduate study, 211
  of women, 213
associations and societies, 344
  guilds, 347
  professional, 346
  trade unions, 348
Aubert, Vilhelm, 584
automation, 7, 35, 500, 502, 542

Barnard, Chester I., 114
Becker, Howard S., 293, 490
Belitsky, Harvey, 257
Ben-David, J., 113
Bendix, Reinhard, 113, 449
Berelson, Bernard, 242
Berger, Bennett M., 38
Bideau, Pierre, 512
Blalock, H. M., Jr., 343
Blanch, Lloyd E., 242
Blau, Peter M., 101, 192, 294
Blood, Jerome W., 490
Bloom, Gordon F., 323
blue-collar workers, 23, 158, 256, 349
Bluestone, Abraham, 217
Bogue, Donald J., 37
Borenstein, Audrey Farrell, 429
Bracey, Howard E., 390

Bradway, John S., 342
Bright, James R., 513
Brown, David G., 249
bureaucracy, 87
  formal and informal organization, 91
  impact on occupations, examples of, 100
  incentives, 97
  occupational organization, 92
  professions in, 101
  recruitment into, 92
  scientists in, 105
  work patterns, 93
Burnham, James, 114
Burns, Robert K., 146, 388, 513
Burnstein, Eugene, 185
Burritt, Bailey B., 119

Caplow, Theodore, 60
career patterns, 266
  achievement, 281
  concepts and definitions, 266
  cosmopolitan-local, 283
  hierarchies, 268
  informal factors, 278
  mobility, 281
  personality and life styles, 286
  professional workers, 270
  success, 280
  types, 288
  vertical mobility, 291
Carey, William N., 367
Carper, James W., 293, 491
Carr-Saunders, Alexander Morris, 77, 411
Centers, Richard, 69, 73
Chamberlain, Neil W., 238
Chaplin, David, 570, 584
Charters, W. W., 474
Chinoy, Ely, 65, 68, 411, 556
Christiansen, John R., 84
Clarke, Alfred C., 185

Coats, Charles H., 108, 293, 343
Coleman, A. Lee, 536
colleagueship, 334, 413
    concept of, 414
    cult, 416
    evaluation, 421
    friendship and, 416
    interaction, 424
    location, 415
    obligations, 419
    recruitment, 417
    rewards, 315
community, 36, 486, 487
Corwin, Ronald G., 133
Coulton, G. G., 117
Counts, George, 165, 169, 171
Coxe, Margery N., 533, 536
Crockett, Harry J., Jr., 64
Crosser, Paul K., 436
Curtis, Richard F., 85

Danielson, Lee E., 403
Davidson, Percy E., 69
Davis, James A., 212, 218
Davis, John H., 535
Davis, Kingsley, 166
Devorak, Eldon J., 162
Dibble, Vernon K., 431
Dickson, William J., 441
Dictionary of Occupational Titles, 21,
    40, 52, 538
Diebold, John, 500
domestic service occupations, 567, 568,
    569
Drucker, Peter, 19, 133, 513
Dubin, Robert, 15
Ducoff, Louis J., 38
Dufty, N. S., 411
Durkheim, Emile, 13, 41
Dynes, Russell R., 217

Eaton, Joseph W., 133
Edwards, Alba M., 14, 19, 83, 122,
    165, 185, 473
employee society, 31, 33
Estey, Martin S., 141
executvies:
    government, 110
    women, 111

farm labor force, 29, 521
Form, William H., 270, 367

Frederick, William, 342
French, Cecil L., 514
Friedmann, Eugene A., 390
Friedmann, Georges, 37
fringe benefits, 306, 312
    assistants and accouterments, 317
    physical facilities as reward, 318
    profit-sharing, 314
    status and prestige, 316
    technical equipment, 315
    type of payment, 309
    vacations and holidays, 313

Gerth, H. H., 112
Ginzberg, Eli, 191, 216
Glaser, Barney, G., 294
Gold, Ray, 447, 585
Goldberg, Ray A., 535
Goldstein, Bernard, 162
Gomberg, William, 584
Gompers, Samuel, 438
Goode, William J., 490
Goodrich, H. D., 488
Gordon, J. E., 263
Gordon, Robert A., 114
Goulder, Alvin W., 93, 96, 294
Grant, J. A. C., 342
Greenberg, Herbert M., 514
Griff, Mason, 430
Gross, Edward, 83, 429, 474
Grunes, Willa Freeman, 198, 199

Hagstrom, Warren, 133
Hall, Oswald, 294, 342, 430
Haller, A. O., 84
Hansen, W. Lee, 324
Hauser, P. M., 60
Havighurst, Robert J., 390
Hawthorne studies, 440
Henle, Peter, 323
Henry, Nelson, 242
Heron, Alexander R., 410
Higbee, Edward, 535
Hilgert, Raymond L., 513
Hirsch, Irvin, 133
Hodge, Robert W., 174
Homans, George C., 496
Hoppock, Robert, 411
Hoos, Ida Russakoff, 513
Howton, F. William, 514
Hughes, Everett C., 34, 133, 491
Huntington, Mary Jean, 490

idea people, 24, 30, 31, 35, 446, 482
ideologies, 431
    and boundary maintenance, 433
    managerial superiority, 435
    nature and dimensions, 431
    and occupational stereotypes, 442
    and stratification, 432
    white-collar, 444
images, 11, 249, 251
Indik, Bernard P., 146
Inkeles, Alex, 161

Jaffe, A. J., 60
Janowitz, Morris, 108, 114, 343, 460
Jehring, J. J., 323
Job:
    enlargement, 34
    hunting, 196, 256
    shifting, 74, 75, 501
    simplification, 34
    training, 225
Jones, Arthur R., Jr., 219, 534

Kahl, Joseph A., 562
Kanel, Don, 474
Kassalow, Everett M., 162
Katz, Daniel, 411, 513
Kaufmann, H., 535
Knapp, Robert H., 488
Kohn, Nathan, 253
Kreisbry, Louis, 185
Kriesberg, Lewis, 514
Kruger, Daniel H., 162, 367, 466, 468
Kuvlesky, William P., 217

Labor force, 45, 48, 230, 237
Lamson, Robert W., 113
Lapp, Ralph E., 32, 38
Larrabee, Eric, 324
Larson, Olaf F., 535
Lathrop, Robert I., 263
Lazarsfield, Paul F., 430
Lenski, Gerhard, 287
Lewis, Lionel S., 168
Lewis, Roy, 33, 43, 104, 367
Levenstein, Aaron, 410
Lieberman, Myron, 162, 367
Lipset, Seymour Martin, 75, 205
Litwak, Eugene, 86, 457
Lyman, Elizabeth L., 411
Lynes, Russell, 584

Mack, Raymond, 442
McGee, Reece J., 263, 429
McGlothlin, William J., 242
McMurry, Robert N., 263
Mahone, Charles H., 219
Mandell, Milton M., 513
Mann, William R., 263
Manpower Development and Training, 471
Marcson, Simon, 294
Marvick, Dwaine, 93
Maude, Angus, 367
Mayer, David, 514
meaning of work, 395
    morale, 406
    reasons for continuing work, 398
    satisfaction, 402
    in urbanized society, 396
    way of life, 399
Merton, Robert K., 38, 491
Messer, Elizabeth F., 389
Metzger, B. L., 323
Metzler, John H., 513
Middleton, Russell, 218
Miller, D. C., 193 217, 270
Miller, Jerry L. L., 217
Mills, C. Wright, 38, 367
mobility, 62, 64, 66, 80, 81, 82, 281
    of American businessmen, 78
    amount of, 74
    career patterns, 76
    intergenerational, 67, 74
    intra-occupational, 77
    national trends, 73
    vertical and horizontal, 66
Moore, W. E., 60
More, D. M., 253
Morse, Nancy C., 398, 513
Mueller, John H., 490

Nash, Dennison J., 490
Niederfrank, E. J., 536
North, C. C., 146
Northrup, Herbert R., 323
Nosow, Sigmund, 367
Nye, Ivan F., 475

occupational aspiration, see aspiration
occupational associations, 345
occupational choice, 196, 201, 202
    concepts of, 190
    community influence on, 208
    family impact on, 456
    impact of religion on, 456

occupational control, 325
  code of ethics, 332
  colleague, 335
  licensing, 328
  power struggle, 337
  rules, 326
  seniority, 330
  social distance, 335
  superordination-subordination, 339
  union, 331
occupational entry, 244, 246
  employment services, 258, 259, 260
  leaving school for work, 245
occupational ideologies, 431, *see also* ideologies
occupational mobility, 62, 64, 66, 67, 74, 80
  age norms, 80
  family, 81
  income, 81
  union membership, 82
occupational projections, 50, 58
occupational remuneration, 296, 298, 301, 307, 315-18, 321
occupational sociology, 13, 14
occupational status and prestige, 164, 169, 170, 174, 175
occupational structure, present, 24
occupational training, 220, 223, 224, 237, 238
  higher education, 229
  professional schools, 231
  types of, 227
occupations and family life, 452
  attitude learning, 456
  decision-making, 455
  inheritance, 457
  in homes, 454
  role models, 457
  unemployment, 471
  wives of occupational men, 458
  women in occupations, 463
  women's marital status, 468
  work group, 453
  working mothers, 466
occupations, concept of, 8, 10
  Christian view, 5
  Greco-Roman view, 3
  Hebrew and Persian view, 4
  historical perspective, 3
  modern doctrines of work, 7
  Reformation view, 6
  Renaissance view, 6
Orzack, Louis H., 217, 400, 484, 490

Page, C. H., 114
Palmer, Gladys, 85
Palmore, Erdman, 389
Parkin, Grace, 263
Parsons, Talcott, 132, 457
Patterson, Florence, 324
Patton, Arch, 324
Pellegrin, Roland J., 293, 343, 514
Polanyi, Michael, 107
prestige, 164, 169, 174, 175, 177-80
professionals, 77, 124, 270, 480
  authority, nature of, 124
  balance of power, 120
  codes of ethics of, 124
  education and training of, 481
  fee-taking, 23
  interdisciplinary behavior, 127
  in labor force, 122
  mobility of, 481
  productivity of, 127
  proliferation of, 118
  recognition of, 126
  role of, 120
  and schools, 231
  self-regulation, 481
  unionization among, 150, 154, 356
professionalization, 115, 125, 129
  environment of, 123
  in the United States, 118

Quarantelli, Enrico, 263

Rainwater, Lee, 363
Rankin, Robert Parks, 474
recruitment, 10, 246-50, 255, 258, 259
Reiss, Albert J., 77
Reissman, Leonard, 294
remuneration, 296, 298, 301, 307, 315-18, 321
retirement, 369
  adjustment, 387
  age norms for, 378
  by occupation, 373, 385
  compulsory, 374
  gradual, 384
  patterns of women's, 386
  pension plans, 370
  preparing for, 375
  reasons for, 372
  Social Security benefits, 371
Reynolds, Lloyd G., 217, 410
Riesman, David, 430
Roe, Anne, 474
Roethlisberger, F. J., 441
Rogers, Everette M., 536

Rogoff, Natalie, 84, 474
Rose, Arnold M., 161, 351
Rosenberg, Bernard, 514
Roy, Donald, 407, 557
Rutzick, Max, 28, 122, 323

Salt, Allan F., 541
Salz, Arthur, 8, 20
Schneider, Eugene V., 324
Schwartzweller, Harry K., 217
scientists, 76
    in bureaucracies, 105
    migratory, 32
Scott, W. Richard, 294
Sewell, William H., 206
Shepard, Herbert A., 343
Sheppard, Harold L., 257
Sherman, Joseph M., 323
Shister, Joseph, 410
Shostak, Arthur, B., 38, 584
Sibley, Elbridge, 474
Simon, Herbert A., 113
Simpson, Richard L., 167, 219
Slocum, Walter L., 193, 195, 216, 536
Smigel, Erwin O., 14, 263
Smith, Ralph J., 133
social origins, 487
Solomon, Benjamin, 146, 513
Sorokin, Pitrim, 83
Spector, Sidney, 342
status, see prestige
Staunton, J. Donald, 510
Stecker, Margaret, 389
Stecklein, John E., 263
Stephenson, Richard M., 217
Stone, John T., 536
Straus, Murray A., 474
Strauss, Anselm L., 294, 363
Strauss, George, 132, 366
Sturmthal, Adolf, 163
Super, Donald, 192, 216, 370, 473

Tannenbaum, Frank, 136
Tannenbaum, Robert, 114
Taussig, F. W., 83
Taylor, Cora E., 61
Taylor, Frederick Winslow, 21, 33, 43, 119, 437
Taylorism, 437, 542
Taylor, Lee, 15, 133, 219, 514, 534, 535
Thielens, Wagner, Jr., 430
Thompson, Daniel C., 294
Thompson, Wayne E., 390
Tilgher, Adriano, 15

Tocqueville, Alexis de, 118
Toynbee, Arnold, 454

unionization, 135, 136
    of blue-collar workers, 158
    boundary maintenance, 139
    extent of, by occupation, 147
    forms of participation, 364
    ideologies, 136
    impact on occupations, examples of, 148
    membership trends, 140
    mobility, 147
    and occupational organization, 143
    of office workers, 157
    of professionals, 356, 360
    of public school teachers, 155, 358
    of white-collar workers, 156, 352
Unwin, George, 118
Uzzell, Odell, 218

Viteles, Morris S., 366
Vollmer, Howard M., 342

Walker, Charles R., 34, 562
Warner, W. Lloyd, 79, 86, 111
Weber, Max, 13, 89, 91
Weinstein, Eugene A., 473
Weiss, Robert S., 398
Westby, David L., 294
Westley, William A., 579, 580
white-collar workers, 23, 156, 352, 444
White, William H., Jr., 458, 460
Whyte, William Foote, 574, 585
Wilensky, Harold, L., 37, 293, 450
Wilson, Logan, 263, 342, 429
Wilson, P. A., 411
Wolf, William G., 323
Wolfbein, Seymour L., 263, 390
Wolffe, Dale, 242
women, 30, 463, 466
    commitment to work, 470
    in labor force, 48, 466
    major occupations, 469
    marital status, 465
    occupation choices, 213
    occupations dominated by, 464
    training for occupational women, 468
    Women's Bureau of the Labor Department, 468
    working cycles of, 465
    working force, 45

Youmans, E. Grant, 294

Zimmerman, Carle C., 535